CATHOLIC CHRISTENDOM VERSUS
REVOLUTIONARY DISORDER

Can the Catholic Church be reconciled with progress, liberalism, and modern civilization? An adequate response to such a question can only be given if we understand what modern civilization is, what the Church is, and what the results of various approaches of the later to the former have been. John Rao's wide ranging and profound writings are indispensable for coming to such an understanding.

—PATER EDMUND WALDSTEIN, O.Cist., lecturer in moral theology, Heiligenkreuz, Austria

Whether you read John Rao's articles or hear him lecture, the experience is exhilarating. At a time when historiography is in something of a melting-pot, Professor Rao is invariably a breath of real fresh air and an exciting source of renewed understanding.

—FR. JOHN HUNWICKE, Senior Research Fellow emeritus, Pusey House, Oxford

Professor Rao's learning, devotion to history, love of the Faith, eye for telling incident, and vivid writing are all on display in his multifaceted presentation of the struggles of the Church in the modern world. Readers will deepen their understanding of the current state of the Church, how it came about, its deep background, and how it can be bettered.

—JAMES KALB, lawyer, writer, and Catholic convert

Dr. John Rao is an extraordinary figure within the contemporary traditionalist movement. This is due to the fact that he is someone who cultivates history philosophically. It is what allows him to evade the all too frequent errors of leniency, conservatism, and Americanism. Moreover, he is not only a profound intellectual but also an enthusiastic and effective systematizer of ideas.

—MIGUEL AYUSO, Ph.D., Professor of Political Science and Constitutional Law, Comillas Pontifical University in Madrid

For the Whole Christ

THE COLLECTED WORKS OF DR. JOHN RAO

VOLUME 1
Catholic Christendom
versus
Revolutionary Disorder

AROUCA PRESS

ISBN: 978-1-990685-41-5 (pbk)
ISBN: 978-1-990685-42-2 (hardcover)

Arouca Press
PO Box 55003
Bridgeport PO
Waterloo, ON N2J 3G0
Canada
www.aroucapress.com
Send inquiries to
info@aroucapress.com

CONTENTS

Revolutionary Modernity and the Devil

NOW AND FOREVER; ONE AND INSEPARABLE

"You are of your father the devil, and the desires of your father you will do. He was a murderer from the beginning, and he stood not in the truth, because truth is not in him. When he speaketh a lie, he speaketh of his own: for he is a liar, and the father thereof" (John 8:44).

TO SAY THAT THE FIRST LECTURE THAT I as a nineteen-year-old college freshman heard Professor Dietrich von Hildebrand deliver for the Roman Forum at Fordham University was startling to me would be an impossible understatement at the very least. Although I was a cradle Catholic, always practiced my Faith, and was indeed very much disturbed by the terrible confusion in the Church accompanying all of my high school years, I was not at all prepared for hearing just how miserable the ecclesiastical situation and its effects on State and society really were. The militant criticism of the Second Vatican Council and the Novus Ordo by von Hildebrand, along with the outraged and total agreement of the turbulent, budding "Traditionalists" in the Keating Hall audience that evening shocked me to the proverbial core. What, I wondered, had I got myself into?

"Don't worry," Dr. William Marra, von Hildebrand's disciple, Fordham colleague, and my dear, departed predecessor as Director of the Roman Forum from its foundation in 1968 down to 1991, assured me; "you will definitely get used to it. And the older you grow, the more you will find that you do not want to waste time mincing words, lest you die before you get the truth across." He was, of course, right; I took his advice to heart, and now, at the age of 72, I could not care less what anyone might think about how straightforwardly I speak and write. The only one who ever gains from reticence in dealing with issues of Church, State and the Social order is Beelzebub—today, more than ever before in history. And this basic fact of life explains the title that I have given to the Preface to this volume, as well as the choice of citation from the Gospel of St. John to illustrate its meaning still further.

I already indicated in the introduction to the *Unrepentant Catholic's Cautionary Calendar* that my entire approach to Global History is one that sees it as a long-term war; a War of the *Eternal Word* against the *mendacious words* of generations of Sophists seeking to emasculate and destroy the effort to transform all things in Christ. The articles in this volume sharpen that battlefield imagery, seeing in the building of Catholic Christendom the pugnacious construction of the kind of castle that the jointly individual and social creatures meant to share a communal life with God and with one another in Eternity were meant to inhabit, and the counterattack of a "revolutionary modernity" determined to raze this fortress as the grotesque work of Satan and Satan's lies. That, as far as I see it, is the "God's honest" Truth, and it profits no one to hide the fraud involved and its psychotic and ultimately damning consequences.

Nevertheless, as St. Augustine made clear to us in *The City of God*, the conflict pitting the two opposing forces of Christ and the Devil, the truthful saving Word and the lying destructive words, is not a clear-cut struggle. Soldiers in both camps can err in their strategies, thereby unwittingly aiding their opponents' cause. They may also continually waver in their commitment, or actually desert the ranks to swell the forces of the enemy, once, twice, and even at the very moment of death: happily so, if moving from the encampment of the evil to that of the good; tragically, should the traffic be in the other direction.

Hence, the need to scrupulously examine the historical record, so as not to whitewash the mistakes and outright sins of the architects and defenders of Catholic Christendom, or the sometimes real and seemingly positive accomplishments of the revolutionary militia, even as one underlines the fact that the former are the often flawed laborers of the Light and the latter the frequently heartbreakingly confused servants of their enemies. Here, too, it profits none of the Children of the Light to ignore their own vices or the misdirected virtues of the many pathetically deceived Children of the Darkness. The nature of the War of the Word and the Words is open to understanding to all with eyes to see; equally so the need for Christian charity in dealing with the all too obvious blindness often afflicting our friends and rejoicing in the sometimes perhaps unintended good deeds of our enemies and "rooting" for their desertion to our camp.

Once again, as also noted in the introduction to the calendar, there may be a certain "overlapping" in a number of the articles to be found in this volume, which are presented in a chronological order. We have decided to allow such repetition, when it appears, because it is itself part of an historical record: that of my own development in appreciation of the argument in question. There are always nuances in the "song" being sung, even when it is accompanied by the unchanging *basso continuo* emphasizing the clash of God and demon. Think of me through these like the tenor in the repertoire of opera stories, repeatedly called out by the audience onto the stage to perform the same aria over and over again "until he gets it right."

Viva Cristo Rey!

Catholicism, Liberalism and the Right
A SKETCH FROM THE 1920S†

This article is based upon a reading of La Civiltà Cattolica
(Naples/Florence/Rome, 1850–present) in the period 1920–1939.
References are to that periodical unless otherwise stated. The
reader is urged to consult the Civiltà *itself for the full comple-*
ment of articles which support the author's argument.

I

CATHOLIC POLITICAL THEORY PRIOR TO
the ascendancy of writers such as John Courtney Murray is
not a field that is widely studied or seriously understood by many
Americans. This is especially true of Catholic political thought
of the nineteenth and early twentieth centuries, a time which
was nevertheless marked by an abundance of careful clerical and
lay analyses of western institutions and aspirations. The shape
of Catholic thought of this period is frequently attributed by
Americans to factors less than intellectual and far from generous
in character, as well as to peculiar aberrations of the Latin mind.
It is accordingly dismissed.

This somewhat gratuitous attitude is maintained (presuming,
that is, that the existence of something identifiable as political
thought is grudgingly admitted) when discussing the relationship
between Catholic political thought and what is known as Catholic
Action. Emphasis is placed upon the Church's pre-disposition, on
non-rational grounds, towards right wing, authoritarian movements,
and her consequent willingness to create, alter or ignore political
and social "doctrines" to encourage them. Alternatively, attention
is directed to the Church's interest in the exercise of raw power,
and to her variable estimation of the importance of her own teachings based upon their momentary ability to promote or to restrain
Roman strength. What non-opportunistic and objective rationale
could possible be conjured to defend the way in which the Vatican
has seemingly urged the development of Catholic political and

---

† First published in *Faith and Reason*, Spring 1983, pp. 9–31

social movements, and then, with baffling frequency, intervened against them? Whether cohesiveness of theory or coherence of thought and action are concerned, many American observers have felt that the Catholic world has little to say for itself.

The purpose of this article is not to argue that Catholic political theory and Catholic Action before the period of important American influence in the Church were necessarily correct and judicious. Neither is it to deny the self-interested, opportunistic, and even purely unintelligent elements that have entered into Catholic formulations and guidelines for action. Instead, it will be limited to a demonstration of three broad points: the fact that theoretical speculation was indeed taken seriously at Rome; that, while firmly anti-liberal, it was not irrationally twisted to serve the needs of the Right; and that apparently opportunistic and inconsistent actions may be partially explained as attempts to prevent what can be described as "back door secularization"—a secularization occasioned by one's seeming friends. The Jesuit journal *La Civiltà Cattolica*, published twice monthly in Rome since 1850, will serve as the reference for illustrating these points; the 1920s will be their proving ground; reactions to two rightist movements with which the Church has been associated—Italian Fascism and l'Action Française—will serve as laboratory specimens.

II

La Civiltà Cattolica is an instructive key to Catholic political thought for several notable reasons. This periodical maintained a reputation for having close, cordial ties with the Vatican, and for serving as one of its mouthpieces. In recompense for seventy years of unswerving support for the papal cause, it had received Vatican funding, enjoyed easy access to the Holy Father, and been granted his public blessing and frequent commendation. Secondly, *La Civiltà Cattolica* had a long-standing commitment to Catholic political and social theory, a mission which it fulfilled by providing reflective essays, satirical articles, novelettes, news commentary, book reviews and verse on every variety of contemporary issue. *Civiltà* writers were influential, if not directly responsible for the inspiration of documents ranging from the *Syllabus of Errors* (1864) to *Rerum Novarum* (1891). Finally, the Jesuit journal was noted for the consistency intentionally cultivated by its editors, a coherence that enables it to be studied as one piece, the work of a particular school of thought.

Such unity and persistence may have been partially due to the clarity of the *Civiltà's* first Jesuit editors, including, most importantly, Padre Luigi Taparelli d'Azeglio (1792–1861). A brother of one of the Risorgimento premiers of the Kingdom of Sardinia, Taparelli was a follower of St. Ignatius admired even by the Society's opponents. His works on the natural law, and his critique of European liberalism as an outlook founded upon a fatal separation of the individual and social character of the human person, exercised an undying influence on *Civiltà* authors. Praised by Leo XIII, Taparelli's memory was also promoted by neo-Thomists throughout Europe, a result of his re-introduction of St. Thomas' writings into Italian seminaries after a long period of disfavor. Taparelli's reputation enjoyed further enhancement in the 1920's after the republication of his main works by the *Civiltà*, the timeliness of his assault on liberalism, and the homage of Pope Pius XI, who had translated some of his writings into German while heading the Ambrosian Library in Milan.[1]

Vatican influence, consistency of purpose, and the reputation of its editors all played a role in elevating *La Civiltà Cattolica* to a position of power in the Catholic world. Its peculiar structure, half intellectual and half commentary on current events, makes it an apt instrument for penetrating the secrets of Catholic thought and its connection with Catholic Action as these were understood in Rome.

III

A European continent devastated by the First World War, decimated by starvation and disease, and troubled by civil disturbances, offered few grounds for general optimism in 1920. Those problems which were not exacerbated by impassioned front-line soldiers returned to unemployment in broken economies, were fuel for the cynic, anxious to cripple all faith in material and moral regeneration.

---

1 R. Jacquin, *Un frère de Massimo d'Azeglio*: le P. Taparelli d'Azeglio 1793–1862 (Paris, 1943); P. Pirri, S. J., ed., Carteggi (*Biblioteca di Storia Italiana Recente 1800–1870*, xiv, 1932); "Il Nostro Centenario," 1949, ii, 7; A. C. Jemolo, *Chiesa e Stato in Italia Negli Ultimi Cento Anni* (Turin, 1948), p. 190; "Le Colpe Della Civiltà Nelle Narbarie Nontemporanee," 1928, ii, 3–15.

The editors of the *Civiltà* were by no means sanguine in the face of such despair. "We foresee more ferocious warfare," they explained as the decade commenced, "more difficult conditions for the good, a more menacing future for society as a whole."[2] Party passions seemed inevitably to accompany civic action, justice in economics to be a utopian dream, and international order a chimera. Meanwhile, the European horizon darkened with the promise of a Bolshevik bloodletting or the victory of American materialism.[3]

Nevertheless, the *Civiltà* encouraged its readers, all hope for a rebirth of Catholic order need not be abandoned. Indeed, the very disappointments of a war that belied certainty in a never-ending progress had radically increased sympathy towards the Church. Moreover, Catholics could take heart from the instruction and inspiration offered to them by a century of Christian political and social writings unprecedented in both their scope and their number; writings among which could be counted the works of Taparelli. Most importantly, Catholics were clear with regard to the source of European decay: liberalism, with its failure to understand that the existence and exercise of authority were essential to the dignity of the individual and the maintenance of a civilized society.[4]

The general culpability of liberalism as an attack upon authority was always central to the journal's outlook. Liberalism, constructed upon an erroneous faith in the individual's ability to achieve the good without the assistance of authority, represented the secularization of an atomistic tendency already present in embryo in the sixteenth-century heresiarchs. It treated the human person as though he were a self-sufficient entity, a citadel threatened only by the evil from without. At first, roused by a rapacious bourgeoisie anxious to reduce Church and State restrictions on the growth and use of personal wealth, liberalism sought merely to prohibit authority over economic matters. Soon, however, more advanced brethren objected not simply to the object of authority's exercise, but to the authority in itself, at least when wielded by men other

---

2 "L'auspizio del Nuovo Anno," 1920, I, 6–7.
3 "Pericoli Sociali dal Liberalismo al Bolschevismo," 1935, I, 97–102; "Impressioni d'America," 1928, I, 251–259; ii, 28–41, 208–222.
4 "La Ristaurazione Morale e la 'Rerum Novarum'," 1920, I, 120–135; "Liberalism in Pena," 1923, ii, 209–218.

than those freely admitted by the autonomous individual. Still more progressive liberals began to include among authorities to be tamed the leaders of subsidiary corporate entities, and even fathers of families. Finally, certain spirits, the most radical of all, could not bring themselves, out of misguided love for the individual, to endure the impudence of what were but intellectual and internal authorities: away with the tyrannies of standards of beauty, of conceptual truths, of the structure of logic and linguistic forms!

Each individual liberal might disapprove of the increased zeal of his next most radical brother-in-arms, but none, accepting the disdain for authority implicit in liberal thought, could develop a convincing rational ground for limiting social wreckage. Cry all that moderate liberalism might do, it "cries against the consequences of principles that it has established."[5] The less radical attacks of the eighteenth century had fertilized the soil for the egoism, passion and off-handed injustice of the twentieth. Present-day madness was explicable after one visit to the schools created by the liberal State but yesterday. The tumbrils carting the Girondins to the embrace of the guillotine rolled through the streets resounding to the hymns of liberty which these partisans of the Revolution had themselves composed. Thus, the ironic end of the liberal experiment is not the benefit of the individual; it is his oppression and destruction.[6]

Three consequences of the liberal assault on authority, three examples of the dangers suffered by the individual as a result of it, were seen to stand out in the most vivid relief after the First World War. The first of these was the passage of legitimate State authority into the hands of partisan groups, each subject to passions which were then molded into grandiose ideological keys to the perfection of society. The *Civiltà* wrote, "Everything has been obscured and overturned due to the lack of a social sense, in order to serve the triumph of individual and collective egoisms." This "abdication of authority" before "private powers"

---

5   "L'Incoerenze e 'Piaghe Sociali' dell'Ora Presente," 1921, I, 100; "Speranze, Timori, e Moniti nell'Allocuzione Pontificia," 1925, I, 20.

6   "La Follia del Naturalismo nel 'Folle Anno' che è Finito," 1920, I, 97–109; "I Moniti Delle Ultime Elezioni," 1921, ii, 385–395; "Liberalismo in Pena," 1923, ii, 209–218; "I Fallimenti del Liberalismo e il 'Colpo di Stato' Nella Spagna," 1923, iv, 97–105; "Le Colpe della Civiltà Nelle Barbarier Contemporanee," 1928, ii, 3–15.

was "the most unhealthy error," detrimental to the satisfaction of legitimate personal needs and goals.[7]

How had this abdication come to pass? A basic assumption of early liberalism had been that the emasculation of the authority of Church and State would "free" the individual, whereas it had, in fact, "freed" only the stronger and better-organized to exploit their fellow-citizens. The theories of democratic liberalism, which recognized the need to give to the weakened State some basis of operation against embryonic anarchism, afforded such powerful partisan groups an effective means of justifying their own extortion and oppression. A "purified" State, one which was not really an authority in the old sense, but simply a mouthpiece for the "will of the people," need not fear degeneration and transformation into an instrument of tyranny. Indeed, its roots in the "will of the people" might entitle it to new mystic powers, to perform all manner of beneficent tasks. For how could "The People" oppress itself?

Easily, the *Civiltà* maintained, since "The People" played little role in the whole process. Any partisan group, whether sincerely or cynically, could manipulate this argument. Incited by a given passion—and liberalism potentially blessed and divinized them all—the "Party" could rush for control of the arms of the weakened State, insisting that it was transmitting into action the "will of the People" for an unquestionable good. Opposition, even from a numerical majority, need not cause special difficulties. It would merely indicate to the Party the lamentable persistence within the population of the influence of former "real" authorities which were, by definition, unacceptable. Such forces had drugged the People into expressing what was actually not its will at all; popular opposition was actually a subconscious plea to crush the remaining oppressors of the individual. The faction, understanding this, interprets what the will of the people would be, were the last vestiges of the influence of older authorities to be eradicated. A State directed by the will of the people, interpreted by the liberating faction, could proceed to the complete destruction of all remaining hostile social institutions. Since potential private usurpers of the functions of the weakened liberal State

7   See note 6; Also, "Nuovi Fallimenti Della Politica," 1922, I, 97–106; "Crisi di Stato e Crisi di Autorità," 1922, iv, 202; "Per il Nuovo Anno ai Nostri Lettori e Amici," 1922, iv, 385–390; "Crisi di Civiltà," 1923, I, 129.

were legion—capitalists, the press, unions, madmen—the hostile institutions destroyed must eventually cover all surviving authorities. Hence, the liberal ends with the individual confronting an oligarchic "pseudo-State" licensed to do whatsoever it pleases in his name, even against his will.

Another aspect of this power-slippage is the fact that the parties created are ideological in character, as is the basic attack on authority. Liberalism can never admit that evil lurks in the heart of the fallen individual himself. Instead, it assumes that his continuing problems must be caused by yet another enemy authority in the thicket, one last obstacle to assuring the Dignity of Man. Each partisan group, inspired by its pet passion, argues that the satisfaction of this desire, and the tumbling of the social fortress preventing its final victory, will inevitably usher in the Millennium. This becomes its article of faith, or, at the very least, its passport through a liberalized Europe seduced by such language. So deeply had the liberal spirit affected the western world that any competing faction refusing to combat its vision directly would find itself promising its own ideological key to social ills, with a faith that no critical evidence could alter. Partisan, ideological Europe could only survive together with liberalism, since it was liberalism's destruction of social authority which alone could pave its highway.[8]

Economic injustice for the individual was a second consequence of the liberal assault upon authority, and this, the journal claimed, had reached a truly climactic stage after the War. Why? Because it now existed in not one but two forms, capitalist and Marxist, both of which crushed the human person. Atomistic liberalism, justifying an individualism which sinful men quite eagerly aimed at material ends, provided the capitalist with his ticket to a destructive journey across nineteenth-century Europe. Capitalism as a whole then firmly insisted that eye had not seen nor ear heard the benefits that would result from economic liberty, from submission to the law of supply and demand. The weakened State collapsed before its desires, or became its ideological tool. Justice to the capitalist was but the assurance that the defenseless and the unambitious received no protection from his demands, and the

---

8 "'Funzione Educativa' e 'Carattere Etico' dello Stato," 1922, iii, 133–146, 217–229; "La Pacificazione in Italia e il Nuovo Appello del Papa," 192, iv, 291–301; "Per il Nuovo Anno ai Nostri Lettori e Amici," 1922, iv, 385–390.

European continent was littered with the results of his "freedom."

Given this background, socialism was a providential scourge for indifference to human suffering. Yet socialism suffered from the same atomistic materialism as did its enemy; it was, in its ideological effects, capitalism writ large. Human beings, in the socialist mind, were indeed nothing more than individual atoms inevitably engaged in conflict on the basis of their economic interests. The goal of the exploited was simply that of combining their strength in order to become the exploiters, crushing the real individual right to private property. Born from materialism, which compares man to the beasts, socialism simultaneously misunderstands the life of the spirit, the dignity of the person and the value of human life. If capitalism destroyed property for the bulk of the population in the name of the individual's unlimited freedom, its bastard socialist child did so under the banner of the community, exacting indignant retribution for parental severity. Moreover, a movement like the socialist, based on the masses of the population, was a microcosm of the liberal State; power within the socialist organization was invariably exercised by an oligarchy of commissars and petty bureaucrats interpreting the membership's will. Attack either socialism or capitalism without understanding the essential question of the importance of authority for the individual, and nothing solid will be accomplished for the true defense of the human person.[9]

A third disaster might also be traced to liberal disdain for authority: exaggerated nationalism and utopian internationalism. If one justifies the autonomy of the individual, the legitimacy of individual passions, a door is opened for maniacs to construct a nation that believes itself to be entitled to violate all moral tenets for self-aggrandizement. Leave the State weakened, and ample opportunity is afforded to individual and partisan groups of patriotic fanatics with their own vision of acceptable expressions of popular will to capture the instruments of government

---

9 "La Parola del Papa e I Capisaldi Della Ristaurazione Sociale Nell'Ora Presente," 1920, ii, 108–118; "Il Congresso del Partito Popolare a Napoli," 1920, ii, 281; "La Passione di Cristo Rinnovellata nella Sua Chiesa," 1921, I, 485–495; "La Pasqua Cristiana e la Concordia Dei Popoli," ii, 3–13; "Per la Pace Industriale," 1922, iv, 12–21; "L'Apostolato Operaio e la Dottrina Sociale Della Chiesa," 1932, iv, 432–440.

for oppressive ends. One need only consider the reprehensible attacks upon priests and nuns of differing nationalities during the War, the vilification of Germans during and after that conflict, and the senseless injustice of the allied nations in the Treaty of Versailles to realize the depths to which national feeling could fall. Who was the ultimate loser in these developments? The individual—taxed, conscripted, brutalized and sacrificed without concern to the needs of a merciless Moloch.[10]

Once again, however, the reaction to this "liberal" error, promoted by utopian internationalists, was equally destructive. The "nation," for such passionate men, becomes the last authority to crush before the commencement of the Year of Jubilee. But the nation, the *Civiltà* maintained, is an essential framework for the development of the individual; it is merely the misinterpretation of its true character in the liberal context of things that ought to be critiqued. Individuals exist as particular creatures of flesh and blood, sharing a language, a family past, customs and real interests with only a limited group of other human beings. Rejection of the nation, and an attempt to replace it with a baseless "League of Nations" with no roots in European society, would simply ensure the appearance of a weak liberal "super State." Power in this organization would flow to the strong and the better-prepared rather than to the people, just as in the liberal State. Thus, a supposedly common international government would be—and was, in fact—the tool of the victorious allies and the financial magnates that controlled them. The errors of the Treaty of Versailles, which had artificially created weak nations, ignored their dangerous proximity to strong ones, and trampled the just interests of the defeated powers, would feed exaggerated nationalism, "and please God that a new and more profound destruction does not take place."[11]

The *Civiltà* editors quite clearly believed that solutions to any given contemporary problems required unification of what had

10 "Errori di Nazionalismo e Nuovi Danni Alle Missioni Cattoliche," 1920, iv, 443–450; "I Moniti del Presente nell'Allocuzione del Santo Padre," 1923, ii, 481–490; "Il Nuovo Invito del Papa Alla Pacificazione Dei Popoli," 1923, iii, 113–123.
11 "Il Grido di Dolore delle Piccole Nazionalità Oppresse," 1921, iii, 245–248; "Feste e Lutti di Guerra," 1921, iv, 289–296; "L'Europa Senza Pace," 1922, i, 311–319; "Nuovi Fallimenti della Politica," 1922, I, 101; "Patria e Patriotismo," 1923, iv, 486.

been put asunder: authority and the individual. Thus, for example, they were quite willing to contemplate State aid to farmers, land reform, and, in the ultimate extreme, expropriation of large holdings in order to combat agricultural indebtedness and semi-peonage. Was this designed to destroy the principle of private property? No. It was intended to promote its widespread dissemination in the context of the common good. Again, recognizing the unbalanced conditions created by capitalism, the editors argued for strong State action in defense of workers, the absence of which excused such potentially dangerous expedients as trade unionism and strikes. Indeed, the *Civiltà* encouraged a Christian syndicalist movement which would organize workers to obtain their rights and seek participation in the ownership and management of industrial concerns. Was this meant to incite a class war against the rich? No. The *Civiltà* wished merely to reiterate the social responsibilities of wealth in a time when the harmonious corporate society of the Middle Ages had disappeared.[12] Finally, on a somewhat different plane, the editors carried on a rather vigorous campaign for a true "Concert of Europe," built upon the successes of European diplomacy after Locarno, and making use of the admittedly flawed League structure. Would this supercede the nation? Again, no, for it was to the particular nation that the European owed his efforts and his loyalty. A "league of nations" would merely serve to overcome problems that the individual, limited peoples of the Continent could not handle on their own.[13]

Catholics had to realize, the *Civiltà* explained, that attempts to deal with any given contemporary difficulty must be made in tandem with a firm intellectual defense of the goodness of authority as such. Liberal atomism must be uprooted. Otherwise, serious obstacles lay in wait for a Catholic restoration of society. Some

---

12 "Compartecipazione Industriale," 1920, I, 401–410; "La Settimana Sociale di Roma," 1921, I, 52–60; "Il Problema della Terra," 1921, ii, 396–411; "Lo Sciopero Secondo la Morale Cattolica," 1921, iv, 409–421, 491–502; 1922, I, 121–129; "Per la Pace Industriale," 1922, iv, 12–21, 237–248, 415–427; "Rassegna Sociale," 1924, I, 325–340; "La Conferenza del Lavoro e la Libertà Sindicale," 1927, iii, 218–227; 1928, iii, 233–243.
13 "Dalla Nota di Benedetto XV al Patto di Locarno per la Pacificazione Dei Popoli," 1925, iv, 385–398; "Lo Spirito Della Chiesa e l'Organizzazione Internazionale Dei Popoli," 1926, iii, 305–317; "Il Problema della Pace Internazionale," 1926, iv, 127–137.

might take the Church's support for the rights of the poor as an indication of the justice of the socialist cause. Others might see in her moderation and her interest in protecting private property a command to encourage the lethargy of the so-called conservatives. Catholics had to be taught that both the Left and the Right, despite superficial similarities with Christian positions on specific matters, were not frameworks within which they could comfortably work. The Left, which often pinpointed the errors of previous less radical liberal movements, and hence might accidentally make common cause with the Catholics, was the direct carrier of the anti-authoritarian seed. The Right, which sensed the importance of authority, and therefore appeared to strike at atomism, did so mainly because its terrified members saw their own self-interests threatened. They established a line beyond which they refused to allow the forces of change to penetrate, regardless of whether or not this boundary was rational or the interests defended were just ones. Catholics could not be the allies of such temporarily frightened atomists and irrationally authoritarian bourgeois. Their battle was with the underlying principles responsible for horrific contemporary conditions. And these, many members of the Right would still dearly love to preserve.[14]

Was a Catholic Party a fit instrument for a restoration of Christian society? The *Civiltà* was firmly convinced that it was perhaps the worst expedient to which a Catholic might turn. A "party" formed in the twentieth century would very easily succumb to the spirit of the times, and begin to compete with its opponents by offering an ideological program for the solution of all manner of problems. If not this, it was highly likely to become rigidly conservative. A "Catholic Party," anxious to win the battle for control of the State, might not only begin to treat the idea of a struggle among different parties as natural,

---

14 "La Parola del Papa e I Capisaldi Della Ristaurazione Sociale," 1920, ii, 108–118; "Il Regno del Papa e il Giornalismo Cattolico," 1923, I, 481–490; "Liberalismo in Pena," 1923, ii, 209–218; "I Fallimenti del Liberalismo e 'il Colpo di Stato' Nella Spagna," 1923, iv, 97–105; "L'Autorità Sociale Secondo la Dottrina Cattolica," 1925, iii, 257; "La Sovranità Universale di Cristo re e I Suoi Fondamenti Teologici," 1925, iii, 481–491; iv, 3–13; "La Rivoluzione Spagnuola e I Suoi Insegnamenti," 1931, ii, 289–298; "Lo Scioglimento della Compagnia di Gesù Nella Spagna," 1932, I, 289–300; "Individualismo Pagano e l'Individualismo Cristiano," 1932, I, 409–423.

but would inevitably demand a party discipline on issues about which Catholics might legitimately disagree. Moreover, parties having a structure and law of their own, party leaders would be tempted to equate the victory of a Catholic Party with the victory of Christianity. Accomplishing nothing, they would hamper the real transformation of all things in Christ.

The *Civiltà* argued that a serious attempt to rebuild society along Catholic lines would have to accomplish several things simultaneously. It would first of all be obliged to ensure the survival and progress of Catholic education, so that society could continue to know what Christianity really entailed. Secondly, it would require the existence of issue-oriented Catholic pressure groups, "Catholic Action," which would promote specific Catholic approaches to a variety of social problems. Such groups, while political in the sense that they would seek to exert pressure on the State, would nevertheless avoid partisanship. Their issue-orientation would prevent their commitment to a given party and thus avoid forcing Catholics to adopt a wide spectrum of positions on topics about which no one need speak specifically as a Christian. It would hinder them from becoming ideological instruments, since they existed to make the State respond to Catholicism, issue by issue, not to concoct a grandiose scheme whereby they became the State and offered their own ideological key to happiness. Hence, Catholics could be brought together politically only on matters of religious importance; no statement need be made on matters about which Christians could disagree, no party discipline exacted on non-essentials.

Finally, Catholics would have to keep their eyes open for statesmen susceptible to pressure from Catholic Action. If men could be found who were not frightened by the use of authority, who disliked the constant struggle for power among parties, and who refused to build an ideology out of their self-interest or their particular political suggestions for dealing with current problems, Europe could entertain hope. Such men might exercise authority as Catholics desired, and not due to some ideological program. Their actions would not have to be interpreted in the context of either Left or Right.[15]

---

15 "'Unione Popolare' e 'Partito Popolare' in Italia," 1920, I, 289–301; "Il Congresso del Partito Popolare a Napoli," 1920, ii, 269–281; "Funzione Educativo," 1922, iii, 217–229; "L'Istruzione Obbligatoria," 1921, iv, 137–149;

IV

Fascism, in its "doctrinal" form, was anathema to the editors of the *Civiltà*, and was condemned by them as being anti-Christian:

> Catholics are not able therefore to approve, much less to support fascism, as they cannot support or approve socialism, both the one and the other being opposed to the most elementary principles of Christianity.[16]

Did fascism believe that authority was divinely instituted, shaped and limited? No, the editors answered. Did it recognize the need to subject individual passions to precepts of right reason and revelation? No. Indeed, it was a movement in which "brutality is allied often with lust and other passions of wayward youths."[17] Was international order one of its more heartfelt concerns? Its encouragement of nationalists like d'Annunzio did not endear it to the *Civiltà* in this regard. Perhaps social justice was a major fascist aim? Hardly. The *gregarii* (fascist comrades) were the Black Hundreds of a dying plutocracy ready to utilize any instrument to protect itself. Fascism was thus the natural home for ex-liberals, ex-socialists and exasperated bourgeois unable to deal with the consequences of their fundamental principles, unwilling to see chaos sweep the land, and hence, forced to deal with their crumbling world by means of frank, willful use of power:

> ... liberalism is always constrained to make up for moral weakness, for the defect of law, with the abuse of material force, and thus to pass from an excess of license to the other extreme of tyranny.
>
> Such we have seen and we still see in the deeds of fascism, even without recognizing it as a direct work of the government, or a specific institution of the 'liberal State' which has, at the very least, tolerated and fomented it.[18]

"La Parola del Papa e l'Azione Cattolica in Italia," 1923, ii, 97–106; "L'Unione Dei Cattolici e la Divisione Dei Partiti in Italia," 1925, I, 385–394; "Political e l'Azione Cattolica," 1926, I, 385–394; "I Principii dell'Educazione Cristiana Nell'Insegnamento del Papa," 1920, ii, 230–231.
16 "La Guerra Fratricidia in Italia e il 'Grido di Pace' del Papa," 1922, iii, 363; "I Torti Dei Partiti e il Dovere Dei Cattolici," 1921, i.
17 "Le Feste Centenarie di Dante e la Gazzare Dei Sovversi in Italia," 1921, iv, 5–6.
18 "La Pasqua Cristiana e la Concordia Dei Popoli," 1921, ii, 3–13; "I Moniti

Nevertheless, the *Civiltà* could not help but see in the fascist movement a possible tool for ultimately restoring the authority of the State, and an unexpected instrument fit to destroy the modern spirit. "Doctrinal" fascism was, to a certain degree, an artificial plant. Many fascists were simply supporters of "action" to end the crisis of paralyzed post-war Italy, and went no further in formulating definite ideological principles. Obedience to the will of the leader, who might then be able to judge the practical steps that had to be taken in order to act effectively, was their single unquestionable axiom. The Duce, whose authority was thus exalted, had shown himself to be a man of enormous organizational ability, who knew how to exploit the deficiencies and errors of both liberalism and socialism, and who could also dominate the population as a whole. This non-ideological fascism, whatever its intellectual flaws, nevertheless struck at anarchic individualism in the population at large. Even the honesty of the fascist glorification of brute force, as opposed to its hidden acceptance by liberalism, could perhaps aid in building a path back to an understanding of the value of social authority:

> The roar of the *fasci* which orders 'enough' to this disorder was like a signal of battle that had to find sympathy and consent in the crowd of tired, disgusted, self-interested, and honest, who, even while applauding the goal of the fascist organizations, did not approve the method.[19]

A consistent *Civiltà* policy, given the two-fold character of fascism, had itself to be somewhat complex. The editors determined that fascism needed to be steered away from any dogmatic statement of its irrational principles, and kept to its "gut" emphasis on action, order and authority. This would deal heavy blows to the spirit of the modern world. Secondly, Catholic Action would have to be developed more vigorously, and Catholic pressure

---

del Papa," 1921, ii, 391; "Le Feste Centenarie," 1921, iv, 6; "Il Trionfo del re Pacifico nel XXVI Congresso Eucharistico di Roma," 1922, ii, 485–495; "Funzione Educativo," 1922, iii, 133–146, 217–229; "L'Unita d'Italia," 1922, iv, 97–110; "Garcia Moreno," 1922, iv, 205–214; "Crisi di Stato e Crisi d'Autorità," 1922, iv, 201.
19 "La Rivoluzione Fascista," 1922, iv, 509; "L'Unità d'Italia," 1922, iv, 97–110; 1923, iv, 289–298; On Nazism, see 1925, iv, 378 and "Il Nazional-socialismo in Germania," 1931, ii, 309–327.

exerted to ensure that Mussolini's practical policies were Catholic in character. Thus, a Catholic order of things could gradually be constructed without the mediation of a Catholic Party which would itself be tempted to accept liberal political presuppositions and to turn the social teachings of the Church into an elaborated partisan ideology. The success of such a policy would, however, require the strictest unity among Catholics, both cleric and lay.

This general approach is clear throughout the journal's pages. Any justification of the paganism, immorality, violence and statolatry of some fascists was vigorously condemned, as much after the March on Rome as before. Such justifications were said merely to demonstrate the ultimate consequences of liberal theories of power and popular sovereignty. Evils that might stem from fascist "doctrines," the murder of Senator Matteoti in 1924 among them, were eagerly identified and connected with their liberal, atomistic roots. The fascist murder was seen as a frank and logical application of principles which liberals and socialists, with their attack on objective truth and their praise of revolution, had been arguing on the theoretical level for decades already.[20]

Similarly, helpful actions of the fascists were extensively praised and combined with exhortations to further good works. Let Mussolini make a reference to the help of God in Parliament, tinged though this might be with Mazzinian pantheism, and the *Civiltà*, seduced, would erupt in expressions of sympathy and hope. Could the *Duce* but cap his triumph over his enemies with a triumph over his own passions! Let the fascists publish works such as that by Giuseppe Bottai, *La Marcia su Roma*, which urged the regulation of the overly violent *gregarii*, and the *Civiltà* was quick to second its wisdom. Let fascism, irritated by liberal and socialist opposition, launch an attack on popular sovereignty, or even on the "protestant" roots of the modern spirit, and the journal's editors took heart that the more balanced and rational advice of

20 "Liberalismo in Pena," 1923, ii, 218; "Fallimenti del Liberalismo e 'un Futuro Ordinamento Costituzionale,'" 1924, iii, 97–110; "La Delinquenza Nella Vita Pubblica e gli Opportuni Moniti Della Chiesa," 1924, iii, 193–206; "Sotto il Velame della Questione Massonica," 1925, iv, 215–230; "Gioaia e Dolori nell'Allocuzione Pontificia," 1926, I, 25–32; "Princiipii di Dottrina Cattolica Circa lo Stato e la Convivenza Civile," 1927, I, 97–106; "La Rinascità Siciliana e la Funzione Sociale dell'Autorità," 1927, ii, 491–504; "I Rinnovati Richiami del Papa," 1927, iii, 15–20.

a Taparelli and the papal social encyclicals might someday be heeded. Fascists were frequently right, they argued. If they could be consistently right on the proper subjects, they might even begin to be right for Catholic reasons.[21]

The task of the *Civiltà* may be clarified by examining its approach to several specific issues. The "statolatry" and basically anti-Christian sentiments of fascism were identified and criticized in such actions as Giovanni Gentile's educational reforms. Gentile did not show any desire to abandon State claims to control over education. The fascist reform suggested the construction of "a new form of monopoly on the part of the pantheistic State."[22] Gentile himself was a Hegelian who believed that advanced students in secondary schools and universities should receive a philosophical education which would radically transform the character of their earlier Catholic education. Nevertheless, the *Civiltà* saw that even in the midst of theoretically bad educational measures, Gentile's reforms granted the Church certain solid benefits. For one thing, at least a primary school Catholic education was encouraged. In practice, the fascists were conceding to the Church more than the liberals had ever done, and with much better grace.[23]

One issue which demonstrates the double-edged character of the regime in the mind of the *Civiltà* was that of fascist syndicalism. Fascism, the journal claimed, had, in a pragmatic maneuver, shed its formerly anti-proletarian image upon obtaining power. Its desire for unity and action led it to condemn the class struggle, and also to sense the need for some kind of cooperative and just industrial system. Lacking this, Italian life would always be darkened by the sullen hostility of a large segment of the population. This seeming recognition of the rights of workingmen offered hope for the reconciliation of management and labor.

The minute, however, that "pragmatic" fascism attempted

21 "La Pacificazione in Italia e il Nuovo Appelo del Papa," 1922, iv, 291–201; "La Rivoluzione Fascista," 1922, iv, 511–512; "I Festeggiamenti e I Problemi del Rinnovamento Fascista," 1923, iv, 289–298.
22 "La Nuova Riforma Scolastica," 1924, I, 385–398, 517.
23 "La Riforma Della Legge Sulle Opere Pie," 1924, ii, 34–40; "Principii di Dottrina Cattolica Circa l'Educazione Della Gioventù," 1926, iv, 193–200; "Il Senatore Gentile e gli 'Allarmi Della Civiltà Cattolica,'" 1926, iv, 442–446; "Il nuovo Codice Penale Italiano," 1927, iii, 482–489; iv, 193–200; 1930, iv, 481–488.

justification of its new, pro-corporative arguments, it revealed its erroneous principles and manufactured an ideological position. "Doctrinal" fascism, founded upon the concept of the Leader whose will is transmitted through the State, conceived of syndicalism as a dependent and monopolistic instrument of the government. Not only would such a "workers' movement" prove to be distasteful to laborers, but, lacking historical roots, it would remain ungainly and uncontrollable, subject to breakdown or easy Bolshevik penetration. The only solution to the industrial problem was a free syndicalism, Catholic in spirit, opposing both the class struggle and the taint of owner or State dominion:

> Just as yesterday Catholics were against Red precursors and masters of monopoly, so also today they remain firm advocates of true liberty in face of the encroachment of fascist exclusivism.
>
> Neither the brutal club of reactionaries nor the paternalistic umbrella of conservatives is useful against the socialist whirlwind. It is necessary to take refuge in a more spacious and solid edifice ... the professional organization.[24]

La Civiltà Cattolica was clearly obliged to defend both Catholic education and Catholic Action along with any toleration of fascism. Teaching of the Catholic ethos and the presence of strong pressure groups were essential to manipulation of a potentially unsound fascist outlook. Hence its critique of the effort to create in the Balilla a compulsory and monopolistic youth movement, completely fascist in character.[25]

The *Civiltà* was under no such compulsion with regard to the Italian Popular Party, whose implicit claim to being the "Catholic Party" it denied. From the very aftermath of the March on Rome, the journal urged the *popolari* not to oppose the fascists in a way that would encumber the real work of the Church in Catholic Action. The *Civiltà* expressed concern that the Popular Party might endanger "a solid national reconstruction," incite certain

---

24 "Fascismo e Sindicalismo," 1923, I, 412–423; "Le Recente Disposizione Dell'Azione Cattolica sul Movimento Professionale Cristiano," 1925, iv, 437, 440.
25 "Il Senatore Gentile e gli 'Allarmi della Civiltà Cattolica,'" 1926, iv, 442–446; "Principii di Dottrina Cattolica Circa l'Educazione Della Gioventù," 1926, iv, 193–200; "L'Accordo fra la Santa Sede e il Governo Italiano per l'Azione Cattolica," 1931, ii, 549–552.

fascists "to return to the deprecated method of violence," and lead more excitable blackshirts to confuse Catholic Action with Dom Sturzo's group, though it "has nothing and ought to have nothing in common with any political direction."[26]

Unfortunately, the journal argued, the *popolari* were pursuing just the sort of policy that revealed the problems of a Catholic Party. Faced with a government legitimately established, open to suggestions from the Church, anxious to restrict the license encouraged by nineteenth-century liberalism and also popular, Catholics ought to count their blessings. They should sense in Mussolini's critique of the liberal State the spirit of their own hostile arguments. Instead, the Popular Party was interested solely in the maintenance of the liberal party system, which was indeed essential to its own narrow partisan goals. An interest in democracy was by no means illicit, but the rise and fall of democratic States, especially hypocritical ones, was not an issue of moral importance upon which the cause of the Church as such depended. It could not be transformed into a Catholic issue. Catholics had a primary concern for the common good, which, as Church doctrine had long taught, was not tied to any particular form of government. It was ironic, the *Civiltà* noted, that Catholic voters, who had been allowed to participate in Italian politics to fight materialist socialists, were now being mobilized by the Popular Party to fight alongside materialist socialists to defend liberal democracy against a government ever more friendly to the Church. Why join with men who showed little sympathy for Catholicism, and who would turn against the Church at the earliest moment, and for the sake of such a non-essential matter as the particular form of Italian political institutions? Because the *popolari* had succumbed to the spirit of the age, and wanted whatever served its particular self-interests to be proclaimed as being dogmatic and inherently Catholic.

The *Civiltà* continued its attack on the *popolari*, despite charges of servility and opportunism, always stressing the same theme. Indeed, opposition seems only to have strengthened the *Civiltà's* bluntness. There was no hope of a Catholic State in Europe under present circumstances, the editors wrote. One had in Italy the second-best thing: a friendly, though admittedly irrational authority,

---

26   "Il IV Congresso del Partito Popolare Italiano," 1923, ii, 272.

one which was open to Catholic influence, and (perhaps most importantly) one which had no intention of abdicating its power. It would be servile to do nothing against an unjust action of this government; it was by no means vile or opportunistic to accept a powerful historical reality, with all its inconveniences—just as one accepted a less than satisfactory marriage or the Third French Republic—and seek to aim it towards the good. A similar approach was necessary, though with less chance of success, under a legally constituted liberal or socialist government. But to commit the Church against a formidable historical reality which seemed disposed to work for the common good, for the sake of the survival of parties and the partisan spirit, was a real betrayal, a secularization of her mission. If the Church appeared to be running the risk of associating herself with fascism by supporting the legal government, this was a fact of life with which she had to live. She would run the equal risk of appearing to support socialism should she oppose Mussolini's regime, and should not, in that case, have the right to claim that her actions were due to a salutary obedience.[27]

The *Civiltà* believed that the Lateran Treaty of 1929 demonstrated the legitimacy of the policy that it had advocated. For modest concessions, great benefits had been gained. Catholicism was recognized as the sole religion of the State, education was in the Church's hands, and, as a result, the old territorial issue had been successfully resolved. Even the sequestration of one *Civiltà* issue, due to the journal's criticism of a ferocious speech by Mussolini in the Parliament interpreting the Concordat in what it considered to be an unacceptable sense, gave little indication of a general change of outlook. Would the Church have gained as much had the government been entrusted to a Catholic Party committed to the partisan spirit of the liberal democratic State? This, the *Civiltà* was convinced, was doubtful.[28]

27 "La Corruzione Della Vita Pubblica e l'Azione Cattolica in Italia," 1924, ii, 481–492; "L'Unione Dei Cattolici e la Divisione Dei Partiti in Italia," 1925, I, 385–394; "La Parte Dei Cattolici Nelle Presente Lotte Dei Partiti Politici in Italia," 1924, iii, 297–306; "L'Eco del Nostro Articolo per la Parte Dei Cattolici Nelle Lotte Politiche," 1924, iii, 481–494; "Crisi di Stato," 1922, iv, 193–204; "Politica e Cattolicismo," 1925, iv, 481–490; "Autorità e Opportunismo Politico," 1928, iv, 385–395; "L'Ora di Dio," 1929, I, 295.
28 "L'Ora di Dio," 1929, I, 293–295; "La 'Conciliazione Italiana' e la

V

L'Action Française, comprising, as it did, a school of thought, an important daily newspaper, and a league for political action, certainly ranks as one of the most significant of rightist movements. Guided by Charles Maurras and his lieutenants, l'Action Française sought the restoration of the legitimate monarchy, the reinvigoration of provincial institutions, the defense of the classical tradition, and the strengthening of the Catholic Church. Such themes were emphasized due to a consciousness of the necessity of strong authority at all levels of human life for the flowering of individual achievement, and because of the conviction that they were, in fact, the historical basis for French greatness. L'Action Française's consequent attack upon anti-clerical legislation won for it numerous adherents among Catholics, giving it great influence in seminaries, at episcopal palaces, and even in the College of Cardinals.[29]

L'Action Française, which seemed to be at one with *La Civiltà Cattolica* in centering its battle round questions of authority, and which was certainly a more pro-Catholic ally than Italian Fascism, was burdened with papal condemnations from 1926–1939. The Jesuit journal tenaciously supported and amplified Rome's position. Identification of the rationale for the *Civiltà's* often bitter attack upon l'Action Française will further help to clarify the question of Church involvement with the Right.

One ground for the Jesuit periodical's assault upon l'Action Française was what it labeled the "exaggerated classicism" penetrating the movement. A pagan sensuality made of some of Maurras' works, and practically all of those of Léon Daudet, a "school of corruption" which even "the worst pages of the lustful d'Annunzio could not surpass."[30] Classical egotism found expression in Maurras' praise of the "strong man," his disdain for the weak, and his willingness to justify such pagan institutions as slavery. The *Civiltà* claimed that the proud spirit of Celsus and Julian the

Riconciliazione della Società con Dio," 1929, I, 481–488; "Pace Christi Italiae Redditi," 1929, iii, 289–294; "Tra 'Ratifichi e Rettifiche'": 'la Parola del Papa,'" 1929, iii, 97–105.
29 "Ancora dell'Action Française,' un po'di Storia," 1927, I, 385–398.
30 "La Polemica Intorno Alla 'Action Française,'" 1928, ii, 142; "Rivista," 1928, I, 145–151.

Apostate ran through Maurras' assertion that the Roman Church had purified with Hellenistic culture what would otherwise have been merely a Jewish slave religion.[31]

So intent were the *Civiltà* editors upon stressing this point that they even tried to depict l'Action Française as a determined opponent of Catholic social teachings. Maurras and his followers, they argued, exalted the material world above the spiritual, coming, then, "to the defense of the possessors of riches, of individual and social force as in paganism." Their gods were "force and capitalism." L'Action Française and the "so-called conservatives" who appreciated it were "all too often deaf to hearing the voice of the Church and backward in practicing it"; they were indifferent to or fearful of "seeing the rights of the people or their social condition improved"; they maintained a spirit "rigidly aristocratic in the worse and anti-Christian sense of the word." The movement was incapable of understanding Christian charity, and, thus, was guilty of a social modernism that rejected the teachings of Leo XIII and Pius XI.[32]

Finally, the *Civiltà* complained that exaggerated classicism fomented the violence associated with l'Action Française. Maurras mobilized youth for political protests "little in conformity with the dignity of Catholic demonstrations."[33] Despite Catholic teachings regarding obedience to the form of government generally accepted in a given nation, he preached the *coup de force*. Most ominously, given the journal's concern for international order, his belief in the sufficiency of strength for the attainment of national ends led him to pressure France into a consistently overbearing and unjust policy towards a humiliated Germany.[34]

---

31   "L'Euivoco dell'Intelligenza nell'Action Française e il Magistero Della Chiesa," 1927, iii, 385–398; "La Crisi dell'Action Française e gli Scritti del Suo Maestro," 1929, iii, 481–494; "Rivista: 'Lo Spirito dell'Action Française' a Proposito di 'Intelligenza' e di 'Mistica,'" 1930, iv, 531–538; See, also, note 30.
32   "L'Euivoco," 1927, iii, 398; "La Lunga Crisi dell'Action Française e le Sue Cause," 1929, iii, 427–428n; "Il 'Libro Giallo' di Una Pretesa Potenza," 1927, iii, 336–337; "Il Primato Spirituale e la Polemica su l'Action Française," 1927, iv, 235–241; Also, notes 30, 31 above.
33   "I Moniti del Papa nella Recente Allocuzione," 1927, I, 26; Also, 1927, iii, 89, 181–182; 1936, I, 436–437.
34   "Lo Spirito," 1930, iv, 535; "La Conferenza di Genova e la Voce del Papa," 1922, ii, 193–202; Also, note 33 above.

Maurrasian positivism complemented and completed the classical element of the movement. It was positivism that really cemented Maurras' materialism, even though his sole interest in the quantitative was cloaked by his respect for it in history and tradition. *Politique d'abord*, the slogan revealing Maurras' conviction that order and stability were primarily dependent upon a political reordering of France, indicated his subordination of all spiritual matters to the return of the King. His demand for a monarchical restoration, innocent in itself, but erroneous should it contradict the Church's admission of the theoretical validity of all governmental systems, demonstrated his secondary concern for religion. Indeed, such a restoration would not necessarily help the Church at all, but, rather, promote "a simple return to the religious and moral conditions of France on the eve of the Revolution."[35] Maurras would protect the Church for political reasons only, "in function of the national interest," and not "for the profound principles of Christian philosophy."[36] The clergy would then be forced to bless monarchism and capitalism, and bear the hatred caused by a "narrow-minded politics of 'conservative at all costs.'"[37] L'Action Française, though anti-liberal, was anti-liberal in an unacceptable fashion:

> In combating liberalism with its false liberties, it passes to the defense of a censurable absolutism or of another form of at least debatable return to the old regime. In defending nationalism, it passes to a condemnation of all forms of 'internationalism,' including the spirit of pacification among peoples, etc. In demanding, in conclusion, the principle of authority, it exaggerates and changes its nature, substituting, for example, the idea of material force and violence for that of moral force, justice and love....[38]

It was, in fact, a secularizing influence, guilty of religious liberalism:

> They have discredited political and social liberalism by giving way to an indeed worse form of liberalism, religious liberalism;

---

35 "La Crisi," 1929, iii, 487; "Ancora," 1927, I, 385–398; "La Lunga Crisi," 1929, iii, 428.
36 "Ancora," 1927, I, 385–398; "L'Euivoco," 1927, iii, 398.
37 "L'Equivoco," 1927, iii, 398; Also, noted 32, above.
38 "La Questione dell'Action Française e le Sue Ripercussione," 1927, I, 297–298.

this is not a good means of serving the cause of a monarchism that wants to reserve for the Catholic religion the first place in society, at least as an element of order and as the best auxiliary of authority.[39]

Catholics, therefore, could agree with members of l'Action Française only in an accidental sense:

These men are indeed able to agree with us in some practical approach, or on some speculative point: as, for example, in rejecting revolutionary liberalism and similar things; but the agreement could never be complete, being determined per se by reasons diverse in motivation and ends opposed in intention.[40]

La Civiltà Cattolica's understanding of Maurras' commitment to capitalism and to pagan immortality was somewhat erroneous. Nevertheless, its attack upon l'Action Française' ideological character, founded upon the necessity of the monarch, was clear. Maurras' followers certainly did see themselves as the "party of the Catholics," at least in the *Civiltà's* conception of the term, and, therefore, deserved criticism from the journal's perspective. If the Italian Popular Party needed to be harnessed due to its commitment to democratic liberalism, then l'Action Française had to be critiqued for its determined support of the monarchy. Catholics did not have to take a stand on such issues. It was precisely the failure of Italian Fascism to insist upon "ideological purity" that allowed the journal to tolerate and support the kind of approach it condemned in l'Action Française. Just as the editors pointed to the malleability of fascist programs in the 1920s as an indication of the justice of the pro-Mussolini stance, so did they emphasize l'Action Française's stubborn reaction to the papal condemnation as a sign of its "doctrinal and practical political modernism." A "Catholic movement" opposing the Church exemplified the secularization frightening the editors.[41]

---

39   Quotation of Pius XI, 1927, ii, 476; Also, I, 145–151; "L'Euivoco," 1927, iii, 385–398; "Lo Spirito," 1930, iv, 531–538.
40   "La Questione," 1927, I, 297–298.
41   "La Questione," 1927, I, 264, 567–569; 1927, iii, 3–14, 352; "I Rinnovati Richiami del Papa Contro le Dottrine Sovvertitrice della Società," 1927, iii, 15–20; "La Polemica," 1928, ii, 135–142; "Il 'Libro Giallo,'" 1927, iii, 329–344; "La Parola Augurale del Papa," 1928, I, 63–64; "Dopo la

Only one element of l'Action Française avoided the *Civiltà's* criticism: the League led by the Catholic, Bernard de Vesins. The League had been designed as a pragmatic pressure group, it did not require a political platform to function, and it had fought good Catholic fights against anti-clericals and masons. It was, in a sense, a Catholic Action organization, since the bulk of its members were practicing Christians. As practicing Christians of "good sense," however, they were urged by the *Civiltà* to cease following "unbelieving and licentious novelists" as leaders. They were acting as Italian Catholics might have done had they taken d'Annunzio as their leader. Catholic Action or secularized partisan organization: there was no other choice.[42]

Three goals were established for this article. It was designed to demonstrate the "serious" character of Catholic thought before the period of major American influence in the Church; to illustrate Catholic autonomy of the Right; and to explain seeming inconsistencies of thought and action on the basis of a fear of back-door secularization coming from the friends of Christianity.

The first of these goals was fulfilled by relating *La Civiltà Cattolica's* critique of liberalism in the 1920s and its specific proposals for effective reforms. Liberalism was seen to have been castigated for its sterility, and social justice to have been tied to a revivification of authority. Such themes were by no means novel to Catholics of the 1920s; they had been passed down to the *Civiltà* from the nineteenth century. Pope John Paul II's simultaneous condemnation of liberation theology and insistence upon social reforms taps a deep well.

The *Civiltà* is a stumbling block to those depicting Catholic thought as being subservient to the political demands of the Right. An authoritarian French movement was obviously judged by as harsh a standard as a liberal "popular party." Different treatment was accorded different rightist organizations. Moreover, even the approval granted to Mussolini was clearly limited in character,

---

Composizione Della Questione Romana," 1929, I, 385–396; "L'Intorno Alla Definizione dell'Azione Cattolica," 1932, I, 121–136; "La Sottomissione dell'Action Française," 1939, iii, 193–202.
42 "La Questione," 1927, I, 292; "Ancora," 1927, I, 385–398; "Il 'Libro Giallo," 1927, iii, 341, 344; "Il Primato Spirituale," 1927, iv, 235–241; Also, 1927, ii, 280–281; 1928, I, 568–569.

the *Civiltà* repeatedly stressing its conviction that "the Right," like "the Left," was the product of "modernism" and "ideology."

Finally, the attribution of seeming inconsistencies to fears of secularization appears to have been justified. *La Civiltà Cattolica* disapproved of entrusting the Catholic message to any movement or party with a broad political vision. The abandonment of the Italian Popular Party and the condemnation of l'Action Française are to a large degree explained by this outlook. In fact, one might argue that the great strategic error of *La Civiltà Cattolica*, given its commitment to the cause of authority, stemmed from its fear of secularization. Condemnation of such movements as l'Action Française did not free the Church from connection with political ideologies. Instead, it simply encouraged French Catholics with fervent democratic convictions. Ultimately, it was from French democratic sources within the Church, nourished, to a certain extent, by American ideas and authors, that the attack upon "authoritarianism" in Catholic political and social thought developed. And this onslaught ended the influence of the *Civiltà* approach entirely.[43]

---

43   See, for example, "Lo Spirito," 1930, iv, 531–538.

2

Louis Veuillot and
Catholic "Intransigence"
A RE-EVALUATION†

NINETEENTH CENTURY CATHOLICISM WAS
troubled by frequently bitter disputes between those encouraging certain accommodations with the spirit of the times and
proponents of a more reserved attitude towards it. Disciples of
the latter school of thought have produced few historians familiar to English-speaking audiences, and, hence, their portrait has
generally been painted by men hostile to their basic perspective.
The likeness that is rendered is not a happy one. Spokesmen for
that which, pejoratively enough, is often labeled the "intransigent"
position, are censured for lack of Christian charity, a want of
discernment, and an attempt to fossilize the Catholic mentality
that leaves it lifeless in the midst of a vigorous modernity.[1]

The summertime of Catholic "intransigence," a period roughly
corresponding to the pontificate of Pius IX (1846–1878), and all
too often rigidly ascribed to his peculiar difficulties with the Risorgimento, has, as its "popular" symbol, Pius' Syllabus of Errors.
A condemnation of eighty contemporary principles, published
on 8 December, 1864, the Syllabus reflects all of the black and
white intensity most disliked in the intransigent position. Serious interest in this much criticized mentality, however, requires
a more penetrating study, an examination of the landscape in
which something like the papal document could thrive, a hunt
for backwoods intransigent game.

An investigation of such indices to Catholic intransigence must
result in a radical alteration of the received view. One learns of a
call for new forms of Catholic action in a changing world, and sees
an innovative apologetic. The distance placed by the intransigent

---

† First published in *Faith and Reason*, Winter 1983, pp. 282–306.

1 R. Aubert, Le Pontificat de Pie IX (*Histoire de l'Eglise*, xxi, 1952), 108–113,
130–131, 224–236.

between the Church and the modern world is understood frequently to be due to his conviction of the inability of contemporary civilization to secure the truly human dignity that it promises, his awareness of its basic principle of contradiction. Finally, one senses that intransigence itself is something in the eye of the beholder, this sin being attributed by its supposed practitioners to the troops of the opposing camp.

A variety of journals, the Jesuit *La Civiltà Cattolica* and *Der Katholik* of Mainz among them, may readily be identified as having been crucial in formulating the concepts expressed in the Syllabus.[2] Perhaps the most vibrant of these is the Parisian daily, *l'Univers*, edited by a man whom contemporaries often felt to be intransigence personified: Louis Veuillot.

Louis Veuillot's biography, as Thureau-Dangin has said, is, in itself, a guide to the battles fought by the Church in mid-nineteenth century Europe.[3] Born of a cooper's family on 11 December, 1813, Veuillot advanced from apprenticeship as a solicitor's clerk in Paris to a career in the Grenzgebiet between journalism and serious literature. His early journalistic work, which began in 1831 and was aided by his support for the July Monarchy, changed drastically in the late 1830's with a journey to Rome and public profession of a renewed Catholic Faith. Veuillot's active life was, thenceforward, composed of two interrelated threads.

One of these centered round an immense amount of literary activity, including novels, devotional works, and satirical social commentary. Perhaps most significant in this realm were his attack on the polished skepticism of the day in *Libres Penseurs* (1846), and a depiction of Catholic and modern Europe in Parfums de Rome (1861) and *Odeurs de Paris* (1866).

A second thread tied in with the journal *l'Univers* and the Catholic political action that it encouraged. *L'Univers* existed from the early 1830's, although Veuillot's appearance in its pages and ascension to its editorial direction dates from the period 1839–1843. Aided by his brother and several trusted colleagues,

---

2 G. Spadolini, "L'Intransigentismo Cattolico: Dalla Civiltà Cattolica al Sillabo," *Rassegna Storica Toscana*, iv, iii–iv (July–December, 1958), passim; G. Krueger, "Der Mainzer Kreis und die Katholische Bewegung," *Preussische Jahrbücher*, cxlviii, iii (June, 1912), 395–414.

3 L. Veuillot, *Mélanges* (*Oeuvres Complete*, iii series, 1933), i, xiii.

he made *l'Univers* a key instrument in the defense of the interests of the Church. For the Committee for the Defense of Religious Freedom, the nucleus of the "Catholic Party" founded in 1845, *l'Univers* supplied the extra-parliamentary propaganda complementing the Comte de Montalembert's (1810–1870) work inside the French legislature. Enduring numerous vicissitudes, *l'Univers* ran afoul of Napoleon III's Italian policy and was suppressed on 29 January, 1860. Veuillot was permitted no part in *Le Monde*, a temporary successor journal, but regained his former position when government policy allowed for resurrection of *l'Univers* in April of 1867. He continued his work until illness silenced him in 1878–1879. Veuillot's services to the Catholic cause were rewarded by his burial in the national expiatory church of Sacre Coeur in 1883.[4] Pope St. Pius X labeled him the model Catholic layman.[5]

Veuillot's importance as a guide to intransigent innovation may be underlined in several ways. The first is by calling attention to the weapons he thought to be essential to a defense of the Church. The editor of *l'Univers*, like other intransigent writers from outside of France, was convinced that he was living in an era whose character required courageously altered forms of Catholic action. It appeared to him to be especially incumbent upon the contemporary layman, who could directly influence the social order, to become the voice protecting Christianity in the political arena:

> To give, to pardon, to make God known and loved—that is the total role of our priests; they do not look for, do not accept any other. Our role, the layman's role, is different; we are in the world, we play politics, and we would like to know who will prevent us?[6]

Crucial to the layman's activities, Veuillot argued, was the development of a Catholic Press. Catholic journalism was a phenomenon "born of the needs of the Church in modern society."[7] Its practitioners were contemporary knights, battling for right in nineteenth-century garb. Hence, Veuillot was prepared to defend its existence not only against the attacks of the secular enemy, but,

---

4 F. Veuillot, Louis Veuillot (Paris, 1913), passim.
5 Ibid., p. 6.
6 L. Veuillot, i, 537.
7 Ibid., v, 358.

on numerous occasions, against bishops who disapproved of the semi-autonomous lay role that it entailed.[8]

Another innovative feature of the intransigent approach, apparent in the writings of Veuillot, is emphasis upon the benefits obtained by men through the establishment of a Christian social order. Catholicism alone, Veuillot claimed, could effect a real improvement in man's lot; it was the sole new and truly radical force that had entered the lists against human misery since the beginning of time. Should Christianity become the formative element in any given society, he insisted, both that society, as well as its individual members, would undergo a transformation elevating them to undreamed of heights.[9]

The individual's prize in the Catholic order of things, Veuillot indicated, was nothing other than divinization. Indeed, he explained, so central was this divinization to the Christian mission that the Church could not help but treat every human person as a potential god.[10] So strong were Veuillot's statements in this regard, that many of his opponents misinterpreted his main argument. This was certainly true in the case of an article in which the "divinization" of the pope was discussed, a thesis which brought down upon him charges of idolatry.[11]

It is interesting to note that similar problems were faced by other intransigent writers, such as the editors of *La Civiltà Cattolica*. They, too, were fascinated by the consequences of the supernatural penetration of the natural world caused by the Incarnation. Hence, they, too, wrote upon the subject of divinization, and in vivid detail upon the concept of the Church as Christ continued in time. The whole doctrine of the Mystical Body can be said to have intrigued them. A great deal remains to be done in order to completely outline the extent to which intransigent interest in these questions encouraged a rebirth of western concern for teachings culminating in Pius XII's encyclical *Mystici Corporis Christi*.[12]

---

8   Ibid., vi, 149–166; vii, 124–129, 367–373; ix, 300–302; xi, 19–21.

9   Ibid., xiv, 4–15; v, 144–151.

10   Ibid., x, 216–218.

11   Ibid.

12   See, for example, "La Passione di Gesù Cristo nella Sua Chiesa," *La Civiltà Cattolica*, vi, ii (1865), 39–57.

Society as a whole was said to undergo manifold improvements under Catholic tutelage. Veuillot's depiction of these reflects the influence of Joseph de Maistre (1753–1821), the doyen of counterrevolutionary thought. Attesting to the Savoyard's extraordinary reputation in nineteenth century French intellectual circles, Veuillot wrote, "When I was born, Joseph de Maistre blew the trumpet and I heard it."[13] He was an unsurpassable, indeed, even an unreachable figure. Veuillot concluded, "It is necessary to place him apart, among the great men, almost among the prophets...."[14]

Veuillot, like de Maistre, did not equate Catholic order with material greatness. He saw in it, however, a guarantee of peace, harmony among the classes, and the victory of both equity and charity. Veuillot repeated the de Maistrean contention that Catholic respect for the human spirit of association promised the existence of a corporate society of numerous authorities affording effective protection against the totalitarian propensities of the neo-pagan state. A community of men on the path to divinization was for Veuillot a polis freed from an insipid materialism and spiritual boredom. It was an entity that would witness a flowering of artistic and cultural achievement "varied to infinity in its imposing entirety."[15]

Modern man, and contemporary society as a whole, had turned away from God. They had rejected contemptuously the idea of supernatural interference in the natural world. It is this general apostasy, and not the specific actions of governments such as those of the First French Republic, that Veuillot, like other intransigents, labeled "The Revolution." Those who did not understand that the whole spirit of rebellion against the extension of Christ's reign on earth was at fault, those who spoke of the Revolution with reference to the period 1789–1815 alone, were destined, Veuillot claimed, to misinterpret its character. Some revolutionary changes were harmless in themselves, while many men and groups who did not necessarily intend to do so assisted the Revolution by practically abetting the spirit of separation from God.[16]

A victory of the revolutionary spirit meant two things for Veuillot, the most important being the inevitable withering of the human

13   L. Veuillot, xi, 120–121.
14   Ibid., xiii, 176.
15   Ibid., i, 334; Also, iii, 304.
16   Ibid., xiii, 447–455; xi, 143–148.

soul. Veuillot seems to have believed that the natural material instincts of men who were once influenced by Christianity but had now escaped its guidance could become totally egotistical and utilitarian in character. One might argue that this was the result of a Catholic emphasis upon the importance of the individual torn from his proper context.[17] Whatever the case may be, the abolition of the Catholic outlook in the modern world had assured the predominance of a "mercantile and savage spirit."[18] Revolutionary definition of freedom as a breaking loose from the bonds of established authorities merely justified the natural reassertion of worldliness.

Yet the withering of the human soul did not stop with this. The spirit of the Revolution had more and more wandered down a democratic direction, developing an obsession with the principle of equality. Here, a false emulation of the Catholic conception of fraternity was at play. Outside of the Christian context, democracy and equality must mean a suspicion of that which could not be attained or understood easily by the majority of men. Veuillot explained, "Vulgarism is the odor, the character, and the inevitable unhappiness of the mob."[19] Hence, the egotism of the de-christianized man would be limited by democratic heavy-handedness to satisfaction only of those desires approved of by the "average man." Such desires would become more and more bland with the gradual disappearance of all vestiges of Christianity's manifold elevating influence.

Finally, Europe found itself prey to and encouraged in acceptance of the Revolution at a time of tremendous scientific and industrial development. The introduction of the machine into all aspects of western life had aroused great hopes for the perfection of European material life. Industrialization, so appealing from this standpoint, required a standardization even more restricting to revolutionary freedom from democracy. It demanded the jettisoning of those human concerns and movements of the individual soul harmful to the discipline and progress of the machine. Ultimately, therefore, the separation of the supernatural and natural realms, the victory of the Revolution, resulted in the triumph of the material and the insipid. "Everywhere," Veuillot insisted, "the reduction of

17 Ibid., vi, 310–325; viii, 562–565.
18 Ibid., xii, 359.
19 Ibid., xiii, 448.

the truth has diminished intelligence, hearts, and even the instinct of life."[20] Western society, stung to the quick, would soon "sail on a sea of platitudes where it will grow immensely bored."[21] Even if the initial violence of the Revolution indicates thought, movement and vigor, its conclusion guarantees staleness and ennui. The chaos disrupting this dull revolutionary society would be a chaos born of mindlessness and despair.

Veuillot illustrated his views with abundant examples from contemporary France. French children, he complained, were being brought up to ridicule orthodoxies of all kinds, whether they be religious, political or literary. Men were made to believe "that the impudence of vice is the summit of virtue";[22] they were taught to communicate in a "dishonored jargon which would draw forth cries of indignation from the most careless writer of one hundred years ago";[23] They had become "barbarians of civilization."[24] Nevertheless, so narrow, petty and bourgeois were the aspirations permitted them, so insistent the need to train them for their little niche in an overly industrialized and commercial world, that this theoretical libertinage became laughable. Frenchmen were no longer even fit to sin:

> Between the sensualists of the past and the sensualists of our day, there is the same difference as between the great lords who ran about the world astonishing it with their prodigalities, and those sons of the enriched of whom one section of Paris sees the splendor and decadence. The first wanted to ruin themselves and did not succumb to it; the latter calculate, are rich, yet succumb without even having known to make a semblance of being magnificent. Everything is lacking to the poverty of our times, including the brilliance and often even the substance of the vices it would like to have.[25]

So numb was the modern Frenchman to the call of glory that a Saint Bernard would find himself able only "to convince a hundred bourgeois to make their Easter Duty," and this, "above all if the

---

20 Ibid., xi, 337.
21 Ibid., xiii, 448.
22 Ibid., xii, 401.
23 Ibid., i, 327.
24 Ibid., xii, 401.
25 Ibid., iv, 2–3; Also, xii, 416–420.

socialists had preached there before [him]."[26] The only extraordinary enterprise for which he could arouse enthusiasm was that of "elevating the world to commercial and industrial civilization," which signified spreading factories, knowledge of banking, and opium to China and India. A terminus to this withering of the soul was clear: the complete abolition of the man of fiber:

> No more men anywhere! The production of man has ceased in France. Some men of more or less complete honesty, but lacking talent; some very incomplete men of talent lacking all honesty; no attachment to any truth, but the most senseless attachment to the most mad errors; no more good sense, except in damning uselessly the impotent and evil works one persists in pursuing; no more pride in the face of anything base, yet puerile and dangerous and even cowardly arrogance in face of all that which one must fear . . . . [27]

Yet France, still prey to revolutionary upheaval, had not tasted the dregs of the cup of spiritual boredom. The United States had had this opportunity, and, therefore, offered a more depressing example of the fate awaiting western man. America, Veuillot argued, had never known the benefits of Catholic community. It was composed of individual, economically-oriented moles, "men without history, without cradles and without tombs; adventurers of both sexes who are not even barbarians."[28] Its cities did not resemble the European polis, because their citizens were "gathered together solely to make one another mutually sweat gold,"[29] and because they "only place in common the flesh from which they nourish machines for making money."[30] It was no wonder, he answered the *Journal des Debats*, that a place like Chicago could be rebuilt as quickly as it was after the great fire, since nothing of lasting importance could ever have been lost in it. The same could be said of the entire nation, were it to disappear in some holocaust. Priests who entered this model land of insipid modernity "go to carry extreme unction to races who are dying and to some savages expatriated from Europe":

---

26 Ibid., v, 186–187.
27 Ibid., ii, 350 (short quotation); xii, 360–361 (extended quotation).
28 Ibid., xi, 333.
29 Ibid.
30 Ibid.

This people does not cry for its dead. It only knows how to cry for money. Fire can grip its cities, but it devours in them neither a monument nor an art object, nor a memory, and the money melted is not money lost at all. One draws it from the ruins; it is often even good business.

One can look at North America and the direction in which it is headed: its rapid progress, owed to the most brutalizing work, has fascinated Europe: but already the true results of this exclusively material progress appear. Barbarism, wicked behavior, bankruptcy, systematic destruction of the natives, imbecilic slavery of the victors, devoted to the most harsh and nauseating life under the yoke of their own machines. America might sink completely into the ocean and the human race would not have lost anything. Not a saint, not an artist, not a thinker—at least if one does not also call thought that aptitude for twisting iron to open pathways to packages.[31]

A second consequence of the Revolution, Veuillot argued, was the establishment of a despotic social order that encouraged this withering of the human spirit. The fact that revolutionaries themselves did not intend such an outcome, but, rather, saw their work as ensuring mankind's liberation, simply emphasized the tragedy of the modern age more poignantly. There was operating in the Revolution a principle of contradiction preventing it from attaining even its most keenly-felt goals. Hence, Veuillot argued, it had to be killed as much for its own sake as for that of society as a whole.[32]

Two features of revolutionary thought contributed to creation of a soul-killing despotism, the first of which was its conception of freedom. The Catholic understood freedom to mean the right to follow the good and to be protected from evil. He could, therefore, demand removal of the restrictions placed upon the activities of a Church which was destined to lead men to eternal glory, while insisting that they be tightened round revolutionaries who could only guide them to perdition. Freedom, for the Catholic, also required the binding of the strong, the cunning, and the ambitious when they manipulate the weak and adversely affect their own spiritual development.

---

31   Ibid., xi, 34; xii, 359–360.
32   Ibid., v, 410–419; vi, 44–68; viii, 271–279; xi, 114–122, 143–148; xii, 333–335; xiii, 15–18, 95–97; xiv, 80–84.

Revolutionaries, on the other hand, equated freedom with the absence of all manner of authoritative restrictions on behavior. They refused to speak of it in terms of the quality and final end of the actions men might perform. Indirectly, therefore, they justified the inevitable exploitation following the simultaneous "freeing" of individuals of varying character and talent, the abuses that "make of this supposed liberation a real and dishonoring slavery"[33] for the bulk of mankind.

Veuillot, like many other intransigents, pointed to that which had happened in the economic order to demonstrate his theory. Catholics, he explained, saw that there were proper and improper uses of economic freedom, correct and incorrect commercial transactions. They recognized that a good deal of pressure must be placed upon the economically strong by society to ensure that their "freedom" not result in their exploitation of the weak. Veuillot was pleased to see organizations developing in France, such as those inspired by Albert de Mun, reminding the rich that their "freedom" was a conditional one, and had to bend to the requirements of the common good.[34]

Revolutionary economic freedom, rather than liberating the whole population, had, instead, liberated only the wealthy element in society, the bourgeoisie. Indeed, "the People," when given the opportunity, had always spoken out against the Revolution, while the bourgeoisie had continuously encouraged it:

> The Revolution is not popular, it is bourgeois. It is the bourgeoisie who made it, has defended it, restored it, continued it, and who, for the unhappiness and ruin of France, will finish it if it can. For fifty years, the assemblies arising from bourgeois suffrage have been revolutionary; they made 1830 and 1848. Placed in control of itself, the people have pronounced against the Revolution; all the great votes of universal suffrage are witness of it, all the titles that the Napoleonic dynasty hold from it, from the first to the last, are counter-revolutionary. The bourgeoisie and the revolutionary spirit sat Louis XVIII on the revolutionary throne of Napoleon; the people and God asked Napoleon I and Napoleon III to sit on the Catholic throne of

---

33 Ibid., vii, 169; v, 17.
34 Ibid., iii, 206–210, 383–390; v, 420–439; ix, 365–371; vii, 161–173; xii, 277–280; xiv, 132–135.

the noble kings of France, protectors of the Church and the poor, magistrates of the nations.[35]

Veuillot had been impressed, as early as 1840, at the beginning of his career with l'Univers, with the industrialization resulting from the "freedom" granted to the bourgeoisie, and the consequent creation of a class of helpless proletariat. He spoke of visiting a factory in the vicinity of Paris, whose "free" owner and wife supported all the correct liberal causes, and whose "free" workers slaved day and night for a pittance in suffocating conditions salubrious only for the machinery. All these "free" employees, broken in spirit, would be put out to pasture like worn-out beasts when sickness or old age dictated.[36] Should the liberated bourgeois invoke the holy name of freedom to defend himself against restriction of his amoral power, then, Veuillot claimed, he ought to be prepared for an eventual — if unfortunate — expression of amoral proletarian liberty:

> I accept that excuse for what it is worth, and I say that the unbelieving poor man can equally use it for himself. He also has become a philosopher, and his philosophy only obliges him when and how well it seems to him to observe the precept which commands him to respect the property of others.[37]

Revolutionary concepts of freedom put society in the hands of the soul-killing bourgeoisie. A second feature of revolutionary thought, its attitude towards government, tended to confirm this domination.

De Maistre had taught Veuillot that serious defense of the common good required a government whose executive possessed a clear, strong, and hence, "regal" character. Such a power was essential for any effective enforcement of community as opposed to particular interests. Monarchies, republics and democracies all rose and fell, to a large degree, due to the extent of this strength and clarity of the executive authority. If the head of the government were not firm, obvious, and therefore regal, all manner of evils could enter the polis. Private interests of great influence might manipulate the weak executive to allow them to oppress the population; "a

---

35   Ibid., ix, 384; Also, xiv, 298–302.
36   Ibid., i, 163–166.
37   Ibid., iii, 306.

horde of Janissaries" would impose upon the nation, "by means of the cudgel, the code of its follies."[38] Meanwhile, appeals and complaints might continue to be directed to a façade-like authority, as though it were still able to effect the common good. The only way that a strong, clear, regal power could be built in a given nation was by hearkening to that country's history and determining which institution or institutions could most efficiently fulfill this role.[39]

Revolutionary thought destroyed all rational hope for a government devoted to attainment of the common good, and it did so in a variety of ways. Perhaps the most important manner in which it worked its negative effect was by asserting the existence of one ideal form of authority, applicable everywhere, regardless of historical circumstances. Since 1815, a parliamentary system modeled after those of England and the United States had frequently been singled out as the sole form fit to aid human progress. Veuillot was particularly convinced that his contemporaries' treatment of America as a guide to solving their own difficulties was dangerous. It assumed the perfection of an infant land, which had not yet been molded by its own traditions and the actions of those "comets" which are called "great men." One did not really know what the results of parliamentary government even in America might be, and one could not know until sufficient time had been given for it to mature. Veuillot personally doubted its quality and its ability to maintain itself:

> Through fisticuffs and slander, by means of a thousand frauds, they [the Americans] manufacture for themselves from day to day governmental tools made purposely to be worn out quickly.... They take a workman, a corporal, a buffalo herder, a pig-skinner, a speculator in newspapers; they place him at the head of the country, under safe guard; they heap outrages upon him, he allows himself a thousand improprieties, and this lasts three years {sic}, thanks to his tricks, when he has sufficient spirit to trick. When he departs, covered with spittle, another replaces him who spat upon his predecessor, and upon whom someone else will spit. This works for them, and it will last until they have become too savage to retain the same leader for three years. They will then create dictators who will perpetuate themselves, or they will devour one another, and the loveliest

38 Ibid., iii, 164.
39 Ibid., v, 339–340.

republic of the world will end by being a strongly disciplined hereditary empire, or a cave and a slaughterhouse.[40]

More significant for Veuillot was the delusion that this developing country, this "tumble of merchants and adventurers who, on the land cleared but yesterday, have neither traditions, nor neighbors, nor boundaries,"[41] could ever serve as a model to civilized France, even when matured. Presuming the validity and effectiveness of the American system in the United States told nothing of its potential career in France. "What does the parliamentary regime in England and America matter to us," Veuillot asked, revealing once more the de Maistrean heritage; "it is necessary to see what it has done, what it is and what it can become here."[42] Elaborate theories might be constructed to insist upon its universal efficacy, "lovely correlations of reciprocal rights and duties traced on paper," checks and balances provided in abundance. Despite all precautions, its dogmatic and a-historical application promised disaster:

> ... all this lovely mechanism, which functioned so easily and so philanthropically in the inventor's study, seems, before long, to be wicked in its use; it becomes disordered, it spreads terror and death around it. Before long, no more remains of it than a pile of debris on a heap of corpses around which, from all points on the horizon, come running the beasts of prey.[43]

Everywhere that "ideal" revolutionary governments were established in disregard of the historical traditions of a nation, they enabled the strong and the ambitious to manipulate them to serve their private interests. In practice, this meant the control of republican and democratic states by the revolutionary-bourgeois element. It was logically impossible for these states to respect the "freedom" of the bulk of their citizens. They must, to take but one example, destroy the Catholic world view which offered a different definition of liberty, regardless of the number of believing Christians under their control. If, somehow, the real will of the non-revolutionary majority triumphed, as it did in the Belgian debate over the autonomy of charitable institutions in 1857, the radical-bourgeois power

---

40 Ibid., xi, 333; v, 497.
41 Ibid., v, 497.
42 Ibid., iv, 362.
43 Ibid., v, 339–340.

regained the upper hand through extra-legal means. And it did so while continuing to maintain the popular image:

> There is no hope of winning by discussion should the majority hold firm against sophisms, ruses, threats: then the windows of the gallery, which are always arranged to look out onto the street, are opened; one cries to the crowd that the majority is betraying the people, that it wants to enchain it, that it wants to brutalize it. The crowd enters, it howls, it boos, it breaks, it silences, it votes: a street carries the motion above all the contrary voices, the majority is changed, the law is made.[44]

"That which liberalism refuses to Catholics in Belgium and everywhere it is in control is the freedom to obey God," Veuillot complained; that which it tolerates is only "the imaginary freedom of animals and rebels."[45] "France is a country conquered by materialism and impiety," he argued, "and materialism and impiety treat it like a conquered country, but one still quivering. Those who resist are destroyed; it is still necessary to treat the others with caution."[46] Veuillot expressed bewilderment after 1870 at the fact that some Frenchmen feared that a legitimist victory would force their attendance at Mass. This kind of pressure, he insisted, was alien to the Catholic approach. In contrast, "the others will make you go where they want; they will impose another hypocrisy that you will not {be able} to disdain."[47]

Nothing was left by revolutionary political thought to permit opposition to the radical-bourgeois manipulation of the modern state. Groundless "divisions of power" were of as paltry a value as an insubstantial commitment to impossibly formless conceptions of rule by all the people:

> Bonaparte re-established religion in spite of freedom: if he had wanted to undo that which he had done, would he have been prevented by freedom? By the freedom of the Church, yes; that is to say, if there were found enough priests and Christians to resist him at the peril of their fortune and their life. By political freedom, no.[48]

---

44 Ibid., vii, 131; Also, v, 280–295; xiv, 298–302.
45 Ibid., vii, 153; Also, vii, 161–173; vi, 440–450.
46 Ibid., ix, 504–512.
47 Ibid., xii, 293.
48 Ibid., v, 331.

There existed no mechanical device by means of which the problem of good and evil, of statesmen with good intentions and tyrants with bad ones, could be avoided. Insofar as purely political protections could be found against the pretensions of a state gone astray, they had to be based upon the existence of independent centers of authority from which resistance could be conducted. The multiform corporate life inspired by Catholic recognition of the goodness of association and authority could—and had—given birth to this type of protection; revolutionary insistence upon atomistic freedom must—and did—destroy it. Revolutionary bourgeois thought dismantles the authority of the subsidiary corporations by relying upon the power of the radicalized state to work its will, leaving that state as the sole remaining viable force in society. Woe to the bourgeoisie should an outraged proletariat seize such a powerful instrument to destroy its class enemy![49]

Catholicism created in all states a multitude of living forces which united individuals in powerful and durable associations, and placed them under shelter from the oppression of power. Protestantism and philosophy demolished all these fortresses of liberty one after the other. Nothing has remained facing the state but individuals impotent in defending themselves against it. Now the socialists propose recognizing the state's rights over the individuals like those which Protestantism and philosophy gave it over the moral persons {i.e., corporations}, which it killed one by one. This is logical: why should it not absorb individuals like it has absorbed all the rest?

An article entitled "Le Canon Rayé," published in 1859, noted that which could happen when an absolute revolutionary power flourished in tandem with banal modern civilization. The nineteenth century, the witness to this phenomenon, would proceed inevitably towards the establishment of a universal state, headed by a charismatic dictator, whose power would rest upon a bureaucratic elite skilled in techniques of manipulation:

> Everywhere the conqueror will find one thing, everywhere the same, the only thing that war and the Revolution will nowhere have overturned: bureaucracy. Everywhere, the bureaux will have prepared the way for him, everywhere they await him with

---

49 Ibid., iii, 304; iv, 345–352.

a servile eagerness. He will support himself on them, the universal Empire will be the administrative Empire par excellence. Adding without end to that precious machinery, he will carry it to a point of incomparable power. Thus perfected, administration will satisfy simultaneously its own genius and the designs of its master in applying itself to two main works: the realization of equality and of material well-being to an unheard degree; the suppression of liberty to an unheard degree.[50]

Men ruled by this system would be much more easily oppressed than at any time in the past. Such facility would be due not so much to the fact that new weapons would give the dictator undreamed instruments of control as to the sad reality that stupefied machine man would approve of his chains, and a dull-witted intelligentsia would bless them. The subjects created by contemporary civilization were, after all, totally distinct from men of preceding generations. "These forces, which today's man possesses," Veuillot wrote, "possess him also; they engage him in weaknesses as unmeasured as his pride; weaknesses which succeed in changing him completely."[51] Men had been transformed into absurdities, beings unable to desire the destiny outlined for them by the Gospel, "too powerful to control the taste for pleasure."[52] The universal Empire would enslave such creatures by providing for their most banal needs:

> The police will take care that one is amused and that its reins never trouble the flesh. The administration will dispense the citizen of all care. It will fix his situation, his habitation, his vocation, his occupations. It will dress him and allot to him the quantity of air that he must breathe. It will have chosen him his mother, it will choose him his temporary wife; it will raise his children; it will take care of him in his illnesses; it will bury and burn his body, and dispose of his ashes in a record box with his name and his number.[53]

As time goes on, this task would become simpler and simpler. A decline in human imagination would entail a destruction of the taste for a variety of pleasures:

50 Ibid., viii, 366–367.
51 Ibid., 364.
52 Ibid.
53 Ibid., 369.

41

But why would he change places and climates? There will not be any more different places or climates, nor any curiosity anywhere. Man will find everywhere the same moderate temperature, the same customs, the same administrative rules, and infallibly the same police taking the same care of him. Everywhere the same language will be spoken, the *bayadères* will everywhere dance the same ballet. The old diversity would be a memory of the old liberty, an outrage to the new equality, a greater outrage to the bureaux which would be suspected of not being able to establish uniformity everywhere. Their pride will not suffer that. Everything will be done in the image of the main city of the Empire and of the world.[54]

Veuillot does not appear to have believed that radical revolutionaries were themselves the most dangerous force facing mid-nineteenth century Catholics. Indeed, one might almost argue that he thought them to possess certain admirable qualities. They, at least, were still vigorously alive, misdirected though their passion might be. They, at least, were serious enough to understand the folly of separation of Church and State, in the sense that they recognized the need to translate their personal beliefs into political and social institutions in order to ensure their survival. Their relative harmlessness also lay in the very offensiveness of their views. Boldly stated, these tended to terrify and repel the population. Radical success required the aid of less fervent and less logical men who might open an unwary nation's doors to the full consequences of the Revolution.

Perhaps the unthinking proponents of machinedom, whose obsession with commercial and industrial development engendered more difficulties for man than it offered solutions to basic human dilemmas, could be singled out as being more fearful in Veuillot's eyes. The degree to which such persons mute revolutionary enthusiasm—indeed, all enthusiasm—to satisfy purely utilitarian demands has already been noted above. Their pragmatism gave them an entry into society denied to seemingly more dangerous radicals, yet they, too, required the Revolution, with its exaggeration of man's natural destiny, in order to prosper.

Nevertheless, Veuillot assigned the role of true villain and most grave threat to those who labeled themselves "conservatives" and

---

54 Ibid.

"Liberal Catholics." Conservatives, he explained, were men who wasted their energies opposing specific manifestations of the Revolution—as, for example, the Reign of Terror—while refusing to combat the infection of naturalism lying behind it. Liberal Catholics, at least at the beginning of their careers, shared the same outlook as true counterrevolutionaries, but reproached them for being too harsh in their criticism of modernity. These liberals blamed their fellow believers for the violent hostility displayed by revolutionaries towards the Church. Both groups opposed the "fanatical," "close-minded" and "uncharitable" tactics of Veuillot and his allies.

The editor of *l'Univers* attributed the gravity of the conservative/ Liberal Catholic threat to three causes. One was the fact that the failure of the conservatives to treat the intellectual context of the Revolution seriously, and the refusal of the liberals to accept the logical necessity of Catholic-revolutionary enmity, forced both to contribute to the general attack upon the human mind. Veuillot complained that it was actually his rational insistence upon close examination of ideas and their consequences which was equated with fanaticism. "Open-mindedness," on the other hand, as he noted in a critique of certain statements made by Albert de Broglie, essentially and ironically involved abandonment of all serious analysis:

> In the islands of Oceania, the savages who fill the office of priests often indulge the whim of declaring that such and such an object is . . . taboo, that is to say, sacred, and from that point no one can touch it under pain of sacrilege and of death. Are we going to accord the same faculty to the flamines of the ideas of '89, and will everything that they have regarded with a pleasurable eye be taboo for the rest of mortals? . . . All revolutionary institutions and all their consequences, whatever they may be, taboo! One must be quiet and adore, or perish! This fetishism is new, at least among Catholics and conservatives.[55]

Veuillot criticized the type of "thinker" and "great man" that must develop from this "moderate" outlook in one frequently cited passage from *Les Libres Penseurs*:

> He is the author of [a] volume, he speaks in it of everything: there lies a title to the Academy of Moral and Political Sciences.

---

55 Ibid., vi, 435; Also, ix, 483–503; vi, 367–373.

It is here that the debate between Leibnitz and Bossuet is definitely settled; it is here that the hidden motives of Descartes are revealed, and that the secret incredulity of the simple Malebranches is demonstrated as clear as day. Here, too, the final word on Voltaire is pronounced, and one sees in it how the author of *Candide* is more spiritual and orthodox than the devout have cared to believe. In a certain section, found towards the middle, the master takes a very objective position in the struggle of the Church with philosophy. The Church would be wrong to complain: the young man does not hate her at all, he is rather good-willed. Without a doubt, 'the priests are not that which a vain people thinks,' but in their doctrines and in their general character there is a goodness that the young man recognizes and confesses. This is not the generosity of a beginner; it is the judgment and sentence of a mature spirit. He is not at all generous, he is wise; he is not dazzled, he knows. The Church rests upon certain needs of the human soul; it has a right to these, it can go that far, but not further! Further lies the superior domain of the reason and philosophy. If the Church had the temerity to breach this limit, it would find the young man there, respectful but inflexible; he would cry to it: Stop! Do not fear that it may pass this limit. This is why he does not approve his friends who are alarmed, and who, 'in the heat of an anger more legitimate than philosophical,' write that all priests are scoundrels, all pious women adulterous, the whole Catholic edifice a heap of impostures. No! Here lies exaggeration. He will deny these hyperboles. He is just, he is calm, he has studied, he has meditated. He sees that the lower class has need of a religion, and the Catholic system seems to him to satisfy better than another that need of the rabble. All this is said in an academic form, without fault of French, without pause, without emphasis . . . citing Kant, Hegel, Schelling, Saint Bonaventure, Thomas Reed, Brockius, Pintus, Chopinetti, and the Third Council of Sardis. He is titular professor, chevalier of the Legion of Honor, intimate of the *Journal des Debats*. He will be married well, his books will be bought for the public libraries, he will be deputy, royal counselor, minister. He is called the hope of philosophy now, he will one day be called its honor. Myself, I call him a turnip.[56]

---

56   L. Dimier, *Les Maîtres de la Contre-Revolution au Dix-Neuvième Siècle* (Paris, 1917), 287–288.

A second reason for viewing conservatives and Liberal Catholics with alarm follows logically from the first. Veuillot argued that a serious opponent of the Revolution, a man who recognized the chasm separating the Catholic and secular world views, had to be what his enemies called "intransigent" in his hostility towards it. Catholic journalism, this *novus organum*, had to be frank, hard-hitting, and consistent in its attack. Adoption of a conciliatory spirit was a miscalculation of even cosmic proportions, in that it sacrificed the souls of existing believers in the gamble for an impossible *entente*. The enemy already had tremendous advantages in this spiritual combat, Catholics finding themselves unconsciously using his language and teaching methods, and open to sweet blandishments at every turn. It was critical to adopt all legitimate weapons to save the home camp from infection, subversion and demoralization. "We are fighting a war," Veuillot concluded, aptly summarizing the concerns of such sister journals as the *Civiltà* as well, "wherein it is always necessary to burn one's ships":

> We see them in the schools, in the midst of a young generation which they water without scruple with all the poisons of error; they have audacity on their faces, mockery in their mouths; they permit us to believe that they have atheism in their hearts. We count their victims by the hundreds, and in our souls themselves there stirs a remnant of their poisons. May God convert them tomorrow! Our task is to escape them today. Finally, will we, out of respect for a small number of mad or wicked men, who, being devoted to the propagation of evil, will always cry that they are being injured when one attacks evil, suffer it to pass and circulate insolently, to carry demoralization along with error into minds, so that the spirits that it will darken will not be able to recover the light, so that the Church, defamed, will not find an immediate defense?[57]

A firm position would prepare the Catholic for battle. "If our voice is not able to make a believer out of an unbeliever," Veuillot argued, "it can make an apostle of a believer, like the stories and good examples of war, like the sound of the trumpet makes a warrior of a soldier."[58] Ultimately, however, it was dictated not by

---

57 L. Veuillot, i, 459 (1st quotation); 462 (1st extended quotation); vi, 372 (2nd extended quotation); Also, i, 427–430; v, 168–261; i, 529–541.
58 Ibid., i, 538.

any utilitarian considerations, but by simple duty. The Catholic's obligation was to proclaim the truth, in season and out of season, and to allow providence to take care of the rest:

> The truth is attacked, it is necessary to save our brother; the land of servitude is evil, the faith is lost therein, the soul is oppressed therein. It does not matter what floods and what dryness separate us from the land promised to our ancestors, and it is necessary to flee servitude. A way will open up under the waves, manna will rain down in the desert![59]

Veuillot claimed that the "dogmatic" moderate and the so-called pragmatic statesman prevent a solid, effective defense against the Revolution. They invite the radical enemy, who would not otherwise have been able to enter, into the camp and demoralize the forces of order. They always doom the society under their spell, preparing their own pathway to the guillotine:

> Those men have been labeled conservatives who, since 1815, have formed the parliamentary majorities that have been seen to fight the revolution, but for the profit of the revolution. The conservative majorities have not conserved anything. Gradually they have delivered everything and have themselves been delivered to the violent minorities that they have seemed to combat, but to which, in reality, they submitted.[60]

The third and final explanation for the conservative/Liberal Catholic danger is the dolorous fact that many of those who first prevented serious analysis of the enemy's thought, and, thus, opened the gates to the Revolution, eventually adopted the enemy's cause as their own. Such an outcome, Veuillot believed, was only to be expected, since vigorous belief always triumphs over the determinedly indecisive.

Two cases may be cited to illustrate Veuillot's arguments. The first concerns the journal *l'Ere Nouvelle* and its support in 1848 for Christian Democracy. Proper treatment of this subject requires a discussion of *l'Univers'* specific political stance.

Veuillot was never a legitimist in the popular sense of the term. True, at times, and especially later in his career, he was a fervent

---

59 Ibid., i, 459.
60 Ibid., xii, 236; Also, xii, 399–402, 445–448; xi, 497–499; xiii, 424–433.

proponent of monarchical restoration in France, but his interest in a specifically legitimist restoration was tied in with his understanding of its utility for the cause of Church and Fatherland.[61] An indifference to political form expressed during the battle for educational freedom conducted during the July Monarchy, when he indicated a willingness to support anyone opposed to the monopoly of the University {the name given to the centralized educational system in France—author's note}, continued to be official policy during Veuillot's long editorship of *l'Univers*.[62] "In the midst of a Europe agitated and upset by the clash of all systems," he wrote in 1848, and could equally have asserted thirty years later, "the Church is not especially absolutist, or monarchist, or republican: she is the Church."[63] Friendship for Catholic ideas was the sole determining factor in *l'Univers'* stance towards any regime:

> ...we reserve our homage and our love for the authority truly worthy of us which, coming out of the present anarchy, marching towards the new destinies of France, a cross in hand, will make it known that it comes from God .... We are only entirely hostile to the radical source of disorder, to impiety, to the vitiation of doctrines, to the frightful degradation of morals.[64]

Take a Don Carlos or a Henri de Bourbon and place him at the head of a legitimate Catholic monarchy: well-founded hopes of good government existed. Veuillot asked after the revolutions of 1848, "Who would not prefer to live under the absolute scepter of Saint Louis than under the fraternal musket of the democrats of Rome, of Berne, or Vienna or of Paris?"[65] Yet, deprive a monarchist state of this driving force and one would see its animation disappear and its defenses against its enemies broken. It was thus that the centralization of Louis XIV prepared the way for revolutionary despotism, that Louis XVIII failed to understand the true character of his age, that legitimists never seemed to attack the central aspects of the Revolution, and that their most favorable opportunities were doomed to failure:

---

61 Ibid., i, 429.
62 Ibid., ii, 7–11.
63 Ibid., iii, 381.
64 Ibid., i, 429; Also, iv, 272–275; v, 493–502.
65 Ibid., iii, 374; Also, x, 454–460; xiii, 15–18; xii, 413–415.

Re-establish the legitimate monarchy, give it a Chamber elected in the most favorable conditions, made up only of the most zealous legitimists themselves; let them impose upon the press draconian laws: there will be an opposition in several months, a Revolution in several years, if one waits several years.[66]

"If there are no more Catholic princes," Veuillot concluded, when once troubled by news of betrayal in the Spanish Carlist camp, "what concern to us are princes!"[67]

The same statements could be made with regard to republican or democratic forms as well. Place a Garcia Moreno, the Catholic Ecuadorian leader, at the head of a republic, and traditions could easily be reconciled with modern developments:

There is the conspicuous and supreme feature that places him beyond comparison: a man of Jesus Christ in the public life, a man of God! A little southern republic has shown us this marvel: a man sufficiently noble, sufficiently strong, and sufficiently intelligent to persevere in the design of being what one calls a 'man of his times.' of studying its sciences, accepting its ways, knowing and following its customs and its laws, and nevertheless not ceasing to be a correct and faithful man of the Gospel; that is to say, a correct and faithful servant of God. Moreover, making his people the same thing when he took control of it; a people correct and faithful in the service of God for all peoples of the earth.[68]

Let democracy be the expression of a Catholic desire to raise the people to their Christian goal of divinization; let democratic rulers respect the Catholic order and permit possible penetration by the Catholic spirit. If this were done, then a system that appeared to be fated to dominate Europe could contribute to that continent's glory. If it were not, then a terrible fate lay in store for the Old World:

Let the democrats be good, just, fearful of God: Democracy is the most beautiful government men can give themselves. Let the democrats be wicked, proud, impious: the society that they will form will only differ from hell in hell's being eternal. This

---

66 Ibid., iv, 314; Also, v, 15–22; iv, 353–363.
67 Ibid., x, 44.
68 Ibid. xiii, 189.

can be said of all the schemes tried among men to reconcile the necessary rights of governors and the inalienable right of the governed. They have been good or evil insofar as the one group or the other have had more or less the feeling of their reciprocal duties.

We have said it and we repeat it: a new era begins, fruit of the long revolutions which have troubled us. Democracy arises and the Church is there, like the mother around the cradle. She protects this infant which has so many enemies, she tries to enlighten this prince which has so many flatterers. Harsh and dangerous education no doubt! But the Church has made others, she has disciplined illegitimates as savage, she has tenderly served and faithfully loved more ungrateful pupils. Will she succeed nevertheless? God knows! If she does not, one trembles to contemplate the future of the world. What will become of these peoples corrupted by independence and each day more rebellious to all authority? What to expect of these unrestrained desires, these mad ambitions, these greedy passions, if not infinite miseries of an anarchy without end, of a despotism without chains, of a war without respite?[69]

In the non-Catholic democracy, "the art of governing reduces to the art of killing."[70] One finds in it "slaves expert in manufacturing masters for themselves, but who do not know how to nor want to destroy slavery."[71]

Veuillot complained of the failure of the editors of *l'Ere Nouvelle*, proponents of "openness" towards the Revolution, to distinguish between prudential and theoretical acceptance of certain of its fruits. He noted the journal's use of the word democracy as a talisman as it tried to convince Catholics that the "will of the People" could never harm them. *L'Ere Nouvelle* ignored the crucial fact that democracy meant differing things to different people:

> Alas! If one at least told us with what kind of democracy Catholicism must reconcile itself! Since, as we have noted, democracy is not one thing, one party, but a word; a deceptive word under which takes refuge and are torn apart one hundred diverse

---

69 Ibid., iii, 374 (1st quotation); ii, 353 (2nd quotation); Also, iii, 197–201; I, 246–250.
70 Ibid., xiv, 322.
71 Ibid., xi, 116.

programs, one hundred different parties, all irreconcilable enemies of one another.[72]

It then made compromises which seemed only to involve Catholic concessions:

> Does one discuss? It agrees with us on the facts, the doctrines, the final ends. At least it does not indicate others. And, nevertheless, it concludes in such a way that all Catholics are astonished or are grieved, while their enemies cry 'bravo.' It has a way of criticizing the revolution which does not make it lose the friendship of the warmest of revolutionaries at all.[73]

Finally, it became clear that, rather than the enemy, it was *l'Ere Nouvelle* which had altered its convictions, assuming that democracy and democracy alone could deal with mankind's "new needs":

> "What! New needs! For new needs, one requires new dogmas! Therefore, the supposed Christian revelation is not complete! Humanity has marched and Christianity remains stationary. Thus, Christianity is not divine! Democracy responds to the new needs of the world: thus true Christianity is democracy. Here is their argument. Why not cut short this dialectic in saying to them [the revolutionaries] immediately that the new need of humanity is simply putting into practice faith, hope and charity?[74]

The Catholic Party, Veuillot concluded at that time, "has not worked twenty years to extirpate monarchical idolatry to seed it anew; it will not any more seed that other idolatry, no less dangerous and degrading, that one has justly called the democratic idolatry."[75]

The second case involved the Comte de Montalembert and the editors and contributors to the journal *Le Correspondant*. Allies of *l'Univers* until the ascendancy of Napoleon III, they became the symbols of Liberal Catholicism to the intransigents. Veuillot complained that Montalembert refused to allow any discussion of the question of the validity of cooperation with revolutionaries and revolutionary institutions. Acceptance of the English parliamentary system, Montalembert's El Dorado, was, Veuillot

---

72   Ibid., iii, 379–380.
73   Ibid., iii, 459.
74   Ibid., iii, 382–383; Also, iii, 161–165.
75   Ibid., iii, 424.

lamented, axiomatic. "He made a crime of simple disagreement of opinion," the editor of *l'Univers* noted, "or even in remaining in an opinion that he had shared and sometimes imposed."[76] Veuillot's allies, like the Jesuits of *La Civiltà Cattolica*, who had regretted Montalembert's refusal even to read the critiques which they had sent to him with almost servile apologies, echoed the same refrain.[77] By definition, Veuillot's camp was attacked as being subjective, uncharitable and in error.[78] The result of this liberal intransigence, Veuillot concluded, was the gradual transformation of the earlier prudential use by the Catholic Party of modern freedoms into an unqualified affirmation of them:

> We said that the Church had a right to the same liberties as everybody, not that everybody had a right to the same liberties as the Church; that all the liberties that we demanded were of natural law and of divine law, good, necessary, legitimate, holy, not that all liberties that were demanded had the same character, the same title, and had to be decreed. Never was our liberty that of the liberals, still less that of the democrats, and never were they unaware of this. Whatever the danger of chilling their friendship, when accidentally and for a moment they were allies; whatever the danger of irritating them as enemies, we—M. de Montalembert and the rest of us—thought that the peril would be infinitely greater accepting or tolerating a single one of their errors. Our conscience demanded this, the interest of our party demanded this. The right tactic for us is to be visibly and always what we are, nothing more, nothing less. We defend a citadel which cannot be taken except when the garrison itself brings in the enemy. Combating with our own arms, we only receive minor wounds. All borrowed armor troubles us and often chokes us.[79]

Veuillot was always sobered by what he thought to be contemporary Europe's singular incapacity to merit the glory entailed by

---

76 Ibid., xi, 423.
77 J. Rao, *La Civiltà Cattolica* as a Background for Understanding Quanta Cura and the Syllabus of Errors (Unpublished Doctoral Dissertation, Oxford, 1977), pp. 120–127.
78 Rao, *La Civiltà Cattolica* as a Background for Understanding Quanta Cura and the Syllabus of Errors (Unpublished Doctoral Dissertation, Oxford, 1977), pp. 120–127.
79 L. Veuillot, v, 276; Also, vii, 266–293; iii, 564–568; iv, 370–376.

a Catholic restoration of the social order. Any society that had known and confessed the living God, and then abandoned Him for trivial rewards, had to offer unpropitious prospects for the forces of renewal. "Society feels itself to be dying," he wrote, and it "feels itself to be ridiculous."[80] Moreover, Europe was ill-served by her leaders. She was "a tragedy represented by mediocre comic actors."[81] These men demonstrated themselves to be bewildered by the appearance of each new—though readily predictable—revolutionary outburst. Their international cooperation was limited to meeting together periodically "to confirm their impotence, and, much more, their scarcely unconscious complicity" in the face of radicalism.[82]

Europe merited chastisement from non-western peoples. Her divine mission, for which she had been amply supplied with material blessings, was "to carry light everywhere, dissolve chains, awaken peoples sleeping in the shadow of death."[83] Instead of fulfilling these functions, she was responsible for ruining native cultures and replacing them with a sterile, materialistic civilization, all body and no soul. Could one not expect that the technology used to expand European power might be turned against the center of Machinedom, so that the rest of the world would come to seek in the old continent itself that which it had refused to share? "The paths are made, the frontiers are pierced, it will come."[84]

Veuillot's sense of the demonic character of modernity ultimately convinced him that reason was not to be the weapon fit to deliver the mortal blow to the Revolution. Reason had already been murdered by it in its rise to power:

> . . . [F]erocious pride is correctly the genius of the Revolution; it has established a control in the world which pleases reason out of the struggle. It has a horror of reason, it gags it, it hunts it, and if it can kill it, it kills it. Prove to it the divinity of Christianity, its intellectual and philosophical reality, its historical reality, its moral and social reality: it wants none of it. That is

---

80 Ibid., xi, 337.
81 Ibid., 336.
82 Ibid., 337.
83 Ibid., 339–340.
84 Ibid.

its reason, and it is the strongest. It has placed a blindfold of impenetrable sophisms on the face of European civilization. It cannot see the heavens, nor hear the thunder.[85]

If the Revolution were ever to be defeated at all, then, unless there were "a miracle, incomparable among all those which the world has seen since the establishment of Christianity," this defeat and the subsequent restoration would have to be completed "in those forges of the night that one calls social chaos."[86] Under these circumstances, only two types of leaders would be suitable for guiding the population back to glory, for loosening the revolutionary blindfold. One of these was poets, who, by disdaining the spirit of the times and cultivating order in the form of art, might kindle the flame of truth in dead souls.[87] More importantly, however, "that blindfold will only be pulled off by the mutilated hands of martyrs."[88]

---

85   Ibid., x, 45–46.
86   Ibid., xi, 338–339.
87   Ibid., vii, 469.
88   Ibid. x, 45–46; Also, viii, 571–576; xii, 333–335; xiv, 80–84.

3

The Barren Harvest of Protestantism[†]

LIBERALS HAVE ALWAYS SAID AMUSING things, but never so sidesplitting as they have done since they lost their knowledge of history. Monks were constantly among their targets, but now they attribute to them statements that only priests of magic-ridden pagan religions could have uttered. They consistently attacked the Inquisition, but their transformation of the Roman Law methods by means of which this worked into trials by ordeals more proper to German barbarians is nothing short of ludicrous. They have metamorphosized Augustines into pro-Nazis and proclaimed Hindu mystics to be mankind's most fervent defenders of individuality. I have even heard environmentalists, justly angered at the rape of nature, condemn Catholicism for being the chief proponent of that scientific utopianism which for centuries was the most cherished child of its enlightened liberal opponents. The only rule operative in this state of confusion seems to be that whatever is currently recognized as being good is, de facto, assigned to non-Catholic sources; that whatever is presently attacked as being bad is written down as a product of the Church.

The five hundredth anniversary of Martin Luther's birth provided liberal Roman Catholics yet another opportunity to join in this clouded ridicule of their Church and to misunderstand her history. It offered them another chance to betray the human race. How shameful, they cried, encouraged by those who love nothing better than a fight within the Christian ranks, that the Church repelled this great Reformation leader. How mindless of Rome, so brutally and sweepingly to have sealed his ideas with the most solemn marks of her disapproval. How joyful, they exulted, that fresh ecumenical winds had finally knocked down the fortress built to keep Luther out.

1984, the year following this outburst of remorse, may be the time to reflect upon just how ill-founded all such breast-beating really was. The Roman Church definitively repelled Luther and his

---

† Unpublished article of 1984.

followers all too slowly. She was often much too gentle and limited in her attack, even in Counter-Reformation days, not grasping how inhuman and universally hideous the consequences of their ideas really were. For a fortress knocked down by Protestantism is not just open to spiritual devastation; it is also one that is vulnerable to rack and ruin in every regard. The defeated defenders of this castle can nurture a bitter satisfaction in the fact that the conquering force ultimately tramples even its own goals underfoot. Indeed, Protestantism's seed yields a totally barren harvest.

The best outline for demonstrating this thesis is provided by the words of my previous sentence themselves: "Protestantism," "seed" and "barren harvest." An examination of each of these in turn will reveal the true horror of last year's ecumenical agape. Hopefully, this article will be helpful in teaching Catholics that truly progressive men interested in the real benefit of mankind must forever band together to reject Protestantism and the barren seed that it sows.

It is essential to begin by insisting that I am not anathematizing Protestants as individuals. Men are always difficult quantities with whom to deal. Even Luther, with his vulgarity, obscenity and pompous boasting, cannot be judged by us, or personally be charged with the developments that I will be cataloguing below. Historians cannot, ultimately, uncover the fullness of human motivation. Men are wont to lie, and, also, to misconstrue their own desires. Human beings are frequently irrational, and, hence, do not apply to their own lives the principles and corollaries of their most beloved theses. The original Protestants operated in a world formed by centuries of Catholic experience, and the power of custom, habit and pure inertia is very strong, indeed. Like Litvinov, the Jewish Soviet Foreign Minister of the 1930s, who crossed himself while boarding airplanes "because he was a Russian," Luther himself contradicted the consequences of his own notions because he was in many ways still a Catholic. Jeremy Bentham is said to have blunted suggestions that utilitarian, democratic rule might give birth to atrocities with the comment: "Englishmen do not act that way." Luther would have attributed my little shop of Protestant horrors to a vivid papist imagination. "Christians," he might have said, "simply do not act that way." He did not see the historical outcome of his concepts' application, and, hence, could not imagine them (until his last, disgruntled apocalyptic days, that is to say. But this is another story, to be tackled in a future article).

Finally, let us remember that practically no one in our unhappy age knows anything at all. Catholics have generally not got the faintest clue as to the meaning of Catholicism; Protestants are no different. Present-day Protestants are as much unwilling victims of Luther's ideas as we Catholics are. They cannot be attacked for supporting what they do not even understand. If ecumenism has been devised to appeal to the good faith of believing Protestants, to guide them lovingly back to the True Church, without rancor and accusation, then ecumenism is a good thing. When Christians are confused, then Rome must be loving and kind.

It is equally essential to point out that one must anathematize Protestantism. Protestantism as an idea stands on its own, unable to be manipulated arbitrarily, incapable of divided feelings and sentimental behavior. Protestantism as an idea is either friendly to Catholicism or not. It is not. It was bad in 1517 and it is worse today. When one meditates upon the foundations of Catholicism, he irons out the kinks and the seemingly dangerous aspects of its machinery. When one meditates upon the foundations of Protestantism, its inner logic makes it destroy Christianity and desolate the world. Ecumenism for the purpose of reconciling Protestantism with the Church is ecumenism with the demon. When Christians are obstinate, then Rome must be firm and authoritative.

What, exactly, is the "seed" of Protestantism? It is not the specific practices and preoccupations of given sects, most of which are either by-products of the basic seed or unimportant eccentricities. Rather, the crucial seed of Protestantism is the doctrine of total depravity. Luther's conviction that human beings are completely corrupted and incapable of pleasing God after Original Sin is the centerpiece of his entire theological edifice. It is only because of his insistence that men can never be purified, either in this world or the next, that the concept of justification by faith alone becomes necessary. If men cannot please God, through good works, the sacraments and sanctifying grace, then their only hope lies in complete abandonment to His will. It is only due to the total depravity doctrine that Scripture becomes the sole possible teacher of Christians. After all, the Church could be shown to have definitively opposed this doctrine throughout her history, while the Bible, freed from Rome's interpretation, might (with a bit of irrational force) be construed to support Lutheran concepts.

Anyone interested in the seed doctrine of Protestantism finds that Luther is ultimately not the man to explain it. Luther, in the final analysis, was a radical with many conservative kinks to him. He had, intellectually at least, a split personality, and does not appear to have been terribly logical. One has the clear impression that he stumbled onto only a few of the consequences of his thought, and these gradually and almost against his will. He seems to have accepted rather than embraced them, if such a distinction can be made. Moreover, his early dependence upon political support for survival quickly limited the development and prestige of Lutheran, or, as it is officially called, Evangelical Christianity.

The real sculptor of the total depravity doctrine is Jean Calvin, founder of Reformed Christianity. Frenchman, lawyer, writer and zealot, Calvin squeezed from the concept almost everything that a man could eke from it while still believing in Christ. Calvin also saw the dangers of the Lutheran political situation, and determined that Reformed Christianity would, if anything, subject the state to religious controls. His prestige thus rose among independent-minded men, and Reformed Christianity became the form of Protestantism that penetrated Europe. Litvinov, when told in Depression New York that snowplows had been abandoned in favor of shovels in order to provide more men with work, asked why spoons were not used to ensure total employment. Protestants, in a sense, asked the same thing. Why ought they to take the Lutheran *hors d'oeuvre* when they could have the Calvinist *entrée*? He who would know the doctrine of total depravity must look to Calvin.

The most important thing to realize about the Protestant seed is that it yields a barren harvest. Protestants thought that the concept of the Creation as a mirror of God robbed the Divinity of His uniqueness and majesty. So did the idea that men were the wounded lords of Creation who, with God's help, might someday be washed as white as snow. The doctrine of total depravity, which humbled the whole of Creation, and men along with it, did so for the purpose of emphasizing the glory of God. It succeeded in accomplishing the opposite. It began by insisting upon a view of the universe so dreary as to make men flee from the harsh God who allowed it as though He were the demon. Instead of magnifying the glory of God, it ended in His rejection. Secondly, the doctrine of total depravity causes those who are formed by it, yet flee from it, to leap back into a rule-less Creation. There exists no way to navigate a course through the Protestant Creation, no path avoiding the bad and leading to the good. All is wicked. True, there are those who take the opportunity to flee from the Protestant God to embrace a universe which they wish to be as perfect as they once thought it to be depraved. Nevertheless, the tendency of secularized Protestantism is to leave men rule-less and ultimately in despair. Ignaz von Döllinger, the nineteenth century German Church historian who later broke with Rome, irritated many followers of the Reform by demonstrating how the doctrines of contemporary Protestant preachers ran totally contrary to the immediate desires of Luther and Calvin. One could go further. The Reformation is in and of itself a principle of contradiction. It destroys man and it destroys God.

This theme may be developed with reference to a body-spirit analogy. Creation, for the sake of my argument, may, somewhat inaccurately be referred to as the "body" of existence, and God as its "spirit." The doctrine of total depravity has sought to humiliate the body, or Creation, for the glorification of the spirit, or God. Its effects have been the abandonment of the spirit, the body's declaration of independence from God, and Creation's collapse into rulelessness. It is essential to examine each of the four aspects of this humiliation in turn.

One might note, to begin with, that the doctrine of total depravity killed the "rhythm" of the body. Christ asked men to use their eyes and their ears to see and to hear. Catholicism did this, and realized that the human body followed certain rhythms. One of these rhythms was that of fasting and feasting. Most civilizations have recognized that men need to fast and to feast in order to answer a two-sided aspect of their character. Needless to say, man's animal nature does tend to pull him towards a desire to sit down to an eternal banquet, but, when he does so, he pays a psychic price that even natural human wisdom has abundantly catalogued. Pagans understood the value of self-sacrifice. Christ demonstrated that renunciation, built upon His abandonment to the Cross, was the pathway to heaven. Catholicism has, therefore, noted in the fast not merely a kind of biological necessity, but an instrument predisposing man to be receptive to, accept and merit sanctifying grace. Lent, and other periods of fast and abstinence, are naturally good for man, and supernaturally still more beneficial.

At the same time, however, life with God is not a fast. It is a heavenly banquet. Christians ought to recognize the joy and glory of living in the presence of the Divine Majesty. The feast day, marked at its mid-point by food and drink, song, dance and general merriment, is necessary as a most-fit means of emphasizing man's future reward. A feast answers man's longing for joyous abandonment, and prefigures the abundant love of God for His children. Carnival may be a somewhat raucous beginning to the Lenten season. The Easter merriment, however, is a perfectly suitable conclusion.

Protestantism's seed doctrine of total depravity attacked this rhythm. It could not see that anything in the human character might give direction to the Christian seeking God. Calvinist Protestantism emphasized the need for a king of permanent fast, not as a means of preparation for sanctifying grace, but because feasting made men believe that the world could provide some pathway to or foretaste of joy. A life of permanent fasting is not, however, a human life. Its dreariness caused men to flee from the Protestant God in horror. When they did, they discovered themselves in a universe which was thought by their ancestors to be depraved, and, thus, had been left ruleless. Imitating Luther himself, who tended towards gluttony, they were logically led to the *table d'hôte*. They behaved in its presence like performers in *La grande bouffe*. They had no measure for their indulgence. They engaged in a permanent feast. But the permanent feast obscures man's understanding even of his natural need to fast. It does so at least until such time as the misery of endless consumption ruins all his happiness. One can ignore the legitimate promptings of the body only at the risk of enormous discontent.

A second way in which the total depravity doctrine works to kill the body, or Creation, is by striking at what may loosely be called its "fuel." This "fuel" comes in two forms, that of thought and that of love.

Catholicism understood that human reason, like every other aspect of man's character, was good, though flawed and limited. It could not help but encourage the work of philosophers and theologians, even while recognizing that they would often err. One could compensate for such error, it argued, by submission to the guidance of the Church on matters of faith and morals.

Protestantism, in the total depravity doctrine, disdained reason along with the rest of Creation. It was frightened by the endless wrangling over philosophical issues that seemed to accompany admission of the value of the human mind, and felt it to be dangerous to a secure faith. It gradually recognized that a preoccupation with dogmatic theology was also harmful, in that it underlined the innumerable disagreements over specifics entertained by the legion of Protestant denominations. Protestantism, therefore, degenerated into a mindless form of Christianity. At best, it exhausted itself in pious practices, moralizing and social work, as though one could long remain in agreement even about their proper character without the active involvement and adhesion of the human mind. At worst, it became an insane religion, whose liturgy encompassed bodily writhings and senseless howling. In either case, the men of thought were shown that they had nothing, really, to tell it.

Those who did think were left with several choices before them. They could pursue their work calmly without reference to religion, being Christians with their left hand and intellectuals with their right. They could themselves reduce thinking to purely utilitarian limits, as though philosophy or theology were primarily practical, in a materialistic sense. Or they could, like those horrified by the permanent fast, flee in horror from the Protestant God. Those that did lose their faith found that they were left with no means whatsoever of rising above the "practical" realm. Faith gone, their reason could not help them. The world of thought for which they abandoned their God was God-forsaken. Again, it was so depraved that it had had no rules given to it. Rules would have meant that reason was itself salvageable. Left on their own, secularized Protestants were like children with too many toys on Christmas morning. They were allowed to play carelessly with their minds. Nothing—not balance, not harmony, nor Aristotelian logic—could really bind them. The intelligent man's adhesion to Protestantism tended to cause him either to assume that his thought should return some kind of cash benefit, or to visit the way station of pride on the road to complete irrationality and true despair.

The doctrine of total depravity also destroyed the fuel of love. It taught, first of all, that man was forever unlovable. Hence, man's love could never touch God, who arbitrarily chose who would live with Him forever. God's Law, according to this doctrine, must be obeyed simply because it was God's Law. It was not carried out because obeying it could ever please God in and of itself, and thus lead man to salvation, even with Christ's sacrifice as its backdrop. Moreover, human love was ultimately reducible by it to a purely material phenomenon, which could never take the form of a sacrament. Even the least radical form of true Protestantism understood that marriage could not be anything other than a contract.

Catholic-dominated nations tend to presume that law and love must correspond. Even though such societies may, at times, appear to be burdened down by a superabundance of laws, these proscriptions are disobeyed *en masse* when the law-love equation is not present. Protestant-influenced nations, in contrast, develop an odd form of legalism that often will not bend to the needs of human beings and to human love. Even though such societies may, at times, appear to be less regulated by law, their reaction to regulations can be rigid and exceptionless.

Two stories may be useful in illustrating my point here. Alice von Hildebrand once told me of traveling on a bus in Italy with her husband. There was a sign in the front of the bus prohibiting smoking. An Italian gentleman sat next to her enjoying a cigar. When Dietrich von Hildebrand pointed to the sign, the man simply shrugged and announced that he paid his taxes. When told, however, that Mrs. Von Hildebrand was physically troubled by smoke, he quickly extinguished his cigar, announcing that that, after all, was a different story.

The second vignette comes from German literature, from a tale entitled "Hans und Heinz Kirch." This is set in a northern German town of the nineteenth century. Heinz and his father Hans quarrel on the eve of the young man's departure on an extended merchant sea voyage. Hans refuses to pay the postage due on his son's first, long-delayed letter home. The disbelieving postman is accosted by Heinz's sweetheart, whom everyone knows. She begs to pay for the letter, read it, and return it. The postman sighs, and says that even the postmaster (even the postmaster!!) cannot allow this. The girl, sadly but submissively, files away without further scene.

Like the Prussians whom I met who were resigned to leaving train windows shut in 95-degree heat because the regulations insisted upon it, the bending of the law to love is understood by her not to be a truly viable possibility.

The loving man soon joined the thinking man and the man who appreciated the rhythm of his body in fleeing in horror from the God responsible for this sort of outlook. When he did so, however, he found himself in the ruleless universe left by the total depravity doctrine. Love lay outside the divine scope of things, and love had no rules when God was abandoned. Hence, men could logically behave in the manner justified by a Protestant friend of mine after he discovered women. This man had been literally disgusted by the most innocent displays of adolescent flirtation in his early youth. When women became a reality to him, however, things changed drastically. I asked him if he intended to marry. He looked at me as though I were a lunatic, and explained that the only thing that interested him was sex. This, of course, was nothing unusual. His views became interesting when I began to question him about his outlook towards sexual morality as a whole. He said that there was none. "Sex," he claimed, "ought to be left in the gutter where it belongs." Those who insist that there is no means of purification in life always tend either toward revulsion to love or ruleless indulgence in lovemaking. Once more, there is no real method of forging a pathway away from the bad and towards the good. Life must be all one or the other.

A third consequence of the doctrine of total depravity involves the stripping away of the body's adornment. Human beings are constructed in such a way as to pull them down into the mud or raise them up to the heavens if they "dress down" or "dress up." When beauty surrounds them, they assert the glory of God and the magnificence of their own destiny. When cheapness, tawdriness and vulgarity surround them, they adjust their understanding of the meaning of existence accordingly.

Catholicism recognizes that the outward forms of Creation are meant to shout *sursum corda* and raise man's heart to God. It understands that it can somehow find the best in food, drink, dress, music, art and architecture to lift man out of the drabness of a day-to-day reality that might otherwise exaggeratedly depress him. This it does in manifold forms. It finds whatever is good in the simple as well as in the grand, the small as well as in the massive, the subdued as well as the explosive, and raises the heart to God in different ways. Counter-Reformation, Baroque civilization, guided by the Jesuits and directed by their devotion to the greater glory of God, lay particular stress on the grandeur to be found in the Creation. It did this to answer the Protestant disdain for the universe. Hence, it filled everything from dress to architecture with vibrancy, color, gold and majestic beauty. Who could not think of the glory of God and of the possibility of Heaven when in a Baroque Church in the Baroque sections of Rome?

Total depravity denied the possibility of this *sursum corda*. Again, nothing on the wicked earth was seen to be capable of leading men to God. Many Protestants, acting on this principle, tried to steal from men all the finery in food, drink, dress, art and other realms that sought to embellish Creation. They stripped the environment of everything that could raise the mind to God. The result was not to glorify God by depriving the world of all that could compete with Him, but to cause His abandonment by depriving the world of all that reflected His beauty.

Some men influenced by the doctrine of total depravity understood that they were being swindled. Nevertheless, when they set about trying to redress their grievances, they did so in an unfortunate manner. A friend tells the story of a boy whose teacher takes him for an outing into town. When the boy questions the teacher about an innocent, attractive young girl that he sees, he is told that she, and everything that she represents, is "the devil." The boys at school ask him of his trip to town when he returns. He explains that the nicest thing that he saw therein was "the devil." Thus, if he is attracted to her, he must abandon God for the demon.

A similar fate awaited other unhappy victims of the total depravity doctrine. They saw a Creation left to be enjoyed by the servants of the demon. They understood the world of beauty to be their domain. Therefore, when attracted to the cultivation of beauty, they noted no choice but that of joining their ranks. Once they began to adorn the body of existence, they felt that they were inevitably working against God. They had become God-forsaken, and were no longer bound by any rules. All sense of proportion, propriety, objective value and reason in general were tossed out of the window. The doctrine of total depravity either leaves the

63

body in a vulgar state due to barrenness, or in a vulgar state due to lack of all classicity and because of atomistic insanity. Man loses in either way. He is dragged down to wallow in the mud.

The fourth and final fashion in which the doctrine of total depravity played havoc with the body was by attacking its structure as such. Catholicism taught men that they were part of a community, the Mystical Body of Christ, guided by the Savior through the Church authorities, and made capable of aiding one another in their path to God. Community and authority were shown to be absolutely essential to man's happiness and end. This Mystical Body was seen to be alive, death in Christ only strengthening a member's ability to act efficaciously within it. Its Cult of the Saints encouraged daily contact with the Immortals, and ensured a constant recognition of the existence of the supernatural. The world beyond was made a palpable reality in the world here and now. All legitimate communities and authorities were told that they, too, in their own fashion, could aid in the perfection of their individual members. They gave flesh to their goals and the virtues required to achieve them in the same palpable way that the Church gave flesh to the Christian message and the Christian way of life.

The immediate effect of the Protestant teaching was to reveal to men their existence as individual atoms, as slaves of an arbitrary God, as creatures incapable of helping one another to reach Heaven. Christianity thus became a purely personal phenomenon. Communities and authorities like the Church and its Bishops were, after all, no less depraved than man was himself. They could not temper an evil which they helped to encourage. "Atomistic" Christianity became a bookish religion, a phenomenon that lost its vibrancy on the date that the last scriptural passage was written. Protestant Christianity, reduced to this lifeless state, ceased to be a sociological force of great importance. Human beings need to see things in flesh and blood, and if they cannot observe a visible Church, with visible prefigurations of an invisible world, then Christianity is not taken seriously by them. Protestantism could not be seen, and it duly sank to secondary importance in the western religious scheme of things.

Alas! Secularized Protestants, wounded by the doctrine of total depravity, found themselves applying the same atomistic principles that had been used to destroy the Church to all authorities and communities around them. If the Church were pretentious in its claims to aid and perfect the individual, so were the guilds, the universities, cities, states, nations and families. All such bodies had to be subjected to individual whim, or even destroyed, in order that the person might face existence alone, as he was meant to do. Since men cannot face existence alone, however, and since they positively require communities and authorities to embody morality and human ends, the results of this general dismantling of the western communal structure has been utterly horrendous. Principles of economic justice, cooperation, learning, neighborliness, patriotism and parental respect have disappeared along with the institutions that gave them flesh. Men without bodies are not men. Human society without communal bodies is not human society. Atomized, secularized Protestant society is, indeed, the abomination of desolation.

Unfortunately, one need not look too far to discover some of the possible consequences of the doctrine of total depravity. The United States is a major example of a country subject to its influence. Our nation is the only crucial western nation that has not gone through an orthodox Christian stage in its development. Protestantism was its religious guide, and Calvinistic Puritanism particularly powerful in its formation. Hence, many aspects of American life reflect the four-fold killing of the body, flight from a harsh God, and plunging into a ruleless Creation that I have noted above.

Demonstrations of this truth can be found all around us. The United States has witnessed the impressive effort to enforce a permanent form of public fasting in the shape of Blue Laws, Prohibition, and similar phenomena. Revulsion by such actions helped to cause a mass exodus from God among Puritan-influenced men and in the Puritan-influenced system of higher education in our country. Rejection of permanent fasting has left us not with a balanced, Catholic view, but with a glorification of permanent consumption, of permanent feasting. A visit to a shopping mall or to urban areas of popular entertainment lead one to the conclusion that we are living a Mardi Gras with no Lent to follow. When this happens, there can be no real enjoyment, because the body's true rhythm is still ignored. The false gaiety of much contemporary

American life is symbolized by the drink once served to a friend of mine. It was not a wine, whose taste might please both God and man. Rather, it was a country stump juice, tasteless, colorless, and odorless, one sip of which sent him flying to the moon. From total abstinence, we have proceeded to total indulgence, without knowing even a minor interval of innocent pleasure.

Similarly, Protestant disdain for true thought has been instrumental in making our country one of the most "practical-minded" on the globe. Serious speculation is often dismissed here as entertaining at best, and insane at worst. Serious issues are frequently addressed by formulae as shallow and simple as advertising slogans. In contrast, practical matters, like dealing in real estate, are transformed into sciences rewarded by degrees. This has had three consequences for thinking men. Some have become Catholics and rediscovered the spiritual life. Many have fled the country to seek comfort elsewhere. Most have adopted the ruleless atomistic thought of secularized Protestantism, felt guilty as a result, and justified their philosophizing with reference to deep and exotic psychic needs.

Love has also suffered its tortures in our land. It is not at all difficult to understand why pornography and perversity are now respectable features of American life. How could a secularized Puritan culture rediscover the sacramental quality of something which it had so long shunned as depraved? Once God's Law disappeared as a restraint, this civilization had nothing left to hold it back. Ironically, one can now buy any debased form of literature in New York City twenty-four hours a day, three hundred and sixty five days a year, while a bottle of wine cannot be sold in stores on Sundays. The pleasure which is always bad is always permitted. The pleasure which can always be used in a proper fashion is not.

And what of the adornment of the body? The United States has constantly had a tradition of denigrating the elaborate as effeminate, and has divinized a drab conformism in dress, music, architecture, art, food and drink. Interestingly enough, as a French visitor once pointed out to me, the only time that many Americans do dress up is when they go to work, as though this were the only sacred liturgy of a practical, consuming population. Again, when the harshness of life developed from such a view became intolerable to those who detested the commonplace, the reaction was as bad as the disease. Functionalism was replaced by the ruleless behavior of psychotic atoms. The adoration of formica and plastic gave way to the adulation of formless sculptures, traditionless trends and atonal music.

Finally, where has there not been a clamor in the United States against substantive authority and community? Where have we not seen demands for a democratization of all institutions, and an abolition of their powers of coercion, both physical and moral? The glory of the atomistic individual is sung by our most important poets, justified by our most famous philosophers, and made inevitable by our obsession with economic growth. We have been punished by an inhuman way of life in our arid suburban shopping malls, on our freeways to nowhere, and in the trendy, childless, apartment houses of our cities.

Catholicism can be said to view the universe as an Unfinished Symphony. It calls an orchestra together under the vaulted hall of the heavens, and explains to the musicians that a composer has given them parts of a magnificent piece that he has prepared, in order to test their ability to play it. It notes that the entire symphony will be given to them only after successful performance of the first movement. The musicians work hard, though some do fall by the wayside. They begin to polish their instruments, put on their finest clothing, and walk with confidence and quiet pride as they realize the quality of the music with which they are dealing. They await the day that they will be given the rest of the piece with humility and with joy. They know that they can finish the Unfinished Symphony.

Protestantism never permits this completion of the symphony. It never permits its completion because it never permits its beginning. The musicians who arrive to audition for it are told that there has been a dreadful misunderstanding. They are assured that the music of the spheres can never be played by men. A disappointment overtakes them, they file out of the hall, and the heavens fall silent forever.

4

Portugal, Austria and Catholic Counterrevolution in Interwar Europe†

INTERWAR EUROPE WITNESSED POLITICAL experimentation on a scale that matched, and in some ways even surpassed that of the quarter century following 1789. Both revolutionary and counterrevolutionary movements, using whole nations as their laboratories, competed for the attention of the European audience. Specifically Catholic counterrevolutionary forces were also permitted their brief day in the twentieth century sunlight.

Portugal and Austria were among the few countries coming under the dominion of groups professing commitment to Christian ideals. They did so under different conditions, through the work of strikingly different men, and in the face of incomparably different obstacles. The language of their commitment varied. Each paid little attention to the successes and failures of the other. Yet both, together, reflect a tradition of Catholic thought that reaches back to Joseph de Maistre (1753–1821), a tradition continuously refreshed amidst nineteenth century struggles with "The Revolution." Studied in tandem, they indicate the common direction of all such thought, the wide divergences of style and emphasis that could exist within it, and, finally, the limitations affecting its potential victory.

Portuguese Catholics felt little affection for the Republic replacing the Braganza Monarchy in 1911. Republican liberalism and anti-clericalism, paralleled by the growing influence of nationalist monarchists like Charles Maurras, sapped whatever good will that may have existed. Opposition to a ubiquitous secularization was fostered by interpretations of the Fatima visions of 1917, which intimated Portugal's special role as a dike against the anti-Christian tide in the modern world. Opportunities opened for believers to combat the revolutionary hydra with the *coup d'état* which in 1926 placed the government in the hands of a junta led by General

---

† First published in *Faith and Reason*, Spring 1985, pp. 1–25.

Gomes da Costa. The entry of Dr. Antonio de Oliveira Salazar (1889–1970) into the government in 1928 as Minister of Finance, and his elevation four years later to the position of Prime Minister, represented a major victory for their cause.

Salazar, who remained in power until 1968, was an ex-seminarian and an influential member of Portuguese Catholic Action. A monkish bachelor all his life, he gained a scholarly reputation as Professor of Economics at the University of Coimbra, whence he was called to political power. Salazar's actions as Prime Minister so impressed many of his fellow believers that, as his own university argued, "the Catholic world acclaims him as its most eminent citizen."[1] American Catholic institutions, such as Fordham, granted honorary degrees to a man whom Coimbra described as the "priest and prophet of the new social order."[2] His reforms continued to be official policy, at least in theory, until the *coup d'état* in 1974 which toppled the regime that he inspired.[3]

Austria, struggling for a *raison d'être* after the collapse of the Dual Monarchy, nurtured an influential Christian social movement under the leadership of the priest-Chancellor, Fr. Ignaz Seipel. It fell firmly into Catholic hands, however, only after the accession of Engelbert Dollfuss (1892–1934) to Seipel's position in 1932. Dollfuss, like Salazar, a practicing Catholic and ex-seminarian, was otherwise quite different in character. A gregarious, indeed, ebullient man, he was born of Tyrolean peasant stock, was happily married, and had served during the war with distinction. Dollfuss was no intellectual, though he did gain some reputation as a specialist on peasant problems for the Christian Socials during the 1920s.

An opportunity for a Catholic counterrevolution in Austria appeared with a parliamentary crisis in 1933, after Dollfuss' assumption of executive power. The president and two vice presidents of the Austrian National Assembly resigned at this time in a dispute concerning a vote taken upon a controversial proposition supported by the German National Party. Parliament lacked legal procedure for filling simultaneous vacancies in all three chairs. The

---

1 Segretariado da Informacao Nacional, Bulletin (August, 1938), p. 20.
2 Ibid.
3 Hugh Kay, *Salazar and Modern Portugal* (New York: Hawthorn, 1969), pp. 1–50 for a description of Salazar's career.

Chancellor took advantage of the inability to reach a compromise to declare the legislature to be a victim of suicide, and to begin administering the country by decree. A moment had arrived for him, as for Salazar, to correct "the mistakes not of fifteen years merely, but of one hundred and fifty years of intellectual and political delusions."[4]

Dollfuss' exuberance made him a danger for the National Socialists, whose desire for political union with Germany was opposed by the Chancellor. The result of their enmity appeared in 1934, with, in Chesterton's words, "a set of horribly arrogant invaders . . . entering a place in disguise and butchering a poor little man . . . who happened to be fighting to keep one little corner of Germany still a part of Christendom."[5] His work was continued, under increasingly impossible conditions, by Dr. Kurt von Schuschnigg, until the Anschluss of 1938.[6]

Salazar was a rigorous political theorist, and, hence, may be invoked to provide the conceptual framework for what is to follow. Austrian divergences with his thought can be indicated when they appear. Certainly, there could be little disagreement regarding the chief goal that Salazar identified for the movement that he led: a root and branch extirpation of the entire liberal-leftist order of things, and, with it, the whole modern *zeitgeist*:[7]

> We are against class warfare, irreligion and disloyalty to one's country; against serfdom, a materialistic conception of life, and might over right. We are antagonistic to all the great heresies of today, all the more because we cannot see that any benefit has accrued through their propagation; for they have rather served the new barbarism by sapping the foundations of our civilization . . . .

---

4   Bundeskommisariat für Heimatdienst, The New Austria (London, 1937), p. 8; Luiz Teixeira, Profile of Salazar (Lisbon: Segretariado da Propaganda Nacional, 1938), p. 63.
5   London Times, 2 August, 1934, editorial page
6   J. D. Gregory, Dollfuss and His Times (London: Hutchinson & Co., Ltd., 1935), pp. 1–100, 189–191; Gordon Brook Shepard, Dollfuss (London: Macmillan & Co., Ltd., 1961), p. 186; Johannes Messner, Dollfuss: An Austrian Patriot (London: Burns, Oates & Washbourne, Ltd., 1935), p. 22; Dr. Kurt von Schuschnigg, My Austria (New York: Alfred A. Knopf, 1938), pp. 93–94.
7   Salazar, Doctrine and Action, translated by Robert Edgar Broughton (London: Faber & Faber, 1940), pp. 26, 29.

We are anti-parliamentarians, anti-democrats, anti-liberals, and we are determined to establish a corporative state.

Further attention must be devoted to three points emphasized in this declaration of intent, all of which eternally recur in Catholic counterrevolutionary literature: the materialism and barbarism engendered by modern political and social thought; the need to replace liberal parliamentary government with a more authoritarian system for the attainment of the common good; and, finally, intimately tied to these first two themes, the "corporative" ideal as the essential key to human freedom.

Modern materialism, Salazar insists, stems, ultimately, from an absurd effort to build a social order upon the foundations of "doubt."[8] This sin, most closely associated with liberal thought, is, he argues, endemic to the Left as a whole, discernable under the most luxuriant ideological foliage. It renders the attempt to fight one branch of "The Revolution" with another of its offshoots a dubious enterprise at best.[9] The abandonment of efforts to uncover the true philosophy of society, through the application of man's natural rational faculties, had not left the West without a reigning *weltanschauung*. It had simply handed it over, by default, to the mindless, yet tyrannical guidance of a utilitarian outlook that emphasized might over right, and bodily needs over spiritual and intellectual ones. [10]

Several examples of irrational and materialistic utilitarianism-by-default may be noted. One is the fact that the average liberal government, after speaking of the impossibility of learning the Truth, finds itself eventually to be compelled to reintroduce some substitute reality on rather flimsy foundations. It recognizes that without this substitute reality, society will crumble. Liberalism was "constrained by its principles to act as if [it] had none"; it was "driven to act inconsistently in order to exist."[11] Hence, the need for "attributing infallibility to the decisions of a parliament, the verdicts of a court, and the acts of an executive power," for creating the myth of democratic wisdom, and shaking the policeman's

---

8 Antonio Ferro, *Salazar: Portugal and Her Leader*, translated by H. de Barros Gomes and John Gibbons (London: Faber & Faber, Ltd., 1939), p. 29.
9 Teixeira, p. 63.
10 *Doctrine and Action*, pp. 24, 269; Teixeira, p. 58.
11 Ibid., p. 269.

nightstick at those unwilling to believe. Instead of remaining subject to a law which sought rational or divine pillars, modern man became the slave of matter, in the form of force. Liberalism and the philosophy of doubt inevitably evoked barbarian sanctions.[12]

A second example of the victory of matter over spirit in the modern world, more blatant than the first, was identified in economic theory and practice. Dr. Salazar discussed this point with reference to Portugal's limited capacity for economic growth.

No reforms, he argued, could transform Lusitania into Eden. Situated on the edge of Europe, poor in mineral deposits and farmlands, Portugal simply lacked opportunities for development on a scale equaling that of the rest of the continent.[13] Still, it was questionable whether contemporary Europe's vision of Eden was, in reality, as enticing as imagined. Her rejection of fixed moral principles gave her a purely quantitative measurement of well-being, a utilitarian standard "detrimental to and beneath human dignity," a subtle infection that ever increased her thirst rather than allowing it to be quenched.[14] European man had been tricked into believing that mountains of artificial and insipid consumer goods had become "dreadful necessities."[15] The "mechanization of life" was his frightful fate. Cities without souls, architecture without animation, luxuries without pleasure were the final, antihuman consequences of the "liberating" philosophy of doubt.[16]

Any truly solicitous regime, Salazar insisted, must turn its energies towards understanding the true, objective foundations of social order. Only when the real order of things was enshrined in law could justice and freedom be assured, and injury to man's rational faculties be avoided. Only when the true order of things guided the government could arbitrary methods forcing irrational substitute realities upon whole populations be rejected, along with "totalitarian concepts . . . which tend to deify the State, the People, a given doctrine or individual."[17] Again, it was useless to argue

---

12 Teixeira, p. 58.
13 Salazar, *The Principles and Work of the Revolution* (Lisbon: Segretariado da Propoganda Nacional, 1943), p. 14.
14 Segretariado da Propoganda Nacional, 1943), p. 14.
15 *Doctrine and Action*, p. 157; Teixeira, p. 51; Christine Garnier, *Salazar: An Intimate Portrait* (New York: Farrar, Strauss & Young, 1954), p. 109.
16 *Doctrine and Action*, p. 156
17 Ibid., p. 154; Ferro, p. 47.

that one might make an error in determining the nature of this real order of things. The price of eliminating possible error was the inevitability of backing, by default, into a barbaric, materialistic and anti-rational nightmare.[18]

Prime Minister Salazar was an academician, an admirer of Maurrasian Integral Nationalism, and highly conscious of the areligious character of the Twentieth Century. Hence, he often emphasized the way in which the Truth that must guide state actions could be determined by rational means. "We wish to organize and strengthen the country by means of principles of authority, order and national tradition," he argued in a characteristic passage, "in harmony with those eternal verities which are, happily, the inheritance of humanity and the sustenance of Christian civilization."[19] The impression given—and it is an impression legitimated by numerous Catholic natural law theorists—is that political science is primarily a secular enterprise. Yet such statements mask the fullness of Salazar's Christian inspiration.

This becomes clearer in his discussion of the need for spiritual awakening. Any lasting political and social improvements, Salazar insisted, any consistent application of the rational faculties, had to be preceded by a spiritual transformation of the individual. "Noisy" modern civilization could not ensure this, nor could Maurras, with his contention that politics was "the great factor in a people's life."[20] Salazar hoped to rebuild the life of the spirit in order to enable our reason to see through the materialist stupidities preventing the attainment of order and peace:[21]

> From a civilization which is returning scientifically to the jungle, we are separated unceasingly by spiritualism—fount, soul, life of our History. We shun feeding the poor with illusions, but we want at all costs to preserve from the wave that is rising in the world the simplicity of life, the purity of customs, the sweetness of feelings, the equilibrium of social reactions, the familiar air,

---

18   Segretariado da Propaganda Nacional, *Portugal: The New State in Theory and in Practice* (Lisbon, 1938), p. 9.

19   *Doctrine and Action*, pp. 96, 207–209, 219–221, 280; *Portugal: The New State*, pp. 9, 12, 17; Ferro, pp. 113, 176, 178, 247–248; Teixeira, pp. 58; Garnier, p. 207.

20   *Doctrine and Action*, p. 229.

21   Ferro, pp. 247–248.

humble but dignified, of Portuguese life—and through these conquests or reconquests of our traditions, social peace.

Yet how was this spiritual transformation to take place? Through clearly Catholic means, in recognition of the Church's role as the "mother of intelligence."[22] Public schools, recognizing "the singular importance of the Catholic religion in the molding of Portuguese character" would "take adequate precautions for overturning the corruption of morals," and teach orthodox doctrine "to pupils whose parents or guardians do not lodge a request to the contrary."[23] Mocidade, the Portuguese Youth Movement, would ensure "that Christian doctrine and morals should be a living force in the minds of the boys, springing from their own personal observation of cause and effect and of conduct of life."[24] Measures long desired by Catholic counterrevolutionaries were the practical path to spiritual renewal. Hence, the Cardinal-Patriarch of Lisbon's enthusiastic endorsement of the regime in 1938:[25]

> There has been, and is, a spiritual renaissance in Portugal. It is a miracle. The soul of the nation is born again in the grace of its people, who are renewing their energies at the source of all life. The Constitution of Portugal, while not officially Catholic, is based on Catholic principles, guaranteeing the freedom of the family, the Church, of education, and by that freedom, encouraging them to grow.

Chancellor Dollfuss and the movement that he led were also convinced that society could not be built upon doubt, and that the materialism of modern Europe was no answer to man's problems. They, too, believed that the spirit had to be reawakened in order to stabilize Austria. The chief difference from the Portuguese—a

---

22 Freppel Cotta, *Economic Planning in Corporative Portugal* (London: P. S. King & Son, Ltd., 1937), p. 185; Ferro, pp. 17, 23–25, 83; A. Salazar, *The Road for the Future* (Lisbon: SIN, 1962), pp. 179, 207; Teixeira, pp. 18, 59; *Doctrine and Action*, pp. 132, 229; Visconde de Alcobaca, *What Portugal Owes to Dr. Salazar: A Debt of Gratitude* (Lisbon: Editorial Imperio, 1935), p. 17; Bulletin (March, 1938), p. 14.

23 Ferro, p. 29; Bulletin, VI (March, 1938), p. 14; SPN, Portugal: *The New State*, p. 14.

24 *Doctrine and Action*, p. 163; Sydney Ehler and John Morrall, eds., *Church and State Through the Centuries* (Westminster, Maryland: The Newman Press, 1954, p. 510; Bulletin (May, 1940), p. 9.

25 Bulletin, (July, 1939), p. 5.

difference dictated by Austria's pressing need for a mass movement strong enough to resist the allure of Nazism—was the more open Catholicity of their enterprise. Dollfuss argued that Austria's new "imperial mission," following the demise of the old Empire, was to give "the example of a real honest attempt at forming a Christian State";[26] to make Catholicism "inherent in our public and political life" and manifest itself "as the formative factor in the development of the State":[27]

> I am convinced that it is the will of a higher power that we should maintain Austria, this land of ours, with its glorious history, though now on a smaller scale; I am convinced that this Austria is to give an example to other nations in the shaping of her public life; that we in this land of Austria have a great and valuable service to render to the German people as a whole. With us, to be German means also to be Christian at the same time. As the German people were once brought by Christianity out of paganism to the highest pitch of civilization, so it is our ambition now once more to realize in our German land a devout, humble, and truly practical Christianity. Perhaps the time may come when what we are striving to bring about in little Austria will also be achieved outside our borders, wherever there is a will and a way.
>
> We intend to renew the spirit of our country in the sign in which western Christendom was delivered from the power of Asia two hundred and fifty years ago; the simple sign of the Christian Cross.

For the Austrians, objective order was to be found in "immutable divine Christian law."[28] Political reforms were secondary, since "only Christ can save men's souls, and only He can help society."[29] "The greatest sin and most heinous crime" that the anti-clericals had committed was that of having trained "masses of the people" to become "irreligious egoists."[30] In recompense, the new Austria would "take care that children in public instructions receive a religious and moral education," and ensure that every teacher be

---

26 Bulletin (March, 1938), p. 14.
27 Shepard, pp. 99, 187; Messner, pp. 96–99.
28 Messner, p. 158; Also, pp. 99, 90, 181; See, in addition, *Doctrine and Action*, p. 246.
29 Schuschnigg, p. 90; Messner, pp. 55, 181.
30 Shepard, p. 187.

trained to "regard it as important that Catholic principles should prevail in the education of the people."[31] To promote the Catholic moral perfection of youth was to promote social improvement and sound statesmanship:[32]

> We want, with the help of grace and the Sacraments, to become better men. If our Catholic Youth Movement is so guided that {the young} will learn to avoid vice, {and} cultivate truly Christian charity from an inner conviction, then they will become a young and healthy source of an entirely Christian nation .... We must arouse within us a truly Christian spirit of endeavor. If we succeed in making ourselves real Christians instead of make-believe Christians, then I have no anxieties about the future.
>
> If they are taught what is the supernatural end of man: if they are told what they must do and what they must avoid; if, above all, they are taught the fundamental precept: 'Love they neighbor as thyself'; if children are brought up not on mere humanitarian slogans, but on Christian principles, so that they may become men of character, men with a sense of responsibility; then the State is most keenly interested in their education .... It is sound statesmanship to foster and encourage a life of religion.
>
> If you, my young friends, talk of taking your part in public life, let me tell you one thing today: just as you can only be a good soldier if you have learned to obey, so you can only take an effective and useful part in public life if you have tested yourselves in the virtues which are in the very blood of the German manhood; if you have honestly tried with the help of the means offered by our religion to become better men ...

Struggle against barbarism and materialism in modern life also meant encouraging only that measure and quality of economic progress that left a nation's spiritual life, intellectual goals and *esprit de corps* intact. Hence, as Salazar indicates, capitalism had to disappear. It had failed to recognize that "the statesman, the judge, the lawyer, the doctor, the priest, the artist, the professor, the man of learning are not mere ornamental flowers of a surface civilization."[33] Liberal capitalism had created "villains," plutocrats who "do not recognize the rights of labor, moral exigencies

---

31 Messner, pp. 62–63.
32 Ibid., p. 162; Ehler and Morrall, p. 503.
33 Messner, pp. 28–29, 162, 178; Also, pp. 12 and 145; Gregory, p. 340.

or the laws of humanity."[34] Economic rules of the game there might be, but it was crucial to remember that these had to bend "in accordance with the community aim," or, as Dollfuss argued, "to the law of love."[35] Individual property, although "a rational imposition of human nature," and "one of the essential bases of social preservation and progress," could not be allowed to work against the nation as a whole.[36] Its use had to be modified in such a way as to aid as many Portuguese as possible to become property owners themselves, and to act in a Portuguese fashion. Portugal, Dr. Salazar claimed, had to be reconstructed into "a more humane and Christian country," where "excessive and inhuman" economic ambitions were discouraged; a "middle land," one "where neither multi-millionaires nor paupers are possible." The best means of restoring property was abandonment of atomistic liberal capitalism in a way that did not encourage its collectivistic, materialist counterpart: socialism.[37]

Two methods of achieving the desired goal were emphasized by the reformers. These corresponded to the two remaining themes indicated above: anti-parliamentarism and restoration of the corporate ideal. Both are so closely entwined as to require their simultaneous discussion.

Anti-parliamentarism is obvious in both the statements and actions of the Austrian and Portuguese reformers. Dollfuss claimed to feel the "finger of God" in an enthusiastic peasant response to his announcement, after the suicide of the Austrian Parliament, that "nobody can say when it will be allowed to take up its dubious activities again."[38] And as far as Dr. Salazar was concerned:[39]

> The truth is that I am profoundly anti-parliamentary. I hate the speeches, the verbosity, the flowing, meaningless interpolations, the way we waste passions, not round any great idea, but just about futilities, vanities, nothingness from the point of any

---

34 Teixeira, p. 50.
35 *Doctrine and Action*, pp. 120–121, 195–198; Messner, pp. 68, 113.
36 Ehler and Morrall, p. 513; Messner, p. 113.
37 Cotta, p. 13 for Charter of National Labor.
38 Ferro, pp. 48–49; Salazar, *Road for the Future*, p. 148, 157–158; *Doctrine and Action*, p. 58.
39 Shepard, pp. 102–103; Schuschnigg, pp. 124, 137–138, 141–142; Dollfuss, p. 108.

national good . . . Of course, there are occasional ideas of value, but it is mostly just fine phrases, just words!

Aversion to liberal parliamentarism was due to the fact that it symbolized the fraudulence of modern claims to defend human freedom. Catholic counterrevolutionary thought understood man to be capable of perfecting his personality, living as he ought to live, and becoming "free" in the traditional sense of the word, only through a recognition of his social nature. The individual's elevation could take place solely in the framework of all the various associations "which spring up and are spontaneously organized in the heart of the nation," these "natural extensions of and supports to human activities":[40]

> Human institutions are not 'chains' for man to break through, impediments hampering the fulfillment of his aims. They are barriers to the vagaries of his liberty, a shelter for the frailty of his nature, a sure guidance amid the hesitations of his conscience, an aid to enable him to obey the laws imposed upon him.
> Each of these "corporations"—families, churches, guilds, etc.—matured man through the duties that they imposed upon him, and the vistas that they opened up to him. Each performed a specific function which could not as effectively be performed by any other body. Each mediated between the individual and the community as a whole, and for the benefit of both.[41]

The State, in this counterrevolutionary system, was meant to be both strong and limited, something which the revolutionary thought to be a paradox. Its guidance by the moral law and human reason rather than by individual whim made its foundation both firm and conscientious. Its submission to an historical community, the nation, which stood above the individual corporations, compelled it to see "everything in the light of its duty and capacity to save the interests of all." The State had to be vigorous enough to make an "unequivocal statement of responsibilities and duties," and to harmonize inevitable clashes among the various

---

40 Ferro, p. 244.
41 SPN, *Portugal: The New State*, p. 7; *Doctrine and Action*, pp. 30, 52, 232–233, 247, 272–273; Salazar, *Salazar, Prime Minister of Portugal Says* (Lisbon: SPN), pp. 28, 32; *Road for the Future*, pp. 83, 138; Ferro, p. 27; Messner, p. 72. Quotation is from Teixeira, *Portugal: The New State*, p. 59.

associations.[42] Yet the very vibrancy of the numerous mediating institutions was a constant protection against the State's becoming Leviathan. One had to be blind to the evidence of history, Dr. Salazar concluded, not to recognize that traditional corporate societies, harmonized through the action of a strong, rational State, had been beneficial to man:[43]

> The medieval institutions, attesting the cooperation between the sovereign and the subject, produced a well-balanced community enjoying the benefits both of liberty and authority. Under the traditional monarchy, a strong government did not run counter to civic freedom, which in politics, economic life, and society ensured the rights of the individual.

Catholics argued that modern "atomism," a "chemical solution of humanity into individuals, into grains of dust equal in value, into particles," had actually ruined prospects for personal and social perfection.[44] This "false conception of individualism," which dismantled corporate life in the name of human liberation, left man in an unnatural, solitary condition.[45] It released him, "manacled and powerless," either into the hands of strong and vicious individuals, who consciously profited from society's destruction, or into the grips of the God-State, which had been called upon to effect the end of corporate life.[46]

Perhaps a better expression of the counterrevolutionary view would be to say that the individual was handed over to a God-State, which was then manipulated by the strong and the vicious. This, indeed, is to many Catholic thinkers what the liberal parliamentary system appeared to guarantee. The liberal State was a "fiction

---

42 *Doctrine and Action*, p. 99; *Principles and Work of the Revolution*, pp. 8–14; SPN, p. 9; Messner, p. 125; Oesterreichischer Bundespressedienst, *The Constitution of the Federal State of Austria* (Vienna, 1937), p. 15.

43 *Doctrine and Action*, p. 183; Schuschnigg, p. 271; Also, *Doctrine and Action*, pp. 59, 96, 126–127, 219, 249, 251, 288–289; *Principles and Work of the Revolution*, pp. 8–14, 24–25; SPN, Portugal: The New State, p. 24; BFH, *The New Austria*, p. 5, Salazar, pp. 91, 107.

44 *Doctrine and Action*, p. 30; Quotation from SPN, *Portugal: The New State*, p. 7.

45 Mgr. Ketteler, in Ralph Bowen, *German Theories of the Corporative State* (New York: McGraw Hill, 1947), p. 85.

46 *Doctrine and Action*, p. 286; Also, pp. 20, 106; Teixeira, p. 41; SPN, *Portugal: The New State*, p. 11.

created chiefly under the erroneous principles of the last century."[47] It created a civil order subject to atomistic individuals "artificially disassociated from the interests and preoccupations which gave them their true place in the social scene."[48] It thus represented no real popular will. Limited by no moral law, it could do what it wished, guided by private and occult groups who were enabled to throw responsibility for their crimes onto "The People" as a whole. Hence, it fashioned the worst of possible systems, one in which the State did not make an unequivocal statement of responsibilities and duties, and one in which the true holders of authority were disguised and could not be held accountable for their actions at all.

Two developments symbolized this degeneration of the State in the eyes of both Salazar and the Austrians. One was the replacement, in the parliamentary order, of true associations by the "Party." The political party was nothing other than a "big employment agency where one struggled to queue up for the distribution of offices awarded when one's party was victorious."[49] The party was anti-national, keeping the population in a "state of feverishness and permanent excitement" which it "wasn't natural to expect from all men at all times."[50] It left the State in a "gloomy and mean melancholy" by magnifying "matters of secondary importance ... into scandals {true or false} that completely absorbed both time and effort." It posed as a friend of the people "to lead them to an agitation which [they] themselves [did] not desire."[51] Parties rejected a specific proposal, as Schuschnigg complained, "not because of its demerits, but simply because it was supported by the other side."[52]

Parties were aided by another negative force, the Press. This stimulated idle "democratic curiosity" in order to sell papers. It betrayed its proper mission to provide "the spiritual food of the

---

47 Teixeira, p. 61; Also, *Doctrine and Action*, pp. 247, 252–253; Salazar, *My Deposition* (Lisbon, 1949), p. 14; Also, Teixeira, p. 59; SPN, *Portugal: The New State*, p. 17.

48 *Doctrine and Action*, p. 120; *Portugal: The New State*, p. 11.

49 SPN, *Portugal: The New State*, p. 11; See, also, *Doctrine and Action*, pp. 106, 292; Schuschnigg, pp. 98–99.

50 Ferro, p. 145; Schuschnigg, p. 25.

51 Garnier, p. 206.

52 *Doctrine and Action*, pp. 92, 247; Also, Mack Walker, ed., *Metternich's Europe* (New York: Walker & Co., 1968), p. 121.

people."[53] Also a tool of "private and occult interests," it helped create a fraudulent public opinion that "complained of evils that do not exist."[54]

The common good dictated the demolition of this system. An "authoritarian government,"[55] a dictatorship of "Reason and Intelligence"[56] was required. Such a government would allow for "no arrangements or compromises."[57] It would be guided by a clearly pinpointed executive who would be set above the entire government and become "the moving force in the life of the State."[58] Executive organs would have "much wider powers than those which they employ at the present time."[59] The State had to be authoritarian, because "in innumerable cases the interest of the Nation and the interests of the regime become practically inseparable."[60] By breaking down the instruments of the liberal State, the dictatorship would be doing a favor to the population as a whole. No longer would government be "slaves to the opinion of the masses, which is different from, and of a much lower category than the true mind of a nation."[61] No longer would the statesman betray his conscience by flattering the stupidity of the mob. Truly popular government required a system which was neither influenced nor directed by the so-called masses, who cheer one day and "may rise up in rebellion next day for equally passing reasons."[62]

Hence, it was crucial to eliminate political parties, control the power of the Press, and abolish parliamentary rule. The first was fairly easy to accomplish. Groups "formed for political aims and organized for the conquest of power and the seizing of the State" were formally abolished.[63] This, as both Salazar and the Austrians insisted, included Catholic political parties as well as others. Such

---

53 Schuschnigg, p. 153; Also, pp. 98–99; Ferro, p. 176; Messner, p. 134; *Road for the Future*, pp. 121, 193; *My Deposition*, p. 13; *Doctrine and Action*, pp. 12, 14, 29, 292; *Salazar, Prime Minister of Portugal Says*, p. 60; Teixeira, p. 41.
54 *Salazar . . . Says*, p. 28; *Doctrine and Action*, pp. 30, 52, 247.
55 Ferro, p. 28.
56 *The New Austria*, p. 5.
57 *Doctrine and Action*, pp. 38, 127.
58 Ibid., p. 143.
59 Ibid., p. 251.
60 *Doctrine and Action*, pp. 99–100.
61 Ibid., pp. 106–107; *Road for the Future*, p. 184.
62 Ferro, p. 34.
63 Ibid., p. 37; Also, Messner, p. 139; *The New Austria*, p. 22.

parties were also subject to the innate corruption of this false institution, and better dispensed with than maintained. Their current members were urged to "transfer their activities to the realm of purely social action."[64] "Even our political phraseology will need revision," Salazar insisted, since "most of the words we are accustomed to use in our politics refer only to the past and will be inapplicable to the present. The old ideas, habits, political machinery and everything else will have to go."[65] Division had to give way to a superior love for the common good:

> We can quite understand that there may be people with an independent outlook, who without necessarily being any members of any political party, would occasionally disagree on this or that point. However, opposition parties, even if they should be friendly and kindly disposed . . . waiting for the Government to fall, are things of the past.
>
> We do believe the party system to be a thing of the past. But we do not think it would be in the interests either of the German peoples in general or the Austrian race in particular to replace the party system with a Party State. . . . If differences of opinion should arise . . . and threaten to cause a split in our ranks, the quarreling parties should shout in one breath: 'Long live our country.'

Similarly, "liberties" had to be regulated "with a view to their effective exercise as real freedoms and not the pomps of an abstract ideal that experience would again show to be unattainable." This entailed censorship.[66] Irritating and unjust to the few serious journalists as this might be, only censorship could ensure the expression of true public opinion.[67] Salazar complained:[68]

> In any case, I think it is very extraordinary that many should be so irritated by the barriers set up by constituted authority (who at least may be supposed to have the welfare of the community at heart) and yet do not raise their voices in protest against

---

64 Ferro, pp. 95–96.
65 Dollfuss, in Shepard, p. 108; Ferro, p. 142.
66 Ferro, pp. 100, 255; Schuschnigg, in Messner, p. 56; Schuschnigg, in *The New Austria*, p. 54; See, also, Ferro, pp. 95–96; *Doctrine and Action*, pp. 90, 144–145; *Road for the Future*, pp. 196, 211–213; Bulletin, XII (April, 1939), p. 6.
67 *Road for the Future*, p. 9.
68 Ibid., p. 142; Ferro, p. 152.

the enslavement of thought by huge capitalist organizations, by private and occult interests, by the brute force of wealth.

Both Salazar and the Austrians were conscious of the dangers of the dictatorship involved. The Portuguese Prime Minister warned of the temptations to which this regime "on the road to fulfillment" might be subject, especially if its officials were not "saints and heroes."[69] It could easily end by becoming a goal in itself.[70] The Austrians sought to establish a "clear dividing line between authoritarian government and forcible dictatorship."[71] "As in the peasant's home, the farmer must rule the household," Dollfuss explained, "so the public administration needs a ruler." Yet, "as in the peasant's household that rule must not be arbitrary if progress is to be made, so also in the government of the state there must be no arbitrary rule."[72] And one thing was clearly recognized by most contemporary Europeans: that the Portuguese and Austrian systems in no way entailed the creation of some reign of terror.[73]

The State's duty was to cry, with Maurras, "all that is national is ours—all this national by virtue of the end in view and of its spirit ..."[74] The State had to resurrect the power and effectiveness of institutions that were central to human and national character. It learned what these were through the natural law and through history. Only by encouraging them could individual madness be prevented, license avoided, and incipient totalitarianism thwarted. Corporations, each in their own field, could do properly what the State could not.

Certainly, both Portugal and Austria were true to their word in leaving the family a wide autonomy. "The basis of all society," Dollfuss declared in 1934, "and especially of every society organized on Christian principles, must be the family."[75] Salazar called it the primary organic element of the political order. The

---

69 Ferro, p. 28.
70 *Doctrine and Action*, pp. 238, 147.
71 Ibid., pp. 81–84.
72 Schuschnigg, p. 271.
73 Messner, p. 135.
74 See *Road for the Future*, p. 209; *Doctrine and Action*, p. 219; Ferro, pp. 65–66, 178 for further Portuguese arguments.
75 *Road for the Future*, p. 168.

Portuguese Constitution insisted that it would do everything to maintain its strength.[76] A "Family Defense League" was developed which sought to counter such concepts as feminism. Public recognition was given to the need for familial control of education.[77] Indeed, Salazar, who was opposed to female participation in civil life in general, encouraged female social action in the realm of education. Hence, his support for the Mother's Movement for National Education.[78] "Everything is based on the family as the [primary] unit of life in society," the Cardinal-Patriarch explained, in praise of the regime.[79]

The Church was also ensured corporate freedom, her autonomy sealed by the Austrian (1933) and Portuguese (1940) Concordats. Canon Law was recognized as binding on priests. Church rights to acquire property were admitted. Taxes could be levied by Church officials. Full and consistent protection was offered to her by the State. Catholics in Portugal were so completely recognized as being part of a unique corporation that divorce was not permitted to them by civil courts. Either they were part of a distinct entity with its own laws and commitments, the State reasoned, or they were not. And if they were not, why, then, had they contracted a canonical marriage in the first place?[80] Austria was seen by many as being so favorable to the Church as to be guided directly from Rome. Schuschnigg attributed this contention completely to anti-clerical sources:[81]

> The idea that the government was getting orders from the Vatican, or that the Vatican sought to exercise influence upon the administration, has been spread by the invention of fantastic stories, the purpose of which was to becloud public opinion, and prepare the ground for a feud against religion which might then be directed to political ends.

---

76 Messner, p. 135.

77 *Doctrine and Action*, p. 101; Ehler and Morrall, p. 510; SPN, *Portugal: The New State*, p. 13.

78 Ferro, pp. 235–237, 301; Bulletin (May, 1940), p. 9; *Doctrine and Action*, p. 209; Ehler and Morrall, p. 510; *Road for the Future*, p. 207; Garnier, pp. 7–8.

79 SPN, *Portugal: The New State*, pp. 14, 54.

80 Bulletin (March, 1938), p. 14.

81 Bulletin, XXVI (May, 1940), pp. 9, 6–7; also, *Doctrine and Action*, pp. 139–140; Ehler and Morrall, pp. 502, 514–515; Ferro, p. 234.

One step that neither country would take was that of officially re-establishing Roman Catholicism as the national religion. This was avoided, partly in recognition of the existence of non-Catholic groups within the body of the nation, and partly due to the desire to avoid resurrecting past conflicts.[82] It was one thing, the argument went, to be guided by the Truth. It was quite another for a single corporate entity, the Church, to be given extraordinary privileges within the State. All that the Church required was the kind of full corporate freedom that corporatism in general promised; nothing more and nothing less. Salazar, criticized severely by many of his fellow Catholics for his failure to relent on this point, defended himself vigorously:[83]

> Such things can and must be so . . . It must be so because political activity corrupts the Church, either when she wields it or suffers its effects, and it is to the general good of all that sacred things and persons be handled as little as possible by profane hands or agitated by mundane interests and passions. I consider it dangerous for the State to arrogate to itself such power that it can violate heaven; equally do I think it unreasonable that the Church, on the grounds of the higher value of spiritual interests, should seek to increase her actions to the point of interfering with those things which the very Gospels declare to belong to Caesar.
>
> Both sides would have failed to have learned the lessons of the past if they had not become aware how privilege can corrupt, how protection can lead to the trimming of essential liberties; how a religious policy can deviate from the defense of the interests of the Church and seek other ends which impair the legitimate action of the State, and which, therefore, the latter cannot countenance.

It is important to grasp the full import of Salazar's argument. This can only be achieved by understanding it in the context of his other pronouncements. Salazar does not mean that the State ought to make believe that Catholic teachings do not concern it. Rather, he is speaking of the serious danger of what I have elsewhere

---

82 Schuschnigg, pp. 256–257; also, p. 269; Dollfuss, p. 233; Messner, pp. 160, 173; Julius Braunthal, *The Tragedy of Austria* (London: Victor Gollancz, Ltd., 1948), pp. 205–208; Cicely Hamilton, *Modern Austria as Seen by an Englishwoman* (London: J. M. Dent & Sons, Ltd., 1935), pp. 84–85.
83 Garnier, pp. 162–164, 168; Teixeira, p. 40.

labeled "back-door secularization," through which Catholic Action becomes too closely tied with purely political parties, decisions or ideologies. Salazar was partly worried that the proclamation of the reestablishment of the Church would convince Catholics that Portugal had been magically purified by this basically rhetorical action alone. The State could then justify all its future decisions by insisting that it was, after all, Catholic, because a document claimed that this was so. All its measures would take on a doctrinal flavor, as though Catholics must agree with them as articles of faith. Similarly, the State could find that its legitimate autonomy would be hampered by the clergy's attempt to guide the so-called Catholic government, even though the priestly charism gave it no special protection in such an enterprise. Better that the Church should devote her energy to putting her own house in order; this alone would give her proper influence over the State, as a teacher. Were she to equate the New Portugal with Catholicism, then the body of the faith would have to be expanded to incorporate positions on all kinds of issues on which the Magisterium had no supernaturally-granted right or need to speak.

One of the most crucial undertakings in the entire enterprise of rebuilding corporate order, one upon which the greatest stress was placed by the reformers, was that of introducing it into economic life.[84] State interference in economics, beyond obvious measures such as the control of foreign investment, ownership of basic industries fundamental to national survival, and general principles regarding minimum wages and maximum prices, could be disastrous. "Real progress can only be achieved when the State is prepared to abandon all forms of activity which can best be performed through private channels," Salazar argued; "the maintenance of healthy social conditions depends on allowing a wide margin of liberty to private initiative . . ."[85] There existed a real danger with bureaucratic regulation that "gradual extension of such control may embrace spiritual and intellectual values, the emotions and family life."[86]

---

84 Bulletin, XXVI (May, 1940), p. 5; Garnier, pp. 162–164, 168; Teixeira, p. 40.
85 Doctrine and Action, pp. 122, 193–194, 343; Ehler and Morrall, p. 513; SPN, Portugal: The New State, p. 12; Teixeira, pp. 48–51.
86 Doctrine and Action, pp. 122, 168, 343.

A modern corporate system, a modified replica of medieval guild life, could, Salazar believed, solve many problems simultaneously. Through it, the State could be enabled "to reap the benefits of all its productive forces and to uphold private property, personal initiative and legitimate competition ... "[87] A commercial life with corporate institutions would mean an "auto-economy," a "self-directed economic system." The State could intervene in this only "to see that the law was duly observed,"[88] and then as a "teacher or trainer," or a "representative of the mass of consumers, whose interests it would harmonize with those of producers."[89] Unrestricted capitalism, Italian and German statism, socialism and communism, might all be avoided in one fell swoop.[90]

The Austrians emphasized the same benefits, but, again, always in a more openly pious tone. "The plan," Kurt von Schuschnigg wrote, was "that by progressive development, the State would be relieved from dealing with those affairs which the corporations were in a position to deal with themselves in their own sphere of influence."[91] Austrian corporatists laid stress on the value of the guild as an instrument for ending the class struggle.[92] Dollfuss indicated that the employer and worker would be linked together in it like the peasant and his helpers round the dinner table after a day's work on the farm. Their union would be still more firm, he added, if, as in the peasant's family, their day were ended with the Rosary. Guild solidarity would ensure the worker's sense of dignity, and, indeed, would give him a kind of property of his own to cherish. The humanity and intimacy provided by the guild, its incorporation of the "law of love,"[93] its efficacy as a religious instrument of perfection, appealed to his Christian conscience.[94] Indeed,

---

87 *Doctrine and Action*, p. 343; Also, pp. 16, 120, 122, 145, 166–167, 196–197, 249, 342; Teixeira, p. 56; *Principles and Work of the Revolution*, p. 24; Cotta, p. 13; Dollfuss, p. 20; Messner, p. 60.
88 *Doctrine and Action*, pp. 22–23; 160.
89 SPN, *Portugal: The New State*, p. 9; *Doctrine and Action*, p. 23.
90 Cotta, p. x; Also, *Doctrine and Action*, pp. 145–146, 161, 342.
91 *Doctrine and Action*, p. 22; Also, pp. 39, 166; *My Deposition*, p. 18; SPN, *Portugal: The New State*, p. 14; Cotta, p. 12; Bulletin (February, 1938), pp. 10–11; (March, 1938), pp. 4–5.
92 Schuschnigg, p. 270.
93 Braunthal, p. 189; Messner, p. 153; also, *Doctrine and Action*, pp. 39, 164.
94 Messner, p. 145.

Dollfuss always associated the Austrian corporative effort with Pope Pius XI's encyclical letter, *Quadragesimo Anno* (1931), which he went so far as to commend to the League of Nations from the speaker's podium at Geneva.[95] This encyclical, he said, contained the "principles of a reform of society which [was] to lead to the overcoming of materialism and the solution of the social question irrespective of religious creed."[96] The end result of corporate order was that "all would take pleasure in [their] work . . . and realize that it {was} harmony and not the stirring up of dissension among men that [made] everybody happy and contented."[97]

Dollfuss claimed that Austria's efforts to realize this seemingly utopian vision would be useless unless "the whole people {became}, as it were, actuated with the new spirit which was] to animate the new Constitution."[98] Yet too many opponents of Catholic corporatism haunted the Austrian political scene to make this saturation possible. National Socialists, for whom Dollfuss' Christian Austrian mission was a serious obstacle to Anschluss, were uncooperative. The Chancellor's non-Catholic allies in the Heimwehr, a nationalist organization which also called for a corporate State, were susceptible to Nazi propaganda, and little moved by religious rhetoric.

Dollfuss exerted much energy trying to win to his cause supporters of the Social Democratic Party whose power he had crushed, and whose leaders viewed him as a "clerico-fascist." "We meet you not with contempt or distrust," he insisted in one of his many speeches to labor.[99] We have established a "fundamentally Christian" constitution, containing "all the elements of the best and purest social philosophy."[100] We wish to provide not merely the necessities of life, but also "the power to believe that Christian charity is truly a living thing which embraces all men."[101] There is, the recurring theme runs, no need for class struggle in a corporate society:[102]

---

95 Messner, pp. 135, 145, 129, 154; Also, 60, 153; Dollfuss, in Gregory, p. 329; Dollfuss, p. 31.
96 Messner, pp. 119, 122; Schuschnigg, p. 213.
97 Schuschnigg, p. 213.
98 Messner, p. 130.
99 Ibid., p. 165.
100 Ibid., p. 74.
101 Ibid., p. 153.
102 Ibid., pp. 67–68.

At a time when the employment of labor was organized wholly according to Liberal and Capitalistic principles, it was intelligible—though unjust according to our Christian conceptions—that on the other side class warfare should have been taken as the basis for the defense of the worker. But if among employers of labor there is a sincere readiness to cooperate in the new political, economic and social constitution, a readiness to take as the foundation of social and economic life the relation of man to man, viewed at a new angle and regarded as the source of mutual duties and obligations, then the antithesis of class warfare no longer exists, and labor must seriously consider whether it is not its duty to show a sincere readiness to cooperate in the new order of things.

The political situation in Austria, as Erik von Kuehnelt-Leddihn once wrote to me, may have made the corporate experiment in that country a "dead letter" from the beginning.[103] The Portuguese, protected by their somewhat isolated geographical position from the vicissitudes of interwar turmoil, had more chance to construct the corporate economic order carefully. Here too, however, results were mixed, any good ones completely negated by the military coup of 1974.

Salazar urged the introduction of the corporate economy slowly, "so as not to try a system which has not yet been adequately tested:[104]

All new establishments which lack experience... must be built up slowly and laboriously. It is always difficult to apply novel principles to old societies with ingrained habits and a different outlook. Indeed, it is so difficult as to appear impossible to those persons who cannot brook delay... Revolutions, to be profound and human, require many years of resolute application and genuine revolutionary laws, for only when the real mind of the people is attained can the movement be said to have reached its objective. In the same way, though it is not absolutely impossible to regulate production, and to set up definite boundaries and channels of development, the effective

---

103   Ibid., 67–68.
104   Braunthal, pp. 186, 194; Joacquin Azpiau, S. J., *The Corporative State*, translated by the Rev. William Bresnaham, OSB (St. Louis: B. Herder Book Co., 1951), pp. 83, 121; *The New Austria*, p. 22; Schuschnigg, pp. 82–137, 208; Hamilton, pp. 25–26; Messner, p. 149 for the Austrian dilemma.

and affective collaboration of the various classes and branches of production in a country where competition and speculation were reckoned inseparable from trade, can be secured only with great difficulty and with endless patience.

A rather detailed framework for this slow but steady establishment of corporative order, an outline frequently altered, was in place by the mid-1930s.[105] "Pre-corporative" programs were undertaken and propaganda campaigns mounted. Ultimately, each given enterprise in industry was to possess a workingman's syndicate (Sindicato Nacional) and an employer's association (Gremio). These would repudiate all the classic instruments of the liberal capitalist order, such as lockouts and strikes, as well as reject the Marxist concept of class warfare. The various syndicates of a specific large-scale industry were to be linked together in "federations," and the employers' associations into "unions." In the last analysis, all together would be joined in a given guild. Functions such as aiding the sick and serving as clearing houses for employment would also be performed by these entities. Labor courts, under the guidance of the National Institution of Labor and Providence, would settle disputes that might develop.

Special institutions, such as the National Foundation for Joy in Work, were also formed, partially to spread propaganda for the New Order. They were created to stimulate "the atmosphere of pure idealism" in which the syndicates were created; "to keep burning the flame of enthusiasm and of confidence which the social concept of the new Corporate State rekindled in the soul of the working classes."[106] Their function was also to "aid the leisure of the Portuguese workers in such a way as to ensure for them the greatest physical development and the raising of their intellectual and moral level."[107] Casas de Povo in rural regions, and Casas dos Pescadores, among fishermen, were designed for similar purposes, the aim of preserving national traditions always being emphasized. Hence, with respect to the latter:[108]

---

105 *Doctrine and Action*, p. 21; Ferro, p. 17.
106 Ferro, p. 276; Morrall and Ehler, p. 513; SPN, *Portugal: The New State*, pp. 38–39, 41; Cotta, pp. 16–17, 19–21, 21–22, 153.
107 Bulletin, I (May, 1937), pp. 8–9; X (February, 1938), pp. 63–64, 77–85; 102–103, 110–111; Cotta, pp. 155–160 164–169.
108 Ferro, p. 19; Cotta, pp. 155–160, 169–171.

With regard to education, it will be the duty of these associations to set up schools for the children of fishermen so as to give them a good all-round education which, in time, will contribute to the raising of their standard of living; local traditions and customs will be piously preserved and proper respect will be paid to those religious beliefs which are so strong in the hearts of the fishing population of Portugal.

Two major problems continuously afflicted the Portuguese in their corporate endeavors. The first was the statism that Salazar himself dreaded. A system designed to lessen State interference in daily life seems to have permitted its intrusions to have grown. This tendency was already clear in the pre-corporative stage of the plan. Ministers of Agriculture and Commerce and Industry were allowed to intervene regularly in corporate life. An Under-secretary of State for Corporations, operating under the aegis of the National Institute for Labor and Providence, was ubiquitous. A Corporative Council that included Salazar and many other ministers became the ultimate watchdog of the entire system. Bureaucratic interference on such a major scale was perhaps inevitable, given the fact that the reformers were attempting to reintroduce artificially something which had grown up spontaneously in the Middle Ages. In any case, they themselves often recognized how "inorganic" their construct was. Salazar admitted that "floods of complaints" came into his office regarding bureaucratic errors and staff inefficiencies. Although he claimed not to be surprised by such criticisms, he did express concern that "they should be repeated without any satisfaction being given."[109]

A second problem, giving the lie to the enthusiastic language of much Portuguese propaganda, was that of lack of cooperation. Salazar indicated, in 1937, that he was pleased enough with the growth of syndicates. These had understandably grasped their aims and duties, given that "those who own little are always unselfish." Gremios, however, he complained, left much to be desired. "Instead of entering into the spirit of the corporative state," he argued, some "may have tried to drive away probably competitors" through their

---

109 SPN, *Portugal: The New State*, pp. 40–41; Ferro, p. 19; Bulletin, II (August, 1937), pp. 11–12; *Doctrine and Action*, pp. 29, 160; Bulletin, I (May, 1937), pp. 8–9; (August, 1938), p. 3; Cotta, pp. 161–163.

structures.[110] Indeed, a number of people, he chided, "have thought that the corporative organization would be a means of multiplying middlemen, removing competition, and safeguarding against all comers the positions acquired by some . . ."[111]

Lack of cooperation in agriculture was especially blatant and irksome. It had proved to be extremely difficult to fit Portuguese agriculture into the corporate structure, due to uncertainty regarding its organization on a geographical or crop basis. By 1937, however, farmers' associations were established on a district foundation. These were then gradually combined into regional entities. Bitterness due to ineffectiveness was always near the surface. Salazar called farmers "by nature selfish and self-sufficing."[112] Farm workers could not see the need for cooperation with those outside of their districts, and landlords would not pay the minimum contribution demanded for participation in the corporate entity. Proprietors, ultimately, were obliged to take part in agricultural bodies, since "in matters of this kind, experience has taught that it is not good enough to trust man's better nature."[113] Still, by the end of the thirties, "no perfect form" of agricultural order had been discovered.[114] None would ever be found.

This renewed corporate order was meant to give a sounder representation of the popular will than any atomistic parliament. Hence, its structure was to be reflected in the political order:[115]

> It is our intention to establish the social and corporative State in close correlation with the natural constitution of society. The families, the parishes, the municipalities, the corporations wherein all citizens co-exist in possession of their fundamental juridical liberties, are the components of the nation and as such should have direct intervention in the constitution of the supreme bodies of the State; this is the most accurate definition of the representative system.
>
> This Constitution must take account of the natural organization of the people, ensure that all estates alike will have an

---

110 *The Road for the Future,* p. 90.
111 Ferro, pp. 20–21.
112 Ibid.
113 Ferro, p. 19.
114 SPN, *Portugal: The New State,* pp. 40–41; Ferro, p. 19.
115 *Portugal: The New State,* p. 40; Also, Bulletin (August, 1937), pp. 11–12; Cotta, p. 103; *Doctrine and Action,* pp. 29, 160, 243.

active part in the conducting of public affairs, while avoiding all those obstructions to legislation arising from the inadequacy of the present Constitution. Such popular representation, being the symbol of the organic life of the community, thus does justice to the State as the visible expression of that organic life.

Accordingly, as the latter develops, the state will more faithfully reflect the nation as an organized whole, while the part played by the individual in the creation of such assemblies will correspond more closely to the part he plays in the national life as head of a family, producer, member of a Church, or in his connection with education, public assistance or sport. This may be described as the 'Policy of Real Life.'

Salazar, for whom parliaments were designed for "ratification of the general fundamentals of juridical rules,"[116] made it clear that this representation would be purely consultative:[117]

In the first place, whatever may be the scope of vested interests in the corporations, there will always be lacking in them the representation of national interests . . . Secondly, because it would be most dangerous without the long preparation acquired by experience, for a particular interest to be defended by, or its activities defined, either by other vested interests or in collusion with them.

The result was that both Portugal and Austria established limited corporative representative institutions. Portugal did not manage to abolish its traditional parliament completely, much to Dr. Salazar's regret:[118]

In fact, a parliament frightens me so much that while I recognize the necessity of our new Constitution, I am just a little afraid of what may come of it. There are three months of the year when you've got to listen to parliamentary debates . . . The present Council of Ministers is good enough for me: it is a small parliament in a way, and it is also useful and does something.

Nevertheless, a Corporative Chamber, including representatives of Lisbon and Oporto, various state administrative agencies, presidents

---

116 *Doctrine and Action*, p. 103; Messner, p. 139; *Doctrine and Action*, p. 39; Also, Ferro, p. 242.
117 *Doctrine and Action*, pp. 99–100.
118 Ibid., p.253.

of corporations and other national interests was created. A ceremonial Head of State, chosen through families, was also established.

Austria formed a Bundesversammlung composed of four distinctive consultative organs representing economic activities, provinces, cultural entities and national interests as a whole. This advised the Bundestag, which was itself made up of representatives of the Bundesversammlung. A ceremonial Head of State, elected by Bürgermeisters from across the country, presided over the whole structure.[119]

New forms of articulating popular interest in government, based on the principle of national solidarity, were also forged.[120] The Mocidade, the Portuguese Legion,[121] and the National Union under Salazar; the Fatherland and Patriotic Fronts in Austria, were all expressions of this desire to stimulate non-partisan concern for the affairs of the nation:[122]

> The National Union was established on a ground sufficiently broad in outlook to admit all Portuguese of good will, irrespective of their political and religious needs, provided only that they should accept the existing institutions and be prepared to defend the principles of our national reconstruction.
>
> Whatever happens ... the National Union must not give up its purely national and patriotic mission and allow itself to become imbued with the spirit of partisanship. It would be criminal and even ridiculous to have yet another party the object of which would be to oppose the principle of party.
>
> The Patriotic Front does not represent a single movement of reconstruction. Freed from the party restrictions of former times, we want to unite all men, irrespective of party, who recognize Austria as their Fatherland, in order to renovate this country constitutionally, socially and economically.
>
> He who wears this ribbon [of the Fatherland Front] pledges himself to bring it about that every individual member and every organization in the Patriotic Front shall have one end in view: Austria.

---

119 Ferro, p. 244.
120 Ehler and Morrall, pp. 503–507; OB, *The Constitution of Austria*, pp. 41–45; SPN, *The Constitution of Portugal*, pp. 24–28, 38–42; Messner, pp. 143–144; Garnier, p. 100.
121 *Road for the Future*, pp. 123–124.
122 Bulletin, (May, 1938), p. 8; SPN, *Portugal: The New State*, p. 50.

The Fatherland Front will be built on the leader principle... The Fatherland Front aims at non-partisan union of all patriotic Austrians to serve the peaceful, cultural and economic development of a free, independent Austrian state.

These groups, like corporate entities and the attempt to develop corporative parliaments, were often ineffective due to statism, partisanship and improper preparation. [123]

There is no doubt that there were enormous problems with the Portuguese and Austrian experiments, from both a Catholic as well as a purely political standpoint. Several of these have been indicated above. They would not have been human experiments if such problems had not existed.

Nevertheless, insofar as anything could be done to Christianize the political order in twentieth-century Austria and Portugal, both these nations attempted it. Insofar as anything could be done to achieve a Catholic cleansing of modernity without falling into the same ideological and intellectual errors as the enemy, Salazar appears to have outlined it.

But ultimately, as this brilliant thinker repeatedly indicated, the Christian statesman faced two almost insurmountable difficulties in a land like his own in the present age. One was the fact that small nations were practically helpless in setting goals for themselves when the large powers were indifferent and hostile to them. And more importantly still, the western world had lost its taste for truth, honor and glory. Perhaps forever. [124]

---

123 *Doctrine and Action*, pp. 133, 109; Messner, pp. 101–102; Braunthal, p. 190; Also, SPN, *Portugal: The New State*, p. 50; Bulletin (May, 1938), p. 8; *The New Austria*, p. 56; Dollfuss, pp. 72–74.
124 Shepard, pp. 107, 168; Schuschnigg, p. 282; Hamilton, pp. 84–85; Braunthal, p. 189.

5

The Divinization of Democracy and the Question of Human Rights†

A NY SERIOUS DISCUSSION OF DEMOCRACY in the West in modern times is an extremely difficult matter, one to be approached in fear and trembling, because it involves treatment of a subject which has taken on a distinctly religious character. The very word "democracy" has become a sacred word in our civilization, the thinker or politician who uses it often demonstrating by his whole demeanor that he believes himself to be elevated by this use into the realm of things divine. Indeed, for many people, democracy and divinity seem to have merged together, so that the victory of the former entails, by definition, the triumph of everything eternally true, eternally good and eternally beautiful: in short, the triumph of God. Democracy has become the Christ—the Way, the Truth and the Life—for a large portion of western mankind. Doubts about this divine role, which have gradually been fading away over the course of the last two hundred years, appear to have been almost entirely dispelled at the time of the Second World War, when democracy was equated with the struggle against Hitler, and the opponent of democracy treated as a Nazi or a fascist fellow-traveler.

I should like to call attention to three exceedingly unfortunate consequences of this divinization of democracy.

First of all, political systems and institutions, precisely because they deal with the realm of mutable, diverse historical realities, ought to be open to critical examination. But democracy's justice and value are accepted as unquestioned dogmas, and serious treatment of its foundations and supposed fruits have been lifted out of the sphere of rational public debate. One ought not to be exhorted to have faith in a political system, bur, rather, to be shown rationally why that system merits trust. Yet the religion of democracy does not allow the use of reason to confirm it. One

† First published in *Mut zur Ethik*, 1997, pp. 311–312.

must adore or perish. Yes, one can complain that "true democracy" is endangered in some confessedly democratic society, but he cannot critically question the value of democracy as such, lest he find himself thrust into the political wilderness. This means that if there are problems with democracy, even with true democracy, no one will be allowed to hear of them. Such silence is hardly a victory for the human intelligence; though ironically, the mythology of democracy associates democratic victory with an expansion of open, tolerant, rational discussion.

Secondly, the dogma of the central importance of democracy as the work of God is so deeply implanted in the consciousness and subconsciousness of the age that the democratic system has ceased to be viewed merely as a practical means to a substantive end. It has become a substantive and higher end itself. Anyone seeking to promote or defend a given cause finds that he is constrained to express his goal in the context of a still greater concern for democracy as the price of gaining a public hearing. Knowing that an opponent can win the advantage over him in open debate by the simple suggestion that he is not sufficiently committed to democracy, he sees that he had best begin his struggle for whatever end he has in mind by showing the world just how democratic that goal really is. Hence, all ends are subordinated to the supreme goal of achieving democracy. One lives, as a result, in an enormous "outcome-based" society in which everyone is educated and all causes are judged in relation to their ability to aid the victory of democracy—the triumph of a machine which ought to be a tool rather than a master.

Thirdly, and most importantly, given the practical concerns of *Mut zur Ethik*, this turning of democracy into the supreme, unquestioned end of human action opens the door to endless misunderstanding and self-deception, as well as to oppression by well-organized ideological or criminally ambitious men and movements. Let us pause for a moment to examine this third point in some greater detail, with reference to the dilemma of conservative-minded people.

All current mainstream western political discussions presume the necessity of democracy. But conservatives are likely to argue that democracy means something much more limited for them than what I have outlined above. They will often claim that for them it means the triumph of some specific goods—like patriotism or the family—which they call a traditional value, and which they believe to be supported by a silent majority that would certainly win out if only "true democracy" were to dominate.

My argument is that modern democracy has been developed and promoted, in theory and in practice, by people who define it in ways that are inimical to values of the sort that conservatives often support; values that have grown out of a specific tradition of classical and Christian roots. For the people who really define its meaning in modern times, democracy is tied together with one or another idea stemming from eighteenth-century enlightenment or romantic visions of the meaning of life. Thus, they may stipulate democracy to be anything whatsoever that the popular will desires, regardless of whether its utterances are moral in the classical-Christian sense or not, because that will is itself considered to be the voice of God. More likely still, they may mean by democracy the victory of a popular will whose consciousness has been raised to overthrow the oppression of centuries of darkness; i.e., the evils of the classical-Christian tradition. In this case, the popular will may not be expressed by a numerical majority, but by a small, enlightened vanguard of the people, speaking in the name of that people's future purified wishes. Such democrats have been aided enthusiastically by the criminally ambitious, who have understood that democracy, operating in tandem with the eighteenth-century attack on corporate authority, offers them enhanced opportunities for pillage. For the criminally ambitious have seen that making everyone equally free allows the strong and the vicious few the chance to assert their will over the weak and the mild many who desperately need the protection of social authorities to give their supposed equality with the more brutal any serious practical meaning. Moreover, it allows them to do so in the very name of the majority whom they are manipulating.

Thus, when conservatives hinge the battle for traditional values of the classical-Christian variety on the need to secure democracy, they are riding on the back of a monster. Conservatives did not create the modern democratic system or the language by which modern democracy promotes itself. They are obliged by the circumstances of history to fight for "true democracy" with presuppositions and battle cries and weapons and on battlefields designed by those who wish to crush the classical-Christian tradition, with its concern for objective truth, goodness and beauty. It is impossible under such circumstances to escape the influence of one's enemies and to properly defend what one wants to defend. One ends by accepting and defending at least part of what it is that the enemy is proposing. And, in fact, what has repeatedly happened through the course of the nineteenth and twentieth centuries is that groups of conservatives, honestly outraged by certain specific revolutionary developments, have raised the banners of defense of traditional values while accepting many of the axioms of the anti-traditional democratic system which is engaged in overthrowing them. Conservatives have thereby baptized the underlying principles of the assault on traditional values, and simply chosen not to recognize the logic that leads from these principles to the outrage that they are fighting at the moment. Certainly this is what has happened to many people in the conservative movement in the United States. Horrified by one or the other evil which is encouraged around them, they nevertheless continue to glorify the revolutionary concepts underlying the American system, and reject the idea that they themselves may be responsible for current nightmares. They do so partly because those ideas and that system have now over two hundred years of history behind them, and, therefore, might also be considered something "traditional." Defense of traditional values is said to be a matter of obvious common sense, and since this is the case, the potential conflict between American traditional values and those of classical-Christian origin is not rigorously investigated. Such an investigation might shake faith in America and divert energy from the struggle for the victory of "true democracy," which would, of course, set everything back on the right path. The result of this mentality is that the steamroller of revolutionary American democracy moves forward relentlessly, and the conservative, in effect, does not understand what runs him over when he is crushed by it yet again.

Think of the problems posed by the divinization of democracy for the question of human rights. Where democracy is lacking, its worshippers argue, human rights also unavoidably suffer. Where human rights are infringed, one can be certain that democracy has been thwarted as well. He who would work for democracy must inevitably promote the cause of human rights, and he who would seek the victory of human rights is obliged, perforce, to join the crusade for democracy.

I do not believe that any such claims are accurate. If the value of democracy is accepted as an article of faith, one cannot critically examine whether it does, in practice, what it claims in theory to do. Again, if democracy is made the prior end in life anyway, human rights will, by definition, mean whatever democracy declares them to be. This then entails following one or another of the different directions that victorious eighteenth-century thought has taken, so that human rights, in practice, might mean a plethora of things: whatever a majority decrees them to be; diverse things to different nations or races or sexes; whatever one individual desires; one thing today and another tomorrow. All of these visions of human rights have been proclaimed by democratic thinkers and democracies, and they have been the outlooks that have shaped the battle over the concept of freedom in the lands ruled by the democratic god.

When conservatives hinge the battle for human rights on democracy, they are, therefore, once again riding on the back of a monster. They are pressed by the immense power of the spirit of the times to accept a definition of human rights that actually destroys everything that is both traditionally and objectively good in a classical-Christian sense. And, once more, what has repeatedly happened through the course of the nineteenth and twentieth centuries is that conservatives have tried to parry assaults on traditional values while defending theories regarding human rights which must erode them. Thus, returning to the United States for an example, conservatives in my country are generally outraged by the claim that one has a right to publish pornography. At the same time, they often consider it necessary to support a tradition of American commitment to an atomistic, anti-authoritarian vision of human rights. This vision has consequences that many of them like when applied to individual economic freedom, but, unfortunately, it is the same concept of rights which logically leads to the demand for the individual freedom to produce pornography. Many American conservatives simply choose not to allow the validity of this logical development, announcing that common sense dictates rejecting pornographic freedoms. They thereby abandon a more serious investigation of the intellectual roots of the problem, and continue to talk of rights in an atomistic, anti-authoritarian way in realms that please them. Their more logical enemies appeal to the same notion of rights, and continue to pursue the breaking down of barriers and taboos in areas that do not please them. Within a few years, the definition of common sense will expand to include the right to pornography that conservatives deny today. By that time, the battle for traditional values will center around another, still more serious issue, and many people will accept the freedom of pornography they once rejected. In fact, after a reasonable period of time, the right to produce pornography will have itself become a tradition. How would one know whether it was a good tradition, a traditional value, and something thereby worthy of defense? By an appeal to theology, philosophy and history? That would involve appealing to a judge other than common sense, a judge other than democracy. Surely Hitler would be lying right around the corner ready to pounce if one did so!

What, then, would be the best manner of defending democracy if what one understands by democracy in a civilization where everything must be presented in a democratic package is actually the defense of some real objective truth or eternal good in a classical-Christian sense? It is, after all, such things which I believe most conservatives truly want to defend. The best thing to do would be to demythologize democracy, to free oneself mentally and spiritually from enslavement to the overbearing democratic god, to reduce democracy once again to the level of a means as opposed to an end, and to subject that means to examination and criticism by reason. If one does so, two remarkable things happen.

To begin with, history is reopened to the observer of society in all its fullness. With history's reopening comes access to the thoughts of millennia regarding the relationship of the essentially mutable world of politics to the unchangeable world of truth, goodness and beauty. An entire army of Hebrews, Greeks, Romans, Medievals, critics of the Enlightenment and teachers of Catholic social doctrine come on to center stage. Through their writings, one starts to realize that all political systems have their benefits and detriments, all have their rises and falls, due to the virtues and vices of their leaders and their peoples, as well as due to the mere circumstances of history; that given the peculiarities of time and place, all can be helpful or unhelpful in achieving the good. One sees that the manipulation of democratic systems by small factions who themselves define the popular will and oppress true majorities has been one of the constant problems of democracy, not an occasional abuse, and that this has been exacerbated by its tie-in with the revolutionary ideologies of the "tradition" of the past few centuries. One learns that it has often been precisely non-democratic governments which have better protected the traditional and good desires of the population, and that, in point of fact, the first time that the silent majority argument was used in recent history was in defense of the legitimate French Monarchy against the Jacobin Democracy of the 1790s.

Secondly, demythologizing democracy enables one to rediscover the true focus needed to secure the proper functioning of the political order and the protection of the individual. That focus cannot be on undying commitment to some mutable institution, to a democracy or to a monarchy, to local government or to world government, since historical needs regularly change what is required in practical terms to do the good. That focus has to be upon the question of what the objective order of things itself demands; what the law of God and of nature necessitates, and what virtues one needs to fulfill it. It is concern for obedience to divine and natural law, with their emphasis upon what the individual owes to others, that has been the real source of western excellence in building order and promoting the perfection of the human person, and not repeated reiteration of the need for popular sovereignty and human rights, with their emphasis upon what is owed to individuals. This is especially true in the modern world, where individuals are defined as grasping bundles of insatiable desires incapable of respecting anything and anybody anyway. Learning what the law is and how to fulfill it is a task that opens up the jewel box of the whole of the glorious tradition of the West, and pinpoints the dangers of working with the flawed vision of the two hundred fifty-year tradition of the Enlightenment.

If one argues that acceptance of my premise would reopen all the acrimonious debates about God and man which the Enlightenment correctly noted have left blood stains throughout the ages, I would still have to insist that we have no choice. If we do not reopen that debate, we will be engaged in an enormous, self-deceptive waste of time. One cannot defeat evil by making believe that the great problem of identifying objective truth and the whole drama of trying to live by that truth on the earth do not exist, or that they can be ignored by means of democratic consensus. The peace that this denial purchases is a peace which cheats the human mind and spirit in their thirst for the highest perfection. It is a peace that has historically been administered by the consciousness-raiser and the criminal. If troubles have arisen in dealing with correctly understanding reality and living in charity with one another in the past, then these troubles can be overcome only in one way: by the painstaking work of trying to understand reality still better, and by trying to live still more charitably, personally, every waking moment of every day. They cannot be overcome through the mechanical functioning of some democratic apparatus which is worshipped as a god and which has generally run out of fuel to boot.

6

The Bad Seed

THE LIBERAL-FASCIST EMBRACE AND
ITS POST-CONCILIAR CONSEQUENCES†

*Use of the word "fascist" as an epithet to castigate anything
one dislikes intensely ought not to blind us to the fact that
there is a real historical phenomenon, active in the Second
World War, to which the label does indeed apply. This article, building upon my essay in the Spring 2001 issue of* The
Latin Mass, *seeks to demonstrate that important aspects of this
fascist phenomenon, developed in the context of that global
conflict, are very much reflected in the Novus Ordo Ecclesiae
by which the inscrutable designs of Providence have allowed
our generation to be tormented. Many a tale needs to be told
to convey the truth of this assertion fully; the discussion that
follows serves merely as a useful introduction to an extremely
delicate and perplexing topic.*

L ET US BEGIN OUR STORY IN THE YEARS
1939–1941, when many Catholics, long convinced of the
innate weaknesses of the liberal bourgeois "Established Disorder,"
expressed little surprise over the victories of Nazi Germany. What
really concerned them was whether Catholicism could find some
way to turn a potentially apocalyptic situation to its own advantage.
Nowhere was this concern confronted so directly as in France,
which became a laboratory in the war years for educational and
evangelical schemes designed to reshape the world in a Catholic
way. One major example of educational experimentation incorporating both Catholic ideas as well as organizational features of
the Ordensburgen, the castle training centers for the new elite of
German youth, was the Ecole Nationale des Cadres at the Château
Bayard above the village of Uriage, near Grenoble. Founded in the
waning months of 1940, it became especially significant by June
of 1941, when the Vichy regime determined to require a session
at the Ecole for all future high government functionaries.

---

† First published in *The Latin Mass* magazine, Fall 2001.

The teachings of a vast array of Catholic luminaries and their fellow travelers were marshalled under the banner of the National Revolution of Pétainist France to play a role in the education offered at Uriage. Still, under the day-to-day direction of Pierre Dunoyer de Segonzac and the guidance of the Study Bureau of Hubert Beuve-Mery, the most potent influences were those of Personalism and what later came to be known as the New Theology.

Emmanuel Mounier is the prime representative of the first of these forces. Editor of the journal *Esprit*, which was dedicated to an elaboration of the personalist vision, Mounier had had prewar contacts with a kaleidoscope of thinkers engaged in similar speculations: Jean Danielou, the future cardinal; Jean Guitton, who would one day become a close friend and advisor to Pope Paul VI; Jacques Maritain, Nicholas Berdyaev and their circle of friends at the former's home outside Paris; Henri Daniel-Rops and his fellow members of the organization Ordre Nouveau (New Order); Belgians inspired by the "spiritualized Socialism" of Henri de Man; proponents of European cooperation like Otto Abetz, the Nazi ambassador to defeated France; and a group of "revolutionary National Socialists" gathered in the early 1930s around the Hitler rivals Gregor and Otto Strasser. Mounier's "communitarian Personalism" was formative in Uriage, even after political problems led to his own removal from the school, through the similar teaching of his friend, Jean Lacroix, and their common master, Jacques Chevalier, Professor at Grenoble and sometime Vichy Minister of Education.

The second crucial influence, that of the budding New Theology, arrived in the Chateau Bayard via the Dominican houses of Saulchoir and Latour-Maubourg, the Jesuit center at Fourvières, the journals *La vie intellectuelle*, *Sept* and *Temps Present*, the French scouting movement and specialized Catholic Action groups stimulated by the labor of Joseph Cardijn with young Christian workers in Belgium. Segonzac and Beuve-Mery had frequented such circles before the war, bringing to Uriage priests like Henri de Lubac, Jean Maydieu, Victor Dillard and Paul Donceour. These men, in turn, introduced students to the writings of Félicité de Lamennais, Henri Bergson, Maurice Blondel, Charles Péguy, Marie-Dominique Chenu, Yves Congar, Karl Adam, Romano Guardini, Charles de Foucauld and, perhaps more importantly than anyone else, Pierre Teilhard de Chardin. Uriage also had links, direct and indirect, with Frs. Louis Joseph Lebret and Jacques Loew, founders of the Catholic social movement, Economie et Humanisme, destined for a significant "progressivist" future.

Through both these conduits, students at the Ecole were familiarized with currents of biblical, historical, spiritual, liturgical and philosophical thought which, while marginal at the moment, would become immensely powerful after the war, and instrumental in guiding the Second Vatican Council and the post-conciliar Church claiming to operate in its name. Again, they were all enthusiastically propagated by a team "ensconced in a chateau up in the mountains with a commission to completely rethink and transform the way France educated its young people."[1]

Transformation of the world, according to the doctrine taught at Uriage, was dependent upon the creation of "persons" as opposed to "individuals." Allow me briefly to remind readers of my last article that "persons" were defined as men who responded to the call of "natural values" which pressed them to surpass in community life their narrow individual desires. One knew that he was dealing with a community dedicated to a natural value constructing true persons whenever he saw that it possessed a discernible "mystique," and that it led to creative, self-sacrificing activity. One day, the "convergence" of all such mystiques would result in the establishment of a community of communities producing, in effect, Super-persons, "the greatest transformation to which humanity has ever submitted." The nightmare of the twentieth century was actually "the bloody birth of a true collective being of men," mysterious indeed, but providential and eminently Catholic. [2]

Catholicism's role in this "convergence" was that of giving witness to the supernatural significance of every natural value, reflected in the mystiques of the active communities of self-sacrificing persons it saw around it, and helping each of them to come to its own innate perfection. It must not sit in judgment of them, because Catholicism itself could not fully know what it really was until everything natural had matured and converged.

1 John Hellman, *The Knight Monks of Vichy France: Uriage, 1940–1945,* McGill, 1997, p. 56.
2 Ibid., p. 178.

Catholicism was part of a multifaceted pilgrimage to God, linked together by intuition and action, whose destination was unclear. What was important at the moment was encouraging deeply willed commitment to self-sacrifice of all sorts.

Hence Uriage's stunning ecumenism, testified to in a myriad of ways. Beginning with Segonzac's ability "to form friendly relations, on the spiritual plane, with Protestants, Catholics, Jews, Moslems, agnostics," since he "preferred (rooted) people ... in their own setting, in their own culture,"[3] it passed through the Uriage Charter's proclamation that "believers and non-believers are, in France, sufficiently impregnated with Christianity that the better among them could meet, beyond revelations and dogmas, at the level of the community of persons, in the same quest for truth, justice and love"[4] and arrived, in Mounier, at full-fledged Teilhardian rapture over the strange growth of the "perfect personal community," where "Love alone would be the bound, and no constraint, no vital or economic interest, no extrinsic institution":[5]

> Surely [development] is slow and long when only average men are working at it. But then heroes, geniuses, a saint come along: a Saint Paul, a Joan of Arc, a Catherine of Siena, a Saint Bernard, or a Lenin, a Hitler and a Mussolini, or a Gandhi, and suddenly everything picks up speed...[H]uman irrationality, the human will, or simply, for the Christian, the Holy Spirit suddenly provides elements which men lacking imagination would never have foreseen.[6]
>
> May the democrat, may the communist, may the fascist push the positive aspirations which inspire their enthusiasm to the limit and plenitude.

As John Hellman explains, "Mounier's belief that there was an element of truth in all strong beliefs coincided with Teilhard's vision of the inevitable spiritualization of humanity."[7]

Let it be emphasized that the message taught at Uriage was not a rational one. Its ultimate justification was intuition and strength

3   Ibid., p. 83.
4   Ibid., p. 59.
5   John Hellman, *Emmanuel Mounier and the New Catholic Left: 1930–1950*, Toronto, 1981, p. 85.
6   Ibid., p. 90.
7   Ibid., p. 128.

of will leading to creative action. Any appeal to logic, either in support or criticism of strongly willed commitment to natural values was dismissed as either belaboring the given, or dangerous, decadent, individualist scholastic pedantry. Better to bury the temptations of a sickly rationalism through the development of the obvious virtue of "manliness," again, defined in completely anti-intellectual ways: the ability to leap onto a moving streetcar; to ride a bicycle up the steep hill to the Ecole like Jacques Chevalier; to look others "straight in the eye" and "shake hands firmly"; to endure the sweat-filled regimen labelled *décrassage* devised for students under the inspiration of General Georges Hébert; to sing enthusiastically around the evening fire in the Great Hall; to know how to "take a woman"; and, always, to feel pride in "work well done." Such manliness was said to have deep spiritual meaning, aspects of which were elaborated in lectures like de Lubac's Ordre Viril, Ordre Chrétien (Virile Order, Christian Order), and Chenu's book, *Pour Etre Heureux, Travaillons Ensemble* ("For Happiness, Let Us Work Together").

Finally, let us note that Uriage's teaching was unabashedly elitist, the particular mystique of the Ecole being that of developing the natural value of leadership. "The select youth of Uriage" were said to be "the first cell of a new world introduced into a worn-out one,"[8] "entrusted with the mission of bringing together the elite from all of the groups that ought to participate in the common task of reconstruction in the same spirit of collaboration."[9] Since they were destined to reveal the eternal supernatural significance of the natural values witnessed to by the mystique of all virile communities, Uriage students were actually priestly figures as well. Each class was consecrated and given a great man's name as a talisman. Segonzac especially "took upon himself a certain sacerdotal role, even regarding the wives and children of his instructors."[10] This entailed also a "separation between the leaders, the lesser leaders, the lesser-lesser leaders, the almost leaders and the not-at-all leaders," irritating some of the interns. "The central team," as one of them indicated, "were gods."[11]

---

8   Hellman, KMV, p. 65.
9   Ibid., p. 63.
10 Ibid., p. 90.
11 Ibid., p. 75.

Fascism was seen by the Uriage gods as a "monstrous prefigura-tion" of the new personalist humanity waiting to be born. It clearly revealed the presence of strong will, virile manliness, self-sacrifice to the community and even, in the context of the war effort, a commitment to the construction of that European-wide order which the leadership thought to be crucial to a more successful unleashing of the creation of spiritualized personalities. Pétain's so-called National Revolution was appreciated both because of its anti-liberal bourgeois character and its freedom from the gross "materialist" aspects of Nazism, racism in particular. Neverthe-less, the deportation of French youth to forced labor camps, the increasing control by Germany of internal Vichy affairs and the outright takeover of the Unoccupied Zone in the latter part of 1942 moved the leadership of the Ecole closer to the growing Resistance Movement. This tendency was matured by December of that year when Uriage's enemies at court managed to have it expelled from the Château Bayard.

But Uriage never did anything haphazardly. Building upon the sense of being a modern version of a band of crusading knights, the exiled Ecole leadership created in 1943 a chivalric Order whose inner circle was bound by special vows of a character that Fr. Maydieu compared spiritually to those of marriage. Members of the Order were to sally forth to show the various elements of the Resistance how to perfect their mystiques in the Uriage manner. Thus, high-level emissaries were sent to contact de Gaulle, and "flying squadrons" into the countryside to guide the maquis so that their deficient mystiques could be "transcended spiritually" and "converge" in the construction of the better world of the personalist-Teilhardian faith.

The enthusiasm with which this labor was undertaken was genuine, especially with respect to the Marxist aspects of the Resistance Movement (Marxism, like Fascism, being another "mon-strous prefiguration" of a happier future). Here, the Order's activ-ity was paralleled by the efforts of priests and bishops trying to understand the "mystique" of workers in labor camps and ordinary French factories, training for the latter purpose being offered under the patronage of the supra-diocesan Mission de France. Uriage teachers were themselves involved in these priestly activities—Fr. Dillard, for example, canonizing the Soviets he encountered in the labor camps, and insisting that all workers were born to their task with specific virtues denied to other people. An Uriage-like openness was everywhere in the air. After all, there were "riches in modern disbelief, in atheist Marxism, for example, which are presently lacking to the fullness of the Christian conscience."[12] Enlightened spirits had "to share the faith in and the mystique of the Revolution and the Great Day (that of the total Christ),"[13] as did one priest who asked to die "turned towards Russia, mother of the proletariat, as towards that mysterious homeland where the Man of the future is being forged."[14]

The sons of Uriage retained their wartime sense of being a priestly nation, a people set apart, chosen to judge which mystiques were and were not acceptable on the pathway to "convergence." Objects of contempt offered themselves aplenty. Soviet apparatchiks did not seem to understand that Marxism was meant to be spiritually transcended. A Stalinist mystique, therefore, had to be jettisoned. American culture was even more hopeless. "The Americans," Beuve-Mery complained, "could prevent us from carrying out the obligatory revolution, and their materialism does not even have the tragic grandeur of the materialism of the totalitarians."[15] Jews were dangerous due to their potential spirit of revenge.[16] Perhaps most of all, however, traditional Catholicism, which, from Uriage days, had feared the "insistence on bringing together men with different 'mystiques' while affecting a 'manly' irritation with clericalism, dogma and the orthodox,"[17] needed to be tossed onto the rubbish heap of contempt.

Mounier is particularly instructive with respect to this growing dismissal of the Church. His vision had always logically involved the possibility of shelving whole realms of Christian scripture, theology and spirituality, should they clash with the "emerging convergence." By the last years of the war, "there was little place for sin, redemption and resurrection in the debate; the central acts of the Christian drama were set aside."[18] Nietzsche's critique

---

12 Emile Poulat, *Les Prêtres–Ouvrières: Naissance et Fin*, Cerf, 1999, p. 408.
13 Ibid., p. 386.
14 Ibid., p. 244.
15 Ibid., p. 213.
16 Ibid., p. 197.
17 Ibid., p. 88.
18 Hellman, *Mounier*, p. 255.

of slavish Christianity now seemed to him to be unanswerable, and he "came to think that Roman Catholicism was an integral part of almost all he hated. Then, when he searched his soul, he discovered that the aspects of himself which he appreciated least were his 'Catholic' traits."[19] Doing what one willed was the *unum necessarium*. Everything rational from the Greek tradition used to support Christianity and dampen the will was execrated as well. If there was anything valuable in the Greco-Christian heritage, it had to come from personalists rebuilding it from scratch; those appealing to the Catholic name and Catholic practice in his day required diagnosis and psychiatric help:

Mounier now flatly denounced old-fashioned Christianity and Christians. Christianity, he wrote, was "conservative, defensive, sulky, afraid of the future." Whether it "collapses in a struggle or sinks slowly in a coma of self-complacency," it was doomed. "Christians," he castigated in even stronger terms in a rhapsodic style worthy of his new master (Nietzsche): "These crooked beings who go forward in life only sidelong with downcast eyes, these ungainly souls, these weighers-up of virtues, these dominical victims, these pious cowards, these lymphatic heroes, these colourless virgins, these vessels of ennui, these bags of syllogisms, these shadows of shadows..."[20]

Metaphysical speculation, Mounier declared, was a characteristic of "lifeless schizoid personalities."... Mounier even referred to intelligence and spirituality as "bodily diseases" and attributed the indecisiveness of many Christians to their ignorance of "how to jump a ditch or strike a blow."... "Modern psychiatry," Mounier wrote, had shed light on the morbid taste for the "spiritual," for "higher things," for the ideal and for effusions of the soul.... Thus, many forms of religious devotion were the result of psychosis, self-deception or vanity. Prayer was often a sign of psychological illness and weakness.[21]

This brings us back to the liturgical question, the liturgy being one of the most important aspects of Christian life that had to change with the emergence of the new personalist order. Uriage was very much permeated with the pastoral emphasis of the more

---

19 Ibid., p. 190.
20 Ibid., p. 191.
21 Ibid., pp. 192–193.

recent liturgical movement, which itself helped to shape its own understanding of the need to accommodate oneself to particular active "mystiques" so as to create self-sacrificing persons. Fr. Maydieu was already celebrating new-style Masses for "friends of Sept" before the war, during which the priest faced the people and provided a French narration.[22] Fr. Doncoeur, terrified that life was passing Catholics by, became enthusiastic for pastoral liturgical developments in Germany as early as 1923. He used the model of games and sports events, as well as the general desire of youth to cooperate as a group, to guide the French scouting movement down a new liturgical direction:

> Games can also be an excellent preparation for worship, which to the little ones appears to be very little different from a game. This should not scandalize us. The word game is not in the child's vocabulary, and particularly in the realm of scouting, it is a synonym for diversion. A game is an action, passionate insofar as it is sincerely played. Well, official worship is eminently sincere. Children sense this. They find satisfaction in this atmosphere of truth. They savor this serious action, wherein all participate, body and soul, this collective and ordained action, similar in nature to those grand modern sports events wherein modern youth finds its discipline and sometimes its mystique. But the little faithful heart senses well that worship is more noble than sports. Worship is the Big Game, the Sacred Game which is being played for the Chief of Chiefs .... Among the troops the Mass is generally a Dialogue Mass at which all actively participate. Certain among them make the offering. The cadets which Father Doncoeur leads each summer with knapsacks across France's roads also have the Dialogue Mass. Gathered before the altar, they respond to the liturgical prayers, make the offering of the host which will be consecrated for them at the Offertory ... [23]

Uriage, concerned as it was with using all communal tools to build persons possessing the "leadership mystique," turned the entire day into a "manly" liturgical experience. Bonfires were lit, backs slapped, virile poems and hymns excogitated, and special pageants mounted. All of these were, of course, inspired by "deep

22   J. Duquesne, quoted in Didier Bonneterre, *Le Mouvment Liturgique*, Fideliter, p. 39.
23   Abbé Aigrain, quoted in Ibid., p. 38.

feeling," and all constituted demands upon the developing persons of the community, rejection of which would have been a breach of Volksgemeinschaft equivalent to an individualist sin against the Holy Spirit. Interestingly enough, all of this participatory, creative and expensive new "natural" liturgical life was being elaborated while Frs. Maydieu, Doncoeur, Chenu, Congar and others were bringing into existence what would be the extremely influential Center for Pastoral Liturgy, designed to effect similar changes on the ecclesiastical level.

Worker-Marxist-Soviet mania from 1942 onwards increased to fever pitch the demand for a liturgy based on pastoral response to particular mystiques. This often played upon Pius XII's well-known willingness to take risks on the pastoral level if success could be demonstrated to emerge from them. Henri Godin's famous work, *France: Pays de Mission?* (1943), outlining worker dechristianization, had created a sense of crisis. Prudence had to be tossed aside. Lack of any precise plan for diving into the worker mystique was attributed to genius and faith in the Spirit. One thing alone was certain: the liturgy and the priesthood were out of sync with the world of labor. All that was associated with what Paul Claudel called the "mass with one's back to the people" had to be abandoned. It had become the precious toy of little minds and bigots who could not understand the New Order coming into being around them. Hence the critique of Fr. Dillard, who dismissed the difficulties of a total rejection of the past, and also took it for granted that the worker clientele would be able to sense the superior spirituality of what we would call a secularized clergy due to the *je ne sais quoi* emanating from its own new mystique:

> My Latin, my liturgy, my mass, my prayer, my sacerdotal orna-ments, all of that made me a being apart, a curious phenomenon, something like a (Greek) pope or a Japanese bonze, of whom there remain still some specimen, provisionally, while waiting for the race to die out.[24]
> Religion as they [the workers] knew it is a type of bigotry for pious women and chic people served by disguised characters who are servants of capitalism ... If we succeed in ridding our religion of the unhealthy elements that encumber it, petty

24 Poulat, p. 329.

superstitions, the bourgeois "go to Mass" hypocrisy, etc. we will find easily with the Spirit of Christ the mystique which we need to re-establish our homeland.[25]

It ought to be obvious by this point that the war and efforts to respond to its challenges gave much greater exposure to many of the ideas, men and expressions of contempt for believers which were instrumental in assembling the *Novus Ordo Ecclesiae*. *Le Monde*, under Beuve-Mery's leadership, has alone been worth thousands of extra mileage en route towards the Omega Point, with automatic upgrades to first-class seats for everyone of the Uriage personalist persuasion. But what are we to conclude about the other argument touched upon at the beginning of this essay? Is there then any validity to the claim of a fascist-like character to the ecclesiastical universe in which we now live and gasp for a breath of the supernatural?

Very little, it would seem, in the minds of those people for whom Fascism means anti-Semitism and racism alone. Participation of many of the architects of the Novus Ordo Ecclesiae in the Resistance Movement and in vigorously anti-Nazi journals like *Témoignage Chrétien*, seems to provide unquestionable protection from any accusation of Fascism whatever, even when such involvement had been preceded by several years of respectable flirtation with Pétain and the National Revolution.

Nevertheless, for those manly spirits ready to leap from streetcars moving towards undiscernable destinations, to sit down in a cafe and to indulge in a little scholastic logic, the issue cannot be dismissed so easily. Fascism is more than Hitler. It is even more than Mussolini, its twentieth-century "founder." It is a phenomenon that emerged out of the same concern to restore a shattered Western social order by appeal to the non-rational will of virile communities stirred to action by charismatic prophets central to the preaching of Lamennais and a whole tradition following from him that was appealed to by the teachers of Uriage. Yes, aspects of contemporary Fascism may have been of secondary importance to the Catholics we have been discussing, but the canonization of submission of the individual to the will of the non-rational community was common to both. What difference

---

25   Ibid., p. 333.

if Catholic-friendly words like "person," and expressions such as the "Mystical Body of Christ" were employed, when rigorous philosophical-theological examination of their meaning was ridiculed as decadent and unnecessary to men with "deep faith" in the emergence of the better world towards which their natural leaders were guiding them?

Nineteenth-century Catholics opposed to Lamennais knew what to expect from his vision, and their critique, present in the writings of men of the day like Louis Veuillot and the Jesuit editors of *La Civiltà Cattolica*, underlined many of the problems of the fascist experience and any Christian personalism related to it as well. Burial in vital community life alone cannot, on its own, produce spiritual "persons" of any supernatural significance. The very conception of the person requires the unique Christian mentality judging the will and action of the "mystiques" from which it is supposed by the men of Uriage to emerge. Forgetfulness of this basic principle was bound to entail the creation of hollow men, swaying according to the vagaries of each and every "vital," willful, all-too-fallen, worldly wind.

This is why the claim to "spiritualize" and "transcend" all of life by basing that transformation on burial in the activity of natural communities is also an empty one. "Spiritualization" of everything natural, as practiced by the thinkers we have been discussing, ends in the naturalization of everything which might have been lifted up to God, had the tools for accomplishing that goal not been rejected, and an opening been given instead to all the gross, banal and frequently inane fantasies to which the human mob always feels its deepest pull. No insistence upon one's innate virtues and natural leadership skills can save those attempting to guide such a false spiritualization from a depressing fall to earth. Hence, the deeply committed Fr. Dillard ended by concluding that his work in the factory was more important than his Mass, and, indeed, that the machine on which he labored itself actually had a soul. [26] Similarly, Mounier's Ascent of Mount Carmel jettisoned prayer for psychoanalysis, while the Monde milieu helped mightily to build a technocratic Europe marked by the same bland, materialist "diversity" of the American pluralist circus

26   Poulat, p. 327.

it so self-righteously condemned. Let us allow the final word to go to Jacques Maritain and his early critique of the direction certain personalists were headed with their understanding of the manner in which life might all be spiritualized. The unique significance of Catholicism was abandoned by their approach, he complained, and the result would be that they would find themselves helpless before any substantive phenomenon, spiritually "barren in the face of a Ramakrishna."[27]

---

27 Hellman, *Mounier*, p. 42.

7

Secular Italy and Catholicism: 1848–1915†

LIBERALISM, NATIONALISM, SOCIALISM AND THE ROMANTIC IDEALIST TEMPTATION

IN MANY RESPECTS, THE HISTORY OF ITALY since the collapse of the Roman Empire has been one of a "Dark Peninsula." True, there are a certain number of bright spots familiar primarily to scholars, while the artistic and dramatic characteristics of ages like the Renaissance are well known even on a popular plane. Nevertheless, much of what happens in Italian History is seen by people, both scholars and laymen alike, through a glass, and very darkly indeed. At the top of the list, in this regard, is the entire, crucially important sphere of religious-secular and Church-State relations, whose study is badly vitiated by ideological and cultural prejudices.

When one is speaking of the Risorgimento and immediate post-Risorgimento eras, both Italian and non-Italian knowledge of the general intellectual, political and social environment, not to speak of the more specific problem of religious-secular clashes, is still, to a large degree, lost in this black hole. Description of the nineteenth century context of Italian life often descends into caricature; indeed, even into cultivation of the most simplistic "good guy—bad guy" myths. This is particularly unfortunate for the sense of historical perspective of Italian-Americans, since the Risorgimento, the decades following thereafter, and the difficulties of Church-State relations accompanying the movement for Italian unification provided the framework and much of the explanation for the Great Migration of the population of the Mezzogiorno to the New World in the period 1890–1914.

---

† First published as a chapter in *Models and Images of Catholicism in Italian and Italian American Life* (Forum Italicum of the Center for Italian Studies at S. U. N. Y. Stony Brook, 2004, pp. 195–230).

Clarifying this nineteenth and early twentieth century context involves first of all noting the reality of an anti-clerical and even outrightly anti-Catholic spirit existing all through Italian history. That spirit was the product of many causes, beginning with a heritage of State absolutism nurtured by the ancient Roman bureaucracy, which continued its influence, even in the most obscure years of the Middle Ages, through the important function fulfilled by such officials as notaries. Hostility to the Church was also fed from the eleventh century onwards by two other factors: the ever-deeper revival of understanding of Roman legal principles, and the increasing lay anger over papal recourse to interdicts, excommunications, and the calling of political crusades against its internal enemies, the most significant of which were those unleashed in the long-lasting struggle to obtain a friendly regime in the Kingdom of the Two Sicilies.

Such stimuli continued to embitter many influential laymen still later, in the Renaissance and Reformation eras, though their irritation was now aroused even further by the involvement of Spanish, Austrian and French dynasties in Italian affairs, and the association of their quarrels with the international Protestant-Catholic battle. Florentine and Venetian anti-Romanism could be extraordinarily heated, as evidenced by the writings of Niccolò Machiavelli in the early 1500s, and the seventeenth century exchanges between Paolo Sarpi and the Roman Curia. Jansenist anti-papal reformism, Enlightenment dismissal of religious interference in natural life in general, and, finally, the Napoleonic reordering of much of Italy along the lines of the secularizing measures of the French Revolution, each with the aid of certain segments of the nobility and bourgeoisie, all played their role in feeding these tendencies down to the era of the Risorgimento. [1]

The strange coalition of monarchists, liberals and moderate nationalists which led the movement for independence and unification, created the Kingdom of Italy in 1861, and then engineered the annexation of Rome in 1870, inherited all of these various

---

1 For an introduction, see Waley, Daniel, *The Italian City-Republics* (London & New York: Longman, 1988); Bouwsma, William J., *Venice and the Defense of Republican Liberty* (Berkeley: University of California, 1968); also, Anderson, in Scott, H. M., ed., *Enlightened Absolutism* (Ann Arbor: University of Michigan, 1990). pp. 37–55.

strains of anti-clericalism and anti-Catholic feeling, giving them a greater chance than ever before to triumph on a peninsula-wide plane. More radically democratic, anarchist, socialist and nationalist groups, opposed as these might be to the particular combination of conservative and liberal secularist forces dominating Italy in the late nineteenth century, could still share with them a basic, vigorous, historically-rooted world view hostile to some or all of the structures and teachings of the Roman Catholic Church. The combustible anti-clerical material was, therefore, abundant and varied.

Moreover, it was stirred to fire heat in the nineteenth century due to another fact of life which was as vexing as it was unexpected: the revival of Catholicism as a consciously supernatural religion after its own bleak flirtation with naturalism in the years preceding the French Revolution. That peculiar tryst had seen the weakening, and, in some cases, entire disappearance of ideas, groups and phenomena long intertwined with the explanation and practice of Catholicism, which now, in the course of the 1800s, came back into active life with renewed élan. These included scholastic theology and philosophy, the Society of Jesus, and popular devotions such as pilgrimages, novenas and eucharistic adoration, all of which were horrifying to the Jansenist, Enlightenment and basic secularist mind, and had confidently been presumed to be dead and buried. Most upsetting of all, the restoration movement in Catholicism in the nineteenth century brought with it a revival and centralization of that papal power which secularists associated with danger to the stability and independence of Italy, and, in certain respects, to a degree that was greater than any known even at the height of the Middle Ages. Noticeable in the pontificate of Pius VII (1800–1823), and more apparent still in that of Gregory XVI (1831–1846), the pace and significance of Catholic rebirth was represented, above all else, by the person and reign of Pius IX (1846–1878).[2]

Four points can be made about the character and pontificate of Pius IX which explain why his figure and labor stood out as symbols of the "Catholic Question" to secularists in the Italy shaped by the Risorgimento. To begin with, the pope was perceived by many supporters of the unification-independence movement as

2   Mayeur, J. M., ed., *Histoire du Christianisme* (Vol. XI, Paris: Desclée, 1995–97), pp. 349–366, also, passim; Rao, John C., *Removing the Blindfold* (Kansas City: Angelus Press, 2014), pp. 6–38.

having betrayed what seemed to be his initial, providentially-guided openness to the success of both its specific goals and their root inspiration. Secondly, Pius IX's charismatic, effusive personality made of him a truly modern public figure, fit for demonization after his initial fall from grace, and even more so after his elevation to the status of confessor by Catholics horrified at the overrunning of the Papal States. Next, the pope's commitment to a clarification of Catholic differences with the Risorgimento, which he understood to be necessary once the misinterpretation of his position had led to revolution and war with Austria in the years 1848–1849, not only entailed the direct attack on liberal and nationalist principles found in the *Syllabus of Errors* (1864), but also began the process of official Church investigation of politically charged social questions. Such concerns were stigmatized by the victorious alliance of moderates as a sign of sympathy for radical revolutionaries and peasant "brigands" operating out of the former Kingdom of the Two Sicilies. A Papacy encouraging discussion of them was a Papacy promoting rebellion and subversion.[3]

Finally, and perhaps most importantly, Pius instituted the *non expedit* rule, the papal policy which, while allowing Catholic participation in local political life, prohibited it on the national level in the new "robber" Kingdom. Calls for a boycott of the central, parliamentary establishment began with the politically aware Catholic Press and not through the Vatican. The *non expedit* had its roots in experiences dating back to the 1850s, when Catholic activists like Dom Giacomo Margotti (1823–1887) saw that legally elected deputies who did not subscribe to liberal nationalist ideals were excluded from the Sardinian Parliament. They soon realized that "when we took part in elections and in many places won a victory, we called down upon ourselves all manner of vexations, and our work went up in smoke."[4] Gradually, however, the Papacy came to share with Catholic activists a determination to turn what was perceived as a temporary abstention from a sham participation in the existing system into a serious preparation for a real participation in a future, better disposed Italy.[5]

3   Mayeur, XI, pp. 272–278, 611–636.
4   Invernizzi, Marco, *Il Movimento Cattolico in Italia* (Milan: Mimep–Docete, 1995), p. 22.
5   Kalyvas, Stathis N., *The Rise of Christian Democracy in Europe* (Ithaca and London: Cornell, 1996), pp. 179–183.

Out of this ripened what secularists eager to build a strong and uncontested Italian State could consider one of the worst of the "rotten" fruits of the *non expedit* policy. "Preparation in abstention" meant the creation of a kind of shadow national government, through the construction and elaboration of a centrally organized and nearly comprehensive Italian "Catholic Action" movement. For, although the Società della Gioventù Italiana (1868) always retained a certain autonomy, a multitude of other Catholic organizations and local parish committees were coordinated by the Opera Dei Congressi e Dei Comitati Cattolici, founded in 1874 and given its definitive name in 1881, into a Kingdom-wide tool of serious importance. As that name indicates, the Opera met in regular congresses and carried out routine work through five permanent sections established in 1884: Organization and Catholic Action, Christian Social Economy, Instruction and Education, Press and Christian Art. A generation or more of Catholic lay leaders was trained by the Opera, with the second section, headed, towards the end of the century, by Giuseppe Toniolo (1845–1918), Professor of Political Economy at the University of Pisa and founder of the Unione Cattolica per gli Studi Sociali, being especially active.[6]

The Opera defined itself as intransigent, since it accepted the Syllabus and the pontifical directives; lay, since it was founded and presided over by laymen; papal, since it concentrated all Catholic efforts and organization in the service of the pope; and hierarchical, since its organization replicated the hierarchical Constitution of the Church.

None of this substantially changed in the 1880s and 1890s. Leo XIII (1878–1903) is frequently depicted as the antithesis to Pius IX, and did, indeed, explore various strategies for dealing with the new Kingdom of Italy. Nevertheless, Leo's whole political approach was consonant with the main lines of the movement for Catholic revival as adopted in his predecessor's reign, and clearly manifested a wish to extend the influence of the Church in daily life still further. Nothing substantive came of dreams of official reconciliation. Leo always insisted upon the retention of some kind of Temporal Power, his diplomatic maneuvering with the new German Empire and other European nations frequently involving speculation regarding its side effects for restoration. His

---

6   Ibid., p. 217.

criticism of the errors accompanying the drive for national unity, as reflected in an address of July 26, 1887, was reminiscent of the anti-Risorgimento articles of *La Civiltà Cattolica* from the 1850s and 1860s, and still quite biting. The Pope maintained the *non expedit* policy, and allied the Church more solidly still with concern for the Social Question through his encyclical letter, *Rerum Novarum* (1891), and its justification of the trade union movement, nuanced though this might have been.[7]

The nature of Catholic political action was, however, transformed considerably under the direction of Pius X (1903–1914). Most remembered for his sanctity, and a doctrinal firmness displayed in his battle against Modernism, this northern-born pope, the first since unification who did not come from the former Papal States, was not as troubled as his two predecessors by the specifics of the Temporal Power question. He was, moreover, a man of pronounced democratic temperament, and impatient with many of the formalities and unwritten traditions guiding the behavior of the aristocratic-minded Leo XIII and Roman Curia, viewing them as obstacles to effective action. All this led to his sympathy for alterations in practical Catholic Action, with major, complicated and perhaps unintended consequences for Church-State relations, as will be catalogued in more detail below.[8]

The Kingdom of Italy confronting these popes was a centralized but constitutional monarchy under the House of Savoy. Although the Court did exercise a certain influence in political affairs, Italy was governed much more by the interplay of forces in its Parliament, its municipalities and in the Press. Before turning to a discussion of the specific attitudes towards the Church and Catholicism expressed by any of these elements of Italian political and social life, it would be wise to take a glance at the different parties and factions shaping their views in more or less organized fashion: the Right and Left factions of the Liberals, the Anarchist-Socialists and the Nationalists.[9]

---

7 Jemolo, Arturo Carlo, *Chiesa e Stato in Italia* (Torino: Einaudi, 1977), pp. 47–79.
8 Ibid., pp. 80–160; Romanto, Gianpaolo, *Pio X* (Milan: Rusconi, 1992), pp. 223–291.
9 Mack Smith, Denis, *Modern Italy* (Ann Arbor: University of Michigan, 1997), pp. 95–108, 157–173.

The many difficulties in understanding the Italian Destra can be clarified by realizing that it is a completely different beast than a rightist element in most other European countries, such as France. No supporters of the Kingdom of Italy could ever be identified as legitimists or proponents of a traditionalist program in which religion played a central role, given that they had accepted and worked for the creation of what was itself in essence a moderate revolutionary State. Real rightists either abstained from participation in the government after 1861, or were extremely few in number, including some nostalgists for pre-1848 Piedmont, or followers of the other, fallen peninsular dynasties. Italian "rightists," like the Count Camillo Cavour (1810–1861), Count Stefano Jacini (1816–1891), and Marco Minghetti (1818–1886), were actually men who had adopted liberal and moderate nationalist principles that had proven to be useful to the strengthening of the power of the House of Savoy, and were in no way averse to a vigorous and multiform utilization of the authority of the State.

1876 saw the end of the dominance of this so-called "Historic Right" in the government of Italy, power then falling into the hands of the Sinistra, which was, as intimated above, simply another segment of the basically liberal party that had created the new nation. Associated at its origins with such pronounced anti-clericals as Urbano Rattazzi (1808–1873), the Left was now directed by Agostino Depretis (1813–1887), a Freemason, like many of the other members of his faction. It was much more wedded to the ideals of the free market and the minimal State than its rightist opponent, and, dimly reflecting its earlier republican tendencies, advocated a modest expansion of the suffrage. Troubled greatly by internal governmental scandals, the mainstream of the Sinistra was worried by the increasing disaffection of the Estrema. This force included intransigents of republican sympathies, radicals focused on the domestic injustices of the new Kingdom rather than the foreign affairs that seemingly obsessed their more temperate leftist confrères, and national heroes such as Giuseppe Garibaldi (1807–1882), who considered themselves to be vaguely socialist in sentiment. In fact, opponents within the Sinistra feared that the Estrema was a potential parliamentary conduit for the expression of all manner of advanced socialist ideas already stirring popular and press circles.

Socialism, one needs to remember, was an extremely broad and ill-defined term for most of the nineteenth century. It included among its supporters people who simply wanted steady work; and others, the developers of the trade union movement, who wanted that steady work to be honorable and justly paid. Socialism also was the goal of the small but active bands of anarchists, intellectually stimulated by the Russian, Mikhail Bakunin (1814–1876), who had come to the peninsula in 1864 and remained there as a force for the next ten years. One segment of that movement, headed by Carlo Cafiero (1846–1892) and Errico Malatesta (1853–1932), formed the Federazione Italiana dell'Internazionale Anarchista (1872), taught its message through various rather short-lived journals, as well as the latter's book, *l'Anarchia* (1891), and aimed down the path of direct action versus the State and other authorities. Another branch shed Bakuninian principles and took up the cudgel of legal action. This group included Andrea Costa (1851–1910), who was elected to the Italian Parliament in 1882 as a result of the Depretis suffrage reform. It ended up working alongside Leonida Bissolati (1857–1920), Anna Kuliscioff (1854–1925), Professor Antonio Labriola (1843–1904), who lectured on Marxism at the University of Rome, Claudio Treves (1869–1933), and Filippo Turati (1857–1932). Its journal of intellect was *Critica Sociale*, founded in 1891, and its political organ the Italian Socialist Party, which emerged in Genova in 1892, three years after the establishment of the Second International in Brussels.

Socialist deputies, upon entering Parliament, did indeed sympathize with the Estrema faction of the Left, especially its so-called radical wing, just as the mainstream of the party feared. Severely tested by government repression from the 1880s onwards, Italian Socialism continued to reflect the mixture of influences leading to its birth; i.e., republican, anarchist, Marxist, trade unionist and pragmatist elements simultaneously. Such a mixture enabled men of widely different temperament and intellectual concerns to express sympathy for it. Not surprisingly, therefore, the party conference of 1900 approved two approaches to achieving the Socialist program, those of Maximalism and Minimalism. Maximalists gathered round Labriola and the idea of a more critical break with the existing order of things;

Minimalists around the parliamentarians and the possibilities of the parliamentary system, with both factions seeking to gain control of the party newspaper, *Avanti!*.

Personalities of extremely individualist bent took part in the growth of a new nationalist movement, leading to the creation of the Italian Nationalist Association in Florence in December of 1910. These included such figures as Francesco Coppola (1878–1957), Enrico Corradini (1865–1931), Luigi Federzoni (1878–1967), Giovanni Papini (1881–1956), Giuseppe Prezzolini (1882–1982), and Scipio Sieghele (1868–1913), publishing in journals like *Il Regno, La Voce, Leonardo* and *L'Idea Nazionale*. Their anger was directed against the "legal" Italy which had abandoned the call to greatness of the Risorgimento era, expressing what they saw to be the deepest sensibilities of the Italian spirit. Legal Italy had dedicated itself in the positivist, materialist, post-Risorgimento decades to the petty ambitions of the unadventurous bourgeoisie, realized through the soul-killing parliamentary machinery identified and attacked by Angelo Camillo de Meis (1817–1891), Gaetano Mosca (1858–1941), Alfredo Oriani (1852–1909), Vilfredo Pareto (1848–1923), and Pasquale Turiello (1836–1902). Nationalists claimed to speak for the "real" Italy, the land and population that had not yet realized its manifest destiny, either by completing itself geographically or in answering the needs of its suffering southern peasantry. Armed conflict would be the means by which Italy would escape from its corrupt legal shell and perfect itself, "redeeming" Italians living within the borders of Austria-Hungary. War would also restore to its rightful Italian owners the old Venetian territories now under Ottoman control, and offer lands to the men of the Mezzogiorno in those parts of Africa, such as Libya, still in need of a European colonial master. What was essential to affect this perfection was true, energetic, charismatic leadership, the kind offered by leftists such as Francesco Crispi (1819–1901), Prime Minister on two occasions in the 1880s and 1890s, but cut off in his labors due to the disaster at Adowa in Abyssinia in 1896. Nationalists, like socialists, gained great sympathy in various strata of Italian society: among former anarchists, admirers of modern technology following Filippo Tommaso Marinetti's (1876–1944) famous *Futurist Manifesto* of 1909, and, ultimately, Italy's most curious literary mixture of quixotic influences, Gabriele d'Annunzio (1863–1938), the author of the jingoist *La Nave*, and future patriotic icon. [10]

All these politically active Italians of the decades preceding and encompassing the Great Migration had present before them the picture of a Church that still maintained and wished to retain a formidable hold upon Italian life; an institution that, nevertheless, experience had shown could contemplate adoption of different strategies in its attempt to survive and prosper. Three positions regarding what to think and do about that Catholic grip and will to power grew up among the members of the various Italian parties, and the Court, Parliament, municipalities and press that they utilized. I will label these the approaches of the "rejecters," the "pragmatists," and the "palingenesists." While a clear theoretical distinction among all three attitudes may easily be traced, there was no iron curtain preventing movement from one to another. It was always especially possible for representatives of the first two approaches to slip into attitudes characteristic of the third.

By "rejecters," I obviously mean those for whom any true reconciliation with the Church and Catholicism as they actually existed was not a serious consideration. Giosuè Carducci (1835–1907), with his Hymn to Satan (1863), might be said to have provided a literary manifesto for the most vehement proponents of this approach, and Pius IX certainly believed the outlook expressed therein to be the logical result of cultivating the secularist doctrines of the "robber Kingdom." Indeed, any overall examination of Italian public life would illustrate that the rejecters' camp still held many cards in its hands in the late nineteenth and early twentieth centuries, and this from the Court down to the level of the man on the street.

To begin with, although King Umberto I (1878–1900) was as friendly as possible in his dealings with the Church under difficult circumstances, and Queen Margherita positively effusive in her demonstrations of religious conviction, Vittorio Emmanuele III (1900–1946) showed an outright disdain for everything Catholic. A man of classically nineteenth century positivist convictions, he avoided religious ceremonies and used only Protestant and Waldensian nurses for his children. Within the confines of his

---

10 Thayer, John A., *Italy and the Great War* (Madison and Milwaukee: University of Wisconsin, 1964), pp. 86–143, pp. 192–233.

very pronounced sense of constitutional decorum, the King demonstrated sympathy for Italian political figures who shared his basic secularism, such as the leftist Giuseppe Zanardelli (1826–1903), who was Prime Minister very early in his reign, and the socialist Leonida Bissolati. Vittorio Emmanuele's public dealings with men of the cloth were limited to the most perfunctory and inescapable level on inevitable state visits throughout the country. It was said that the only religious building that he inaugurated during his reign was the Synagogue of Rome.

Moreover, the King was also close to Masonry, which had opened itself to penetration by a much more determined secularism in the latter part of the nineteenth century, once belief in some kind of Supreme Being had been struck from the requirements for membership. Masonry was a strong force in most elite Italian circles, its significance increased by the fact that politicians in all Latin countries often found masonic lodges to be suitable settings in which the members of the loose party coalitions of the day might privately and quietly come to compromises which would be difficult to arrange in the public eye. Zanardelli, under whose name the penal code of 1889 chastising priests for "abuses" connected with their ministry was promulgated, was a prominent Masonic anti-clerical, as was Ernesto Nathan (1845–1921), the Mayor of Rome at the time of the troubled commemoration of the fiftieth anniversary of the creation of the Kingdom in 1911.[11]

Vexations emerging from the Council of Ministers, Parliament and municipal governments, as well as from all political factions, from the Right to the Socialists, were still extremely common after the initial spate of anti-clerical legislation promulgated at the time of the establishment of the Kingdom, and then expanded and extended to the Eternal City after 1870. Thus, Prime Minister Francesco Crispi was responsible both for the removal of the Duke Leopoldo Torlonia (1853–1918), Mayor of Rome in 1887, as punishment for his enthusiastic message of congratulations to Pope Leo on the occasion of the latter's priestly jubilee, as well as for the creation of the electoral machinery that would wrest the

---

11 For Risorgimento anti-clericalism, see Pellicciari, Angela, *Risorgimento da Rescrivere* (Milan: Ares, 1998); Pellicciari, Angela, *L'Altro Risorgimento* (Casale Monferrato: Piemme, 2000); Jemolo, pp. 101–109; Mack Smith, 202–203.

city's government from the hands of Catholics and philo-Catholics. Prominent statesmen often wished to prosecute those suggesting that further changes, such as the obtaining of international guarantees for the Papacy, were required for the peace of Church and State in Italy. The penal code of 1889 was followed by a law on pious legacies of July 17, 1890, and the Zanardelli-Cocco Ortu proposal for legalizing divorce of 20 February, 1902. All these were bitterly opposed by the Church, using the parish and Opera organization to mobilize petitions against them. In fact, the entire decade preceding the First World War was filled with polemic, favorable and hostile, regarding governmental measures concerning everything from control of primary school education and the place of religious instruction within it, to supervision of seminary educational reforms, the rights of Catholic organizations to be represented in governmental councils, and the criminal pursuit of those contracting a religious marriage before passing through a civil ceremony. The speech of Ernesto Nathan, on September 20, 1910, praising the superiority of that lay civilization which had triumphed in the Eternal City in 1870 and would be celebrated in the Roman exposition of the following year, was typical of much anti-Catholic municipal rhetoric, arousing the protests of Pius X himself, and contributing to the decision to prohibit Catholic mayors from participating in the commemorations in the capital in 1911.

Probably the most important of ministerial interferences in the life of the Church took place in the troubled atmosphere of the last decade of the century. It was at this time that agricultural hardships led to the revolts in 1893 of the Sicilian *fasci*, disturbances among peasants in other parts of the peninsula, and, ultimately, to the 1898 riots in Rome, Florence and Milan. Disorder was quelled with particular ferocity in the Lombard metropolis in May of 1898. Crispi and his subsequent imitators, the Marchese di Rudinì (1839–1908) and General Luigi Pelloux (1839–1924), struck hard on such occasions at all those groups perceived as being friendly to "Socialism," including the supposedly "red" leaning Catholics. May 27, 1898 saw the Marchese di Rudinì ordering the close of practically all of the constituent associations of the Opera dei Congressi, three thousand in number, the prohibition of numerous Catholic journals, and even the arrest of leaders of the Catholic movement, like Davide Albertario (1838–1902).

Anti-clerical journalists representing all political factions from the Right to the Socialists still plied their wares to a sizeable audience, with stories ranging from the classic uncovering of unnatural clerical lusts to Church persecution of intelligent and courageous dissenters. Stories of this kind were to be found in *Il Secolo, Gazzetta del Popolo, Messaggero, Vita* and *Avanti!*, as well as in journalistic "histories," such as Benito Mussolini's (1883–1945) biography of Jan Huss. Perhaps most blatant in this regard was *L'Asino*, subtitled *è il popolo, utile, paziente, e bastonato*, run by Guido Podrecca (1865–1923) and Gabriele Galantara (1865–1937), and won over to the socialist camp soon after its creation in 1892. Such journals helped to unleash the kind of anti-Catholic incidents marring the transfer of the remains of Pius IX to San Lorenzo in 1882, the dedication of the statue of Giordano Bruno in the Campo dei Fiori in 1889, the commemoration in 1892 of the discovery of America by Christopher Columbus in 1492, and the fiftieth anniversary of the foundation of the Kingdom of Italy in 1911, the *"anno di lutto,"* as *La Civiltà Cattolica* called it in protest against its pronounced anti-clerical character. Writers like Jessie White Mario (1832–1906), in *La Riforma*, and articles in *La Nuova Antologia*, spread the notion that the Church, more than any other force, lay behind the revolts of the 1890s. Many others taught the simple positivism and scientism that played an important role in Social Darwinism and Marxism, following their counterparts in the rest of Europe in dividing the world into the camps of those infallibly aiding progress and those hindering it, and taking it for granted that the opening of every new train station indicated a victory over obscurantist religion.[12]

Nevertheless, even contemporary observers noted that under the threat of more pressing problems, open, direct, persistent "excommunication of Catholicism" was very much on the decline as the old century turned into the new. What always remained strong, however, was the psychological obstacle preventing some people who came from a background of hostility to the Roman Church from moving from a passion for her destruction to a serious contemplation of an alliance with her in the face of new dilemmas. This potentially inhibited all those of Jansenist or other anti-papal

---

12   See Jemolo's whole discussion of the problem, pp. 47–160.

religious heritage, survivors of the most heated Church-State battles of the Risorgimento, industrialists involved in a capitalist development which was indifferent to the problems of those whom it displaced and disgruntled, and even the children of families living in fervently Catholic areas, for whom anti-clericalism became, as Jemolo notes, a non-conformist necessity. It helps to explain the desire of press moguls like Luigi Albertini (1847–1941), with his *Corriere della Sera*, to try as best they could to act as though Catholicism simply did not exist at all.

One example of a political figure of this type is the Baron Sydney Sonnino (1847–1922), half Jewish, raised as a Protestant, rightist in temperament, proponent of a powerful lay state, painfully aware of the weaknesses of the "legal" organs of the new Kingdom in the face of the "real" problems of the South in particular, and yet lacking substantive psychological stimulus to engage in anything other than half-hearted bridging of the secular-religious abyss. Such men were souls in agony. Sonnino was very much on the hunt for a means of building deeper support for an Italy which possessed little in the way of solid historical and emotional roots, but in a manner that could circumvent the need to treat Catholicism and the Church as equal partners in the enterprise. [13]

A late nineteenth and early twentieth century activist eager for a non-Catholic intellectual position that might come to his aid in constructing a stronger, secular-minded Italy generally found the crude positivism of the day unappealing and insufficient to his needs. It was this intransigent and simplistic materialism which was brutally criticized by Benedetto Croce (1866–1952) in "A proposito del Positivismo Italiano," in his journal, *La Critica*, in 1905. Practically all the existing parties in 1900 paid court to such positivism, the Estrema and the Socialists in perhaps the most pronounced fashion; and in consequence all might intellectually be found desperately wanting. [14]

Serious men could, however, turn to another fountain from which to drink, that which was fed by the broad stream of nineteenth century thought which may be labeled Romantic Idealism. This outlook reflected a heady combination of concerns for feeling,

---

13   Thayer, 59, 69–70, 79, 89, 124–126, 174–175, 210; Jemolo, pp. 76, 96, 106, 132, 148, 149.
14   Jemolo, pp. 87–94.

passion, freedom, will and identification with the masses, presented in a charismatic, prophetic and seemingly spiritual framework that nevertheless could also justify the exercise of the most brutal, physical force. It emphasized the importance of the individual as a means of underlining the superiority and dignity of the human person against mechanist insistence upon inflexible mathematical and scientific laws, and the need to display individual "energy" and "action" in order to confirm the justice of a man's convictions. Discussion of various aspects of Romantic Idealism entails what might appear to be a lengthy digression from a precise historical argument into a hazy realm of philosophical and psychological speculation, but it is one which I believe greatly assists in clarifying the confused international climate of opinion from which the more thoughtful Italian strain of anti-Catholicism gained much of its intellectual inspiration. I will, therefore, take the liberty of steering Italian History into this speculative continental whirlpool, in the hopes of drawing substantive, if mystifying, fruit from it by the end of the chapter.

Perhaps the most potent of the variety of sources of Romantic Idealism can be found in the writings of the Swiss thinker Jean-Jacques Rousseau (1712–1778). Rousseau felt himself to be the prophet of an infallible mission based upon his certain possession of "virtue." For Rousseau, virtue was not something which was attained, even if only in part, by personal action, as a Catholic might think. Rather, it was a "state of being" completely separate from each of man's activities but one: that of sincerely stripping himself of all that was not "natural"; i.e., all that was not spontaneous to him, the non-spontaneous being identified by Rousseau as masquerade, pretension and hypocrisy. This stripping-down action he considered himself to have successfully performed, especially when answering critics of his behavior in his *Confessions* (published posthumously, 1782), where he revealed to the world everything deepest within his soul, without consideration for the effect that such disclosure might have upon his personal fortunes. Having through such an action become "virtuous," Rousseau had no further need to be ashamed of deeds that others thought to be reprehensible; deeds which he himself would have considered to be reprehensible in a "non-virtuous" man who did not openly proclaim a consistent commitment to spontaneous "nature." Rousseau had come to terms with himself as the consistently passionate, natural man; Rousseau was, therefore, good. He was also perfect, because truth and virtue could not help but allow the completely liberated person to reach complete self-fulfillment.[15]

More than this, however, Rousseau was actually Everyman. Anyone who sincerely stripped himself down to his natural state, and thus became truthful, virtuous and free, as Rousseau had done, would have to be indistinguishable from him. This is why the various lovers in his widely-read nouvelle *Héloise* (1761) are actually only loving themselves as they see their images in other people, and the teacher in his enormously influential *Emile* (1761) can be said by Rousseau to both liberate the child and make the youth into himself at one and the same time. For "the whole art of the master is hiding this constraint under the veil of pleasure or of diversion in such a way that they think they want everything that one obliges them to do.... There is no subjection so perfect as the one which retains the appearance of liberty; thus one captivates the very will itself ."[16] Conversely, anyone who is not Rousseau-like, anyone who criticizes him and his actions, anyone who fails to pity him in his trials, is neither free, nor virtuous, nor truthful. In fact, he is not human. Blum describes the situation well in commenting on Rousseau's discussion of himself as the "spectator-animal" contemplating the pointless being; the "suffering animal."[17]

The Spectator animal was denied pleasurable pity in regarding the suffering animal because the suffering animal was evil and hence unworthy of sympathy. Since Rousseau knew that mankind was, like him, good, he was forced to the awful but inevitable realization that the creatures who treated him so heartlessly were not really people at all, that the key to the mystery was that "my contemporaries were but mechanical beings in regard to me who acted only by impulsion and whose actions I could calculate only by the laws of movement." He was now really alone, the only human being left amid a throng of automatons; the human race existed solely in him.

---

15   See Blum's whole discussion of Rousseau's thought: Blum, Carol, *Rousseau and the Republic of Virtue* (Ithaca: Cornell, 1986), pp. 27–132.
16   *Rousseau*, in Blum, p. 67.
17   Ibid., p. 99.

Rousseau was convinced that the non-virtuous and non-human world around him was basically hostile to the effort to perfect it. The duty of Everyman-Rousseau was to make that world into himself or cause it to disappear before it do him any further damage. The question of an initial flaw undermining the value of this entire argument could not even be imagined; the sincere, virtuous, free, liberated Everyman was free from error. No discussion concerning the ground and justification of this underlying truth was permissible. It was a self-evident given. Doubt regarding his position would in effect mean allowing the sham world of the hypocrite to influence him once more. A critique of his obvious rejection of the doctrine of Original Sin, such as that offered by Archbishop Christophe Beaumont of Paris, had no meaning in the Rousseauian universe whatsoever. It simply proved the fact that the prelate, by belief and profession a slave of a supernatural religion, was not thinking naturally. He was not really human. Logically speaking, he was one of the suffering animals for whom no sympathy could be felt, and who could be eliminated.[18]

A Rousseau-like conviction of the infallibility of the free, non-hypocritical, virtuous, natural man, and the simultaneous reliability of this perfect being as the key to understanding the Will of the People, was so endemic to nineteenth century revolutionary thought as to defy any attempt to exhaust depiction of its incidence. It regularly appears in literature, in the novels of men like Hugo and Stendhal, in appeals to the example of Napoleon, and in the manifestos of the leaders of liberal, democratic, nationalist, anarchist and utopian or Marxist socialist movements. We are constantly told that proponents of one cause or another are "sincere" (i.e., spontaneous, non-hypocritical and natural) in their beliefs, and, therefore, virtuous and infallible; that their sincerity is revealed by an energy and consistency of often inconsistent and passionate action that only the Enemy of the People, destined for the rubbish heap of history, could fail to recognize as being good. Again, others cannot be judged by the same standard as the Rousseauian Hero if they are not incorporated into that Hero's Mystical Body—his immediate entourage, or the organization that he has created to carry out his and, by definition, the People's

18   Ibid.

will. Thus, for Hugo, the revolt of "The People" accepting his message is redemptive; the revolt of the mass of the inhabitants of the Vendée (or the Italian resisters to the French revolutionary invasion in the 1790s) is a vile riot. The massacres perpetrated by the former are redemptive; a tap on the finger by the latter in self-defense is the most wretched of crimes. Elimination of the Enemy of the People is a cleansing by the actively virtuous, perhaps the most noble of spiritual measures in an obscurantist universe that uses a supposedly supernatural spiritual sense as yet another justification for base, hypocritical sham.[19]

Italy was very sensitive and open to all these arguments. In fact, it developed a love affair with romantic, idealist maxims of Rousseauian flavor. The ground for them had long been prepared by the Jansenists, who were unshakeably convinced of the infallibility of their interpretation of Catholicism, and outraged by the suffering that they had endured at the hands of papally-backed hypocrites for remaining true to their (self-evident) virtuous state. Jansenists were themselves an influence in Rousseau's understanding of Christianity in his brief period of flirtation with the Roman Church. It comes as no surprise that Pisa, in that Grand Duchy of Tuscany which was perhaps the most important center for the dissemination of Jansenist ideas in Italy, was already an eighteenth-century foyer for the spread of the Swiss radical's teaching as well, and one that influenced Filippo Buonarotti (1761–1837), the first great Italian revolutionary agitator, active in the life of Carboneria. The attraction of Napoleon as the charismatic man for all seasons, whose Energy and Action justified his transforming the world around him, was strong in Italy. Much of the peninsula had been swept up in the general-consul-emperor's whirlwind, and many of its bourgeois inhabitants were given new ambitions through the influence of his revolutionary changes, which were favorable to their interests.[20]

Giuseppe Mazzini (1805–1872), the foremost Italian nationalist thinker and organizer, grounded his certainties about God, man, nationhood and democracy in a theism whose precise roots have been hotly debated by different historians. Whatever their roots,

19 Billington, James H., *Fire in the Minds of Men* (New York: Basic, 1980), pp. 155–157, 206–226, 234–242.
20 Ibid., pp. 88, 98, 149–150, 206–226; 248.

they were backed by infallible, prophetic utterances that exude the omnipresent Rousseauian motifs, and the conviction that energy and action are the sure signposts guiding men to truth.[21] Italian nationalists of even a moderate spirit had little difficulty proclaiming the indefectibility of their program in similar fashion. Massimo d'Azeglio (1798–1866) and the editors of *Il Cimento*, for example, thought that they could adequately defend themselves against the charge of unwittingly unleashing an amoral nationalist crusade with which the Jesuits of the Roman journal, *La Civiltà Cattolica*, taxed them, by pointing to the sincerity, generosity and ipso facto correctness of the Risorgimento's intentions.[22] Even Italian Marxism in its most positivist form spoke frequently not with the voice of science, but with that of the author of the Confessions—prophetic, charismatic, natural and absolutely certain of accurately representing the popular will.[23] To be an educated non-Catholic Italian, as to be an educated, non-Catholic European, was to breathe a climate of opinion permeated by ideas best expressed by Rousseau. To be a Catholic, in the mind of someone raised in this *zeitgeist*, was to be the proponent of an unnatural, hypocritical religion disguising base motivations under the cover of the supernatural, and to appeal to a counter-source of infallibility that could only make him an enemy of spirit, freedom and the people at one and the same time. And even Catholics themselves were affected by this atmosphere, through the writings and example of the Abbé Félicité de Lamennais (1782–1854), whose *Paroles d'un Croyant* "directly inspired Mazzini's Faith and the Future of 1835, which he considered his best work."[24]

But, here, someone might object that Rousseauian influences in Italy were far overshadowed by those coming from Georg Wilhelm Friedrich Hegel (1770–1831). Indeed, no one can deny that Hegel had an enormous and much more demonstrable vogue in official circles of both the Risorgimento and the new Kingdom of Italy. Hegel's books were smuggled into prisons in pre-unification

21 See, for example, Mazzini, Giuseppe, *Address to Pope Pius IX on His Encyclical Letter* (London, 1865), p. 3.
22 See Il Cimento, (Torino, 1852–1855), vi, ii (1855), 110–111; Taparelli, in Pirri, P., ed., *Carteggi* (Milan: Biblioteca della Storia Italiana Recente, xiv, 1932), pp. 182–185.
23 Thayer, pp. 89–91.
24 Billington, p. 161.

days for the inspiration and encouragement of righteous suffering nationalists, who needed to be shown that history would vindicate them. His ideas were promoted through the work of Francesco de Sanctis (1817–1883), Minister of Education in the 1870's, and the academic and literary circles in Naples surrounding Bertrando Spaventa (1817–1883) and his brother, Silvio (1822–1893). Their influence was central to the development of the greatest of Italy's early twentieth century intellectuals, Benedetto Croce and Giovanni Gentile (1875–1944). Mikhail Bakunin, the seminal anarchist teacher, sang paeans to his Hegelian heritage, while no self-conscious Marxist, like Labriola, a student of the Spaventas, could do anything but confirm the German's significance as well.[25]

Be this as it may, Hegel's argument, in practice, is, nevertheless, a variation on the theme dear to Rousseau. It presumes that nature is shaped by a spiritual principle of freedom, incarnating and working itself out in history through the clash of energetic manifestations and counter-epiphanies, as these are charismatically revealed and commented upon by the Prussian professor. Hegel proclaimed the nineteenth century standard bearer for spiritually propelled action-for-freedom to be the coercive authority of the modern State. His teachings were, therefore, immensely useful in defending the righteousness of the Italian Risorgimento doctrine of the necessity of building, through violence, a unified, independent State. They were also handy in support of the measures of Italian rightist lay authorities who valued the "transcendent" qualities of that institution in its battles with a Church, a pope and a Syllabus of Errors which they saw as hopelessly out of touch with the world of the truly spiritual and undeniably infallible. The combined Risorgimento-rightist appeal to spirit and freedom on the one hand, and encouragement of secularization and police repression on the other, proved to be a potent tool for confusing the more logical, Aristotelian, Catholic mind seeking cogent arguments to oppose it. Anyone interested in the complications of the intellectual battle thus unleashed should consult the exchanges between Luigi Taparelli d'Azeglio (1793–1862) of La Civiltà Cattolica and Bertrando Spaventa.[26]

---

25 Thayer, pp. 49, 53, 128–138, 188, 199; Mack Smith, 236, 240.
26 Spaventa, in Gentile, Giovanni, ed., La Politica Dei Gesuiti (Milan: 1911), pp. 278–300; Taparelli d'Azeglio, in La Civiltà Cattolica, ii, viii (1854), passim.

Practical consequences are especially noticeable when these theories were applied to the issue of education. Hegelian adulation of the use of the State to achieve freedom in a way that was offensive to Catholics was omnipresent in journals and parliamentary reports from the 1850s through the 1870s, and underlay much of what was done in this realm thereafter. "Unregenerated" people were said not to be allowed the opportunity to succumb to the temptation of entrusting their children to the care of monks and nuns. Antonio Gallenga (1810–1895), writing in *Il Cimento* in June of 1855, well demonstrated the kind of approach that Catholics loathed, when he claimed for the State the total right to educate, religious being kept from this task until the people had been given "the discernment of good and evil." Up till the moment that "national regeneration" was completed, he insisted, the State had the duty to exercise, "let us say it frankly, the tyranny of educating." A proper State required "the unity in one person of the attributes of highest magistrate and supreme pontiff," in order to root out the long centuries of servitude with which the Church was associated. It was useless to cite the example of England and America as models of freedom, he concluded, since in these countries, nothing positive was demanded from the individual:[27]

But here among us the citizen is the property of the State: the law of conscription binds them to the soil of the fatherland during the most florid period of their life. The State has therefore the right and the duty of exercising over him an almost paternal tutelage. It would scarcely be able to consider him responsible to the laws of the land if it neglected or permitted others to pervert its moral and political education. That State that did not claim for itself the sole right for educating would only half understand the duty of legislator.

And Hegel, after all, was himself but a product of the other wing of the anti-mechanist tradition, that which was shaped by one of the greatest of Rousseau's contemporary admirers, Immanuel Kant (1724–1804). Kant, awakened by David Hume (1711–1776) from his "dogmatic slumbers," was as concerned as the Genevan prophet for rebuilding order upon nature, and a nature that could not be expressed by conforming oneself to the faulty information coming

27 Gallenga, *Il Cimento*, v, xii (1855), 1080, for extended quotation; otherwise, 1079–1081.

from outside the human person. He, too, was ultimately forced back upon an assertion of the infallible, sincere, non-hypocritical will that universalizes and proves itself in energetic action. However traditional the kind of order that Kant might have thought would emerge from this process, it seems to me that its practical, historical effect was to give carte blanche to different thinkers to assert varied and conflicting universalizing wills as infallible guides to order in a universe lacking objective (hypocritical?) scientific and logical laws: the natural, passionate, irrational individual; the conspiratorial, nationalist organization guided by the charismatic, spontaneous prophet; or the State shaped by the liberated, the strong-willed, and the consistently energetic men of action.

All the concepts discussed above responded to something embedded in the Italian anti-Catholic's mindset. Hence, Italian admirers of the lay State trained in Hegel's thought were always potentially open to Kantian or Rousseauian influences, while the same is true the other way around. Even the appearance of certain more traditional rightist treatises on the library shelves of turn of the century non-Catholic Italians has generally to be understood in the context of an attempt to utilize them to romantic idealist purpose. This is why Italian thinkers eager to escape the barren silliness of mechanist positivism were susceptible to the arguments of other Europeans groping in the same direction, but finding it impossible to do so without falling into the Rousseauian-Kantian anti-mechanist camp; men of "energy" and "action" like Henri Bergson (1859–1941), with his concept of *élan vital*, or Georges Sorel (1847–1922), in his Reflections on Violence (1908).[28] This is why one can find in the statements of all the varied inheritors of Romantic Idealism a frequently unconscious mixture of what would appear to be conflicting themes: on the one hand, devotion to an anarchic freedom based on a non-hypocritical energetic action which defines consistency as firm commitment to willfulness and the changeability of personal whim or a spiritualized "history"; on the other, an appeal to the use of State organs of physical repression to destroy that liberty in those deemed incorrigibly tied to a slave mentality. And, finally, this is also why none of them ever really raises himself to an appreciation of a truly spiritual

---

28   Thayer, pp. 13, 106, 133–141, 195–198, 201, 258. 388–389; Billington, pp. 425–427.

Catholic position. For Romantic Idealism, of both Rousseauian and Kantian-Hegelian origins, is itself a by-product of the same naturalist, anti-Catholic, Enlightenment outlook that gave birth to mechanist positivism; a *weltanschauung* which was held together, at its outset, only by a seemingly transcendental Deism begging to be logically refuted and brought down entirely to earth.

Several factors were thus coming together in the late nineteenth and early twentieth centuries to indicate the possible creation of new, lay movements that could conceivably bring together the many heads of Romantic Idealism, and, in particular, the combination of irrational will with private violence or coercive state power. Anarchism of the anti-parliamentary Errico Malatesta variety, as well as that promoted by part of the syndicalist movement, intent on escaping Marxist mechanism and finding some immediate tool by means of which to wipe out the corruption of authority, were very much susceptible to such developments. So was the more impatient strain of Socialism, represented, among others, by Benito Mussolini. Both of these sources provided recruits for the force that would most effectively profit from the latest appeal to energy and action, the new Italian nationalist movement. And this, in turn, would pave the way for the emasculation of Parliament in 1915, and the victory of fascist *squadrismo* after the First World War. D'Annunzio, the Futurists, and other nationalist devotees all worshipped at the shrine of a fascinating and explicit anarchic cult of violence and coercion which sometimes reached absolutely grotesque proportions, the profoundly anti-Catholic character of which was not lost on them:[29]

... the Nationalists could hardly preach of the mysterious powers of war and violence without rejecting the Christian view of peace and humility. A D'Annunzian, Nietzschean pose of neopaganism was very much in evidence among the imperialists. Papini in the Leonardo indulged in this, scoffing at what he called *pecorismo nazareno.* Corradini spoke of Christianity as "pathological and economic," whereas life consisted of conquest and struggle. In this, Papini and Corradini, as well as D'Annunzio, were capitalizing on Carducci's 'Romanism' as expressed in the Odi Barbare long after Carducci himself had abandoned the idea as artistically sterile.

---

29   Thayer, p. 202.

Nevertheless, the winds of the times seemed more to be blowing away from the "rejecters" and their efforts to circumvent Catholicism, towards the second position, that of the "pragmatists," those who wished to reach some open reconciliation with the Church and the Catholic position in society. Although this tendency claimed much of its constituency from men who were either indifferent to religion or merely disgruntled by the more exaggerated manifestations of clerical power, it also included individuals of firm anti-Catholic belief who were convinced that the deeper importance of other questions required a practical change of policy on their part. One could find supporters of the pragmatic viewpoint among practically all of the forces active in Italian political life.[30]

By 1876, rightists had become greatly concerned about the potential demagogic effects stemming from the Left's proposal of an expansion of the suffrage, modest though this actually was, and the weakening of State power accompanying its more pronounced espousal of free market principles. They turned, in consequence, to urgent appeals to Catholics to abandon the *non expedit* policy, and join their "natural allies" in a campaign against a resurgent "Jacobinism." Problems arose from what the orthodox judged to be the dubious professions of Catholicism coming from some men of the Right, as well as from the impossibility of accepting their infallible, spiritualized Hegelian State as the final arbiter of what constituted abuses in governmental *contretemps* with Church. It was difficult for Catholics to forget the mass of anti-clerical legislation passed between 1861 and 1876 under rightist auspices, and the fact that Minghetti had himself boasted, when faced with criticism on this score from the Left, of the high level of royal interference with the free action of the Papacy and Catholic organizations during his tenure as Prime Minister. Additionally, insofar as Catholics were active politically, on the local level, they found themselves more in tune with the leftists, and sharing with them a desire for an extension of the suffrage.

In fact, that historically anti-clerical Left proved itself to be open and pragmatic in national matters also, as its awareness of the weaknesses of the new Kingdom, which they desperately wanted to play a major international role, became more vivid. The Left did nothing to harm the *modus vivendi* for cohabitation with the

---

30   Jemolo, pp. 47–160; Thayer, pp. 124–133; Mack Smith, pp. 78–232.

Papacy which followed Pius IX's rejection of the Law of Guarantees of 1871. Even Zanardelli, whose anti-clerical convictions we have already noted, refused to entertain the suggestion of more rabid opponents of the Church, who wanted those bringing up new plans for reconciliation prosecuted. As the social crisis matured, leftists hoped that Catholic concern for private property and order would be a tool for bringing the Church into unified action with them versus Anarchism and Socialism.

In this, they were joined by a former member of the Estrema, Francesco Crispi. Crispi, a Freemason of deist convictions who had opposed the Law of Guarantees, had warned Bismarck and Gambetta of the international danger of the Papacy in 1876, and had sacked Torlonia as late as 1887, gradually emerged as the leader of the effort to form an alliance with Catholics in defense of the established order. He refused to take part in the ceremonies inaugurating the creation of an organization honoring the atheist Giordano Bruno in 1889, and claimed, now, to be happy with the system of practical cohabitation with the Church which maintained the existing equilibrium. Other anti-clerical heirs of Angelo Brofferio (1804–1866), Giuseppe Ferrari (1811–1876), Francesco Domenico Guerrazzi (1804–1873), and Ferdinando Petruccelli della Gattina (1815–1890) in the Estrema faction could still be venomous, however. And this fact, along with serious moral concerns for the social responsibility of property, doubts regarding the commitment to free-enterprise of a party that had begun by confiscating Church property, conviction that materialist socialism was merely a development of the same naturalism that had produced materialist capitalism, and fears of merely being used by a basically unaltered Crispi, led Catholic activists and prelates to back away from the Prime Minister's advances. His sharp reaction to their recalcitrance, as the crises of the 1890s increased, seemed to justify their reluctance.

Anarchism was closed to offers of cooperation with an authoritarian Church, but the still vague socialist movement allowed for some pragmatic proposals to emerge from its undefined ranks. The young Francesco Saverio Nitti (1868–1953), the future radical statesman, invited the Church, in *Il Socialismo Cattolico* (1891), to consider the way in which friendship for the socialist cause would benefit it. Despite the violent rants of *l'Asino*, disdain for cooperation with outrightly religious organizations, and the often bitter ridicule by socialist workers of their Catholic comrades, the party was never officially hostile to individual believers. Bissolati, Turati and Treves all made it abundantly clear that such issues troubling Catholics as the divorce proposal of 1902 were purely upper-class bourgeois concerns. Still, the reality of the role of materialist Marxist principles in the socialist movement, and the potential competition for control of the masses that its growing organization threatened, made activists like Toniolo and Romolo Murri (1870–1944) more concerned to draw stimulus and lessons from it for the purpose of better opposing it.

Liberals of both rightist and leftist complexion made new efforts to obtain pragmatic cooperation from Catholics in the period of social calming following the assassination of Umberto I at the hands of the anarchist, Gaetano Bresci, in 1900. These were the years most associated with the dominance of that dispassionate, peace-loving, Piedmontese supporter of the organs of legal Italy, Giovanni Giolitti (1842–1928). Giolitti was open to compromises with Catholics, but saw no need for any dramatic reconciliation as a prelude to joint action. *La Nuova Antologia*, which had published articles in favor of repression, turned away from an approach that seemed to menace all freedom of association. Rightists, by now, generally lacked the old Risorgimento interest in Church matters, perhaps due to an indifference to all theological and philosophical issues that would have seemed impossible to a Cavour, a Bettino Ricasoli (1809–1880) or a Ruggiero Bonghi (1826–1895). Indifference was demonstrated by their general lack of concern for the Modernist Controversy, which they considered to be an internal Church issue, and one that interested the State only insofar as it required defense of the civil rights of those who were excommunicated by the pope. The American example of Church-State relations, already appreciated by Crispi in the 1890s, was held up to ever further praise. A group of senators, disturbed by radicalism and socialism, began to pursue Church assistance versus enemies of individual freedom and property, while putting Catholics on warning regarding such "utopians" in their ranks as Toniolo and Murri. More modest proposals for divorce were presented by leftists in Parliament, while old rightists like Sonnino rejected the divorce project entirely. Alessandro Fortis (1841–1909), a Prime Minister from the ranks of the Estrema, was even willing to appoint the Marchese Nerio Malvezzi, "a Catholic ... who dared to say that the Law of Guarantees had not closed the Roman Question," into his cabinet in 1905, although he paid for it with opposition bringing his ministry down. [31]

While Liberals appealed to Catholics to join them against madcap colonial ventures, proponents of precisely such enterprises also made their voices heard by the second decade of the new century. Not all nationalists labeled the Church a divisive, effeminate institution, or were averse to exploring ties to it. Pragmatist proponents of conciliation could appeal to a joint nationalist-Catholic disdain for a legal Italy shutting out the legitimate demands of the real nation. Some of those favoring North African colonization also argued that this would solve the social problem of the Mezzogiorno, which troubled Catholic reformers as well. Nationalists were pleased by the reality of support from prelates, priests and laymen, especially children of old Catholic families, and hoped to build upon the interpretation of the war with the Ottomans over Libya that broke out in October, 1911 as a Crusade against Islam. [32]

The chief practical method by means of which Italian governments accomplished the work of accommodation was that of *trasformismo*. This term, utilized by Agostino Depretis in 1876 to describe efforts to work with, and "transform" the existing rightist government into one which reflected the will of its new, but divided, leftist masters, had a history in Italy extending back to the days of the Count Cavour. Giolitti was one of its master practitioners in the period before the First World War. *Trasformismo* sought to avoid radical divisions by, in effect, co-opting the representatives of all important political movements, well-established or embryonic, and winning them over to actions acceptable to the governmental majority. If the most energetic "enemy" figures could be won over to support the ruling coalition, the troops that they commanded would be left without leadership. While functioning nicely to maintain stability, successful *trasformismo* prevented the voice of serious opposition from being effectively heard in the organs of "legal" Italy even more than limited suffrage did. Pragmatists might appreciate it, but it was detested by men of strong conviction in the Estrema, as well as the more uncompromising Socialists,

31   Jemolo, pp. 131–132.
32   Ibid., pp. 153–154; Thayer, pp. 201–230.

Nationalists and Catholics, all of whom often viewed it as the most cynical tool of a thoroughly cynical parliamentary system.[33]

More thoughtful pragmatists could easily find themselves becoming supporters of the third position, that of the "palingenesists." Palingenesis, formed from the Greek words "again" and "birth," was the idea that a new and much better society was "emerging" in the nineteenth century, one that was destined to develop out of the earlier forces dominating western life, and one that would eliminate past divisions in a higher unity releasing energy for ever happier and humane projects. Such a vision rejected the pessimism of the apocalyptic thought popular in some religious-minded circles of the day, and reflected much more the hope for a "third age of humanity," "the arrival of the age of gold under the sign of universal fraternity through social justice," redolent of the prophecies of Joachim of Fiore.[34] Palingenesis could be appealing to any defender of "modern" ideas who still possessed a spiritual sense and did not want to jettison his personal Christian baggage and that of European civilization as a whole.

One group of people extremely interested in palingenesis and the uncovering of its mysteries was the Saint-Simonians: Claude Henri de Saint Simon (1760–1825), Barthélemy Enfantin (1796–1864), Saint-Amand Bazard (1791–1832), Auguste Comte (1798–1857), and their many fellow-travellers, like Charles Fourrier (1772–1837). Horrified by the violence and rejection of social order represented by the Revolution, the Saint-Simonians set out to illustrate the laws underlying community life, and the principles by means of which it had grown and developed organically through the ages. In this manner, they could show how one historical era had been the prelude for the next, and how the teachings of Jesus, the cult of the Virgin, a hierarchical priesthood, a liturgy and many other elements of western civilization still had a role, transfigured though it might now be, in modern life. Liberals, democrats and nationalists all around Europe could, and did, all tap into palingenesist visions, along with fervent supporters of more particular causes dear to one or another nineteenth-century group.[35]

---

33   Mack Smith, pp. 103–107, 123–128; Thayer, pp. 44–45, 48, 66–67, 82–83, 112, 130, 139, 141, 149, 372.
34   Mayeur, X, p. 864.
35   Ibid., pp. 837–904; Billington, pp. 217–224.

Catholics also responded to palingenesist arguments. To understand why is to have to turn once again to the figure Lamennais and his Rousseauian respect for the sparks unleashed by the non-hypocritical, natural order of things. Lammenais' connection to the energy syndrome was "traditionalism," that philosophical-political school which disdained the role of reason in grasping the truth, and, for that matter, in passing on the Faith as well. For Lammenais and traditionalists as a whole, the truth could not be understood, and the faith could not be taught, rationally; rather, they were handed down by the power of the very nature of things themselves, by means of a solid society's culture, institutions and people. For traditionalists, the Revolution's basic untruthfulness was evident in that, in order to accomplish its program for the salvation of France and her people, it had tried, against the opposition of the majority of those people, to destroy the culture and traditional institutions whose energy had created and defined France and Europe in the first place.

Problems for Lamennais came from the fact that one part of the tradition—the Catholic part—was not as active as it had to be. It itself lacked energy. If it continued to lack energy, then it would run the risk of not shaping the environment and not passing down the truth in the only way that truth effectively could be transmitted: namely, through society and social action. Hence, the need to shake institutions and people out of their torpor and "indifference," and restore their desire to fight energetically for what was true. The Essay on Indifference, his first important work, was really not an apology for the Catholic Faith; it was much more a call to energetic action.

Torpor could scarcely be hounded out of the Catholic soul if the Church as an institution were unable to function as she must. Thus, the Papacy, so cruelly harassed by the Enlightenment and the Revolution, had to have its just and full powers appreciated and restored. In addition, the Church in each nation had to be unchained for action under papal guidance. Unleash the Papacy and the national Church together, and indifference would retreat. With the retreat of indifference would come the willingness to commit energy to struggle, and with more energetic struggle would come advancement in truth.

Unfortunately, both the traditional monarchy and the national episcopacy fettered by it themselves lacked commitment to truth and the requisite courageous energy to free the Church. Casting about for an alternative force to lead the defense of traditional culture and Catholicism within the nation, Lamennais was led, ironically, to an untraditional conclusion. The Catholic People, which as a whole had also been unjustly and absurdly enchained by a legitimate monarchy playing the Enlightenment game, became, almost by default, the pillar on which to energize the tradition, politically and socially, inside the nation.

But here yet another unexpected problem intervened. The Papacy failed to see the truth. The very institution whose energies Lamennais was most seeking to release, and which would have most benefited by the liberation of the Church from the legitimist State through the work of the Catholic People, rejected his logic. It had lacked energy and erred. This left the Catholic People as a whole on their own as the sole defenders of the Truth within a given nation, a "silent majority" destined now to do its work even in opposition to those who were thought but yesterday to be its leaders. Palingenesis gave Lamennais the means to explain this phenomenon. In *Paroles d'un Croyant*, he argued that "the republicans of our days would have been the most ardent disciples of Christ eighteen centuries ago," thus, in effect, teaching that contemporary Catholics should see in them the best guides to the meaning of Christianity in the nineteenth century.[36]

Two themes appearing more clearly than any others in the nineteenth century palingenesist vision were adopted by Lamennais. One insisted that the age that was "emerging" from the European past was one that would overcome the confessional differences of what Lamennais called a mere "diplomatic Christianity." The third epoch of Humanity would see society enjoying the communion of a universal religion transcending an historical Faith which had outlived its usefulness, whose standard-bearers, again, as Lamennais noted, would be the People:[37]

> How far we still are from that religion of devotion, of self-forgetfulness for the good of all; in sum, of that fraternity of which one speaks so much! I only find it in the People; the People surround the cradle of the future, just as the shepherds

36 Mayeur, p. 848; also, pp. 837–904. See also the complete discussion in Bowman, Frank Paul, 1987, *Le Christ des Barricades* (Paris: Cerf).
37 Mayeur p. 866.

at Bethlehem surrounded that of the God about to be born. Blessings on the little ones, the simple of heart. It is those who will save the world.

Moreover, the age emerging out of the Christian past would be "socialist" in character. We have seen that the precise definition of "Socialism" in the nineteenth century was a tricky question at the very best, given the wide variety of understandings and aspirations then attached to it, but the idea that it involved a concern for economic inequality and social injustice was universal. Secularists, spiritualists, Protestants and Catholics alike were involved in Socialism's birth and evolution. For our purposes, one ought to note that Catholics like Philippe Ballanche (1776–1847) and Philippe Buchez (1796–1865) were fervent proponents of the concept of the emergence of Christianity into Socialism, the former seeing the essence of the Christian mission as the abolition of inequality in his day, and the latter elevating the Revolution, Robespierre and the People into the instruments of a constant battle against tyranny until the great day of the final liberation of all should arrive. Similar themes were elaborated in the Catholic Parisian journal, *L'Ere Nouvelle*, of 1848. And Lamennais himself also evoked some of the language of the Socialist palingenesists in his commentaries on the Gospel of Mark, which he read as a kind of allegory of his own historical fate.[38]

Mazzini and Garibaldi were sympathetic to the palingenesist approach, the former having been deeply influenced by Lamennais, and both men having traveled in Saint-Simonian circles. The founder of Young Italy sought to turn the former priest from violent revolutionary writing to violent revolutionary action. Mazzini reproached him for his inactivity by letter from London, urging him, at the very least, to lead a regenerated priesthood basing itself purely on God's love, to guide a "Church of Precursors which I should like to see you found while waiting for the People to rise," one that would embrace the heavens and the earth:[39]

Why do you only write books? Humanity awaits something more from you . . . Do not deceive yourself, Lamennais, we need action. The thought of God is action; it is only by action that

---

38 Ibid., p. 892.
39 Ibid., p. 893, Billington, pp. 161, 217–224.

it is incarnated in us . . . . So long as you will be alone, you will only be a philosopher and a moralist in the eyes of the masses; it is as a priest that you must appear before it, a priest of the future, of the epoch which is beginning, of that new religious manifestation of which you have a presentiment, and which must inevitably end in that new heaven and new earth which Luther glimpsed three centuries ago without being able to attain it, since the time had not yet come.

Lamennais' influence in Catholic Action, even after his excommunication, was immense. Liberal Catholicism was founded by men who came from his camp and expressed openness to the "energetic" reform movements of their day, while claiming to reject the theoretical principles that had brought him into ill repute with the Papacy. His ideas, the ideas of a palingenesis connected with expressions of energy and action, and the Romantic Idealism lying behind them, revived, again, in Catholic circles, in Italy as elsewhere, in the 1890s and 1900s, through the example of movements like the Sillon, the development of Modernism, and the influence of writings like Maurice Blondel's (1861–1949) treatise, *Action.* They would continue, despite papal condemnation, to gain further strength after the First World War.[40] Mazzinians, Risorgimento nationalists in general, and men of the Right in particular, expressed a mix of Liberal Catholic, Hegelian and Saint-Simonian sentiments that easily fit into a palingenesist perspective. Even Croce, an a-religious defender of lay culture with no place for true transcendence in his vision, gave a palingenesist timbre to some of his comments in *La Filosofia della Pratica*, by speaking of the religious man as the philosopher's little brother. His one-time collaborator on *La Critica*, Giovanni Gentile, dabbled in efforts at reconciliation with Catholic thought, claimed appreciation for the logic of men like the *Civiltà* editor, Luigi Taparelli d'Azeglio, but happily jettisoned earlier Church doctrine which had been superceded by the demands of modern "energies."[41] In short, there

---

40 Petit, pp. 15, 135, 192–197, 200, 211; See, also, Dubarle, D., ed., *Le Modernisme* (Paris:Beauchesne, 1980); Meinvielle, J., *De Lamennais a Maritain* (Paris: La Cité Catholique, 1949). and Sarasella, Daniela, *Modernismo* (Milan: Editrice Bibliografica 1995).
41 Jemolo, pp. 91–95; Gentile, pp. ix–xiii; Minghetti, Marco, *Miei Ricordi* (Three Volumes, Turin, 1888–1892), Vol. iii, 17–18; passim.

was always some support in Italy for the idea of the "emergence" of a "higher" religious viewpoint, and this from both Catholic and secularist starting points.

Whether for pragmatic or palingenesist reasons, many Italian Catholics were eager for a change in the Church's prohibition of participation in national political life from the 1860s onwards. Aside from the movement of "patriotic priests" of the Risorgimento era, one can note the yearnings of such prominent writers as Fr. Carlo Curci (1810–1892), a former editor of the determinedly anti-unification *La Civiltà Cattolica*, who paid for his change of heart about reconciliation and alliance with the more conservative elements within the government by expulsion from the Society of Jesus. Other enthusiasts included the contributors to the Florentine journal, *La Rassegna Nazionale*, founded by Count Stefano Jacini, a rightist statesman, in 1879, which sought to bring both Catholic and moderate non-Catholic thinkers together, and the novelist, Antonio Fogazzaro (1842–1911). Hopes were particularly high among these men in 1886–1887, as can be seen in the exchange of ideas on this issue between Monsignor Geremia Bonomelli (1831–1914), the Bishop of Cremona, and Leo XIII, and their expectations following the pope's conciliatory letter of May, 1887, *Episcoporum Ordinem*. Church participation in the public sorrow for the colonial losses at Dogali in Abyssinia (1887), Father Luigi Tosti's (1811–1897) pamphlet, *La Conciliazione*, with its exuberant prophecies for reconciliation in 1888, and the joy of many Catholics over the friendly expressions of King Umberto I (1878–1900) on the occasion of Leo's priestly jubilee, all attest to a similar hope for change. We have seen how these dreams came to naught in the tense social atmosphere of the late 1880s and 1890s.

By the late 1890s, however, many more activists within the Opera Dei Congressi were seriously divided over their future attitude towards participation in national politics. One group insisted upon continuing business as usual, neither compromising with the existing authorities, nor opposing them in politics directly, lest the Socialists, whom it considered to be simply the more radical child of an erring liberal parent, pick up the pieces in a bitter public conflict with the government. A second force, many-headed in character, thought that business as usual was no longer opportune. One of its constituent elements, from 1899 onwards, wished boldly to declare liberal economic policies to be erroneous and immoral, and longed for the creation of a distinctly popular political party. Although priests like Don Romolo Murri were prominent in its ranks, it was nevertheless convinced that its social concerns would give it a broad appeal beyond the immediate camp of believers that would require operation outside the constraints of the ecclesiastical hierarchy.

Another faction, which came to be known as the clerico-moderates, wished, by 1908, to take advantage of the signs of a weakening of liberal opposition to the Church to see if a broader "conservative party" might be created. Catholic abstention from national politics would end, and leaders who had been prepared during that abstention could move forward to exercise direct influence over Italian political life. This group included the old conciliarists around La Rassegna Nazionale, younger proponents of cooperation such as Filippo Meda (1869–1939). and, eventually, even the editors of La Civiltà Cattolica, which began to speak sympathetically of the work of leftist Prime Ministers like Luigi Luzzatti (1841–1927) and the need for devotion to the Italian Army.[42]

Papal involvement with these three approaches became more intense after the turn of the century. To begin with, Leo XIII, on January 18th, 1901, published the encyclical letter *Graves de Communi*, in which he made it clear that he was not in favor of the creation of a distinctly Catholic mass party in Italy. This may well have been because of his recognition of a recrudescence of Mennaisian tendencies, in France as well as in Italy. If the words "Christian Democracy" were employed at all, Leo insisted, they could only legitimately be employed to indicate "a beneficent Christian action in favor of the people"; not as a statement committing the Church *qua* Church to a party involved in democratic politics. Moreover, as the first of its two names emphasized, "Christian Democracy" could only exist with reference to a grounding in the Christian Faith; a direct appeal for the votes of non-Catholics was thereby excluded. Even what today would be called a "preferential option for the poor" was dismissed as unacceptable by the pope, since a true concept of "the People" had to include all social classes, coordinated into one harmonious

---

42   Jemolo, pp. 47–160; Invernizzi, Il Movimento Cattolico, pp. 15–58.

whole. Leo did, however, praise those who were engaged in a democratic action that did all it could to lessen the sufferings of the ordinary man.

But papal action did not end here. It was further stimulated by an intensification of the debate within the Opera. In September of 1902, Giovanni Grosoli, a man who was rather favorable to the more social-minded democratic elements of the movement who were looking forward to the eventual creation of a political party, became President of that organization. At the XIX Congress in Bologna, from November 10–13, 1903, it became clear that the supporters of Grosoli and the much more committed Christian Democrat, Romolo Murri, had gained the edge over the faction which was eager to continue abstention from politics and maintain a joint anti-liberal and anti-socialist approach. An imprudent circular from Grosoli indicating that "old questions," presumably such as those surrounding the Temporal Power, no longer mattered that much to contemporary Catholics, stirred a second intervention, this time by the new pope, Pius X. While personally content to let the Temporal Power issue die, he was disturbed by what he considered to be the Opera's lay-clerical insubordination to higher ecclesiastical authority. It was dissolved, by order of the Secretary of State, Merry del Val (1865–1930), on July 28, 1904. Section II, dealing with Social Economy, was alone maintained to emphasize the fact that "beneficent action in favor of the people" was not being punished by this severe measure.

Pius X, like Leo XIII, clearly disliked the idea of a creating a distinct, Italian Christian Democratic Party appealing for non-Catholic support. He, too, felt threatened by Mennaisian concepts. This can be seen not only by his condemnation of the French Sillon, but also by his reproach of Bonomelli of Cremona, who had begun to praise the separation of Church and State, and his chastisement of Romolo Murri, the journal, *Cultura Sociale*, the Lega Democratica Italiana, and every other initiative that envisaged a democratic cooperation of officially constituted Catholic organizations with non-Catholics who were inspired by the concept of "social justice" rather than by religion.

Still, Catholics, by the time of the general election of 1904, had already shown little respect for the *non expedit*. Pius X's restructuring of the Catholic Movement on June 11, 1905, with the publication of an encyclical letter, *Il Fermo Proposito*, took account of this. Section II of the Opera became the Unione Economico-Sociale dei Cattolici Italiani. An Unione Popolare tra i Cattolici d'Italia was established on the model of the German Volksverein. Most importantly, however, the Unione Elettorale Cattolica Italiana, designed to prepare Catholics for participation in political life on the national level, also now made an appearance. With the "business as usual" position abandoned and the hopes for a Catholic Party squelched, Rome ended by opting for the clerico-moderate line, pushing the Unione Elettorale towards the kind of contractual agreement with more conservative-minded liberals already utilized in other countries. While the *non expedit* remained on the books, *Il Fermo Proposito* empowered bishops to dispense from its strictures, and it was quite clear to everyone that its days were numbered, officially, as well as on the practical level.[43]

The great chance to put the plan into operation came with the introduction of universal male suffrage, which Giolitti felt could no longer be resisted, in 1913. This increased the value and impact of the Catholic vote for "conservatives," resulting in the famous and highly successful "Pact" of 1913 of the President of the Unione, Vincenzo Ottorino Gentiloni (1865–1916) with the Giolittan Liberals; an "alliance" that some moderate Nationalists would also not have been averse to joining. Seven "commandments" laid out by the Unione were subscribed to by a large number of individual Liberal candidates for office, all of them assuring support for Catholic policies in exchange for Catholic votes. The *non expedit* was lifted entirely to allow election of the men in question, guaranteeing victory for over two hundred deputies.

Revealed by a variety of sources, ranging from the *Corriere della Sera* to *La Civiltà Cattolica*, the Gentiloni Pact aroused the last anti-clerical storm of the period with which this article is concerned. A mass of Rightists, Leftists, Estrema supporters of both republican and radical hues and Nationalists took up the cudgel in defense of secularist principles. These included Sonnino,

---

43 Kalyvas, p. 89 ; Invernizzi, *L'Unione Elettorale*, pp. 11–20; Jemolo, pp. 108, 122; Mack Smith, 251–252; Invernizzi, *Il movimento cattolico*, pp. 15–58; Agócs, Sándor, *The Troubled Origins of the Italian Catholic Labour Movement* (Detroit: Wayne State, 1988), pp. 165–199; Launay, Marcel, *La Papauté à l'Aube du XX Siècle* (Paris: Cerf, 1997), pp. 106–111, 183–191.

Albertini, Luzzatti, two future Prime Ministers, Antonio Salandra (1853–1931) and Vittorio Emmanuele Orlando (1860–1952), most of the Press, and numerous student organizations. The State was endangered by its ancient enemy once more. Much was made of the address of Antonio Rossi, the Archbishop of Udine, at the VIII Settimana Sociale at Milan, in November–December, 1913, as proof of the evils that cooperation could engender for the civil authority. Rossi had merely argued that the Temporal Power issue could be adequately resolved through adding international backing to the Law of Guarantees. This reopening of what secularists considered to be the closed Roman Question, was said to show a rebelliousness and even lack of patriotism which was a portent of the further clericalist demands that Catholics emboldened by the Pact were sure to make. Men like Meda, who had been elected to Parliament in 1909, protested that Catholic patriotism was in no way in question; the problem was simply that honest Italian citizens had decided that they need not view themselves merely as bulwarks against Socialism, and wanted a reconciliation and political participation that would fully protect their religious rights. Still, the anti-clerical outcry was so great that Giolitti tried to repair the damage to his government by reviving the call for enforcement of civil before religious marriage. In doing so, he alienated the Catholics alongside his other enemies. With the radicals of the Estrema especially angry, the fourth Giolittan Ministry thus came to an end.[44]

Nevertheless, the Church's option for the clerico-moderate position held firm, and, with it, a desire to influence an Italy governed by conservative-minded Liberals of basically capitalist mentality. It was this encouragement of candidates of the industrialist interests that aroused Estrema complaints regarding the Gentiloni Pact as much as any anti-clerical sentiment. In fact, the same *sous-text* alarmed men of Christian democratic sympathies like Murri and Dom Luigi Sturzo (1871–1959) as well.[45] As time went on, the answer of the call for cooperation with Italians of moderate liberal background would lead to the "emergence" of a clerico-moderate, Liberal Catholicism. This, like Lamennais, would come to insist

---

44 Jemolo, pp. 132–139; Invernizzi, *L'Unione*, pp. 24–38; Agócs, pp. 165–199.
45 Invernizzi, *L'Unione*, pp. 33–36; Agócs, pp. 197–198.

upon a pragmatic separation of Church and State that rendered the Catholic doctrine on that issue theoretical and harmless. It would also subscribe to a palingenesist "higher" religion of all men of good will reducing the anti-modernist Catholicism of Pius X to the world of the catechism; a world that could conveniently be forgotten when dealing with the "real world" of practical politics. This "rebirth" of Catholicism could overcome quarrels of Church and State by effectively bending the former to the demands of the "higher religion" of the latter, whose value was demonstrated by its "energetic" practical "action" for peace and prosperity. But it would also encourage those whose understanding of palingenesis required a new Catholicism which was much more democratic or socialist in character, one allying itself with liberation theologies of varied types. All this, however, is the stuff of another chapter in another book.

What concerns us here is the Italian environment out of which the migrants to the United States from the Mezzogiorno arrived. These were mostly peasants lacking formal education, religious as well as secular, that would have introduced them to the complications of the problems discussed above. Such problems did, indeed, affect them, secularization and liberal economic theories playing a serious role in the rural disruptions in the former Kingdom of the Two Sicilies. Interestingly enough, the American experience to which the uprooted southern peasantry would be exposed, the experience praised by men like Crispi, was one that was guided by a vision of pragmatic pluralism whose attitude towards religion and Church-State relations had much in common with ideas and experiments that were important in Italy. Their New World Order, when transported as a model to the Republic of Italy (and the globe) after the Second World War, was to find a soil in which it could easily take root and grow; whether for good or for ill, time alone will tell.

8

An Introductory
Anti-Capitalist Manifesto[†]

No other forces are to be recognized except those which reside in matter, and all the rectitude and excellence of morality ought to be placed in the accumulation and increase of riches by every possible means, and the gratification of pleasure. (Error #58, Pius IX, *Syllabus of Errors*, 1864)

A SPECTRE IS HAUNTING TRADITIONAL Catholicism: the cult of Enlightenment capitalism and its ideology of the unrestrained free market. I find the influence of this sect in American Catholic circles to be historically frustrating, intellectually offensive, and spiritually devastating. It is historically frustrating in its blithe indifference to the dramatic nineteenth century battle during which the basic Catholic complaints against modern capitalism were first cogently expressed and accepted by the Church. It is intellectually offensive insofar as it neglects the serious Catholic anti-capitalist critique, often reducing it to a purely romantic flirtation with pre-industrial life. It is spiritually devastating, because worship of the unrestrained market drives a stake into the very heart of the Catholic vision, erecting an impenetrable intellectual barrier to the transformation of individual and society in Christ, and turning sincere Catholic believers into schizophrenic practitioners of a blatant practical Modernism.

Allow me to begin by insisting that this short article could easily have been called "Been There, Done That" or "Nothing New Under the Sun." This is due to the fact that the entire contemporary debate concerning the acceptability and catholicity of the unrestrained market is in no way a groundbreaking one. It was already conducted in Catholic circles a century and a half ago, and with clearly anti-capitalist results. Anyone looking for the precise details of this old dispute and the names of the people involved in it can consult my book, *Removing the Blindfold* (Angelus Press, 2014). My goal, here, is a much more modest one; that of merely

[†] Unpublished article (2004).

opening Catholic eyes to the general history of this nineteenth-century dialogue and the issues which were truly central to it. The sad fact that this needs to be done at all indicates just how complete the victory of the anti-traditionalist position in Roman Catholic circles has been.

Although discussions of the relationship of capitalism and Catholicism began in the first part of the 1800s, it really took the Revolutions of 1848, and especially the Parisian social and economic uprising called the June Days, to intensify them. Crucial to this intensified discussion was the attempt by certain segments of the liberal capitalist bourgeoisie to forge an alliance with long-time Catholic opponents who seemed to be as horrified as they were by the appearance in June of 1848 of a socialist threat to property. Creation of a unified anti-socialist Party of Order, such liberals argued, should be the overriding goal of all morally upright and far-sighted men.

One troublesome condition for the sealing of this alliance was demanded, however: obliteration of much of the intellectual and historical record of the previous one hundred years. While Catholics would be permitted by their new friends to pursue criticisms of those Enlightenment and French revolutionary principles which produced socialism, they would be obliged to abandon objections to any of the very same precepts which had fashioned liberal capitalism. Obvious "common sense" was said to dictate a joint liberal-Catholic polemic versus the socialist evil. Continued Catholic anti-capitalist attacks would, on the other hand, represent an inexplicable, pointless, peevish waste of intellectual energy, and merely aid the destructive advance of the palpable Red Menace.

Now some of our Catholic ancestors were only first awakened to the problems of modernity by the disturbances of the "June Days." Shocked by the open critiques of property accompanying this uprising, they did not investigate its deeper causes and really quite variegated and often even traditionalist complaints. Instead, many lunged for the liberal capitalist bait with enthusiasm and joined, fervently, in the common crusade against socialism. They obligingly condemned as intransigent obscurantists and shameless rabble rousers those of their fellow-believers who refused to jettison the broader philosophical and historical battle with Enlightenment liberalism.

But such "intransigents" were unmoved by the "common sense" onslaught of the Party of Order. They insisted that any coherent response to contemporary evils had to emphasize the truth that liberal capitalism and socialism were actually blood brothers; that both had exactly the same atomistic, naturalist Enlightenment roots; that the arguments of the liberal capitalists had actually given intellectual birth to the doctrines of the socialists; that capitalist excesses had provided psychological stimulus to the desperate spirit of the June Days.

Catholic social doctrine, beginning with the negative attacks of Pius IX's *Syllabus of Errors* (1864) and the positive guidance of Leo XIII's (1878–1903) encyclicals, emerged out of this intense, post-1848 debate. It is true, as critics of this social doctrine note, that its teaching is in many respects a sketchy and tolerant one. It does indeed allow for a kaleidoscope of practical responses to modern economic conditions, ranging from calls to scrap the liberal capitalist system entirely to acceptance of the basic framework which this system has created and vigorously maintained as a prudential necessity. Still, there is no doubt whatsoever that the Church deemed the "intransigents" to be correct on one absolutely crucial matter: the need to reject the principle of the unrestrained free market as a morally reprehensible standard. This rejection rings loud and clear through every papal statement on social issues. To paraphrase a certain American Catholic weekly, the Church decided that no one could be a sincere Catholic and a supporter of the unrestrained free market simultaneously.

Germany, Austria, Italy, France, Belgium, the Netherlands, Switzerland and even the United Kingdom were all centers for this nineteenth century debate. As intimated above, the bulk of those anti-capitalist thinkers whose ideas really had an influence on the *Syllabus* and the Leonine encyclicals were not at all obsessed with a return to an idyllic life on a feudal manor filled with altruistic barons and voluntarily servile peasants. All realized that capitalist investment in modern industry was yielding a greater productivity than man had ever known before. A number were fully aware of benefits emerging from industrialization, and convinced that, having entered down its pathway, there was no easy, charitable way out of it either. Nevertheless, personal experiences with the unrestrained free market and its justification (often obtained in a period of exile in 1848 in Britain or famished Ireland) convinced them that modern capitalism was an ideologically revolutionary force which also had the capacity for causing an enormous amount of unneeded suffering for mankind.

Let us take the arguments of *La Civiltà Cattolica*, the "intransigent" Jesuit journal published in Rome after 1850, as an example of the critique I am relating. Its editors, men like Luigi Taparelli d'Azeglio, Carlo Curci, and Matteo Liberatore, examined the Enlightenment capitalist system from many different standpoints and in a massive number of articles stretching over many decades. One line of their criticism, jointly philosophical, theological, historical, sociological and psychological in character, ran as follows.

Western civilization grew up emphasizing the existence of an objective order of nature, the importance of individual freedom within that order, and the need for individuals to be enlightened as to the character of nature and freedom through the guidance of authoritative societies like the family and the State. Western thinkers argued that individuals, left to their own devices, simply could not properly see all that needs to be seen to understand either the objective order of things or the essence of human liberty. Individual knowledge and personal freedom could only be perfected though life in community. Social beings alone could become wise and free. Unaided, anti-social individuals could possess but a fragmented, flawed science of nature and knowledge of their place within it. They would thus be condemned to use their liberty to destroy themselves as well as the people around them.

Such ideas, already shaped by the ancient Greeks, really only gained historical clout due to the Incarnation and Redemption. Christ provided supernatural teaching and medicine to heal the weaknesses and flaws of a natural world which had chosen to mar itself through sin. His message confirmed an order and purpose to things that even the best of non-believers were tempted intellectually to question and practically to contradict. His labors for the salvation of human persons underlined the central value of the individual to the plan of God. His demand for individual submission to Him and to His Mystical Body placed a supernatural stamp upon the importance of authoritative communal guidance of men. Christ taught that it was only through full membership and participation in supernatural society, only, in effect, by choosing to see Creation through God's eyes, that individuals and societies could fully understand nature and use it fittingly. The Incarnation gave men the ability to use nature to serve the God who had created it to the utmost degree, raising their consciousness of the intrinsic value and responsibility of all of nature's specific tools, from its sciences to its temporal authorities, as it did so. Without the supernatural grace of God, imparted through a socially powerful Church, individuals could not suitably understand and exploit what they seemed to be capable of knowing and putting to use even on purely natural grounds alone.

Any economist formed by these influences would know that he could not base his knowledge of the functioning of the market upon his unaided, atomistic reason and desires alone. He would realize that his economic reasoning and decisions must be informed by the deeper wisdom gained by actively living under the authoritative guidance of family, fraternal and professional organizations, and the State; by actively living under the supernatural moral authority of the Church; by ultimately seeing economic needs through the eyes provided by all of nature's tools and those of nature's Creator and Redeemer as well.

Such an economist would enter into his studies with his eyes wide open. He would be aware that his discipline is not merely the science of gaining wealth, but of gaining wealth in union with all other natural and supernatural requirements. He would understand that he could not promote behavior which might, at least in the short run, make men wealthier, if it would be better for them and for their neighbors, in the long run, to act differently. Again, he would recognize that what this "better" meant would have to be defined by taking stock of a variety of factors that the collective natural and supernatural wisdom of the ages deemed to be important: a balance of agriculture and industry; neighborhood stability and access to the necessities of life; stewardship of the environment; defense of deeply-rooted customs and the beautiful achievements of high cultures; the demands of justice and charity; the need to transform all things in Christ so as to aid man's quest for eternal salvation. The truly wise economist would teach that men were not free to gain wealth obtained at the expense of leveling the Roman Forum to create more parking spaces for easier shopping at the Wal-Marts of the Eternal City; of turning patriotic celebrations and sacred festivals into nothing other than elaborate occasions for purchase and consumption; of marketing whatever might satisfy the wishes of revelers participating in Gay Pride Week. Simply put, the truly wise economist would see that man does not live by bread alone, nor does it profit him if he gains the whole world and loses his soul in the process. He would encourage wise social authorities to use all their strength to oppose the victory of an economic materialism, even if this were democratically supported by 99% of the population.

Enlightenment thought, *La Civiltà Cattolica* argued, is flawed because it violates all the above western philosophical and Catholic theological precepts, thereby blinding its proponents to the truth. Its atomistic freedom reduces men to precisely that unaided, anti-social condition which the previous development of our civilization had condemned as parochial and self-destructive. Its naturalism compounds the problem by prohibiting consideration of God's plan for His Creation and man's eternal destiny in secular matters as unpardonably invasive.

Enlightenment man thus lives and acts in a world whose every basic daily motions, both mundane and serious, are cut off from their final purpose. The "sciences" produced by Enlightenment freedom and naturalism are, therefore, studies that uncover nothing other than the laws of an incomplete nature, and a fallen one to boot. These sciences are then studied for incomplete, fallen reasons, chiefly to gain power over the world as it is so as to provide some immediate satisfaction perceived as being good by flawed individuals. Such "sciences" obstinately refuse to admit the possibility of learning how to change and heal nature through reason, revelation and grace; they dedicate their practitioners to the encouragement of limitation and weakness. Ideological and arrogant in their self-sufficient rationalism, they close themselves off to all criticism of their errors, responding to much rational evidence in irrational ways. Hence, the above-mentioned appeal to the dictates of an unexamined "common sense." Hence, their frequent calls for a consciousness-raising which would transform the unenlightened into creatures able to distinguish natural data which is acceptable from that which is strictly *verboten*. Hence, also, the infallible trump card utilized by every sophist relying on psychological and rhetorical rather than rational tools to influence the mob:

consideration of the respective success rates of the enlightened and the obscurantists in exploiting a world governed by unrestrained Original Sin.

All Enlightenment atomists and naturalists teach flawed, iron-clad, materially satisfying "scientific laws of nature" to which they demand unquestioning submission from the Church and Christian believers. Nevertheless, they differ as to what these laws are, merrily lambasting their fellow *illuminati* with as much rhetorical disdain as they do the retrograde Catholic community. Prince Otto von Bismarck of Prussia and Count Camillo Cavour of Sardinia saw that the rules of Machtpolitik yielded their states an immediately greater power and wealth than any nation following the guidelines of a St. Louis IX or a Pius IX might expect. Therefore, they insisted that Church doctrine bend to its "natural laws" and political science. Piety could be no excuse for neglecting the demands of a Machtpolitik whose victories might even be presented to believers as reflecting the higher will of God. Sexual libertines had proof positive that the unrestrained pursuit of physical satisfaction could result in much more immediate carnal rewards. Therefore, Church doctrine had to bend to accept the "science" of seduction, and perhaps encourage experts to raise the sexual consciousness of religious critics to make them, too, act more naturally. Liberal bourgeois capitalists witnessed the way in which the totally free market produced vast wealth for clever entrepreneurs. *Voilà*, a revelation of the infallible framework for a naturalist economic science before which western philosophy and Catholic theology must kneel and worship. Regardless of such differences in emphasis, the "free" individual operating under the spell of all of these "sciences" is everywhere the same: a self-limiting, parochial being; a willful, passionate child who specializes in learning how to get more toys for himself than the other kids around him, regardless or whether he needs or benefits from them. He wants what he wants when he wants it, and no mommy or daddy is going to force him to give up his rattle and learn the meaning of true virtue.

By now, it should be clear that the kinds of Catholic criticisms represented by journals like *La Civiltà Cattolica* have nothing whatsoever to do with adulating the early morning collection of eggs and the milking of cows. They are partly the product of a philosophical, historical and sociological study. More importantly still, they are the result of a Catholic Incarnational vision that battles coherently versus all Declarations of Independence from God's creative and redemptive plan, including those concerning economic methodology and morality.

When applied to the current traditionalist flirtation with capitalism, this nineteenth century critique must suggest a whole battery of soul-wrenching concerns: the fact that Catholics are separating daily individual choices regarding economic matters from their impact upon our eternal destiny; that Catholics are reducing market issues to the realm of the morally indifferent, and judging right and wrong on the basis of success in manipulating fallen nature alone; that Catholics are reading history on the basis of a Liberation Theology of the Market that sees the transformation of all things in capitalism as being infinitely more important, in practice, than transformation in Christ. This is frightening, because it is Modernism pure and simple, and in a realm where everyone has his daily temptations, and most of us, unfortunately, our price. Allow such a vision to triumph in Catholic circles and worries about the morality of Machtpolitik and sexual libertinism must logically disappear as well. Christian behavior will eventually mean nothing. Eternal salvation will be viewed as a reward for a lifetime of orthodox recitation of a purely intellectual and inconsequential Creed after our days in a morally indifferent playground have ended.

Many of the early supporters of erroneous ideas do not desire the consequences that flow from them. Martin Luther did not want the principles of Protestantism to aid radical enthusiasts. America's Founders did not plan for the influence of Karl Rove. Cavour and Bismarck might have laughed away the prospect of a Hitler, and sexual libertines the universal spread of gross pornography. Liberal bourgeois capitalists of the mid-nineteenth century would, perhaps, have run headlong from massive shopping malls destructive to more restrictive forms of village and city economic life. And, certainly, most recent traditionalist defenders of the unrestrained market whom I know do not wish to destroy what remains of Christian morality and Christendom.

The fact that so many heretics and ideologues do not wish bad things to happen is a proof of the continued hold of traditional beliefs and conservative presuppositions regarding personal behavior upon them. But it is also a demonstration of the failure of their logic. Regardless of the will or the choice of the Founders of any erroneous school of thought, the ideas that they espouse are what they are and spread their inevitable subversive poison. Some men, like the Anabaptists and Unitarians of Luther's and Calvin's days, accept that logic straightaway. Nevertheless, the bulk of humanity requires time to do so; time, the slow dissolution of the beliefs and behavior which block radicalism, and the construction of a society which fully shapes people not on the basis of its Founders' irrational conservative scruples, but their corrosive rational principles.

Enlightenment freedom and naturalism lead, logically, to the creation of radical, passionate men who care nothing for long-standing traditions and objective morality. The logic of Enlightenment capitalism, as men like Michael Novak exult, is to create a new kind of man who thinks and acts differently than citizens of traditional western Christendom. These new men will ensure that the pattern of capitalist industrial development in twenty-first century Africa and Latin America is different than that guided by more traditionally-minded individuals still shaped by the Christian remnants of eighteenth-century Britain. These new men will not define or practice a "charity" that can correct social imbalances in the same way as older Catholic believers could. These new men will adore the anti-social, anti-historical, materialist way of life, and, if they are Catholic in name, make of the Traditional Mass and the Traditional Faith an after-hours parlor sport for those engaged in what really counts in a democratic, capitalist universe: making big-time bucks and spending them on often useless or destructive toys.

One of the sad realities of life today is that this new capitalist man seems already to dominate the global scene through a version of the Enlightenment revolutionary vision which cannot be altered without untold dislocation and horror. I believe that that dislocation will nevertheless come, and not from the outside, but from the system's own implosion. It is understandable that many may find this notion difficult to accept, both because the system, by its very nature, discourages intellectual investigation of its problems (See "Why Catholics Cannot Defend Themselves," www.romanforum.org), and because a mere two hundred years of

Enlightenment capitalist history may not yet have been enough time for its full disruptive potential to display itself. Both Reason and Faith indicate that its judgment day must come. In the meantime, traditionalist Catholics can at least be put on warning against praising a force that barters away their true freedom, their true knowledge, the true, redeemed order of nature and the moral concerns of their true Faith for a killing on the market. Christ came to save us from the Fall; not to preach encouragement of Original Sin as the only sound basis for economic security and personal liberation.

9

The Ancient Roots of the Anti-Catholic Mentality†

AN INTRODUCTION TO THE HISTORY OF THE "BLACK LEGENDS"

REPEATED, DISMISSIVE, SELF-ASSURED calls for "closure" and "moving on" after one or another horrendous event in our personal and public lives clearly highlight some of the most salient features of contemporary culture: its dislike and downright fear of preoccupation with matters of profound significance; its love affair with immediate, superficial experiences which can be jettisoned, daily, along with yesterday's newspaper; its absolute certainty of the approval by its shallow populations of a "no-nonsense" dispatch of the basic stuff of human existence; and, finally, its insistence that pandering to surface phenomenon at the expense of thought-provoking reflection is not a frivolity, but actually the only truly weighty and useful approach that men and women who embrace real life with joy can entertain.

Catholicism, of course, can never be satisfied with this narrowing of human horizons to the concerns of the moment alone. A Catholic mentality uses serious events as a springboard for grave and sometimes very long-lasting meditation; it considers obsession with the petty, changing data of life to be unhealthy, a psychological flaw blinding people to the need to study the great matters, positive and negative, that shape reality; it knows, fears and resists sinful man's penchant for fleeing from the exalted to the vulgar; and it is convinced that it is only under the guidance of its broader outlook that the meaning of individual and social life can be fully grasped and become practically fruitful.

This conflict of mindset is one of the many reasons why contemporary culture loathes Catholicism. Unfortunately, the very nature of that mindset also tells modern society that it has achieved "closure" on the subject of its troubled relationship with the Church

† First published in the *Una Voce America Newsletter*, Summer 2004–Spring 2005.

as a whole. It thus prohibits modernity from studying whence its hatred and the varied elements underlying it have emerged, where they have led, and what they really signify. Hence, our age's self-satisfied reliance on a set of unexamined "Black Legends" to explain and reject its Catholic enemy, and then "move on." After all, knowledge of Catholicism's true character would require a fuss and bother which modernity's dominant, shallow ideology orders it to direct elsewhere.

Anyone studying the modern preference for the shallow over the profound, its general war against Christendom, and its willing acceptance of ignorant Black Legends to dismiss the "absurdity" and ultimate "irrelevance" of its opponent must begin his labors in the ancient, pagan world. For the spirit of anti-Catholicism is older than our religion itself. It began being shaped long before the Christian Era was born, in the Classical Greece of the Fifth and Fourth Centuries B. C., especially in the period of the Peloponnesian War and its dismal aftermath (431–336 B. C.). This is because Greece, as the home of the first insightful discussion of the meaning and practice of education, *paideia*, called forth that primary battle between those concerned with substantial and surface phenomenon, which Catholic Christianity then intensified and brought down more effectively to the level of the ordinary man.

Epic, lyric and dramatic poets were the first teachers of Hellas. They sought answers to the basic issues of life by asking aesthetic questions, queries regarding the meaning of beauty. Aesthetic preoccupations led them to tackle the problem of how best to educate for a knowledge and possession of "the Beautiful." That hunt for the tools essential to a primarily aesthetic formation slowly uncovered the need for consultation with, and guidance from, a variety of different sources: the individual and his immediate desires, the family and its long-term requirements for stability, and the demands of the *polis*, the city-state, in its search for attainment of a common as opposed to a merely individual or familial "beautiful" life.

The reputation of the *polis* as an aesthetic, educative, guiding force was enormous at the end of the Persian Wars (490–479 B. C.). Athens and Sparta, its two greatest contemporary representatives, had assured its prestige by winning a victory over the most impressive power in the world, before which, in contrast, a number of important individuals and purely family-dominated Greek lands had cowered. Such an unexpected but clear triumph made it appear that the community-focused *polis* could, in effect, accomplish anything. It was for this reason that Aeschylus (525–456 B. C.), in his *Oristeia* trilogy, has an unending cycle of superhuman vengeance and counter-vengeance concluded through *polis*-shaped (i.e., political) judicial action. Beauty, education and the *polis*, one might have said; now and forever; one and inseparable.

Unfortunately, however, it was precisely the same cherished *polis* of Athens and Sparta which revealed insane, self-destructive passions and limitations during and after the Peloponnesian War, thereby stimulating further discussion of the basic tools required for a proper education for possession of beauty. Control of the renewed dialogue passed out of the hands of the poets alone, who had said everything that they could possibly say on all sides of this issue of *paideia* by the time of Euripides (480–406 B. C.). Greece now even witnessed the emergence of a quite different approach towards education, along the lines suggested by the first philosophers, the so-called pre-Socratics, who wished to replace an aesthetic understanding of man and nature with one founded firmly upon knowledge of the material structure of the universe, its constituent "scientific" elements.

Pre-Socratic approaches to life and education proved to be too radical a break with the traditional aesthetic vision for the mainstream Greek world to accept. They were rejected, in particular, by two schools of thought which were themselves destined to lock horns in mortal combat. One of these schools was that of the Sophists, men concerned with rhetoric, the successful use of language, who, in effect, argued that the old-line aesthetic method was correct, but that it needed to be organized, taught and followed much more rigorously if it were to become a sure foundation for the individual and society. The other was the school of Socrates (469–399 B. C.), who, while also retaining much of the traditional aesthetic approach to education, recognized a need to critique, transform and elevate it. The battle that this entailed was catalogued for us not by Socrates but by his most brilliant pupil, Plato (427–347 B. C.), in his struggle with Isocrates (436–338 B. C.), perhaps the most self-conscious proponent of the sophistic, rhetorical approach.

Plato's great achievement as a philosopher and as an educator was that of demonstrating that the classical Greek formation of an individual for the possession of the beautiful required an understanding both of the nature of goodness as well as of the underlying truths of the universe towards which the pre-Socratics seemed to be groping. He showed Socrates, his model teacher, to be a "soul doctor," a man who demanded the cure of moral and intellectual flaws in his continued hunt for aesthetic perfection. Education for beauty in the fullest possible sense was, Plato insisted, a project drawing the individual closer and closer to God, the measure of all things, shaping his soul as an image or icon of the divine as he advanced. Every tool that the Greeks had come to consider to be important, the *polis* included, had a crucial role to play in this all-encompassing, life-long enterprise. Nevertheless, those valuable tools were all flawed. Paradoxically, they themselves required correction and improvement at the hands of the individual "icons" that they helped to shape. This meant that soul doctoring could be a confusing and immensely difficult task, involving much meditation and self-questioning; an enterprise which could not help but appear to be a pointless, frustrating detour to those on a perpetual hunt for "get possession of beauty quick" schemes.

"Pointlessly frustrating" was certainly the criticism attached to Platonic education by Isocrates, who claimed the title of philosopher with as great a fervor as his fellow Athenian did. Still, apt student of the Sophist Gorgias that he was, Isocrates understood philosophy to be a wisdom that only the trained rhetorician could possibly grasp and use properly. His definition of any Good or Truth underlying the Beautiful had to differ considerably from that of the Socratics in consequence.

For Isocrates, there was no question of seriously critiquing, transforming, and possibly even rejecting the preoccupations of the ordinary man. Man was the measure of all things, and unquestionably correct in his "common sense" concern for obtaining the riches, power and fame that he knew would yield the beautiful life. The average individual's sole problem was a technical one: he could not relate one justifiable common-sense experience to another, and thereby understand how best to exploit and satisfy them regularly and comprehensively. His efforts to explain his reactions to daily problems both to himself as well as to others proved to be "dumb" ones. It was effective words, and the arguments shaped through them, that were lacking to him. Only the well-trained rhetorician, the master of words, could clarify the full depth of common-sense experiences, show where they were headed, and stir people to do what was necessary to fulfill their promise. The Good and the True are, therefore, ultimately nothing other than "appropriate" explanations and developments of those common-sense reactions to the raw stuff of daily life which are themselves absolutely infallible guides to the possession of Beauty.

To take but one simple example, the average person might be said to have eminently justifiable, positive, common-sense reactions to the powerful experience of sexual passion. Nevertheless, without the right words and arguments to explain his "opinions" regarding this formidable *force de la nature*, he is not able to relate the meaning of his experience properly even to himself. Pragmatic efforts to gain the full promise of sexuality and cause it to work together with other experiences about which he has positive "opinions" are even further out of his reach. It is the rhetorician who illuminates Everyman through the use of appropriate and stimulating words, demonstrating the key to sexual understanding and its link with the multitude of other desirable goals. Everyman knows that the rhetorician is speaking appropriately when he sees how clearly and consistently his advice responds to his own preoccupations, and how the self-assurance of the master of words is crowned with the success for which he longs. Hence, Isocrates' recognition of his need to underline the simplicity, lucidity, harmony of purpose, confidence and material achievements of his pupils, while contrasting them with the cranky detours, self-criticisms, bitter divisions, and practical failures of the Socratics.

Isocrates longed to prove rhetoric's ability to gain possession of the Beautiful on a grand, world scale. In order for him to find the key to such great success, the philosopher/rhetorician had to begin with the study of the raw experiences and the common-sense reaction to them, not merely of an individual, but of an entire people, since a city-state or nation alone could conceivably become a driving force in global events. The work of Herodotus (484–424 B. C.), Thucydides (mid-400s B. C.–403 B. C.?), Xenophon (430 B. C.?–355 B. C.?), and others offered guidelines as how to how such historical data might be collected. Rhetoricians like Isocrates saw one of their tasks as being that of explaining to a population the appropriate greatness to which its otherwise "dumb" historical experiences were calling it. History thus came very early under rhetorical purview and influence, partly to its profit, since it became more readable and effective, but very often to its severe detriment, being transformed into a tool of propaganda.

From the raw history of his environment, Isocrates claimed to learn a number of important principles: that there actually was a Greek people, united by a shared culture, Hellenism; that the essence of Hellenism was the development of the illuminating, life-giving and unifying "word"; that the universal value accruing from appropriate use of the word gave the Greece which possessed knowledge of its significance a world-wide cultural mission; that this universal vocation had been shown to involve the sea, struggle against Persia, and imperial expansion; and that Hellenist destiny would require a simultaneous concern for the "good old days" of the foundation of the Greek spirit and the institutions giving clout to it, as well as for shaping a loyal population obedient to any vigorous strongman who might guide it to its contemporary fulfillment, all stirred to positive political roles by the vital words of the creative rhetorical genius.

But philosophy, as defined by Isocrates, constitutes a gigantic circle, manipulated by the rhetorician who, through the clever use of appealing words and images, seizes control of the familiar concerns of the average man or State and runs with them where he wills. Common sense experience is pronounced the infallible basis for action simply because it is declared to be common sense experience and the infallible basis for action. Successful attainment of riches and power is said to prove the appropriateness of the rhetorician's guidance of Everyman to the beautiful life because possession of riches and power is presented as axiomatic proof that beauty is in his grasp. Respect for the "good old days," current strongmen and obedient populations is essential because denial of such reverence would be tantamount to putting into doubt the destiny for whose fulfillment the rhetorician insists these forces exist in the first place. Absolutely no questioning of "common sense," "success," the "historic mission" and the consistency of the tools required for its realization can be contemplated, lest this lead to the unacceptable argument that common sense, success, the historical mission and its vital tools were themselves problematic. Isocrates, as Werner Jaeger notes, makes a virtue out of abandoning any deeper investigation of the meaning of life once he has shaped what for him appears to be a rhetorically beautiful "point of view" with a chance of obtaining a successful outcome. That "point of view," if attractive, must be accepted as Truth itself. With this, the debate is over. Closure has been achieved. One must move on to accomplishment of the Great Promise, or face the wrath of the rhetorician and the outraged nature whose infallible voice he has proclaimed himself to be.

And the rhetorician is powerful indeed. He knows that he can count on the support of individual, family, or polis-wide "common sense" passions in his call for their immediate satisfaction. He senses the understandable and well-nigh universal fear that Socratic self-criticism would paralyze action, preventing exploitation of favorable opportunities to fulfill desire, causing men to "lose out" on success, perhaps even to the very moment of death. The rhetorician, with his mastery of words, can paint the profound, life-determining, "either-or" option offered to men by Sophists and Socratics in all of its dramatic colors, but weighted to his advantage. Afterwards, any Socratic who calls the average man to logical, painful soul-searching at the possible expense of satisfying immediate passion becomes a sitting duck for rhetorical abuse. He lends himself to the accusation of representing both a crackpot idealism, indifferent to the obvious demands of human nature, as well as a cynical opposition to the successes of "real men," whom he cannot emulate, bitterly envies, and wishes to destroy in consequence.

Plato was himself a literary genius, sensitive to the power of purely rhetorical arguments over the average man, and the need to respond to them "beautifully" to demonstrate their flaws. He did so reply, by showing the pure rhetorician to be a self-deluding failure. Contrary to what such a man argued, his influence arose precisely from his inability to educate those whom he claimed to be illuminating. For Plato, the "word" spoken by the rhetorician styling himself to be a philosopher could itself never rise above "dumb" opinion, and merely illustrated a trained man's ability effectively to flatter peoples' fancies. Rhetoricians possessed what he called a "knack" of appealing to a particular appetite, like that of a cook in a fast-food restaurant, ignoring entirely the question of whether such an admittedly successful flattery and knack ought to have been indulged in the first place. The successful rhetorician deceives himself into thinking that he is superior to his "wordless" audience, but he is simply more effectively thick than it is. His words resemble an overbearing and endlessly repeated rock rhythm in a room filled with impressionable, but musically illiterate hedonists. They fail to elevate, just as any tool that uses man, rather than God, as the measure of all things falls miserably short of its pretensions. Anyone responding to the "either-or" option confronting him by choosing for the rhetorician would, therefore, be voting for eternal mediocrity and blindness. Sadly, precisely due to the rhetorician's observable knack for maintaining power over the vulgar mob, the pathetic outcome of such a wrong choice could conceivably be hidden from its victims forever. False rhetorical philosophers needed only to do two things: enthusiastically to invent ever "new" surface variants on the proven appealing slogans to keep men thinking that fulfillment of the brilliant promise of the Empty Life lay just around the corner; and constantly to drill into a benumbed population's mind the fear of the "dead-end" impotence that the Socratic hunt for a more profound goal would ensure.

One of Plato's painful labors was that of explaining instances of this seeming Socratic impotence, the disaster of his own political missions to Dion in Sicily in 388 and 367 being primary among them. Such shipwrecks, he argued, were not attributable to philosophy's innate inability to navigate effectively. Rather, they were simply another confirmation of the difficulty and very infancy of the task that the real lover of Beauty, Goodness and Truth had set for himself. Yes, he admitted, philosophy needed the aid of rhetoric, of the lesser "word" to explain itself successfully to a world filled with ambiguous though powerful passions, and convince it to change its ways. But that secondary "word" must always be subordinated to a deeper Word, the Logos towards whose ultimate knowledge it was meant to be employed. Alas, at least in Plato's own day, it had proven to be "hard to find the creator and father of the world," and "impossible to describe his nature publicly." Men could not yet be guided properly to the divine imitation that would definitely perfect them and give them possession of the Beautiful. As dilemmas went, this certainly was a killer, and Plato feared that it would remain an unresolved one unless "some God" came to the earth to unravel it.

Faulty or not, the ideas of his opponents helped to form that mixed Greek/Middle Eastern/Latin civilization which we call the Hellenistic World. This new reality did demonstrate the literal value of the Greek language, whose superiority in transmitting manifold, complex concepts was universally recognized. It also reflected all of the potential practical consequences of a cosmos shaped by a purely rhetorical "word" alone. For Hellenistic Civilization was one that did indeed work for the "common sense" benefit of men, though only of those "vigorous strong men" praised by the rhetorician as essential for fulfillment of its mission. These leaders learned to create and manipulate powerful state machinery for the purpose of keeping the "dumb" mass of the population in submission. "Doers of great deeds," from Alexander through to the Caesars and the Senatorial Aristocracy of the Roman Empire that worked with them, were willing to tolerate satisfaction of certain specific, immediate desires of the multi-cultural, pluralist world over which they ruled. Still, this had to be at the price of its constituent elements accepting "closure" regarding matters that might disturb what really counted: the personal power, wealth and fame of the victors.

Rhetoricians were very active from the 300s B. C. through the 300s A. D., providing the Hellenistic cosmos, or *ecumene*, the arguments proving that the debate over who possessed the things that made life beautiful, and what those things were, was over. They contributed mightily to efforts to overcome "parochial" religious "superstitions" whose concerns might threaten the status quo. Such integration of divisive elements involved publicizing the need to submit to and adore the superior divinity of the State apparatus and the self-made men who dominated it. "Closure" had been achieved in the realm of the gods as well as that of men, and the "word" could now "move on."

It moved on by devoting itself to legal and civil service careers, and to sickly praise or boring, encyclopedic chronicling of the existing, unchangeable order of things, thereby sharing in any trickle-down benefits its Divine Masters permitted. It moved on by finding substantial employment producing that esoteric, archaic and pointless heap of pretty sounds and properly placed commas adulated by exclusivist literary circles. Failing that, it moved on by churning out pornographic material for the gross diversions of a rabble ever tempted to accept subordination and abandon true enlightenment for cheap material satiety. The spiral downward from the more sophisticated "apologetic" writings and literary achievements of earlier Hellenistic regimes to the servile, pedantic and vulgar *oeuvre* of much of the so-called Second Sophistic of the 2nd through 4th Centuries, A. D. is instructive. It reminds one anew of Plato's argument that word merchants indifferent to true philosophy were destined to a low-class butchering of even their own art and talent. One need only consult the biographies and stories to be found in Aulius Gellius' (123–165) *Attic Nights*, the 2nd Philostratus' (c. 170–248) *Lives of the Sophists*, Eunapius' (346-414) *Lives of the Philosophers and Sophists*, Diogenes Laertius' (no later than 200s) *Lives of Eminent Philosophers*, and Athenaeus of Naucratis' (200s) *Doctors at Dinner* to test the validity of his hypothesis.

Ironically, however, solid philosophy itself ended by adapting nicely to the depressing, conformist, "common sense" rules established by a degenerate, power-worshipping, rhetorically justified cosmos. This was partially due to certain innate weaknesses of schools of thought like Stoicism. Stoic insistence on the purposeful structure of the universe, in the absence of a concept of sin, tempted it into treating accommodation to the successful status quo as though it were obedience to the will of God. Acceptance of the idea of universal purposefulness also convinced many Stoics that crude popular experiences of reality, including truly offensive superstitious practices, should be approached seriously as well, even if often only as fuel for more "sophisticated" (dare we say "appropriate"?) explanations of their deeper meaning. Indeed, even Plato's passionate rhetorical embrace of the use of allegory to explain complex truths could be called upon to defend this dressing up of popular opinion. Finally, Neo-Platonists, with their admittedly exalted discussion of the existence of a Hierarchy of Being leading to the final, divine, unchangeable principle of the universe, also became propagandists for the powers that be. They were fearful that any disorder and alteration in the political and social world could open the path to what they considered to be a totally unacceptable conception of change, willfulness and unpredictable action on the part of the very Godhead itself.

It was at this point, however, that the Divinity whom Plato said might have to intervene in human events to resolve the dilemma of possession of Beauty did just that: He intervened. Through the Incarnation, the establishment of the Church, and the offer of the gifts of Faith and Grace, God called men to complete the march to the fullness of wisdom and individual "divinization." He thus injected a vibrant new force into the "stable" ancient cosmos. Christians were summoned to reject "closure." They were told that they could not "move on" under the old rules. The debate over what was required to complete life's voyage had to be reopened. All the tools of antiquity needed to be re-examined, and, if found to be lacking, transformed through Christian Light. But from the standpoint of those willingly imprisoned in a familiar, rhetorically justified strait-jacket, this meant that a revolutionary Monster had leaped into their Peaceable Kingdom.

Hence, the emergence of a strange alliance, a kind of United Nations of the Status Quo, co-opting all who were contented, for varied reasons, with "closure," and repelled by rabble-rousers who would not allow men to "move on" to "get the real job of life done." Participants in this alliance were legion. They included the many-headed tribe of legal and literary rhetoricians; those philosophers who were convinced that the existing, dominant order must necessarily be the true one, and others worried about the turmoil that the personal Christian God could bring into a universe where everything had been hung so carefully on its proper, immovable peg; the ordinary man, whether highborn or low, fearful lest satisfaction of his customary pointless or lewd appetites be disturbed by an exhortation to avoid sin and strive for higher rewards. Heretical Christians eventually sought membership in this alliance, too, such as those Gnostics, expelled from the Church for following up on the teaching of their greatest teacher, Mani (200s A. D.), who urged them to use language to deconstruct the message of salvation and reshape it to suit their own nature-hating purposes. Even Church authorities themselves could be found in its ranks, as time-serving bishops saw how their restraint of Christian militancy could be useful to the status quo, gaining for them all the paybacks enjoyed by earlier rhetorical lap dogs of the regime.

Our United Nations of the Status Quo pursued its program with a variety of eminently successful tools. One of these was a conspiracy of silence; many of the great literary men of the late Roman period wrote as though Christianity simply did not exist and would therefore quietly go away. This approach was complemented by an attempt to hide a clear understanding of the real substance and history of our religion. To that end, all obviously popular and beneficial Christian fruits were attributed to anti-Christian beliefs and labors, Christianity being held responsible only for what was deemed dangerous to the State and to the passions of the men of common sense. Rhetorical ability and fervor embellished this entire mish-mashed story. In short, the United Nations of the Status Quo developed the stuff of what would become a library of dramatic Black Legends, the full flavor of which I will present in future articles. Whenever circumstances permitted, these Black Legends could now be brought before the eyes of the Established Authorities, with the accompanying demand that force be applied to re-establish the wonderful world of productive closure anew.

Great strength was shown by this rhetorically-armed alliance through its ability to appeal to the aforementioned "either-or" option. It called men irresistibly to the same overwhelming choice: support "either" its point of view, rooted in common sense desire, protection of order and successful pandering to the familiar, obvious joys of the great and small; "or" enter onto the Christian path, with its paradise "seen through a glass, darkly," its self-denial, and the endless disruption that Christ said His sword had brought into the world. With this "either-or" alternative, it continually tempted the resolve not only of the clueless, but also that of the faithful. For, ultimately, not one of us is infallibly protected from doubt.

Strength came as well from the rhetorical refusal to admit that qualitative questions were at stake here, requiring it to find different, more substantive justifications for promotion of its position. Each time any given argument on its behalf did not work, it simply called forth a handy "new deal" out of its full, one-dimensional, surface bag of tricks—this being "new" only in the sense that it varied a word or an image to describe its ever-monotonous qualitative sameness. Each readily available "new deal" or "new frontier" could then be proclaimed some specially brilliant chance for gaining the Beautiful Life that meaning-obsessed Christians would have men critique and lose. Hence, the same, unchanging, underlying appeal to common sense, the spirit and institutions of the Good Old Days, the great men and loyal, obedient populations needed to assure the fulfillment of the Mission, the limited passions of the vulgar mob, and the importance of silencing or misinterpreting "naive" and "cynical" questioning of the golden opportunity could be repeated in a billion varied forms. But an anti-Christian Pragmatism, Foundation and Imperial Mission are just as dangerous if pursued by pagan rulers or those appealing to the Manifest Destiny of the United States as standard bearer for freedom-loving mankind on the lookout for a good deal. The world has heard it all before, sugared differently according to taste, if not with chocolate topping, then with vanilla or mocha.

Given the fact that this United Nations could draw arguments, at will, from all of its many diverse constituent elements, it was also armed with the capacity seriously to confuse anyone honestly seeking to counter its assault. For just when a more logical mind might think that he was debating successfully on a relatively sophisticated historical plane, the UNSQ could level an argument drawn from and appealing to its truly vulgar supporters. This change of tactics would require a corresponding alteration of defensive strategy from the Christian, a lowering to the demagogic level. That modification could then itself, in turn, be condemned by insisting that dialogue take place on the rigorous philosophical or refined aesthetic plane favored by still other members of the alliance. If the befuddled Christian, always responding to attack, and never taking the initiative in this cat and mouse game, sought to discuss the absurdity of constantly changing the basic character of the argumentation, the customary rhetorical sigh of frustration could be audibly emitted. For, once again, as with Plato, time was being demanded for a diversion from the real task of "moving on" in order to satisfy the unrewarding, abstract speculations of impotent, loser "enemies of mankind." In the Kingdom of the Illogical it is the wily one who generally calls the shots. And in doing so, he drives the sane man mad.

Still, our United Nations of the Status Quo was not without its weaknesses. Like the modern exemplar from which I have drawn its name, its varied members were their own Soviet Unions and United States of Americas, temporarily united in opposing a common foe, but ever poised to fight out irreconcilable differences should their joint combat someday cease. Rhetoricians supporting one "beautiful vision" serving the established authorities were girded therein against any upstart colleagues who might begin touting another; philosophers unwilling to be used purely for intellectual ornamental purposes chafed under rhetorical domination; have-nots envious of the people who had "made it" could rise up to satisfy the fullness of their own uncontrollable passions. "Time Bomb" might be a better name for this alliance, since, the exaggerated fancies of conspiratorial theorists notwithstanding, no absolutely reliable, indissoluble glue held its members miraculously together.

But could their divisions be exploited for Catholic benefit, so that the Black Legends they created, and through which they all prospered, might be uncovered and effectively refuted? Catholic History offers an ambiguous answer to that question. Instances of victorious Christian battling of powerful, rhetorically-crafted lies are available, but, sadly, they are buried amidst many more indications of dismal failure in this enterprise. I intend to investigate a variety of such examples over the course of articles to come.

One fact seems absolutely clear to me in plowing through the divided evidence of the historical record of the Catholic resistance. Cleverly constructed Black Legends, fueled by half truths and outright lies, can only be overturned by a Christianity that accepts all the lessons of the Incarnation, and honestly uses the full arsenal of tools that God and nature provide to protect itself. A Christianity that roots its supernatural "newness" in the whole of God's nature would not hunt for answers to its problems in the immediate experiences of its own time-bound world, but in all of divine and human history. In doing so, it would come to appreciate that it must fight its enemies not just with abstract theological arguments, even when these are supported by the philosophical strength that comes from the Socratics. It would also embrace the just use of rhetoric in all of its forms, which Plato himself saw a need to snatch from the hands of rootless Sophists. In short, only a full, Incarnational Truth, seeking the Good, gaining full, supernatural possession of the Beautiful, and living a life of active imitation of God through transformation in Christ can prevent a premature "closure" in a world tempted by the lesser "word." Only this can "move on" to restore the Christian Order that we have seen torn down around us by men possessed by the libido for the ugly.

10

Half the Business of Destruction Done†

POPULAR PERCEPTION OF HISTORICAL developments often lags far behind the time of their actual occurrence. Thus, most people look upon the twentieth century as the age of de-catholicization of social life, when, in fact, the current era has merely hosted a further unfolding of a phenomenon ravaging the western world long before the 1900s. Even those aware of this particular error of perception frequently fail to pinpoint the movement of de-christianization in Catholic lands early enough, associating it only with the French Revolution and its aftermath. Nevertheless, the whole of the program — and, more importantly still, the spirit — of the assault on the Christian order were visible everywhere in the pre-revolutionary Catholic world, with half the business of destruction done before a single vote had been cast for delegations to the Estates-General.

Let us note at the outset that some — even much — of what might pass at first glance for eighteenth-century dechristianization is not really such in the final analysis. Christendom, with its many diverse corporate elements, ranging from parish sodalities to guilds, religious and crusading orders, universities, international confraternities, and up to the different branches of the royal and papal courts themselves, does, after all, provide shelter for an all too numerous collection of human concerns and ambitions, alongside and closely intermingled with those which are divine. It is always tempting to enlist theology in the defense and promotion of what might be merely self-interested goals, thus lending an exalted, sacred flavor to something unjustifiably parochial and even totally natural in character. An attack on ramparts which serve to protect purely or mostly human treasures, but which are nevertheless held together with much theological cement, may seem to be an assault on Christendom. In practice, however, it could actually be an aid in the liberation of the sacred from decadent secularizing incrustations. What is hidebound, overblown and

---

† First published on the *Seattle Catholic* website (December 28, 2004).

grasping is not inherently Christian due to a long-term association with the Christian name. A lunge at the customary and grandiose, while risky, is not necessarily a thrust at the Christian heart itself.

Many servants of eighteenth-century governments in Catholic Europe were convinced of the desperate need to implement certain educational, scientific, economic, administrative and legal changes for the benefit of society at large. Very frequently, some immediate disaster hardened their determination to implement them. Ecclesiastical privileges and financial exemptions of labyrinthine proportions often stood in their way, alongside the corporate prerogatives of countless secular institutions. Did the State have any right to seek to modify this situation? Was a dismantling of specific aspects of the existing corporate order, religious as well as secular, ever justifiable? It is difficult to answer this question with an uncompromising "no" without jeopardizing the very raison d'être of the civil authority; without baptizing and declaring essential to the plan of God everything that every corporate body with some tie to the Church or to a Christian-inspired tradition has at one time or another succeeded in doing.

Nevertheless, pre-revolutionary statesmen went further than the mere assertion of the necessary role of the State in coordinating a corporate society for the sake of the common good, and thereby engaging in a salutary humbling of parochial self-interests decorated with theological icing. Many passed beyond the limits of an arrogant unilateral reform program which could have been totally justifiable if undertaken in cooperation with the Church. An impressive number of statesmen ventured into the work of ridding everyday life of truly indispensable sacred elements; supernatural influences which could not be eliminated without Christianity itself disappearing from the public arena.

Some of the stimulus for this unacceptable secularization can be laid directly at the door of the openly anti-Christian Enlightenment. Still, outrightly enlightened influences ought not to be overestimated, especially at the beginning of the reform movement. Enough enticement to secularization emerged out of disputes among Christians themselves, as well as from a contemporary reinterpretation of the pursuit of quite mundane goals as the most laudable of religious enterprises. These earlier non-Enlightenment factors, generally unknown outside of academic circles, need to be addressed before any others. Three subjects in particular call for closer investigation: missionary quarrels in China; the political and material successes of Britain and Prussia, and the arguments used to promote and justify them; and, finally, the late seventeenth and eighteenth-century school of "Reform Catholicism."

China provided a focus of European discussion of evangelization from the mid-1600s onwards. It was at that time that Jesuit missionary tactics, approved by the Papacy but contested even within the Society itself, were brought vigorously into question by Spanish Dominicans and Franciscans who were also toiling in the Chinese vineyard. The debate raged on into the next century, eventually involving mendicants, ordinary Jesuits, members of the Society working as scholar-courtiers in the Imperial City, the Sorbonne, disciples of the Paris Mission Seminary active as Vicars Apostolic in the Asian theater, and the Congregation for the Propagation of the Faith and Papacy themselves. Their dispute exposed educated Europeans to the backbiting prevalent among many of those responsible for spreading the Gospel of Love. More importantly still, it also pointed to the possibility of the existence of a successful "atheistic" society.

This latter theme emerged from the debate over the specifics of the so-called "Chinese Rites" —ceremonies in honor of Confucius and the ancestral dead —and the suitability for Christian use of the native names for God. Were such rites merely natural marks of honor akin to saluting a flag, or were they acts of pagan worship? Were the terms used by the Chinese to describe their divinity valid starting points from which to leap to the God of Abraham, Isaac and Jacob? Or were they dead ends pulling the Christian vision downwards into a pantheistic-materialistic swamp? What about Confucianism itself, the grand system underlying the whole ethos of the Empire and its administration? Did it involve Taoist and Buddhist speculations and practices? If so, were these susceptible to allegorical Christian interpretation or editing, along the lines of what Catholic thinkers and missionaries had done with much Greek, Roman and barbarian thought and custom? Was the entire Confucianist school basically a pagan religious construct or a secular philosophical-ethical system fitting together happily with the comparably powerful and positivist Chinese legal tradition?

A number of participants in the debate about Confucianism, the names of God, and the Chinese Rites in general emphasized an underlying atheism in the dominant native political-social vision. But here, as the Jesuit Le Comte worriedly noted, lay both exaggeration and a danger with consequences far beyond any related specifically to Chinese issues. European theologians had always insisted that atheism was actually an unthinkable position, every man having the instinct of God written in his soul. Disbelief was ascribed by them to a pure perversion of the will, and one that made any ordered society impossible. But if one accepted the notion that atheism was thinkable in the sophisticated Chinese intellectual world, and that it sustained the greatest non-European society, the whole apologetic of the necessity of religion for ordered community life would be shaken. Indeed, with the decisions taken against the Jesuit approach in China from the time of Pope Clement XI (1700–1721) to Benedict XIV (1740–1758), it was so shaken. As Alan Kors writes:

> In the heat of the polemic ... positions lost their nuances, and a concert of voices insisted that what most educated French took to be the most learned minds of the most civilized nation outside Europe were 'atheists' pure and simple ... Its own Church would come to insist that this was not a theoretical possibility, but a historical fact. If one accepted the widely circulated view of the excellence of Confucian ethics and the official determination by both Rome and the Faculty of Theology at Paris that Confucianism was atheistic, this conclusion followed ineluctably (Phillips, p. 247; see reading list at end of essay).

Admittedly, proto-Enlightenment thinkers like Pierre Bayle (1647–1706), in his *Pensées Diverses sur la Comète* (1683) and *Dictionnaire Historique et Critique* (1696), were also arguing for the possibility of an atheistic society, one that was perhaps better ordered than any Christian counterpart, in Bayle's case, as part of a general plea for religious toleration. Nevertheless, China played a more important role in initially popularizing the argument. More than 130 books on the subject —an astonishing number for the time —were published in France alone between 1660 and 1714. Voltaire (1694–1778) gave testimony to its secularizing implications by breaking with the traditional western manner of discussing the history of the world in relation to the history of salvation, beginning his own global historical study with China.

Here, the atheistic society was not only shown to be possible, but (erroneously) given priority in time as well.

Still, questions regarding atheism could only be a tool to batter the Church intellectually in the early eighteenth century. Few people were actually earnest evangelical atheists. Voltaire was certainly not among them. In practice, secularization could not be brought about at that moment through an openly atheistic onslaught. More mundane —and therefore more tempting —paths to secularization were required, and Christianity itself summoned to bestow its approval upon the process to render it respectable. Discussion of these developments lead us directly to the extraordinary growth of and admiration for Britain and Prussia in eighteenth century Europe.

The most powerful and generally effective psychological argument in favor of any position is the argument from success. If something is successful, its justification is accepted by most people in history as a given; if it is not successful, it is overwhelmingly suspect. Everything Britain touched from the time of the War of the Spanish Succession (1701–1714) seemed to turn to political and literal gold. Prussia appeared to be similarly blessed, and at no time more than in the reign of Frederick II "the Great" (1740–1786), son of the "soldier-king," Frederick William I (1713–1740). What, the rest of Europe asked, was their secret?

On the one hand, that secret was nothing other than the willingness to seize each political and material opportunity that offered itself; to apply all of one's available strength to exploit it, regardless of obstacles arising from existing alliances or generally agreed-upon norms of international behavior. One cannot help but share the contemporary astonishment at mid-century British diplomatic and commercial audacity, provoking Spain, France and Austria without just cause, and then reacting with moral indignation when these countries responded in kind. Neither are the cynical admission of Frederick the Great that truth plays no role in the governance of men, nor his sudden aggression against Austria in Silesia without their own peculiar grandeur. The outrage of Louis XV (1715–1774) over illegitimate British colonial incursions in the Americas and Frederician diplomatic shenanigans, as well as Maria Theresa's (1740–1780) horror at the Prussian king's eagerness to dismember Poland, were interpreted by many contemporaries merely as the bewilderment or hypocrisy of outmaneuvered decaying powers. The telling French expression, "to work for the King of Prussia," indicating laboring without pay, and originating out of experiences with Frederick during the War of the Austrian Succession (1740–1748), once again underlines the basic attitude of the rest of Europe to both Britain and Prussia: no matter what we do, they win.

Another element central to our concerns here also entered into the British-Prussian secret: the enlisting of religion in the work of redirecting man's primary attention towards the attainment of natural goods; the gaining of a Christian blessing upon such a central change of focus as a sign of supernatural approval as well. Victory in this enterprise involved both a quieting of religious controversy and the turning of "common sense" and "natural virtues" conducive to procuring power and wealth into the only true means of knowing, loving and serving God in our world of sin.

A general British retreat from open religious controversy in the eighteenth century is certainly understandable. Memories of nearly two hundred years of unpleasant political and social consequences stemming from such disputes were painfully vivid. Moreover, given the fact that all contemporary Christians seemed to share a common code of morals and manners which, in practice, they shockingly neglected, it is also understandable that concerned men might argue for the primary importance of a public campaign to reform and uplift basic behavior. Finally, the impressive emergence of the Press in the reign of Queen Anne (1702–1714) explains the central function this medium began to exercise in the switch of attention from Scripture and sacraments to morals and manners.

Nowhere was the connection of the quieting of religious controversy, the interest in a reform of behavior, and the importance of the Press clearer than in the work of the two periodicals, *The Tatler* and *The Spectator*, brought out by the joint effort of Joseph Addison (1672–1719) and Sir Richard Steele (1672–1729) in the years between 1709 and 1714. Readers of these journals were exposed, week after week, to social and behavioral commentaries, in the latter through representatives of the worlds of commerce, the army, the town, and the country gentry, presented by one Mr. Spectator, an observer of the London scene. Both periodicals served as models for manifold imitators on the European Continent, such as the *Hamburg Patriot* and *Il Caffè* of Milan.

What one finds in *The Tatler*, and even more in *The Spectator*, is the insistence upon the need for men of "common sense" to gather together without religious rancor and cooperatively undertake the truly moral business of bettering themselves and their surrounding societies. The fact that such journals would generally be read in public places like coffee houses emphasized still further the need for moral men to develop friendly manners, keep passions down, avoid grating on one another's nerves, and thereby allow the very establishment in which one was thinking and speaking peacefully to survive.

A similar emphasis upon the prevention of divisive controversy and dedication to good-mannered cooperative ventures of obvious personal and social value could be found in the varied reading clubs and scientific-agricultural-commercial "patriotic" societies founded in Britain and Ireland in the late seventeenth century. Already promoted by Sir Francis Bacon (1561–1626), these included the Royal Society (1660), the Society for the Improvement of Husbandry, Agriculture and Other Useful Arts of Dublin (1731), and, one might add, the Freemasons (1717) also. Here, the class distinctions operative outside such circles could, just as in cafes, temporarily be suspended for the good of all. Here, then, were truly God-blessed confraternities and sodalities, "religious orders" with a purpose. In such communities, swords were literally beaten into plowshares through practical achievement. In such an environment, men could begin an honest, practical ascent of Mount Carmel. For, if the scientist and the practical entrepreneur whose discernible fruits could be weighed and measured and imitated with mathematical exactitude were not in union with God and His plan for the world, who was? Squabbling missionaries in China? Did not Sir Isaac Newton (1642–1727), head of the Royal Society from 1703, and humble student of the laws of motion and their practical consequences, point the way to true service of the God who presided over nature's mysteries and the men He commands us to love infinitely better than quibblers battling over the Divine names and the suitability of honoring Confucius?

Prussia also feared religious controversy as the pathway to disaster. Its population at the time of the proclamation of the kingdom in 1701 was basically Lutheran. Its ruling House of Hohenzollern, in contrast, was Calvinist. Unity could only be made possible by deemphasizing doctrine. Pietism, a movement within the Lutheran camp, became the chief instrument in this dynasty-friendly enterprise.

Pietism's essential concern was commitment to a Christianity which could visibly be recognized as being a vibrant force in the lives of men. Such a Christianity was, its supporters claimed, obscured or even totally smothered by the highly credal denominations and ceremonial practices of a politicized Europe. Hence, Pietists stressed the need for a true faith born of the experience of each individual and judged with reference to that faith's obvious fruits. The path of Pietism is generally understood to have moved from the work of Englishmen like William Ames (1576–1633), author of *The Marrow of Theology* (1627), over to the Dutch Republic through Willliam Teelinck (1579–1629), Gisbertius Voetius (1589–1679), and Jadocus Lodensteyn (1620–1677), and into the German Lutheran world with Johann Arndt (1555–1621), Philipp Jakob Spener (1635–1705), August Hermann Francke (1663–1725), and Nicolaus Graf von Zinzendorf (1700–1760). Spener's book, *Pia Desideria* (1675), gave the movement its lasting name.

But this one name covers a diversity of approaches. Pietism could end in very traditional territory. It influenced men like John Wesley (1703–1791), who gained from it a general concern for an internal conversion active in love for one's neighbor which did not shun ordinary organized Church structures and ceremonies. A Pietism of the Wesleyan Methodist variety could easily open a man to the practice of good works on a natural level while still retaining a central goal of mystical union with God that tapped into the mainline of Christian contemplative history.

What concerns us here is the quite distinct Pietism of Francke, the chief protégé of Spener. Francke was appointed Professor of Near Eastern Languages at the University of Halle in Prussia in 1692. Francke's Pietism, unlike Wesley's, and, for that matter, unlike Spener's as well, was very much tied in with the need to overcome a personal experience of despair and disbelief, which struck with particular fury at one moment in his life and threatened constantly to return. He became convinced that God would give him the sense of His presence and the peace that indicates forgiveness of sin only if he developed an intensely disciplined and constant activity on behalf of the good of his neighbor. He would know that he was persevering on the right track if his labors were crowned with success. Success could not help but witness to God's blessing. Lack of success, inactivity and failure to maintain the inner personal discipline needed to sustain one's enterprise promised a return of existential anxiety.

Francke's Pietist work, which he wished to serve as a model for a worldwide Christian renewal, involved the creation at Halle of what are referred to as the Anstalten or Frankesche Stiftungen, various institutions at whose core lay clearly charitable ventures like a well-developed orphanage. Since charitable endeavors required money to survive, however, Francke's foundations also encompassed commercial organizations designed to procure needed funds. Educational projects intended to form men with the iron-like inner discipline that could sustain constant commitment to enterprise and the service of one's neighbor also played a crucial role in his labor at Halle. Francke provided Lebens-Regeln to guide them, rules which emphasized the task of breaking the individual's self-will and rebuilding it the way his own conversion experience demonstrated God unquestionably wanted.

Charitable, commercial and educational Anstalten moved forward vigorously under Francke's direction from the 1690s onwards. They were fortunate in finding favor with Frederick William I, who had himself undergone a similar conversion experience independently of Francke. He, like his father, Frederick I (1688/1701–1713) before him, sought some means of unifying religiously divided Prussians, but instead of attempting this through Lutheran-Calvinist credal or ceremonial union, began to place his hope in Pietist-inspired commitment to common, practical Christian activism. By the 1720s, he was eagerly promoting the Anstalten, and incorporating Francke's educational ideals into his own plans for the general instruction of the entire Prussian population.

For Frederick William as for Francke, a self-disciplined, constantly active citizenry, alert to the good of one's neighbors in society-at-large, needed to be successful to demonstrate its retention of God's favor. A man in Frederick William's position, and with his responsibilities, needed to see their success reflected in the growth and benefit of the Kingdom of Prussia. Christian action on behalf of one's neighbor in society, must, to a large and indeed primary degree, mean the co-operation of all individuals and groups in the development of the Prussian State, whose every victory would mean a further confirmation of divine approval.

Prussia, like other German states, was already familiar with "cameralism," a set of studies designed to form administrators who could better manage governmental resources and performance. Halle Pietism taught the cameralist the God-given duty lying behind his work, while simultaneously passing down to all Prussians in their various stations in life an inner sense of personal responsibility for sharing in the bureaucrat's task. Pietism bestowed the blessings of Heaven upon all the manifold labors undertaken by the active citizen in the City of Man, with its highest approbation of work on behalf of the State. Francke's educational methodology, with its complex system of surveillance of pupils and insight into their psychology, ensured that the lesson of the moral importance of such labors would stick for life. Mobilization of the clergy as a teacher of morals and a morals police seemed to Frederick William to be the most suitable means of drilling the Pietist message into the population-at-large. It, too, had to learn and utilize the Francke spirit and method systematically, and turn away from unproductive theological dispute that would immorally weaken the State in the process.

A British-Prussian Christianity shorn of doctrinal clarity, centered around practical moral achievement and friendly manners, and aimed at a common action of immediate, obvious, successful benefit to one's neighbor, proved to be susceptible to more powerful secularizing tendencies than many of its original proponents perhaps expected. The more the world of God was shunned as the realm of the controversial, the more that the world of nature taught what was pleasing to the Almighty and deemed to be successful in His eyes on its terms alone. Moreover, the reading of the meaning of nature and the teachings of natural experiences changed once Christian doctrine began to lose its hold on people. What was taken as common sense and natural law and virtue by a first generation that still knew Christian teaching but simply ceased to engage in theological dispute over its significance was no longer the same as that of a second generation lacking doctrinal formation and prohibited from seeking it under the penalty of being "divisive." The commands of God which were learned from nature alone were then registered and carried out by groups or individuals who retained a strong conviction of divine guidance in their secular activities, regardless of whether these fit together with traditional Christian considerations of what was socially acceptable and good. And who would know what traditional Christian considerations were any longer anyway? For history, alongside doctrinal disputation, would also have to be discarded or reinterpreted to rid it of its potentially dangerous effects on the success-and-unity oriented personality.

In such an environment, whoever had the strongest feelings and the most powerful will to enforce them became the voice of Heaven in nature and of true "tradition" themselves. In Britain, this amounted to a shared dominance of different secular, materially-minded groups and interests; in Prussia, to the victory of the bureaucratic State. No appeal could readily be made in either case to any supernatural force transcending such powers since God had already been appealed to by them in a nature liberated from metaphysical considerations. Recourse to a divine message coming from beyond nature could, again, axiomatically be dismissed as "divisive," and, hence, immoral; un-Christian even. The initial work of naturalizing the supernatural having been undertaken within a Christian idiom and in Christian circles, this bridge to the Enlightenment and its concerns could be completed without the sharp anti-clericalism emerging in countries like France. Prussian thinkers such as Christian Wolff (1679–1754) are instructive in tracing the path from a Christian-sounding discussion of life truly rooted in the supernatural to one that in fact draws its inspiration from nature and natural tools almost exclusively.

British and Prussian influence, practical and "spiritual," are crucial to understanding pre-revolutionary secularization in lands ostensibly loyal to the Roman Church as well. Still, their impact must be noted in tandem with another late seventeenth and eighteenth-century force: that which is often referred to by historians as "Reform Catholicism."

Reform Catholicism included in its ranks a wide variety of different but interrelated groups, united publicly chiefly by a dislike for the Society of Jesus. Oratorians objected, among other things, to the nature of Jesuit education, priding themselves on their colleges' greater openness to useful natural sciences, and, hence, to the achievements of René Descartes (1596–1650) and Isaac Newton. Men like Ludovico Antonio Muratori (1672–1750), the Italian priest-historian, whose *Della Regolata Divozione Dei Cristianti*

(1747) was "the classic statement of Catholic reforming ideals in the eighteenth century" (Chadwick, in Scott, p. 59), opposed the emphasis upon grand liturgical ceremonies and public devotions encouraged by Jesuit Baroque culture. These he deemed to be an obstacle to the Pietist-like inner moral development, fed by a solid Scripture-based education, and confirmed in useful productive activities which he supported. Jesuit understandings of the relationship of grace and free will were targeted not only by Dominican Thomists, but also by Augustinian friars, the latter influenced by the *Historia Pelagiana* and *Vindiciae Augustinianae* of their confrère, Cardinal Enrico Noris (1631–1704). Reforming bishops, extolling the memory of the anti-Jesuit episcopal activity of Juan Palafox y Mendoza (1600–1659) of Puebla in Mexico, saw in the Society the symbol of all self-interested regular clergy sabotaging the legitimate power of local Ordinaries and work of diocesan priests.

Regalist defenders of the "dignity" of the monarchy, and its primary responsibility for the guidance of a kingdom's spiritual environment, often aided the work of reformers. They loathed the Ultramontanism associated with the Jesuits, and the papally-dominated national churches that the Society's "Romanism" would encourage. In fact, regalist concerns seems to have been the chief motivating factor in the reform programs of many Italians, particularly graduates of the University of Pavia, like the Tuscan-Neapolitan statesman Bernardo Tanucci (1678–1783). It also strongly influenced the contemporary Electors Emmerich Joseph (1707–1774) of Mainz and Clemens Wenceslaus (1739–1812) of Trier, bishops of the Roman Church though they were. The episcopal-regalist camp was further strengthened by the writings of a wide group of reforming canonists, beginning with Zega-Bernard van Espen (1646–1728), author of the *Ius Ecclesiasticum Universum* (1700) in the Lowlands, and passing through Johann Kaspar Barthel (1697–1771) and Georg Christoph Neller (1709–1783) down to Johann Nikolaus von Hontheim (1701–1790), auxiliary Bishop of Trier, who wrote underneath the pseudonym of Justinus Febronius. Such canonists rejected Ultramontanism and encouraged bishops to defy Rome on the grounds of their intrinsic worth as "popes in their own dioceses." They also stressed the State's divinely given right to concern itself with religion, and the logic of a secular institution responsible for control over all aspects of man's nature taking charge of "natural" spiritual needs. Nature's God required nature's civil policeman, aided by what in effect would be an army of ministers of that natural religion formerly known as Christianity.

Behind the varied wings of Reform Catholicism, an entire army of French, Belgian, Dutch, German, Italian and Spanish Jansenists maneuvered, bringing with them a program which had snowballed since the time of the publication of Cornelius Jansen's (1585–1638) *Augustinus* (1640/1641). Jansenism, by the eighteenth century, entailed support for a Calvinizing theology of grace involving rigorous penitential practices and reticence to receive communion; disdain for a devotional life and mystical theology encouraging hopes for union with God; a desire for a Church guided by that segment of the lower clergy and laity which had not accepted papal-episcopal condemnations of the movement; an unparalleled talent for underground organization, for propaganda and for spreading doctrinal deviations under the rubric of engaging in purely pastoral activities; and, of course, unvarying antipathy towards the Jesuits and everything associated with them.

All aspects of Reform Catholicism were visible and influential in Rome from the late 1600s onwards. Oratorians of the Chiesa Nuova provided ready recruits for its ranks, a major center for whose meetings was in the so-called Circolo dell'Archetto. Reform Catholicism was certainly prevalent by the reign of Pope Benedict XIV (1740–1758), who himself, as a canonist, could be counted in its ranks, along with his Cardinal Secretary of State, Gonzaga, and numerous other Princes of the Church, heads of religious orders, and clerical scholars. One would not be far off the mark in saying that Rome herself seemed to be embarrassed at Catholic "inadequacy" as a spiritual force, and calling out for help from more serious students of nature to remedy this scandal.

Economic resentment, defeat in war and natural disasters drove most Catholic lands down the pathway of reform by the middle years of the eighteenth century. For Portugal and Spain, inability to resist British commercial pressures at home and in the Americas were major incitements to change. Austria shared similar anti-British sentiments since the reign of Charles VI (1711–1740). She was, however, pushed to tinkering with her own system more by her bad military showing, first against the Ottoman Empire in the

1730s, and even more versus Prussia in the War of the Austrian Succession and the subsequent Seven Years' War (1757–1763). Severe crop failures which seemed unnecessarily destructive, given the state of contemporary science and technology, urged certain Italian and German lands down the same direction. France responded to comparable stimuli, though her complicated story requires special treatment in another article.

In all the cases cited above, the success stories of rival Britain and Prussia offered themselves as models for reforming activity. Maria Theresa (1740–1780) began such changes in Austria. Joseph II (co-ruler, 1765–1780; sole ruler, 1780–1790) and the Austrian Chancellor, Wenzel Anton Kaunitz (1711–1794), who had imbibed cameralist-pietist principles in foreign schools, were still more vigorous promoters of Hapsburg administrative, fiscal and educational changes along Prussian lines. Austrian Prussophilia also influenced smaller German states, many of which had already made tentative moves down the same highway, following the model of cooperative activity offered by the Dublin Society. Prussian methods and ideas penetrated from Hapsburg Austria into its lands in Italy, though the entire peninsula was itself filled with men like the Neapolitan, Antonio Genovesi (1713–1769), who pointed to the English experience for their primary guidance.

Portugal's secularization under José I (1750–1777) is forever associated with the influence of his Prime Minister, Sebastiao José de Carvalho e Melo (1699–1782), known as the Count of Oeiras from 1759, and the Marquis de Pombal after 1770. Pombal became a member of a British-style "confraternity" established by the Ericeiras Family, the Academia dos Illustrados, in 1733. He drank in more British influence during his diplomatic work in London (1739–1744), at which time he was admitted to the Royal Society. Pombal completed his education during a second assignment in Vienna in the 1740s, just as Prussian fever was taking hold of the Hapsburg Crown.

King Charles III of Spain (1759–1788) already gained a reputation as a reformer while ruler of the Two Sicilies (1734–1759). His work in Italy was aided and continued by men like the regalist, Tanucci. In Spain, other allies also proved to be useful in the effort to redirect society to the primary goal of practical, constructive labor. One of them, Pedro Rodriguez de Campomanes (1723–1803), in his *Discourse on the Encouragement of Popular Industry* (1774) argued for the universal spread of the English-style cooperative movement as the best means of promoting economic efficiency. This movement was mediated in Spain through organizations such as the Basque Economic Society of Friends of the Country, founded in 1763.

Wherever Regalists took up the banner of practical regeneration, they found that Reform Catholics of various stripes would enthusiastically fall in step alongside them, often pressing them to advance still further in their assault. Oratorians like the Portuguese Luís António Verney (1713–1792), whose *O Verdadeiro Metodo de Estudiar* (1746) had called for the introduction of a type of instruction "intended to be useful to the Republic and to the Church commensurate to the style and necessity of Portugal" (Scott, p. lo4), was of central assistance to Pombal's educational policies. The Spanish bishops José Clíment (1706–1781) and Felipe Bertrám (1704–1783), as well as the Benedictine Benito Jeronimo Feijoo (1676–1764), author of the *Teatro Critico Universal*, proved valuable to Charles III's reform program, in education as well as in other fields of activity. Johann Ignaz Felbiger (1724–1788), Augustinian Abbot of Sagan in Prussian Silesia and noted educational reformer, was imported to Vienna in 1774 to supervise the alterations in Austria, which provided its own Benedictine apologist for change in the person of Franz Stephan Rautenstrauch (1734–1785). Muratori's influence over reform fever was palpable. Two of his disciples, Johann Joseph Trautson (1751–1757) and Christoph Anton Migazzi (1757–1803), who ensured the translation of the Italian's major work into German in 1763, became Archbishops of Vienna, and, thus, advisors to reforming Hapsburgs.

Jansenists were not far behind Muratori in impact. A Jansenist trio — the natural law theorist Carlo Antonio Martini (1726–1800), along with Maria Theresa's physician, Gerard van Swieten (1700–1762), and confessor, Ignaz Müller (1713–1782) —were most conspicuous in Austria. The University of Pavia was a conduit for practical Jansenist support of reform in Italy, though its most famous active proponent was the Bishop of Pistoia and Prato, Scipione de'Ricci (1741–1809), himself a close collaborator of the secularizing Grand Duke Leopold of Tuscany (1765–1790). Jansenists from the reform circles of Feijoo, Clíment, Bertrám and the historian-philosopher, Gregorio Mayáns y Siscar (1699–1781), flourished in Spain and assisted Charles III's activities there.

Rome herself frequently stimulated or accepted reform fever, depending upon pope and pontificate. Encyclicals on varied matters signaled papal support for change. Concordat after concordat, some forced, some bought, still others willingly conceded, abandoned Church prerogatives to State authorities in Spain, Portugal, Sardinia and elsewhere. Once again, the practical reformer might be excused for thinking that the Papacy itself saw the justice of securing or submitting to secular help in order to control a voracious regular clergy and a self-interested traditional lay elite that led people away from useful activity both divine and human.

But what reforms were actually undertaken? As noted at the beginning of this article, many were of an administrative, fiscal and legal character, concerned with bureaucratic efficiency, tax collection and the reduction of expenses. Even if generally unilateral and insensitive in their planning and implementation, they did not necessarily impinge upon the essential spiritual rights of the Church. Where unjust, they were often unjust regarding primarily secular matters. Moreover, it must be admitted that certain changes that even did impinge upon the spiritual realm ultimately helped to alleviate undeniable abuses which Trent itself had sought to address, one of them being the exaggeratedly early and easy entry into religious life.

Other reforms, however, entailed unbearable tightening of regalist restrictions on all Church activities, spiritual as well as secular, according to the naturalist, secularizing plan. Unacceptable measures included the almost total destruction of the Jesuits, the abolition of contemplative monasteries, the abolition of "unproductive" feast days, devotions, and liturgical ceremonies, the prohibition of confraternities not engaged in "practical" work as ipso facto useless, the expropriation of properties supporting such "pointless" groups and their activities, the civil usurpation of controls over marriage questions, and State direction of seminary education. This last reform, in places like Austria, was integral to the overall effort of the civil authority to train the secular clergy as a Pietist morals police in the Prussian manner, and the consequent need to prohibit non-governmental (especially Papal) spiritual influence over the formation of priests. Such changes were repeatedly promoted and implemented by prince-bishops as well as lay rulers, while popes like Clement XIV (1769–1774) cooperated, willingly and unwillingly, in radical reform. They savaged the Jesuits and avoided "insulting" the "spiritual" activities of the secularizing Catholic monarchs of Europe by abandoning the traditional Holy Thursday catalogue of State abuses in the religious sphere altogether.

Whatever the specific measures dictated by reform fever, its truly offensive aspect was the spirit in which they were adopted: an ultimately closed-minded and self-interested spirit which, nevertheless passed itself off as a public-minded, philanthropic attack on obscurantism. Pombal's *Deducção Chronólogica Analítica* and *Relação Abbreviada* laid all secular problems at the doorstep of a Church dominated by Jesuit irrationality, and this at a time when fellow reformers like Joseph II were scattering scholarly Bollandist libraries as useless scrap paper, and van Swieten rejecting the Jesuit-encouraged use of smallpox vaccine. Love of mankind led reformers simultaneously to deep anguish over religious intolerance and summary condemnation of many, many Jesuit priests to a decades-long living death in monstrous Portuguese prisons. Numerous popular anti-reform protests were attributed to Jesuit conspiracy alone, and brutally suppressed on that basis. Meanwhile, "the People" as a whole were said to benefit by capitalist battening on a "practical" end of price controls in grain, the tossing of aged contemplatives into the street, and the prohibition of evening outdoor diversions that kept men up too late at night, limiting their sleep, and, hence, their following morning's productivity. The "reform movement" rejected contemptuously and out of hand the idea that Catholic Christianity had the ability to say anything sensible and practical. Catholicism was there to learn, not to teach, and the teaching it was obliged to swallow displayed that same union of sweet rhetoric, practical cruelty and bourgeois money-grubbing which has been a central characteristic of most revolutionary movements since the twelfth century.

All of this leads us to note that outright, root-and-branch enemies of the Christian name were also active in the mid to late century reform movement. Indeed, by the 1750s, Enlightenment supporters and Freemasons were operating at every level of government and practically everywhere. A few of them were playing with the "atheistic" China model much more seriously than their precursors might have done in 1700. Interestingly enough, Voltaire found it easy to utilize the writings of Reform Catholics in his more radical, post-1750 work, and men such as Joseph von Sonnenfels (1733–1817), one of Joseph II's educational czars, could move back and forth from the Reform Catholic to the anti-Catholic Enlightenment camp without notable difficulty.

Many of the proponents of practical change and Reform Catholicism were, however, ultimately quite well-meaning believers. Upon seeing that governmental reform was moving down an openly anti-Christian direction, they became honestly frightened for the future. Archbishop Migazzi and Maria Theresa, contemplating the work of her more radical son, Joseph II, were among them. Pope Pius VI (1775–1799), another reformer, also became alarmed over its unfolding consequences, his famous journey to Vienna in 1782 to urge the Austrian Emperor to retract his de-christianizing Edict of Toleration, illustrating the extent of his alarm. Unfortunately, objections of repentant pragmatists and reformers got almost nowhere. The Migazzis of the movement had badly underestimated the way in which their own confused intellectual and spiritual statements had deprived them of logical consistency when wishing to bridle more radical elements. The pre-revolutionary Revolution could not be halted by their action. Mass resistance in places like Belgium, stimulated by a mixture of "gut" parochial and religious feeling, did much more to stop it. So did the later horror over the excesses of the Terror of Republican France, and the full-scale, profound nineteenth century re-examination of the issues of Church-State-society relations. Still, by that time, the whole Catholic understanding of political and social life and its relation to God had received a tremendous and seemingly irrevocable jolt.

What lessons ought we Catholics today learn from this story of the pre-revolutionary Revolution? Four come to mind, all of them important to mention, though none of them, as is true of many serious historical judgments, are particularly surprising.

First among these lessons is the crucial need for a clear and full understanding of the entirety of our tradition. It is only through complete knowledge that we can know what is essential to Catholicism, what is transitory, and what has elbowed its way into Christendom for an easier ride to its own peculiar destination. Failure to be rigorous in this matter can lead us to make hasty and dangerous alliances with predatory "friends." It can also cause us to draw equally sudden and perilous conclusions once we understand and withdraw from compromised positions. Many Catholics had so misunderstood their own tradition that they themselves had helped to construct the Regalist vision of exaggerated State power. They then tried to "correct" their mistake in the nineteenth century through the singularly more egregious error of rejecting all proper union of Church and State whatsoever. Neglect of the full riches of tradition assures Christian failure to make the right distinctions and to judge accurately between erroneous and correct Church and State activity.

Secondly, while recognizing the scandal of heretical ideas and influences entering into serious disputes regarding the Faith and the pastoral methods designed to spread it, we must nevertheless remind ourselves repeatedly of the need to conduct our quarrels with the maximum of self-awareness and charitable restraint. Apostolic activity can never be based on the desire purely for winning points for one's camp. The eighteenth-century European reaction to the China dispute shows that the population-at-large will recognize and be repelled by the vicious backbiting predominating in a battle fought in the wrong spirit, ignore the serious issues at stake, and fall prey to the machinations of enemies wishing to use our flaws for their own benefit.

Thirdly, Catholics must rigorously strive to avoid succumbing to the spirit of the times, the *zeitgeist*. This is not a simple matter. It is easy to oppose and be outraged by those who did not reject the *zeitgeist* of another era; it is extraordinarily more difficult to escape one's own, and often even to begin to identify it properly. Fallen men have a natural tendency to justify what is useful to them. Catholics, as all other natural, fallen men, have to examine themselves regularly to see if they, too, are not engaged in the process of baptizing whatever the governing ethos of the day promises will give them practical material and political success. Barriers against the eighteenth century British-Prussian recipe for worldly success are particularly important to erect because, *mutatis mutandis*, it is that same model which tempts Catholics today, almost everywhere, in the triumphalist ideology of global American Pluralism. When those barriers are dismantled, the consequences go far beyond a simple change in "style" regarding secondary matters of "practical" daily life. A full-scale attack on the Faith comes free of charge along with the superficial benefits of the *zeitgeist*.

Finally, seeing that failure to understand the whole Catholic tradition leaves us in a vulnerable position, that lack of charity in our own ranks can teach lessons destructive to our cause, and that abandonment to the modern *zeitgeist* of success goes beyond a simple common sense practicality into dechristianization (or rather, makes dechristianization seem commonsensical and practical), let us always remember what that secularization ultimately entails. Iced in a sugary language of progress, goodness, happiness and freedom, it is and always will be a mere love affair with power. This was true of eighteenth century Britain and Prussia as well as of the "moderate" Enlightenment encouraged by and encouraging them. It is altogether too true of America and its global imitators today. As Gawthrop notes, focusing on Prussian Pietism, but expanding his argument into a critique of the whole modern dilemma:

> In light of the demonstrated connections and affinities between Lutheran Pietism and Anglo-American Puritanism, it should be evident that these psychocultural tensions, which have haunted German history in perhaps an archetypal way, are endemic in the very nature of modernity itself. Although the Prusso-German path toward modernization was characterized by an unusual degree of primacy given the collective state power, its deeper significance will elude us if we fail to focus on the Promethean lust for material power that serves as the deepest common drive behind all modern Western cultures. Thus, when we look upon such figures as August Hermann Francke and Frederick William I, we should not simply dismiss them as embodying something alien, but rather see them as possible reflections of ourselves (p. 284).

FURTHER READING:

Bordet, L., *St. Philip Neri and the Roman Society of His Times* (Sheed and Ward, 1932).

Gawthrop, R., *Pietism and the Making of Eighteenth Century Prussia* (Cambridge, 1993).

Gay, P., *The Enlightenment* (Norton, 1969).

Hildesheimer, F., *Il giansenismo* (San Paolo, 1994).

Phillips, H., *Church and Culture in Seventeenth-Century France* (Cambridge, 1997).

Scott, H.M., *Enlightened Absolutism* (Michigan, 1990).

Lamennais, Rousseau and the New Catholic Order†

A GOOD CASE COULD BE MADE FOR ENTI-
tling a history of modern Catholicism *The Age of the Abbé
Félicité de Lamennais* (1782–1854). Son of a Breton bourgeois
family ennobled one year before the outbreak of the Revolution,
Lamennais left a profound and permanent mark on the life of the
Church. On the one hand, he stimulated studies and activities
which contributed mightily to a healthy Catholic self-conscious-
ness and growth. On the other, he promoted certain exceedingly
dangerous doctrines at the heart of the current crisis, not only of
our religion but of our entire civilization.

Lamennais was ordained a priest in 1816. The success the following year of the first volume of his *Essay on Indifference in
Matters of Religion* (four volumes, 1817–1823) caused many to
view him as a modern-day Church Father. His enthusiasm for a
revitalization of the Papacy and the episcopacy, clerical and lay
political and social action, an impregnation of the State, education, the economic order, music and art with a religious sense, a
mobilization of the press as a teaching tool, and an organization
of Catholic energies on the international level quickly resonated
throughout the European world.

The young priest's charisma can be measured by the quality
of the men drawn to the Congregation of St. Peter, which he
assembled at his estate of La Chênaie to study methods for resuscitating dormant Christendom. The Mennaisiens, as they were
often contemptuously labeled by their opponents, included in
their ranks a large number of those who were to play major roles
in all fields, lay and clerical, for many decades to come. Among
these were Charles de Montalembert (1810–1870), future leader
of that "Catholic Party" which fought for freedom of education
in the French Parliament during the July Monarchy (1830–1848);

† First published on the *Seattle Catholic* website (February 1, 2005).

Charles de Coux (1787–1864), social thinker and professor of economics at the University of Louvain; Jean Baptiste Lacordaire (1802–1861), who was instrumental in reestablishing the Dominican Order in France; Prosper Guéranger (1805–1875), Benedictine founder and proponent of liturgical reform; Olympe Philippe Gerbet (1798–1864), the theologian of the movement and Bishop of Perpignan; Alexis-François Rio (1797–1874), author of *De la Poésie Chrétienne* (1836); and René Rohrbacher (1789–1856), the Church historian.

Yet despite the brilliant careers of such disciples, Lamennais' own position within the Roman Catholic world was soon destroyed. His theories regarding Church-State relations—one of the keystones of his labors—were rejected in Gregory XVI's (1831–1846) encyclical letter *Mirari Vos* (August 15, 1832). He himself was personally excommunicated by the same pontiff through *Singulari Nos* (June 21, 1834). Lamennais died in 1854, unreconciled with the Church. What evil spirit, his admirers have wondered, could possibly have induced Rome symbolically to burn this male Joan of Arc at the stake, and precisely at the moment when he was pointing the way to a true liberation of the Catholic genius?

Certainly, an "evil spirit" that actually saw a great deal of good in much of what Lamennais had to say. Neither his vocal critique of the manipulation of religion by existing European states, nor his concern for a freedom of association, exploration of a variety of new disciplines, and openness to untraditional systems of government came under papal attack. Gregory XVI, the demonized scourge of Lamennais, himself dedicated the Papacy to a liberation of the Church from secular domination in *Commissum Divinitas* (May 17, 1835). He supported the famous German activist campaign protesting the Prussian government's imprisonment of Archbishop Clemens August von Droste zu Vischering (1773–1845) of Cologne after that prelate tried to enforce canonical requirements regarding mixed marriages. The same pontiff recognized the Latin American republics which had revolted against the legitimate Spanish monarchy and worked with the liberal-catholic Belgian Union. Moreover, Gregory never required Mennaisiens who had broken with their master to abandon the practical activist paths that he had marked out for them, politically controversial though these might be. Neither did he rein in Catholics, Jesuits prominent among them, who developed contacts with representatives of "modern" schools of philosophical, political and social thought. If a masculine Joan of Arc had been symbolically burned at the stake, many of the followers of his cult seemed to be thriving nicely.

Where, then, did the *real* problem lie? In Lamennais' "liberation" of a Catholicism which was actually a new and different Faith than that of his Breton forebears; in his support for a belief system that seemed, at first glance, to exalt the supernatural, but ended by tossing it into a secular house of contradictory horrors from which it could never escape. For this "modern Church Father" did not ultimately base his religion upon the Apostolic Faith. Instead, he refashioned that Faith in a manner that reflects both the form of Enlightenment naturalism espoused by Jean-Jacques Rousseau (1712–1778) as well as the evolutionary concept of change through *palingenesis*.

Rousseau, perhaps the most readable and influential of eighteenth-century writers, followed the Enlightenment injunction to found all judgments upon an honest observation of nature and nature alone. Unlike those *philosophes* who observed in nature the reign of objective mathematical and scientific laws, however, his studies revealed a universe inhabited by energetically "feeling" individuals whose real character could never be uncovered by books or laboratory experiments detached from men's inner passions. Rousseau insisted that anyone wishing to join him in becoming a true observer of life had to begin by examining himself to see if he were honestly speaking and acting in line with his spontaneous nature, however passionate and non-rational this might prove to be. Such an investigation required an abandonment of all the masks, pretensions and hypocrisies which men embraced in order to "fit with the program" dictated by tyrannical, external, passion-challenged forces operating in the name of objective reason. Once an individual succeeded in breaking his chains and getting in touch with his real self, he became natural, and, through nature's innate value, correspondingly "virtuous."

Virtue, for Rousseau, was not something built through the repetition of petty, daily, "good" actions. Rather, it was attained by entering into the aforementioned ontological state of being a liberated "natural man." Rousseau reached this natural, virtuous condition through his *Confessions* (published posthumously, 1782). Here, he revealed to the world all his deepest, passionate, non-rational feelings and their effect on his actions, without consideration for the effect such disclosure might have upon public opinion and his personal fortunes. Having thus accepted himself, he became virtuous, and need not be ashamed of deeds that others thought to be reprehensible; deeds which would, indeed, still be blame-worthy if done by men seeking praise from the artificial, outside, "objective" world. Rousseau could permit himself no rationalist post-mortem on the validity of his deeply-felt virtue. All "looking back" amounted to a renewed embrace of the unjustifiable rules of a soul-killing artifice and duplicity.

Moreover, natural virtue transformed Rousseau into Everyman. Nature possessed integrity. It was all of one piece, honest and good, and could not help but speak with a single voice. Therefore, others who sincerely stripped themselves of the obstacles stand-ing in the way of expression of their spontaneous natural feeling would inevitably be indistinguishable from, and united fraternally with Rousseau. It is this indistinguishability which ensures that the various lovers in his widely-read *Nouvelle Héloise* (1761) are actually only loving themselves in other people, and the teacher in his enormously influential educational treatise, the *Emile* (1761), can be said by Rousseau to both ensure the child's self-fulfillment and yet remake him totally in the tutor's image at one and the same time. (Blum, p. 67). Conversely, anyone who was not Rousseau-like, anyone who criticized Everyman's feelings and spontaneous actions, anyone who failed to pity him in his trials, revealed him-self as being unnatural. The critic could therefore be neither free, nor virtuous, nor truthful. In fact, he could not even be labeled human, and did not deserve any fraternal consideration whatsoever. Blum describes the situation well in commenting on Rousseau's discussion of himself as the "spectator-animal" contemplating the suffering of one such pointless being.

> The Spectator animal was denied pleasurable pity in regard-ing the suffering animal because the suffering animal was evil and hence unworthy of sympathy. Since Rousseau knew that mankind was, like him, good, he was forced to the awful but inevitable realization that the creatures who treated him so heartlessly were not really people at all, that the key to the

mystery was that 'my contemporaries were but mechanical beings in regard to me who acted only by impulsion and whose actions I could calculate only by the laws of movement.' He was now really alone, the only human being left amid a throng of automatons; the human race existed solely in him (Ibid., p. 99).

Unfortunately, that non-virtuous and non-human world had shown regularly that it was dedicated to Rousseau's destruction. The pressing duty of Everyman was, therefore, to remake a dangerous, aggressive universe in his own image. Failing this, he had to annihilate it before it could cause him any further damage. There could, again, be no doubt about this either/or choice. As the voice of a holistic, harmonious nature, Rousseau possessed infallibility. The sincere, natural, virtuous, free, liberated Everyman simply could not possibly err. Any personal hesitation regarding his position would once more reveal continued susceptibility to the sham world of hostile, rationalist hypocrisy that the virtuous man must categorically reject and move vigorously to obliterate.

One final, exceedingly important point. Although totally earthbound in his approach, Rousseau's emphasis on the overriding importance of non-rational feeling and passion in human life does give his "natural world" a certain unpredictably mysterious glow. Rousseau's "nature" is indefinable, and fueled by seemingly superhuman feelings that continually shock and awe. Hence, while no one would view the mechanical-minded naturalism of many of his Enlightenment opponents as being somehow "spiritual," many people have been led to see Rousseauian naturalism in precisely this light. Instead of being viewed as merely the wilder version of the same earth-bound vision shared by all *philosophes*, it has often been depicted as open to sacralizing influences that the mathematician and scientist cannot allow. Many enthusiasts have even gone so far as to limit the very definition of the spiritual to the kind of universe within which Rousseau works, equating the presence of God and of His blessing only with the existence of strong feelings, and the vital, energetic, conquering action they release. Terrible error indeed! For anyone succumbing to such a temptation blocks himself off entirely from access to what Catholics believe to be the true source of the spiritual: supernatural truths and supernatural grace coming from outside of limited, created nature and the human persons inhabiting it. Anyone falling victim to this kind of "spirituality" refuses to permit God to be what the adjective supernatural indicates that He is: *above* His handiwork. Moreover, he loses all ability to see that his flights of deeply felt enthusiasm may be caused merely by madness or adolescent hormonal activity.

Rousseau-like statements of one form or another make an appearance in the writings of practically all revolutionary thinkers of the nineteenth century. One finds them in the novels of Victor Hugo and Stendhal, in the political proclamations of the leaders of democratic and nationalist movements, and in the manifestos of the representatives of varied forms of contemporary socialism. One is constantly told that the proponents of The Cause are "feeling" men who have sincerely got in touch with their true nature, and thus possess a virtue, an infallibility, and a kind of spiritual excellence that only dead souls could fail to recognize. One regularly learns that Enemies of the People cannot be judged by the same standard as the revolutionary Hero if they do not subscribe to his Teaching and are not incorporated into his Mystical Body. Thus, for Hugo, the revolt of the People accepting the Hero's message is redemptive; the rebellion of the inhabitants of the Vendée is a vile riot. The massacres perpetrated by the former are Christ-like; a tap on the finger by the latter is the most wretched of crimes. Virtue lies all on one side, however animalistic its actions may be; animalism on the other, however rational and peaceful the behavior of its victimized supporters.

Lamennais served as one of Rousseau's chief conduits into the Catholic world. His path to becoming a passionate, natural, virtuous, infallible, heroic, revolutionary Rousseauian Everyman was first paved by acceptance of the concept of "traditionalism." Traditionalism, in the nineteenth century, did not mean what it popularly signifies today. In Lamennais' day, it identified a philosophical-theological outlook disdaining the role of reason both in grasping truth and teaching the Faith. Truth, for Lamennais and nineteenth century traditionalists as a whole, was learned by individuals as social beings, under the active guidance of the historical institutions at the very core of society's "nature." In effect, it was the wholehearted opening to the vital force of these institutions which created believing, energetic Catholic Peoples. Truths lying behind institutional vitality were passed down through the process of living in the society which they formed. The Revolution's battle versus truth was effective not because of any rational struggle against ideas, but due to its temporarily successful efforts to crush two crucial traditional institutions, the Church and the Monarchy, whose unified active energies had led the society of men to live and accept the Faith. If Church and Monarchy were ravaged, spiritual life and knowledge of the truth were also destined to be lost. Individuals could not be expected to understand the doctrines of the Faith as independent thinking atoms.

But here Lamennais encountered a terrible paradox. The Church, restored to legal institutional life after the Revolution, was not acting as the vital social force that she must be in order to have the desired effect. She ran the awful risk of not really electrifying men's social existence, and thus not passing down the message of Faith. It was necessary to shake Church structures out of their formalistic torpor and revive their will to give vital witness to the truth. This was ultimately the point of the *Essay on Indifference*, which was not a call for devotion to the intellectually-enunciated doctrines of the Catholic Faith, but, rather, a condemnation of half-hearted or lazy commitment preventing that "felt" witnessing to the truth which alone could be effective.

Committed, sincere witness could scarcely be offered if basic Church institutions were unable to live in accord with their own true "nature." Thus, the Papacy, so thoroughly emasculated by the Enlightenment and the Revolution, had to have its integral rights and powers fully recognized and revived. Similarly, each national episcopacy had to be freed to follow its proper path under papal guidance. Place the Papacy and national episcopacies back in touch with their supernaturally "natural" character, and the spontaneous energetic life that would flow through their arteries would end religious indifference. The result would be an electrified, creative civilization of believing social individuals.

Lamennais had seen in the traditional Bourbon Monarchy of the French Restoration (1814–1830) the force most apt to work together with the Church as a battery charging Christian society and Christian man. He was a fervent contributor to legitimist journals such as *Le Conservateur* and *Le Drapeau Blanc*. Gradually, however, the young priest became convinced that the monarchy actually had either little interest in or ability to do what was necessary to electrify Catholic civilization. It had turned its back on its own historical nature and mission. One strong segment of legitimist opinion, represented most vigorously by François de Reynaud, the comte de Montlosier (1755–1838), in his *Mémoire à Consulter sur un Système Religieux et Politique Tendant à Renverser la Religion, la Société et le Trône* (1826), was vigorously hostile to the idea of a Church living a spontaneous, independent life alongside a believing Monarchy. Even more upsetting to Lamennais was the French Church authorities' apparent connivance in this betrayal. Legitimists, Lamennais began to think, sacrificed or redefined Church goals to suit their own unnatural and self-destructive ends. Catholics were culpable in trusting and even adulating these misguided secularist Pied Pipers. His reaction, in 1828, was to argue for a total end to a union of the deluded, abused Church with the unnaturally manipulative legitimist State. Separation alone could guarantee the former a chance to get back in touch with her real nature and do her job as it ought to be done if the Faith were to survive.

1830 saw a Catholic-Liberal Union in Belgium triumphantly overthrow a legitimist Dutch monarch who had proven to be harmful to both their quite different interests. France also succumbed to revolutionary fever that fateful year, replacing the legitimist Charles X with the liberal Orleanist Louis-Philippe. Lammenais seized what he considered to be a general providential moment to found an outspoken journal, *L'Avenir (The Future)*, whose first issue appeared on October 16, 1830, under the motto "God and Liberty." *L'Avenir* was designed to become the mouthpiece of an international coalition of vital Catholics, a Holy Alliance of Peoples. Through its work, believers themselves would achieve what the old union of self-interested legitimist State and deceived national Church could or would not accomplish. In other words, if hypocritical or emasculated monarchies and episcopacies refused to undertake the necessary labor of getting in touch with their true nature and reanimating Christian society, then sincere, unpretentious, committed, believing Peoples as a whole would themselves energetically propel Church and State in Catholic nations to do their duty.

Opposition from powerful circles in France and elsewhere was nevertheless so strong that the embattled Lamennais felt the need for papal confirmation of his vision. He thus temporarily suspended publication of *L'Avenir* in November of 1831, and set off with Lacordaire and Montalembert on a Roman "pilgrimage of liberty" to gain the blessing of Pope Gregory XVI. But despite the support of the Theatine philosopher, Fr. Gioacchino Ventura (1792–1861), and even of several cardinals, Rome proved to be unfavorable to his message. One by one, the "pilgrims of liberty" read the handwriting on the wall and left, Lamennais the last of all. The axe began to fall shortly thereafter, with *Mirari Vos*. Then, following two years of further controversy regarding *L'Avenir*, Mennaisien enthusiasm for the Polish rebellion against Tsarist Russia, and the publication of Lamennais' controversial *Paroles d'un Croyant*, came the aforementioned excommunication.

Our pilgrim of liberty was shocked. First, the French episcopacy had proven to be useless. Now the Papacy, the institution destined to benefit the most from an end to unnatural, legitimist State controls and episcopal collaborationism, had rejected the summons to vitality. The sincere, European-wide coalition of traditional-minded Catholic People was thus left entirely to its own energies if Christianity were to survive and prosper. Lamennais called upon this Silent Catholic Majority to take up the task of teaching the Faith through the example of its vital living of its message, even in opposition to the pronouncements of its erstwhile international leader, dethroned by his public display of "indifference."

A counterrevolutionary defense of the Faith now seemed, ironically, to be based upon a concept very much resembling the revolutionary principle of popular sovereignty. Lamennais had little trouble admitting as much, as he had by this point come to believe that vitality itself was a sure sign of the divine presence. Already in 1829, in *Progress of the Revolution*, he noted that the energetic fervor with which revolutionaries supported the doctrine of popular sovereignty demonstrated that there must be something solid and good behind it. Upheaval in 1830 merely confirmed him in this conviction. All that seemed to be lacking to the revolutionary vision was a recognition that the truths taught by an energetic populace were not purely earthly ones. Vital Catholic Peoples possessed supernatural truths to which they had to testify, and would be able to give witness more effectively through further, democratic, revolutionary changes.

This brings us to the second influence on Lamennais, that of the concept of *palingenesis*. Formed from the Greek words "again" and "birth," palingenesis was the notion that a "Third Age of Humanity" was emerging in the nineteenth century out of traditional western forces that many thought erroneously to be dead. Palingenesis was appealing to all defenders of modern ideas who still possessed a spiritual sense and did not want to jettison the entire Christian baggage of European civilization. These included men like Claude Henri de Saint Simon (1760–1825), Charles Fourrier (1772–1837), Barthélemy Enfantin (1796–1864), Saint-Amand Bazard (1791–1832), and Auguste Comte (1798–1857). Such thinkers, horrified by destructive revolutionary violence, sought to illustrate how modernity could grow and develop, organically and peacefully, through the ages. They showed how one vital historical era was inevitably the prelude to the next; how the teachings of Jesus, the cult of the Virgin, a hierarchical priesthood, a liturgy and many other elements of western civilization still played an energetic, though transfigured role in modern life.

Lamennais shared this palingenesist vision. Contemporary Catholicism, as far as he was concerned, was deeply flawed. "How far," he bitterly lamented, "we still are from that religion of devotion, of self-forgetfulness for the good of all; in sum, of that fraternity of which one speaks so much!" (Mayeur, X, p. 866). Nevertheless, historical Christianity had performed its basic task well. Its earlier vitality had prepared the way for a syncretist, universal religion which would electrify the Third Age of Humanity. If the familiar historic Faith were now dying, it was only because it was meant to be reborn in this new and better form.

Sincere, energetic, believing Catholic Peoples were to be the midwives of that birth. Following Adam Mickiewicz (1798–1855), poet and religious philosopher, and his friends, Alexander Towianski (1795–1878) and Julius Slowacki (1809–1849), Lamennais believed that Catholic Poland was pointing the route to the future. For, as Mickiewicz demonstrated in his *Book of the Nation and of the Polish Pilgrims* (1834), the preface for which was written by Montalembert, the contemporary revival of the seemingly dead Polish people was making it into the Christ among nations. Poland was destined to carry forward and improve upon the salvific mission of the Savior, uniting all peoples and religions into a new, common worship of the Almighty, transforming and perfecting a praiseworthy but superannuated Catholicism. (Ibid., pp. 860–863).

This Third Age of Humanity would usher in a socio-political order both republican and socialist in character; an "age of gold under the sign of universal fraternity through social justice" (Ibid., X, p. 864). The energy behind the republican movement illustrated its divine favor, proving that "the republicans of our days would have been the most ardent disciples of Christ eighteen centuries ago" (Ibid., X, p. 848). A similar statement could be made regarding socialism; that contemporary socialists would have been the original Christians as well. Republicanism and socialism would not only set right the injustices suffered by the People in a changing, industrializing Europe; they would also avenge the humiliations that Lamennais, palingenesist facilitator, had himself received at the hands of a vicious but dying Establishment (Ibid. p. 892). Eventually, they would be responsible for other developments as immeasurably exciting and mystical as they were incredibly vague in their Mennaisien formulation.

Europe, according to Lamennais, faced a stark choice between hope and despair. It could either place its faith in the People and palingenesis, or it would be delivered over to Nihilism. "There will be no more middle way between faith and nothingness," he wrote to de Maistre with respect to the dilemma facing the world-in-birth; "Everything is extreme today. There is no dwelling place in between" (Billington, p. 123).

The choice for Faith was, however, complicated by the horrible fact that the Catholic Peoples themselves seemed to lack the requisite energy to accept, live and thereby teach the activist, palingenesist program. They, too, were resistant to the command to get in touch with their true nature, indifferent to performance of the tasks vital to their role, and even susceptible to the continued influence of the hypocritical, artificial ecclesiastical and political authorities around them. Still, there was a way out of this nightmare. If the Catholic Peoples remained unconscious, then their unquestionable message could still be expressed, temporarily, by an enlightened Prophet, a Rousseauian Everyman. Lamennais was that man. He must himself speak for the "dumb" Catholic Peoples and work to raise their consciousness from its unnatural torpor. He must destroy those who would stand in the way of their maturation.

Hence, his openness to Giuseppe Mazzini's (1809–1872) call to leadership of a regenerated, God-loving priesthood; a vanguard that would establish the new heaven and the new earth; a "Church of Precursors which I should like to see you found while waiting for the People to rise" (Mayeur, X, p. 893).

> Why do you only write books? Humanity awaits something more from you . . . Do not deceive yourself, Lamennais, we need action. The thought of God is action; it is only by action that it is incarnated in us . . . So long as you will be alone, you will only be a philosopher and a moralist in the eyes of the masses; it is as a priest that you must appear before it, a priest of the future, of the epoch which is beginning, of that new religious manifestation of which you have a presentiment, and which must inevitably end in that new heaven and new earth which Luther glimpsed three centuries ago without being able to attain it, since the time had not yet come (Ibid.).

We are now in a much better position to understand the depth of the problem behind the project central to our "Joan of Arc's" ecclesiastical condemnation: his call for a total separation of Church and State. Mennaisien separation, quite simply put, is a monstrous fraud, made possible by the convoluted reasoning of Rousseauian naturalism. That fraud has been remarkably successful, convincing the average thinking man that separation finally ensures the possibility for a liberated Church to operate according to her own spiritual nature in a free and properly focused State. Yet, under the cover of a public Church-State divorce, it actually ensures that these two institutions are more dangerously fused together than ever before in Christian History; that they are both placed under far more devastating secularist, demagogic control than at the most corrupt moments of traditional regimes professing an official union.

Unnatural fusion comes from the fact that, for the first time, in the revolutionary universe, ultimate authority in both institutions lies in exactly the same hands: those of "the People's Prophet." This man (or party) understands that People's true character and desires. He must do everything in his power to arouse it to an awareness of what he knows they unconsciously long to know and destroy anyone standing in his path. The reason why Lamennais does not have to worry about clashes between an independent Church and State on matters where their jurisdiction over creatures of body and soul intersect is because a collision, in his system, cannot possibly take place. How could there be any tension of authorities when all power is invested in the hands of the Everyman-Prophet, from whose judgments only the Rousseauian Enemy of the People might think of making appeal? And how could any such Enemy, non-human as he is, be permitted to point out the incredible swindle that was being perpetrated, or treated seriously if he succeeded in having his animalistic voice heard? What Lamennais had illegitimately and surreptitiously linked together, let no dehumanized supporter of a dignified public union put asunder.

Vulgar, secularist demagoguery triumphs in the Third Age of Humanity due to Church and State submission to an Everyman-Prophet/Party whose decisions are rooted in a willfulness disguised as the height and limit of spirituality. Ultimately, it is only energetic passion and vital will which are king in the land shaped by the new Christianity that they represent. Religion, republicanism and socialism mean what the Prophet/Party want them to mean. When the victory of the Spirit is lauded by Lamennais and his disciples, one can be absolutely certain that this will surely entail, on the contrary, a total immersion in what everyone sane recognizes to be either irrational willfulness or its ideological justification. When they condemn Gregory XVI's supposed slavishness to secularism, they are really criticizing the pope's efforts to enunciate a truly supernatural sense of Christian evangelization, its consequences, and the difficulties of defending it effectively in a world of sinful men, both hypocritical and "sincere."

Quicksand lies everywhere in Lamennais' Rousseauian Third Age of Humanity. One thing always dissolves into another within it. Spiritual truths are grounded in commitment to passion and will. Energetic Catholic Peoples opposed to palingenesis are condemned for their lethargy. Getting in touch with their true nature requires annihilation of what they themselves believe that nature to be. A single individual speaks infallibly and democratically for an entire hostile People armed with rational arguments and enthusiastically eager to crush his wishes. Contradiction after contradiction piles up. Whoever unmasks the deceptions somehow proves his own artifice and dissembling hypocrisy, voluntarily resigns from the human race, and justifies his future obliteration at the hands of the Prophet of the humble and the weak.

Despite his condemnation, Lamennais' negative influence has come back again and again to haunt the Catholic world, today much more than in the 1830's. "Defeated" by Gregory XVI, it was promoted in more "prudent" form in the Liberal Catholicism of the 1850s and 1860s, and then more determinedly again in the Sillon of the 1890s and 1900s. Driven underground by Pius X, it re-emerged with reference to natural law analogies in Integral Humanism from the 1930s onwards. Its mystical adulation both of the fraternal community as well as the individual or elite raising its sleeping consciousness was reaffirmed by Personalism at the same time. Liberation Theology took up the torch shortly thereafter. Teilhard de Chardin (1881–1955) provided its palingenesist evolutionism a further biological-spiritual support. Triumphant Americanist Pluralism, with its exaltation of thoughtless action, has served as an effective ally, and a seemingly all-conquering one since 1945. Each time the Mennaisien spirit returns, it announces itself to be strikingly new, startlingly energetic, invincible, and yet, predictably, the humble victim of persecuting forces. Every time it appears, it raises the banner of the primacy of the Spirit, and proceeds to reduce the Christian mission to a set of pressing political imperatives. Over and over again, it insists that it is ushering in an age of Christian victory and Catholic freedom, though the greater its successes, the less there is anything distinctly Christian about it, and the more that the very word Catholic tends to disappear entirely from its lexicon.

Many of the proponents of the faith of Lamennais, like Lamennais himself, have been exceedingly gifted men with valid criticisms of Church life, and imaginative, workable solutions to specific problems. They, like Lamennais, have thus drawn serious Catholics into their orbit. And once within it, the creed that they oblige everyone to profess in the energetic People, the Prophet who must rouse it from its lethargy, and the forcible witness that it is then compelled to give to a "spontaneously" emerging, universalist Christian culture poisons all that they do.

Perhaps Lamennais' remarks to Joseph de Maistre were true; that, in modern times, there would be no middle ground; that only extremes could function. Unfortunately, the extreme represented by this new faith, and shared in varied forms by other groups in contemporary western society, reduces in the long run to an apotheosis of the independence and freedom of the sincere, vital individual masquerading the Triumph of the Will. That "will," unchecked by true Christian faith and grace, leads its possessor and the society that he victimizes into an eternal abyss of meaningless passion. To cite the title of an article in *La Civiltà Cattolica*, the choice was and still is one that is simple: either God is King, with a true freedom, or Man is King, based on the use of raw power alone.

FURTHER READING:

Billington, J.H., *Fire in the Minds of Men* (Basic Books, 1980)

Blum, C., *Rousseau and the Republic of Virtue* (Cornell, 1986)

Jedin, H. and Dolan, J., eds., *History of the Church* (VII. VIII, IX, Crossroads, 1981)

Mayeur, J., *Histoire du Christianisme* (X/XI, Desclée, 1995/1997)

School Days†

R EDISCOVERY IS THE BEST WORD TO CHAR-
acterize the experience of a great number of committed
Catholics of the 1800s. Throughout the post-French revolutionary
Catholic world, thinkers and activists of impressive caliber demonstrated a desire to learn, develop and put into practice themes and
customs which had been buried by decades and even centuries
of Jansenist, naturalist and simple parochial neglect. Depending
upon energy, taste and imagination, this drive led them back to
the Fathers of the Church, to the medieval scholastics, and to a
mystical, devotional and liturgical life rich in lessons for both the
Catholic community and individuals. The centers of re-discovery—
German, Italian and French, for the most part—were lay/clerical
circles of believers, religious confraternities, orders restored after
the devastation of the Revolution, university faculties, and groups
gathering around those journals and newspapers that seemed to
spring up everywhere in the course of the nineteenth century.

It was out of this movement of rediscovery that the approach of
what some have called the "Roman School" was formed. Although
it is impossible in a single article to name all of this "School's"
founders and proponents, one can at least orient himself historically
and geographically by referring to those segments of the scholarly
and popular press of the years from the 1830s to the 1870s which
were actively engaged in popularizing it. Anyone wishing to grasp
the character of the Roman School at its origins should examine
the pages of *Der Katholik*, the *Historisch-Politische Blätter*, and
Archiv für Katholisches Kirchenrecht in the German world; *La
Civiltà Cattolica* in Italy; *L'Univers/Le Monde* in France; and
the *Dublin Review* in the United Kingdom.

Five themes may be said to have provided the "curriculum" of
the Roman School, the most basic of which was an insistence upon
the impossibility of understanding anything "natural" without reference both to nature's future supernatural destiny as well as the

---

† First published on the *Seattle Catholic* website (March 15, 2005).

supernatural life surging through it now as a consequence of the Incarnation. The work of the editors of *La Civiltà Cattolica* and of Cardinal Louis Pie (1815–1880), Bishop of Poitiers, is extremely informative in this regard. Try as modern man might, Pie argued at Lourdes in 1876, he could never escape the fact that he lived in a world created and redeemed at the behest of a supernatural will. "The supernatural is finished," he quoted nineteenth century man as gloating. "Well, look here, then! The supernatural pours out, overflows, sweats from the sand and from the rock, spurts out from the source, and rolls along on the long folds of the living waves of a river of prayers, of chants and of light" (Mayeur, XI, p. 350). Similarly, the reality of the supernatural, its impact, its demands, and the folly of denying it, could be seen in politics, economics and every other aspect of human life. The enemy of the supernatural, Cardinal Pie noted, thought that he was the friend of nature; instead he was actually nature's most aggressive enemy, and an ignorant one to boot.

Central to this theme of natural-supernatural interaction was the role of the Church as Christ continued in time. For the Romanists, the Church was Jesus in action on earth today, possessing a spiritual significance far surpassing anything obviously natural in her structure. Discussion of the Church in this context enabled the Roman School to place the functions of pope, bishop and priest in a different light than a purely juridical treatment of their responsibilities would allow; to stress their character as "other-Christs" active in the world. Romanists underlined the same theme in explaining every other "fleshly" aspect of the Church's activity, from the most sacramental to the most mundane. A correct understanding of the Church as Christ-continued, Liberatore wrote in the *Civiltà*, would so transform one's appreciation of her that "the very carriages of the cardinals would change their appearance in your eyes" (*Civiltà Cattolica*, i, 7, 533). The Church was the chief manifestation of the supernatural's penetration of the natural world and the chief instrument for awakening consciousness of the practical meaning of that penetration.

Such a concept, while fed from many sources, was especially nourished by the ideas of Johann Adam Möhler of the University of Tübingen, whose works Giovanni Perrone (1794–1876), professor at the Gregorian in Rome from 1824–1863, made known to many of his influential students: Carlo Passaglia (1812–1887), Clemens Schrader (1820–1875), and Johannes Baptist Franzelin (1816–1886). Perrone was also a channel of Möhler's ecclesiology to the Jesuit editors of *La Civiltà Cattolica*: Luigi Taparelli d'Azeglio (1793–1862), Matteo Liberatore (1810–1892), and Carlo Maria Curci (1809–1891). Year after year, these Jesuits churned out articles dealing with the consequences of the concepts of natural-supernatural interaction and of the Church as Christ-continued for all aspects of life. "Official" acceptance of the entire argument took many decades. Pius X's adoption of the motto "to transform all things in Christ" and *Mystici Corporis*, the 1943 encyclical letter of Pope Pius XII on the subject of the Mystical Body, clearly illustrated its ultimate impact.

A second theme intimately connected with the doctrine of the interaction of nature and the supernatural was that of a spirituality emphasizing the friendship offered man by God, and the ascent to the divine to which every individual was invited. On a theoretical level, such a theme entailed emphasis upon the concept of individual divinization in Christ. This, again, was a favorite topic of the editors of the *Civiltà*, who persistently argued that membership in the Church meant participation in the life of the God-Man, and hence in every conceivable perfection; human freedom and human personality thereby being raised to heights undreamed of by any rationalist. On a popular level, the theme of friendship and closeness to God, attained through humble union with the God-Man, brought with it a victory for the anti-Jansenist moral theology of Alphonsus Liguori (1696–1787), which recognized the importance of human labor in the upward path. Brunone Lanteri (1759–1830), inspirer of the lay/clerical Amicizie Cattoliche in Italy, Cardinal Thomas Marie Gousset (1792–1866), Archbishop of Rheims, in his *Justification de la Théologie du Bienheureux A. M. de Liguori* of 1832, in France, and the Redemptorists everywhere all waged vigorous combat for the victory of Liguorian thought. Its triumphant march was accompanied by a revivification and expansion of a variety of devotions providing flesh and blood manifestations of spiritual realities loathed by Jansenist and Enlightened Catholics of the previous era.

Nothing illustrated the divinization of a part of nature through incorporation into the life of a Divine Person better than devotion to the Sacred Heart of Jesus. This devotion, hated by the Jansenists perhaps more than any other, enjoyed enormous popularity wherever the Roman School gained influence. One can follow its recovery, from strength to strength, in the fortunes of the Apostolate of Prayer, begun in 1844, in the pages of *The Sacred Heart Messenger* (1861), in the ceremony of the consecration of the world to the Sacred Heart in 1875, and in Leo XIII's encyclical letter, *Annum Sacrum*, of May 25, 1899. A very un-Jansenist devotion to the saints was similarly encouraged by the Roman School, with the exaltation of Marian practices heading the list. The cults of the Sacred Heart of Mary, of Mary as Mediatrix, of the Miraculous Medal, of Our Lady of La Salette (1846) and of Lourdes (1858), along with Leo XIII's fifteen encyclicals on the Rosary and the publication of the previously ignored works of Louis Grignion de Montfort (1673–1716), all testify to the importance Marian devotion attained in the course of the century. Finally, the practice of going on pilgrimage to traditional holy places was fervently revived after having been a special target for abuse in the 1700s. Restoration of the pilgrimage to revere the Holy Coat of Trier in 1844, which attracted hundreds of thousands of participants, and the use of the very modern tool of the railroad to reach pilgrimage sites, especially impressed contemporaries as unexpected but unquestionable signs of changing times.

Perhaps most important — and anti-Jansenist — of all was the renewed nineteenth-century interest in the Eucharist as the prime means of uniting natural man with a supernatural God. Eucharistic emphasis led to the call for an earlier introduction to and more frequent reception of the Sacrament. *La très sainte communion* of Gaston de Ségur (1820–1881) was one of the many significant works encouraging such practices. Proponents of the Roman School were also active supporters of public Adoration of the Eucharist, both perpetual and nocturnal adoration spreading everywhere with papal approval in the years after 1850. Eucharistic Congresses, involving processions, adoration and theological conferences, also began in the 1870s through the work of Marie Tamisier (1834–1910), Gaston de Ségur and others. These gradually became international affairs, the Eucharistic Congress of Jerusalem in 1893 foreshadowing the world-wide significance they would attain in the 1900s.

Liturgical revival inevitably accompanied that of eucharistic devotion. Conviction of the powerful role that the liturgy was meant to play in the life of the whole Christian community and in that of each of its individual members became a major theme for Benedictine spirituality, its starting point being the work of Dom Guéranger and his *Année Liturgique* (1841). A liturgical movement grew from its original center in Solesmes (1838) to the associated abbeys of Beuron (1862), in Germany, under Marius Wolter (1825–1890), and Maredsous (1872), in Belgium, with its great liturgist, Gerard van Caloen (1853–1932). It was at Maredsous that the first influential *Missel des fidèles* was published in 1871, fourteen years after the last papal condemnation of such a translation of the Mass into the vernacular, and twenty-six before prohibition was quietly dropped in 1897. Eucharistic and liturgical revival were given powerful support through Pius X's endorsement of early and frequent reception of the Sacrament by a laity which knew, prayed and sang the Mass together.

Neo-scholasticism was a third element in the Roman School's approach. A return to the teaching of the scholastics had been advocated since the first half of the century, when men like Taparelli d'Azeglio became convinced that only a grounding in a well-organized body of Christian thought would provide the Catholic student with a means to accurately digest and judge the complexity of the modern anti-religious intellect. Similar concerns motivated Bishop Wilhelm Emmanuel von Ketteler (1811–1877) of Mainz, who was also certain that modern social problems could be efficiently addressed in a more Catholic manner if tackled logically with scholastic rigor. Italy and Germany thus became major centers for reviving scholastic studies, which, far from being merely neglected in Catholic circles during the course of the previous century, had often positively been prohibited. Neo-scholastics such as Joseph Kleutgen (1811–1883), author of *Die Theologie/ Philosophie der Vorzeit Verteidigt*, became extremely active by the time of the First Vatican Council.

Although the neo-scholastic renaissance involved study of many of the different thinkers of the twelfth and thirteenth centuries, most of those engaged in it became convinced of the superiority of St. Thomas and of the commentaries on St. Thomas produced in the sixteenth century by Cardinal Cajetan (1469–1534). Leo

XIII, through his encyclical letter *Aeterni Patris* of August 4th, 1879, and his patronage of the Leonine edition of the works of the Angelic Doctor (1882), gave to Thomistic studies pride of place in the Catholic world. Journal after journal, and Catholic center after Catholic center, including the great Catholic University of Louvain in Belgium, began to dedicate itself to intellectual work in this tradition, the *Accademia Romana di San Tommaso*, established 1880, providing the model for much of their labor.

A fourth theme, and the one justifying the designation of the School as a whole as "Roman," was an emphasis upon the role of the Papacy in every aspect of Church life, and a concomitant movement towards administrative centralization. This was inspired by theological considerations, admiration for the sufferings of Pius VI and Pius VII at the hands of the republican and Napoleonic governments, concern for efficacious action in a world of ever more centralized, revolutionary, anti-Catholic political and social forces, and frustration with the inadequacies of local ecclesiastical authorities. Stirred by Joseph de Maistre (1754–1821), Félicité de Lamennais (1782–1854) and the Mennaisiens in general, a neo-ultramontanist movement began, aided also by Protestant converts to Catholicism and a host of priests angry for one reason or another at their local Ordinaries. Neo-ultramontanism's enlistment of the Papacy in its plans dates from 1831 onwards, though it really had to await the reign of Pius IX (1846–1878) before arrival at the center of the papal stage. The First Vatican Council and the proclamation of the dogma of papal infallibility demonstrated its victorious progress most dramatically. Vatican One also pointed the way to an extensive editing of canon law in a neo-ultramontanist sense, completed in 1917, emphasizing an ever-greater centralization of Catholic activities under the Holy See.

Finally, the Roman School was charged with a sense of mission. It was convinced that it had a message for the world that could complete and exalt all of nature, a message whose neglect could only result in both supernatural and natural disaster. Catholic dogma had a supernatural and natural *telos* which could only be fulfilled if Christ were made the King of Society at large and of individuals personally. An early witness to this conviction can be seen in the Mennaisien Olympe Philippe Gerbet's (1798–1864) book, *Considérations sur le Dogme Générateur de la foi Catholique*

(1829). Later ones appear in the writings of Juan Donoso Cortes (1809–1853) and of the editors of *La Civiltà Cattolica*. The sense of urgency and drama felt by all of them is well depicted in one major article of that Roman Jesuit journal: *O Dio re Colla Libertà, o L'uomo re Colla Forza.* ("Either God as King with Liberty, or Man as King Through Force"). Catholics had to transform the world in Christ, or the world would be handed over to the perverted free will of libertine tyrants to destroy as they pleased, and sooner rather than later.

Two consequences flowed from this fifth of the Roman School's themes. One was that, given the political and social activity connected with transforming the world in Christ, the laity, the natural militants in secular society, had to be looked to as the Church's chief agents in ordinary daily Catholic Action. The call to arms of the laity was a nineteenth century mobilization, and the proponents of the Roman School were very much the recruiting sergeants. A second consequence was the great care and suspicion with which modern man and modern civilization had to be approached, given their rejection of the reality of the supernatural as an active and positive element in natural life. Modernity, to the Roman School, meant a desire to barricade oneself in nature alone—naturalism; and naturalism meant the destruction of the human personality and all of the perfections offered to civilization by God. Romanists could thus enthusiastically defend proposition number 80 of the Syllabus of Errors, which enunciated the impossibility of a reconciliation of the Roman Pontiff with "liberalism, progress, and modern civilization." Such a reconciliation meant the embrace of slavery to self-deluding will and technologically-advanced barbarism. A laity armed with knowledge and grace was therefore called to a joint offensive-defensive action. Many Romanists allowed it wide scope for tactical experimentation in pursuit of victory, while urging retreat into Catholic fortresses should success be denied.

There were, indeed, flaws in the approach of the Roman School which its friends ignore or deny at their own peril. In fact, insofar as these flaws *were* ignored or denied, they grew to undermine the very foundations of the School itself. Let us briefly pause, therefore, to glance at some of them, and in a way that parallels the main themes outlined above.

A conviction of the reality of the interaction of the natural and the supernatural may have encouraged many proponents of the Roman School dangerously to over-rely on supra-rational explanations for historical events. Hence, to take but a single example, the sense that "war in heaven," with apocalyptic overtones, was guiding the course of nineteenth-century human history, seems to have been one of the factors contributing to French Catholic inaction and resignation to the passage of anti-clerical legislation during the early years of the Third Republic, from 1877 through the 1880s. History, to some Romanists, seemed to belong to God alone, and God was therefore seen to be the physician for history's problems, either directly or through the medium of a providential personality, such as a sacred monarch. Human organization to head off disaster could be construed almost as an insult to salvific supernatural forces. But no discernable miracles were forthcoming, and a Catholic defeat which perhaps need not have taken place ensued. France was not the only land where some believers' response to defeat involved retreat into a ghetto to await a retribution which they thought would surely fall upon the enemy from on high. Thankfully, numerous French Catholic luminaries, such as Albert de Mun (1841–1914), rejected this pious defeatism, and helped to prepare the way for the activism of the following century. The assistance of many more men would have been required to turn the tide in his own day.

It may also be argued that the Roman School was so concerned for illustrating the interaction of the supernatural and the natural in the Church institutionally that a number of its most prominent spokesmen gradually ignored the consequences of the Incarnation for the individual believer. While it is true that the reality of the divine element in the visible, hierarchical structure of the Church is in itself so awesome as to take away the breath of the reverent believer, it is equally true that a complete understanding of the divine role of this hierarchical institution requires meditation on the transformation in Christ of each of its constituent members. Romanists certainly did not *begin* by neglecting individual "divinization," as consultation of the articles of *La Civiltà Cattolica* clearly indicates. Nevertheless, such meditations as those of its Jesuit editors may have lessened as the nineteenth century moved into the twentieth. But this is hard to say. Only further study of

Romanist journals of the time period—which is sadly lacking—would be able to tell for certain.

Again, it does appear to be true to say that the rediscovery of an incarnational piety eventually took precedence over the rediscovery of other aspects of the Catholic past, thus placing the need for a scriptural, patristic and general revival of knowledge of the theological and historical sources of the Faith in still greater relief. Contemporary apparitions came to resonate more in the minds of some individuals than the words of the Gospel or that of Councils and Popes. Ironically, the piety which is thus exalted is actually weakened, in the long run, if it is emphasized at the expense of familiarity with the apostolic and ecclesiastical testimony from which its very justification and value is derived. In other words, neglect of the ground of the Faith in exchange for an exclusive or exaggerated commitment to a particular pious practice, even one which has the highest backing of the Church, may well bring that specific practice itself into question over time. Critics of the Roman School claim that the piety thus inspired was an egotistical one, centered upon individual devotions and stressing self-sanctification at the expense of a more balanced appreciation of the unity of all believers in that communal enterprise of adoration of the True God from which personal sanctification flows. This self-centeredness was then said to stand as an obstacle to true liturgical revival. One might well note in passing, however, that such a complaint seems to contradict or at least weaken the argument that adulation of the character of the Church gradually obscured interest in personal union with Christ.

A third potential defect of the Roman School, and an ironic one, is its rationalism. Despite the fact that the Enlightenment and its heritage are often popularly thought to have been rationalist in character, the "Age of Reason" was, in fact, reductionist in its arguments, allowing scope for only one kind of experimental reasoning to flourish. This experimental reasoning soon began to understand human life as something hopelessly enchained to passion, will, subjective value judgment and irrationality. Nineteenth century Catholicism, on the other hand, was one of the few forces defending the objective value and significance of the human reason as such. The First Vatican Council gave eloquent testimony to this fact with its Dogmatic Constitution Concerning the Catholic Faith, which reiterated the Church's belief that reason could prove the existence of God.

The problem lay not in this defense of reason, but in the tendency by the end of the century and the beginning of the next to focus on one specific line of speculative reasoning—Thomist—to the exclusion of other philosophical approaches. This exclusivity was accompanied by a neglect of historical and other studies which would have helped to reveal the inadequacy of such a development. Thus, it was often only with great difficulty, and with accusations of suspicious orthodoxy to boot, that one could speak of the historical context in which men like St. Thomas Aquinas wrote, suggest that this context necessarily limited the completeness of their work, and argue that their labor could well be complemented by the efforts of other thinkers of other eras. To say that the method and writings of St. Thomas are not in and of themselves *completely* sufficient, to argue that they do not by themselves *alone* give the fullest possible expression to the Christian Faith, to discuss the historical circumstances in which St. Thomas labored and how these may have limited the scope of the questions to which he directed his attention, is not at all the same as saying that Thomism is wrong or beside the point. Similarly, to say that knowledge of Christian dogma might grow beyond the manner in which St. Thomas expressed it is not the same thing as denying to dogma an objective, God-given content, any more than appreciation of St. Thomas's doctrinal use of Aristotelian language amounts to a denial of the divine character of the non-Aristotelian doctrinal statements of the Apostles. Still, such inferences *were* often drawn by many members of the Roman School, with the consequence that *any* non-Thomistic, biblical, patristic, experiential or historically-based exploration of the Faith, was often condemned as "Modernist" or intrinsically invalid. This proved to be especially unfortunate when clever students, realizing the gaps in their education, confronted less than gifted teachers who failed to address real problems in a substantive way, and yet presented their work as "authoritative." It was under circumstances such as these, by the 1890s, that students were seduced by true heretics with superior teaching skills and charismatic personalities—men such as the scriptural scholar Alfred Loisy (1857–1940).

Neo-ultramontanism also had its negative side which, alas, has become clearer to traditionalist Catholics in recent times. Like all centralizing movements, it caused problems at the diocesan level, hampering the development of local initiative. This was not so much due to the disturbing but ultimately salutary rocking of the many rather listless parochial boats of the day, as it was to a gradual encouragement of the hope that Rome could handle all future problems on its own. When Rome could not do so, or when Rome itself became a source of confusion, local clerical and lay stimulus to confront debilitating crises was often therefore missing.

Moreover, the manner in which the definition of Papal Infallibility was "resolved" at Vatican One was itself problematic. Official plans had called for a general schema on the nature of the Church to be discussed and promulgated at the Council, and it was into this schema that the issue of Papal Infallibility was introduced. Difficulties arose, however, due to intense lobbying for and against the doctrine, inside and outside the Council. Problems also accompanied the lifting of the discussion of Papal Infallibility from the basic explanatory framework in which it was embedded, and treating it on its own—first, and out of context. The storm grew more violent still. When it was calmed, the resulting definition in no way met the expectations of more fervent Infallibilists. Fallout from the Franco-Prussian War then shut the Holy Synod down, leaving the schema on the Church a schema alone. Vatican One did indeed bequeath the Catholic world a real understanding of the importance of papal power and prerogatives, but failed adequately to explain how these were to be practiced, and what relation they had with the work of ordinary bishops in their own dioceses. It especially left a certain confusion about how Infallibility applied to the use of the Ordinary Magisterium, feeding that constant debate that we have witnessed for one hundred thirty four years over whether or not it actually had been invoked in specific matters. Parenthetically, however, in defense of the Council's procedure, one ought to note that all such synods have tended to treat issues as they arose, in the envelope of ecclesiastical crisis. All have thus left terrible conundrums for posterity. Still, the confusion was real, and many Romanists acted, unjustifiably, as though the maximalist position which had definitely not been adopted by the Council was the one that "real Catholics," in practice, were obliged to accept anyway.

Fifthly, the call for transformation of everything in Christ through the activity of a mobilized laity had the undesired consequence of promoting laicization within the Church. Such difficulties were not new. They have always followed upon attempts to achieve a deeper understanding of what the Christian life entails for all the members of the Church. They have, in fact, manifested themselves repeatedly since the tenth century, at which time the first serious attempts were made to dig deeper into the meaning and repercussions of the Incarnation. Roots of the dilemma go back far indeed, and the issue itself is examined in more detail in the next chapter.

Suffice it to say, at the moment, the laity became more conscious, through the work of the Roman School, of its own mission and responsibilities. That consciousness opened it to a willingness to judge its ecclesiastical guides and their performance as spiritual leaders. Such judging led to many laymen and laywomen presuming that the Teaching Church had, herself, to be taught, and to be taught from the bottom up by the faithful as a whole. Hence, ironically, a Jansenist presbyterianism broke through the armor of Romanist neo-ultramontanism. Moreover, dangerous Mennaisien influences reappeared through the medium of the Roman School as well as through that of its enemies, the democratic (though ultramontanist) laity claiming the right to command insufficiently intransigent priests and prelates in the new age that was a-dawning.

Harshness of spirit and tone, attribution of nothing but bad motivation and hidden heresy to opponents, and stubborn conviction of the necessity and goodness of their own approach were, indeed, not absent from the work of many prominent standard bearers of the Roman School. This was true of laity and clergy, high and low, alike. Denunciation and calls for papal support of the denouncers accompanied the growth of the movement throughout the nineteenth century and into the next.

But where did this spirit come from? It definitely did not come from Rome. Rather, it too, to a large degree, was the inheritance of that prophetic brutality of the Mennaisiens, lamented from the 1820s onwards by many bishops, including those who were not hostile to much that the disciples of Lamennais had to say and offer. Although his followers may well have condemned and abandoned their master, many seem to have found his whole brutal, prophetic deportment more difficult to reject. Anyone interested in investigating this question further can do so by examining the rough tactics utilized by Mennaisien reformers in order to rid French seminaries of Gallican texts and to introduce the Roman Liturgy into French dioceses with different ancient traditions.

A number of the criticisms of the Roman School outlined above can be discovered in the writings of some of its most prominent members—the editors of *La Civiltà Cattolica* and *l'Univers*, theologians of the caliber of Cardinal Pie and Cardinal Victor Dechamps (1810–1883) of Malines; neo-scholastics like Joseph Kleutgen; liturgists such as Dom Guéranger; the historian, Ludwig von Pastor; and Popes Leo XIII and Pius X—and often in very unexpected ways indeed. Hence, the fervent ultramontanists, Pie and Dechamps, were among the most harsh judges of exaggerations of the procedure and apologetics of the infallibalists at the First Vatican Council; the neo-scholastic Kleutgen demonstrated an awareness of the importance of history and mystical theology; Pastor presented individual nefarious popes in his "apologetic" history in anything but an apologetic manner; the "authoritarian legalist," Pius X, was the man who actually, in practice, democratized the Roman Curia and encouraged the revivification of the understanding of the liturgy as the communal prayer of the Church; and the Thomist Leo XIII did more for historical and scriptural studies than any pontiff of the century. In fact, Leo's insouciance regarding potential dangers emerging from uncontrolled studies underlines the absence of authoritative intervention during his long, centralizing pontificate:

> There are some restless and worried spirits who press the Roman Congregations to pronounce upon still doubtful questions. I oppose this, I stop them, because it is necessary not to prevent the intelligent from working. It is necessary to leave them the leisure to hesitate and even to err. The Truth can only win by this. The Church will always arrive in time to put them back onto the right path (Jedin and Dolan, IX, p. 330).

Perhaps the case of Dietrich von Hildebrand in the twentieth century illustrates the point most clearly. Von Hildebrand spent much of his professional life criticizing the dominant neo-scholasticism of his contemporaries, pious practices obscuring the primary focus on adoration of the Godhead essential to true transformation in Christ, failures to appreciate the riches of the liturgy, and the dangers of the militant lay spirit running amok. Yet while doing so, he never, for one moment, considered himself to be anything other than a fervent supporter of a Roman School of thought. In fact, a meditation upon the example of von Hildebrand and all the other figures noted above, might lead one to reach the conclusion that the Roman School was actually a conglomerate of potentially contradictory tendencies, some of which definitely rose to the fore, though without destroying the others entirely. More than anything else, what then would appear faulty in its "curriculum" was a certain lack of coordination and rigorous self-examination, accompanied by a want of nuance and humor on the part of some neo-scholastics and exaggerated neo-ultramontanists holding important academic and curial positions.

But let us now turn to the opposition.

In indicating a nineteenth century *anti-Roman* complex, I do not intend to speak of men who merely disagreed with certain features of the Roman School's approach, and happened to have frequent contact with those militantly rejecting it, figures like John Henry Newman (1801–1890) and Fr. Marie Joseph Lagrange (1855–1938). Newman was indeed concerned for the history of the development of doctrine in a way that appeared to give him more in common with anti-speculative historians than with the anti-historical theologians increasingly dominating the papal entourage by the time of Pius X. Lagrange did indeed lament the exegetical backwardness of many powerful leaders of the Roman School, who began to cause him severe difficulties when they fully realized where he was headed with his own scriptural studies by the time of the International Congress of Fribourg in 1897. Anti-Romanists admittedly did like to claim both of these men as sympathizers. Nevertheless, we have already seen that "card carrying" Romanists themselves could utter similar criticisms. Moreover, the attack by Newman on the kind of liberal theology which would later evolve into what is called Modernism, and the assault by Lagrange on Loisy's dogmatic refusal to allow even the possibility of a perception of supernatural activity in the natural world, created an iron curtain between their attitudes and the one that I am identifying here. Newman and Lagrange were men who thought with the Church, were sometimes unjustly treated by fellow Catholics, and whose intelligent criticisms required patience and perspicacity equal to their own to digest. One has to look elsewhere to locate the real center of opposition.

The truly committed foes of the Roman School in the nineteenth century were a formidable lot, even if (for a time) defeated. Many of them were heirs of Enlightenment and Jansenist ideas about the relationship of nature and the supernatural, piety, theological methodology, the Papacy, and Catholic militancy in general. Others were supporters of condemned Mennaisien views concerning democracy and the need to submit to "vital" contemporary forces, spokesmen for the supremacy of a *purely* historical or scriptural approach to truth, or one basing itself on philosophical systems allowing no room whatsoever for speculative theology. Such thinkers bemoaned the Church's loss of esteem in the eyes of an "energetic," modern, secular world which the Romanists condemned. Nationalists also formed an important part of the serious nineteenth-century anti-Roman complex. Roman universalism represented for them an obstacle to a full appreciation of the truths taught by the individual genius of each ethnic group; "truths" which somehow regularly seemed to emphasize the enlightened, Jansenist, democratic, vitalist and anti-speculative attitudes indicated above.

More specifically, followers of the "Kantian" Georges Hermes (1775–1831) and "Hegelian" Anton Günther (1783–1863), both of whom ran into certain troubles with the Holy See, helped to form the nineteenth-century anti-Roman complex in Germany. They were joined by a few angry historians, the most famous being Ignaz von Döllinger (1799–1890). Döllinger resented the growing flirtation of many of his fellow countrymen with what he irrationally dismissed as an outdated scholastic theology. His speech on "The Past and Present of Theology" at the Congress of Munich in September of 1863 was a declaration of war upon the Roman School. Döllinger's anti-scholastic historicism had a great impact upon vehement anti-Romanists outside of Germany as well, Lord John Acton (1834–1902) prominent among them. Many of the disciples of Günther and Döllinger formed the backbone of the schismatic Old Catholic Church, which refused to accept the decree of Vatican One on Papal Infallibility. Admirers of the Protestant biblical exegesis of David Strauss (1808–1874) and Ferdinand Christian Baur (1792–1860) increased the numbers of the anti-Roman camp. So did governmental bureaucrats upset by the ecclesiastical autonomy demanded by Romanists, and moralists convinced that their anti-Jansenist spirituality would shape a vulgarized, superstitious and lazy Catholic flock. Those stirred by German national feeling were not averse to calling in the secular authority to support their positions when they believed that such intervention could guarantee them victory—hence, the Old Catholic encouragement of German states engaging in Kulturkampf in the 1870s.

The French anti-Roman complex was created by an alliance between Gallicans and certain Mennaisiens which would have been deemed inconceivable before 1850. Gallican-minded bishops had, up till that point, been deeply angered by the assault on their seminaries and their liturgies by the neo-ultramontanism of which the Mennaisiens had been a major stimulus. Such bishops, however, generally supported French governmental policies, whatever they might be. Thus, when the Second Empire entered the lists against militant, anti-modernist "Romanism," they were gradually able to make common cause with Mennaisiens like the Liberal Catholic, Charles de Montalembert (1810–1870). Montalembert's speech on liberal concepts of freedom and separation of Church and State at the Congress of Malines of 1863 had the same impact, *mutatis mutandis*, as that of Döllinger at Munich. Although French bishops tended to be restrained in their outright anti-Romanism, some, like Henri Louis Maret (1805–1884), were quite openly eager to fight attempts by the Romanists to free the Church and Catholics from complete submission to the civil law. Again, as in Germany, they were joined by bureaucrats and Jansenists who lamented the turn of the tide against naturalism and enlightened piety. It was only gradually that the biblical criticism of a Joseph Ernest Renan (1823–1895), perfected by the work of men such as Alfred Loisy, and Kantian-based philosophical approaches populated the ranks of the anti-Romanists with a different clientele. French influences, along with those coming from Germany, were then central to the formation of the anti-Roman complex in other countries, Italy and the United Kingdom prominent among them.

All-out foes of the Roman School were by no means always self-interested or off-target in their attacks. However, they differed from scholars like Newman and Lagrange in that their perspicacity was seriously marred by a bitterness and an arrogance that were as unedifying—if not, indeed, much more so—than anything they ascribed to their opposition. Every defeat rankled with them, justified or not. One sees in their writings and actions a desire for vengeance at the first available opportunity. One can almost imagine a collective unclenching of teeth in the graves of anti-Romanists across Christendom during the 1960s, as one ecclesiastical change after another apparently vindicated their own position.

Conspiratorial myth-making was one of the anti-Romanist fortés. This is a bit ironic. Here were men who satirized as overblown and a-historical all efforts by speculative thinkers to tie together theological principles, historical developments, and pastoral approaches in modern times into some cohesive intelligible whole; men whose dislike of speculation contributed mightily to killing that speculative schema on the Church at Vatican One which would have made the infallibility decree more cohesive, comprehensible and efficacious. And yet they insisted upon belief in the existence of a murky, age-old intellectual-political plot, led by intransigent Jesuits and their scholastic drones, responsible for every setback and defeat that they and progress-loving peoples everywhere experienced. One would be tempted to say—as Modernists do when rejecting Pius X's attack upon them as members of a unified alliance—that there would be no "Roman School" to criticize at all were it not for the work anti-Romanists did in bringing its disparate elements together into what was actually an artificial and illusory union.

Though it is tempting to argue that the Roman School existed only in the minds of its opponents, there were clearly those who relished the title of Romanist and felt a spirit of camaraderie with others of like mind. Let us therefore, if only for their sakes, admit its substantial reality. Insofar as it did exist, however, it was, as indicated repeatedly above, both a more divided and a much more nuanced and positive force than its opponents from the 1800s onwards have made it out to be. What is most striking about the picture painted of the Roman School by the twentieth century anti-Roman complex is just how much its strong and weak features are simultaneously neglected by it. Why should this be the case? A conscious desire on the part of the anti-Romanists to distort "Romanism" cannot be excluded as an hypothesis, though the effort to prove and document this would require a book-length study. In any case, there is another, ironic explanation for the shortcomings of the critique which is readily available.

It is, once again, fair to say that the dominant Romanists did not give to historical studies the importance that they deserved, and that despite the School's birth in a rediscovery of the Christian past. Nevertheless, infinitely more damage has been done to Church History in the long run by the anti-Romanists of our own day. This is due to the fact that contemporary anti-Romanists have embedded the appreciation for a rigorous historical methodology which they inherited from their nineteenth century ancestors in that overall Modernist vision of life which glorifies will, action and prophetic democracy. And this vision has the contrary effect of justifying a complete disdain for the "dead past." In other words, twentieth century anti-Romanists teach us a great deal, in practical terms, about how to research and write history in a superior manner, but they also have given us all the reasons for not bothering to take up that historical activity in the first place! History, like metaphysics, is a block to a completely vital, action-centered, liberated life. It provides too many lessons, too many models to follow, all of which hamper guidance from one's own creative will, whose veracity and goodness is proven through success. A Mennaisien faith in an emerging, evolving Christianity, taught by the People and its Prophets, provides another impulse to look forward and ignore what lies behind.

Actually, the same result follows with respect to other studies neglected or treated with restraint by the Roman School, such as sociology. A powerful stimulus to rigorous sociological work is given by the critics, but fitted into that view of life which (to paraphrase James Burnham's critique of Eleanor Roosevelt) dissolves every solid bit of evidence in a murky goo of directionless will and democratic rapture. In the last analysis, the anti-Romanists of our own day seat us upon a mountain of data, and then tell us to make our judgments on the basis of what we "will" and "feel"; — whatever succeeds in giving us that which we desire. They then appeal to our "faith-in-the-future" to revive our flagging spirits when unhappiness ensues.

Where does all this lead us with respect to an accurate historical appreciation of the Roman School? Into a black hole. For the anti-Romanist foot soldier of modernity, history is really only valid in so far as it can help to guide us to a confidence in will, action and democratic faith. Historical research into an understanding of the growth of this confidence is undertaken and praised, and, given the Roman School's basic failure to support such confidence-building, much attention is devoted to its terrible error in this regard. Positive teachings of the Roman School, which explain the reasons for its theological and philosophical stance, are ignored as a useless waste of vital human time and energy. Any of its true flaws that might impact badly on the modern vitalist argument are tossed into the abyss along with them.

Creative historical writing thus becomes the rule. To hate the Roman School is to know it; to know it in its fullness is beside the point. One all-too-famous history of the reign of Pope Pius IX devotes pages to a description of the "vital" and "forward-looking" journal *l'Ere Nouvelle*, which lasted but briefly in 1848, while it pays scant attention to *La Civiltà Cattolica*, founded in 1850, and still published today. This is because *La Civiltà Cattolica* testified to the positive character of the anti-modern Roman School. I, personally, had discussions at Oxford with a scholar who criticized vehemently the "obscurantist" character of that journal, while at the same time I was enjoying the privilege of cutting open large numbers of the thousand pages of its volumes for the fifteen year period from 1850–1865, thus, presumably, becoming the first man actually to read them in the university library as well. I would not be surprised if the same were true for students in other libraries elsewhere. The committed opponents of the Roman School have no interest in its history as such; a scholar making a painstaking case for its achievements according to the best rules of the modern historiography to which they themselves ascribe is lost in space. A public formed in the spirit of willful, democratic, prophetic action has no time for him. It has more vital, energetic, important things to do than finding out the simple, boring truth.

The result is that very few people have any idea of the positive accomplishments of the Roman School. They know little or nothing about its concern for the doctrine of the Mystical Body of Christ and of individual divinization, concepts partly inspired by men like Möhler, whom proponents of the New Theology of the 1930s and 1940s claimed to be rediscovering for the first time. They know little or nothing of the Roman School's sustained fight for Catholic universalism against arrogant, condescending, secularist, modernist imperialists. They leave buried in scholarly texts the record of the Romanist battle versus nationalist parochialism, alongside rabid, chauvinist, progressive pronouncements which would make most twenty-first century liberals shudder. They are, in short, ignorant of the central nature of the struggle of the Roman School against modernity, which was a fight for human freedom and dignity against the fraudulent gods of democracy and arbitrary willfulness.

Similarly, few people are aware of what I think to be the greatest (though unwitting) flaw of the Roman School: namely, its tendency, in seeking to galvanize the entire Catholic population, to open the backdoor to the carping presbyterianism and lay, democratic, Mennaisien spirit which I discuss in the next chapter. And, finally, almost no one recognizes that the anti-Roman complex is really not new at all; that a great deal of what it stands for, both in general and in its specifics, concerning themes ranging from Church organization to liturgy to the relationship of the ecclesiastical authority to the State and to common law, is actually resurrected Enlightenment and Jansenist theology, philosophy and pastoral vision, gussied up in ball gowns designed by Lamennais.

I have often quoted Louis Veuillot's observation that Catholics grow worse the farther they stray from their beliefs, while their opponents grow worse the more faithful they stay to theirs. Something similar might be said for the proponents of the Roman School and their enemies. The spirit of the Roman School contained within it the stimulus to the rediscovery and development of the whole Catholic Tradition; the narrowness and bitterness of a number of its followers led them away from that high road down limiting and even self-destructive byways. The critical spirit of many of the enemies of the Roman School, on the other hand, enabled them to pass down immensely valuable insights to their present-day heirs. But that critical outlook was set to work in minds shaped essentially by bitterness, Jansenism, and an adulation of the will, energetic action of whatever variety, and the religion of democracy. Such minds were poisoned, and their Catholic

Faith badly obscured, provoking understandably vigorous, though sometimes disjointed, and often equally acerbic reactions from Romanists. A retreat from the cult of modernity would put the specifics of the criticisms of the anti-Roman camp into rational perspective. The Roman School needed better and more fully-rounded Romans, something which merely critical opponents could have helped to produce. It did not need a full-scale dismantling, and the establishment of a company of enlightened, Jansenist, Mennaisien cheerleaders in the campus of the saints.

FURTHER READING:

Butler, C., *The Vatican Council* (Newman, 1962)

Gough, A., *Paris and Rome. The Gallican Church and the Ultramontane Campaign* (Oxford, 1986)

Jedin, H., and Dolan, J., *History of the Church* (Vols. VII, VIII, IX, Crossroads, 1981)

Mayeur, J.M., ed., *Histoire du Christianisme* (Vols. X, XI, Desclée, 1995/1997)

Rao, J., *Removing the Blindfold* (Angelus Press, 2014)

13

All Borrowed Armor Chokes Us[†]

AN HISTORICAL INTRODUCTION TO
THE PROBLEMS OF CATHOLIC ACTION

ONE OF THE GREATEST MISTAKES OF OUR arrogant age is to think that the past has little to teach it. We Catholics should know better, and formulate our practical daily judgments with a respect for the lessons of our whole, rich, historical tradition. Problems connected with the defense of Catholicism in the political realm are no exception, and in this particular regard, the experience of the nineteenth-century Catholic revival should be of special interest to faithful observers with eyes to see.

Many nineteenth century believers, their consciousness raised by the troubles of the French Revolution and Napoleonic Wars (1789–1815), were outraged by the absence of Catholic influence over political and social life. They realized that believers had not been permitted to speak and act as real Catholics already for decades before the revolutionary disruptions in France. This silencing of the Catholic voice had not only prevented them from living as faithful Christians. Worse, still, it had created an atmosphere in which it was difficult for believers to discover what the teachings of the Church that affected them as individuals and social beings actually were in the first place.

Sadly, the most powerful of the contemporary culprits muzzling the Catholic voice were the self-proclaimed friends and protectors of Christendom: legitimist "sacred monarchies." In 1815, these had formed a "Holy Alliance," supposedly to fight the revolutionary demons of the Continent on behalf of Christianity itself. But this familiar "sacred union" *controlled* rather than protected Catholicism, subordinating spiritual concerns to secular ones. Its chains were strongest where Protestants or Orthodox were the legitimate sacred monarchs, as in Prussia and Russia. Nevertheless, they were often equally observable under Catholic rulers as well, whose goals were frequently inspired by the very Enlightenment that

---

† First published on the *Seattle Catholic* website (July 9, 2005).

had helped to foment the French Revolution. Moreover, clerical political activity under "friendly" sacred monarchies had led to an unseemly service of two masters, with the secular superior getting better attention than the spiritual, and a consequent secularization of the Church's own personnel.

Realization of these unhappy truths caused nineteenth century Catholics to pay greater attention to a definition of the distinct character and primary responsibilities of political and religious authorities alike. They did not do so for the sake of encouraging "separation" of Church and State. Such a separation, given the joint spiritual-physical nature of the beings ruled over by each, was deemed to be a theoretical and practical impossibility anyway. Rather, they were eager to determine exactly how a necessary Catholic influence could be exercised without either impairing the State's just prerogatives or the Church's own supernatural mission.

Many thinkers, clerics prominent among them, began to argue that the traditional dilemma might be resolved by seeking protection for religion from the political and social action of the mass of the Catholic laity. The laity, by definition, had different self-interested concerns than the clergy. As a mass force, it was neither an integral part of the government, nor directly moved by the more suspicious personal aims of its secular rulers. Action by mobilized lay pressure groups would keep the clergy's hands clean of everything but the dogmatic and spiritual guidance which its charism justly involved. That guidance could then itself be improved through cooperative clerical initiatives stimulating better teaching on the part of priests and bishops. Should clerical and lay associations operate as planned, true Catholic doctrine would have an impact on society in a proper fashion. At the very least, clerical politicians would be repressed, and lay activists who were tempted to engage in dubious battles with the government for tainted self-interested reasons would not compromise the prestige and mission of the Teaching Church as such.

Germany's role in encouraging this call to the formation of Catholic associations dedicated to "Catholic Action" was seminal. It began in various lay/clerical "circles," such as that of Princess Adele Amalie Gallitsyn in Münster already in the 1770s, and others in Bonn, Landshut, Mainz, Munich and Vienna by the next century. France and Belgium played an important part in the birth of the movement as well, starting with the Abbé Félicité de Lamennais' Congregation of St. Peter and the Belgian Catholic Union in the 1820s. Countless other clerical and lay societies were added, ranging from the communities of Dom Prosper Guéranger to Pauline Jaricot's Society for the Propagation of the Faith, and Frédéric Ozanam's Conferences of St. Vincent de Paul.

Catholic Action's potential political clout was soon obvious. France witnessed it in the form of a determined resistance to regulations hindering the establishment of new religious congregations and their use in a school system opened to Catholic guidance. In Germany, it was manifested by activist transformation of instances of governmental repression into major *causes célèbres*. The most famous of these was stirred by the publication of Joseph Görres' *Athanasius* (1838), and Karl Ernst Jarcke's numerous articles in the *Historisch-politische Blätter*. It underlined the significance of the imprisonment of Archbishop Clemens August von Droste zu Vischering (1773–1845) of Cologne for his insistence upon application of canonical marriage regulations in legitimist Prussia. Such unfamiliar political outspokenness evoked Gallican and Febronian outrage, and led to embittered demands for a return to humble acceptance of the religious policies of the sacred monarchies.

By now, many activists had begun to believe that legitimist "friends" could do the cause of Catholic liberty no discernible good. Perhaps friendship with groups promising the creation of free, responsive institutions might succeed in breaking the chains on a salutary Catholic Action? An opportunity to form just such an alliance with liberals was offered through the 1830 Revolution in Belgium. This was followed by the contemplation of possible *ententes cordiales* with a variety of liberal, democratic and nationalist forces in Italy, France and Germany, culminating in the heady hopes engendered by the Revolutions of 1848.

Certainly the movement to promote the formation of properly motivated Catholic associations, lay and clerical, *did* gain further steam in those nations adopting liberal or democratic political institutions in the latter nineteenth century. A glance at the situation in Germany during and after the Revolution of March, 1848 is instructive in this regard. March brought with it the establishment in Mainz of the Pius Association for Religious Freedom, named after the new Roman Pontiff, Pius IX. Five months later, there were several hundred branches of this Piusverein. Their first general meeting took place in Mainz on October 1st, at which time a universal German Catholic Association was created. This then held seventeen Catholic Conferences in the years between 1850 and 1870, giving birth to many more subsidiary organizations, including charitable ones modeled on Ozanam's Conferences of St. Vincent de Paul, Adolf Kolping's Workingmens' Aid Association, an aesthetic institute promoting the mystical-artistic ideas of the Nazarenes, the Görres Society, dedicated to scholarly and educational activity, and committees for the Defense of the Papal States and the founding of a Catholic University. The clergy also took advantage of revolutionary chain-rattling to liberate their teaching mission from rigid state control. Ground-breaking episcopal conferences were held at Würzburg from October 22–November 16, 1848 and in Vienna by the spring of 1849. Both the Austrian Concordat of 1855 and the 1867 regularization of meetings of the German bishops at Fulda and Freising testify to an ever-growing recognition of the need for an episcopal independence and cooperation guaranteeing effective Catholic teaching regarding political as well as other matters.

Unfortunately, however, the proponents of liberal constitutional government also proved to be false friends. The "freedom" that they were willing to grant to Catholics to defend their "rights" turned out to have an Enlightenment-shaped definition involving certain conditions which were impossible for the faithful both to accept and to fulfill. Activists began to realize that liberal constitutionalism was designed to ensure the victory of an anti-Catholic faction using the word "freedom" to whitewash and justify its continuation of an even more effective state repression in new, hypocritical ways. Crises were already visible in the liberal governments functioning in France and Belgium in the 1830s and 1840s. These multiplied and intensified throughout Europe in the second half of the nineteenth century, affecting Italy, the German countries, the Netherlands, and then Belgium and France anew. Sometimes they focused on a single issue, especially that of education. Very frequently, however, the crisis was a universal one, striking not only at education but at the existence of the religious orders engaged in it, the ability of Church authorities to control their dioceses and parishes, the general freedom of association, and the very right of individual Catholics to speak out on any political matter whatsoever: in short, to use the German term, due to a full-scale Kulturkampf, or "culture war."

Catholic reaction to such measures was often very impressive. Lay Catholics were particularly incensed over school issues, which directly touched the average family. "They are not going to have it, the beautiful souls of children," Flemish peasants sang (Kalyvas, p. 62). "The generosity and ardor of the Catholics surpassed everything imaginable," one observer of the Belgian scene reported. "Almost every Catholic meeting which I attended at that time," a witness of Austrian passion noted, "was a fiery furnace for the souls, from which a torrent of sparks and flames of holy enthusiasm was generated; a powerful forge, in which the armaments were hardened for a battle for the Cross which now threatened from all sides" (Ibid., pp. 97–98). The liberal-fomented "School Wars" were seen by Catholics as the first step towards the complete destruction of the Church. If secularists succeeded in destroying Catholic education, one activist noted, "the church will then be a building with four walls, whose interior, as the liberals count on, will become emptier with every decade." (Ibid., p. 62).

Catholic lay associations were often called upon by self-conscious teaching hierarchies to fight the good fight in these battles. Thus, Belgian prelates summoned the laity to three seminal organizing congresses in Mâlines in 1863, 1864 and 1867, culminating in the formation of a Fédération des Cercles Catholiques in 1868. After collective appeals for repeal of nefarious educational laws were ignored, the organized hierarchy and laity moved on to stronger action: teachers by resigning their positions in public schools, parents by refusing to send their children to them, and priests by denying the sacraments to anyone who failed to toe the designated line. A private Catholic school system was planned, and a campaign launched to pay for it. By 1880, this network was in place and had managed to garner the majority of Belgian students. Its creation provoked still more anti-clerical legislation. Committees of resistance of all kinds were then formed, with the Catholic press publicizing a petition signed by 317,000 against the repressive educational legislation.

After similar episcopal action, Dutch Catholics also focused on the building up of a primary school network. One ought to note that their organizational vigor was matched, if not surpassed, by pious Calvinists. Abraham Kuyper's league against school reform, and his newspaper, *De Standaard*, joined with Catholics in a massive petition movement demanding repeal of the Netherland's detested 1878 decrees on secular education. At a time when the entire Dutch electorate was limited to around 100,000 voters, Kuyper's petition collected 305,000 signatures; its Catholic counterpart an additional 164,000 names.

Popular reaction to the cultural wars in Austria came with demonstrations in favor of the Venerable Bishop Franz Rudigier of Linz, imprisoned in 1869 for his vociferous opposition to the changes of the newly liberal government of the Empire. Various lay organizations came into being at this moment, with Karl von Vogelsang's newspaper, *Das Vaterland*, drawing up a complex battle strategy for the future, economically, socially and politically.

Perhaps most impressive was the organizational fever initially excited by the *Kulturkampf* in the German Empire, leading to the formation of the Katholische Frauenbund, Katholische Mütterverein, Katholische Kaufmännische Vereinigung, and a large number of youth, student and teacher groups. Growth in the Catholic Press was enormous, the *Kölnische Volkszeitung* and the Berlin *Germania* being the giants of the media. Most famous of all the associations formed after 1870 was the Volksverein für das Katholische Deutschland (1890), whose stronghold was the Rhineland, and whose secretaries, Franz Hitze and August Pieper, presided over a vast membership undertaking all manner of tasks on behalf of the Catholic population.

Catholic associations seeking not just to overturn anti-clerical legislation but also to replace it with Church-friendly laws often first approached existing "conservative parties" to serve as their agents. Such parties would be offered what were in essence contracts. The network of active Catholic associations would do much of the propaganda and legwork for the election of conservative deputies to parliament, with the proviso that these, when winning office, would follow Catholic bidding on state matters touching upon religion.

Results rarely matched expectations. Conservatives were too inclined to negotiate with immovable enemies of the Catholic cause. Gradually, Catholic activists came to loathe conservatives as "doubtful friends," people who were happy to have the support of a religious electorate, but only to twist that backing to serve their own narrow purposes. It thus became clear, as the Italian activist,

Ruggiero Bonghi, said in 1879, that this "exchange between Catholics and Conservatives is a great error and is very suspect" (Ibid., p. 225); that "Catholic feeling is not necessarily conservative, and conservative feeling is not necessarily Catholic" (Ibid.). Catholics were not alone in this bitterness, either. The Dutch Calvinist leader and fellow-traveler Kuyper insisted that the battle being fought by all religious people was also "against conservatism; not conservatism of a specific brand but against conservatism of every description" (Ibid.). Although in many places they called themselves Rightists, conservatives were soon understood to be merely "liberals who had been mugged." Conservatives were men who shared with liberals the same basic Enlightenment principles, especially with regard to the concept of economic freedom, but who had simply become more cautious about their implementation in most other realms. Hence the activist temptation to move from contractual agreements to the establishment of consciously Catholic parties of their own (See also Ibid., pp. 258–259).

Perhaps the first clear instance of such a venture was the "Committee for the Defense of Religious Freedom," promoted by Charles de Montalembert and Louis Veuillot's Parisian daily newspaper, *l'Univers*. This elected 144 representatives to the French Parliament in the 1840s. Another example of early political development was the "Catholic Club," composed of various prelates, clerics and laymen, which was formed at the German revolutionary Frankfurt Assembly of 1848. A third initiative was the Prussian "Catholic Faction," founded in 1851 by August Reichensperger, his brother Peter, and Hermann von Malinckrodt for the purpose of defending the freedoms enshrined in the religious clauses of their Kingdom's Constitution and protected until the cultural war twenty years later.

After 1870, these rather loosely organized factions began to tighten up. Catholics from Prussia formed the Center Party, which also functioned in the new, democratically elected, imperial *Reichstag*. The increasing severity of the Kulturkampf legislation from 1872 onwards made the party's fortune, since the devastation of the Catholic hierarchy and priesthood during these very difficult years necessitated what amounted to a temporary assumption of church guidance by the active laity.

Belgium, in 1884, saw the formation of the Union Nationale pour le Redressement des Griefs as a temporary "war machine against liberalism" and its secularist educational laws. Although this still desired to work with conservatives, it nevertheless aimed to "absolutely prevent the return to power of an autonomous Right, which would not take into account, as it did [not] in the past, the demands of the Catholic world." The electoral campaign "was animated, enthusiastic, marked by religious mysticism," and helped enormously by the various Catholic associations. Results were spectacular. June, 1884 saw a triumph over the Liberals which was "more a massacre than a defeat," and the hated laws were repealed (See Ibid., p. 191).

In the Netherlands, Kuyper formed the Antirevolutionary Party, its Declaration of Principles proclaiming consistent resistance to the world of 1789. Catholics, under the guidance of Fr. Hermann Shaepman, were by that time also building a "war machine" of their own out of a federation of local groupings. Despite enormous disagreements and even hatreds, an *Unio Mystica* of Catholics and Protestants was proclaimed by Kuyper in 1888 (Ibid., p. 194). Both denominations coordinated their support for candidates. The Conservative Party broke up under the pressure, and, just as in Belgium, the Liberals were soundly trounced. Calvinists and Catholics then continued to share power, ensuring their separate, autonomous free development, though the "party" formed by the latter remained an amorphous entity until some years into the next century.

As early as 1868 the Austrian newspaper *Das Vaterland* had called for an "anti-liberal confederation" of all those who "suffered from the financial and material consequences of the recently adopted system" (Ibid., p. 200). A coalition was indeed formed in 1887, holding a convention the following year whose importance was grasped by Karl Lueger, the head of the Vienna democrats. *Das Vaterland* promoted Lueger's leadership of the coalition, and suggested the name Christian Social Party to designate it. In 1890, the parliamentary leader of the traditional conservatives, Alois Liechtenstein, "grew weary of his lack of tactical success" and joined the Christian Socials. By 1897 a permanent central party bureaucracy was firmly established (Ibid., p. 202).

Troubles, however, did not cease. Parties often had troubled relations with the complex network of active Catholic lay and clerical associations, which they viewed as competitors for ultimate direction of the Catholic movement. Much more significantly, however, Catholic associations expressed the concerns of an ever-greater assortment of social groups with divergent interests and agendas, especially economic ones. This complicated the life of a Catholic Party enormously, forcing it to take stands regarding given positions which might satisfy one element of its clientele but horrify another. As Joseph Edmund Jörg noted, "any attempt to construct a detailed political program would be injurious and perhaps fatal to the Party" (Ibid., p. 236). Bismarck claimed that "there are not two souls in the Center but seven ideological tendencies which portray all the colours of the political rainbow from the most extreme right to the radical left" (Ibid., p. 237). Hence, raising the banner of the Church in Danger was the only means of assuring internal unity. It became ever more difficult to hoist that flag when the Kulturkampf in Germany eventually eased, and the more each internal group demanded doctrinal confirmation of its principles from Rome.

Parties also showed a propensity to easy acceptance of new "false friends." Once they had found some way through their initial difficulties and begun to function more smoothly in a given nation, they all too frequently valued their institutional survival more than the purposes for which they were created. When working in a liberal constitutional system, they tended to treat the rules of that system, hostile though they might be, as givens, accepting limitations upon and modification of Catholic expectations. If laboring in a more democratic environment, they began to praise the will of "The People," no matter how rabidly nationalistic, racist, Marxist, libertine or fraudulently manipulated this could be. Criticism might be met by insisting that everything the "religious party" accepted and promoted was ipso facto Catholic; as though its claim to be the "Catholic Party" protected it from error in its political defense of Christianity; as though an idea or policy which was notoriously secular and bad could become sacred and good through its magic wand. Victories by opposing parties might then bring down upon Catholics a persecution for supporting positions that really had nothing to do with their Faith at all, but only partisan self-interest.

That parties, Catholic and non-Catholic, were indeed succumbing to such temptations was clear. The Center Party defined religious truth ever more broadly in order to win elections.

"Confessional party leaders such as Julius Bachem were repeatedly attacked for setting aside the Catholic basis of the most important organization of German Catholicism in order to substitute a so-called non-denominational Christian basis as the party's guiding philosophy" (Ibid., p. 248). "Catholics must appeal to the ideas on which modern society is based in order to vindicate their belief," Etienne Lamy, one of the French Catholic democratic leaders, argued in 1896 (Ibid., p. 232). An Austrian Christian Social spokesman put it most succinctly a bit later: "in politics the only thing that counted was success" (Ibid.).

Many laymen were dangerously insistent upon their role as *religious leaders*. Archbishop Victor Dechamps complained to the pope of two prominent and politically active lay Belgian Catholics, both "fervent and good soldiers," but problematic since they "want to command within the church" (Ibid., p. 40). Italian lay activists often ended up "giving directives to bishops, provoking frequent complaint" (Ibid.). *Le Temps* in 1881 labeled the French activist, Albert de Mun, "a lay bishop who undertakes . . . a political campaign, and who finds nothing better than to address the authentic bishop like a master" (Ibid., p. 45). One priest bitterly criticized the special pretensions of journalists, noting their claim to a right to resolve doctrinal disputes. "Is not that a stunning victory for laicism?" (Ibid., p. 46), he wondered. Worse still, organizations sometimes moved from liberal constitutionalism and democratic politics to calls for internal Church reform on their bases. Austrian prelates, for example, were told that they "must cease to act autocratically" (Ibid., p. 40) or face the consequences of the wrath of a more conscious democratic populace.

Another problem for Catholic parties came from the hierarchy's dislike of participation of the lower clergy in their affairs. Special circumstances were one thing, bishops reiterated; a general permission for clerical involvement, however, was quite another matter. The bishops' chief grievance—that political activity took priests away from their primary spiritual responsibilities, and also gave them a power base enabling them to speak to their clerical superiors as equals or even inferiors—was more than understandable. The Bishop of Trier was not alone in lamenting, in 1873, that his subordinate clergy were simultaneously guilty of absenteeism and monitoring his own behavior for political correctness (Ibid.).

Complaints on the part of the hierarchy regarding lay and clerical activism were rejected by many in the Catholic Movement as a sign of the high clergy's tradition of timidity, outright cowardice, or hypocritical protection of its own unacceptable political position. There are, indeed, a number of cases where all these accusations appear to be valid, perhaps most clearly in Austria-Hungary (Ibid., pp. 91, 98, 179). Still, practical examples of episcopal failure should not blind us to the fact that the general critique of the Catholic Movement by the late nineteenth century was the same as that which its founders itself had made of the earlier Catholic political position! Sacred monarchies of the past had bent religious concerns to parochial secular considerations. Clergy had played too great a role within them, sullying their spiritual mission along the way. Now, out of an initial desire to fight precisely such corruption, the sacred political party had emerged, twisting Catholic goals to the divinized requirements of anti-clerical liberal constitutions, willful Peoples, and the charismatic party leaders and journalists interpreting the "true meaning" of their desires, sometimes claiming to be the voice of the Holy Spirit in doing so. The Divine Right of the past had not just reappeared; it had resurfaced compounded, with laymen and secularized clerics claiming to protect a twisted understanding of human freedom and progress along with their own political advantage and a corrupted Catholic Faith.

What was Rome's reaction to this ferment? Discussion of Roman relations with Austria, Germany, Belgium and France would offer nuanced answers to that question. All should be looked at to understand Vatican policy accurately. For my purposes at the moment, however, it is sufficient to bring up the Holy See's attitude towards the above developments in the context of a more detailed examination of the Italian Catholic Action experience.

Italy's introduction to lay-clerical associations began with Brunone Lanteri's early nineteenth century revival of pre-revolutionary Amicizie Cattoliche. Many Catholic newspapers aided this work from the 1820s onwards, the most influential of which was *La Civiltà Cattolica*, which began publication in 1850. The creation of an extensive network of Catholic associations was seen by most of these journals to be the only means of making the wishes of the "real country" known in the unnatural situation established by the proclamation of the Kingdom of Italy in 1861. This was due to the fact that that Kingdom's liberal constitution limited the number of people who could vote to a miniscule percentage of the population, based upon property ownership and wealth, and insisted that its representatives act only in an "enlightened" manner. Where Catholic deputies had been validly elected, as in 1857, in what was then the Kingdom of Sardinia, they had been excluded as unacceptable because they were Catholic and therefore unenlightened. An exasperated Catholic witness noted, "When we took part in elections and in many places won a victory, we called down upon ourselves all manner of vexations, and our work went up in smoke" (Invernizzi, p. 22). The real, long-lasting backdrop for the famous *non expedit*, the papal prohibition of Catholic participation in the political life of the Kingdom on the national, as opposed to local level, was not aggression against the Temporal Power. It was the recognition that participation under current conditions would be a sham. Hence, it was better to stand apart, and, as the *Osservatore Romano* noted in 1880, prepare for *real* participation in the future by temporary abstention from the existing fraudulent system.

This temporary abstention presupposed serious work outside of legal, constitutional national politics. It was to the end of laboring effectively as a kind of parallel government that the vast bulk of Catholic organizations and local parish committees came to be coordinated by the Opera Dei Congressi e Dei Comitati Cattolici, founded in 1874 and given its definitive name in 1881. The Opera met in regular congresses and aided the work of local groups through five permanent sections established in 1884: Organization and Catholic Action, Christian Social Economy, Instruction and Education, Press and Christian Art. The second section, headed at the end of the reign of Leo XIII by Giuseppe Toniolo, founder of the Unione Cattolica per gli Studi Sociali, was especially active.

By the late 1890s, however, Opera leaders were seriously divided over future initiatives. One group insisted upon continuing business as usual, neither compromising with the existing liberal authorities nor opposing them in politics directly, lest the socialists pick up the pieces in a bitter national political campaign. Another faction, which came to be known as the clerico-moderates, wished to take advantage of certain liberal invitations to form a broad "conservative party" which could then confront the common danger of socialist extremism. Catholic abstention from national politics would thus end, and leaders who had been prepared during that abstention could move forward to exercise direct influence over Italian political life. Yet a third force, many-headed in character, considered business-as-usual as no longer opportune, but viewed the clerico-moderate position as a sell-out to the anti-Catholic conservatism of the "liberals who had been mugged." One of this third force's constituent elements wished boldly to declare liberal economic policies to be materialist and immoral. Some proponents longed for the creation of a distinctly popular Catholic political party. They presumed that such a party would also have a broad appeal beyond the immediate camp of the believers, to open-minded socialists in particular, and would therefore have to operate with significant freedom from the ecclesiastical hierarchy. Priests, Don Romolo Murri prominent among them, played a role within its ranks. Friction among these contesting components of the *Opera* was stirred by brutal government repression of both socialist and Catholic organizations in the midst of the riotous years of the 1890s, as well as by the failure of the dominant proponents of the business-as-usual approach to make more of an issue of injustices that they, too, abhorred.

At this point, the Papacy became deeply involved. Papal intervention was a two-step affair. It began on January 18th, 1901, with Leo XIII's publication of the encyclical letter *Graves de Communi*, which rejected the creation of a distinctly Catholic Italian democratic party. If the words "Christian Democracy" were employed at all, he insisted, they could only legitimately be used to indicate "a beneficent Christian action in favor of the people," not a commitment of the Church to democratic politics. Moreover, as the first of its two words emphasized, "Christian Democracy" could only exist with reference to a grounding in the Christian Faith; cooperation with those of democratic spirit who were materialist socialists was thereby excluded. Even what today would be called a "preferential option for the poor" was dismissed as objectionable by the pope, since a true concept of "the People" had to include all social classes, coordinated into one harmonious whole.

A second intervention came in the aftermath of the XIX Congress of the Opera in Bologna, November 10–13, 1903. Romolo Murri, with a certain support from Giovanni Grosoli, President of the organization, had gained the edge over the older faction eager to continue abstention from national politics in Bologna. An imprudent circular from Grosoli then argued that "old questions," presumably including the issue of the Temporal Power, no longer mattered that much to contemporary Catholics, who were thus freed to confront more serious matters. Although personally content to let the Temporal Power issue die, the new pontiff, Pius X, was disturbed by what he considered to be the Opera's lay-clerical insubordination, and dissolved it on July 28, 1904. Only Section II, dealing with Social Economy, was maintained, in order to emphasize the fact that "beneficent action in favor of the people" was still approved.

The Italian Catholic Movement was then entirely restructured on June 11, 1905, with the publication of an encyclical letter, *Il Fermo Proposito*. Section II of the Opera became the Unione Economico-Sociale dei Cattolici Italiani. An Unione Popolare tra i Cattolici d'Italia was established on the model of the Volksverein, along with an Unione Elettorale Cattolica Italiana, designed to prepare Catholics for gradual active participation in national political life. In practice, with the hopes for a Catholic Party squelched and the "business as usual" position abandoned, Rome had opted for the clerico-moderate line. The Unione Elettorale gradually pursued the kind of contractual agreement with conservatives utilized in other countries. Its great chance to put this plan into effective operation came with the introduction of universal male suffrage in the next decade, increasing the impact of the pro-Catholic vote and resulting in the famous "Pact" of 1911 of the President of the Unione, Vincenzo Ottorino Gentiloni with the conservative elements of the liberal party guided by Giovanni Giolitti.

Romolo Murri, disturbed by this development, moved on to build a Lega Democratica Italiana, open to direct cooperation with socialists in a way that seemed to indicate democracy's superiority to the Faith as a guide to political life. Such an impression was confirmed by Murri's calls for an internal democratization of the Church. He was formally expelled from the Catholic Movement and eventually excommunicated. Nevertheless, Christian Democrats still quietly remained within the official camp, hoping one day to be able to build a mass party that could address itself outside as well as inside Catholic circles, and continue to allow a joint lay-clerical political activity. Don Luigi Sturzo emerged as the leader of what became the Italian Popular Party, and, after its demise under Mussolini, the Christian Democratic Party of Alcide de Gasperi. This latter formation, sometimes criticized by the Papacy and sometimes prodded by it, would then go on to preside over the most successful secularization of Italian life in the peninsula's history.

Surely, by this point, the problems facing Catholic Action must be clear. But what can we possibly conclude from all their complexity? Three things, as far as I can determine, the first of which is that it has proven to be very hard to deal with the revolutionary policies emerging from the Enlightenment and the monarchies, liberal constitutional governments and democracies that implement them. These have changed daily life more radically than anything since the beginning of history. It took the Catholic world seven hundred years to come to terms with the barbarian invasions and begin successfully to jell the German tribes together with Graeco-Roman civilization. It should come as no surprise that it has taken more than two hundred fifty years to deal with political and social predicaments posed by a still more powerful invader.

A second lesson is that it will *never* be possible for the Church and for Catholics to discover an infallible system for dealing with the political and social realm. It has been part of the modern error to presume that some foolproof mechanism can be discovered through which the difficulty of discovering and doing the right thing in each and every new situation might be avoided; to dispense men, in effect, from the labor of living. It cannot. No constitution and no political system are free from manipulation by the noonday devils; no individual from the work required to avoid their seductive appeal. Prudent experimentation, guided by the unchangeable moral teaching of the Church, seems as though it must always be the order of the day in times of crisis and change. It was a good thing for the nineteenth century to have undertaken that experimentation; it would be equally judicious for twenty-first century Catholics to learn from its dilemmas in their own activities.

Thirdly, this flexibility regarding systems dictates that when Catholics participate directly in politics, they do so as free men who understand that the systems within which they work are *not* their Savior, that they *will* tempt them to abandon a Social Teaching which inevitably disturbs venal self-interest, and that, unfortunately, they have regularly found Catholics easy targets for worshipping at their shrines and twisting their own Faith in order to do so. Flexibility also dictates that when Catholics judge participation in an existing political system to be a sham, they conscientiously organize their abstention from it in a positive way, so as to prepare themselves to handle national and international affairs responsibly in the future.

Allow me to end with a special warning to Catholics in America. The United States is a vulnerable nation, subject to the vagaries of human action and human history, just as any other polity in the long record of the human race. It is no more divine than any other nation or any other system. It has had an historical beginning and it will also have an historical end. Everything written above applies to the present situation of Catholics in the United States even more than elsewhere in contemporary life, precisely because the forces tempting Catholics to believe in its divinity and benign character are immensely powerful and growing ever stronger. No nation and no system can be our Mother. Only the Church is our mother, and, as Louis Veuillot said, Catholic Truth alone can guide us to safe political action in the flux of changing historical conditions:

> The right tactic for us is to be visibly and always what we are, nothing more, nothing less. We defend a citadel which cannot be taken except when the garrison itself brings in the enemy. Combatting with our own arms, we only receive minor wounds. All borrowed armor troubles us and often chokes us.

FURTHER READING

Jedin, H. and Dolan, J., eds., *History of the Church* (Vols.VII, VIII, IX, Crossroad, 1981)

Invernizzi, M., *Il Movimento Cattolico in Italia* (Mimep-Docete, 1995)

Kalyvas, S.N., *The Rise of Christian Democracy in Europe* (Cornell, 1966)

Mayeur, J.M., ed., *Histoire du Christianisme* (X/XI, Desclée, 1995/1997)

Veuillot, L., *Mélanges* (*Oeuvres Completes*, iii series, 1933)

14

A Message From Bethlehem

LORD ACTON TENDS TO CORRUPT†

L ORD ACTON (1834–1902) WAS A NINETEENTH-
century English historian, a Liberal Catholic who intensely
disliked the counterrevolutionary direction down which the Church
was headed under the leadership of Blessed Pius IX. He is a hero
to many modern men and women who share his Enlightenment
outlook on society, politics, and especially the meaning of freedom. These include the directors of a powerful and well-heeled
American think tank, the Acton Institute, which has an enormous
influence in Catholic circles around the entire western world.

Acton is most well known through his teaching that power tends
to corrupt, and absolute power to corrupt absolutely. This dictum,
repeated by constitutionalists and libertarians alike, is supposed to
force those of us who justify Church and State use of power to face
honestly the unpleasant truth about ourselves: that we are on the
low road to becoming despicable tyrants or friends of tyranny. But
it seems to me that a solid Catholic analysis of the Power Dictum
leads to a quite different conclusion: that it is actually this teaching
of Lord Acton which tends to corrupt, and the absolute dedication
to promotion of his beliefs, represented by foundations like the
Acton Institute, which corrupts absolutely. For the Actonian PD,
in practice, reflects a Gnostic and Manichean vision totally incompatible with the one taught by the holy babe born in Bethlehem.

Gnosticism is an ancient world view which argues that matter is
evil and brought into being through the work of wicked demigods.
It is the antithesis of the Christian belief that Creation is the loving
gift of a good God who even offered it redemption once human
sin caused His supernatural plan to go astray. Mani (216–276), a
third-century Persian religious leader, gave his name to the most
successful Gnostic movement known to history. Manicheanism has
owed its strength through the ages to the writings and organizational ability of its founder and his disciples. Both have promoted

† First published in *The Remnant* (December 31, 2005).

251

an extremely effective strategy of superficially accepting the varied religious and cultural beliefs they encounter in their missionary labors, and then deconstructing and redefining them to serve their own subversive purposes.

Manichean Gnostics were very powerful in certain parts of Western Europe in the early Thirteenth Century. Many Christians were fooled by their policy of subtle cooption of familiar religious language to teach a message alien to orthodox Catholicism. But the Manichean Mayor of a well-known central Italian town found to his chagrin that one of his fellow-citizens had hit upon a sure-fire way of checkmating otherwise highly successful Gnostic maneuvers. The city was Assisi; the citizen, St. Francis; his tool, the crèche. St. Francis knew that thoroughgoing Gnostics cringed at the thought of everything connected with childbirth and its announcement of the arrival of yet another lump of wicked matter into the universe. He counted on the fact that Manicheans from Assisi would turn away in disgust at the sight of the crèche, just as they literally spat at the feet of all pregnant women crossing their path. And when they did so, they would proclaim themselves to be implacable enemies to truly believing Christians, all of whom reacted lovingly to the babe in the crib, even when they could not grasp the import of intellectual attacks on the Incarnation.

The message of that Incarnation is one of the need to redirect the entirety of fallen Creation to the glorification of God. Such a redirection is made possible through what St. Irenaeus calls the "recapitulation" of everything in Christ, the Word Incarnate. This recapitulation entailed Christ's "gathering up" of each and every aspect of existence into one sublime effort to nurture and raise human persons to eternal life with the Trinity. That enterprise required recognition and redemption of all natural goods and relationships, in the manifold ways that history had developed and meshed them together, and with due respect for the intricate hierarchy of earthly and supernatural values.

A number of the great Church Fathers of the fourth and fifth centuries, the Cappadocian St. Gregory of Nyssa prominent among them, were fully awakened to what this message meant for Greco-Roman culture. They showed how an opening to the teaching of the Babe born in Bethlehem involved a new study of the thoughts and achievements of their civilization, from the time of Homer onwards, to see whether they might be mobilized to aid the task of salvation. What was required for the success of such an enterprise, they realized, was a docility to supernatural correction of their natural culture's flaws, and a readiness to allow grace to guide its insights to uses much more exalted that anything it was capable of imagining when left purely to its own earthly devices.

One of the most important elements of the Greco-Roman Tradition that the mainline of the Church Fathers appreciated and sought to mobilize for Christ was its clear sense of the importance of familial and state authority. The value of such authority for identifying and gaining possession of all that was beautiful in human life, the evils befalling men who fled from its corrective application, and its troublesome and seemingly insoluble problems, were brilliantly presented in the writings of the great men of classical culture, its Hesiods, Solon the Lawgivers, Platos and Aristotles.

Far from rejecting their brilliant insights, Christianity, with its teaching of submission to the authority of the Babe of Bethlehem, seemed to the Church Fathers to confirm them. Greco-Roman Christians were compelled to study, purify, complete and transform what their forbears had already said and done in this realm. The Christian task was one of showing how a disciplining and coordination of all of the natural authorities developed by complex and troublesome human experience under the supernatural authority of the Incarnate Word and His Church could assure an infinitely more successful movement towards the True, Good and Beautiful; a march from darkness to light which would be sublimely beneficial for society as a whole, all of its individual members, and the very holders of authority themselves.

Men and women presented with the opportunity or need to wield a social authority built upon natural Greco-Roman foundations and purified by Christian teaching and grace, do not tend to be corrupted by it. What they tend to become, instead, is much more aware of the enormity of the burden that such authority places upon them to serve those subject to their control. Yes, it is very possible that this heightened sense of awareness may then lead them into a sinful hunt for ways of fleeing clear responsibilities, or cynical and hypocritical masquerading of abuse of power. On the other hand, it is also very possible that it will guide them down the pathway to sanctity.

Those who meditate on the lessons of the crèche know that Mary and Joseph are there to press them down this road to holiness through willing acceptance of authority. The blessed couple of Bethlehem said "yes" to a sublime authority over Christ which they exercised for quite some time, raising the God-Man to adulthood and providing us the model for the Holy Family in the process. All parents and fathers of nations who embrace their varied forms of social authority under analogous circumstances cam be transformed in Christ and attain personal perfection through their decision. They can become ever more conscious of flaws they need to overcome in order to fulfill their responsibilities to their charges properly. They can, under the pressure of that responsibility, become ever more aware of inner talents that they had no previous knowledge of possessing.

Nineteenth century counterrevolutionary Catholics were part of a movement of rediscovery of the fullness of the Christian past leading them back to the insights of Church Fathers regarding the message of the Incarnation and the consequences for human perfection of the full cooperation of nature and grace. They eagerly applied what they learned to one of the burning questions of their own day, the relationship of authority and individual freedom. Article after article in journals such as the Jesuit review, *La Civiltà Cattolica*, emphasized the conviction that strong natural and supernatural authority was a precondition for the perfection of personal liberty as well as all other human goods. For obedience to the fullness of authority was bound to ensure the fullest opportunity for self-correction and introduction to the Truth that really set men free. Rejection or limitation of the fullness of authority, on the other hand, entailed an opening to passion and a stubborn commitment to ignorance which was certain to work in favor of the strong, at the expense of the weak, but to the ultimate disadvantage and perdition of both.

> "When the right of command, or authority, is exercised in all its fullness, then all individuals, even the most weak, may use in all fullness their own rights; with the result that the fullness of liberty corresponds precisely to the fullness of authority...." (Taparelli, "Di Una Apologia Cattolica degli Ordini Rappresentativi," ii, 1, 1853, 273n).

"And the truth is that this freedom, as any other unlimited liberty not circumscribed by anything, is nothing other than the privilege agreed upon for the strong to assassinate the weak. In this case, the freedom of the strong is offended, since he is given the arbitrary ability to abuse his faculty, and the freedom of the weak is offended, as he remains the undefended victim of the abuse" (Curci, "Una Censura della Stampa," iii, 1, 1856, 387).

Contemporary Catholics who have been led by their respect for the Incarnation to become conscious of the sublime importance of social authority for the work of raising society and men to God have precious little opportunity to wield this tool in any influential manner. What small authority they still possess, whether over themselves, their families, or their friends, should, however, be exercised to hammer out warnings against all dangers threatening corruption of mind and soul. And hence we return to what this article announced at the outset: the need to identify Lord Acton's tendency to corrupt, and Institutes absolutely dedicated to spreading his ideas to corrupt absolutely.

A full discussion of the problem represented by Acton would require a theological, philosophical and historical analysis of Protestantism and the Enlightenment, as well as an examination of the all too great influence these have had even in Catholic circles in the past few centuries. Suffice it to say, for the moment, that he, like the mainstream of heretical modern man, cannot endure nature as God really created it, nor the still more exalted goal given to it through Christ's Redemption. Acton is particularly revolted by the crucial, positive role played in Creation and Redemption by social authority, both natural and supernatural. He wants to get rid of this role, and, in order to do so, he maligns it as something which tends to aim its possessors towards corruption.

But it is necessary at this point to note something very central to the particular corruption toward which the Actonian system actually tends. Acton speaks of "power" and not "authority." If what he really intended to say was that a raw, stubborn, unbending power tended to corrupt, he would have been correct, and would not have encountered the criticism that he did from nineteenth century counterrevolutionary opponents in the Catholic camp. Unfortunately, what Acton meant by "power" was precisely the activity of that mesh of social authorities, guided by a sense of philosophical and religious responsibilities and hierarchical organization, developed by Greco-Roman culture and Catholic thinkers tying natural wisdom together with the message of the Incarnation. It was this mesh that had, through its tendency to heighten awareness of the burden and the exalted mission of authority, tamed illicit strength and hemmed in its possible misuse at the hands of passionate and ignorant men. What Acton was, in fact, urging, in his assault on a social authority incorrectly identified as raw power, was a flight from an accurate and responsible use of a tool demanded by God and well developed, as a "seed of the Logos," in the natural world of Greece and Rome. What he was really calling for was the creation of a social jungle in which the kind of truly raw power that ultimately destroys both the strong and weak would happily flourish. This wicked power, which definitely does tend to corrupt, and, if absolute, corrupt absolutely, would then be limited by absolutely nothing substantive. How could it be otherwise? For every effective attempt to control its evil would involve the use of authority of some kind or another, be it philosophical, religious or traditional, and would be condemned by Acton as a step backwards into tyranny! The irony of this position is only surprising to someone unaware of the whole syllabus of ironies of the modern world that Acton loved so deeply. Remember, just to take one other example, that this civilization is one that praises Luther as a glorious founder of the modern commitment to human liberty, yet he believed that the concept of free will was a total absurdity.

I identified Acton's position as a Gnostic one. On second glance, this appears to me as unfair to the Gnostics. They were much more logical in their approach. Acton is a selective and illogical enemy of nature as it really is, aiming his ire primarily at the essential tool of authority. It would, therefore, perhaps be better to label him a semi-Gnostic. But I stand by the comparison of the Acton Institute, dedicated to the spread of his ideas in the Catholic world, with Manicheanism. Like so many other "conservative" Catholic organizations today, it works with familiar Christian language. It can even defend itself against the charge of Gnosticism by pointing out how much it loves money. Meanwhile, it systematically works to deconstruct the essence of the Christian message and redirect it to the service of its own subversive purpose: the equation of our

Faith with an unnatural, semi-Gnostic, Enlightenment concept of a self-destructive freedom destined to ensure the victory of the strong over the weak. For this is the ultimate goal of Acton's contemporary followers: to make it seem that God created and redeemed the world in order to make it safe for the exercise of a raw power masquerading as true freedom.

If the sole consequence of an individual's exercise of intellectual or spiritual authority today were to be the enlightenment of merely one other person to the tendency to corruption represented by Actonian thinking, this, to my mind, would be sufficient to justify his entire existence. Dangerous as that thinking is, it can still be defeated by the liberation of a handful of souls who understand the real power for transformation of the world contained by the Catholic message. And if a Catholic who senses its dangers despairs of finding the right arguments to lead a friend or family member away from it, let him take his student in this Christmas season to look at a crèche. Do Mary and Joseph really look like a libertarian mother and foster-father? Are they where they are because of their rejection of the authority of the Roman State? Does that Christ Child seem to be a victim of parents whose power over Him was bound to corrupt them, or one who wants us to be subject to the commands of His mother as much as He was?

15
Catholic Social Thought: Europe†

"REDISCOVERY" IS A GOOD WORD TO CHARacterize the experience of committed Catholics of the 1800s. Thinkers and activists demonstrated a desire to learn and put into practice themes and customs which had been buried by over a hundred years of Jansenist and Enlightenment neglect. This drive led them back to the Fathers of the Church, to the medieval scholastics, and to a mystical, devotional and liturgical life rich in lessons for both the Catholic community and individuals alike. The centers of rediscovery—German, French, Italian and Belgian for the most part—were mixed lay-clerical circles, religious orders restored after the devastation of the Revolution, university and seminary faculties, and the editorial offices of the journals and newspapers that seemed to spring up everywhere in the course of the nineteenth century.

Revival of the Catholic spirit entailed renewed recognition of the need for spiritual interaction with the political and social world as well. Zealous thinkers argued that the influence of Catholic belief was especially important to their own confused and rapidly changing century. Crucial to development in this respect was the work of the Savoyard writer, Joseph de Maistre (1753–1821), and his disciple, the Abbé Félicité de Lamennais (1782–1854), both of whom were convinced that secularist modern society could not help but self-destruct. Equally important work was done by thinkers exploring the consequences of the doctrines of the Incarnation and the Mystical Body of Christ, such as Johann Adam Möhler (1796–1838) and a myriad of anti-Enlightenment intellectuals and artists stirred by the Romantic Movement. Germany was particularly significant in this regard, due to the impact of the circles which had grown up in Mainz, Tübingen, Landshut, Munich and other cities in fields ranging from catechesis to politics. Though less known, the numerous Italian Amicizie Cattoliche were producing similar fruits.

---

† An entry for the *Encyclopedia of Catholic Social Thought, Social Science, and Social Policy* (Scarecrow Press, 2007)

Social Catholicism, in the sense of a movement addressing the problems of economic dislocation and pauperization connected with the Industrial Revolution, had many sources. Commentaries on migrations and urban riots, observations of dechristianization among workers, studies of prison conditions, and repeated efforts of ordinary Christians to improve the effectiveness of traditional concepts of charity all played their role in its gradual emergence. Here, too, international cross-fertilization was common, with German Protestant activities in what was referred to in Evangelical circles as the "Inner Mission" exercising a certain influence as well.

Among those active in the early stages of such developments were, in France, the Viscount Jean Paul Villeneuve-Bargemont (1784–1850), author of the *Traité de l'Economie Politique Chrétienne* (1837), Frédéric Ozanam (1813–1853), one of the founders of the Society of St. Vincent de Paul, Frédéric Le Play (1806–1882), with his Société Internationale des Hautes Études d'Économie Sociale, and Armand de Melun (1807–1877), promoter of innumerable social initiatives; in Germany, the Baden activist, Franz Josef von Buss (1803–1878), author of *Fabrikrede*, Adolf Kolping (1813–1865), who was deeply concerned with the conditions of migrant workers, and Bishop Wilhelm Emmanuel von Ketteler (1811–1877) of Mainz, whose *Die Arbeiterfrage und das Christentum* (1864) was seminal for many Catholics throughout Europe; in Italy, Frs. Carlo Curci (1809–1891), Matteo Liberatore (1810–1892), and Luigi Taparelli d'Azeglio (1793–1862), the Jesuit editors of *La Civiltà Cattolica*, which dedicated hundreds of pages to systematic critiques of existing economic conditions; and, in the Lowlands, Edouard Ducpetiaux (1804–1868), one of the founders of the independent Kingdom of Belgium.

All those convinced of the necessity of spiritually influencing social life emphasized the urgency of escaping the web of controls preventing freedom of political action established by enlightened absolutists, revolutionaries and the Napoleonic system alike. They did so often at the price of bitter confrontations with the police. The arrest and imprisonment of Archbishop Clemens August von Droste zu Vischering (1773–1845) of Cologne in the 1830s was one of the most significant of these *causes célèbres*.The reality of continued state restrictions explains why Pope Pius IX's (1846–1878) amnesty to political opponents, and the anti-absolutism of the Revolutions of 1848, were greeted with such enthusiasm by Catholic activists. Both portended an end to regulations and a new era of freedom from which they believed a revived Catholicism could not help but benefit. Nevertheless, the Revolutions of 1848, rather than working unfailingly for the benefit of Catholics, uncovered more problems that the youthful movement had to face, both internal as well as external. Discussion of three of these will allow us to grasp the shape of European Catholic Social Thought through the 1920s.

First of all, the Revolutions of 1848 made it clear that the word "freedom" was defined differently by Catholics than by other opponents of absolutist restrictions, such as liberals, democrats and nationalists. Political and social consequences of these differences had to be clarified by competent authorities, the Papacy being called upon to address the issue. The end result of this process of clarification was not simply the "negative" condemnations of Pius IX's Syllabus of Errors (1864), but also the more "positive," elaborated work of the whole corpus of Social Encyclicals and related pronouncements of Leo XIII (1878–1903), Pius X (1903–1914), Benedict XV (1914–1922), Pius XI (1922–1939) and Pius XII (1939–1958). Here, one finds reiterated, in varied forms, two basic themes of the entire Catholic revival: the need to deal with all human actions with reference to man's simultaneous natural-supernatural and individual-social character, and the self-destructive flaw of all types of naturalist thinking. These themes are developed with reference to a myriad of specific political and social issues. Along with this process of clarification came the work of definition of the Petrine Power underlying such efforts, symbolized, most importantly, by the First Vatican Council's definition of Papal Infallibility in 1870.

A second factor placed in higher relief by the Revolutions of 1848 and their aftermath were the differences of approach within the Catholic Movement itself. Here, the figure of Lammenais is of crucial significance. Lamennais' growing conviction that the catholicization of society required guidance by "the People," aroused by charismatic teachers to an energy and activity revealing the unquestionable presence of the infallible Spirit of God, led to the French priest's condemnation by Pope Gregory XVI (1831–1846). Nevertheless, his importance for developing initiatives and attracting enthusiastic followers made him the spiritual and intellectual father of large numbers of nineteenth century activists throughout Europe. Liberal Catholicism, represented most illustriously by a former follower, the Comte Charles de Montalembert (1810–1870), although steering clear of acceptance of Lamennais' principles, retained, in practice, much of his spirit of openness to vital contemporary movements, and impatience with those critical of them, such as Louis Veuillot (1813–1883) and his Parisian daily, *l'Univers*.

A third battle involved the question of the structure of the Catholic Movement. One pathway it followed was that of the creation of a network of pressure groups which could be mobilized for political combat whenever clear issues of spiritual importance emerged. Action by mobilized lay pressure groups had the benefit of keeping the Church's hands clean of everything but the dogmatic and spiritual guidance which her charism justly involved, and evoking that guidance only when the religious and political spheres truly touched one another. Thus, should pressure groups prove to be engaged in battle for their own particular causes in self-interested or less spiritually charged matters, the prestige and mission of the Church and clergy would not thereby be compromised.

Some tentative steps towards the formation of Catholic political parties were taken already in the years after 1830. Loose organization characterized all such groups. Still, despite their growth, the Church authorities, and with them, conservative forces in general, were frightened by mass confessional political parties. A severe crisis was usually required as a spur to the acceptance of militancy. These crises were offered aplenty in the course of the second half of the nineteenth century. Sometimes, they were set off because of one particular issue, especially freedom of education. Very frequently, however, the crisis was a general one, striking not only at education, but at the existence of the religious orders engaged in it, the ability of Church authorities to control their parishes, priests and seminaries, communication of bishops with the Papacy, marriage regulations, the right to form charitable organizations and the general freedom of association and right to speak out on any political matter whatsoever: in short, to use the German term, due to a full-scale Kulturkampf, or "culture war."

Catholic associations seeking to overturn liberal legislation often first approached existing conservative parties as their agents.

Such parties would be offered what were in essence contracts: the network of active Catholic associations would do much of the propaganda and legwork for the election of conservative deputies to parliament, with the proviso that these, when winning office, would do Catholic bidding on state matters touching upon religion. Results rarely matched the expectations, convincing many that the time had come to seek direct control of the State. One of the most important models for outright political action was the German Catholic Centre Party, which earned much of its prestige fending off the worst of Bismarck's attacks on the Church in the course of the 1870s. Belgian, Dutch and Austrian Catholics took much inspiration for their own political movements from its early militancy.

Major problems plagued the Catholic association and political movement with greater intensity from the 1870s onwards. One of these was the rivalry between the leadership of Catholic political parties and that of the associations that aided them. Certainly the Catholic Centre Party and the Volksverein für das Katholische Deutschland, founded in 1890 and developed under the able leadership of Franz Hitze (1851–1921) as an umbrella for a myriad of subsidiary groups with literally millions of adherents, sometimes eyed one another suspiciously. This was partly due to the fact that the association movement gave Catholic voice to an ever-greater variety of social groups with different interests, many of which were at sword point on a purely natural level. Pressure was thus placed upon a Catholic Party to take up positions which might satisfy one part of its clientele and horrify another. Especially problematic was the confusion created by the diversity of Catholic associations concerned with economic issues.

Basic, troubling questions were posed from the very beginning of the history of this type of Social Catholicism: whether one's activities on behalf of the poor was curative or preventive; should they be aimed at stirring individuals or institutions to labor on behalf of the needy; which institutions, sacred and secular, might be involved in such a charitable enterprise; and if one could cooperate in this venture with non-Catholics, should these happen to express ideas that coincided with certain concerns of orthodox believers. Three basic positions, all of which continued to be supported well into the twentieth century, quickly were established.

One of these was conservative, presuming that the existing liberal capitalist system, reformed to deal with the problems of chronic European pauperism, would continue to be the normal framework for economic life. Charles Perin (1815–1890), Professor of Economics at the University of Louvain from 1845–1881, and author of *De la Richesse dans les Sociétés Chrétiennes* (1861), as well as Bishop C. E. Freppel of Angers (1827–1891), were significant defenders of this approach.

A second group considered the liberal capitalist system to be so vitiated by the Enlightenment as to require its radical overhaul. Some of these "radicals" urged the elaboration of a more socially minded "corporate" order, inspired by medieval economic life, though expanded and adapted to the exigencies of an industrialized age. Among the proponents of such radical revision were, in Italy, the editors of *La Civiltà Cattolica*; in the German world, Karl von Vogelsang (1818–1890), editor of the Viennese newspaper, *Vaterland* (1874), his Austrian collaborator Alois zu Liechtenstein (1846–1920), the German Karl zu Löwenstein (1834–1921) and the Berlin journal, *Germania*; and in France, Albert de Mun (1841–1913) and René de La Tour du Pin (1834–1924), both of whom became influenced by German Catholic social thought while prisoners during the Franco-Prussian War.

These more radical attacks on the existing liberal capitalist system also involved recognition of the reality of a "working class." Such an awareness can be found in Henry Cardinal Manning (1808–1892), who was often called upon as a negotiator in labor disputes, the wealthy French entrepreneur, Léon Harmel (1829–1915), author of *Catéchisme au Patron* (1889) and De Mun and La Tour du Pin, with their Cercles Catholiques d'Ouvriers (1871). Numerous clerical activists in Belgium and the Netherlands, and men like Hitze in Germany, began to understand the necessity of a truly independent labor movement as well. The Syndicat des Employés du Commerce et de l'Industrie (1887), out of which later emerged the Confédération Française des Travailleurs Chrétiens, and the Christliche Gewerkvereine Deutschlands, sought to organize workers without upper class assistance.

An outrightly socialist vision provided a third, and even more revolutionary approach to economic issues, which flourished in the border regions of the acceptable and the heretical. This fringe of the

Catholic movement emerged from religious minded Saint-Simonians, some of the followers of Lamennais, and a number of the Polish emigrés who fled to France after the rebellion against Russia in 1830. It grew in conjunction with the theory of palingenesis, taken from the words "born" and "anew," which argued that the external representation of the "seed" of Christianity, contained in the Gospels, had periodically "died," merely to be revived in new and better form, Socialism representing its latest and best expression.

By the latter nineteenth century, newspapers, study groups, mutual aid societies and elaborate organizations of bewildering variety were pressing the Church as a whole for approval of their respective approaches. Their fervor was heated still further in the late 1880s an early 1890s, due to the Marxist-Trade Unions alliance creating the Second International and Social Democratic Parties, the commitment of the German Imperial Government to far-ranging social and economic reforms, and the pro-labor statements of the young Wilhelm II. Entities like the Fribourg Union Catholique d'Études Socials et Économiques put together sessions which tried to resolve the most serious of divisions so as to build a united Catholic front on such matters.

Rerum Novarum (1891), the great social encyclical of Pope Leo XIII, emerged out of this potpourri. Clearly the work of a committee on which Matteo Liberatore and others struggled, it tried to reconcile a variety of viewpoints. Rejecting all economic solutions that did not recognize man's joint natural-supernatural and individual-social character, it could thus be seen to be critical of both liberal capitalism and Marxist socialism. It admitted the right of the State to enter the economic arena, as well as the possibility of workers organizing for their self-protection. Rather than stifling debate, however, Catholics interested in social issues became still more eager to determine the limits of government intervention, the suitability of denominational or non-confessional unions, and the permissibility of going out on strike. Pius X found himself regularly confronted with these issues and attempts to resolve them.

Such divisions troubled Catholic political parties, whose leaders were, moreover, painfully aware of being outside of the mainstream of European society. Thoughtful political activists wanted to advance beyond a minimal protection of basic Catholic needs to an exercise of a real Christian influence over the whole of life. The important question in the long run was to prove to be whether or not this influence could be gained without losing the soul of the Catholic Social Movement. For entering the mainstream involved creating a party bureaucracy with an elite of parliamentary representatives whose primary concerns were often merely gaining and retaining power, and finding ways to appeal for the votes of people inspired by democratic, Marxist, nationalist and racist issues, which many prelates and believers thought might involve an abandonment or redefinition of the Faith. "Confessional party leaders such as Julius Bachem (1845–1918) were repeatedly attacked for setting aside the Catholic basis of the most important organization of German Catholicism in order to substitute a so-called non-denominational Christian basis as the party's guiding philosophy" (Kalyvas, p. 232). An Austrian Christian Social spokesman confirmed their fears when he succinctly noted: "in politics the only thing that counted was success" (Ibid., p. 232).

Italy was prey to special tensions. Here, the *non expedit* policy, the papal prohibition of Catholic participation in national political life, had barred the creation of a political party. It did so because the government had clearly refused to allow Catholic deputies who rejected the Kingdom's liberal nationalist program to be seated in Parliament anyway. Italian Catholics like Giuseppe Toniolo (1845–1918), founder of the Unione Cattolica per gli Studi Sociali, were active in the Opera Dei Congressi e Dei Comitati Cattolici (1874), where they prepared, in what was a kind of shadow government, for future guidance of a better disposed country. By the 1890s and 1900s, some activists, either worried or encouraged by the advance of Socialism, wished for a modification of the *non expedit* in order to enable them to join, depending upon their viewpoint, either with pro-government liberals or worker movements in a joint battle against a common perceived threat. Others, horrified by what seemed to them to be the temptation to accept the anti-Catholic economic principles inspiring both of these groups, thought that the time had come for the creation of a distinctly Catholic political party appealing democratically to the voters at large.

It was at this point that the Papacy intervened, first under Leo XIII, with the encyclical letter *Graves de Communi* (1901), which condemned the idea of a political party and limited the use of the term "Christian Democracy" to "a beneficent Christian action in favor of the people," and then with Pius X's *Il Fermo Proposito* (1905). This completely restructured the Opera, creating what was now called Catholic Action, and allowing for resort to the kind of contractual agreement with conservatives utilized, usually unsatisfactorily, in other countries. It was only after the war, in 1919, with the creation of Don Luigi Sturzo's (1871–1959) Partito Popolare, that a distinct partisan movement was created. This, too, however, was chastised for succumbing to secularizing tendencies, and abandoned by Rome when a seemingly friendly fascist government sought resolution of outstanding ecclesiastical problems, culminating in the Lateran Accords of 1929.

The collapse of traditional monarchies, the influence of Marxism-Leninism, the competing corporative theories of fascist governments, and the double blow of inflation and depression stimulated Catholics to still more concerted efforts in political and social matters in the interwar period. Expansion was aided by a noticeable increase of papal interest in current issues, as witnessed by Pius XI's allocutions and his renowned encyclical letter, *Quadragesimo Anno* (1931). This latter document, like *Rerum Novarum*, gave encouragement to both liberal reformers and corporatist pathfinders, while warning against Soviet Communism and the bureaucratic heavy-handedness accompanying fascist efforts to build national solidarity. Certain of the smaller European nations, such as Portugal and Austria, were guided by men and movements who had themselves been shaped by Catholic corporatist thought. Papal disdain for outrightly Catholic political movements had to be nuanced in the Austria of Engelbert Dollfuss (1892–1934), since an insistence here upon the letter of the law could lead to a deadly victory of National Socialist enemies of the Church.

Exceedingly important in the interwar period was a new debate over the structure of Catholic Action. Hierarchical Catholic Action, based on parish and diocesan organizations, controlled by pastor, bishop and Pope, had been promoted by Pius X and Pius XI, and was the rule in countries like Italy. Pius XI sought to protect the work of ecclesiastically-controlled lay groups against governmental assault by means of Concordats. Quite different, though also supported by the Papacy, was what was referred to as Specialized Catholic Action, which argued that re-christianization could only succeed by approaching distinct groups in distinct ways, a favored slogan being that of "like evangelizing like." Specialized Catholic Action's most famous representative was the Jeunesse Ouvrière Chrétienne, founded by Fr. Joseph Cardijn (1886–1967) in Brussels in 1924, and expanding from Belgium into France swiftly thereafter. This initiative was thrown into shock at the outbreak of the Second World War, when believing soldiers confronted the almost overwhelming lack of Christian spirit among troops of all nations. That shock was intensified by the brutality of the experiences of many activists in labor and concentration camps, including their appreciation of the self-sacrifice and altruism of Marxist and ordinary Russian inmates.

Personal experience contributed to a linkage with the philosophical school called Personalism. Personalism, promoted by a wide variety of often clashing thinkers ranging from Jacques Maritain (1882–1973) to Emmanuel Mounier (1905–1950), emerged from principles familiar to the student of Lamennais, including a favorable judgment of all cultures and movements reflecting a special "energy" or "mystique" indicating the presence of the fount of all vitality, the Holy Spirit. The increasingly radical arguments of many Personalists were that the Christian activist had to abandon his distinct intellectual and cultural training in order to dive enthusiastically into the work of the group to which he believed himself to be called. Fears concerning fragmentation and secularization were allayed by arguments coming from Pierre Teilhard de Chardin (1881–1955), who emphasized the spiritual movement of all such activities towards a common God-directed purpose.

Many Personalists were at first attracted to the energy of the fascist youth movements, although never to their racist arguments. In France, they were enthusiastic about the National Revolution promoted by the Vichy government. The Mission de France, established by the French episcopacy in 1943 to deal in unique ways with the wartime working class population, and stimulated still further by Henri Godin's (1906–1944) book, *France: Pays de Mission?* (1943), also attracted their attention. Personalism played a major role in justifying the Worker Priest Movement, which, after the war, led a number of clerics so to dedicate themselves to contemporary European labor activities as to take a leading part in "energetic" communist union activity. Their apostolate was suspended by Pius XII in the course of the 1950s, a suspension confirmed by John XXIII soon after ascending to the throne of Peter, but lifted by Paul VI shortly thereafter.

A number of those who emerged out of the junction of specialized Catholic Action with Personalism, such as Louis-Joseph Lebret (1897–1966), were crucially important for building the Liberation Theology movement in South America, which became especially important in countries like Brazil by the 1960s and favorable to the "energetic" model of Fidel Castro's Cuban Revolution. This juncture was then popularized in European universities and seminaries. Considerations emerging from the union of Specialized Catholic Action and Personalism also helped shape John XXIII's encyclical letters *Mater et Magistra* (1961) and *Pacem in Terris* (1963), the Constitution *Gaudium et Spes* of Second Vatican Council, Paul VI's *Popolorum Progressio* (1967) and the social teaching of John Paul II.

In any case, while the main lines of historical Catholic Social Thought are still reaffirmed in papal pronouncements, the idea that openly confessional organizations could not penetrate and understand contemporary energies and mystiques played an enormous role in their voluntary postwar abandonment of the label "Catholic." This process was encouraged by certain European episcopacies which had long before criticized influential organizations which called themselves Catholic, but managed to escape direct diocesan control. Much "Catholic" social thought and action, today, therefore, continue not under the banner of the Church, but as sub-categories of broader philosophical, political and sociological studies and movements.

BIBLIOGRAPHY

Arbuthnott, A., *Joseph Cardijn* (London, 1966).
Bowman, F. P., *Le Christ des Barricades* (Cerf, 1987).
Cholvy, G., *Jeunesses Chrétiennes au xxe Siècle* (Ouvrières, 1991).
Elbow, M., *French Corporative Theory, 1789–1948* (New York, 1948).
Fattorini, E., *I Cattolici Tedeschi dall'Intransigenza alla Modernità, 1870–1953* (Morcelliana, 1997)
Hellman, J., *Emmanuel Mounier and the New Catholic Left* (McGill-Queens, 1997).
Hoeffner, J., *Wilhelm Emmanuel von Ketteler und die Kathholische Sozialbewegung im 19. Jahrhundert* (Wiesbaden, 1962).

Jedin, H., and Dolan, J., eds., *History of the Church* (VII, VIII, IX, X, Crossroad, 1981).

Jemolo, A.C., *Chiesa e Stato in Italia dalla Unificazione agli Anni Settanta* (Einaudi, 1970).

Kalyvas, S.N., *The Rise of Christian Democracy in Europe* (Cornell, 1996).

Launay, M., *Le Syndicalisme Chrétien en France de 1885 à nos Jours* (Desclée, 1984).

Mayeur, J.M. et al., *Histoire du Christianisme* (X, XI, XII, XIII, Desclée, 1995–2001).

Moody, J.N., ed., *Church and Society. Catholic Social and Political Thought and Movements, 1789–1950* (New York, 1953).

Poulat, E., *Les Prêtres Ouvrièrs* (Cerf, 1999).

16

La Civiltà Cattolica[†]

L *A CIVILTÀ CATTOLICA*, A JOURNAL EDITED
by priests of the Society of Jesus, began publication in April
of 1850, for a short time in Naples, but ultimately in Rome. Its
lengthy issues, which appeared twice monthly, were planned as
part of an orderly discussion of the foundations, nature and benefits
of Catholic culture. Each issue came to include theological, philosophical, scientific, historical, sociological and polemical articles,
as well as a book review, a chronicle of world events, and fictional
pieces. The editors wrote, "Sometimes the same truth comes to
you exposed by one author as a theory, implanted by another in
a dialogue, rendered evident and almost physically palpable by a
third in a short story" (Series I, Volume 2, p. 14).

The original editors of *La Civiltà Cattolica*, including Revs.
Carlo Maria Curci (1809–1891), Matteo Liberatore (1810–1892),
and Luigi Taparelli d'Azeglio (1793–1862), were scholars, literary
men and political activists. Their chief concern, in developing a
comprehensive theory of the nature of Catholic civilization, was
to avoid shallow, time-bound discussions of the consequences of
the French Revolution, the Revolutions of 1848, and the growth of
European liberalism, capitalism, socialism and nationalism; instead
placing them within the broader context of the centuries-long
battle of religious and secular minded world views. In pursuance
of this goal, they developed many sub-themes:

• the need to understand the Catholic vision through a deeper
study of the doctrines of the Incarnation and the Mystical Body
of Christ.

• the complementarity of social authority and the individual
person in the attainment of order, human freedom and dignity.

• the disaster of a modern world view, emerging out of Protestantism, the Enlightenment and the Revolution, which had locked
authority and the individual in an unnatural combat against one
another to the detriment of both.

---

† An entry for the *Encyclopedia of Catholic Social Thought, Social Science,
and Social Policy* (Scarecrow Press, 2007).

• the practical political and social consequences of a choice for either the Catholic or the Modern outlook in everything from the nature of government to the question of workers' rights in a world shaken by the Industrial Revolution.

• the importance of clarifying the terrible contemporary mis-understanding of the Christian and contemporary relationship to Progress and Liberty by means of precisely the kind of systematic teaching that the journal encouraged, utilizing a long-neglected, logical, revitalized scholastic philosophy.

• the value of a strengthened Papacy in fighting an ever more widespread, international, revolutionary secularism.

While written only in Italian, its substantive articles, ecclesias-tical backing and aggressive promotion gave the *Civiltà* enormous influence in the entire Catholic world. It was extremely significant in shaping both Pius IX's Syllabus of Errors (1864), as well as that Catholic Social Doctrine reflected in the avalanche of Encyclicals from the pontificate of Leo XIII onwards. The *Civiltà's* conviction that supernatural religion was the primary force working for the perfection of natural life gained it bitter enemies from everyone who insisted that particular constitutional, democratic, national-ist, utilitarian or racist systems were the first building blocks of Progress, and that anyone who refused to recognize this axiomatic reality was hopelessly "intransigent."

BIBLIOGRAPHY

Jemolo, A.C., *Chiesa e Stato in Italia negli ultimi cento anni* (Torino, 1948).

Memorie della Civiltà Cattolica (Roma, 1855).

Rao, J., *Removing the Blindfold* (Kansas City, 2014).

17

THE TALLINN LECTURES
Introduction†
IN SEARCH OF EUROPE'S CULTURAL IDENTITY

INTRODUCTION

I. THE "ANTI-EUROPEANS"?

Some years ago, two good British friends of mine found themselves called upon to cast their ballots on an issue involving closer cooperation with what was then called the European Community. As they went to the polling station, they both told me that they had decided to vote "against Europe."

Now these two friends were, indeed, as British as they could possibly have been. Nevertheless, to my mind, they were simultaneously representative of everything positive that European culture in general signified. Proud of their own nation, they lacked all trace of a closed, parochial spirit. They had benefited from that traditional classical education once common to the British Isles and the whole of the Continent, and cultivated extensive business and personal ties with France, Italy and Germany. How is it, then, that two such fine examples of the specific British contribution to the broader Old World achievement could convince themselves that they were somehow "anti-Europe," and therefore "anti-Europeans?" One valuable source to consult in finding an answer to that question is the nineteenth century movement of Catholic revival and its passion for rediscovering the fullness of the Christian European cultural achievement. (For this revival, see J. M. Mayeur et. al, eds., *Histoire du Christianisme*, Desclée, Vols. XI, XII, 1995–1997; also, John C. Rao, *Removing the Blindfold*, Angelus Press, 2014; and Chapter 12 of this volume, "School Days").

---

† Lecture given at the TriaLogos Festival in Tallinn, Estonia on September 24, 2007.

II. NINETEENTH CENTURY CATHOLICS AND THE PROBLEM OF
LANGUAGE

Throughout the post-French Revolutionary Catholic world, thinkers and activists of impressive caliber demonstrated a desire to learn, develop and put into practice themes and customs which had been buried by decades and even centuries of Jansenist, naturalist and simple pastoral neglect.

Depending upon energy, taste and imagination, this drive led them back to the Fathers of the Church, to the medieval scholastics, and to a mystical, devotional and liturgical life rich in lessons for both the Catholic community and individuals. The centers of re-discovery — German, Italian, and French, for the most part — were lay and clerical circles of believers, religious confraternities, orders restored after the devastation of the Revolution, university faculties, and groups gathering around those journals and newspapers that seemed to spring up everywhere in the course of the nineteenth century.

La Civiltà Cattolica, a Jesuit journal of international impact founded in Rome in 1850, was of central significance in this broad and effective movement. It sought to deal, comprehensively, with all of the issues brought up by the Enlightenment, the French Revolution and their aftermath, as well as the response that Catholics must offer to them. The biggest difficulty that it faced, the journal's editors noted from the very outset, was the problem of language.

Why language? Because they recognized that Catholic themes, such as the order and value of all of nature; and words like freedom, which had been cherished and developed from late ancient times through the Baroque Era had been seized by the enemies of the Faith and redefined for their own anti-Christian use. So successful had the efforts of these opponents of Catholicism been that their seized themes and words had dominated the common parlance and penetrated deeply into the mentality of the general population. The result was that they were taken for granted by the average man as being obviously and unquestionably true.

Anyone who wished to fight the supporters of the Enlightenment and prove that they had actually distorted the language — to the detriment of the world around them and their own self-deception as well — was therefore obliged to begin his work with the basics. He had to examine all the disfigured themes and words to demonstrate their older and totally diverse meaning. "Almost everything will have to be reconstituted anew," the *Civiltà* concluded, "since almost everything has been deformed and tampered with" ("Il Giornalismo Moderno," *La Civiltà Cattolica*, Series I, Volume 1, 1850, pp. 14–15).

Unfortunately, the anti-Enlightenment activist had to be prepared for enormous practical difficulties in undertaking such a task. His enemies would be fighting him every step of the way and with a clear linguistic advantage. Moreover, the average man, incapable of taking the time required for comprehending the rationale behind this massive work of reconstruction, could easily lose interest in it or, worse still, actually condemn it as a dangerous nuisance demanding impossible and economically destructive changes in his familiar thought patterns and daily behavior.

If the editors of *La Civiltà Cattolica* were still alive, so that I might express to them my English friends' conviction that they were "anti-Europeans," I know what their response would be. They would ask many questions about the definition of "Europe" and seek to determine who had seized control of that word to define it in the particular manner they had done. The *Civiltà* editors would suggest that my friends were perhaps not "anti-European" at all, but merely opposed to a precise vision of Europe that was a deformed and self-deluding one. And they would then tell them to prepare themselves to face a barrage of harsh criticism if they should dare to bring up the very possibility of there being a conception of Europe different from the one presented as an unquestionable "given" by the contemporary masters of the common parlance.

We today are not pressed to cast a ballot for or against "Europe." We therefore have the chance to delve more fully into precisely what that word "Europe" might mean; to go "In Search of Europe's Identity" with greater leisure and scientific openness to the truth. In the spirit of *La Civiltà Cattolica*, I should argue that we set to work to exploit this happy opportunity by asking ourselves four questions of crucial importance to our task: 1) What do we mean by a search? 2) How do we define an identity? 3) What, precisely, is Europe's identity? And, finally, returning to the drama faced by my English friends, 4) What was the character of the "Europe" which they were called upon to accept, were they unquestionably "anti-European" for rejecting it, and are we as guilty as they were for adopting a similar critical attitude to "Europe" today?

III. WHAT IS INVOLVED IN THE SEARCH?

Our first question may seem a rather strange one, and yet it must immediately be posed in a world which for several centuries has suffered from the ravages of intellectual reductionism and ideology. What is involved in an intellectual search of any variety? Are we honestly permitted to utilize all the tools that intelligent men and women through the ages have come to appreciate as being necessary to conducting a hunt for answers to problems of great political, social and personal importance? May we gather and consult everything—scientific evidence, historical and cultural information, psychological studies of medical, literary and spiritual character, and philosophical and theological judgments—hat the mind and soul have judged valuable to a complete understanding of human affairs? If some of these tools have been excluded from our search, on what basis have they not been permitted to play their role? What might be gained or lost by abandoning them? Who might benefit or suffer from that abandonment?

IV. WHAT DO WE MEAN BY THE SEARCH FOR AN IDENTITY?

Our next query is, what do we mean by a search for the identity of something existing in nature? This question lies at the very heart of the western philosophical debate, and the answer to it is of crucial practical significance in every realm. Have we exhausted our ability to identify a man, a woman, an animal, a political and social order or whatever else might grasp our attention once we have recounted individual bits of data; individual "facts" concerning the subject under study that have made an immediate impression upon our eyes and ears; data and facts which can and do often change from one moment to the next? Could an identification on this basis somehow be flawed? And, if flawed, is it possible to correct what our senses immediately tell us, to distinguish between what is changeable and unchangeable in that which we are examining; to distinguish between what is truly natural and what is a misperception of the natural?

If we think that it is theoretically possible to identify flaws, what would our practical methodology for uncovering such flaws involve? Would it be based upon a hunt for the "essence" of a man, a woman, an animal, or a continental political and social order? Could "accidental" flaws of something natural be corrected according to its deeper, inner "reason" or "logos?" If so, what specific tools would we employ to determine what that essence is, and how to use it as a model? Once again, as noted above, would we utilize every instrument that intelligent men and women have come to appreciate through the course of history to reach our goal? Or would we perhaps seek to make sense out of the mountain of data that nature presents to our eyes and ears with reference to some simple, internal principle for identifying the essence of a thing: a mind already structured to interpret data that it has not yet encountered according to fixed rules; a strongly felt sentiment; even an act of pure imagination and will?

Finally, if, after all of this effort, we come to the conclusion that it is not possible to reach any accurate identification of the essences of things around us, would we abandon the search entirely and prohibit others from engaging in what we have come to believe is an impractical "waste of time?" Would we enter into a "contract" with one another and decide upon a "make-believe" identification of the nature of things so as to avoid despair, get on with the business of ordinary day-to-day life, and maintain some social order? And, once again, what would be gained or lost, and who would benefit or suffer from any of the positions discussed above?

V. WHAT DO WE MEAN BY THE SEARCH FOR EUROPE'S IDENTITY?

Our first two questions are obviously related to a third: what does our search for Europe's identity entail? Is it the hunt merely for accumulated material data concerning a particular parcel of land as it exists now and will change, perhaps drastically, one, ten or fifty years from now? Does it involve accumulating past material data impacting on its present character as well? Should one go beyond the purely material sphere and investigate the identity of Europe by examining her whole psyche? What specific role should history, literature, philosophy and theology play in such an enterprise?

Then, again, must whatever is discovered about Europe be accepted "as it is," or is it at least theoretically possible to identify flaws in her character? Can these possible flaws be corrected, in order to complete and fulfill any underlying "potential" she might seem to possess? If so, would such correction be made with reference to "essences" — such as the notion of "human nature" and its dictates regarding law, freedom and dignity — now made applicable to European political and social life? Could reference to God and His plan, and any place Europe might have under His Providence be seriously considered and publicly discussed? Would correction of Europe's flaws be based only upon an innate internal principle of organization or a strongly felt sentiment or an act of pure imagination and will? If the search for Europe's deeper identity were deemed an utterly meaningless enterprise which "practical" men of "common sense" ought to abandon, should any existential fears about the meaning of life flowing from this nihilism be calmed through a "social contract" erecting what amounts to a "make-believe" truth and order? And, yet once more, what would be gained or lost, and who would benefit or suffer by any such decisions?

VI. SEIZING THE WORD "EUROPE" TO CONSTRUCT AN ANTI-CHRISTIAN SOCIETY

We are now in a position to return to the drama faced by my English friends, identify the "Europe" concerning which they were called upon to vote, and judge the justice of their feeling that they were unquestionably "anti-European" for opposing it.

Let it suffice to say for the moment that I am convinced that my friends were only voting against a very particular vision of "Europe"; a "Europe" whose name has been seized to promote a specific understanding of what the continent should be, and what must be changed to allow her to fulfill the destiny ascribed to her. The European "order" promoted by this vision is built upon the will of the strongest elements in contemporary society. It is an order which will not permit itself to be corrected with reference to rational scientific and psychological evidence or any metaphysical guidelines whatsoever. Irrationally materialist, hostile to religion, and subject to constant flux, it is a vision which is ultimately incapable of identifying anything, including, ultimately, the "Europe" it insists that we believe it cherishes.

This particular vision of "Europe" has had a very successful career. Its proponents have consistently and skillfully associated it rhetorically with everything that westerners continue to view as being "good," while cleverly linking opposition to its progress with all that westerners continue to identify as being "evil." They have hindered dialogue by limiting the tools which one is permitted to

use to search for the continent's true identity, by unjustly condemning expansion of the debate as inevitably conducive to religious war and genocide, and also by ridiculing attempts to keep
the discussion alive as a nostalgic and economically impractical
waste of time. Hence, the errors, self-interests, and even criminal
actions prospering under "Europe's" unquestioned aegis remain
dangerously hidden.

In the following three essays I will go in search of Europe's
identity by 1) Showing that it is an exploration whose character
has been shaped by western battles concerning ways and means
of understanding life in general, rooted in the ancient Greek confrontation of philosophy and rhetoric; 2) That this ancient battle
was made more intense by the arrival of Christianity and the
evolution of the struggle over the meaning of the word "natural"
into a conflict between those seeking to correct and transform all
things in Christ and what I should like to call a "Grand Coalition on behalf of the unexamined life"; and, finally, 3) That the
Christian vision of life, the search for the identity of the continent,
and the perfection of the true character of Europe are all in the
greatest danger in our time. This is due to the powerful modern
tendency to justify thought and action on the basis of a willful
"voluntarism" and appeal to "vitality" and "success" working in
tandem with the secular religion of Americanist Pluralism.

One final comment before beginning. These conferences are not
intended as detailed academic papers, but as a broad introduction
to an enormous issue of theological, philosophical, historical, literary, political, economic, and sociological character. They form part
of a larger work, still in preparation, entitled The War Between
the Words and the Word. The foundation for that project can be
found both in my study of the nineteenth century Catholic revival
movement, published in 2014 as Removing the Blindfold (Angelus
Press) as well as in related articles in this volume and available
online (For the Whole Christ, jcrao.freeshell.org). I will identify
other indispensable sources for my argument in subsequent essays.

18

THE TALLINN LECTURES

I. Sophist Blindfold or Escape from the Cave?†

THE BASIC EITHER-OR OPTION

MANY OF THE GREAT MEN OF THE WEST-ern past warned against too easy an acceptance of the lessons of immediate sensual and emotional experiences, fearing that their powerful impact would divert necessary attention away from the thought and reflection which could place them in their proper perspective. Any unquestioning love affair with the messages sent by the intense sensations of ordinary daily existence would, they argued, ensure loss of a deeper understanding of the meaning of life and how to pursue that meaning and fulfill it. A romance of this kind would only guarantee indulgence in what was superficial, deceptive and ultimately completely self-destructive.

Nevertheless, the dominant forces of the contemporary western world encourage just such a passion. In varying ways, they all insist that voluntary abandonment to the teaching of surface phenomena, far from being a frivolity, is actually the only realistic approach to existence that men and women can possibly embrace. Anyone seeking meaning, fulfillment and joy in life must energetically fight off that temptation to deeper thought and reflection which prevents "closure" and "moving on" to satisfaction of the ever changing and evolving messages of immediate sensation.

Study of the roots of the militant modern preference for the shallow over the profound must begin in the ancient, pagan world. For the conscious encouragement of a spirit favoring "closure" and "moving on" over "stepping back" and "reflecting" is already notice-able in the Classical Greece of the Fifth and Fourth Centuries B. C., especially in the eye-opening period of the Peloponnesian War and its dismal aftermath (431–336 B. C.). This is because

† Lecture given at the TriaLogos Festival in Tallinn, Estonia, on September 26, 2007.

Greece, as the home of the first insightful discussion of the meaning and practice of education, *paideia*, inevitably provoked the original vocal battle between those primarily valuing either the lessons of surface phenomenon or the hunt for underlying and more nuanced truth. (The following discussion on the battle of Socratics and Sophists is based on the work of Werner Jaeger, *Paideia: The Ideals of Greek Culture*, Oxford, 1986, 3 Volumes)

Epic, lyric and dramatic poets were the first teachers of Hellas. They sought answers to the basic issues of life by asking aesthetic questions; by making queries regarding the meaning of beauty. Aesthetic preoccupations led them to tackle the problem of how best to educate for a knowledge and possession of "the Beautiful." That hunt for the tools essential to a primarily aesthetic formation gradually became "holistic." It slowly uncovered the need for consultation with, and guidance from, a variety of different sources: the individual and his immediate desires, the family and its long-term requirements for stability, and, perhaps most importantly, the demands of the polis, the city-state, in its search for attainment of a common as opposed to a merely individual or familial "beautiful" life.

The reputation of the polis as an aesthetic, educative, guiding force was enormous at the end of the Persian Wars (490–479 B. C.). Athens and Sparta, its two greatest contemporary representatives, had assured their polis' prestige by winning a victory over the most impressive power in the world; a force before which, in startling contrast, a number of important individuals and purely family-dominated Greek lands had humiliatingly cowered. Such an unexpected but clear triumph made it appear that the community-focused polis could, in effect, accomplish absolutely anything.

It was for this reason that Aeschylus (525–456 B. C.), in his *Oristeia* trilogy, has an unending cycle of superhuman vengeance and counter-vengeance concluded through polis-shaped (i.e., political) judicial action. Beauty, education and the polis, one might have said; now and forever; one and inseparable.

Unfortunately, however, it was precisely the same cherished polis of Athens and Sparta which revealed insane, self-destructive passions and limitations during and after the Peloponnesian War, thereby stimulating further debate regarding the basic tools required for a proper education designed to gain possession of the beautiful. Control of the renewed dialogue passed out of the hands of the poets alone, who had said everything that they could possibly say on all sides of this issue of *paideia* by the time of Euripides (480–406 B. C.).

Greece, even before this moment, had witnessed the emergence of a quite different approach towards education, along the lines suggested by the first philosophers, the so-called pre-Socratics. These thinkers wished to replace an aesthetic understanding of man and nature with one founded firmly upon knowledge of the material structure of the universe itself; a "scientific" knowledge of its constituent elements. But pre-Socratic approaches to life and education proved to be too radical a break with the traditional aesthetic vision for the mainstream Greek world to accept. They were rejected, in particular, by two schools of thought both active in the war and post-war period, which were themselves destined to lock horns in mortal combat.

One of these schools was that of the Sophists, men concerned with rhetoric, the successful use of language. Sophists, in effect, argued that the old-line aesthetic approach to hunting for the Beautiful was correct, but that it needed to be organized, taught and followed much more rigorously if it were to become a sure foundation for the individual, the family and society. The other school was that of Socrates (469–399 B. C.), who, while also retaining much of the traditional aesthetic approach to education, felt a call to critique, transform and elevate it. The battle that this entailed was related for us not by Socrates himself but by his most brilliant pupil, Plato (427–347 B. C.). And Plato reveals the nature of the conflict in his debate with Isocrates (436–338 B. C.), perhaps the most self-conscious and instructive proponent of the opposing, sophistic, rhetorical approach.

Plato's great achievement as a philosopher and as an educator was one of demonstrating that the classical Greek formation of an individual for the possession of the beautiful required an under-standing both of the nature of goodness as well as of the underlying truths of the universe for which the pre-Socratics were groping. He presented Socrates, his model teacher, as a "soul doctor," a man who sought the cure of moral and intellectual flaws in his continued hunt for aesthetic perfection. Education for beauty in the fullest possible sense was indeed a holistic project, Plato insisted, but an exciting and dramatic one, drawing the individual closer and closer to God, the measure of all things, shaping his soul as an image or icon of the divine as he advanced.

Every tool that the Greeks had come to consider to be important—the polis included—had a crucial role to play in this all-encompassing, life-long enterprise. Nevertheless, those valuable tools were flawed, each and every one of them. Paradoxically, the means of education themselves required correction and improvement at the hands of the individual "icons" that they helped to shape. Soul doctoring could be a perplexing, immensely difficult, exhausting task, involving much meditation and self-questioning. And such an enterprise could not help but appear to be a pointless, frustrating detour to those on a perpetual hunt for "get possession of beauty quick" schemes; those interested in "closure" and "moving on."

"Pointlessly frustrating" was certainly the criticism attached to Platonic education by Isocrates, who claimed the title of philosopher with as great a sense of justice and fervor as his fellow Athenian did. Still, apt student of the Sophist Gorgias that he was, Isocrates understood philosophy to be a wisdom that only the trained rhetorician could possibly grasp and use properly. This inevitably meant that his definition of any Good or Truth underlying the Beautiful would differ considerably from the one given to them by Socratics eager to pass beyond the borders of rhetoric alone.

For Isocrates, there was no question of seriously critiquing, transforming and possibly even rejecting the immediate emotional and sensual experiences and preoccupations of the ordinary man. Man was the measure of all things, and unquestionably correct in his urgent, common-sense appreciation of the importance of obtaining the riches, power and fame that he obviously knew would yield the beautiful life. The average individual's sole problem was a technical one: he could not relate one, justifiable, obvious, common-sense experience to another, and thereby understand how best to exploit and satisfy them regularly and comprehensively. His efforts to explain his reactions to daily problems, both to himself as well as to others, proved to be "dumb" ones. It was effective words, and the arguments shaped through them, which were lacking to the average man. Only the well trained rhetorician, the master of words, could clarify the full depth of immediate feelings and experiences, show where they were headed, and stir people to do what was necessary to fulfill their promise. The Good and the True were, therefore, ultimately nothing other than "appropriate" explanations and developments of those obvious and common-sense reactions to the raw stuff of daily life which are themselves absolutely infallible guides to the possession of Beauty.

To take but one simple example, the average person might be said to have an eminently justifiable, positive, common-sense reaction to the powerful feeling and experience of sexual passion. Nevertheless, without the right words and arguments to explain his "opinions" regarding this formidable *force de la nature*, he is not able to relate the meaning of his reaction to experience properly; not even to himself. Pragmatic efforts to gain the full promise of sexuality and cause it to work together with other deeply felt experiences about which he has positive "opinions" are even further out of his reach. It is the rhetorician who illuminates Everyman through the use of appropriate and stimulating words, demonstrating the key to sexual understanding and its link with the multitude of other desirable goals.

But how will Everyman know that the rhetorician is "speaking appropriately?" The answer to this question is also an obvious one. For the master rhetorician's advice will not only "sound right"; clearly, consistently and self-assuredly responding to the average individual's personal sense of the obvious truth of his own preoccupations, and where, more or less, those concerns are headed. Beyond that, it will prove itself by being crowned with success. Hence, Isocrates' recognition of his need to underline the simplicity, lucidity, harmony of purpose, confidence, and material achievements of his pupils, while contrasting them with the cranky and unfathomable detours, self-criticisms, bitter divisions, and practical failures of the Socratics.

Isocrates longed to prove rhetoric's ability to gain possession of the Beautiful on a grand, world scale. In order for him to find the key to such great success, the philosopher/rhetorician had to begin with the study of the raw experiences and the common-sense reaction to them not merely of an individual, but of an entire people, since only a city-state or nation could conceivably become a long-term driving force in global events. The work of

Herodotus (484–424 B. C.), Thucydides (mid-400s–403 B. C.?), Xenophon (430?–355 B. C.?) and others offered guidelines as to how such historical data might be collected. Rhetoricians like Isocrates saw one of their tasks as being that of explaining to a population the appropriate greatness to which its otherwise "dumb" historical experiences were calling it. History thus came very early under rhetorical purview and influence, partly to its profit, since it became more readable, dramatic and effective, but very often to its severe detriment, being transformed into a tool for propaganda.

From the raw history of his environment, Isocrates claimed to learn a number of important principles: that there actually was a Greek people, united by a shared culture, Hellenism; that the essence of Hellenism was the development of the illuminating, life-giving, and unifying "word"; that the universal value accruing from appropriate use of "the word" gave to a Greece which possessed knowledge of its significance a world-wide cultural mission; and, finally, that this universal vocation had been shown to involve the sea, struggle against Persia, and imperial expansion.

Fulfillment of future Hellenist destiny would require two things simultaneously. On the one hand, it was crucial to maintain a constant respect for the "good old days" of the foundation of the Greek spirit and the institutions giving clout to it. On the other, it was necessary to shape a loyal population obedient to any vigorous strongman who might guide that spirit to the discharge of its contemporary mission. Moreover, the institutions embodying the spirit of the good old days, the strongman giving them clout and the populations obedient to his fist, were to be stirred to their appropriate political roles through the vital words of the creative rhetorical genius.

But "philosophy," as defined by Isocrates, can easily constitute a gigantic circle, manipulated by the rhetorician who, through the clever use of appealing words and images, may seize control of the familiar concerns of the average man or State and run with them where he wills. Common sense experience is pronounced the infallible basis for action simply because the experience appealed to is declared "common sensical" and an infallible basis for action. Successful attainment of riches and power is said to prove the appropriateness of the rhetorician's understanding of the beautiful life and ability to guide Everyman to fulfill its promise because possession of riches and power is presented as unquestionable, axiomatic proof that beauty has indeed been grasped. Respect for the "good old days," contemporary strongmen and obedient populations are essential, because denial of such esteem to any one of these elements would rip apart the "beautiful" rhetorical image tying together ancient roots with present hopes and future destiny, mass popularity and elite power. And all those aspects of "the vision" were necessary, since experience had proven them necessary to construct the career of the master of words, whose success worked to guarantee the validity of their union.

Absolutely no questioning of "obvious experience," "common sense," "success," the "historic mission" and the consistency of the tools required for its realization could be contemplated, lest this lead to the unacceptable argument that obvious experience, common sense, success, the historical mission and its vital tools were themselves somewhat problematic. Isocrates makes a virtue out of abandoning any deeper investigation of the meaning of life once he has shaped what for him appears to be a rhetorically beautiful "point of view" with a chance of obtaining a successful outcome. That "point of view," if attractive and potentially useful, must be accepted as though it were Truth itself. With this, the debate is over. Closure has been achieved. One must move on to accomplishment of the Great Promise, or face the wrath of the rhetorician and the outraged nature whose infallible voice he has infallibly proclaimed himself to be.

And the rhetorician is powerful. He knows that his words have "the ring of truth." He knows that he can count on the support of immediately-felt, individual, family or polis-wide "common sense" passions in his call for their immediate satisfaction. He senses the understandable and well-nigh universal fear that acceptance of Socratic self-criticism would paralyze swift action, thus preventing exploitation of favorable opportunities to fulfill desire, and causing men to "lose out" on success, perhaps even up to the very moment of death. The rhetorician, with his mastery of words, can paint the profound, life-determining, "either-or" option offered to men by Sophists and Socratics in all of its dramatic colors, though clearly weighted to his advantage. After he has skillfully organized the picture as he wishes, any Socratic who calls the average man to logical, painful soul-searching at the possible expense of satisfying urgent passion becomes a sitting duck for his rhetorical abuse. A Platonic philosopher would all too easily lend himself to the accusation of representing both a crackpot idealism, indifferent to the obvious demands of human nature, as well as a cynical opposition to the successes of "real men" whom he cannot emulate, bitterly envies, and wishes to destroy in consequence.

Plato was not just a Socratic philosopher but a literary genius in his own right, sensitive to the power of purely rhetorical arguments over the average man, and the need to respond to them "beautifully" to demonstrate their flaws. He did so reply, by depicting the pure rhetorician as an ultimately self-deluding failure. Yes, Plato argued, the Sophist rhetorician was influential. But contrary to his claim that that influence came from his role as a wise man teaching individuals and states what the beautiful was all about and how to get possession of it, the impact actually and ironically was exercised precisely due to his inability to educate those whom he professed to be illuminating. For the "word" spoken by the rhetorician styling himself to be a philosopher could itself never rise above "dumb" opinion. It merely illustrated the trained man's ability effectively to flatter people's fancies. Rhetoricians possessed what Plato called a "knack" of appealing to a particular appetite, like that of a cook in a fast-food restaurant, ignoring entirely the question of whether such an admittedly successful flattery and knack ought to have been indulged in the first place.

The successful rhetorician deceives himself into thinking that he is superior to his "wordless" audience, but he is simply more effectively "thick and stupid" than it is. His words resemble an overbearing and endlessly repeated rock rhythm in a room filled with impressionable, but musically illiterate, hedonists. They fail to elevate, just as any tool that uses man rather than God as the measure of all things falls miserably short of its pretensions. Anyone responding to the "either-or" option confronting him by choosing for the rhetorician would, therefore, be voting for eternal mediocrity and blindness. Sadly, precisely due to the rhetorician's observable knack for maintaining power over the vulgar mob, the pathetic outcome of such a wrong choice could conceivably be hidden from its victims forever. False rhetorical "philosophers" only needed to do two things: 1) enthusiastically to invent ever "new" surface variants on the proven appealing slogans to keep men thinking that fulfillment of the brilliant promise of the Empty Life lay just around the corner; and, 2) constantly to drill into a benumbed population's mind the fear of the "dead-end" impotence that the Socratic hunt for a more profound goal would ensure.

One of Plato's painful labors was that of explaining embarrassing instances of this seeming Socratic impotence, the disaster of his own political missions to Dion in Sicily in 388 and 367 being primary among them. Such shipwrecks, he insisted, were not attributable to true philosophy's innate inability to navigate effectively. Rather, they were simply another confirmation of the difficulty and very infancy of the task that the real lover of Beauty, Goodness and Truth had set for himself. Yes, he admitted, philosophy needed the aid of rhetoric, of the lesser "word" to explain itself successfully to a world filled with ambiguous though powerful passions, and to convince it to change its ways. But that secondary "word" must always be subordinated to a deeper Word, the Logos towards whose ultimate knowledge it was meant to be employed. Alas, at least in Plato's own day, it had proven to be "hard to find the creator and father of the world," and "impossible to describe his nature publicly." Men could not yet be guided properly to the divine imitation that would definitely perfect them and give them possession of the Beautiful. As dilemmas went, this certainly was a killer, and Plato feared that it would remain an unresolved one unless "some God" came to the earth to unravel it.

Faulty or not, the ideas of his opponents did more than those of the Socratics to form that mixed Greek/Middle Eastern/Latin civilization which we call the Hellenistic world. This new reality certainly did demonstrate the literal value of the Greek language, whose superiority in transmitting manifold, complex concepts became universally recognized. It also reflected all of the potential practical consequences of a cosmos shaped by a purely rhetorical "word" alone. For Hellenistic civilization was one that did indeed work for the "common sense" benefit of those "vigorous strongmen" praised by the rhetorician as essential for fulfillment of its mission. These leaders learned to create and manipulate powerful state machinery for the purpose of keeping the "dumb" mass of the population in obedient submission. Such "doers of great deeds," from

Alexander through to the Caesars and the Senatorial Aristocracy of the Roman Empire that worked with them, were even willing to tolerate satisfaction of certain specific, immediate desires of the multi-cultural, pluralist world over which they ruled, so long as its constituent elements accepted "closure" regarding matters that might disturb what really counted: the personal power, wealth and fame of the victors. And rhetoricians galore gained a decent income justifying the order thus created. (For this discussion, see Peter Green, *Alexander to Actium. The Historical Evolution of the Hellenistic Age*, University of California, 1993; Also, Peter Brown, *The World of Late Antiquity, 150–700*, Harcourt Brace, 1971; Moses Hadas, *A History of Greek Literature* and *A History of Latin Literature*, Columbia University, 1950 & 1952; Hans Jonas, *The Gnostic Religion*, Beacon, 1963; Jean Mayeur et al., eds., *Histoire du Christianisme*, Volume 1, Desclée, 2000)

Rhetoricians were very active from the 300s B. C. through the 300s A. D., providing the Hellenistic cosmos, or *ecumene*, the arguments proving that the debate over who possessed the things that made life beautiful, and what those things were, was over. They contributed mightily to efforts to overcome "parochial" religious "superstitions" whose concerns might threaten the Status Quo. Such integration of divisive elements involved publicizing the need to submit to and adore the divinity of the State apparatus and the self-made men who dominated it. "Closure" had been achieved in the realm of the gods as well as that of men, and the "word" could now "move on" to "get the ordinary job of living done."

It moved on by devoting itself to legal and civil service careers, and to sickly praise or boring, encyclopedic chronicling of the existing, unchangeable order of things, thereby sharing in any trickle-down benefits the Divine Rulers supposedly in the service of a Great Vision permitted. It moved on by finding substantial employment producing that esoteric, archaic and pointless heap of pretty sounds and properly placed commas adulated by exclusivist literary circles. Failing that, it moved on by churning out pornographic material for the gross diversions of a rabble ever tempted to accept subordination and abandon true enlightenment for cheap material satiety.

The spiral downward from the more sophisticated "apologetic" writings and literary achievements of earlier Hellenistic regimes to the servile, pedantic and vulgar *oeuvre* of much of the so-called Second Sophistic of the 2nd through 4th Centuries, A. D. is instructive. Plato, for one, would not have been surprised by the decline, since he had argued that word merchants indifferent to true philosophy were destined to a low-class butchering of even their own legitimate art and talent. One need only consult the biographies and stories to be found in Aulius Gellius' (123–165) *Attic Nights*, the 2nd Philostratus' (c. 170–248) *Lives of the Sophists*, Eunapius' (346–414) *Lives of the Philosophers and Sophists*, Diogenes Laertius' (no later than 200s) *Lives of Eminent Philosophers*, and Athenaeus of Naucratis' (200s) *Doctors at Dinner* to test the validity of his hypothesis.

But what about the Socratic opposition? What about their war with immediate appearances and superficial judgment? Did not the grasping of the Hellenistic Monarchies far surpass that of Athens and Sparta at the time of the height of the Peloponnesian War and its aftermath, when Socrates himself had shown that the call to possession of a flawed Beauty could never, in the long-run, satisfy either the population or the very tyrants misleading it? Was there not a fraud to be identified and corrected here? Or had some mystery of iniquity done its job, quieting the outrage of the true philosopher?

Alas, philosophy had generally been tamed, adapting itself nicely to the depressing, conformist, "common sense" rules established and rhetorically justified by a combination of power-worshipping adventurers and sophists. This was partially due to certain innate weaknesses of the Socratics and subsequent powerful, related schools of thought like Stoicism. Aristotelians retreated into their cubbyholes of knowledge, working in spheres that did not have to bring up the big questions disturbing to the Status Quo. Neo-Platonists, even while conducting a truly exalted discussion of the Hierarchy of Being leading to clarification of the final, divine, unchangeable principle of the universe, also became propagandists for the powers that be. They were fearful that any disorder and alteration in the political and social world could open the path to what they considered to be a totally unacceptable conception of change, willfulness and unpredictable action affecting one's notion of the character of the very Godhead itself. Stoic insistence on the purpose-filled structure of the universe tempted it, in the absence of a concept of sin, into treating accommodation to the successful status quo as though it were obedience to the will of God. Acceptance of the idea of the purpose lying behind every aspect of natural life also convinced many Stoics that crude popular experiences of reality, including truly offensive superstitious practices, should be approached seriously as well. Plato's effective rhetorical use of allegory could be called upon, though in reverse, to show the more "sophisticated" (dare we say "appropriate?") meaning expressed through their vulgar exterior peculiarities.

But none of this would work if the populations thus "guided" by the rhetoricians and their allies did not in some way respond to the song which was sung to them. This the majority of them seem to have done, dealing with the bewildering change backed by willful men and their propagandists by going on vacation to a never-never-land where native beliefs and customs which did not shake the Established Order could still be maintained. Many ancient Greeks, Romans and Near Easterners took this holiday of denial, stunned as they were by the innovations accompanying the multicultural empires shaping their world beginning with the conquests of Alexander the Great (336–323 B. C.) and continuing down to the eve of the victory of Christianity. Once arriving in never-never-land, they often even denied that anything new and dangerous had actually entered into their lives at all. In order to obtain permission for traditionalist never-never-land games, however, the visitors to these varied ancient playgrounds had to collaborate with the existing system and its rulers on those matters that really guided their practical lives. Forget about simply avoiding anything which might give offense to the powers that be. Personal security required that they enthusiastically praise the divinity of the Establishment oppressing them. And this they readily did: over and over again.

Beyond that, collaboration for the truly powerful might entail the shouldering of active obligations to the divine monarchs of the age before rushing home to the more pleasant task of cultivating impotence. Collaboration, for the weak, might mean just working, paying taxes, and never transgressing the sacred wall separating private fantasy from social and political reality. Most collaborators kept the wheels of the regime machinery going because they did not wish to risk their necks by openly opposing it; some since they had become so used to its gears that they took them for granted as an unquestionable given, maintaining ties with their own oppressed traditions through pure inertia. A few of those who collaborated were fully co-opted by their masters. They became fervent propagandists for the new order, alongside the official rhetorical class, even hoping to be accepted into its inner circles.

Of course, not everyone confronted by bewildering change, backed by force and justified through rhetorical bombast, went down the escapist-collaborationist path. A respectable number reacted to such transformations by militantly taking up arms against them, and this often outside of those legitimate structures of their societies which had cowardly or unthinkingly opted for an accommodating posture. But such a path was fraught with danger as well. On the one hand lay the overwhelming power of the existing order of things. On the other, stood the tendency of initial opponents of the Status Quo eager for success so to adopt the same approach as their enemies as to become indistinguishable from them. Such men masqueraded their transformation by unceasingly referring back to their past glories, seeking to hide their treason through reiteration of their former, justified designation as "defenders of the faith." One can point most effectively in this regard to the change of the Maccabees from Jewish martyrs and confessors into typical Hellenistic tyrants.

All this is not to say that that those tyrants and their propagandists were necessarily "fulfilled" human persons. How could they be, unless one truly believes that their pathway is indeed the pathway to individual perfection? Plato himself insisted that the tyrant had to be the least contented of all men. And, in point of fact, the elite of the Status Quo were shot through with discontent, and not just that expressed by material dissatisfaction. Some of the elite themselves retreated into the never-never-lands of the ineffectual philosophical clubs. Others "went native," seeking meaning in the local gods of conquered lands, gods whose labors could be construed, through Hellenism, to signify something much more universal than Egyptians or Mesopotamians had ever thought possible. A few even went so far as to adore the strangest god of all, the god of the Jews. But the Status Quo remained unchanged through it all.

Something "other," the intervention of "some god," as Plato indicated, was needed in order to fight this unchangeable beast. Only the intervention of a force from the outside could inject new strength into sufficiently large numbers of the "dumb" population— which, by this point, included not only ordinary individuals but the philosophers as well—and elevate and stiffen its awareness of the real Drama of Truth in which they were players, and strike some fear into the opposition. That new force arrived with the Incarnation. And with the arrival of the Incarnation, a War Between the Words and the Word truly began in earnest.

19

THE TALLINN LECTURES
II. Christianity and Naturalism†
THE EUROPEAN PURSUIT OF HEAVEN & HELL

A. CHRISTIANITY — THE ACCEPTANCE, CORRECTION,
TRANSFORMATION AND ENCOURAGEMENT OF
POPULAR BELIEF IN THE VALUE OF NATURE

The Greeks were clearly open to nature's "voice." Nevertheless, a number of the greatest of the Hellenes became convinced that a proper opening to the cosmos and a discovery of the true path to gaining possession of its beauty, required looking behind the shallow surface of things to understand their broader and deeper messages: their inner "reason" or "logos." We have noted that signs of a spirit both accepting and yet more intensely questioning can be found in Homer, the work of lyric poets such as Solon the Lawgiver, the classical dramatists, the first philosophers, and finally and most importantly, in the discussions of the Socratics.

Among the many lessons that Greek civilization learned through this receptive but inquiring outlook, two stand out as being of special importance because of their relationship to Christianity. The first was the need, on the one hand, for communal life and social authority in order to achieve the individual's perfection, and the simultaneous necessity, on the other, for individual perfection so as to appreciate the correct use of community and its authoritative agents. A second lesson, stressed in an emphatic way by Plato and his followers, was the value of continuing the hunt for an ever-greater infusion of intellectual and spiritual "light." More and more light was essential for the proper understanding of exactly how the individual and society were to resolve the seemingly insoluble dilemma outlined by lesson number one: i.e., that of achieving a joint individual and social perfection. Plato himself had suggested that perhaps some new divine light might

---

† Lecture given at the TriaLogos Festival in Tallinn, Estonia, on September 27, 2007.

have to penetrate into the shadows of the aspiring soul and the communities in which he lived before a satisfactory result could ever be obtained.

It was some centuries later, during the first decades of the Roman Principate, that the closed cosmos of the post-Alexandrine Hellenistic World was tossed history's greatest and most beneficent "curveball." At that time, the Father of Lights indeed did intervene in the world, through the Incarnation of His Son, the Second Person of the Blessed Trinity, as Jesus Christ, the God-Man. The Incarnation presented the individual in particular and society in general with fresh "light"; a new factor to deal with in each and every one of their daily calculations about the meaning of life and how to fulfill it. Both were now obliged to accept or to reject the permanent presence in life of a natural force which also claimed that it was divine; divine, that is to say, in a supernatural, and thus qualitatively different manner than Hellenistic rulers were considered to be divinities. Society and the individual had to come to terms with a God who worked to provide access to the supremely True, Good and Beautiful in a personal, flesh-and-blood fashion, through two tightly linked bodies: the physical, human body of the God-Man Jesus Christ to begin with, and that of His Mystical Body, His Church, thereafter.

The Light coming from the Incarnation through Christ and His Church teaches wholehearted acceptance of the purpose and value of the natural world that God Himself created out of the deepest supernatural love. But that Light also teaches that mankind, marred by our first parents' bad use of freedom—Original Sin—has a fallen tendency to be guided by the dictates of what might be called a "raw paganism." This raw paganism pushes men to an unquestioning acceptance of the mere appearance of things; to an indulgence in the immediate passions and quickly perceived needs of both individuals and communities. Such appearances, passions and needs were unquestioningly accepted by the "raw" pagan world because they just "were there" and were thus supposedly "obvious" to everyone.

Christianity joined its voice with that of the great Hellenes who argued that nature cannot be accepted "as it is," and must be probed for an understanding of its deeper messages instead. For Christianity also saw that much of what individuals and societies passionately desire are reflections not of truly natural longings but, rather, of unnatural perceptions concerning what the world around them can and ought to give them. Like its Socratic precursor, it taught that giving in to these passions is dangerous for the community and for the individual alike, deforming their real natural character still further. Hence the need for correction of flawed perceptions regarding nature and the consequences of acting unthinkingly upon their dictates.

But Christian correction is of a different order than that offered by even the best of the Greeks. It recognizes that nature is marred because the bad use of freedom has brought sin into the world, and because that sin affects man and society more deeply than the poets and the Socratics could have imagined. Sin's corrupting consequences are so serious that they can even lead those seeking honestly to probe the inner meaning of the things of nature to make mistakes, and thereby guide the individual and his communities further astray.

Thus, for Christianity, a full correction of a fallen nature's flaws can only be obtained through membership in the society of Christ and the Mystical Body which is His Church. For, once again, life in Christ and His Church offers supernatural community and supernatural light: a new and qualitatively different kind of community and light; the final community and the final infusion of Light required to complete the individual's knowledge of both himself and the rest of nature. Such community and such Light not only accept and correct the created universe; they also elevate and transform the natural world which responds to their teaching and their gift of new life.

They do so because they grant the individual and the natural societies in which they live the possibility of seeing all of nature and their specific roles and responsibilities within them through the eyes of Christ; in the way that God sees them. Such sight gives to men and society the opportunity to grasp and complete the coordination of the hierarchy of values in a supremely coherent, rational, though rationally unfathomable manner. It is this vision that permits the individual, the most dignified part of nature, to become all that he can be, and each community and activity in which he participates to fulfill its potential along with him, thereby overcoming Plato's dilemma. This joint individual and social perfection creates a truly diverse "multiplicity in unity" mirroring and prefiguring the still greater perfection and diversity of eternal life. It thus can bring a responsive universe to as superhuman a perfection as is possible for a created and dependent cosmos, preparing men and women for the full life of an eternity with God to experience.

The emergence of such perfection and diversity in unity cannot be predicted in some legalist or mechanist fashion, and this for two basic reasons. First of all, precisely because individuals and societies are indeed all so unique, and new persons are continually being born into them—persons who act, historically, in their own particular way—no ironclad formula for their precise correction and transformation within the Mystical Body of Christ can ever be provided. Individuals and societies are participants in a kind of dance whose basic character and rhythms are indeed known, but whose exact execution cannot be foretold until it is performed; and this again and again until the end of time.

Secondly, the continued reality of sin allows for the possibility that the entire ballroom of life can be willfully disrupted by anyone at each and every moment, and in many varying ways. This cannot help but render the Christian transformation of nature, with all of its exalted consequences, an unpredictable and quite fragile Drama of Truth, Goodness and Beauty. Hence, the essential need for Christians to be vigilant and insistent. They must be vigilant to make certain that every single natural tool available to man for the fulfillment of God's plan always be honored and utilized, with none of them ever arbitrarily abandoned as somehow historically obsolete and superfluous. They must be insistent on an energetic effort completely to evangelize all individuals and all societies, since any attempt to keep the Truth and its full consequences for oneself alone would display a lack of charity working mightily against the will of God and one's own self-perfection as well.

Christianity clearly practiced what it preached regarding the value of Creation, as can readily be seen in the employment that it made of the past natural achievements of the classical Greco-Roman world. So reverently did it utilize Socratic philosophy that it can be said to have given that small and often timid group of men who were attempting to use their Reason to understand and take possession of the beauty of the natural world the courage really to believe in and act upon what they had learned. Moreover, the light, grace and supernatural strength of the Incarnation allowed Christianity to perfect and order all of the powerful natural tools of a popular religion in order to spread the otherwise "elitist" philosophical enterprise and give this courage to believe in and act upon its conclusions to the mass of the population. Faith, in other words, brought Reason to fruition.

Catholic grasp of the full meaning of the Incarnation and its consequences for nature deepened enormously over the centuries. Although it is impossible for me in this short talk to speak of that historical development of doctrine in detail, I can at least mention some of the key figures and events central to it: 1) the Church Apologists and Fathers. These included men like St. Justin Martyr (100s, A. D.) with his teaching concerning the existence of pre-Christian "Seeds of the Logos," brought to completion by the Incarnation, as well as those great Cappadocian Doctors (300s) who were deeply concerned for the harmonization of the whole of classical culture with Christian Revelation; 2) St. Maximus the Confessor (600s), whose interpretation of the hierarchy of values demonstrated the intrinsic importance of each of nature's varied elements, from lowest to highest, in reflecting the glory of the Creator God; 3) the Iconoclast Controversy (700s–800s), which led to a recognition both of nature's general iconic role, as well as the fact that its "symbolic" existence truly points to and means something eternally substantive and real; 4) the effort to transform everyone and everything in Christ promoted by the medieval reform movement, from the period of monastic revival in the 900s through the work of Pope Innocent III and St. Francis of Assisi in the 1200s; 5) the fight of the Catholic Reformation of the 1500s and 1600s for the correction and exaltation of nature, nobly represented by the Society of Jesus in its dedication of all life to "the greater glory of God"; and, finally, 6) the nineteenth century movement of Catholic revival following the devastation wrought by Regalism, Jansenism, the naturalist Enlightenment and the secularization of society of the 1700s, even before the events of the French Revolution. (For a deeper study of the above argument, students should examine Emile Mersch, *The Whole Christ*, Herder, 1949; and Werner

Jaeger, *Early Christianity and Greek Paideia*, Harvard, 1961; Also, George Goyau, *L'Allemagne Religieuse*, Le Catholicisme, Paris, 1905, four volumes; J. M. Mayeur et al., eds., *Histoire du Christianisme*, Desclée, 1990–2000, thirteen volumes; John Rao, *Removing the Blindfold*, Angelus Press, 2014).

B. THE GRAND COALITION ON BEHALF OF THE UNEXAMINED LIFE

Christianity, from the standpoint of the many conscious and unconscious followers of Isocrates who wished to give an "appropriate explanation" of human experience and aspiration based upon the acceptance of nature "as it is," thus had to appear to be an infinitely more hideous and dangerous force than Plato, with his limited, elite audience. Here was another voice rejecting immediate satisfaction of individual and communal desires, and demanding correction of nature "as it is"; a voice with much greater popular appeal, and with new and much more mysterious arguments involving the transformation of Creation as part of a work of personal sanctification leading individuals to eternal perfection and satisfaction.

Varied groups hostile to Christianity thus began almost immediately to create what might be called a Grand Coalition on Behalf of the Unexamined Life; or, perhaps better still, a Grand Coalition in Defense of the Natural Status Quo. This Grand Coalition was composed of all those who insisted upon putting limits on questions concerning nature's flaws, not to speak of actions aimed at their possible correction.

Gnostics who thought that nothing good could ever be done with anything in nature—either "as it is" or through some utterly impossible correction of its hideous and total depravity—were obvious and active members of this alliance. Still, we are primarily concerned here with the less extreme elements which chiefly swelled its ranks. These members included everyone from the average "raw pagan" individual and community wishing easy justification for their self-interested actions, to those philosophers disturbed by the injection of a popular universal religion into their closed, elitist, intellectual clubhouse. Rhetorically-skilled "Word Merchants" joined the Grand Coalition as well. Their formidable talents were needed to prevent the opening of a fresh discussion of the validity of satisfying the "obvious" needs of the strong men of the ancient world. Word Merchants had profitably served such masters for centuries and thus had their own self-interested motives for calling upon the physical assistance of divinized rulers to crush a Christian foe posing them a common threat. (See, for the above, Hans Jonas, *The Gnostic Religion*, Beacon, 1963; Marta Sordi, *The Christians and the Roman Empire*, Routledge, 1998; R. L. Wilkens, *The Christians as the Romans Saw Them*, Yale, 1984; Also, *Histoire du Christianisme*, Volume 1, 2000).

All of the "either/or" arguments applied against Plato were resurrected by such non-gnostic Coalition members with telling effect in this new, more intense anti-Christian context. Those who accepted Catholicism were depicted as almost inhuman "losers"; as a kind of "third race," neither male nor female, dehumanized by their rage against "real life" and its obvious pleasures. Anti-Christians accepting nature "as it is," were again shown to be the "winners" in life's game, their status as true philosophers proven by "successes" whose clear definition and value could, yet once more, never seriously be discussed and questioned.

Although the Catholic vision did gain official acceptance by the Roman Empire and its successor states in the West, and this powerful Grand Coalition seemed to go "underground" from the Fifth through the Eleventh Centuries, the Church never won anything close to a complete victory over it. How could she have done so? Christians also had to fight a ceaseless battle against that strong temptation to accept nature "as it is" which was presented them by their opponents. For the struggle to correct and transform nature was a war against tendencies rooted in each and every flawed human heart; rooted in endless sentimental ties to flawed or simply incomplete customs and habits passed down to Christians along with everyone else from time immemorial. In many cases, it took long centuries before believers realized the extent to which their own unexamined presuppositions about life blinded them to the fullness of the correction taught and made possible by the Incarnation. In fact, the complete transformation in Christ to which it calls all men remains in many ways still unperceived by the faithful as much as by non-believers today.

What happened from the 1000s onwards is well described by that Nineteenth and Twentieth Century Catholic revival movement already mentioned above. Emerging out of various clerical and lay circles and benefiting from the support of the Papacy after the shock of the Revolutions of 1848, this movement shared its age's interest in exploring the historical development of ideas and institutions. Its effort to understand the disastrous loss of Faith in the century preceding 1789, and the easy assimilation by Catholics themselves of one or the other manifestations of the Enlightenment vision of life, led many of its proponents to study just how the Grand Coalition had been reconstituted. This work of reconstitution they described as an anti-Incarnational Crusade, spurred on, in the first instance, by the heightened rage of the supporters of nature "as it is" over the medieval successes of Catholicism in transforming all things in Christ.

The Grand Coalition on Behalf of the Unexamined Life slowly came back into existence by seeking to turn against Christianity one after the other of the natural tools that Catholics themselves had claimed for their own use and transformed into instruments employed for the greater glory of God: "Seeds of the Logos" ranging from Socratic Philosophy and Roman Law to the corpus of Greco-Roman literature. It did so by emphasizing the natural self-sufficiency of each of these tools and, hence, their freedom from the pronouncements of the "Incarnational Law" that had been elaborated by Catholics over the centuries to correct and transform them.

More and more, from the Renaissance beginning in the Fourteenth Century through the Enlightenment of the Eighteenth, the theme of Mother Nature as a whole and her need for freedom from judgment by any outside force was "seized" upon to fight the full Catholic vision. But just as Plato's elevation of the status of philosophy had forced Isocrates to abandon the more humdrum and vocational definition the sophists had previously given to it, the propagandists of the Grand Coalition were forced to operate within the context of the exalted Catholic call to transformation and perfection of nature. Hence, the Grand Coalition's initial glorification of the sublime order and purpose of the universe, along with its emphasis upon the peculiar dignity of the individual human person as a microcosm of cosmic magnificence.

Acceptance of nature "as it is," on its own terms and presumably sinless, was now said to offer the possibility of understanding the universe's true (enhanced) order and putting that (exalted) order to use to secure the (infinitely greater) dignity of the individual human persons living within it. On the other hand, the need for nature's transformation through correction of its supposed flaws was identified both as an assault upon its integrity and potential and an insult to the skill of the Creator God in constructing it in the first place. Once more, acceptance of nature "as it is" was justified on the grounds of an evident common sense that laughed away as a pointless waste of time the need for deeper philosophical and theological discussion of the appearance of things. (For the above, see George de la Garde, *La Naissance de l'Esprit Laique au Declin du Moyen Age*, Beatrices, 1934, three volumes; Also, Carl Becker, *The Heavenly City of the Eighteenth Century Philosophers*, Yale, 1932; Christopher Dawson, *The Dividing of Christendom*, Sheed & Ward, 1965; Peter Gay, *The Enlightenment: The Rise of Modern Paganism*, Norton, 1977; John Rao, *Removing the Blindfold*, Angelus Press, 2014; and Chapter 10 of this volume, "Half the Business of Destruction Done").

New "Word Merchants," fishing in ancient rhetorical waters, learned and even improved upon the skills enabling them to propagandize the growing anti-incarnational cause with an effectiveness similar to that of the anti-Socratic movement of past times and the early persecution of the Church. Just as might have been expected, the late ancient depiction of the Christian as the ultimate "loser," the man who questions the obvious gifts of existence, re-emerged from the netherworld. That battery of "Black Legends," already created in paleo-Christian times and playing on the theme of Christianity as the Enemy of the Natural Order, the Natural Man and Nature's God, was resurrected, expanded upon and refined. All of Isocrates' arguments against Plato came back to life along with them. These were augmented with horror stories outlining the ghoulish character of that wicked period when the Christian Beast imposed upon a beneficent nature its ugly and unnatural reign of terror. Even though these legends and the arguments confirming them were generally contrived and actually hid the central either/or issue—whether nature ought to be accepted "as it is" or not, and what the consequences of one's answer to this question really were—they gained a widespread credibility.

One crucial reason for their credibility was the extremely clever manner in which they were now presented: simultaneously high-minded and grand in scope while starkly simple and popular in form. Yet again, just as Isocrates needed to have a high-minded structure for his vision, given Plato's raising of a world view to a new, more elevated, coherent plane, high-mindedness in a high-minded, Incarnation-steeped environment was a requirement for the Black Legends. High-minded grandeur was achieved by once more "seizing images" evoking the nobility of an anti-incarnational spirit contested tooth-and-nail by a base and wicked Christian opponent; gripping, magnificent images of enduring significance, detailing the Struggle for Freedom and Dignity against Catholic Slavery and Human Self-Debasement.

Simplicity was added to grandeur by incarnating this eschatological battle of obvious good versus palpable evil in easily recognizable and contrasting stereotypes: e.g., noble, persecuted, naturalist philosophers, scientists, crusading journalists and freedom fighters on the one hand; stupid, obscurantist, often insane, conspiratorial, tyrannical, persecuting popes, priests, monks, mother superiors, mystics, scholastics and all their lay slaves or cynical masters on the other.

Popularity was then pursued by promotion of the grand, seized image, incarnated in simplistic, embattled stereotypes, through a mixture of demonstrably appealing forms: in songs, novels and pamphlets; on stage; in rabble-rousing, press-guided *causes célèbres*; through the *bons mots* of upper class salons translated by their influential *habitués* into grounds for dealing decisive socio-political blows against the Catholic Sect; by means of a brutal ridicule which avoided substantive argument the more that it hammered the believer into the mud. Points were even effectively scored and high-minded lessons popularly taught through a selective silence, which subtly showed that Catholics and Catholicism were not to be mentioned by rational men when topics of political or social importance were under serious discussion.

Responses to Black Legends constructed in this fashion are always terribly tedious and time-consuming. Remember that the very meaning of common words which teach the wisdom and goodness of the enemy, and the idiocy and evil of Catholics, have themselves been consistently seized and battered into acceptable shape along with the particular image which the mythmakers have embraced. Catholics entering the fray after the damage has been done find that they need to convince the population to re-examine the way in which each and every term has been defined by their enemies in order to uncover the game that they are play-ing. The public's mind already has been molded according to the anti-incarnational spirit, and thus takes the existing, anti-Catholic meaning of words like "freedom," "dignity" and "love" for granted as being the absolutely obvious dictate of "common sense."

If one argues that any given "seized image" is founded upon historical inaccuracies, its artisans may well claim that it is not the literal meaning of a specific event which ultimately counts, but the absolutely valid "Mission Statement" which the rhetorically reconstructed historical "record" embodies. After all, only super-ficial, obscurantist pedants would adore all the petty particulars of a dead past!

Then, should the Catholic apologist still refuse to surrender, and boldly attack the fundamental truth of that Mission State-ment, its "real" historical foundation, with all of the previously ridiculed trivial details, will be reasserted and further dissemi-nated. Rational Catholic refutation of the veracity of the Mis-sion Statement will once again be buried under heaps of familiar, dubious, exaggerated, stereotypical illustrations of ultramontan-ist stupidity and brutality of proven popular appeal. Even men and women without firm views on the issues in question will be entertained by the dramatic "historical" wrapping in which the Black Legends are presented, and pass by their scholarly, point-by-point denial with a deep and drawn-out yawn. The average man, both the basically intelligent as well as the hopelessly ignorant, will instinctively draw from the legendary well whenever called upon to make some passing comment on Catholic thought and behavior, or carry out his ordinary daily actions, many of them of immensely practical importance.

Moreover, seized images and their Mission Statements, cari-catures and the popular tools used to drive them home, all have an accordion-like flexibility. They can readily be changed, based upon what temporarily "works" most effectively against the hated Catholic enemy. By the time believers finally realize how histori-cally and intellectually false one particular assault upon them is; at the moment they understand the exact way in which Catholics are stereotyped through caricatures cleverly disseminated; just

when they discover a workable means of popularly and successfully answering (and ridiculing) their opponents themselves; the
seized image and the Mission Statement its stereotypes embody
are changed: sometimes slightly, sometimes drastically. Catholics
are then left to direct their artillery against a fortress which their
enemies have completely dismantled and abandoned as strategi-
cally insignificant.

Catholic thinkers, smarting from the blows delivered by the
Enlightenment and the Revolution, came to see that eighteenth
century Christians had been overwhelmed by the naturalist Black
Legend attack upon them. They had become so demoralized that
they themselves had adopted much of the language of their opponents, seeking to defend their religion by actually enlisting in the
crusade to end its supposed supernatural humbug. This placed
them in an impossible, indeed pathetic, situation, making them
appear to hover between the illogical and the hypocritical. Such an
awkward position was then easily exploited by revolutionary activists appealing to Rousseau's emphasis upon "sincerity" as the path
to the truly natural life. One has only to look at the confrontation
between a believing but baffled Catholic like Louis XVI and his
Rousseau-inspired persecutors to grasp how such confusion could
be exploited to create the impression of hypocrisy and deception.
(Useful for the above as well as for later illustrations of the phe-
nomenon are James H. Billington, *Fire in the Minds of Men*, Basic
Books, 1980; Carol Blum, *Rousseau and the Republic of Virtue*,
Cornell, 1986; William J. Bouwsma, *Venice and the Defense of
Republican Liberty*, California, 1968; R. Darnton, *The Literary
Underground of the Old Regime*, Harvard, 1982; M. Leroy, *Le
Mythe Jesuite de Béranger à Michelet*, PUF, 1992, J. W. Merrick,
*The Desacralization of the French Monarchy in the Eighteenth
Century*, Louisiana State, 1990; Philips, H., *Church and Culture
in Seventeenth-Century France*, Harvard, 1997; Chapter 32 of this
volume, "He Who Loses the Past, Loses the Present"; Chapter 10
of this volume, "Half the Business of Destruction Done"; H. M.
Scott, *Enlightenment Absolutism*, University of Michigan, 1990;
and, perhaps most importantly, D. Van Kley, *The Religious Origins
of the French Revolution*, Yale, 1996).

Proponents of Catholic revival understood that Church effectiveness could only be assured by a return to a wholehearted

embrace of her supernatural origin in the Incarnation and a full appreciation of what that Incarnation brings along with it in its train. They saw that the more that Catholics grasped the significance of the Incarnation, the more clearly they would realize just how their mystery-steeped, God-centered Faith, while primarily focused on the worship of the Almighty and the task of individual salvation, nevertheless also worked indirectly to perfect the whole of the natural world. The Catholic who was fully conscious of the accepting, correcting and transforming function of the Incarnation would more confidently and joyfully rejoice in the knowledge that his Faith and the grace that it offered put all the diversity and riches of the universe at his fingertips; that it enabled individuals to obtain everything that life promised: eternally, with God in Heaven, but also here, upon the earth, and this to the greatest degree that his frail, mortal, dependent character permitted. Hence, these passages from *La Civiltà Cattolica*:

> God ... has established one sole order composed of two parts: nature exalted by grace, and grace vivifying nature. He has not confused these two orders, but He has coordinated them. One force alone is the model and one thing alone the motive principle and ultimate end of divine creation: Christ ... All of the rest is subordinated to Him. The goal of human existence is to form the Mystical Body of this Christ, of this Head of the elect, of this Eternal Priest, of this King of the immortal Kingdom, and the society of those who will eternally glorify him. ("The Encyclical of 8 December," *La Civiltà Cattolica*, Series VI, Volume 1, 1865, 287–288).

> Therefore, the faithful believer, in loving and exalting the Church, directly loves and exalts the glory of God, and sacrificing himself for her makes a sacrifice to God: that is to say, not for a good which is extrinsic and alien to him, but for a good which is in the greatest manner his own, and which is the sole good that can make him truly blessed. Therefore, in doing this, he is neither abandoning himself nor annihilating his own personality, but perfecting it and rendering it sublime, making it worthy of the possession of God, his ultimate and irreplaceable end, principle and terminus from which each and every one of his goods proceeds and reaches its conclusion. ("The Restoration of Human Personality Through Christianity," Ibid., Series I, Volume 2, 1850, 536)

The legitimate consequences not only for the individual but also for society and both individual and social happiness [are thus] the greatest that can possibly be enjoyed upon this earth. ("Social Happiness," Ibid., Series I, Volume 4, 1850, 578)

Increased recognition of "Incarnational Law" would inevitably bring with it a much firmer assertion of the fraud and uselessness of the determinedly anti-incarnational message of the Grand Coalition. Naturalism, with its warm embrace of an earthly status quo, marred by sin, as a "self-evident, practical guide to life," would be clearly identified as a force putting awakened Catholic man to sleep regarding the complete potential and multiform character of the universe that God intended men to inhabit and enjoy. Along with gnosticism and all the other anti-incarnational visions taught throughout the ages, it would be indisputably shown to cheapen and diminish the individual; to prevent him from properly using Creation to obtain eternal life, while encouraging him to embrace earthly "goods" which unfailingly proved to be peripheral, ephemeral, or utterly meaningless and repulsive shadows.

The supporters of the Catholic revival insisted that in fact, the victory of naturalism in the modern world led directly to the opposite conclusion anticipated by its most sincere proponents. Honestly convinced members of the Grand Coalition thought that naturalism would inevitably yield a deeper understanding of the order of the universe and individual human dignity. But such things were really gifts of the message and grace of the Incarnation. Without Catholic belief in the purpose and value of nature; without the grace which gives to otherwise weak human persons the courage not only to look consistently beyond the appearances of things to their deeper inner reason or "logos," but also to act upon their conclusions, men would generally yield to their immediate perceptions and temptations. They would be much more likely to disregard the practical consequences of their best rational speculations. In fact, they would be even more likely to do so in a period of return to nature "as it is." For the noble Socratic hunt for form and meaning in nature would appear to those looking for a "second childhood" to have been hideously deformed through its adoption and baptism by the hated Catholic world. In fact, all Reason would eventually be lost alongside Faith.

Once they abolished the supernatural realm and returned to pagan rationalism, the modernizers of society found that they could not stop. They had to continue their demolition, beginning with the moral truths that serve as a foundation for the existence and order of society, and then society's whole natural organic structure.... All that remains to do now is to have the individual unlearn all the essences of things, deny all the laws of logic, and burrow into the Night of complete ignorance in order that he be said to reach the apex of perfect liberty. ("The State and the Fatherland," Ibid., Series I, Volume 7, 1851, 45; "The Guests of Casorate," Ibid., Series II, Volume 1, 1853, 31)

In practice, as the history of naturalism since its very inception revealed, men and women working with the same "basic common sense" began to see in nature different and very contrasting things. For some, nature was perceived to be a machine whose apparatus and laws could be explained through one or another simple "key" to its functioning. Such "mechanists" had no appreciation for human freedom or for any special dignity of what could be merely programmed, individual human "machine parts." Others saw in the universe a realm of freedom, diversity, rights and will, and thus tended to dismiss the intrinsic value of any overriding natural law guaranteeing man's ultimate meaning and purpose, or the community life and social authority embodying this law in practical forms. For such "atomistic" thinkers, the innate character of law, community and authority is to work to smother the free natural spirit.

Doubt regarding man's ability to understand nature's structure was strengthened by any number of different factors, including the writings of *philosophes* like David Hume, who argued that examination of the outside world could yield a history of empirical observation, but not itself establish permanent scientific "laws." The potential fatalism and nihilism threatened by this and other humbling views of empiricism were "checked," and a "make-believe" certainty about nature's order and individual dignity maintained, through a combination of philosophical willfulness and appeal to practical success. Some writers sought to build law and order upon the "strongly felt reality" of the "non-hypocritical," "natural" man; the man who could confidently legislate for all the universe and simultaneously purge the external world of any "insincere" and hence "unnatural" obstacles to human freedom. Such ideas were expressed in two contrasting but complementary ways by Jean-Jacques Rousseau and Immanuel Kant. Other Enlightenment thinkers simply chose to act "as if" historically evolved systems which seemed to them to work to protect property, reason and order, were in harmony with nature, reconciling them with individual liberty by attributing their foundation to free contractual agreement. Both groups promised life, liberty, property and happiness to those who were true to sincere sentiment or the foundation contract. Future pragmatic success would then put the seal of nature upon their theoretical arguments.

Success was also an important confirming element in the arguments of many supporters of eighteenth- century Christian Pietism. This was a potent force in a Prussia and a Britain blessed after 1740 by one political and military triumph after another. Pietists, like naturalists, denigrated the importance of Christian doctrine, but for different reasons, chiefly because discussing theology held up Protestant divisions for public Catholic ridicule. Both ended, however, in making "whatever worked" in a fallen universe appear as though it were an essential guideline for human life. Hence the possibility of building an unholy alliance in which "might makes right" could be presented both as the product of "common sense" and as the will of God.

Given the fact the "obvious meaning of nature" was construed in so many different forms, the Grand Coalition was in many respects a very badly split alliance. Nevertheless, all of its members were united in their desire to prevent supernatural religious doctrines from having an impact on political and social life. Moreover, they were also bound by their basic reliance on willful as opposed to rational choice of their underlying principles (a "voluntarism" leading some to Pietism, others to a freedom-drunk atomism) and their appeal to success (one of the terms for which is "vitalism") to justify their respective preferences. Even those who thought that nature was a law-filled machine, whose central "key" could be scientifically discovered and exploited, willed rather than reasoned their way to this reductionism and claimed validity for their viewpoint on the basis of the active, successful, vital control of nature and men that application of it entailed. One or the other aspect of this "voluntarism" and "vitalism" then entered into the standard operating procedure of every revolutionary movement from the late eighteenth century onwards: from a relatively peaceful Liberalism to Democratic Nationalism, Anarchism and Marxism-Leninism. (See Becker, Op. Cit., Gawthrop, R., *Pietism and the Making of Eighteenth Century Prussia*, Cambridge, 1993; Rao, *Removing the Blindfold*, Angelus Press, 2014). Louis Veuillot, the mid-nineteenth century editor of the Catholic journal *l'Univers*, summed up the foundation of the naturalist-revolutionary position in this way:

> ... [F]erocious pride is correctly the genius of the Revolution; it has established a control in the world which pleases reason out of the struggle. It has a horror of reason, it gags it, it hunts it, and if it can kill it, it kills it. Prove to it the divinity of Christianity, its intellectual and philosophical reality, its historical reality, its moral and social reality: it wants none of it. That is its reason, and it is the strongest. It has placed a blindfold of impenetrable sophisms on the face of European civilization. It cannot see the heavens, nor hear the thunder. (L. Veuillot, *Mélanges*, from *Oeuvres Complete*, Paris, iii series, 1933, x, 45–46; On Veuillot, see John Rao, "Louis Veuillot and Catholic 'Intransigence': A Re-Evaluation," *Faith and Reason*, Winter, 1983, pp. 282–306)

By the mid-nineteenth century, supporters of the Catholic revival were convinced that the Grand Coalition working for the laws of a fallen nature against the laws of a supposedly unnatural incarnational religion could be said to be composed of two main groups of members: 1) truly sincere but irrational ideological believers in the uncorrected and untransformed powers of nature "as it is"; and, 2) cynics who utilized this vision, which ultimately reduced life to a struggle of willful, power-hungry naturalists, for the purpose of aiding their lives of vice and crime. Both these elements were said to be served by Word Merchants. Their work was needed by the ideologue to masquerade the perversion of high ideals caused by his appeal to the help of the vicious and the criminal to bring his new, more natural order into existence. But Word Merchant labor was also essential to the vicious and the criminal, so as to associate their willful, cynical and wicked deeds with their ideological ally's "noble" cause. Both ideologues and criminals tended to become like unto one another due to their need to cooperate for success, although temporary, explosive suspensions of their alliance were always possible whenever the clear differences between their opposing goals became too blatantly apparent. Still, neither could rid himself of the other without risking defeat. If the Catholic Drama of Truth involved a mysterious but glorious "dance," these pathetic gyrations of the differing members of the Grand Coalition ensured their performance of a *danse macabre*.

Since the modern appeal to unaided and uncorrected "feeling," "history and contract," "vitality" and "success" was trapped in the fallen natural realm, it could not help but be highly self-deceptive and self-destructive. Nineteenth century Catholics argued that there had already been a noteworthy spiraling downward of the thought and behavior of men appealing to such principles; a progressive degeneration of the environment wherever their precepts had been heeded. Efforts to reconstruct order and freedom upon these bases would spiral downwards to still more false perceptions about life, into ever more vulgar and violent moral and social practices, and attempts both transparent and subtle for cutting off discussion of the mistake that had been made and the path back to sanity. Nature would unquestionably fall into the deepest and sickest slumber, with the strongest and yet most dreary and drab "felt reality" winning out in the end. Hence, the *Civiltà's* description of the situation:

> Starting with the words 'I am free' and their new-found spirit of independence, men began to believe in the infallibility of whatever seemed natural to them, and then to call 'nature' everything that is sickness and weakness; to want sickness and weakness to be encouraged instead of healed; to suppose that encouraging weakness makes men healthier and happy; to conclude, finally, that human nature [conceived of as sickness and weakness] possesses the means to render man and society blissful on earth—and this without faith, grace, authority or supernatural community—since 'nature' gives us the feeling that it must be so. ("Modern Representative Government," *La Civiltà Cattolica*, Series I, Volume 6, 1851, 497–498)

> All societies at all times have seen wickedness and wicked people, ambitious and oppressed men. But when such wickedness

and oppression were only born from the passions, the guilty man, free as he was to dominate his passions through the use of reason, began to come to his senses almost as soon as he put his mind to it. Modern society, in contrast, entertains principles and theories that are at the root of the evil. Hence, the more a man reasons the more he is constrained to oppress society, and, vice versa, the more society is oppressed, the better logicians the oppressors are. ("Epilogue," Ibid., Series I, Volume ii, 1852, 438)

Louis Veuillot shares this bleak *Civiltà* judgment:

Between the sensualists of the past and the sensualists of our day, there is the same difference as between the great lords who ran about the world astonishing it with their prodigalities, and those sons of the enriched of whom one section of Paris sees the splendor and decadence. The first wanted to ruin themselves and did not succumb to it; the latter calculate, are rich, yet succumb without even having known to make a semblance of being magnificent. Everything is lacking to the poverty of our times, including the brilliance and often even the substance of the vices it would like to have. (Op. Cit., iv, 2–3)

No more men anywhere! The production of man has ceased in France. Some men of more or less complete honesty, but lacking talent; some very incomplete men of talent lacking all honesty; no attachment to any truth, but the most senseless attachment to the most mad errors; no more good sense, except in damning uselessly the impotent and evil works one persists in pursuing; no more pride in the face of anything base, yet puerile and dangerous and even cowardly arrogance in face of all that which one must fear . . . . (Ibid., xii, 360–361)

He was particularly worried about what an America steeped in Enlightenment principles would do to aid naturalist degeneration:

This people does not cry for its dead. It only knows how to cry for money. Fire can grip its cities, but it devours in them neither a monument nor an art object, nor a memory, and the money melted is not money lost at all. One draws it from the ruins; it is often even good business. (Ibid., xi, 34)

One can look at North America and the direction in which it is headed: its rapid progress, owed to the most brutalizing work, has fascinated Europe: but already the true results of this exclusively material progress appear. Barbarism, wicked behavior, bankruptcy, systematic destruction of the natives, imbecilic slavery of the victors, devoted to the most harsh and nauseating life under the yoke of their own machines. America might sink completely into the ocean and the human race would not have lost anything. Not a saint, not an artist, not a thinker—at least if one does not also call thought that aptitude for twisting iron to open pathways to packages. (Ibid., xii, 359–360)

Veuillot's final conclusion was that all would end with the conquest of the globe by an Empire of the World, a world both bureaucratic and consumerist, where platitudes would reign and deep ennui would be treated with cheap and boring pleasures:

Everywhere the conqueror will find one thing, everywhere the same, the only thing that war and the Revolution will nowhere have overturned: bureaucracy. Everywhere, the bureau will have prepared the way for him, everywhere they await him with a servile eagerness. He will support himself on them, the universal Empire will be the administrative Empire *par excellence*. Adding without end to that precious machinery, he will carry it to a point of incomparable power. Thus perfected, administration will satisfy simultaneously its own genius and the designs of its master in applying itself to two main works: the realization of equality and of material well-being to an unheard degree; the suppression of liberty to an unheard degree. (Ibid., viii, 366–367)

The police will take care that one is amused and that its reins never trouble the flesh. The administration will dispense the citizen of all care. It will fix his situation, his habitation, his vocation, his occupations. It will dress him and allot to him the quantity of air that he must breathe. It will have chosen him his mother, it will choose him his temporary wife; it will raise his children; it will take care of him in his illnesses; it will bury and burn his body, and dispose of his ashes in a record box with his name and his number. (Ibid., 369)

But why would he change places and climates? There will not be any more different places or climates, nor any curiosity anywhere. Man will find everywhere the same moderate temperature, the same customs, the same administrative rules, and infallibly the same police taking the same care of him. Everywhere the same language will be spoken, the *bayadères* will everywhere dance the same ballet. The old diversity would be a memory of the old liberty, an outrage to the new equality, a greater outrage to the bureau which would be suspected of not being able to establish uniformity everywhere. Their pride will not suffer that. Everything will be done in the image of the main city of the Empire and of the world. (Ibid.)

C. THE REVIVAL OF THE EITHER-OR BATTLE

Only a return to the incarnational vision of accepting, correcting, elevating and transforming nature could awaken the world, human communities, and the individual person to an understanding and realization of their full potential and real diversity. A militant commitment to pursuit of this recovery, to the removing of the blindfold shutting out the light of reason and faith, and to the importance of spreading the acquired knowledge throughout all classes of society was required. Such militancy had to be accompanied by a realistic sense of the difficulties of the task ahead, the most importance of which was, as we saw in the first lecture of this series, the control that the naturalists had gained over the language; control over the popular definition of the words central to the issue in question; control over words such as "nature," "natural law," "freedom," "individual dignity" and "progress."

The Catholic revival movement gained the full support of the Papacy in the wake of the 1848 Revolutions in Italy, France, the German Confederation and Hungary. These disturbances began as a love feast, an agape where all differences were thought capable of resolution through sincerity and general appeals to freedom. They ended in deep disillusionment and awareness of the need for much greater clarification of the exact positions of Catholics and the varied naturalist schools of Liberalism, Democratic Nationalism and Socialism.

A Catholic work of clarification began with the "negative" condemnations of naturalism and its manifold consequences to be found in Blessed Pius IX's *Syllabus of Errors* (1864). It continued with the "positive" guidance to be found in what became known as Catholic Social Doctrine, formulated from the time of the pontificate of Leo XIII (1878–1903) onwards. Those militants following its dictates took many pathways, developing what was referred to as the Inner and the Outer Missions, the first dedicated

313

to revivifying already Christian lands devastated by naturalism; the second to the work of first conversion in Africa and Asia.

If we apply the arguments of these thinkers and activists to the theme of our conference, we can summarize their conclusions in the following way: Either Christ or uncorrected Nature would be the King of Europe. The victory of Christ would see a Europe whose natural potential could be fulfilled in line with the proper hierarchy of spiritual and rational values, and thus with the greatest possible role for the freedom, dignity and diversity of each of the nations composing it and their individual citizens as well. Any international political structure (which, let it be noted, the editors of the *Civiltà* took for granted was coming) emerging in a Europe with Christ as her King would be one whose first political and social principle would be attainment of the common good of all; a principle which would end in the intense and brilliant diversity of in unity which Dante describes in the last section of the *Paradiso*.

In stark contrast, the victory of uncorrected Nature would bring incalculable disasters in its train: the annihilation of the human spirit, willful greed in material concerns, disconnected uses of Europe's natural blessings, disdain for and persecution of true national distinctions and the individual citizens of each country. The foresightedness of these mid-nineteenth century thinkers was such that they even understood how the consequences of nature as King would include abortion, euthanasia, racial engineering and genocide. Europe would be dominated by disordered forces which placed freedom for national ethnic groups or anarchic individuals in a higher and unwarranted place in the hierarchy of values, higher than commitment to the common good, with endless war and revolution the inescapable fate of the continent. Any internationalism that an uncorrected nature would dictate to right such wrongs would simply foster new vices and crimes. Europe would find herself oppressed by dull-witted but strong-willed masters who would always present their crimes as the victory of Nature, Reason, Freedom, Dignity and Progress.

> While man commands, nothing can reassure the conscience of the subject who obeys, neither with regard to the truth presupposed in the command, nor with regard to justice. Obedience without such persuasion would not be the obedience of man,

because not rational, and, therefore, not voluntary. It cannot, therefore, be obtained without the force either of arms or of deceitful intelligence. The liberty of the ruled, either violated or deceived, will always be tampered with. Therefore, while man is king only as man, he will govern with force. ("Either God as King with Freedom or Man as King with Force," *La Civiltà Cattolica*, Series II, Volume 3, 1853, 618)

Now I have demonstrated one hundred times in the course of these articles that pagan civilization is a regression for humanity, its liberty entailing the most shameful slavery and the liquidation of the human personality, absorbed by the omnipotence of the God-State. Therefore, even without my saying it, anyone can see by himself that modern liberalism, under the fiction of promoting liberty, tends to destroy it; under the shadow of desiring progress, it desires barbarism . . . . It is not aversion to liberty or sympathies for despotism that lead the Church to fight their wicked efforts . . . . Rather it is the love it feels for true liberty, its native repugnance for all kinds of despotism, the mission it has from God to save the personal independence of man that inspires it, and urges it to such a battle. ("Does Human Personality Have Anything to Fear From the Church," Ibid., Series I, Volume 2, 1850, 540–541)

Even a sleeping, inactive Church was an irritant to the supporters of the natural status quo. If nothing else, at least such a half-dead body still weakly suggested the possibility of an alternative to "unquestionable" guidelines for human existence. A truly awakened, militant Bride of Christ, however, was a much more threatening phenomenon. A force of this kind must inevitably be viewed by the defenders of nature as king "as it is" as an intolerable assault on the good life. Thus, the *Civiltà* argued, it was logical that they felt obliged to meet an active Catholic challenge by unleashing a total war to eradicate such an intrusive, unnatural (and reborn) monster.

This intolerance must extend everywhere in the measure that the supernatural claims to transform human nature, which accompanies a man wherever he extends his influence. This is why I added that the supernatural principle must be excluded from all of humanity. ("Naturalism," Ibid., Series I, Volume 4, 1850, 452)

Hence, it was no surprise that the latter half of the nineteenth century saw the outbreak in numerous countries of what in Germany was labeled a Culture War against awakened Catholicism. (See Chapter 13, "All Borrowed Armor Chokes Us"). This war has so far led to a Catholic rout. We will examine the peculiar reasons for that defeat, one that involved a subversion and radical dilution of the Church's discernible but "depraved" sociological influence, in the next chapter.

20

THE TALLINN LECTURES
III. Vitalism & Americanist Pluralism†
SMILING AS CHRISTIAN EUROPE DIES

A. VITALISM, VOLUNTARISM & THE EMASCULATION OF THE CATHOLIC MOVEMENT

Despite the vigor of the movement of Catholic revival, many if not most believers continued to display their susceptibility to naturalist temptations. Some gave in to these temptations on the intellectual level, thus openly and willingly joining the naturalist camp. But even when Catholics did not necessarily accept naturalist theory, they often acted in daily life as though they had done so, becoming practical naturalists.

In one way or another, therefore, Catholics could be found supporting all of the various forms of naturalist thought and practice discussed in the previous lecture. These ranged from a mechanism that valued uniformity over diversity to an atomism that worshiped individual freedom, whatever the negative consequences this liberty might have for the survival of objective law and morality.

All Catholic naturalists, conscious and unconscious, shared in the basic voluntarism underlying one "natural" choice as opposed to another; a voluntarism which called itself rational, while possessing all of the characteristics of a Faith; an unexamined Faith; a Fideism. Like their secularist counterparts, they allowed no room for their Faith-disguised-as-Reason to enter into the kind of rational dialogue regarding its validity nurtured by the Catholic Tradition. Instead, they, too, appealed to "success" as a criterion for judging the ultimate truth of their willful option.

I should like to begin by discussing a more complex phenomenon: the transformation of a significant group of Catholics active in the Incarnation-centered revival movement into vitalist-voluntarist proponents of the acceptance of nature "as it is." Once this melancholy

---

† Lecture given at the TriaLogos Festival in Tallinn, Estonia, on September 28, 2007.

development has been outlined, I will add to it a treatment of the worldwide, postwar impact of Americanist Pluralism. At that point, we will finally be able to grasp the fullness of the problem we face today if we seek to defend a broad European identity respectful of the integrity of each of its constituent national parts.

The great early leader of fervent Catholic activists making the changeover to the vitalist-voluntarist camp was the Abbé Felicité de Lamennais (1782–1854). His significance in this regard, from the 1820s onwards, cannot be exaggerated. Lamennais was the priest-apologist who became the great conduit for transmitting the message of Rousseau to the Catholic world in the early 1800s. Filled with love for The People as the vibrant, energetic Voice of God, Lamennais at first thought that the legitimate monarchy was the political vehicle for translating its sacred wishes into reality. When the monarchy failed him, he turned to the Pope as the God-People's political and social agent. With papal rejection of the notion of the People as the source of Truth, Lamennais then looked to a purely secular democratic system as the infallible translator of God's will into practice. But since even the supposedly vital People did not seem to possess much enthusiasm for the sacred task he had identified for them, Lamennais realized that it fell to him, as Prophet, to take up this task. He saw that he had been called by God to raise the People's slumbering spiritual consciousness and reveal the new and higher stage of political democratic development to which the history of Catholicism was inevitably leading it.

The Prophet's "official" influence in the Catholic world ended with his excommunication in the 1830s. Nevertheless, his initial followers, both orthodox and heterodox, were to be found everywhere within it, some retaining merely his prophetic fervor, others his precise prophetic vision in more subtle "liberal" Catholic form. His impact on the secular world continued unabated. In union with many of the other religious syncretists, nationalists and utopian reformers of the first half of the nineteenth century, he spent the rest of his life preaching the final realization of the Catholic spirit through its rebirth in a secularist, democratic, anti-Catholic form (See Chapter 11 of this volume, "Lamennais, Rousseau and the New Catholic Order"; Frank Paul Bowman, *Le Christ des Barricades*, Cerf, 1987; J. Meinvielle, *De Lamennais a Maritain*, La Cité Catholique, 1949).

I am most interested at this time, however, in the work of a group of figures from the 1890s through the 1930s who at first glance would not seem to have been at all influenced by Lamennais' approach. These were the activists involved in the Outer and Inner Missions—missionaries in Asia and Africa on the one hand, and Catholic political, labor and youth movement leaders on the other—discussed in the previous chapter. All such activists were honest militants who shared the sense of urgency central to the movement of Catholic revival. All, in consequence, were men and women who were desperate for success.

Unfortunately, the Outer Missionaries were worn down by their many failures, amazed at the resistance of native religions and cultures to the Catholic message, and disturbed by signs of their revitalization even in places where they had long seemed nearly extinct. Inner Missionaries were still more demoralized. They were shocked by their pre-1914 political failures, their frontline service during the First World War, and the terrible social disruptions accompanying that conflict's end and aftermath. All three experiences had demonstrated to them the weakness of their distinctly Catholic impact upon the average voter and soldier. Most of these apparently "typical" Europeans had proved to be totally indifferent to the Faith, and yet capable of being roused to enthusiastic action by energetic lieutenants in the trenches and political radicals at home. Such military and civilian leaders, as well as the communities that they shaped, seemed to possess an extraordinary vitality. Where did it come from? Why did Catholic Outer and Inner Missionaries lack the strength that a wide variety of non-Catholic militants possessed?

A translation of the concerns of Catholic activists into theoretical arguments was undertaken in the 1920s and 1930s by a kaleidoscope of thinkers calling themselves Personalists. Personalists ultimately went down numerous, divergent directions. Nevertheless, the mainline, in the interwar period, either consciously or unconsciously adopted positions going back to Lamennais and, through Lamennais, to Rousseau, to Kant, and to the Pietist Tradition.

Catholic activists, the Personalists lamented, despite their claims to be community-minded, actually thought and spoke much more like the eighteenth-century individualist rationalists they were said to oppose. In practice, all of their arguments were designed to appeal to isolated human atoms, and this on a one-dimensional, purely intellectual, boring scholastic level. Hence the conviction on the part of the flesh and blood men and women to whom they addressed themselves that in dealing with Catholics they were dealing with teachers who were dead to the fullness of existence; cerebral academics; professional note-takers; disembodied "losers."

The Holy Spirit, the Personalists continued, could never be an advocate of such lifeless creatures and the Gospel as they preached it. He manifested Himself in history through those vital, energetic leaders and communities whose successes impressed the "dead" Catholic activists themselves. This was due to the fact that God wanted human beings to perfect their personalities, and they could only accomplish this perfection, becoming full "persons" rather than desiccated "individuals," through participation in precisely such energetically led circles.

Should Catholics really wish to have an impact in life, what they had to do was to "dive into" the already vital, successful, "person-shaping" communities which they hoped to influence. Their work would then be one of "witnessing"; i.e., using their Catholic presence to help these vibrant, Spirit-favored societies to complete and perfect their unique "mystiques."

In order to "witness" properly, believers had to shed whatever stood in the way of their enthusiastic cooperation with the mystiques in question: namely, their substantive Catholic formation, with all of its presuppositions about how to express what was True, Good and Beautiful. Yes, these vital communities might seem, at first glance, to be in many ways hostile to one another in belief and behavior. Nevertheless, their success proved that they all had the Holy Spirit behind them. Therefore, one could have absolute faith that their contemporary, outwardly clashing mystiques would somehow providentially "converge" in the future. Hence, these comments of Emmanuel Mounier, one of the most important of the thinkers in question:

> Surely [development] is slow and long when only average men are working at it. But then heroes, geniuses, a saint come along: a Saint Paul, a Joan of Arc, a Catherine of Siena, a Saint Bernard, or a Lenin, a Hitler and a Mussolini, or a Gandhi, and suddenly everything picks up speed...[H]uman irrationality, the human will, or simply, for the Christian, the Holy Spirit suddenly provides elements which men lacking imagination would never have

foreseen... May the democrat, may the communist, may the fascist push the positive aspirations which inspire their enthusiasm to the limit and plenitude. (John Hellman, *Emmanuel Mounier and the New Catholic Left*: 1930–1950, Toronto, 1981, p. 90)

Such personalist arguments found a serious hearing in Catholic educational, political, youth and labor movements in the 1920s, 1930s and afterwards. Their acceptance did not affect merely these circles' vision of their ultimate purpose and *modus operandi*. It also worked to justify a sea change in that Catholic liturgical movement which had formed part of the revival of the previous century. Many of the leaders of the liturgical renaissance now began to claim that their principal task was that of learning how to respond to the Spirit manifesting Himself in the different mystiques of vital communities. For a true "witnessing" would require developing a form of divine worship peculiar to the spiritual genius of each of these providential entities.

From the standpoint of the older theorists of the nineteenth century Catholic revival, hunting for a "success" that could only be gained by "witnessing" to a Holy Spirit who was willfully said by His prophetic interpreters to endorse everything "vital" and energetic in contemporary communities was a recipe for total disaster. Abandoning all that one knew from the Catholic, incarnational vision in order to open the mind and heart to vital "mystiques" meant nothing other than consciously diving into "slumbering" nature. It entailed limiting God's message and activity in the world to the voice of nature "as it is," and not admitting His supernatural role as corrector and transformer of nature's flaws. The believer would be left with no means of judging whether the particular manifestations of nature confronting him were true or false, good or bad, beautiful or ugly ones.

In the final analysis, such "witnessing" involved giving oneself over to and blessing a modern "natural" world ruled by people with an agenda: the agenda of power-hungry ideologues, libertines and criminals whose rhetoricians used Isocrates' "appropriate words" to justify erroneous and evil actions and cut off real, substantive criticism of them as though it were some pointless waste of time. Such "witnessing" amounted to a baptism of the false and ever more vulgar perceptions of the strongest and most arrogant "activists" of the place and the moment. Should the liturgy be dragged into this enterprise, it would mandate a tailoring of worship to however many self-deluded or cynical voices of Reason, Freedom, Progress and the People might succeed in imposing their corrupt wishes on the communities which they manipulated. It would require a constant retailoring of divine worship to respond to the changing and progressively degenerating demands of the strongest wills. It would demand a self-censorship and silence whenever the true Catholic spirit broke through and suggested that God was being mocked and men in need of supernatural redemption were being cheated.

A study of those involved in the Personalist campaign yields a Who's Who of the liturgical and postwar European unification movements. It also serves as an introduction to many of the liberal and radical *periti* at Vatican II and related, post-conciliar "experts." Investigation of the vital, successful communities to whose mystiques such people thought they must give witness is also quite revealing. One discovers an early sympathy for Fascism and its cult of vital action and successful application of strength. This was accompanied by liturgical experimentation with much respect for the Leadership Principle and expressions of paramilitary camaraderie. A major and very instructive example of such Fascist-like fervor can be seen in the program and lifestyle fostered at the elite training center established at the castle of Uriage near Grenoble, with the aid of the Vichy government in France.

Studies of the development of Personalist influence also make it clear that this was matched by an ever-growing contempt for the entire theological, philosophical, liturgical and general cultural tradition of Catholicism. How could this not be so? We have by now repeatedly noted that that tradition encouraged too strong of a critique of diving into a contemporary world marred by naturalism not to be viewed as a most dangerous pest indeed. So angry with this "cranky" tradition was Emmanuel Mounier that he even argued that the only man who had come close to understanding how flawed it really was, and how Catholicism must be regenerated, was the Nihilist prophet, Friedrich Nietzsche:

> Nietzsche's critique of slavish Christianity now seemed to him to be unanswerable, and he 'came to think that Roman Catholicism was an integral part of almost all he hated. Then, when he searched his soul, he discovered that the aspects of himself which he appreciated least were his Catholic traits' (Ibid., p. 190).

Doing what one willed was the *unum necessarium*. Everything rational from the Greek tradition used to support Christianity and dampen the will was execrated as well. If there was anything valuable in the Greco-Christian heritage, it had to come from personalists rebuilding it from scratch; those appealing to the Catholic name and Catholic practice in his day required diagnosis and psychiatric help. Mounier now flatly denounced old-fashioned Christianity and Christians. Christianity, he wrote, was 'conservative, defensive, sulky, afraid of the future.' Whether it 'collapses in a struggle or sinks slowly in a coma of self-complacency,' it was doomed. 'Christians,' he castigated in even stronger terms in a rhapsodic style worthy of his new master (Nietzsche): 'These crooked beings who go forward in life only sidelong with downcast eyes, these ungainly souls, these weighers-up of virtues, these dominical victims, these pious cowards, these lymphatic heroes, these colourless virgins, these vessels of ennui, these bags of syllogisms, these shadows of shadows . . .' (Ibid., p. 191).

Metaphysical speculation, Mounier declared, was a characteristic of 'lifeless schizoid personalities.'. . . Mounier even referred to intelligence and spirituality as 'bodily diseases' and attributed the indecisiveness of many Christians to their ignorance of 'how to jump a ditch or strike a blow.'...'Modern psychiatry,' Mounier wrote, had shed light on the morbid taste for the 'spiritual," for 'higher things,' for the ideal and for effusions of the soul . . . Thus, many forms of religious devotion were the result of psychosis, self-deception or vanity. Prayer was often a sign of psychological illness and weakness. (Ibid., pp. 192–193; all of the above from Chapter 6 of this volume, "The Bad Seed")

But the dominant National Socialist strain of Fascism was unavoidably and unacceptably tied to the Volksprinzip, and Personalists, despite their other temptations, never succumbed to that of modern racism. Even more significantly, Fascism had not proved to be vital enough to win the Second World War, losing whatever credibility as an engine of success that it had once possessed. The prize in that conflict had been carried off by the Soviet Union and the United States. One might legitimately conclude that Marxist-Leninist and Americanist Pluralist communities were those possessing the greatest vigor, successful energy, and stamp of approval of the Holy Spirit. These communities had their own

Word Merchants working day and night to encourage such an attitude; to find the "appropriate words" to equate everything non-Marxist-Leninist or non-Pluralist with Fascism, and therefore with evil incarnate. Catholic doctrines and achievements of the European Catholic past were generally non-Marxist and non-Pluralist. It was therefore only a matter of time before they were both identified with the Fascist disease.

Both conviction and prudence told the Personalists that a swift change of allegiance was definitely in order. The preference of most of them was for the vitalist Marxist-Leninist victor, due to the more obvious communal and collectivist character of the Soviet system. A number of men active in the Catholic Personalist movements mentioned above had learned to respect the "energy" of Marxism-Leninism due to their experiences with Soviet citizens and European Communists in labor camps in Germany. Those who had not "enjoyed" this opportunity, schooled themselves in the same experience through participation in the worker priest experiment of the late 1940s and 1950s. Liturgists from both groups then sought to tailor worship to the needs expressed in such Spirit-guided communist *milieux*. Just how accurate their perceptions were regarding their atmosphere is of course highly debatable, given the willful voluntarism that constantly fuels their thought and action.

Liberation Theology is instructive in this regard. A number of extremely important Personalists were at the center of its birth and development; hence, their call to dive into vital Marxist-Leninist communities the world over in order to witness and perfect their mystiques. Liberation Theologians, like their immediate Personalist precursors, insisted that responding to the clear message of these Marxist communities required the dismantling of every obstacle that a deadening, individualistic, Catholic rationalist tradition might place in their way. But the Catholic peoples of Latin America who were supposed to be the generating force behind the vital needs expressed through such vibrant communities seemed stubbornly attached to beliefs and practices which they ought to have been in the forefront of rejecting. Such stubbornness indicated the need for a little consciousness-raising of the kind which Lamennais had been the first important Catholic to prescribe. Consciousness-raising was to be accomplished by hearkening to the "appropriate words" of the Liberation Theologian, who explained to the People that which, in its heart of hearts, it really loved and wanted. Such work could be done in "base communities." Here, an unacceptable Catholic vitalism might be replaced by the acceptable, unquestionable vitalism willed by the prophets of Marxism-Leninism but disguised as the *Diktat* of the Holy Spirit (for all the above, see John Hellman, Op. Cit., plus his *The Knight Monks of Vichy*: Uriage, 1940–1945, McGill, 1997; J. Meinvielle, Op. Cit.; Emile Poulat, *Les Pretres-Ouvrieres: Naissance et Fin*, Cerf, 1999; also, Chapter 6 of this volume, "The Bad Seed"; Chapter 13, "All Borrowed Armor Chokes Us"; John Rao, "The Good War and the Rite War," Latin Mass Magazine, Spring, 2001)

B. AMERICANIST PLURALISM

Even those entranced by Marxism-Leninism had to admit that the impact of America's vital energy was evident everywhere in the postwar world. A number of Catholic personalists therefore argued for the need to "dive into" and help perfect the American community and those shaped by it. But what, exactly, were the underlying principles and standard operating procedure of that community? And what would a Catholic "witness" to its peculiar "mystique" really mean in practice?

Americans like to speak of their nation as a "young" one, and contrast it favorably with the decadent countries of the Old World. But the American nation is as much a product as a European land of all of the ancient battles and modern naturalist developments that we have been discussing. America's Founding Fathers worked in an environment deeply affected by the loss of Christian Faith and its transformation into a secularist tool. The system that they created also very much reflects the concerns of the final, Enlightenment stage of modern naturalism: including all of its doubts regarding both speculative and empirical Reason, and, hence, all of its temptations to rebuild order on foundations that one "makes believe" are objectively true.

The Founding Fathers and their successors built their "make-believe" objective order first and foremost upon America's British heritage. This was quite a schizophrenic legacy by the late eighteenth century. It certainly included Christianity, chiefly in the form of Anglicanism and Puritan Protestantism. But it also involved the Enlightenment, primarily in the manner that former

Anglicans and Puritans who had lost their Faith presented it. These converts to the naturalist camp often used the Christian-inspired language with which they were familiar to promote their new, anti-Christian goals. Whether they intended this or not, such speech soothed those who remained believers and blinded them as to where, exactly, their familiar-sounding doctrines might actually lead in the future.

Even the Founders were aware that there was a troublesome reality that their *novus ordo saeclorum* was obliged immediately to confront. This was the presence in the United States of a kaleidoscope of different ethnic groups and religious convictions. That presence grew still more complex and troublesome with the mass migrations of the nineteenth and early twentieth centuries. The fullness of the make-believe order of the American Pluralist system emerged out of attempts to harmonize the reality of a multicultural society with the basic conservatism of the Anglican *via media*, the radicalism of Puritanism, and the naturalism of an Enlightenment of both Anglican and Puritan flavor. Its theory and "mystique" were firmly in place by the late 1890s. What they claimed was that America had discovered the formula for providing a peaceful, ordered community out of a society guaranteeing freedom to all of God's (or Nature's) divided children. America thus offered mankind throughout the globe its "last and best hope" for a liberty, tranquility and happiness greater than any ever known in human history.

Unfortunately, "diving into" the Americanist Pluralist mystique helps merely to bring to fruition another version of vulgar, materialist and uniform disorder, whipped into some semblance of make-believe unity through the will of the strongest. It aids in the perfection of that type of bland, organized willfulness predicted by nineteenth century Catholic thinkers, but in a more successful and seductive way than they could ever have imagined. Those who are interested in a deeper, more detailed discussion of Americanist Pluralism and its (temporarily) successful employment of Original Sin as the central building block of individual and social life should consult my articles, "Americanism and the Collapse of the Church in the United States," "Why Catholics Cannot Defend Themselves," "Founding Fathers and Church Fathers," "To Promote Dialogue, Fight American Pluralism," and many other articles, all to be found on the "For the Whole Christ" website (jcrao.freeshell.

org). All I propose to do here is to outline the main lines of the perversion and the confusion that this system perpetrates.

Let it suffice to say for now that the "freedom" and the "order" that one obtains through it are a purely naturalist freedom and order based upon the peculiar and often contradictory Christian and Enlightenment factors forming American culture. Its naturalism is bewildering to the believer because, as noted above, so many Americans used—and still use—Christian language to describe, praise and promote a set of anti-Christian purposes. It is baffling also because it has to cater to both radical and conservative naturalist tastes at one and the same time.

Hence, the American is told that he has the radical freedom that a secularized Puritan might wish him to have, a freedom that "sounds Christian" because it can easily be related to its fundamental Protestant roots. But in order to practice this freedom in a way that does not disturb the order preferred by Enlightenment conservatives, he learns that liberty actually has to be utilized in a way that avoids "divisiveness"; in a fashion that "integrates" its practitioner into an order composed of endless varieties of "non-divisive, integrating individualists."

Americans learn that the "freedom" of communities, such as the Catholic Church, is subject to the influence of Puritan and secularized Puritan ideas regarding liberty. Freedom, under these circumstances, means only the freedom given for individual members of a religious society to rip their communal authority to shreds. All attempts to hold onto communal authority could be nothing other than assaults on freedom detested by the anti-institutional God of Protestantism and the anti-institutional Nature of the liberty-loving Enlightenment. Freedom for religious communities—for all communities, as far as more radical thinkers are concerned—amounts to nothing other than the freedom to be impotent and to self-destruct. James Madison, the chief author of the American Constitution, quite openly rejoices in this truth, arguing for the need to "multiply factions" within existing, strong communities so as to paralyze their ability to mobilize their followers and actually shape the American political and social order.

Individuals and communities are ultimately given a two-fold teaching regarding the relationship of freedom and order. On the one hand, they are pressed to divide serious free thought from serious free action. On the other, they are encouraged to build whatever unity can exist upon a positive materialist use of their freedom. In the final analysis, the freedom granted to men and communities under the Americanist Pluralist "mystique" is merely the freedom to be materialists in a myriad of fashions. To take but one example, freedom for a Chinese must never be understood as allowing him to harmonize the American system with Confucianist principles. It does mean, however, that he can open as many restaurants as he might see fit, thereby contributing to the rich diversity of American life.

But this cheap form of freedom offers no more substantial block to sinful misuse than reliance on "common sense" prevents adherence to unnatural errors. It has within it an innate tendency to degenerate, and, with that degeneration, to ensure construction of an "order" based upon the dictates of the strongest practitioners of materialist freedom: libertines and criminals. Such criminals maintain their alliance with the Americanist Pluralist ideologue and the Word Merchant in order to justify and ennoble their oppression of the weak. All together guarantee that the system gradually "spirals downward," ending in that boring, corrupted sameness identified by Louis Veuillot as a chief characteristic of the "Empire of the World."

None of these essential problems of the American Pluralist mystique can even begin to be discussed. That mystique prohibits all criticism of its theory and its practice. If, for example, a person wishes to employ all of the various tools western man has developed over the course of the ages for discussing the validity of its definition of the meaning of individual and social life, all of these tools, one by one, including theology, philosophy, history, psychology and sociology, will be dismissed as both impractical and intrinsically dangerous. A desire to use them will be said to illustrate nothing other than a lack of "obvious common sense" on the part of the foolish, impractical, "loser" critic. Do such tools help one to make money or keep the peace? On the contrary, all they do is bring up disruptive fantasies encouraging divisiveness and disturbing profits.

If, on the other hand, one seeks to demonstrate the long-term practical dangers of the Americanist Pluralist mystique, and especially its degeneration into a reign of "might makes right" disguised as the victory of freedom, its totally unquestionable "godliness" will be called up to smother the dialogue. The critic will be accused of lacking Faith in its divine nature and mandate; as revealed, let us remember, through the all too arbitrary Will of the Founding Fathers. Here he is condemned for his cynical rejection of the "last and best hope" for individual freedom and social peace, and his consequent lack of charity for suffering humanity.

Should the critic then return to theory, and identify the Americanist Pluralist Faith as a voluntarist, irrational fideism masquerading a purely materialist conception of life, he will be brutally brought back down to the practical level once again. Now, with complete disregard for the change in tactic, he will be assaulted for his childish naiveté; his hopeless idealism in the midst of a jungle universe guided by the War of All Against All. Surely only a "loser" envious of the success of his betters would think that life was susceptible to guidance by his utopian spiritual babble!

But what if our critic persists in his position and emphasizes the fact that he has been the subject of an irrational attack, accused simultaneously of being both a faithless cynic and impractically (but enviously) naïve? Why, then he will become the kind of "public nuisance" promoting unpleasant, logical consequences of first principles that David Hume deplored and Ralph Waldo Emerson considered to be the infallible sign of a "petty mind." The Word Merchants will be called onto center stage to find as many "appropriate words" as possible to brutalize this Enemy of the People. Truth will not matter in their campaign against him. He will be dismissed as an obvious lunatic. Moreover, since Americanist Pluralism fought the good fight against the Fascists, he will also be denounced as a Nazi; an anti-Semite; a defender of genocide. Terrorism being the system's current manifestation of evil, the critic will also be painted as a probable Al Quaeda, "Islamo-Fascist" supporter. Why, this deranged, extremist Loser is the kind of man who most likely wishes that Estonia were still within the Soviet Bloc as well!

Few have the stamina to reach this final stage of unsuccessful dialogue. The schizophrenia brought on by Americanist Pluralist refusal to allow serious thought to be transmitted into action will have deconstructed most potential critics' spirit from the very outset. Others will have been daunted by the number of tools that have to be marshaled to uncover the system's fraud and its bewildering *modus operandi*. Should a hardy few possess the will to fight the good fight still longer, they too shall eventually be forced to abandon the struggle due to the materialist environment created by the system in question. That environment demands work and ever more work in order merely to survive. Even the strongest opponent, over time, will be simply too exhausted to indulge the luxury of criticizing the system in the few hours of repose left to him by it each day. Hence, mankind's "last, best hope" retains its undeserved image, its victims never learn of its poisons, and it can continue to wreak its all too predictable havoc again and again, in country after hapless country.

Equivocal use of Christian language on behalf of a happy vision of order and freedom, accompanied by the appeal of potential success in the New World, seduced many Roman Catholic immigrants into the camp of Americanist Pluralism in the years between 1890 and the present. Accepting its precepts seemed to be a "no lose" proposition. The appearance of openness, prosperity and tranquility similarly entranced the exhausted and demoralized Europeans of the 1940s, with those resisting the Americanist Pluralist embrace easily anathematized as unregenerate Fascist remnants.

But what happens both to Catholics and to non-Catholic Europeans still at least partly historically shaped by Catholicism once they "dive into" this mystique, "witness" to it, and then "bring it to perfection?" Neither has any hope of survival as a distinct force or culture. They are both obliged to destroy whatever distinguishes themselves as Catholics and Europeans in order to practice a "non-divisive, integrating, materialist freedom," and then to repeat, as a dogma, the belief that they have never experienced such great liberty and so exalted a sense of human dignity. They are both obliged to dismantle what is most essential to their character, especially what has been corrected and transformed through the message of the Incarnation, in order to "fit in" to a jungle society which they must praise repeatedly as the most beautifully ordered in history. They are condemned to see their children treat this dismantling and emasculation as the obvious fulfillment of the real Catholic and the real European potential. They are condemned to hear their offspring repeat Black Legends which denigrate truly Catholic and European heroes as villains, and adulate anti-Catholics and opponents of past, substantive European culture as brave champions of the March of Progress. And they are obliged to accept the fact that the focus of this dismantling and emasculation of true human achievement will change along with whoever is the strongest ideologue, libertine and criminal of the moment and whatever it is that he wishes. Today, that focus is on making certain that Catholics and Europeans be morally outraged only over whatever does not build bigger and more globally-oriented business enterprises. It is also focused on mocking "outmoded" concerns over just and unjust international conflicts, or humane treatment of prisoners of war.

"Diving into" the mystique of Marxism was a terrible thing. Nevertheless, that mystique was so patently fraudulent that it possessed a built-in destructive element. If one compares it to a drink, it offered a beverage which contained a poison one could taste and therefore wish to reject before it reached the point of destroying absolutely everyone who touched it. "Diving into" the Americanist Pluralist mystique is not quite the same phenomenon. It is like taking a poisoned cocktail that does still have something of a familiar, pleasant taste to it and seems, for a while, to provide what it promises: tranquility and satisfaction of personal desire. One does not realize, until the very moment that he reaches the bottom of the glass, that there is nothing really there, and that the poison has done its job. The individual members of all of the desiccated, "free," meaningless communities who drink the Americanist Pluralist poison—the members of the Catholic Pluralist Club, the European Pluralist Club, and the Estonian Pluralist Club—smile and toast their murderer as they die.

How, then, do we end this discussion? What can we say that we must do to go in search of Europe's identity? This is a simple question with a simple answer. We must go in search of that identity by going in search of Christ and the meaning of Christ's Incarnation. With our eyes fixed on Christ, we gain both Faith and Reason along with all of the complex and eminently useful tools they provide for us for learning the True, the Good and the Beautiful. Through the application of these tools, we gain a diversity that comes from unity in the Creator God; a solid unity; not a make-believe unity emerging from a twisted vision of freedom and order.

The choice in front of us is exactly the same which the editors of *La Civiltà Cattolica* posited in the middle of the nineteenth century: either Christ as King, with both order and the diversity of true freedom, or Man and Nature as King with a make-believe order, with the tyranny of the strong, and with the destruction of that magnificent bouquet of different cultures which Europe once seemed willing to offer to her God. My friends in England who thought that they were "anti-European" turned out merely to be voting for the first of these options.

Our hopes of making Christ the King seem very limited today. Still, success is not our primary concern as active individuals. Our primary concern is to know, to love and to serve God. Let us therefore concentrate on these first things and leave His Providence to grant our labors their just rewards. Certain factors are working to our benefit as we undertake this mission. The self-deluded ideologues, criminals, and ordinary, confused members of the Coalition on Behalf of the Unexamined Life remain divided. They do, at times, battle with one another and thus bring harm to their common naturalist cause. Moreover, even if the majority of men throughout the globe were to persist in mocking God, God cannot unceasingly be mocked. The nature which He created, even though fallen and marred in its beauty, still tells of His glory. It will always offer starting points for thoughtful men and women to develop "Seeds of the Logos" leading individuals and societies back to reality. Nature will strike against its false naturalist friends and a deceived mankind which tries to push it too far, demanding from it what it cannot give. And it will do so with the aid of the Almighty Himself.

Try as modern man might, Cardinal Louis Pie (1815–1880), Bishop of Poitiers, argued at Lourdes in 1876, he can never escape the fact that he lives in a world created and redeemed at the behest of a supernatural will. "The supernatural is finished," he quotes nineteenth century man as gloating. "Well, look here, then! The supernatural pours out, overflows, sweats from the sand and from the rock, spurts out from the source, and rolls along on the long folds of the living waves of a river of prayers, of chants and of light." (Mayeur, Op. Cit., XI, p. 350).

21

A View From Rocco's

PROFESSOR GRADGRIND'S MAGISTERIUM
& RECENT CATHOLIC MODERNISM[†]

"There are times when an elevated spirit is a true infirmity. No one understands it. It even passes for a kind of parochialism."
(Chateaubriand)

MY CLOSEST FRIENDS AT ROCCO'S ARE generally looking pretty gloomy these days. They attribute their gloom to the fact that the newspapers are filled with reports of big-buck bonuses, while nothing in their own personal economic lives seems to be in any way improving. Some people, they lament, are clearly "making it." Why can't they be among them?

Alas, poor souls! They do not realize that "making it" for them is utterly impossible. "Making it" would entail *remaking* themselves according to the revolutionary dictates of Professor Gradgrind's Magisterium, and this they are in no way ready to do. Nor should they do so, whatever the wisdom of the moment might dictate.

Who is Professor Thomas Gradgrind? He is one of the main characters in Charles Dickens' *Hard Times* (1854), and an enthusiastic collaborator in the construction of the new capitalist, industrialized, "making it" Britain of the nineteenth century. What is his Magisterium? It is a teaching regarding the character of an autonomous natural order of things; a very specific example of what we Catholics would broadly call Modernism.

Gradgrind as educator considers himself bound to raise children to understand and obey laws of nature built upon obvious "facts" that no one under any circumstances can even question, much less disobey. Let us allow Dickens to introduce us to him and to his educational philosophy as he sets to work in a classroom filled with students:

Now, what I want is, Facts. Teach these boys and girls nothing but Facts. Facts alone are wanted in life. Plant nothing else,

† First published in *The Remnant* (November 15, 2009).

and root out everything else. You can only form the minds of reasoning animals upon Facts: nothing else will ever be of any service to them. This is the principle on which I bring up my own children, and this is the principle on which I bring up these children. Stick to Facts, sir! In this life, we want nothing but Facts, sir; nothing but Facts!...

The speaker, and the schoolmaster, and the third grown person present, all backed a little, and swept with their eyes the inclined plane of little vessels then and there arranged in order, ready to have imperial gallons of facts poured into them until they were full to the brim.

Teaching the Facts about the laws of nature was ultimately rather easy for Professor Gradgrind. It did not involve anything more than teaching knowledge of a simple machine closed in upon and content with itself:

Thomas Gradgrind, sir. A man of realities. A man of facts and calculations. A man who proceeds upon the principle that two and two are four, and nothing over, and who is not to be talked into allowing for anything over. Thomas Gradgrind, sir — peremptorily Thomas —Thomas Gradgrind. With a rule and a pair of scales, and the multiplication table always in his pocket, sir, ready to weigh and measure any parcel of human nature and tell you exactly what it comes to. It is a mere question of figures, a case of simple arithmetic.

Gradgrind's instruction came at a price, however. His Magisterium required that whatever other non-mechanical Facts had shaped his students in the past be ruthlessly purged from their benighted souls:

Thomas Gradgrind now presented Thomas Gradgrind to the little pitchers before him, who were to be filled so full of facts. Indeed, as he eagerly sparkled at them from the cellarage before mentioned, he seemed a kind of cannon loaded to the muzzle with facts, and prepared to blow them clean out of the regions of childhood at one discharge. He seemed a galvanizing apparatus, too, charged with a grim mechanical substitute for the tender young imaginations that were to be stormed away.

An opening to the mechanical Facts bought at this price of a closing to knowledge of a different and perhaps broader quality could be utterly baffling to those multi-dimensional fools whom

Gradgrind was dedicated to enlightening. Hence the circus girl
Sissy's confusion regarding how to respond to the Professor's command to define a horse—an animal that to her was everything from
mere beast to noble symbol. And hence, also, Gradgrind's sense that
her discomfiture confirms the truth of his mechanical wisdom. He
triumphantly appeals to one of the pupils he has already remade
to definitively resolve the issue of ignorance and enlightenment:

> "Girl number twenty," said Mr. Gradgrind, squarely pointing
> with his square forefinger... "Let me see. What is your father?"
> "He belongs to the horse-riding, if you please, sir."
> Mr. Gradgrind frowned, and waved off the objectionable
> calling with his hand.
> "We don't want to know anything about that, here. You mustn't
> tell us about that, here. Your father breaks horses, don't he?"
> "If you please, sir, when they can get any to break, they do
> break horses in the ring, sir."
> "You mustn't tell us about the ring, here. Very well, then.
> Describe your father as a horsebreaker. He doctors sick horses,
> I dare say?"
> "Oh yes, sir."
> "Very well, then. He is a veterinary surgeon, a farrier, and
> horsebreaker. Give me your definition of a horse."
> (Sissy Jupe thrown into the greatest alarm by this demand.)
> "Girl number twenty unable to define a horse!" said Mr.
> Gradgrind, for the general behoof of all the little pitchers. "Girl
> number twenty possessed of no facts, in reference to one of
> the commonest of animals! Some boy's definition of a horse.
> Bitzer, yours."

Finally, in one quite extraordinary passage, Dickens offers a
Platonic judgment on the final results of Professor Gradgrind's
Magisterium and the remaking of human beings that it involves.
The extra, broader—and possibly higher—illumination that Sissy
might have brought to those buried in her modernist cave of a classroom, where only a little light involving simple mechanical Facts
shone, cannot be permitted to penetrate. Thus, Bitzer, the student
called upon to enlighten her, is seen to be not only in desperate
need of further light himself, but also stripped of whatever visible
defining features he probably once possessed. Gradgrind, the self-
proclaimed Master of Them That Know, therefore reveals to us that
he has no clue concerning real darkness or enlightenment at all:

The square finger, moving here and there, lighted suddenly on Bitzer, perhaps because he chanced to sit in the same ray of sunlight which, darting in at one of the bare windows of the intensely white-washed room, irradiated Sissy. For, the boys and girls sat on the face of the inclined plane in two compact bodies, divided up the centre by a narrow interval; and Sissy, being at the corner of a row on the sunny side, came in for the beginning of a sunbeam, of which Bitzer, being at the corner of a row on the other side, a few rows in advance, caught the end. But, whereas the girl was so dark-eyed and dark-haired, that she seemed to receive a deeper and more lustrous colour from the sun, when it shone upon her, the boy was so light-eyed and light-haired that the self-same rays appeared to draw out of him what little colour he ever possessed. His cold eyes would hardly have been eyes, but for the short ends of lashes which, by bringing them into immediate contrast with something paler than themselves, expressed their form. His short-cropped hair might have been a mere continuation of the sandy freckles on his forehead and face. His skin was so unwholesomely deficient in the natural tinge, that he looked as though, if he were cut, he would bleed white.

"Bitzer," said Thomas Gradgrind. "Your definition of a horse."

"Quadruped. Graminivorous. Forty teeth, namely twenty-four grinders, four eye-teeth, and twelve incisive. Sheds coat in the spring; in marshy countries, sheds hoofs, too. Hoofs hard, but requiring to be shod with iron. Age known by marks in mouth." Thus (and much more) Bitzer.

"Now girl number twenty," said Mr. Gradgrind. "You know what a horse is."

Professor Thomas Gradgrind, as presented by Dickens, is one of the all too many arrogant ideologues emerging out of the eighteenth century's so-called Enlightenment. All Enlightenment thinkers insist upon building their knowledge of the universe and man's role within it upon "nature" and the "facts" of natural life. Never mind that their notorious disagreements over what these "obvious" natural facts might be—class struggle, laws of supply and demand, race, sex, national identity—have caused contemporary societies shaped by them to endure psychological and physical suffering of a subtlety and intensity unknown to earlier human beings. Each proponent of each and every varied, Enlightenment-inspired key to nature's teaching and the human liberation that

336

must come from acceptance of it has been absolutely and arrogantly certain that his school possesses the sole rational, infallible path to Freedom and Progress.

It is this certainty that requires a program of revolutionary remaking of men and women, clearly described in the 1700s in Jean Jacques Rousseau's *Confessions*, the *Emile*, and the *Social Contract*. Natural man is declared trapped in an unnatural condition. He needs urgently to be returned to life in a natural way. Souls who offer resistance to nature and nature's laws must be subject to a consciousness-raising education awakening them to their true natural selves and the well-being that they still so pathetically reject. None of their continued calls for nuance or consideration of other, broader facts in making decisions regarding both nature's rules as well as individual and social happiness can be rationally addressed. Reason, by definition, is on the side of the man of Enlightenment alone. Unnaturalness, and therefore irrationality and even non-humanness as a whole, are the lot of his opponents. The arguments of those in unquestioned need of being remade must be either ignored or ridiculed. When, as has all too often happened in the last few centuries, the revolutionary Will to Power that underlies the whole Enlightenment vision of intelligence triumphs, and a remaking of human beings is actually undertaken, the Gradgrinds succeed in giving the world the appearance of operating as they say it does. In the name of nature's laws, they cut off sources of light that draw from the whole of nature—not just the ideologue's portion of it—essential facts to teach us. They make natural men as unnatural as they are capable of becoming. And since the Gradgrinds are the masters of the dessiccated and unnatural world and individuals they create—i.e., the ones who "make it"—they have yet another argument for rejecting further criticism of their vision. Critics are envious losers in addition to being mentally incompetent. As neat Sophist approaches go, this Enlightenment pedagogue's program is probably unmatchable.

Now my good friends at Rocco's are "Sissys" as opposed to "Bitzers." They are bewildered by the Gradgrind Magisterium and resist being remade according to its teachings. If they were to "make it" in a world shaped by its principles—say, by winning the lottery, which is the only way they could do so—they would find

337

that they would be still more miserable than they were beforehand. They are too natural, normal, and, I would argue, too unconsciously Catholic in their mentality, to do violence to their souls either as "losers" or "winners." I feel very sorry for them, and ultimately for all of us, in consequence, and this for three reasons.

First of all, I feel sorry for them because we *do* live in a world ruled by the Gradgrind Magisterium. Moreover, we live in a country that has found a seemingly foolproof way to propagate its teachings while convincing almost everyone that we have not been revolutionized by them one bit at all. It has been the particular genius of the Anglo-American Enlightenment—which Chris Ferrara and I have spent years explaining in these pages and elsewhere—to continue to allow people the freedom to present their own varied magisterial teachings for the guidance of their little, impotent, cocktail party worlds, while insisting that they live their practical political, social and economic lives in line with Thomas Gradgrind's vision of reality.

Secondly, I feel sorry for my friends for not realizing that it is only Catholicism that can provide them the arguments to understand their predicament fully; that only Catholicism can end their tongue-tied, Sissy-like bewilderment in the face of the sophistic arguments and power of their naturalist "liberators."

It has been the particular genius of the anti-Enlightenment Catholic movement of the post-revolutionary era to spell out with greater discernment than ever before what it is that is wrong with Gradgrindism in all of its forms, ancient and modern, violent and Anglo-American. What that counterrevolutionary movement has taught us is that the "facts" of nature are always those of a world where evil is mixed with good and perceived by limited individuals open to error and sin. This means that the perceived natural "facts" are often not those of nature as such but of erroneous and fallen aspects of it: the errors of a narrow vision which tell us that might makes right; the fallen, selfish, materialist concerns that lead us to take advantage of the sins of the world to ride roughshod over everything else that our better selves warn us to avoid. And this, in consequence, demands two things: 1) that what is narrow in our natural vision be corrected by broader factual information; and 2) since "every good and perfect gift comes from above, from the Father of lights," that the facts regarding nature, seen under

338

the full sunshine of supernatural truth, always be recognized as trumping those of Gradgrind's half-blind Magisterium.

All those who prefer to view nature with blinders on, refusing the "boat-rocking" effect brought about by correcting what is narrow and parochial through the dictates of what is broader and higher, place a dead weight on the human mind and spirit. They form a depressingly similar force throughout the ages; what I like to call a Grand Coalition of the fallen natural Status Quo. A truly open mind helps to crush this Coalition's influence, but one cannot possess such an open mind and explain its conclusions coherently without the divine wisdom and ultimate organizing principles provided by the Catholic Faith. Again, most of my friends at Rocco's do not have that faith.

Finally, I feel sorry for all of us that Catholic Modernists—just another name for the naturalists I have been describing—seem to have gained the upper hand in the United States among the "salt of the earth" here; namely, conservatives and traditionalists. Prominent among Modernism's recent supporters are libertarians, all of whom insist upon the bending of the classical and Catholic tradition, politically and morally, to a naturalist economic order explained by simple, mechanical, uncontestable, Gradgrind-like "facts." Such Modernists tend to treat all criticism of their narrow facts as either the product of naive minds eager to return to a society where Everyman milks a cow for a living (certainly not my decidedly urbanite vision of existence); or, all too predictably, as the envy of losers who just do not know how to "make it" in a totally sensible market environment. The truth that we critics loathe the kind of world that has been constructed by these "facts" as a one-dimensional and unnatural zoo does not seem to be taken as anything other than a sign of our need for revolutionary consciousness-raising and further re-education.

These Catholic Modernists have convinced otherwise solid believers that Gradgrind's Magisterium is the Magisterium of the Roman Catholic Church. Many well-meaning conservative and traditionalist Catholics in the United States, justifiably proud of their loyalty to Catholic dogma, have thus proven decidedly unwilling to examine whether these dogmas really mean anything serious in their daily economic, social and political activities; whether they really rock the boat of a fallen status quo.

339

While looking for abstruse philosophical and esoteric explanations of Modernism and the way it has corrupted the Catholic Faith in our day, they have lost sight of the very essence of Modernism: once again, the treatment of nature as a closed system, sufficient unto itself, whose laws can be understood on its own terms, without reference to its marred character and its desperate need for redemption. While holding up the Catholic banner, they have welcomed the modernist libertarian invader, his naturalism, and the teachings of his Gradgrind Magisterium into their souls.

Some Catholics, suspicious that not all may be well with the libertarian vision, seem to be terrified into silence by the sheer number and specificity of the works that these Modernists produce. They ought to take heart from Aristotle's explanation of how the discerning rational mind can spot a quack and avoid his ministrations without being a knowledgeable surgeon himself. Catholics should realize that libertarians are quack doctors, and precisely because they are not operating with all of the knowledge that they need in order to make sensible statements about their chosen field of endeavor. They can write as many books as they want to on every economic issue imaginable, from the role of the Federal Reserve to the value of strip malls, and even make some solid points along the way. Nevertheless, there is no way that anyone can take any of these specific insights seriously until they abandon their embrace of the Gradgrind Magisterium and subject their "facts" to correction and consideration alongside non-economic natural concerns and divine truth. Until they do so, they will always be "Bitzers": sucked dry of everything valuable they might have to say. No one should lose a night's sleep worrying how to answer their massive but blind economic data. One should worry, instead, about how to counteract the damage this narrow knowledge is causing in the souls of its victims.

All of which brings me full circle, back to my *Stammtisch* and my friends at the cafe. Rocco's clientele is not unique. There is a world out there filled with normal but bewildered people who are not "making it," wonder why this is the case, and have a gut but unformed feeling that man does not live by "making it" through enslavement to a stunted soulless vision of nature alone. All such people deserve the chance to learn how they can really "make it" in a *truly* natural world. What they require is knowledge of the full Facts of Life.

Only the "boat-rocking" fullness of a Catholicism that teaches that nature needs the light of supernatural truth and grace to unfold its real innate glories and explain its sad problems can answer that need. Our latest crop of Catholic Modernists cannot do this work because their teaching tool is Gradgrind's Magisterium. Let us respond to the hunger of a world that senses there is something wrong with the natural status quo with the teachings of the broader and higher Catholic Magisterium. And let us ignore the modernist libertarian taunt that we display our economic ignorance in doing so. Such taunts are only to be expected. For Chauteaubriand is wrong. Those who would shove mankind back into the darkness of the cave and fasten a blindfold over its eyes *always*, at every moment in history, make the effort to lift minds and hearts to the light appear ridiculous.

The Crucial Seductive Error
of an Error-Filled Modernity[†]

HISTORY AS AN ACADEMIC DISCIPLINE
seeks to uncover the many complex factors playing a role
in shaping the lives of free men of mind, soul and body in an
ever-changing temporal order. Being an art as well, it also involves
discovering suitable techniques for driving home the main lesson to
be learned from the study of intricate past events, and, by seizing
hold of the attention and imagination of men, to move them to
some desirable action. If the historian ignores the complexity, he
presents his audience with a false picture of reality. If he does not
find a way to reduce the complexity to some kind of comprehensible
unity, he loses the teaching entirely, and his listeners along with it.

What this requires of me, as an historian dealing with the topic
in question here, is, first of all, an insistence upon the fact that the
errors of the modern world are legion, that their active agents have
been many, and that some of them have often been as unconscious
and self-destructive in their labors as others have been deliberate
and clear-headed. But driving home the main point to be learned
from the complex mayhem of modernity demands assertion of one
unifying truth: that all of the manifold errors of the modern world
can legitimately be reduced to a single underlying flaw. And this is
a rejection of precisely the doctrine of the Kingship of Jesus Christ.

Such a reduction can be justified because the doctrine of the
Kingship of Jesus Christ pays homage to each and every one of the
truths that affect our lives, ultimately placing all of them on their
proper rung in the hierarchy of values. Supernaturally revealed
though that doctrine is, it is also the jewel in the crown of all of the
teachings regarding the natural world that men of reason and genius,
eager to discover the real meaning of things, began to formulate
already before the Incarnation of the Word in time. It confirms,
corrects and exalts them all, serving as their most powerful and

---

[†] Lecture given at the 2011 Angelus Press Conference in Kansas City,
Missouri.

sole reliable shield and buckler. Let us briefly review the impact of this "sum of all truths," with reference both to Revelation and past historical developments, before returning to the complexities and the tragic seductive strength of the main problem before us now: its rejection by what we call the spirit of "modernity."

We know that the universe, as a whole, and in each and every one of its innumerable parts, is a work of God that He Himself found to be good. Any human attempt to come to grips with the world and man's role within it must therefore attest to the glory of their Creator. The conscious *rational* effort to discover the truths of the universe began with a Greek world that came to emphasize three points crucial to their intellectual enterprise: 1) that first appearances regarding things natural were often highly deceptive, and that what was therefore needed was to look for their underlying meaning—their *logos*—in order to be able to appreciate their proper purpose; 2) that individual men could learn and achieve nothing solid, and would even actually destroy themselves, if they did not realize that their personal development and perfection was a social enterprise, involving their participation in social life and their obedience to social authority; and, 3) given that the "good society" required for the development and perfection of individuals must itself be created by good individuals, men seemed to be trapped in a vicious circle that could only be broken if, as Plato said in *The Laws*, "some God" came to save them.

One of the reasons that the True God *did* come to save men was to reveal the conditions for using nature properly. Those conditions involved submission to Christ's supernatural teaching, His kingship, and His reign. Entry into the supremely good society created by membership in Christ, and obedience to His authority therein, provided the guidance and the grace needed to overcome a natural world wounded by human sinfulness and the temptation of fallen individuals to accept its false appearances rather than its substantive truths. The social authority of Christ and His Church, His Mystical Body, simultaneously offered both individual men as well as the temporal societies in which they lived the means of correcting their errors, allowing both to complete and perfect one another. In doing so, it turned all of nature into a tool for the realization of man's final supernatural end: eternal life with God. In and under Christ, as the second century Apologists so clearly indicated, all truths and all institutions could finally be made to work together harmoniously and effectively, with each gaining a much greater confidence in its particular value than it could ever have possessed without the appearance of the Savior in time and firm adherence to His teaching. In other words, they had to believe in Christ in order seriously to *believe* even in what their reason already told them about themselves.

But a focus on the rejection of the concept of the Social Kingship of Christ as the crucial modern error is more than simply justifiable; it is also an absolute practical necessity. Why? Because our enemies have promoted modernity's alternative to the reign of Our Lord and Savior as their own key principle, and they have done so and with a rhetorical genius whose seductive message believers themselves have repeatedly shown a propensity to accept and even somehow to baptize as eminently orthodox. Let us now turn our attention to that modern alternative, uncovering, as we do so, its seductive character, and the horror of succumbing to its apparent charms.

Modernity lives, or rather dies, by related versions of the same basic naturalist myth, whose various aspects were fleshed out over a long stretch of time. This myth describes the world's awakening to an ever-deeper understanding of nature through reliance on its own unaided teachings alone. As a result of that awakening, it claims that man was rendered capable not only of grasping nature's laws, but also the essence of the State, society, and the individual human person. In learning the laws of nature and political order, and the dignity and rights of man along with them, modernity supposedly found the real key to social and individual harmony. It became the simultaneous defender of law and order on the one hand and the fullness of the rights of a natural human freedom and diversity on the other. So great were the consequences that one might even entertain the hope of the lion lying down with the lamb! But far from opening man's ears to "the music of the spheres," modernity has actually guaranteed the creation of socio-political systems that deaden societies and individuals to all higher spiritual and aesthetic considerations whatsoever.

Rather than first tackling the question of the fraud in and of itself, I should like to begin approaching the spirit of modernity by discussing what I believe to be the basic reason for its success: its adoption of a strategy invented at the very beginning of the hunt for the Logos, whose greatest achievement was the transformation of the justification of passion and will into a seemingly high-minded vision. Profoundly anti-Socratic Sophists developed this strategy, which was most thoroughly expressed by the great rhetorician, Isocrates (436–338 B. C.) in his many battles with Plato. I think it is very important to explore that strategy in detail at its ancient roots in order to emphasize the truth that the demon that plagues us today has been lurking about for millennia. Besides, learning of modernity's actual antiquity is one potent means of debunking its claim to be something "new" and "fresh."

For Isocrates, there was no question of seriously critiquing, transforming and possibly even rejecting the immediate emotional and sensual experiences and preoccupations of the ordinary man. Man was the measure of all things, and unquestionably correct in his urgent, common-sense appreciation of the importance of obtaining the riches, power and fame that he *obviously* knew would yield the beautiful life. The average individual's sole problem was a *technical* one: he could not relate one, justifiable, obvious, common-sense experience to another, and thereby understand how best to exploit and satisfy them regularly and comprehensively. His efforts to explain his reactions to daily problems, both to himself as well as to others, proved to be "dumb" ones. It was effective words, and the arguments shaped through them, which were lacking to the average man. Only the well-trained rhetorician, the master of words, could clarify the full depth of immediate feelings and experiences, show where they were headed, and stir people to do what was necessary to fulfill their promise. The Good and the True were, therefore, ultimately nothing other than "appropriate explanations" of reality, and developments of those obvious and common-sense reactions to the raw stuff of daily life that are themselves absolutely infallible guides to the possession of Beauty.

But how would Everyman know that the rhetorician was "speaking appropriately" about reality? The answer to this question was also an obvious one. For the master rhetorician's advice would not only "sound right," clearly, consistently and self-assuredly responding to the average individual's personal sense of the obvious truth of his own preoccupations, and where, more or less, those concerns are headed. Beyond that, it would prove itself by being crowned with clear material success. Hence, Isocrates' need to underline the simplicity, lucidity, harmony of purpose, confidence and material achievements of *his* pupils, while contrasting them with the cranky and ultimately unfathomable detours, self-criticisms, bitter divisions and practical failures of the Socratics.

Still, Isocrates realized that Plato had placed the discussion of nature, the State and the individual on such a higher plane that the rhetorician was now obliged to drive his argument home with a "philosophy"; a vision that was equally universal and noble sounding. He offered such a philosophical vision by hunting for the Foundational Principle of Greek society and the mission that corresponded to it. These he outlined in his discussion of Hellenism: the knowledge of "words" as such, rather than understanding of the Logos or "Word" behind things, and the need to spread this eastward, into the Persian Empire.

Fulfillment of future Hellenist destiny would require two things simultaneously. On the one hand, it would be crucial to maintain a constant respect for the "good old days" of the foundation of the Greek spirit and the institutions giving clout to it. On the other, it would be necessary to shape a loyal population obedient to any vigorous hero who might guide that spirit to the discharge of its contemporary mission. Moreover, the institutions embodying the spirit of the good old days, the strong man giving them clout, and the populations obedient to his *fiat* were to be stirred to their appropriate political roles through the creative rhetorical genius, who grasped the essence of Hellenism through his vital knowledge of and skill with words.

But "philosophy," as defined by Isocrates, constitutes a gigantic circle, manipulated by the rhetorician who, through the clever use of appealing words and images, seizes control of the familiar concerns of the average man or State and runs with them where he wills. Common sense experience is pronounced the infallible basis for action simply because the experience appealed to is arbitrarily declared "common sense-filled" and thus an infallible basis for a man's work. Successful attainment of riches and power is said to prove the appropriateness of the rhetorician's understanding of the beautiful life, and guidance of Everyman to fulfillment of its promise, because possession of riches and power is presented as unquestionable, axiomatic proof that beauty has indeed been grasped hold of. Respect for the "good old days," contemporary strong men and obedient populations are essential because denial of such esteem to any one of these elements would rip apart the "beautiful" rhetorical image tying together ancient roots with present hopes and future destiny, mass popularity and elite power. And all those aspects of "the vision" were essential, since experience had proven them necessary to construct the career of the master of words, whose personal success worked to guarantee the validity of their union.

Absolutely no questioning of "obvious experience," "common sense," "success," the "historic mission," and the consistency of the tools required for its realization can be contemplated, lest this lead to the unacceptable argument that obvious experience, common sense, success, the historical mission and its vital tools were themselves somewhat problematic. Isocrates, as Werner Jaeger notes, makes a virtue out of abandoning any deeper investigation of the meaning of life once he has shaped what for him appears to be a rhetorically beautiful "point of view" with a chance of obtaining a successful outcome. That "point of view," if attractive and potentially useful, *must* be accepted as though it were Truth itself. With this, the debate is over. Closure has been achieved. One must move on to accomplishment of the Great Promise, or face the wrath of the rhetorician and the outraged nature whose unerring voice he has infallibly proclaimed himself to be.

And the rhetorician *is* powerful. He knows that his words do have "the ring of truth." He is sure that he can count on the support of immediately felt, individual, family or polis-wide "common sense" passions in his call for their immediate satisfaction. He senses the understandable and well-nigh universal fear that acceptance of Socratic self-criticism would paralyze swift action, thus preventing exploitation of favorable opportunities to fulfill desire and causing men to "lose out" on success, perhaps even up to the very moment of death. The rhetorician, with his mastery of words, can paint the profound, life-determining, "either-or" option offered to men by Sophists and Socratics in all of its dramatic colors, though clearly weighted to his advantage. After he has skillfully organized the picture as he wishes, any Socratic who calls the average man to logical, painful soul-searching at the possible expense of satisfying urgent passion becomes a sitting duck for his rhetorical abuse. A Platonic philosopher would all too easily lend himself to the accusation of representing both a crackpot idealism, indifferent to the obvious demands of human nature, as well as a cynical opposition to the successes of "real men," whom he cannot emulate, bitterly envies, and wishes to destroy in consequence.

Plato argued that the successful rhetorician may deceive himself into thinking that he is superior to his "wordless" audience, but he is simply more effectively "thick" than it is. His words resemble an overbearing and endlessly repeated rock rhythm in a room filled with impressionable but musically illiterate hedonists. They fail to elevate, just as any tool that uses man, rather than God, as the measure of all things falls miserably short of its pretensions. Anyone responding to the "either-or" option confronting him by choosing for the rhetorician would, therefore, be voting for eternal mediocrity and blindness. Sadly, precisely due to the rhetorician's observable knack for maintaining power over the vulgar mob, the pathetic outcome of such a wrong choice could conceivably be hidden from its victims forever. False rhetorical "philosophers" needed only to do two things: 1) enthusiastically to invent ever "new" surface variants on the proven appealing slogans to keep men thinking that fulfillment of the brilliant promise of the Empty Life lay just around the corner; and, 2) constantly to drill into a benumbed population's mind the fear of the "dead-end" impotence that the Socratic hunt for a more profound goal would ensure.

If the efforts of the Socratics to look behind the outward and generally false appearances of things in order to discover their inner "logos" were bitterly resisted by those who wished to follow the demands of "nature as is," the followers of the Word Incarnate enraged them all the more. As noted above, Christ provided the logos-hunters infinitely greater support in their effort to get at the truth, guiding it through the work of His Mystical Body, the Church, with her militant insistence upon a universal submission to His Kingship. All those who for whatever reason could not endure looking beyond the "business as usual" concerns of an unrepentant world joined in a common war to bring the Christian beast to heel: a Grand Coalition in aid of the maintenance of the fallen natural Status Quo. Heirs of those Sophists who used their talents to ridicule the Socratic enterprise did the same with the

Christians, dismissing them as "enemies of mankind" and—to resort to modern American parlance—"losers" to boot.

Due to the public conversion of the Roman Empire, and the subsequent evangelization of the barbarian invaders of the Christianized world, the Grand Coalition of the Status Quo was forced to go "underground." Its membership, however, grew in number and boldness in proportion to the commitment of the Church to announce to the world that the Kingdom of God really was at hand, and that its arrival affected all of human life. By the Twelfth Century it was ready to "come out of the closet" and openly contest the Catholic vision, as well as all of those natural ancient allies that had found their home in the bosom of the Church.

Sad to say, enemies of the Kingship of Christ have always been able to count upon assistance even from among otherwise firmly orthodox believers. This has been true for many different reasons. Grasping exactly what the correction and transformation of all of nature would mean, and then fighting ingrained personal and social customs and authorities preventing the taking of its requirements seriously were not precisely easy tasks from the very outset. When progress in knowledge was gradually made, growing Catholic appreciation for the intrinsic dignity of the earthly tools and institutions to which they were most attached tempted men and women to exaggerate their unique importance to the exclusion of all of the others around them. Given a simultaneous misdirection of the developed Catholic sense of the supreme importance of the individual, such tunnel vision was now backed by a personal willfulness more pronounced in its reductionism than anything known in the ancient world. That willfulness was ready to baptize whatever it wished, not only as something eminently Catholic, but often even as the *unum necessarium*. It could believe this all the more firmly to the degree that Church authorities failed to do their necessary corrective work, allowed such errors to take root as "new traditions," that then turned into articles of Faith. And to make matters worse, anger and frustration over missteps and outright malfeasance on the part of the popes, bishops and priests responsible for effecting beneficent Christian change brought discredit upon the whole project. None of these factors contributing to limiting the true Kingship of Christ can be neglected if we are fully to understand and deal with our own dilemma today.

What happened, therefore, from the High Middle Ages onwards, is that Catholics themselves, alongside outright members of the Grand Coalition of the Status Quo, ended up latching onto the ancient defense of "nature as is" for their own mistaken and misguided purposes. What this was eventually to entail was a dismantling of the entire corrective and transforming mission of the Word in history. But such an enterprise also had to become an attack on the whole Socratic project, whose underlying goals and whose enemies were, *mutatis mutandis*, similar to those of the Christians, and certainly had been co-opted by the latter. This was to leave as the guide for human action precisely what the Socratics had fought against from the very beginning of the hunt for the Logos: reliance solely on the data provided by "obvious" passion and first impression. And this inevitably ended by serving the interests of the strongest "heroic" wills in society, as justified by clever "word merchants," with reference to loyalty to "foundation principles."

Moreover, just as the Socratic Revolution did not allow Isocrates the opportunity to press for a return to the unexamined life without an appropriately noble explanation for doing so, no one, after having experienced the infinitely greater effort to transform the world in Christ, could retreat from the higher plane on which the Church's argument had been made without a rich rhetorical cover story that was presented as a theological or philosophical vision. This took two basic forms, the first appearing in the Thirteenth Century, the second slightly later. Both "alternate good stories" worked for a long period of time in sometimes friendly, sometimes quite hostile pursuit of the same anti-Catholic, anti-Socratic goal, until the second finally gained the dominant role. Both were expressed in a variety of nuanced ways that "worked" for different audiences. Both played on fallen man's desire to be rid of a religious and rational message that sought to restrain satisfaction of his manifold immediate passions, while answering his post-Christian need to appear to be virtuous as he continued with a career of sin.

Alternate good story number one chastised the Catholic (and Socratic) outlook for having betrayed the true Christian Foundation and Mission. These were said to be discernible through Scripture alone, and only capable of being recaptured through a return to that poor, humble, basically fleshless Apostolic Church that the storytellers insisted Holy Writ required. The writings of men like Marsilius of Padua (c. 1270–1342), William of Ockham (c. 1288–1348), and, ultimately, Martin Luther (1483–1546) cannot help but show us where all this was leading, whether they wanted it to go there or not: to an unexamined natural order ruled only through the triumph of the strongest will. All of the writers in question excoriated a papal-guided Church with practical muscle, seeking to correct and transform things in Christ. All of them, in different ways, stripped nature of the tools required for judging social and individual action.

For Marsilius and William, any such corrective effort, interfering as it did with the activity of the sole Defender of the Peace, the Roman Emperor, the heroic agent entrusted by them with the mission of securing a return to the Christian Foundation Principles, was the chief cause for disorder in nature. Marsilius made of the law, both natural and positive, whatever it was that a man had to do in order not to be hung by the Emperor; William insisted upon the limitations of Reason, stressed the overriding importance of Divine Will in learning all truths, and then made it impossible for us to know what this would be, in practical political and social life, except through the natural will of the existing authorities. Luther, who could not count on imperial aid in returning to the "original intent" of the Christian Foundation, gave this power over to the local sovereign, who thus became a "necessity bishop." And through his doctrine of the total depravity of all of nature, he left the chaos around us, and anyone who would try to guide it, with no clear tools for doing so whatsoever.

Luther, despite his handing of the jungle of nature over to political lion tamers, was actually a bridge to alternate good story number two, in which the heroes bringing about the return to the Foundational Principles were the rhetoricians themselves; the men of letters, the preachers, the prophetic ideologues stirring men to the destruction of the idols terrifying them into enchaining their free action. But this second myth differed from the first in abandoning the Christian Foundation theme entirely, and chastising the Catholic-Socratic outlook for betraying the fundamental teachings of Mother Nature, whose basic principles were said to be there for anyone with bare common sense to grasp. The choice now was either that for Catholicism (and the "unnatural," helpless, poverty-stricken disorder its vision ensured), or for Mother Nature, along with the strength, riches and peace that she provided.

Unfortunately, those opting for Mother Nature found that their common-sense grasp of her fundamental principles actually led them down many opposing directions. Some saw her to be a machine, filled with obvious, ironclad "natural laws," often reducible to one magical "key," whether economic, biological or sexual in character. Others saw in her the realm of diversity, the playground of endless diverse passions and dreams, an ever-increasing number of which had to be protected as crystal-clear "natural rights." But although the preferential options for "natural law" or "natural right" seemed to be in total contradiction, they both actually reduced to similar willful choices that accepted no correction from any outside "judge" that might limit or reject their desire to manipulate nature as they saw fit. Machine-like or libertine in character, they both reflected a common disdain for the teaching of the "logos of things."

Anyone longing to discover natural law and order under these circumstances had to nuance his "vision" by following in one way or another the equally willful advice given by Jean-Jacques Rousseau (1712–1778). Law and order, for Rousseau, came through construction of the natural, virtuous society. But natural virtue was not something built through the repetition of the petty, daily, "good" actions praised by the outside world. Rather, one attained it by entering into that ontological state of being a liberated "natural man." Rousseau reached this natural, virtuous condition through his *Confessions* (published posthumously, 1782). Here, he revealed to the world all his deepest, passionate, non-rational feelings and their effect on his actions, without consideration for the effect such disclosure might have upon public opinion and his own personal fame and fortune. Having thus accepted his natural self, he became virtuous, and no longer ashamed of deeds that others thought reprehensible; deeds that would, indeed, still be truly blameworthy if done by men seeking praise from the artificial, outside, "objective" world. Once virtuous, Rousseau could permit himself no rationalist post-mortem on the validity of his deeply-felt goodness. All "looking back" amounted to a renewed embrace of the unjustifiable rules of a soul-killing artifice and duplicity.

His hunt to be natural not only made him virtuous; it also transformed Rousseau into Everyman. Nature possessed integrity. It was all of one piece, honest and good, and could not help but speak with a single voice. Therefore, others who sincerely stripped themselves of the obstacles standing in the way of their right to express their spontaneous natural feeling would inevitably be indistinguishable from, and united fraternally with Rousseau. It is this indistinguishable character that ensured that the various lovers in his widely-read *Nouvelle Héloise* (1761) were actually only loving themselves in other people, and the teacher in his enormously influential educational treatise, the *Emile* (1761), could be said by Rousseau to both ensure the child's self-fulfillment and yet remake him totally in the tutor's image at one and the same time. Conversely, anyone who was not Rousseau-like, anyone who criticized Everyman's feelings and spontaneous actions, anyone who failed to pity him in his trials, revealed himself as being unnatural. He could thus be neither free, nor virtuous, nor truthful. In fact, he could not even be labeled human, and did not deserve any fraternal consideration whatsoever.

Rousseau was convinced that the non-virtuous and non-human world around him was stubbornly hostile to the effort to perfect it. The duty of Everyman-Rousseau was either to transform that world into his image, or cause it to disappear before it could do him any further damage. Once again, the question of a possible initial flaw undermining the value of his entire argument could not even be imagined; the sincere, virtuous, free, liberated Everyman was necessarily free from error. No discussion concerning the ground and justification of this underlying truth was permissible. It was a self-evident given. Doubt regarding his position would in effect mean allowing the sham world of the hypocrite to influence him once more. It was either one or the other; natural virtue or self-doubting vice in their fullness.

Orthodox Catholic defense against the first of the alternate good stories discussed above, with its high-minded "return" to the supposed "foundation" principles of the Apostolic Church, was, to begin with, fitful. The Catholic Reformation nevertheless represented a major effort to restore commitment to the need for acceptance, correction and transformation of all of nature in and through Christ and His Mystical Body. Internal opposition to what modern critics have called "Tridentine Catholicism" remained strong, however, most vividly in the battle of puritanical Jansenists against the work of the Society of Jesus. And in the Eighteenth Century, they were joined by many Catholic clerics and laymen who had become overawed by the arguments and the successes of the so-called "moderate" proponents of the second "alternate good story."

These were the Newtonians, the Whigs, and the Pietists of Britain and Prussia. Eager to escape the outright atheism of the radical naturalists, and therefore seemingly "godly" in their approach, such men insisted upon avoiding doctrinal battles and focusing on universally accepted Christian themes and guidelines for practical action which they claimed were rooted in natural "common sense" anyway. Moderates also argued that any fears regarding whether or not one was doing God's work in life could be determined by seeing if He crowned one's efforts with natural "success."

Britain and Prussia had much success in the 1700s. Catholic States not wanting to be "losers" followed their lead, and much of the Church, willy-nilly, accommodated and even enthusiastically imitated them. But even if the name of God might indeed be regularly on their successful lips, this was a Deity who blessed whatever "worked" for individuals and societies in the temporal order—something Isocrates could easily have accepted. He was not the King of the universe who corrected and transformed the accomplishments of the "successful" when they ran counter to what was honestly True, Good and Beautiful. This was an impotent God who obeyed the "laws" of nature, the state of whose health could no longer be examined by believers, lest their doctrinal squabbles disrupt the smooth machine of society and supposedly aid the cause of atheism to boot.

But impotence was not in the program of a Catholicism that came to rediscover itself in the course of the 1800s. Throughout the post-French revolutionary world, Catholic thinkers and activists demonstrated a desire to learn, develop and put into practice principles that had been buried by decades and even centuries of naturalist influence, Jansenist rejection of "Jesuitical" attempts to raise all things to the greater glory of God, and simple, rut-like, parochial neglect. The centers of re-discovery—German, Italian and French for the most part—were lay/clerical circles of believers, religious confraternities, orders restored after the devastation of the

Revolution, university faculties, and groups gathering round those journals and newspapers that seemed to spring up everywhere in the course of the nineteenth century. A number of the themes that we have already repeatedly emphasized in today's lecture stand out in this movement of rediscovery, the most basic of which is, once again, an insistence upon the impossibility of understanding and perfecting anything in nature without reference to its supernatural end and the grace surging through individuals and societies as a consequence of the Incarnation of the Word. For, as the Roman Jesuit journal, *La Civiltà Cattolica*, put it:

> God ... has established one sole order composed of two parts: nature exalted by grace, and grace vivifying nature. He has not confused these two orders, but He has coordinated them. One force alone is the model and one thing alone the motive principle and ultimate end of divine creation: Christ ... All the rest is subordinated to Him. The goal of human existence is to form the Mystical Body of this Christ, of this Head of the elect, of this Eternal Priest, of this King of the immortal Kingdom, and the society of those who will eternally glorify Him.

Catholic thinkers saw that modernity, in barricading man in nature alone, had cut him off from his final purpose in life and thus completely misunderstood human personality and the means of perfecting it. Liberal modernists interpreted that naturalism in an individualist manner, with an emphasis upon "freedom" that destroyed man's social character and ensured the triumph of the will of a materialist and ultimately self-destructive oligarchy over the weak mass of the population. But it opened itself up to other willful forces eager to dominate the world based on different interpretations of nature's supposed meaning and goals. Hence, Marxism, though sharing the same materialism as liberalism, exaggerated man's natural social character and thus destroyed his individuality. Therefore, despite all of its claims to assure Order, Progress and Liberty, modern naturalism could not help but guarantee the opposite result: the creation of a realm of confusion, where neither society nor the individual understood its true character, where violence reigned, and where "freedom" and "success" were defined by the will of the strongest, whoever they might be. Again, in the *Civiltà's* words:

The truth is that the universe is the work of an infinite wisdom of which no man can change the nature, although he may be free to deny it. The nature that is denied by man through thought and doctrine is then denied by him also in practice. A man's struggling with nature is an insane war against God, wherein the mortal cannot hope to triumph, but, rather, is certain to be defeated. To concede, therefore, to all men the freedom to wage this war, to blindfold their eyes so that they may not see their sores, their defeats; to concede the freedom of error to oppress the truth, may well be the momentary delirium of blinded intellects and the suicide of frenetic societies; but it can never be the durable basis of civilization, never the hoped-for foundation of a new society.

Starting with the words "I am free" and their new-found spirit of independence, men began to believe in the infallibility of whatever seemed natural to them, and then to call "nature" everything that is sickness and weakness; to want sickness and weakness to be encouraged instead of healed; to suppose that encouraging weakness makes men healthier and happy; to conclude, finally, that human nature {conceived of as sickness and weakness} possesses the means to render man and society blissful on earth, and this without faith, grace, authority or supernatural community... since "nature" gives us the feeling that it must be so.

Let us say it then frankly: all social unity must collapse and be routed as soon as the Protestant principle is introduced and reigns therein. And the reasons reduce all to one. Admitting the Lutheran principle, it is impossible to have any true idea of right. Protestants may well be able, owing to logical incoherence or by accident, to admit some principle of right in their society. But this will be the effect of a habit, of an accident, of a lack of reasoning, of natural honesty in their inclinations, or of some other similarly fortuitous conditions affecting this or that individual. But the nature of the Protestant principle, that nature which sooner or later finally produces its inevitable effects, renders absolutely impossible the idea of right, and, in consequence, of social unity.

... No, there is no more unity for this destructive demon. The mind was liberated, through freethinking, from the yoke of a God who speaks to man; through individual criticism, from the yoke of reason; through Popular Sovereignty, from that of any authority; through the right to suicide, from the yoke of all fear. Any society—the communion of the soul with God in the

356

Church, of the people with their prince in the polis, of a wife with her husband in the family, of the body with the soul in the individual—is devastated any time social bonds are measured against the impulse of a passion, against a "right," against a desire for pleasure. Each society is devastated in its primary governing entity. It is thrown into the hands of a crazed man whose will is arbitrary. This is the ultimate consequence of the Protestant principle of independence.

. . . Force. Let us say it straightforwardly. Let us repeat it with daring. Force is the only social instrument left to the Protestant who wishes to be logical. And since the sole means of salvation becomes a right in society, the right in Protestant society is force.

And the truth is that this freedom, as any other unlimited liberty not circumscribed by anything, is nothing other than the privilege agreed upon for the strong to assassinate the weak. In this case, the freedom of the strong party is offended, since he is given the arbitrary ability to abuse his faculty, and the freedom of the weak party is offended, as he remains the undefended victim of that abuse.

In fact, all of the thinkers of the nineteenth century Catholic revival were convinced that the "music of the spheres" that was heard under modern circumstances would be either the insane ravings of the mentally ill or the ever more base drumbeats played by libertines or criminals stirring up passions and fear among the "natural men" that they were oppressing in the name of liberty. Which of these approaches would gain the final victory they could not say. Nevertheless, they envisaged the development of a worldwide criminal and pleasure-seeking order, ever loyal to the fraudulent concept of the freedom and the rights of increasingly boring "natural men," and working through a mishmash of capitalism, socialism, advanced scientific technology, bureaucracy, and charismatic dictatorship. Louis Veuillot (1813–1883), editor of the Catholic daily, *l'Univers*, gave us this prediction of drab, global, materialist pragmatism and socialist bureaucracy very well in his vision of what he called the coming Empire of the World.

Everywhere, the conqueror [of the world] will find one thing, everywhere the same, the only thing that war and the Revolution will nowhere have overturned: bureaucracy. Everywhere the bureau will have prepared the way for him; everywhere they await him with a servile eagerness. He will support himself on them. The universal Empire will be the administrative Empire par excellence. Adding without end to that precious machinery, he will carry it to a point of incomparable power. Thus perfected, administration will satisfy simultaneously its own genius and the design of its master in applying itself to two main works: the realization of equality and of material well-being to an unheard-of degree; the suppression of liberty to an unheard-of degree.

Men ruled by this system would be much more easily oppressed than at any time in the past. Such facility would be due, not so much to the fact that new weapons would give its dictator undreamed-of instruments of control, as to the sad reality that stupefied, machine-like man would approve of his chains, and a dull-witted intelligentsia would bless them. The men produced by modern civilization would be totally distinct from men of preceding ages. "These powers that present-day man possesses," Veuillot wrote, "possess him also; they engage him in weaknesses as unmeasured as his pride, weaknesses that succeed in changing him completely." Ironically, they also left him "too powerful to control the taste for pleasure." Man thus became a being unable even to begin to desire the destiny intended for him by God. The universal Empire would enslave such creatures by providing for their most banal needs.

> The police will take care that one is amused and that its reins never trouble the flesh. The administration will dispense the citizen of all care. It will fix his situation, his habitation, his vocation, his occupations. It will dress him and allot to him the quantity of air that he must breathe. It will have chosen him his mother; it will choose him his temporary wife; it will raise his children; it will take care of him in his illnesses; it will bury and burn his body, and dispose of his ashes in a record box with his name and his number.

And as time went on, this task would become simpler and simpler. A decline in human imagination would entail a destruction of the taste for a variety of pleasures.

> But why would he change places and climates? There will no longer be different places or climates, or any curiosity anywhere. Man will everywhere find the same moderate temperature, the same customs, the same administrative rules, and infallibly the same police taking the same care of him. Everywhere the same language will be spoken, the same *bayadères* will everywhere

dance the same ballet. The old diversity will be a memory of the old liberty, an outrage to the new equality, a greater outrage to the bureau, which would be suspected of not being able to establish uniformity everywhere. Their pride will not suffer that. Everything will be done in the image of the main city of the Empire and of the World.

This being the case, the movement of Catholic rediscovery was charged with a sense of mission. It was convinced that Christianity and Christianity alone possessed the truth that could complete and exalt all of nature. This message had to be made manifest in politics, economics and every other aspect of human life, and that could only happen if Christ were recognized as the King of Society at large and of individuals personally. The sense of urgency and drama felt by activists is well depicted in one major article of the *Civiltà*: *O dio re colla libertà, o l'uomo re colla forza.* ("Either God Will be King with Liberty, or Man Will be King Through Force"). Catholics had to correct and transform the world in Christ, or the world would be handed over to the perverted free will of varied groups and individuals to destroy as they pleased; and sooner rather than later.

The history of the Church is replete with examples of intellectually and militantly active stimuli emerging from "below" to awaken believers to the fullness of the Christian mission and the dangers threatening it. Nevertheless, nothing fully and properly Catholic can ever be achieved unless the Papacy is enlisted in a movement of revival. Reformers understand that truth and pressed insistently for an expansion of the teaching and pastoral activity of the Holy See over Christendom as a whole. It was precisely this that took place from the reign of Blessed Pius IX (1846–1878) onwards, first through documents such as the *Syllabus of Errors* (1864), that clearly identified the errors of modernity, and then through the encyclicals of Pope Leo XIII (1878–1903), that contrasted them with the basic Catholic position on issues of all kinds, beginning with the relationship of natural reason to theology, and ending with the specifics of confronting contemporary political, social, and economic life.

Libertas (June 20, 1888) is a classic of the latter genre; a *Summa* of all of the themes regarding the hunt for the proper understanding of nature tackled from the very beginning of this lecture in presenting the battle of Isocrates and Plato. That makes sense, for three specific reasons. First of all, because the question of whether "freedom" from supernatural and natural authority of all kinds aids or destroys individual and social life is at the heart of our discussion of the Kingship of Christ and its rejection. Secondly, due to the fact that Leo XIII was not the creator of the ideas to which he gives clear, magisterial support, but was himself a product of the nineteenth century revival movement that so brilliantly emphasized them. And, finally, because it was that movement that grasped the long-term historical development of the problem before us, guiding academics like myself to see their ancient, pre-Christian roots in the process. Without the Leonine encyclicals, the influence of the nineteenth century movement to accept, correct and transform all aspects of the jointly individual and social life of men in nature would not have had the impact it deserved; but without that movement there would have been no encyclicals promoting the universal reign of Christ at all.

Given that worldly activity was the sphere of the laity, the work of promoting the Social Kingship of Christ generally had to be its responsibility. The call to arms of the laity was very much a nineteenth century mobilization, with the prophets of Catholic rediscovery having been the initial recruiting sergeants and Blessed Pius IX and Leo XIII their authoritative voice. After 1848, practical guidelines for fulfilling its mission were clearly laid out. So long as the principle of striving to construct a Catholic society (the so-called *thesis*) were clearly maintained, a wide scope for tactical experimentation (the *hypothesis*) in pursuit of victory was permitted. Should experimentation threaten to subvert the principle of the Kingship of Christ, however, a retreat from an exposed front would be in order.

Convinced naturalist members of the Grand Coalition of the Status Quo obviously could not accept such a revival of the Catholic claim to correct and transform social life. Hence, the outbreak of those "culture wars" that began in the latter half of the nineteenth century. In Germany and Austria, Catholic political activity was somewhat effective in defending the Church. In Italy, where the liberal system more rigorously blocked religious influence, a policy of neither voting for nor serving as officials on the national level was adopted. Catholics "participated" in national social life by "abstaining" from a political fraud and preparing for a return to power in their own "shadow government." Unfortunately, however, the perennial temptation of Catholics to become fellow travelers of the Grand Coalition of the Status Quo and the "business as usual" demands of "nature as is" proved once again to be very strong indeed.

The tragic story of the Abbé Félicité de Lamennais (1782–1854), one of the great early figures in the Catholic revival movement, already illustrates all too clearly the problems to come. What he did was to base his argument for the transformation of all things in Christ in a Faith that ultimately took a radical Rousseau-like naturalist form. The Faith, for Lamennais, was ingrained in the whole tradition of a Catholic people. One might say that he thought it had become "second nature" to it, guaranteeing it a comforting infallibility.

At first, he believed this meant that a traditional, legitimist, Catholic "people's king" would unfailingly protect religion. It was when the Bourbon government seemed to strangle the Church's voice, sometimes even in alliance with liberals, and French bishops failed to vigorously oppose such activity, that he transferred all his deceived hopes to a separation of Church and State that he thought would release Catholic energies and ensure Christ's reign over society. Lamennais confidently turned to the pope, as another voice of tradition, to support this new "obvious" truth. When the pope himself proved to be a disappointment, the bastion of the Faith became the People at large.

Unfortunately, the people were as yet "asleep" to their mission, and had to be awakened to it by the one man who had stripped himself of all obstacles to listening to the voice of infallible Tradition: Lamennais himself. Having reached this point, and having been excommunicated for it, he gradually abandoned the Faith entirely. By the time Lamennais died, he had become the prophet of a universal democratic religion of the People as the voice of God. "Separation" for him then became the means of a new political-spiritual union, whose goals were defined by the religious prophet whose consciousness had been properly raised and who could therefore show the People at large what God wanted them to say. Isocrates had returned in Catholic form. True supernatural correction and transformation of nature had found another enemy, with an alternative good story to sell his wares.

Fear of the "radical" socialist movement eventually led many continental liberals to emphasize their moderate "conservatism," abandon their anti-Catholic religious attacks, and make an appeal to men of faith to join in a common defense of private property against "godless communism." The one catch here was that Catholics were summoned to accept the liberal contention that socialism was the only real modern danger, and that liberalism should be baptized as "godly" in consequence. This argument was rejected by the so-called "intransigent" wing of the Catholic movement of rediscovery, which reiterated liberalism's foundation in the same modern naturalist rejection of the Kingship of Christ as socialism, and its inevitable encouragement, whether consciously or unconsciously, of all willful, anti-religious, irrational, materialist visions of life.

In fact, if some liberals moved towards "conservatism," and even dropped the name "liberal" altogether, others followed the dictates of their irrational materialist will down a socialist direction. Some of these liberal socialists also began to make an appeal for Catholic support, emphasizing their agreement with religious attacks on the anti-social individualism of the "conservatives." Intransigents rejected their appeal for the same reasons as they did that of the friends of uncontrolled individual property. Catholic understandings of freedom and community, they argued, were based upon an acceptance of the corrective and transforming guidance of Christ and all of the societies that worked together with His Mystical Body. They could never be founded upon modern naturalist ideas separating individual and social concerns from one another, and "liberating" both from the dictates of Faith and Reason.

But, once again, there were fellow travelers who disagreed with the intransigents. Most of the intellectual opposition emerged from the camp of Lamennais. This led to the formation of the school of Liberal Catholicism, whose most famous proponent was the Count Charles de Montalembert (1810–1870). His argument for continued cooperation with liberalism took several forms, with its more radical expression rooted in the principle of *palingenesis*. This claimed that Catholicism was reborn anew in each age in different form. Catholicism had to be liberal in the modern age because the modern age had made of liberalism a practical necessity. But Liberal Catholicism could not remain united. Given the innate confusions of liberalism itself, Catholics who cooperated with it split in the same way as their non-religious brethren. Some became liberal conservatives, treating individual freedom, and especially economic freedom, as the most important of political goals for god-fearing Catholics to support. Others followed the path leading to liberal socialist programs and emphasized the concerns of the god-beloved masses above all others.

A much more mundane opposition to the intransigent vision of striving for the Kingship of Christ also existed, this one emerging from the ranks of Catholic parties and movements. It made perfect sense that these preferred a more democratic political and social order as a means of escaping the control of naturalist, materialist, capitalist oligarchies. But they themselves proved to be susceptible to naturalism in pursuing their democratic politics. Here, the problem was the same as that described by Max Weber in discussing the German Social Democrats: the creation of the party "functionary" and the desire to succeed in order to justify the group's existence and continue to have a secure position. What this meant was that Catholic democratic-minded activists, rather than seeking to correct and transform the world around them, were tempted to appeal to every popular movement, from extreme nationalism to socialism, just to keep themselves in business.

Pius IX already condemned the intellectual arguments of Liberal Catholics in the Syllabus of Errors and other documents of the latter part of his reign. More radical developments of their themes continued to be rejected throughout the following pontificates of Leo XIII and St. Pius X, both through the growth of Catholic social theory as well as through the campaign against Modernism, culminating in the attack on the democratic Sillon movement in 1910. Political and social currents eager to cooperate with popular non-Catholic groups were also reined in at the same time.

On the other hand, the Church seemed more and more to be giving practical support to that anti-socialist, "liberal conservative" position that claimed to disown its revolutionary past and extend a hand of friendship to Catholics. This certainly was the noticeable effect of reining in desires to create a popular Catholic political party in Italy before World War One. Moreover, one of the major consequences of that wretched conflict was to intensify this "practical conservatism." Horrified by the growth of Soviet Marxism, the Church was more ready than ever to cooperate with liberals whose perhaps even greater terror before the Bolshevik threat was driving them to contemplate alliance with anyone and everyone. The Lateran Accords with Fascist Italy was a deal with liberal conservatives who had come to terms with Mussolini as well. Cooperation with outright Catholic parties was generally only supported—as with Dollfuss in Austria—when no other force was available to effectively fight what were considered to be really dangerous opponents.

"Intransigents" continued to warn that support of a "practical liberal conservatism" would bring many "false friends" along with it. It would inevitably involve compromises with oligarchies, intellectual support for more radical logical development of naturalist principles, and a degeneration of the supernatural sense of Catholics living purely "pragmatic" naturalist lives, today just as much as in the pre-revolutionary era. I would argue that their warning was prophetic. For any distinctive "Catholic before all else" position, truly dedicated to assuring the Kingship of Christ, was very soon to be destroyed by cooperation with the most powerful of "liberal conservative" appeals: that of American Pluralism.

In order to understand how American Pluralism gained its hold over believers, it is first necessary to return to the European Catholic activists and thinkers noted above, but in their post-World War I manifestation. These activists were missionaries spreading the Kingship of Christ in Asia and Africa on the one hand, and Catholic political, labor and youth movement leaders on the other. All were honest militants who shared the sense of urgency central to the movement of Catholic revival. And all, in consequence, were men and women who, once again, were desperate for success in the battle for Christian and against naturalist guidance of life.

Unfortunately, these missionaries were worn down by their many failures, amazed at the resistance of native religions and cultures to the Catholic message, and disturbed by signs of their revitalization even in places where they had long seemed nearly extinct. Political, labor and youth leaders were still more demoralized. Their frontline service during the First World War and the political revolutions following it shocked them, demonstrating as they did the weakness of the impact of their distinctly Catholic labors upon the average soldier and citizen. Europeans, they saw, while indifferent to the Faith, could clearly be roused to enthusiastic action by energetic lieutenants in the trenches and political radicals at home. These military and civilian leaders, as well as the communities that they shaped, seemed to possess an extraordinary vitality. Where did it come from? Why did Catholics lack the strength that a wide variety of non-Catholic militants possessed?

A translation of the concerns of Catholic activists into theoretical arguments was undertaken in the 1920s and 1930s by a kaleidoscope of thinkers calling themselves personalists. Personalists ultimately went down numerous, divergent directions. Nevertheless, the main-line, in the interwar period, either consciously or unconsciously adopted positions going back to Lamennais and, through Lamennais, to Rousseau, to Kant, and to the "moderate" Pietist naturalists of Protestant provenance. Catholic activists, the personalists lamented, despite their claims to be community-minded, actually thought and spoke much more like the eighteenth-century individualist-minded naturalists they were said to oppose. In practice, all of their arguments were designed to appeal to isolated human atoms, and this on a one-dimensional, purely intellectual, boring scholastic level. Hence the conviction on the part of the flesh and blood men and women to whom they addressed themselves that in dealing with Catholics, they were dealing with teachers who were dead to the fullness of existence; cerebral academics; professional note-takers; disembodied "losers."

The Holy Spirit, the personalists continued, could never be an advocate of such lifeless creatures and the Gospel as they preached it. He manifested Himself in history through those vital, energetic leaders and communities whose successes impressed the "dead" Catholic activists themselves. This was due to the fact that God wanted human beings to perfect their personalities, and that they could only accomplish this perfection, becoming full "persons" rather than desiccated "individuals," through participation in precisely such energetically-led circles.

Should Catholics really wish to have an impact in life, what they had to do was to "dive into" the already vital, successful, "person-shaping" communities that they hoped to influence. Their work would then be one of "witnessing"; i.e., using their Catholic presence to help these vibrant, Spirit-favored societies to complete and perfect their unique "mystiques."

In order to "witness" properly, believers had to shed whatever stood in the way of their enthusiastic cooperation with the mystiques in question: namely, their substantive Catholic formation, with all of its presuppositions about how to express what was True, Good and Beautiful. Yes, these vital communities might seem, at first glance, to be in many ways hostile to one another in belief and behavior. Nevertheless, their success proved that they all had the Holy Spirit behind them. Therefore, one could have absolute faith that their contemporary, outwardly clashing mystiques would somehow providentially "converge" in the future. In short, the victory of the Kingship of Christ would be assured by abandoning thinking about what it might actually mean and what it might entail in the way of correction of the outside world. This kind of logos-hunting an Isocrates could applaud.

Such personalist arguments found a serious hearing in Catholic educational, political, youth and labor movements in the 1920s, 1930s and afterwards. Their acceptance did not affect merely these circles' vision of their ultimate purpose and *modus operandi*. It also worked to justify a sea change in that Catholic liturgical movement which had formed part of the revival of the previous century and sought to "lift up men's hearts" by aiming them firmly on God. Many of the leaders of the liturgical renaissance now began to claim that their principal task was that of learning how to respond to the Spirit manifesting Himself in the different mystiques of vital natural communities. For a true "witnessing" would require developing a form of divine worship peculiar to the spiritual genius of each of these providential entities. Men would worship God by examining themselves.

From the standpoint of the nineteenth century theorists of Christ's social kingship, hunting for a "success" that could only be gained by "witnessing" to a Holy Spirit who was *willfully* said by His prophetic interpreters to endorse everything "vital" and energetic in contemporary communities was a recipe for total disaster. Abandoning all that one knew from the Catholic vision in order to open the mind and heart to vital "mystiques" meant nothing other than consciously diving into "slumbering" nature. It entailed limiting God's message and activity in the world to the voice of nature "as it is," and not admitting His supernatural role as corrector and transformer of nature's flaws. The believer would be left with no means of judging whether the particular manifestations of nature confronting him were true or false, good or bad, beautiful or ugly ones.

In the final analysis, such "witnessing" involved giving oneself over to and blessing a modern "natural" world ruled by people with an agenda: the agenda of power-hungry ideologues, libertines and criminals whose rhetoricians justified erroneous and evil actions and cut off real, substantive criticism of them as though it were some pointless waste of time. Such "witnessing" amounted to a baptism of the false and ever more vulgar perceptions of the strongest and most arrogant "activists" of the place and the moment. It involved preparing Veuillot's "Empire of the World" and stripping oneself of defenses against it, once again, in true Sophist-like fashion.

A study of those involved in the personalist campaign yields a Who's Who of the liturgical and postwar European unification movements. It also serves as an introduction to many of the liberal and radical *periti* at Vatican II and related, postconciliar "experts." Studies of the development of personalist influence also make it clear that this was matched by an ever-growing contempt for the entire theological, philosophical, liturgical and general cultural tradition of Catholicism. How could this not be so? We have by now repeatedly noted that that tradition encouraged too strong of a critique of diving into a contemporary world marred by naturalism. How could it not be viewed as a most dangerous pest indeed?

Fascism, as a vibrant movement, was appealing to most personalists. But the dominant National Socialist strain of Fascism was unavoidably and unacceptably tied to the *Volksprinzip*, and personalists, despite their other temptations, never succumbed to that of modern racism. Even more significantly, Fascism had not proved to be vital enough to win the Second World War, losing whatever credibility as an engine of success that it had once possessed. The prize in that conflict had been carried off by the Soviet Union and the United States. One might legitimately conclude that Marxist-Leninist and American-guided communities were those possessing the greatest vigor, successful energy, and stamp of approval of the Holy Spirit. These communities had their own "word merchants" working day and night to encourage such an attitude; to find the right slogans to equate everything non-Marxist-Leninist or non-American with Fascism, and Fascism with National Socialism and thus with evil incarnate. Catholic doctrines and achievements of the European Catholic past were generally non-Marxist and non-American. It was therefore only a matter of time before they were both identified with the National Socialist racist disease.

Both conviction and prudence told the personalists that a swift change of allegiance was definitely in order. The preference of most of them was for the vitalist Marxist-Leninist victor, due to the more obvious communal and collectivist character of the Soviet system. A number of men active in the Catholic personalist movements mentioned above had learned to respect the "energy" of Marxism-Leninism due to their experiences with Soviet citizens and European Communists in labor camps in Germany. Those who had not "enjoyed" this opportunity schooled themselves in the same experience through participation in the worker-priest experiment of the late 1940s and 1950s. Liturgists from both groups then sought to tailor worship to the needs expressed in such Spirit-guided communist milieu. Just how accurate their perceptions were regarding their "vital" atmosphere is, of course, highly debatable, given the willful voluntarism that constantly fuels their thought and action. The postwar history of the Liberation Theology movement is very instructive in this regard.

Even those entranced by Marxism-Leninism had to admit that the impact of America's vital energy was evident everywhere in the postwar world. A number of Catholic personalists therefore argued for the need to "dive into" and help perfect the American community and those shaped by it. But what, exactly, were the underlying principles and standard operating procedure of that community? And what would a Catholic "witness" to its peculiar "mystique" really mean in practice?

James Madison, the father of the American Constitution, made it clear that the "multiplication of factions" in a religiously diverse United States was a desirable goal. It would render them all uniformly impotent to effect change, and thereby protect the goals of the "moderate" naturalist Whig-like oligarchy—in effect, "liberal conservatives"—dominating the new system.

But the country that Madison built the Constitution to rule was a land that was also deeply influenced by Puritanism; a Puritanism that had fallen subject to naturalist ideas that led it to expand its religious individualism to a secularist concern for radical personal "freedom" in all spheres. This convert to the naturalist camp used its Christian-inspired language to promote its new, non-Christian goals. Whether intended or not, such speech soothed those who remained believers and blinded them as to where, exactly, their familiar-sounding doctrines might actually lead in the future. Moreover, the United States, by the latter part of the nineteenth century, was home to a kaleidoscope of ethnic groups and religious convictions much broader than that of Britain, making the work of reducing them to impotence a more intense and complex project.

The American system—that which in the post-World War II era came to be known as Pluralism—emerged out of attempts to harmonize the reality of a potentially chaotic multicultural society with the "liberal conservative" desire for the order of a Whig-like oligarchy, the radicalism of Puritanism, and a naturalism both Whig and Puritan in flavor. Its theory and "mystique" were firmly in place by the late 1890s. What they claimed was that America's Founders had discovered the formula for providing a peaceful, ordered community out of a society guaranteeing freedom to all of God's (or Nature's) divided children. America thus offered mankind throughout the globe its "last and best hope" for a liberty, tranquility and happiness greater than any ever known in human history. A new, alternative good story had thus been born.

"Diving into" this system meant gaining the radical freedom that secularized Puritans might wish someone to have, a freedom that "sounds Christian" because it can easily be related to its fundamental Protestant roots. But in order to practice this freedom in a way that does not disturb the order preferred by liberal conservatives, the man exercising it learns that liberty actually has to be utilized in a way that promotes "order" and avoids "divisiveness"; i.e., in a fashion that "integrates" its practitioner into an order composed of endless varieties of "non-divisive, integrating individualists."

Catholics incorporated into this system learn that Church "freedom" is subject to the influence of Puritan and secularized Puritan ideas regarding liberty. Freedom, under these circumstances, means only the freedom given for individual members of a religious society to rip their communal authority to shreds. All attempts to hold onto Church authority could be nothing other than assaults on "real freedom," condemnable in the eyes of the anti-institutional God of Protestantism and the anti-institutional Nature of the liberty-loving Enlightenment. Freedom for all communities, religious or otherwise, once again, amounts to nothing other than the freedom to be impotent and to self-destruct.

Individuals, like communities, are ultimately given a two-fold teaching regarding the relationship of freedom and order. On the one hand, they are pressed to divide serious free thought from serious free action, renouncing any attempt to shape the society in which they live according to their convictions. On the other, they are encouraged to build whatever unity is permitted to exist upon a positive *materialist* use of their freedom that all can agree upon. In the final analysis, the freedom granted to men and communities under the American Pluralist "mystique" is merely the freedom to be naturalist materialists in a myriad of fashions.

Such freedom worked against preserving the oligarchy that dominated at the moment of the American "founding" in the form that it wanted at that moment. For such a cheap vision of "liberty" offers no more substantial block to sinful misuse than reliance on "common sense" prevents adherence to unnatural errors. Once again, it has within it an innate tendency to degenerate, and, with that degeneration, to ensure construction of an "order" based upon the dictates of the strongest practitioners of materialist freedom: libertines and criminals. Such criminals maintain their alliance with the American Pluralist ideologue and the rhetorical word merchant in order to justify and ennoble their oppression of the weak. All together guarantee that the system gradually "spirals downward," ending, once again, in that boring, corrupted sameness identified by Veuillot, as a chief characteristic of the coming "Empire of the World."

None of these essential problems of the American Pluralist mystique can even begin to be discussed by critics, since that mystique prohibits criticism of its theory and its practice. If a Catholic wishes to employ all of the various tools western Christian man has developed over the course of the ages for discussing the validity of its definition of the meaning of individual and social life, all of these tools, one by one, including theology, philosophy, history, psychology and sociology, will be dismissed as both impractical and intrinsically dangerous. A desire to use them will be said to illustrate nothing other than a lack of "obvious common sense" on the part of the foolish, impractical, "loser" critic. Do such tools help one to make money or keep the peace? On the contrary, all they do is bring up disruptive fantasies encouraging divisiveness and disturbing profits.

If, on the other hand, a Catholic seeks to demonstrate the long-term *practical* dangers of the American Pluralist mystique, and especially its degeneration into a reign of "might makes right" *disguised* as the victory of freedom, its totally unquestionable "godliness" will be called up by liberal conservatives and bewildered believers to smother the dialogue. The critic will be accused of lacking Faith in its Christian nature and mandate . . . as revealed through the all too arbitrary *will* of the Founding Fathers. Here the Catholic is condemned for his cynical rejection of the God-given "last and best hope" for individual freedom and social peace, and his consequent lack of charity for suffering humanity.

Should he then return to theory, and identify the American Pluralist Faith as a willful, irrational fideism masquerading a purely materialist conception of life and the victory of an oligarchy, he will be brutally brought back down to the practical level once again. Now, with complete disregard for the change in tactic, he will be assaulted for his childish naiveté; his hopeless idealism in the midst of a jungle universe guided by the War of All Against All. Surely only a Catholic "loser" envious of the success of his betters would think that life was susceptible to guidance by his utopian spiritual babble!

But what if our Catholic critic persists in his position and emphasizes the fact that he has been the subject of an irrational attack, accused simultaneously of being both a faithless cynic and impractically (but also enviously) naïve? Why, then, he will become the kind of "public nuisance" promoting unpleasant, logical consequences of first principles that David Hume deplored and Ralph Waldo Emerson considered the infallible sign of a "petty mind." The word merchants will be called onto center stage to find as many "appropriate words" as possible to brutalize him as an Enemy of the People. Truth will not matter in their campaign against him. He will be dismissed as an obvious lunatic. Moreover, since American Pluralism fought the good fight against the Fascists, he will also be denounced as a Nazi; an anti-Semite; a defender of genocide. Terrorism being the system's current manifestation of evil, the critic will also be painted as a probable Al Quaeda, "Islamo-Fascist" supporter. Isocrates could not have prepared this scenario any better.

Few Catholic supporters of the Kingship of Christ will have the stamina to reach this final stage of unsuccessful dialogue. The schizophrenia brought on by American Pluralist refusal to allow serious thought to be transmitted into action will have deconstructed most potential critics' spirit from the very outset. The number of tools that have to be marshaled to uncover the system's fraud and its bewildering *modus operandi* will have daunted other critics. Should a hardy few possess the will to fight the good fight still longer, they, too, shall eventually be forced to abandon the struggle due to the naturalist, materialist environment created by the system in question. That environment demands work and ever more work in order merely to survive. Even the strongest defender of the Kingship of Christ, over time, will be simply too exhausted to indulge the luxury of criticizing the system in the few hours of repose left to him by it each day. Hence, mankind's "last, best hope" retains its undeserved image, its victims never learn of its poisons, and it can continue to wreak its all too predictable havoc again and again and again, in country after hapless country.

Equivocal use of Christian language on behalf of a happy vision of order and freedom, accompanied by the appeal of potential success in the New World seduced many Roman Catholic immigrants to the United States into the camp of American Pluralism in the years between 1890 and the present. Accepting its precepts seemed to be a "no-lose" proposition. The appearance of openness, prosperity and tranquility similarly entranced the exhausted and demoralized Europeans of the post World War II era, with those resisting the American embrace easily anathematized as unregenerate Fascist remnants by pluralists and personalists alike.

What happens to Catholics once they "dive into" this American, Pluralist, liberal-conservative mystique, "witness" to it, and then "bring it to perfection"? They have no hope of survival as a distinct force or culture, much less one that can work for the Social Kingship of Christ. They are obliged to both destroy whatever distinguishes themselves as Catholics in order to practice a "non-divisive, integrating, materialist freedom," and then to repeat, as a dogma, the belief that they have never before experienced such great liberty and so exalted a sense of human dignity. They are forced to dismantle what is most essential to their character, especially what has been corrected and transformed through the message of the Incarnation, in order to "fit in" to a jungle society which they must praise repeatedly as the most beautifully ordered in history. They are condemned to see their children treat this dismantling and emasculation as the obvious fulfillment of the *real* Catholic potential. They are condemned to hear their offspring repeat Black Legends which denigrate truly Catholic heroes as villains, and adulate anti-Catholics as brave champions of the March of Progress. And they are conditioned to accept the fact that the focus of this dismantling and emasculation of true human achievement will change along with whoever is the strongest ideologue, libertine and criminal of the moment and whatever it is that he wishes. Today, that focus is on making certain that Catholics be morally outraged only over whatever does not build bigger and more globally oriented business enterprises. It is also focused on mocking "outmoded" concerns over just and unjust international conflicts, or humane treatment of prisoners of war, or anything that disturbs the plans of the State of Israel.

"Diving into" the mystique of naturalist Marxism was a terrible thing. Nevertheless, that mystique was so patently fraudulent that it possessed a built-in destructive element. If one compares it to a drink, it offered a beverage that contained a poison one could taste and therefore wish to reject before it reached the point of destroying absolutely everyone who touched it. "Diving into" the American Pluralist mystique is not quite the same phenomenon. It is like taking a poisoned cocktail that does still have something of a familiar, pleasant taste to it and seems, for a while, to provide what it promises: tranquility and satisfaction of personal desire. One does not realize, until the very moment that he reaches the bottom of the glass, that there is nothing really there, and that the poison has done its job. The individual members of the desiccated, "free," meaningless Catholic Pluralist "Club" smile and toast their murderer as they die.

The basic problem with Pluralism, from the standpoint of the supporter of the Kingship of Christ, is that the natural law and order and the natural rights that it assures are not those fit for human beings. It has no room for the tools of Faith and Reason through which law and rights are clarified. They can be "reconciled" with one another for two reasons only. First of all, because Pluralism has ensured the victory of the will of the strongest contemporary jungle animal: uncorrected, individualist materialism, as interpreted by American storytellers. And, secondly, because this victorious beast allows no criticism of its fundamental principles, thus permitting it to claim that the entire globe enjoys its peace and order in perfect freedom and happiness. It is *the* chief representative of the central seductive revolutionary error of an error-filled modernity.

Our basic problem, as orthodox American Roman Catholics, is convincing ourselves, as well as others, that the dominant vision guiding our country, and the world, is a fraudulent myth, and one that has exercised a seductive appeal upon us; that it is merely the latest version of a rhetorical tall tale concocted in ancient times in order to justify Original Sin and use it as the "natural" building block for order; that it destroys social life and the individual along with it; that it has no rational message to transmit, and, still less, nothing to offer those pursuing the Social Kingship of Christ. For, as Louis Veuillot says:

> ... [F]erocious pride is correctly the genius of the Revolution; it has established a control in the world which pleases reason out of the struggle. It has a horror of reason, it gags it, it hunts it, and if it can kill it, it kills it. Prove to it the divinity of Christianity, its intellectual and philosophical reality, its historical reality, its moral and social reality: *it wants none of it*. That is its reason, and it is the strongest. It has placed a blindfold of impenetrable sophisms on the face of European civilization. It cannot see the heavens, nor hear the thunder.

Let us pray that we can find the strength to break with naturalism's most effective tool in history, even if only internally, so that we will cease praising the alternative good story of the enemy and rediscover, once again, the fullness of the corrective and transforming message of the Social Kingship of Christ. Let us pray that Rome will once again aid us firmly in this enterprise. We have nothing to lose but our self-destruction. *Écrasez l'infâme.* Viva Cristo Rey!

23

Christendom, Naturalism and the New World Order[†]

"WHERE THERE IS NO VISION," THE PROV-
erbs tells us, "the people perish." What the people really
need, of course, is not just any vision, but one that is true. And in
discussing this theme with respect to nature, its laws, global order,
and the rights of the individual in relation to them, it will come
as no surprise to anyone that I believe that such a true vision is
readily available for consultation and effective guidance. It is the
vision provided by those whom we may call the philosophers of
Christendom; a vision which, due to its sublimity, is in some way
always "still under construction."

This vision began to take shape before Christ, through the work
of the Socratics, in their hunt to uncover the essential meaning of
things, which they understood to be buried beneath the weight
of willful social and individual passions and seemingly venerable
customs. So crucial and valuable to man was their rational labor
that the Church Fathers saw that it represented a "seed" of the
Divine Logos, the Creator Word, surviving even after Original
Sin. The Fathers insisted that all such seeds led men away from
unquestioningly accepting "nature as is," encouraging a desire for
increasingly more light in order to grasp the laws of the universe
and the individual's relationship to them. As firmly believing
Christians, they were convinced that the light cast by the Incarnation of the creating and redeeming Word in history offered
the final illumination that the best of these ancient thinkers had
eagerly longed to obtain.

A joint Christian and Socratic investigation of nature, law and
the individual was then enhanced still further through later historical developments: the rediscovery of missing ancient philosophical
and legal texts providing a much clearer picture of classical Greco-
Roman thought; a medieval Church reform movement that both

[†] First published in *Verbo* (Madrid, Spain) in 2011.

stressed the fullness of the impact that the supernatural Word was supposed to have on every aspect of natural social and individual life, as well as undertook the pastoral work to give this practical meaning; the Catholic Reformation, with its call for the use of all Creation for the greater glory of God; and the revival of the militant spirit of Christianity in the Nineteenth Century following the disaster of the French Revolution. What emerged out of all these developments was a firm conviction of the basic unity and harmony of the individual human person with all aspects of nature and its supernatural Creator. As the Roman Jesuit journal, La Civiltà Cattolica, noted in the 1860s:[1]

> God ... has established one sole order composed of two parts: nature exalted by grace, and grace vivifying nature. He has not confused these two orders, but He has coordinated them. One force alone is the model and one thing alone the motive principle and ultimate end of divine creation: Christ ... All the rest is subordinated to Him. The goal of human existence is to form the Mystical Body of this Christ, of this Head of the elect, of this Eternal Priest, of this King of the immortal Kingdom, and the society of those who will eternally glorify Him.

It was, therefore, ultimately by focusing on Christ, the Word Incarnate, and seeing all of life through His eyes, that nature as a whole, and the individual in particular, were to be understood. As the teaching on the Seeds of the Word clearly indicated, and the reality of the entrance of God Himself into his fallen Creation confirmed, what viewing life in Christ entailed was an acceptance of the innate value of everything in nature, while simultaneously recognizing its fall from its intended state, and the necessity of its correction and transformation through the Revelation and grace coming into history with the Savior of mankind.

Allowing Christ to "inform" nature, as insisted by James of Viterbo (1255–1308), the Augustinian Archbishop of Naples, a follower of St. Thomas Aquinas (1225–1274) and a pioneer student of ecclesiology, had the effect of placing every one of its constituent elements in its correct rung on the hierarchy of values.[2] Having

---

1 Liberatore, "L'Enciclica dell'8 Dicembre," La Civiltà Cattolica, vi, 1 (1865), 287–288.
2 For the following argument, see Georges de Lagarde, La Naissance de l'Esprit Laïque au Declin du Moyen Age (Béatrice-Nauwelaerts, Five Volumes,

thus been properly ordered—"ordained"—each of these elements possessed a more accurate sense of the necessity and justice of its peculiar mission, both natural and supernatural, a correspondingly more secure awareness of its own innate dignity, and a stronger confidence in going about its work.

As a Faith that teaches the need to evangelize the whole of the human race in Christ, Catholicism has always nurtured a vision of the basic unity of mankind. As a believer in the value of seeds of the Logos, its supernatural universalism was combined together with a powerful inclination to consider the Roman imperial order as the natural model for human political organization. The rediscovery of Aristotle's scientific works in the High Middle Ages, with their revelation of real mechanisms built into an overall cosmic order that thinking men must learn to grasp and apply in guiding human action, seemed to confirm still further the validity of this Catholic universalism.

Medieval rediscovery of the fullness of Roman Law also awakened Catholics to the concept of an imperial public authority that took its right to rule as a self-evident given. If accepted purely on its own terms, what this could have done was to "liberate" any potential universal Christian ruler from all obstacles to acceptance of the "majesty of his laws" and the peace and order secured through them. But the great thirteenth century speculative philosophers and theologians who were intellectual representatives of the reform movement of the era knew that they had to digest this particular Seed of the Logos in conjunction with all the others that nature offered, and, most importantly, in light of the teaching of the Word Incarnate through His Mystical Body.

What this meant to them, especially at that particular moment in time, was mulling over the lessons of Roman Law in union with what they were simultaneously learning from the recaptured texts of Aristotle. Aristotle, like Plato, in examining the character of his own State, the Greek polis, tied its work together with a broader discussion of nature as a whole. He demonstrated that the public authority's title to rule and its field of action were rooted in the individual's innate need for fraternal unity, and this not just for

---

1934, 1956–1962), especially I (*Bilan du XIII Siècle*) and II (*Secteur Social de la Scolastique*) for the discussion of Roman Law and Aristotle. On James of Viterbo, see I, *passim*; II, 121–131.

the satisfaction of his obvious material demands, but also in order that he might communicate crucial aspects of his personality to other human beings. Hence, the scholastic recognition that the State, the majesty of its laws, and the peace and order that emerged from its authority and prestige could only be rendered worthy of respect insofar as it acted in the service of what was a fraternal, common good, rooted in the laws of nature in general, and different from any particular good. Appropriation of Aristotle's hunt for the "logos" behind the outer shell of a State thus allowed them to give to Roman Law an understanding of its value and purpose that its native Founders themselves never possessed.

Secondly, the Faith and Reason-filled openness of the greatest of these philosophers of Christendom to all that their eyes could see clearly indicated to them that the world in which they lived was not one with a single universal public authority. It was a multiform corporate society, with everything from individual nations to merchant guilds influencing its *modus operandi*. Any universal Christian State that might operate in such an atmosphere would have to negotiate constantly for guidance of society as a whole with this intricate network of corporate entities, representing claims to control of men and protecting varied parochial customs enshrined in innumerable oral and written statements of rights and privileges. Since this corporate order was there, and since it was clearly functional and appreciated by men, this meant that it, too, had to be accepted as a valid message from nature. And what that message related was that society had to embody the individual's fraternal spirit in manifold form. The public authority of any universal Roman State could not act on its own in the service of the common good.

Finally, a profound Christian Faith informed these teachers of Christendom that a complex natural order could only fully learn of its common good by digesting the lessons of the Revelation of the Incarnate Word of God. This Revelation confirmed the value of Reason, and both together provided much in the way of specific moral guidance to the defenders of this fleshed-out common good. But the single most significant political and social teaching that the Faith as such offered to society was that everything done in the name of the common good had to be done for the ultimate benefit of free, distinct, individual human persons. It was they

378

who were the jewels in Christ's crown; it was they and they alone who alone would live eternally with God. Even if pursuing the common good certainly at times required their personal temporal sacrifices, those sacrifices themselves had in some way to work for their higher, eternal, individual good.

In sum, our philosophers of Christendom presented us with a vision of a complex universal order possessed of unchanging natural laws reflecting a hierarchy of values that simultaneously aided in the perfection of distinct individual human persons with all of their particular differences. Respect for natural law inevitably entailed respect for what might be called "natural rights," so long as one recognized that these "rights" were always contingent; contingent, that is, upon acceptance of and obedience to the divine plan of a Creator of the universe who gave the individual such a magnificent role to play in the drama of truth in the first place.

On the immediate human level, this work of God, this aesthetic masterpiece, was also shown to involve a delicate dance of natural and positive laws, the State, corporate societies, and free individuals. That dance of life was a dramatic one because it was always affected by the appearance of new, distinct individuals in history, and since it could be disrupted by free beings capable of sinful interference with God's plan every moment of every day. It could only be performed properly if continuously guided by the corrective and transforming teaching and grace that comes from Christ in His Mystical Body. The key to harmony on Christendom's ballroom floor was for all participants in this truthful, dramatic, dance of life—individual, State, and a many-faceted corporate society—to open themselves to "the sense of the universal"; to "not separate goodness from power"; to learn, as Gilles of Rome (c. 1243–1316), another follower of St. Thomas said, that, of all forces in life, "love and charity have the maximum unifying and conjoining strength."[3]

One of the most important of the militant Catholic thinkers of the Nineteenth Century, Luigi Taparelli d'Azeglio (1793–1862), an editor of *La Civiltà Cattolica* and author of a major text on the natural law, the *Saggio Teoretico di Dritto Naturale Appoggiato sul Fatto,* expressed exactly the same themes in modern times. He, too, believed that the universal aims of the Christian mission involved at the very least a preferential option for a global political society.

3   De Lagarde, *Op. cit.,* II, 321.

Moreover, he was convinced that closer communication and economic interdependency were making such a global society much more of a reality in his own day than every before. Insofar as such a society did come into existence, and were to function justly, its standard operating procedure, according to Taparelli, would have to reflect the principles noted above. It would inevitably need a public, State authority. But that international authority would be obliged to act for the common good of its constituent parts, which were distinct nations, with their own States and complex corporate orders, composed of individuals meant to share eternal life with God. There could be no universal common good that did not simultaneously allow these building blocks of international society to express their innate fraternal needs, which, once again, far from being purely material, were cultural, spiritual, and unending in their significance.

In other words, a justifiable modern global order had to respect supernatural as well as natural law and the innate mission and dignity of each of its constituent elements. And every aspect of that order—public international authority, nation-States, corporate societies and individuals—always had be ready for correction and transformation in Christ. They and their desires could never be accepted "as is," left to wander freely where they might. Were any of these principles to be ignored, Taparelli warned, then the unbridled national passions of the most powerful part of the growing international order, guided purely by the dictates of *Machtpolitik*, would inevitably shape global unity according to their disordered and uncorrected whims.

Yes, the true vision that would be needed to guide a universal Christendom came to us through a union of the revealed Deposit of Faith with human Reason that was open to all the natural data of God's creation. But precisely because such a true vision involved correcting and transforming the messages offered to us by our very powerful fallen passions and the impact that they have on both our minds and our bodies, its triumph has been very difficult to assure. Hence, myths that actually flattered and encouraged uncorrected social and individual desires found their way into human heads and hearts. And, unfortunately, it has generally been these that have provided the vision that actually does guide the people and has led them to perdition in the process.

Modern western society lives—or, rather, dies—by related versions of the same basic naturalist myth, whose various aspects were fleshed out over a long stretch of time, beginning with the very opening of the Socratic enterprise and continuing down to the present. This myth describes the West's awakening to an ever-deeper understanding of nature in all its fullness. As a result of that awakening, it claims that western man was rendered capable not only of grasping nature's laws, but also the essence of the State and society, and the individual human person. In learning the laws of nature and political order, and the dignity and rights of man along with them, modern western society supposedly found the real key to social and individual harmony. It became the simultaneous Defender of Law and Order on the one hand and the fullness of the rights of a natural human freedom and diversity on the other. So great were the consequences that one might even entertain the hope of the lion lying down with the lamb, with both together peacefully listening to "the music of the spheres."

But the price that the West has had to pay for accepting and propagating this myth is much too high; higher than any paid by ancient Egyptians who rather magnificently explained their political and social system with reference to the biographies of Osiros, Isis and Horus. Despite its noble-sounding claims, the naturalism underlying the varied forms of the same basic modern myth guarantees that it can never understand the true laws of the universe and of natural society, nor the real character of the dignity, freedom and unique distinctions of each and every human person. And far from opening man's ears to "the music of the spheres," it guarantees the creation of socio-political systems that deaden societies and individuals to all higher spiritual and aesthetic considerations. Just as Calgacus complains with respect to the consequences of Agricola's campaign in ancient Britain, mythic modern western society "creates a desert and calls it peace."[4] Be that as it may, as naturalist myths go, the one guiding our world has been a clever, long-lasting and highly successful one.

Rather than tackling directly the question of the fraud in and of itself, I should like to approach this by discussing what I believe to be the basic reason for its success: its adoption of a strategy

---

4   Tacitus, *Agricola*, 30.4.

invented at the very beginning of the hunt for the Logos, whose greatest achievement was the transformation of the justification of passion and will into a seemingly high-minded vision. Profoundly anti-Socratic Sophists developed this strategy, which was most thoroughly expressed by the great rhetorician, Isocrates (436–338 B. C.) in his many battles with Plato.[5]

For Isocrates, there was no question of seriously critiquing, transforming and possibly even rejecting the immediate emotional and sensual experiences and preoccupations of the ordinary man. Man was the measure of all things, and unquestionably correct in his urgent, common-sense appreciation of the importance of obtaining the riches, power and fame that he *obviously* knew would yield the beautiful life. The average individual's sole problem was a *technical* one: he could not relate one, justifiable, obvious, common sense experience to another, and thereby understand how best to exploit and satisfy them regularly and comprehensively. His efforts to explain his reactions to daily problems, both to himself as well as to others, proved to be "dumb" ones. It was effective words, and the arguments shaped through them, which were lacking to the average man. Only the well trained rhetorician, the master of words, could clarify the full depth of immediate feelings and experiences, show where they were headed, and stir people to do what was necessary to fulfill their promise. The Good and the True were, therefore, ultimately nothing other than "appropriate explanations" of reality, and developments of those obvious and common sense reactions to the raw stuff of daily life that are themselves absolutely infallible guides to the possession of Beauty.

But how would Everyman know that the rhetorician was "speaking appropriately" about reality? The answer to this question was also an obvious one. For the master rhetorician's advice would not only "sound right"; clearly, consistently and self-assuredly responding to the average individual's personal sense of the obvious truth of his own preoccupations, and where, more or less, those concerns are headed. Beyond that, it would prove itself by being crowned with clear material success. Hence, Isocrates' need to underline the simplicity, lucidity, harmony of purpose, confidence and material

---

5   For the following discussion, see the brilliant work of W. Jaeger, *Paideia* (Oxford, Three Volumes, 1965), particularly Volume III (*The Conflict of Cultural Ideals in the Age of Plato*), 132–262.

achievements of *his* pupils, while contrasting them with the cranky and ultimately unfathomable detours, self-criticisms, bitter divisions, and practical failures of the Socratics.

Still, Isocrates realized that Plato had placed the discussion of nature, the State and the individual on such a higher plane that the rhetorician was now obliged to drive his argument home with a "philosophy"; a vision that was equally universal and noble sounding. He offered such a philosophical vision by hunting for the Foundation Principle of Greek society and the mission that corresponded to it. These he outlined in his discussion of Hellenism: the knowledge of "words" as such, rather than understanding of the Logos or "Word" behind things, and the need to spread this eastward.

Fulfillment of future Hellenist destiny would require two things simultaneously. On the one hand, it would be crucial to maintain a constant respect for the "good old days" of the foundation of the Greek spirit and the institutions giving clout to it. On the other, it would be necessary to shape a loyal population obedient to any vigorous hero who might guide that spirit to the discharge of its contemporary mission. Moreover, the institutions embodying the spirit of the good old days, the strong man giving them clout, and the populations obedient to his *fiat* were to be stirred to their appropriate political roles through the creative rhetorical genius, who grasped the essence of Hellenism through his vital knowledge of and skill with words.

But philosophy, as defined by Isocrates, constitutes a gigantic circle, manipulated by the rhetorician who, through the clever use of appealing words and images, seizes control of the familiar concerns of the average man or State and runs with them where he wills. Common-sense experience is pronounced the infallible basis for action simply because the experience appealed to is arbitrarily declared "common sense-filled" and thus an infallible basis for a man's work. Successful attainment of riches and power is said to prove the appropriateness of the rhetorician's understanding of the beautiful life, and guidance of Everyman to fulfillment of its promise, because possession of riches and power is presented as unquestionable, axiomatic proof that beauty has indeed been grasped hold of. Respect for the "good old days," contemporary strong men, and obedient populations are essential because denial of such esteem to any one of these elements would rip apart the "beautiful" rhetorical image tying together ancient roots with present hopes and future destiny, mass popularity and elite power. And all those aspects of "the vision" were essential, since experience had proven them necessary to construct the career of the master of words, whose personal success worked to guarantee the validity of their union.

Absolutely no questioning of "obvious experience," "common sense," "success," the "historic mission," and the consistency of the tools required for its realization can be contemplated, lest this lead to the unacceptable argument that obvious experience, common sense, success, the historical mission and its vital tools were themselves somewhat problematic. Isocrates, as Werner Jaeger notes, makes a virtue out of abandoning any deeper investigation of the meaning of life once he has shaped what for him appears to be a rhetorically beautiful "point of view" with a chance of obtaining a successful outcome. That "point of view," if attractive and potentially useful, *must* be accepted as though it were Truth itself. With this, the debate is over. Closure has been achieved. One must move on to accomplishment of the Great Promise, or face the wrath of the rhetorician and the outraged nature whose unerring voice he has infallibly proclaimed himself to be.

And the rhetorician *is* powerful. He knows that his words do have "the ring of truth." He is sure that he can count on the support of immediately felt, individual, family or polis-wide "common sense" passions in his call for their immediate satisfaction. He senses the understandable and well-nigh universal fear that acceptance of Socratic self-criticism would paralyze swift action, thus preventing exploitation of favorable opportunities to fulfill desire and causing men to "lose out" on success, perhaps even up to the very moment of death. The rhetorician, with his mastery of words, can paint the profound, life-determining, "either-or" option offered to men by Sophists and Socratics in all of its dramatic colors, though clearly weighted to his advantage. After he has skillfully organized the picture as he wishes, any Socratic who calls the average man to logical, painful soul-searching at the possible expense of satisfying urgent passion becomes a sitting duck for his rhetorical abuse. A Platonic philosopher would all too easily lend himself to the accusation of representing both a crackpot idealism, indifferent to the obvious demands of human nature, as well as a cynical opposition to the successes of "real men," whom he cannot emulate, bitterly envies, and wishes to destroy in consequence.

Plato argued that the successful rhetorician may deceive himself into thinking that he is superior to his "wordless" audience, but he is simply more effectively "thick" than it is. His words resemble an overbearing and endlessly repeated rock rhythm in a room filled with impressionable, but musically illiterate hedonists. They fail to elevate, just as any tool that uses man, rather than God, as the measure of all things falls miserably short of its pretensions. Anyone responding to the "either-or" option confronting him by choosing for the rhetorician would, therefore, be voting for eternal mediocrity and blindness. Sadly, precisely due to the rhetorician's observable knack for maintaining power over the vulgar mob, the pathetic outcome of such a wrong choice could conceivably be hidden from its victims forever. False rhetorical "philosophers" needed only to do two things: 1) enthusiastically to invent ever "new" surface variants on the proven appealing slogans to keep men thinking that fulfillment of the brilliant promise of the Empty Life lay just around the corner; and 2) constantly to drill into a benumbed population's mind the fear of the "dead-end" impotence that the Socratic hunt for a more profound goal would ensure.

The opponents of Christendom latched onto this ancient defense of "nature as is" for their own purposes. What this was to entail was a dismantling of the entire corrective and transforming mission of the Word in history; the fullness of the message of Christ and Christ continued-in-time, His Mystical Body, the Catholic Church. But such an enterprise also had to become an attack on the whole Socratic project, whose underlying goals and whose enemies were, *mutatis mutandis*, the same as those of the Christians. This was to leave as the guide for human action precisely what the Socratics had fought against from the very outset of the hunt for the Logos: reliance solely on the data provided by "obvious" passion and first impression. And this inevitably ended by serving the interests of the strongest "heroic" wills in society, as justified by clever "word merchants," with reference to loyalty to "Foundation principles."

Moreover, just as the Socratic Revolution did not allow Isocrates the opportunity to press for a return to the unexamined life without an appropriately noble explanation for doing so, no one, after having experienced the infinitely greater effort to transform the world in Christ, could retreat from the higher plane on which the Church's argument had been made without a rich rhetorical cover story that was presented as a theological or philosophical vision. This took two basic forms, the first appearing in the late Thirteenth Century, the second slightly later. Both "cover story visions" worked for a long period of time in sometimes friendly, sometimes quite hostile pursuit of the same anti-Catholic, anti-Socratic goal, until the latter finally gained the dominant role. Both were expressed in a variety of nuanced ways that "worked" for different audiences. Both played on fallen man's desire to be rid of a religious and rational message that sought to restrain satisfaction of his manifold immediate passions, while answering his post-Christian need to appear to be virtuous as he continued with a career of sin.

Cover story vision number one chastised the Catholic-Socratic outlook for having betrayed the true Christian Foundation and Mission. These were said to be taught through Scripture alone, and only capable of being recaptured through a return to that poor, humble, basically fleshless Apostolic Church that the storytellers insisted Holy Writ required. The writings of storytellers like Marsilius of Padua (c. 1270–1342), William of Ockham (c. 1288–1348), and, ultimately, Martin Luther (1483–1546) cannot help but show us where all this was leading: to an unexamined natural order ruled only through the triumph of the strongest will. All of the writers in question excoriated a papal-guided Church with practical muscle, seeking to correct and transform things in Christ. All of them, in different ways, stripped nature of the tools required for judging social and individual action.

For Marsilius and William, any such corrective effort, interfering as it did with the activity of the sole Defender of the Peace, the Roman Emperor, the heroic agent entrusted by them with the mission of securing a return to the Christian Foundation Principles, was the chief cause for disorder in nature. Marsilius made of the law, both natural and positive, whatever it was that a man had to do in order not to be hung by the Emperor; William insisted upon the limitations of Reason, stressed the overriding importance of Divine Will in learning all truths, and then made it impossible for us to know what this would be, in practical political and social life, except through the natural will of the existing authorities.[6] Luther, who could not count on imperial aid in returning to the "original intent" of the Christian Foundation, gave this power over to the local sovereign, who thus became a "necessity bishop." And through his doctrine of the total depravity of all of nature, he left the jungle world around us, and anyone who would try to guide it, with no clear tools for doing so whatsoever. As the great English Church historian, Philip Hughes, says:[7]

> It is the surrender to despair, in the name of greater simplicity, which 'simplicity' is presented as the road back to primitive truth and the good life ... All those anti-intellectualist, anti-institutional forces that had plagued and hindered the medieval Church for centuries ... were now stabilized, institutionalized in the new reformed Christian Church. Enthronement of the will as the supreme human faculty; hostility to the activity of the intelligence in spiritual matters and in doctrine; the ideal of a Christian perfection that is independent of sacraments and independent of the authoritative teaching of clerics; of sanctity attainable through one's own self-sufficing spiritual activities; denial of the truth that Christianity, like man, is a social thing; all the crude, backwoods, obscurantist theories bred of the degrading pride that comes with chosen ignorance, the pride of men ignorant because unable to be wise except through the wisdom of others, now have their fling.

Luther, despite his handing of the jungle of nature over to political lion tamers, was actually a bridge to cover story vision number two, in which the heroes bringing about the return to the Foundation Principles were the rhetoricians themselves: the men of letters, the preachers, the prophetic ideologues stirring men to the destruction of the idols terrifying them into enchaining their free action. But this second myth differed from the first in abandoning the Christian Foundation theme entirely, and chastising the Catholic-Socratic outlook for betraying the fundamental teachings

---

6 For Marsilius, see de Lagarde, III (*Le Defensor Pacis*); For Ockham, see de Lagarde, IV (*Guillaume D'Ockham: Defense de L'Empire*) and V (*Guillaume D'Ockham: Critique des Structures Ecclésiales*)
7 Philip Hughes, *A History of the Church* (Sheed & Ward, Three Volumes, 1949), III, 529.

of Mother Nature, whose basic principles were said to be there for anyone with bare common sense to grasp. The choice now was either that for Catholicism and the unnatural, helpless, poverty-stricken disorder its vision ensured, or for Mother Nature, along with the strength, riches and peace that she provided.

Unfortunately, those opting for Mother Nature found that their common-sense grasp of her fundamental principles led them down many opposing directions. Some saw her to be a machine, filled with obvious, ironclad "natural laws," often reducible to one magical "key," whether economic, biological or sexual in character. Others saw in her the realm of diversity, the playground of endless diverse passions and dreams, an ever-increasing number of which had to be protected as crystal-clear "natural rights." But although the preferential options for "natural law" or "natural right" seemed to be in total contradiction, they both actually reduced to similar willful choices that accepted no correction from any outside "judge" that might limit or reject their desire to manipulate nature as they saw fit. Machine-like or libertine in character, they both reflected a disdain for the "Logos of things" well expressed in the early history of cover story vision number two through the career of a Renaissance humanist like Pietro Aretino (1492–1556):[8]

> Untrammeled by convention, dominated by instinct, swept along by his nature, fulfilling his fate with the agility of an acrobat, yet true to his inner essence, his mysterious *virtù;* this was the compulsive image which Renaissance man created for himself... In no other man of this age is the image more sharply mirrored than in Pietro Aretino, the first Bohemian. "I am a free man," Aretino wrote, "I do not need to copy Petrarch or Boccaccio. My own genius is enough. Let others worry themselves about style and so cease to be themselves. Without a master, without a model, without a guide, without artifice, I go to work and earn my living, my well-being, and my fame. What do I need more? With a good quill and a few sheets of paper I mock the universe."

Anyone longing to discover natural law and order under these circumstances had to nuance his "vision" by in one way or another following the equally willful advice given by Jean-Jacques Rousseau

8   John H. Plumb, *The Italian Renaissance* (American Heritage Library, 1986) pp. 115–116.

(1712–1778).[9] Law and order, for Rousseau, came through construction of the natural, virtuous society. But natural virtue was not something built through the repetition of the petty, daily, "good" actions praised by the outside world. Rather, one attained it by entering into that ontological state of being a liberated "natural man." Rousseau reached this natural, virtuous condition through his *Confessions* (published posthumously, 1782). Here, he revealed to the world all his deepest, passionate, non-rational feelings and their effect on his actions, without consideration for the effect such disclosure might have upon public opinion and his own personal fame and fortune. Having thus accepted his natural self, he became virtuous, and no longer ashamed of deeds that others thought to be reprehensible; deeds that would, indeed, still be truly blameworthy if done by men seeking praise from the artificial, outside, "objective" world. Once virtuous, Rousseau could permit himself no rationalist post-mortem on the validity of his deeply felt goodness. All "looking back" amounted to a renewed embrace of the unjustifiable rules of a soul-killing artifice and duplicity.

His right to be natural not only translated into virtue, but also transformed Rousseau into Everyman. Nature possessed integrity. It was all of one piece, honest and good, and could not help but speak with a single voice. Therefore, others who sincerely stripped themselves of the obstacles standing in the way of their right to express their spontaneous natural feeling would inevitably be indistinguishable from, and united fraternally with Rousseau. It is this indistinguishable character that ensured that the various lovers in his widely-read *Nouvelle Héloise* (1761) were actually only loving themselves in other people, and the teacher in his enormously influential educational treatise, the *Emile* (1761), could be said by Rousseau to both ensure the child's self-fulfillment and yet remake him totally in the tutor's image at one and the same time.

Conversely, anyone who was not Rousseau-like, anyone who criticized Everyman's feelings and spontaneous actions, anyone who failed to pity him in his trials, revealed himself as being unnatural. He could thus be neither free, nor virtuous, nor truthful. In fact, he could not even be labeled human, and did not deserve

---

9   On Rousseau, see Carol Blum, *Rousseau and the Republic of Virtue* (Cornell, 1986).

any fraternal consideration whatsoever. Carol Blum describes the situation well in commenting on Rousseau's discussion of himself as the "spectator-animal" contemplating the suffering of one such pointless being.[10]

The Spectator animal was denied pleasurable pity in regarding the suffering animal because the suffering animal was evil and hence unworthy of sympathy. Since Rousseau knew that mankind was, like him, good, he was forced to the awful but inevitable realization that the creatures who treated him so heartlessly were not really people at all, that the key to the mystery was that 'my contemporaries were but mechanical beings in regard to me who acted only by impulsion and whose actions I could calculate only by the laws of movement.' He was now really alone, the only human being left amid a throng of automatons; the human race existed solely in him.

Rousseau was convinced that the non-virtuous and non-human world around him was stubbornly hostile to the effort to perfect it. The duty of Everyman-Rousseau was to transform that world into him himself, or cause it to disappear before it do him any further damage. Once again, the question of a possible initial flaw undermining the value of his entire argument could not even be imagined; the sincere, virtuous, free, liberated Everyman was necessarily free from error. No discussion concerning the ground and justification of this underlying truth was permissible. It was a self-evident given. Doubt regarding his position would in effect mean allowing the sham world of the hypocrite to influence him once more. It was either one or the other; natural virtue or self-doubting vice in their fullness.

Catholic attempts to fight off these two cover story visions, with their high-minded "returns" to their respective Foundation principles, were fitful. The Catholic Reformation represented a major effort to recapture recognition of the need for acceptance, correction, and transformation of all of nature in and through Christ, which was the sole means by which natural law and the supreme dignity of the individual, his "natural rights," if you will, could firmly be held together. Nevertheless, by the Eighteenth Century, Catholics were so cowed by the arguments and the successes

---

10 Blum, *Op.cit.*, p. 99.

of their opponents that they too, for all intents and purposes, had abandoned their Word-based vision in exchange for a "practical," moralistic Christianity that seemed more in line with the call to return to the teachings of "natural common sense." It was only through a re-examination of the whole of the Catholic Tradition under the impact of revolutionary changes that led to the serious, militant revival of the Nineteenth Century. With that meditation came a new realization of what fallen natural men, exercising their uncorrected perceptions of nature, its laws and their rights, actually did to society at large. Again, let us hear Taparelli d'Azeglio:[11]

> Starting with the words "I am free" and their new-found spirit of independence, men began to believe in the infallibility of whatever seemed natural to them, and then to call "nature" everything that is sickness and weakness; to want sickness and weakness to be encouraged instead of healed; to suppose that encouraging weakness makes men healthier and happy; to conclude, finally, that human nature [conceived of as sickness and weakness] possesses the means to render man and society blissful on earth, and this without faith, grace, authority or supernatural community... since "nature" gives us the feeling that it must be so.
> The truth is that the universe is the work of an infinite wisdom of which no man can change the nature, although he may be free to deny it. The nature that is denied by man through thought and doctrine is then denied by him also in practice. A man's struggling with nature is an insane war against God, wherein the mortal cannot hope to triumph, but, rather, is certain to be defeated. To concede, therefore, to all men the freedom to wage this war, to blindfold their eyes so that they may not see their sores, their defeats; to concede the freedom of error to oppress the truth, may well be the momentary delirium of blinded intellects and the suicide of frenetic societies; but it can never be the durable basis of civilization, never the hoped-for foundation of a new society.

Discussing this nightmare in relation to that "Protestant principle" of individual independence from social authority underlying the whole development of modern naturalist atomism, Taparelli repeatedly stressed that it must lead to a social disorder that could only be controlled through the triumph of the will of the strongest.

---

11   *La Civiltà Cattolica*, I, 6 (1851), 497–498; III, 5 (1857), 17.

Man always required order to live. And what this meant was that in the naturalist and individualist society that followed hot on Protestantism's heels, "might made right":[12]

> Let us say it then frankly: all social unity must collapse and be routed as soon as the Protestant principle is introduced and reigns therein. And the reasons reduce all to one. Admitting the Lutheran principle, it is impossible to have any true idea of right. Protestants may well be able, owing to logical incoherence or by accident, to admit some principle of right in their society. But this will be the effect of a habit, of an accident, of a lack of reasoning, of natural honesty in their inclinations, or of some other similarly fortuitous conditions affecting this or that individual. But the nature of the Protestant principle, that nature which sooner or later finally produces its inevitable effects, renders absolutely impossible the idea of right, and, in consequence, of social unity.
> . . . No, there is no more unity for this destructive demon. The mind was liberated, through freethinking, from the yoke of a God who speaks to man; through individual criticism, from the yoke of reason; through Popular Sovereignty, from that of any authority; through the right to suicide, from the yoke of all fear. Any society—the communion of the soul with God in the Church, of the people with their prince in the polis, of a wife with her husband in the family, of the body with the soul in the individual—is devastated any time social bonds are measured against the impulse of a passion, against a "right," against a desire for pleasure. Each society is devastated in its primary governing entity. It is thrown into the hands of a crazed man whose will is arbitrary. This is the ultimate consequence of the Protestant principle of independence.
> . . . Force. Let us say it straightforwardly. Let us repeat it with daring. Force is the only social instrument left to the Protestant who wishes to be logical. And since the sole means of salvation becomes a right in society, the right in Protestant society is force.

And, sad to say, a social order in which "might made right" was one in which the "freedom" and the "natural rights" that were granted men were nothing other than a license for the strong to oppress the weak:[13]

---

12 *La Civiltà Cattolica*, I, 2 (1850), 265; I, 5 (1851), 412; I, 2 (1850), 406.
13 *La Civiltà Cattolica*, III, 1 (1856), 387; VI, 1 (1865), 222–223; VI, 5 (1866), 9–10.

And the truth is that this freedom, as any other unlimited liberty not circumscribed by anything, is nothing other than the privilege agreed upon for the strong to assassinate the weak. In this case, the freedom of the strong party is offended, since he is given the arbitrary ability to abuse his faculty, and the freedom of the weak party is offended, as he remains the undefended victim of that abuse.

What did these developments signify for the global world order that Taparelli saw rapidly emerging in his own time? We have already noted what he was afraid would happen: that it would be dominated by the passions of the strongest willful nation. This, he feared, would then utilize its will to define nature, the laws of nature, and natural rights and freedom in whatever way that it saw fit. Given its refusal to allow any correction and transformation of its definition in Christ, its global judgments would be presented as doctrinal formulations for its weak victims to accept unquestioningly. Anyone criticizing them would be stigmatized as unbearable opponents of obvious natural order, peace and freedom.

All of the thinkers of the nineteenth century Catholic revival were convinced that the music of the spheres that was heard under these circumstances would be either the insane ravings of the mentally ill or the ever more base drum beats played by libertines or criminals stirring up passions and fear among the "natural men" that they were oppressing. Which of these approaches would gain the final victory they could not say. Nevertheless, they envisaged a worldwide criminal and pleasure-seeking order, ever loyal to the fraudulent concept of the freedom and the rights of increasingly boring "natural men," and working through a mishmash of capitalism, socialism, advanced scientific technology, bureaucracy and charismatic dictatorship. Veuillot's vision of what he called the Empire of the World sums up this prediction of drab, global, materialist pragmatism and socialist bureaucracy very well. [14]

Everywhere, the conqueror [of the world] will find one thing, everywhere the same, the only thing that war and the Revolution will nowhere have overturned: bureaucracy. Everywhere the bureau will have prepared the way for him; everywhere

---

14 Louis Veuillot, *Mélanges* (*Oeuvres Complete*, iii series, Paris, 1933), VIII, 366–367.

they await him with a servile eagerness. He will support himself on them. The universal Empire will be the administrative Empire par excellence. Adding without end to that precious machinery, he will carry it to a point of incomparable power. Thus perfected, administration will satisfy simultaneously its own genius and the design of its master in applying itself to two main works: the realization of equality and of material well-being to an unheard-of degree; the suppression of liberty to an unheard-of degree.

Men ruled by this system would be much more easily oppressed than at any time in the past. Such facility would be due, not so much to the fact that new weapons would give its dictator undreamed-of instruments of control, as to the sad reality that stupefied, machine-like man would approve of his chains, and a dull-witted intelligentsia would bless them. The men produced by modern civilization would be totally distinct from men of preceding ages. "These powers that present-day man possesses," Veuillot wrote, "possess him also; they engage him in weaknesses as unmeasured as his pride, weaknesses that succeed in changing him completely." Ironically, they also left him "too powerful to control the taste for pleasure." Man thus became a being unable even to begin to desire the destiny intended for him by God. The universal Empire would enslave such creatures by providing for their most banal needs. [15]

> The police will take care that one is amused and that its reins never trouble the flesh. The administration will dispense the citizen of all care. It will fix his situation, his habitation, his vocation, his occupations. It will dress him and allot to him the quantity of air that he must breathe. It will have chosen him his mother; it will choose him his temporary wife; it will raise his children; it will take care of him in his illnesses; it will bury and burn his body, and dispose of his ashes in a record box with his name and his number.

And as time went on, this task would become simpler and simpler. A decline in human imagination would entail a destruction of the taste for a variety of pleasures. [16]

---

15 Ibid., VIII, 364.
16 Louis Veuillot, *Op. cit.*, VIII, 369.

But why would he change places and climates? There will no longer be different places or climates, or any curiosity anywhere. Man will everywhere find the same moderate temperature, the same customs, the same administrative rules, and infallibly the same police taking the same care of him. Everywhere the same language will be spoken, the same *bayadères* will everywhere dance the same ballet. The old diversity will be a memory of the old liberty, an outrage to the new equality, a greater outrage to the bureau, which would be suspected of not being able to establish uniformity everywhere. Their pride will not suffer that. Everything will be done in the image of the main city of the Empire and of the World.

Pluralism is the dominant variant on the basic western naturalist myth, by means of which the people perish in our own day. It has, to a large degree, actually constructed a universal Empire of the World. Moreover, pluralism has one of the grandest cover stories ever invented, involving all of the features outlined by Isocrates in his battle with Plato. This is backed, in its homeland, the United States, with reference to the will of the Founders of the universal Empire. It places an especially heavy emphasis upon the either-or option: *either* pluralism, with peace, order, prosperity and free-dom, *or* the brutal, mindless, totalitarian, warmongering, genocidal, poverty-stricken death camp assured by any vision hunting for the Logos of things, with that of Catholicism at the top of the list of this Axis of Evil. The lion lies down with the lamb in the pluralist paradise, with all the natural rights that insane human minds can imagine gaining *droit de cité* in its nature-friendly order without danger of disturbance by the natural law. Pluralism is thus Marsilius' Defender of Peace *par excellence*.

The basic problem with Pluralism is that the natural law and order and the natural rights that it assures are not those fit for human beings. It has no room for the tools through which law and rights are clarified. They can be "reconciled" with one another for two reasons only. First of all, because Pluralism has ensured the victory of the will of the strongest contemporary jungle animal: uncorrected, individualist materialism, as interpreted by American storytellers. And, secondly, because this victorious beast allows no criticism of its fundamental principles, permitting it to claim that the entire globe enjoys its peace and order in perfect freedom and happiness.

Our basic problem, as Catholics, is convincing ourselves, as well as others, that the vision it presents is a fraudulent myth; that it is merely the latest version of a rhetorical tall tale concocted in ancient times in order to justify Original Sin and its use as the building block for order. In the final analysis, it has nothing rational to tell us about nature, natural law and natural rights. For as Louis Veuillot says: [17]

> ... [F]erocious pride is correctly the genius of the Revolution; it has established a control in the world which pleases reason out of the struggle. It has a horror of reason, it gags it, it hunts it, and if it can kill it, it kills it. Prove to it the divinity of Christianity, its intellectual and philosophical reality, its historical reality, its moral and social reality: *it wants none of it*. That is its reason, and it is the strongest. It has placed a blindfold of impenetrable sophisms on the face of European civilization. It cannot see the heavens, nor hear the thunder.

---

17   L. Veuillot, *Op. Cit.*, X, 45–46.

24

Catholic Social Doctrine†

A CENTRAL THEME OF CHRIST'S PREACH-
ing is the fact that "the Kingdom of God is at hand." What
this means is that Christ's Kingship over the universe does not
refer merely to the end times, His future judgment of the world,
and His eternal reign in heaven. It means that the Incarnation of
the Second Person of the Blessed Trinity as the God-man Jesus
Christ has shaken all of nature out of its wounded, sinful rut,
beginning here and now, whether that "here and now" concerns
the Roman Empire of the First Century or the American Empire
of the Twenty First. What, exactly, such "shaking up" entails in
a broad socio-political sense is the subject dealt with by Catholic
Social Doctrine.

Although this doctrine was a work in construction throughout Church History, the day of its *systematic* development really
dawned only in the Nineteenth Century. This was because studies
undertaken by nineteenth century Catholic thinkers horrified by
the consequences of the French Revolution of 1789 made them
realize that the terrible assault on Christian order that it represented had far deeper roots. Modern anti-Christian errors, they
understood, were the product of a rejection of the full significance
of the Incarnation on the part of complacent Catholics, Protestants,
Jansenists and naturalist Enlightenment *philosophes* alike; a rejection reaching back into the latter Middle Ages. Rediscovering that
full significance led them to probe the lessons of the Fathers of
the Church, the medieval scholastics, and the mystical, devotional
and liturgical life of the Catholic community, and merge them
together into a more effective guide to the practical correction
and transformation of the wounded natural world. The centers
of rediscovery—German, French, Italian and Belgian for the most
part—were mixed lay-clerical circles, religious orders, university
and seminary faculties, and the editorial offices of the journals
and newspapers that seemed to spring up everywhere at the time.

† First published in *The Angelus* (January 2012).

Eminently Catholic in spirit, this movement of ideas and action could not rest until it had gained the backing of the Papacy for its labors. This, it solidly obtained during the reign of Blessed Pius IX (1846–1878).

It obtained papal support, however, at a time when proponents of a kaleidoscope of political, economic and social ideas—Right and Left, conservative and liberal, moderate and radical—were all trying to seduce Catholics into their ranks. Under these circumstances, a clarification of truly Catholic as opposed to dubious and non-Catholic principles underlying all socio-political issues was crucial. The end result of this process of clarification is to be found both in the "negative" condemnations of Blessed Pius IX's Syllabus of Errors (1864) as well as in the "positive" work of the whole corpus of Social Encyclicals and related pronouncements of Leo XIII (1878–1903), St. Pius X (1903–1914), Benedict XV (1914–1922), Pius XI (1922–1939) and Pius XII (1939–1958). Here, one finds repeatedly reiterated, in varied forms and with respect to a myriad of practical matters, the three basic themes of Catholic Social Doctrine.

The first of these is the need to deal with all human actions with reference to man's two-fold character, both natural and supernatural. Catholics, the Social Doctrine teaches, cannot accomplish anything of temporal value without realizing that nature is the gracious gift of God, that natural Reason must therefore be cherished, and that the pursuit of natural well-being is a positive good. On the other hand, nature is terribly wounded through sin, and men find it difficult even to believe and act upon what their Reason tells them to be true. Faith and grace coming from the supernatural realm give them the courage to do what nature itself dictates. Faith also confirms the complementary relationship of the individual and authoritative community life, a truth that classical Greek and Roman wisdom grasped imperfectly, demonstrating that personal perfection can only take place in a social framework, both natural and supernatural, with participation in the society of Christ and His Church as the center, crown and guarantor of it all. Through Faith and grace, nature's strengths become stronger, its fallen misconceptions of its supposed "laws" are unmasked as delusions, and the temporal well-being that it pursues is shaped in a way that aids the perfection of virtue and the attainment of eternal life with God.

A second principle concerns the practical implementation of Catholic Social Doctrine. Here, the guiding rule became the "thesis-hypothesis" distinction. The thesis concerns the Catholic teaching in its full integrity, which clearly allows a great deal of scope to nature and natural Reason, and this with respect to the *structures* of government, economic order and social institutions in general. The hypothesis refers to existing historical situations that may be less than optimal for attainment of the thesis and even downright contrary to its precepts. Catholics were told that prudence could compel them to accept the reality of an existing, unpalatable hypothesis, so long as this did not seduce them into considering it as a normative and therefore cause them to abandon their work for the Kingship of Christ.

That brings us to the third principle: the urgent need for militant Catholic lay action. Opponents of the Kingship of Christ might argue that they were friends of nature, eager to prevent its distortion at the hands of a supernatural "invader." But these modern naturalists could not even agree on what the nature they wanted to "save" was all about. Some of them insisted upon seeing in nature a mechanism with inexorable laws that reduced the individual human person to a machine part, lacking all freedom of action. Others demanded that nature be viewed as a realm of pure freedom and diversity, lacking in all existential meaning and authoritative moral direction. Both groups created political, economic and social institutions in line with their reductionist principles, and destroyed the individual and the natural social environment in consequence. Ultimately, willfulness was the guiding principle behind those who chose to rule the universe through mechanical "natural laws" and those who chose to open it to the chaos ensured by granting everyone and everything "natural rights." The future was crystal clear: either Christ would be King of the universe, with existential meaning and individual freedom protected; or willful, strong men would be King, with tyranny and the eventual destruction of the oppressors along with their victims. The clergy were there to teach, guide and offer sacramental grace. It was the laity's task to fight for Christ on the natural level, and to rule over the political and social order. Treating the Second Vatican Council as the "liberator" of the laity is to be one hundred years behind the times. Such liberation came with "integrist" popes and lay leaders.

Ultimately, the guidance given by the Papacy in the development of Catholic Social Doctrine has been offered in very broad strokes. Hence, one can see in encyclicals of Leo XIII such as *Immortale Dei* (1885) and *Rerum Novarum* (1891) a firm insistence on the need to build a State and a social order that can indeed pursue communal and individual well being, but only with a respect for both together, and through moral actions that would save rather than damn political leaders, property owners and workers alike. No government and no economic order is ever permitted to take "might makes right," "power politics," "Reason of State," "national exceptionalism," "laws of supply and demand," "economic freedom," or "inevitable class struggle" seriously. All these principles are equally condemnable by the Catholic *thesis*, and Catholic lay activists must be on guard against seduction by them in any *hypothetical* political compromises that they might be compelled to make with their proponents.

On the *rational* level, men can justly argue whether or not a monarchy, a constitutional system or a democracy is best suited to a given country's pursuit of temporal order, as well as its communal and individual well-being. They can *rationally* militate for a capitalist or a more socially organized corporate economic system. And arguments and militants of extremely diverse types filled the Catholic world all through the latter part of the nineteenth and the whole of the twentieth century. Into the precise details of these arguments and the organizational work giving flesh to them, Catholic Social Doctrine, *qua* authoritative Church teaching, could not go.

On the other hand, the broad, supernatural, moral and thesis-hypothesis guidelines forming that doctrine's backbone nevertheless still packed an enormous wallop. They struck directly at anyone who insisted that *his* State and *his* economic principles could not be corrected and transformed through the teaching and Kingship of Christ. They identified him as a self-proclaimed enemy of God and nature. In fact, the Church rather quickly realized that political parties calling themselves "Catholic" and "Christian" had a tendency to go down this direction, baptizing anything they did as self-evidently orthodox. It was for that reason that, special local problems aside, she favored the work of Catholic Action "lobbies" tied clearly to specific issues of obvious doctrinal and moral importance.

The postwar world has shown the wisdom of this approach, as Christian Democratic Parties, using the Council and its spirit as a justification, have themselves presided over the dismantling of Catholic influence over States, economic systems and individual behavior in general. While the Church often still today reaffirms the main lines of Catholic Social Doctrine in *theory*—as she does on other doctrinal matters—their teaching has been rendered basically meaningless on the practical level. The *Zeitgeist* and the spirit of a particular land rules Catholic Social Doctrine as it rules Catholic episcopacies and the laity. *Immortale Dei* and *Rerum Novarum* may continue to be praised, but it is Liberation Theology (both that of Marxists and of American Libertarians), Third World Theology and the demands of American exceptionalism that command doctrinal priority in the political and social sphere. If I might paraphrase the title of an article that I wrote for *The Remnant* some years ago, the scoreboard for Catholic Social Doctrine in any battle with contemporary socio-political "mystiques' would read the following: *Zeitgeist*, 666; Catholic Social Doctrine, o.

BIBLIOGRAPHY FOR FURTHER STUDY

Arbuthnott, A., *Joseph Cardijn* (London, 1966).
Bowman, F. P., *Le Christ des Barricades* (Cerf, 1987).
Cholvy, G., *Jeunesses Chrétiennes au XXE Siècle* (Ouvrières, 1991).
Elbow, M., *French Corporative Theory, 1789–1948* (New York, 1948).
Fattorini, E., *I Cattolici Tedeschi dall'Intransigenza Alla Modernità, 1870–1953* (Morcelliana, 1997)
Hellman, J., *Emmanuel Mounier and the New Catholic Left* (McGill-Queens, 1997).
Hoeffner, J., *Wilhelm Emmanuel von Ketteler und die Kathholische Sozialbewegung im 19. Jahrhundert* (Wiesbaden, 1962).
Jedin, H., and Dolan, J., eds., *History of the Church* (VII, VIII, IX, X, Crossroad, 1981).
Jemolo, A.C., *Chiesa e Stato in Italia dalla Unificazione agli Anni Settanta* (Einaudi, 1970).
Kalyvas, S.N., *The Rise of Christian Democracy in Europe* (Cornell, 1996).
Launay, M., *Le Syndicalisme Chrétien en France de 1885 à nos Jours* (Desclée, 1984).

Mayeur, J.M. et al., *Histoire du Christianisme* (X, XI, XII, XIII, Desclée, 1995–2001).

Moody, J.N., ed., *Church and Society. Catholic Social and Political Thought and Movements, 1789–1950* (New York, 1953).

Poulat, E., *Les Prêtres Ouvrièrs* (Cerf, 1999).

Rao, J., *Removing the Blindfold* (Angelus Press, 2014).

25

The Individual, the Family
and Catholic Corporate Society†

M ODERN MAN IS DEEPLY CONFUSED
regarding the proper relationship of the individual, the
family and society in general. This is understandable, given that
contemporary civilization is primarily the product of a revolutionary naturalism that seeks to understand life apart from God and
His law. While appearing to respect the inherent value of the
world and its wonders, modernity rejects the Christian teachings
that gave men the ability to deal harmoniously and positively with
nature's rich and complex character in the first place. This tragic
"dropping of the pilot" has made its supposedly nature-friendly
order of things a many-headed beast, a house divided against
itself, with its various elements in total and constant war with one
another. Only an opening to Catholic Truth can once again join
together all the aspects of nature that modern naturalist civilization
has torn asunder. What does this have to tell us?

Sacred History and Catholic Tradition both emphasize the
primary significance of the human person in God's plan. It is clear
from the account of Creation in Genesis that it is through Adam
that all of nature is marshaled to fulfill the divine will. So important
is the individual in the teaching of Christ that "every hair on his
head is numbered," and the Good Shepherd leaves His flock in
order to find one sheep who has gone astray. The Church Fathers,
grasping the full significance of a salvation that comes through the
Incarnation of the second Person of the Trinity in one sole God-
Man, Jesus Christ, marvel at the ultimate "divinization" that this
offers to the individual who faithfully lives his life in union with
his Savior. The Canon of the Mass makes the same point. It was
in defense of the supreme value of the individual, immortal soul
that the great scholastics of the Middle Ages fought their battles
against the impersonal, fatalistic vision of Averroes. It was in

---

† First published in *The Angelus* (March/April 2012).

recognition of the centrality of each distinct human person in the ultimate scheme of things that Dante, in the *Paradiso*, shows the individual in heaven shining forth with a clarity and distinction much greater than he possessed while still alive.

But it is equally clear that even if the individual human person is the "apple of God's eye," *he can only be saved as a social being.* His salvation and divinization come through membership in Christ; a Christ whose corrective and transforming authority, teaching and grace is essential in a universe where human freedom led not merely to an Original Sin weakening all of mankind, but the constant possibility of further error and evil behavior. And that membership in a corrective and transforming Christ is made palpable until the end of time through membership in His Mystical Body, His Church; His supernatural continuation in the natural realm after His own death and Resurrection.

It is precisely in discussing the individual's salvation through membership in a jointly supernatural and natural Christ and Mystical Body that we enter into the realm of social theory. For Catholic Tradition, building upon what emerges from the message of the Sacred Scriptures, has insisted that all of nature has its crucial part to play in this work of raising the individual to eternal life with God. Everything in nature, as St. Ignatius of Antioch teaches, has been "recapitulated" and redeemed in Christ. Nothing that God has created is superfluous to His plan, and nothing somehow becomes superannuated as the centuries advance. Everything thought, written, painted, sculpted and sung to the greater glory of God under the corrective and transforming grace of Christ and His Church is of crucial importance in the work of personal salvation and divinization. And anything done for the benefit of a man's final end reverberates back on his temporal existence, illuminating its purpose and enhancing its character as well.

Highest on the list of natural aids to the individual's path to heaven with positive temporal effects are earthly social institutions. The Greeks already understood society's secular benefits, with Solon the Lawgiver (c. 638–558 B. C.), the first great western political thinker—and, instructively, a poet to boot—demonstrating that individuals, left to their own devices, destroy not only their neighbors but themselves in the process. They needed guidance through the authoritative, coordinating power of the Greek *polis*, or State. For man, as Aristotle magisterially summarizes Solon's point, is *essentially* a social, political animal.

Greeks and Romans gave to the social authority of a monolithic State too exclusive an importance. What Catholic Christianity did, with a bit of practical historical aid from the Germanic and Slavic disruption of the ancient order of things, was threefold in character: it made it clear that the State required the corrective and transforming guidance of the supernatural authority of the Church; that other natural, non-governmental social institutions, equally subject to the teachings of the Mystical Body, were involved in the enterprise of chaining the individual's destructive tendencies; and that all of these societies together were ultimately intended for the *positive* benefit of distinct human persons and their divinization in Christ.

It is the family that is undoubtedly the first and most basic of these crucial, natural, authoritative societies aiding the attainment of the individual's supernatural end. Only through the union of a man and a woman can a human person exist. That union gives him the basic natural building blocks with which he must operate for the rest of his life. What happens to him in the bosom of his family, especially in the earliest years of his own existence as well as those in which he shapes the growth of his offspring, is more significant than anything else in his development of an understanding of individual needs, flaws to be corrected, and talents and virtues that can and must be cultivated. In other words, when considering things in the order of nature, "it takes a family," first and foremost, to set a creature of God on that proper path to eternal life that aids him temporally also.

On the other hand, it takes *more* than a family to do so. It does, indeed "take a village." Families are as subject to error and sin as anything else that is human. In fact, it was in recognition of the selfishness and trampling of the just demands of others on the part of powerful Greek families that men like Solon contemplated the need for political reform to begin with. A Roman or Confucianist *paterfamilias* could be a monstrous tyrant crushing the true dignity of the individual members of the family unit in their temporal pilgrimage to God. Hence, the need for the family's correction by other social authorities: those of Church and State together.

Still, it takes more than a village represented by a monolithic Church and State alone to complete nature's social influence in assisting attainment of the individual's supernatural end and simultaneously improving his temporal existence. It takes every other kind of authoritative social institution dedicated to a valid natural or supernatural human activity involving more than one individual: varied religious organizations within the Mystical Body, diverse organs for the exercise of communal political power, fraternal and charitable associations, economic guilds, schools and universities and many others besides them.

All of these "corporations"—the traditional word for any authoritative society, taken from the Latin for a body—together produced that Catholic "society of societies" or "corporate order" that thrived in the Middle Ages. All, together with the family, the most basic corporate society, under the coordinating authority of the manifold organs of Church and State, not only gave practical assistance to individuals but also helped to reveal to them their flaws and develop their talents and virtues in different, unique and irreplaceable manners. All, therefore, were God-given aids to personal natural benefits as well as personal salvation and divinization in Christ. In short, corporate social authorities, beginning with that of the family, in union with Church and State authority, are a blessing for the individual and his temporal freedom, rights and dignity, making for a fruitful passage through nature to eternal life with God. As the Jesuit journal, La Civiltà Cattolica, repeatedly noted in its development of Catholic Social Doctrine in the nineteenth century, the fullness of liberty and the fullness of life only exist in union with the fullness of social authority of all kinds. Without the latter, the willful strong oppress the weak, to the ultimate physical and spiritual detriment of both.

Catholic Christendom gave to natural social authorities and to the individual an exalted sense of their importance and their role in life. But what this also meant, should an institution or a human person sinfully rebel against the overriding need for the correction, coordination and transformation of all things in Christ—as they often did, even in the best of times—was an enhanced, exaggerated sense of their autonomous value. It is this rebellion and exaggeration that eventually, by the seventeenth and eighteenth centuries, gave birth to modern naturalism. And modern naturalism, as intimated at the beginning of my article, claimed to be able to maintain the Catholic validation of all aspects of nature for the benefit of the individual human person, but without the aid of Christ.

It has amply demonstrated that it simply cannot accomplish this task. Naturalists have disagreed intensely over what "nature" actually teaches us. One branch of the naturalist family has insisted that the universe is a realm of infinite diversity, and has therefore emphasized the supremacy of the individual's freedom, his "natural rights," and his "dignity," with no concern for his potential sinfulness. Another has argued that the universe is a machine, guided by inexorable "natural laws." For the former, law, order, society and authority are not only subordinate to the will of endlessly diverse individuals, but their innate and dangerous enemies as well. For the latter, the individual human person is nothing more than an automaton; one piece of equipment among many in a well-oiled cosmic engine. There is no such thing as individual freedom, with peculiarities of the human person, but kinks in the machinery that must, if necessary, ruthlessly be suppressed for the sake of order, and by whichever social institution it thinks most suitable for doing so, to the detriment of the work of all the others.

Both of these forms of naturalism have by now committed suicide, at least on the rational level; the mechanists because of endless debate over what, exactly, makes their machine of the universe tick, and the atomists because their position ultimately finds any meaningful definition of truth an assault on personal "choice." Historically, their varied supporters have arbitrarily demanded an unqualified belief in what it is that they teach. This they back by reference to the "will" of forces ranging from the leaders of revolutionary movements to that of the Founding Fathers.

Only an opening to the full message of the Faith can repair the naturalist damage. Alas, Catholics themselves generally fail to take the lead in this much-needed enterprise. They also have fallen prey to the naturalist temptation, at least in their practical, day-to-day lives. Although some do seem to view nature as though it were driven by one or the other mechanical force whose gears need to be oiled by one favored social institution and authority, most believing American Catholics have pitched their tents in the other naturalist camp. They talk as though the individual, left purely to his own devices, is entrusted with the fulfillment of God's plan in nature. If they are willing to make concessions to some social guidance, it is only to that given by the family. Involvement of any other authoritative institution beyond the family—the State in particular—is anathema to them.

This is not a Catholic position, but a development of modern naturalism, destructive on the natural as well as the supernatural level. Salvation is individual. Individuals primarily concerned to gain eternal life are given a holistic grasp of existence that enables them to create a better natural world than those who are not. But individuals are social beings. It takes a family to save them supernaturally and guide them temporally. It also takes a village, a complex corporate society and coordination by the State. And, above all else, it takes obedience to a Church that recognizes the role and relationship of all of these together.

26

Two Books, One Common Purpose, and the Catholic Fraternal Spirit†

WRITING AN ARTICLE ABOUT ONE'S OWN newly published book is neither the most common nor even the most respectable means of arousing interest in its value. The reason why I think that it is actually necessary for me to do so here is twofold: to begin with, because talking about my book allows me to praise a second work which underlines the same crucially important common theme; and, secondly, since it gives me the opportunity to make a statement about the spirit of Catholic fraternity that I believe to be essential to the future revival of civilized society in an age of deadly crisis.

Let me begin by rushing in foolishly "where wise men never go" in order openly to promote my own long-time intellectual labor of love. This has now come to fruition in a work called *Black Legends and the Light of the World: The War of Words with the Incarnate Word*, published by The Remnant Press. Based upon my lectures at the Roman Forum Summer Symposium in Gardone Riviera in northern Italy from 1993–2011, this book is a study of the whole of the history of the Catholic Church, from the "Seeds of the Logos" to our own post-conciliar Dark Age.

Black Legends is a thematic study rather than a purely chronological treatment of the events of two millennia. Briefly put, it explains the high and low points of Church History with reference to an unending war waged against Christianity throughout the centuries. The Great War in question is one fought by everyone angry at the boat-rocking disruption of "business as usual" brought about by a religion that demands correction and transformation of each and every aspect of a fallen world and its individual inhabitants in Christ. It is a war whose first blood was actually shed before the Incarnation in the stubborn battle in defense of an unchanging, fallen, "natural" status quo offered by the Sophists against a handful of truth-hungry Socratic philosophers. It is a

† First published in *The Latin Mass* magazine (Summer 2012).

war that was rendered truly brutal and thoroughgoing with the arrival of Christianity, and this due to the justifiable fears of the many heirs of the Sophists concerning the more universal and practical appeal of the Word made flesh and His Mystical Body.

My contention in *Black Legends* is that the Church prospers in that Great War when she honestly and wholeheartedly follows the *fullness* of the message of the Incarnation, a message that teaches the need to mobilize *everything* natural and supernatural to lead men to eternal life with God. Such a total mobilization means enthusiastic acceptance of the value of all the arms that the Creator God has placed at a Catholic's disposal: philosophy, theology, rhetoric, art and literature, along with the social authority of Church and State, with nothing excluded or somehow super-annuated, to fight those who revel in fallen nature "as it is." And, thankfully, as this book happily points out, there have been a number of moments in Church History when such a total mobilization has indeed taken place.

Alas, however, the many units fighting against correction and transformation of man and nature in Christ are a powerful lot, and *Black Legends* shows that their most potent weapon against The Incarnate Word has been nature-bound "words" and "word merchandizing." I call this octopus-like army of word merchants *The Grand Coalition of the Status Quo* and demonstrate that it has relied on exactly the same armaments since the pre-Christian battles of the Sophists and Socratics. It has not changed these arms precisely because they have proven to be so terribly effective.

The Grand Coalition's offensive of "words" against "The Incarnate Word" has been two-pronged. On the one hand, it has promoted "black legends" about the pointless, life-wasting destructiveness of Christianity, accusing it of being not only "unnatural" and "inhuman" but also even dangerous to a "proper" belief in God. On the other hand, and in recognition of the undeniable successes of this Christian troublemaker, the Grand Coalition has pulled another rhetorical ace from its sleeve. Instead of always attacking the religion of the Incarnate Word directly, it has also repeatedly sought to destroy its influence by defusing its impact; through the use of alternative "nice stories" about what Christianity "really means" that impoverish or totally emasculate its corrective and transforming mission; tall tales that do still resort to "black legends," but in order to libel orthodox, boat-rocking Catholics, now treated as enemies of Christ's "true teaching."

If Catholics embrace such "nice stories" and join in promoting "black legends" attacking the full message of their Faith and its honest militants, the cause of the Church suffers disastrously. Unfortunately, as *Black Legends* makes painfully clear, sinful Catholics, from the highest to the lowest ranks, both clerical and lay, have all too regularly done just this. They have frequently baptized as "Catholic" ideas and pastoral strategies that have actually served the purposes of those lovers of "business as usual" who will not accept correction and transformation in Christ. It is this tragically repetitive feature of Church History that has forced solid Catholic prelates, thinkers, lay activists and saints to work again and again to "remove the blindfold" from befuddled believers' eyes, awakening them to the fact that their standard operating procedure is often merely that of *the customary routine of a fallen natural world out to destroy them.* This is tragic, as Pope St. Gregory VII lamented, because it is only the Truth that sets men free, not beliefs and customs whose stubborn persistence give them what amounts merely to a deceptive aura of permanent merit.

Black Legends brings this story of the battle of words against the Incarnate Word down to our own day, which is so much shaped by the ideas of the naturalist "Enlightenment." In its so-called radical form, the Enlightenment fights against a supernatural correction and transformation of man and nature through an open assault on religion and a greater reliance on the use of "black legends." In its supposedly more moderate form, it does exactly the same thing, but by means of "nice, impoverishing, emasculating stories" reducing Catholics to a cheering squad for the Grand Coalition of the Status Quo. In a nation born of the Moderate Enlightenment, this has meant seeking to convince believers that the American understanding of "liberty" and Catholic freedom are one and the same thing; that 33 A. D. and 1776 A. D. work together to provide "mankind's last and best hope," with the edge going to the latter; and that a pluralist minded Catholic Clubhouse with no ability to rock anybody's "business as usual" boat is the best guarantee for the success of the Church Militant that has ever existed.

This brings me to the second work mentioned at the beginning of this article as justification for a discussion of my own tome. That book is Christopher Ferrara's *Liberty: The God That Failed.* If my volume has any value, it is precisely because it points readers to his more detailed and more immediately crucial work; and may he write many more like it! Both *Liberty* and *Black Legends* share one and the same common purpose: the unmasking of fraudulent beliefs presented as godly, benevolent and pragmatic. And, in fact, as we wrote them, the two of us realized more and more that they were providentially meant to go together.

"An epochal achievement" is the only phrase that I can think of to characterize *Liberty: The God That Failed* accurately. The historical research behind it is brilliant. Its findings are both myth-shattering and unanswerable. They are driven home with apostolic zeal and a lawyer's razor-sharp logic. Finally, and very importantly from the standpoint of a "call to action," the whole volume is "reader-friendly" in the extreme. In fact, aside from its specific Catholic merits, it should be utilized in a classroom as a model of approachable scholarly work.

But specific Catholic merits it has a-plenty, so much so that every Catholic eager to understand the socio-political nightmare in which we find ourselves in the modern world owes it to himself to read this brilliant book. Why? Because Chris, as intimated above, so clearly uncovers a still current self-destructive fraud: that of the "American" definition of "liberty" emerging from the theories of the so-called Moderate Enlightenment, along with its claim that it is the key to a peaceful and just social order friendly to sound religious belief and the satisfaction of the wishes of the mass of men.

He does this on the theoretical level through an analysis of the ideas and impact on the American Founders and their successors of the vision of the socio-political thinker perhaps most associated with the Moderate Enlightenment: John Locke. Demonstrating Locke's accommodation of Thomas Hobbes' approach to fit the sensibilities of the "proper," anti-monarchical, property-hungry, Whig aristocracy of his day. Chris calls this amalgam "Hobbeslocke." He indicates that the Moderate Enlightenment is really nothing other than a "nice story" preparing the way for its more radical cousin and his further progress. American Moderate Enlightenment "liberty" does nothing other than bring Hobbes' monarchical willfulness into the hands of "the right individuals," who still pay lip service to God so long as He keeps his distance from their "business as usual."

But such "reasonable men" cannot keep liberty from falling into the lap of others more willful still and less concerned for singing traditional Protestant hymns before using their common sense to go out and wrack rents. Ultimately, what this "liberty" amounts to is a license for the strongest individuals to seize opportunities to satisfy their material passions; to institutionalize Original Sin and seek to use it as a pillar of social order. What the author so well details in his description of the Lockean influence on the American Regime is what our mutual friend, Dr. Danilo Castellano, succinctly summarized as the English thinker's chief flaw: his reduction of all of life to the level of the individual, destroying society in the process, and then his destruction of the individual, reducing him to nothing other than a bundle of desires.

Liberty: The God That Failed also excels in dealing with the practical historical fortunes of "freedom" in America. Chris introduces us to a colonial revolutionary cabal that displays an innovative (and quite violent) understanding of how to invent and manipulate public opinion in support of a World Turned Upside Down that aids only the *paucis felicibus*: its own members. But he also makes it clear that a number of these inventive manipulators were themselves self-deceived and perhaps even manipulated in turn. They were led by their own logic from 1787 onwards to ensure that the blessings of liberty would grow in tandem with a state more centralized than any British monarch had ever imagined, and a society infinitely more atheist in character than those willing to praise a God who left them alone had originally intended. Their "moderation" produced radicalism as smoothly as the nineteenth century children of the Founders asked why their fathers' will should not mean what their progeny "chose" it to mean. For whatever the original generation of American revolutionaries might have thought Lockean "liberty" to entail, its true colors were ever more obvious as Washingtons evolved into Lincolns: its role as a tool suitable for the strongest men to get what they wanted, either ideologically or materially, from the naïve masses under the rubric of allowing everyone to be free.

One of the most interesting parts of Chris' work is his discussion of the South. Many traditionalists realize that Lincoln's understanding of liberty was problematic in an Enlightenment way, but this book underlines the fact that the supporters of the "Old South" shared the same flawed vision. Like conservatives, neo-conservatives, and libertarians of our own day, both North and South simply wanted liberty to mean what they wanted it to mean. Instructive also in this regard is the author's discussion of the way in which southerners like Robert E. Lee seem to have interpreted northern victory as a Hegelian-like demonstration of the "testing" of liberty and its further evolution. In short, what the North meant by liberty had been proven correct by the Triumph of the Will.

Another highly instructive section of this always illuminating work is that which treats of a highly laudable post-Civil War association of Protestants dedicated to the healing of America's "Original Sin": its understanding of "liberty." Their analysis was the same as that of Chris. Behind the author's poignant description of the failure of their efforts to amend the Constitution to acknowledge the need for submission to God so as to arrive at a sound definition of liberty and construct a properly structured free society, one can sense his rage that contemporary Catholics are generally not as perceptive as these earlier separated brethren. Most continue to praise a liberty that works to destroy them despite evidence of the kind of ill-treatment that "liberty" meted out to Catholics (read the author's account of the San Patrizios in the Mexican War!) from the very outset; even in the land of liberty's supposedly more pristine pre-Civil War era.

Mention of these "outside" fellow travelers brings me to my second point: that concerning Catholic fraternity. Chris and I are close friends. I constantly learn from him and from his research and he graciously says that the same is true for him concerning my own labors. I believe that this is because we are both operating according to the true rules of Catholic fraternity expressed so well by the late Dr. William Marra: the recognition that we, as individual Catholics, are all limited; that we are not ourselves the voice of the Church and need correction; that we all need to listen to one another with great care, and this more especially in an era and in a society that has precisely been marred by the enormous egotism and self-seeking promoted by a system that gives its blessings on individual passion and thereby institutionalizes the effects of Original Sin.

Early Catholics realized that because nature was not totally depraved by sin, there were "Seeds of the Logos" with which they could happily work. Among these were the seeds planted by pagan

Socratics seeking to use their natural rational abilities to discover what was True, Good and Beautiful. Their labors helped mightily to rock the boat of the Grand Coalition of the Status Quo, and this earned them a warm welcome into the Catholic camp. There, they could be heard, weighed, corrected and transformed through the superior wisdom and grace of Christ's Mystical Body.

We have to recognize that just as there were Protestant opponents of the Original Sin of America in the nineteenth century with something worth hearing, similar "outsiders" hunting for the Truth are still wandering through the ruins of our own "free" civilization today. Some of these outsiders remain blinded by black legends regarding Catholicism and do not understand that they are looking for what the Catholic Faith has to offer. They may also have something important to tell *us* as we correct *their* errors. Indeed, we may actually need their help to remove the blindfold from the vast number of contemporary Catholics believing "nice stories" about the godly character of an American liberty that actually compels them to emasculate their true Faith.

Only a Catholic fraternal love, open to the fullness of the Truth and yet aware of the difficulties of individual "paths to Rome" can bring such tasks to fruition. And that Catholic fraternal spirit calls us to accomplish this "gathering in" of serious seekers of the Truth with ever-greater urgency in the face of a crisis of civilization on the global level that could well move from intellectual to material conflict. As Ernst Jünger, discussing the same need to abandon a self-deceptive worldview for a deeper knowledge of the Truth that *Liberty: The God That Failed* and *Black Legends* address, one wrote that intellectual preparation must precede effective action. And it has to be more solid than ever before in an infinitely more dangerous world.

"Now battle had to be joined, and therefore men were needed to restore a new order, and new theologians as well, to whom the evil was manifest from its outward phenomena down to its most subtle roots; then the time would come for the first stroke of the consecrated sword, piercing the darkness like a lightning flash. For this reason, individuals had the duty of living in alliance with others, gathering the treasure of a new rule of law. But the alliance had to be stronger than before, and they more conscious of it." (Ernst Jünger, *Auf den Marmorklippen*, XX)

27

An Interview with the Author of
Liberty, The God That Failed[†]

Editor's Note: The following is an interview conducted by Dr. John C. Rao with Christopher A. Ferrara, author of Liberty, the God That Failed.

JR: Let's begin, appropriately enough, with your title, and the mention of "liberty" and coercion together. Is that the essence of the failure of this "god"? Its reliance on police action to force men to be "free"?

CF: That is part of it, of course. The book demonstrates that "Liberty" has never arrived at any place in its long march through the nations except at the point of a gun. The book exposes the utter myth of Liberty—essentially the overthrow of monarchy and any form of the perennial alliance between Church and State—as the result of spontaneous popular uprisings of downtrodden masses, yearning to be free from "the tyranny of popes and kings." The age of democratic revolution, as one chapter explains, merely replaced old yokes with new and far heavier ones. But more than this, the book traces how Liberty was first reified—given a kind of concrete being, such as Lady Liberty or Liberty Tree—and then deified, that is, literally hailed as a goddess. This was more than a trope of the 18th century style of rhetoric, albeit less than a worship of divinity as such. Think of Liberty treated this way as a kind of demiurge or emanation of the divine. In fact, there is a goddess Liberty of pagan Roman provenance who is the model for the goddess celebrated by the colonial radicals of 1776. Her likeness as seen on a Roman coin also appears in the Statue of Liberty.

JR: What about a second issue brought up by your title, that of secular "myth making" and the assault on the earlier existing sacred tradition. Are you dealing here with a new, sincere religious vision? Or are you confronting a conscious fraud?

† First published in *The Distributist Review* (November 11, 2012). *Liberty, The God That Failed* is available from Angelico Press.

CF: If we accept Becker's thesis of a new "heavenly city" that represents the Enlightenment's persistence in the Christian vision radically altered to exclude Christ—and I do not accept that thesis at all—then one could speak of a sincere religious vision. But the behavior of the ideologues who practiced revolution in 1776 and thereafter belies sincerity and bespeaks hypocrisy and fraud—as their own contemporary critics protested. The book develops the evidence of this hypocrisy and fraud beyond serious dispute, showing that Liberty has always been just Power by another name—but a new form of power, the "will of the people," that knows none of the restraints imposed by the Christian political tradition with its divine dictate that we must obey God rather than men.

JR: If fraud is involved in this unified development, who is it that gains from it? Or do the beneficiaries change over time? In other words, do Locke, Obama and everyone in between serve the cause of the same or different people?

CF: Broadly speaking, the same sort of people. That is, the people who proclaim their service of Liberty while they exercise Power and revel in its perquisites with voluptuous abandon. There is no better example of this than Thomas Jefferson, the very Apostle of Liberty: a slave-owner who deplored slavery, a supposed champion of "limited government" whose entire career is marked by one dictatorial move after another, including a tyrannical embargo of American shipping during his second term, during which he deployed the American military against American citizens. And this long before Lincoln supposedly destroyed the illusory "Jeffersonian democracy" that Jefferson himself never practiced. The book rather relentlessly documents Jefferson's career in this regard, perhaps with a thoroughness not seen in other books treating of this subject. Another of the dozens of examples presented in the book: Jefferson's plan, which he defended throughout his life, for the state-sponsored forcible deportation of black slave children in order to kill off the black population in America, thus ending the problem of the black man's inconvenient presence among the white beneficiaries of the Revolution. Today, of course, we have the same sort of person in Obama. He is a fanatical advocate of the mass murder of his own people in the womb, preferably with state subsidies. As Martin Luther King declared, abortion is "killing populations. It's killing generations and certainly the population that is most impacted by abortion in America is the black community. So I feel that as a civil rights leader I have a responsibility to proclaim that black Americans are being exterminated by the genocidal acts of abortion." Like Jefferson—like so many American Presidents—Obama is a Liberty-preaching tyrant of dimensions unknown in the Christian centuries. Here is a man it costs a billion dollars a year to maintain, who lives in a mansion and has a fleet of private jets and helicopters, who takes multi-million dollar vacations at our expense, who can destroy the world by authorizing the launch of nuclear missiles, who holds the power over life and death in his hands via Presidential pardon, and who presides over a government whose tentacles extend into every area of human existence. But thank God the Founders overthrew King George! Now we have Liberty! And taxation with representation!

JR: So what is it that disturbs you more—the fraud or the nature of the fraud?

CF: As a lawyer and writer, the fraud. I loathe sophistical and disingenuous arguments and the hoary myths that modernity tells about itself. They keep me up at night. I feel driven to destroy them. As a citizen, it is the nature of the fraud, which is the life we must endure under the heavy secular yokes of the state and federal governments that "we the People"—meaning, "we the revolutionary elites"—supposedly "conceived in Liberty," which wield powers and make demands on ordinary people that no mere Christian king could even dream of.

JR: One historical question suggested by the title before moving on. You start with Locke, but in the text Hobbes comes up as well. That indicates you believe the ideology of liberty to have earlier roots.

CF: Yes, it is in Hobbes, whom Locke made more palatable while pretending to deplore "Hobbesism." But it appears much earlier, in germinal form, in the thought of such as William of Ockham, Marsilius of Padua, Machiavelli, and the rather obscure Juan de Mariana, the Jesuit outlier whose works were burned by his own order. Hobbes and Locke, however, put it all together: the state of nature, man's natural "absolute" freedom, the demotion of natural law in favor of a new, crabbed conception of rights, the subjugation of Church by state (which Hobbes achieves by having the monarch usurp the role of Pope and Locke by simply separating the two powers completely), the social compact as the source of political authority, the right to revolution. And, of course, "the sovereign will of the people"—meaning the sovereign will of those who oppress the people in their name in completely unprecedented ways—precisely because they claim to represent the popular will.

JR: I was struck by your description of the highly sophisticated co-option of the role of "voice of the people" by what amounted to a small number of American revolutionaries eager for independence. It sounds more "modern," "radical," and even Bolshevik than one would normally think. Were the revolutionaries innovators in this misrepresentation of their numerical strength? Is it just in the nature of the liberty-seeking beast? Did they actually believe it?

CF: Some may have believed it, others may have persuaded themselves that they believed it, and still others, such as Madison in Federalist No. 40, quite cynically declared that they represented the will of the people no matter what the people would actually have willed if given a say in the matter.This indeed is the nature of the beast: its claim to absolute authority based on the "consent" of those it purports to govern by consent. Yet how is it that any popular attempt to revoke that mythical consent is invariably met by lethal force?

JR: Given all of the shenanigans that you describe, is there any way to separate the Constitution as a legal and administrative document out from its service on behalf of the god of Liberty?

CF: Yes there is! The last chapter of the book explores exactly how this could be done. And the Church has never condemned democracy per se. My book is thus not a brief for the restoration of monarchy, even if I would much prefer it personally and, in fact, the imperial Presidency exemplified by Obama is nothing but an elective monarchy. By the way, even the radical libertarian Hans Hermann Hoppe, in his *Democracy: The God that Failed* (his title inspired my title) concedes that Christian monarchs were far more respectful of the rights of their subjects than modern democratic regimes.

JR: You catalogue Jeffersonian Republicans acting as Washingtonian Federalists and vice-versa. How aware were they of serving the same god of Liberty and its contradictory message? When you speak of some of them as disappointed with the results of the Revolution, were they really penitent for supporting it, or did they just claim that they did not "choose" that the situation developed in unpleasant ways?

CF: The Federalists and the Republicans alike claimed to be the loyal servitors of Liberty. Those who later repented, repented of the outcome, not the idea of Liberty. A few, however, such as Benjamin Rush, seemed to actually repent of the Enlightenment itself, finally conceding that only the Gospel could serve as the foundation of the good State—which is exactly the conception of social order the Revolution had destroyed. There is a chapter devoted to these varying repentances. But you will find none of these latter penitents among the first rank of the Founders.

JR: Let me ask your opinion on a side question that has always interested me. The Founding Fathers and the Old Guard Bolsheviks were generally educated and cosmopolitan men. They both created systems that were then conducive to domination by much more parochial-minded Jacksons and Stalins. Do you think that the "priesthood" serving the god of Liberty inevitably suffers from this kind of degeneration?

CF: An important insight. Yes, the boldly conceived revolutionary vehicle that will transform and elevate the human race inevitably falls under the control of lowly, crass and shallow demagogues, Obama being the latest example.

JR: While we are on this subject of devolution, how about the line of development from men like Benjamin Franklin to Abraham Lincoln? Both seem to have been convinced of the need for a civil religion of liberty to replace the sacred religion of Christianity. Is the new secular religion they support unchangeable, or do you see a development of doctrine along the way?

CF: The worship of the nation-state as the ground of social order, as the new mystical body to replace the Mystical Body of Christendom, is the prime dogma of Liberty as religion. The dogma leads to development in the form of an ever-expanding catalogue of "rights" that "the people" clamor for, which now includes mass murder in the womb and the "marriage" of members of the same sex. In this development, the concept of rights loses what Pierre Manent calls its "ontological density," and becomes simply whatever the hell people would like to do or whatever judges say they should be able to do. And all of this "development" becomes part of the Liberty catechism in keeping with the other prime dogma: Locke's Law of Toleration, which ensures that no "private" religious belief shall be "imposed" by law. Of course, the demotion of revealed religion to ineffectual private opinion is itself a theological judgment that undergirds the modern nation-state, making it no less a confessional state than the Christian commonwealth it supersedes. The political scientist Ralph Hancock has called this the "anti-theology" of the State.

JR: Still thinking of Lincoln, is he the pivotal figure for the survival of the Union that most historians seem to think? In other words, no Lincoln, no Civil War? What would have been the fate of the god of Liberty without him?

CF: Such counterfactuals are difficult to assess. If Buchanan had been President, and if we are to take him at his word in his farewell address, he would have let the Southern states walk away. But it is hard to believe that even Buchanan would have done nothing to respond to the seizure of all federal forts, arsenals, mints, courthouses and other federal properties by Confederate forces, the firing on Fort Sumter, the aiding and abetting of armed insurrection in Baltimore, and the establishment of a rival federal government asserting jurisdiction over half the United States and Mississippi, beginning just across the Potomac from the White House. The Southern romantic claim that Lincoln started the war is simply laughable. It was the Lynchburg Virginian newspaper that admitted the fact of history concerning the aims of the Confederacy, one year after the bombardment of Sumter: "We dared a revolution, and provoked a war." Granted, the fire-breathing politicians of the South predicted a short and rather bloodless conflict, but then politicians always lie or mislead "We the People." And then they promptly exempt themselves from the wars they provoke, while the common man—as you say, John—is told to "march and pay." In any case, even if the South had succeeded, we would have two federal leviathans on the same continent instead of one. Confederate Vice President Stephens openly declared that it was the intention of the Confederate government—a new federal government, not a mere voluntary league of states—to be "the controlling power on this continent." In other words, a new nation-state, modeled on the one from which the Southern states had seceded, including a Confederate Constitution—borrowed verbatim from the United States Constitution—that separated Church and State, forbade any religious test for office, and provided for the supremacy of Confederate law over the law of the Confederate states in cases of conflict.

JR: You go into great detail to indicate that the South offered homage to the god of Liberty alongside the North. Is it exactly the same god? A heretical "Arian" or "Monophysite" version? Or is it just that there is a different, restricted elite that benefits from the fruits of freedom, South as opposed to North?

CF: The latter; I call it "Southern-fried Liberty." As I have just noted, the Union and Confederate Constitutions were practically identical, including a supremacy clause, used to enforce the Confederate military draft against state opposition in the Confederacy; the first draft in American history, by the way. Both sides invoked the Founders and the Spirit of 1776. The Confederate Seal featured George Washington on his horse. Confederate leaders spoke again and again of their "second American Revolution." Indeed, no less than Robert E. Lee declared just before the war that "secession is nothing but revolution." Think of the Civil War as Liberty without slaves versus Liberty with slaves: the matter and anti-matter of Liberty, colliding with immense destructive force. But then, when it was all over, Lee, Davis, Stephens and other Southern leaders said, in essence, "Never mind. We are all one country again." Just like that! The book explores what I call "The Great Never Mind."

JR: There seems to be a certain Hegelian spirit that emerges from what both Abraham Lincoln and Robert E. Lee say about the Civil War; in other words, "liberty" is tested in battle and he who arises victorious from the field of combat is to be accepted as its true standard-bearer and interpreter. Do you think that "struggle" and "survival of the fittest" might be more essential to the religion of Liberty than anything substantive that it can offer to its believers?

CF: Exactly so! It was as if the Confederacy vanished like a soap bubble once the South failed the test of strength. After it was over, Lee swore an oath of allegiance to the Union, declaring: "I will, in like manner, abide by and faithfully support all laws and proclamations which have been made during the existing rebellion with reference to the emancipation of slaves, so help me God." And the same Lee who had written before the war that "secession is nothing but revolution," wrote to the arch-liberal and anti-Romanist Lord Acton—a great enthusiast for secession and the Confederacy—that "the judgment of reason has been displaced by the arbitrament of war, waged for the purpose as avowed of maintaining the union of the states." Referring to the "fratricidal war which has taken place," Lee told Acton that the South "now accepts in good faith its constitutional results." So, for Lee and other Southern leaders, the Civil War was just one massive arbitration proceeding. And since the South lost the arbitration, it was time to resume union with the North again. As Lee chided one correspondent in 1867: "Madam, do not train up your children in hostility to the government of the United States. Remember we are all one country now. Dismiss from your mind all sectional feeling, and bring them up to be Americans." Just like that! And this after nearly 700,000 essentially pointless deaths. Lee even went so far as to declare in the year of his own death that "...I am rejoiced that slavery is abolished. I believe it will be greatly for the interests of the South.... I would cheerfully have lost all I have lost by the war, and have suffered all I have suffered, to have this object attained." Then why did the South secede in the first place, for the professed reason—the primary source documents are undeniable on this point—that the institution of slavery had to be defended against Northern threats? Even Jefferson Davis would declare: "The past is dead; let it bury its dead, its hopes, its aspirations; before you lies the future—a future full of hope and golden promise; a future of expanding national glory, before which all the world shall stand amazed. Let me beseech you to lay aside all rancor, all bitter sectional feeling, and take your place in the ranks of those who will bring about a consummation devoutly to be wished—a reunited country." In that case, what was the point of the secession?

JR: Your discussion of the late nineteenth-century Protestant critics of the American Foundation and its "original sin" of ignoring God is very interesting and thoroughgoing. Was there any indication on their part of the role that Protestantism itself may have played in creating the god of Liberty?

CF: Excellent question. No, unfortunately they seemed oblivious to the fatal defect in their own religion. Hence their fascinating campaign to amend the Constitution to acknowledge—believe it or not—the social kingship of Christ, to which I devote a chapter, succumbed to its own inconsistency, which was inherent to the Protestant conception of sovereignty.

JR: From what you say, it strikes me that the only obstacle to the radicalization of the American god of Liberty is the continued struggle of such religious-minded critics against its logical development from its more moderate-sounding envelope. Am I wrong in arguing this, or do you see a real connection between Anglo-American liberty and continental European radicalism that only the persistence of Christian opposition prevents becoming crystal clear?

CF: European radicalism is Anglo-American Liberty in its direct confrontation with a Catholic social order of centuries' standing that was never present in America. R. R. Palmer and others have noted that the American Revolution would have been as bloody as the French if not for the lack of any serious religious opposition to revolution in the colonies. The Anglican loyalists, weak opponents of the radicals to begin with, were driven from the country and never returned, unlike the French loyalists who were slaughtered in the Vendee or those who later made possible the Bourbon Restoration.

JR: That, of course brings up the question of Catholics. If I remember correctly, they first come up prominently in your book with reference to the San Patrizio brigade in the Mexican War, and as victims of "liberty." Why are such historical experiences as those of the San Patrizios so unknown to American Catholics? Do they have two conflicting religious affiliations? Are they worshipers of the God of Abraham, Isaac and Jacob on the one hand and the god of Liberty on the other? Or do they place more faith in the Founding Fathers than the Church Fathers?

CF: Pierre Manent has put it best: In America, as in every Western polity, we are expected to be "atheists under the one God, the God in whom we believe." This is the intolerable paradox that the partisans of Liberty have foisted upon us—and with spectacular success. They have hypnotized an entire civilization, which need only awaken from its trance in order to realize the ridiculousness of its situation.

JR: Modern conservatives are always talking about getting back to the roots and the Original Intent of the Founding Fathers. It is clear from your book that Original Intent serves an anti-Catholic and secularizing cause. Does that mean that modern conservatives are anti-Catholic secularists? Or do they simply refuse to admit that $1 + 1 = 2$?

CF: I would say that in principle they are anti-Catholic secularists, while emotionally they would deny the charge and view anti-Catholicism with horror or at least disapproval. And yes, they refuse to admit that 1 plus 1 makes two. Like the libertarians, they never cease to denounce the excesses of the very State arising from the Liberty they never cease to praise.

JR: You describe tarring and feathering as a favored tool of the Sons of Liberty in the revolutionary era. Don't you think that the disciples of liberty in our own day will tar and feather your book? And perhaps you along with it?

CF: Anything to stimulate sales! Please direct post-mortem payments to my estate.

JR: If Liberty is the god that failed, how is it that many people, neo-conservatives and libertarians prominent among them, seem to think that the religion of American liberty is on the verge of worldwide triumph?

CF: That was the delusion of the Roman Republic just before its fall.

JR: Your book is one of the most illuminating, well-researched and reader-friendly that I have ever enjoyed. Like all superb scholarly works, it indicates a much wider substructure. You must have a lot more material on the subject of liberty and its discontents, maybe dealing with matters beyond the borders of America. Are you planning a follow-up work?

CF: Yes, a second volume was already substantially written when this book appeared. It traces Liberty's march through the nations after 1776, and ultimately its march into the Catholic Church through the bronze doors of Saint Peter's at Vatican II—provoking ecclesial chaos of unprecedented proportions. God willing, the second volume will find its way into print within the next two years. Maybe sooner, if my publisher pushes hard enough.

28

Representative Democracy
ITS GENESIS AND DEVELOPMENT[†]

WHENEVER I HAVE TO GIVE A TALK ON the present theme, two quite contradictory names immediately come to mind: Woodrow Wilson and Louis-Ferdinand Céline. Although one does not normally hear these two men mentioned together, and for good reason, both are very useful for making clear just how different judgments regarding the reality of representative democracy can be. For Wilson, making the world safe for such a system of government was tantamount to guaranteeing social order, eternal peace and personal happiness. For Céline, as one of his characters in *Journey to the End of the Night* explains, all that the victory of modern representative democracy ensured was the personal financial destruction of the average man and his permanent mobilization for perpetual conflict as well.

One of the best ways of shedding light upon these contradictory judgments, along with the emergence and value of representative democracy as a form of government in and of itself, is with reference to the writings of the Jesuit educator and writer, Luigi Prospero Taparelli d'Azeglio, S. J. (1793–1862). Born into an aristocratic Piedmontese family, Taparelli's initial fame rested upon his tenure as Rector of the Roman College (1824–1829) and his influential *Saggio Teoretico di Dritto Naturale Appoggiato sul Fatto* (1840). His later career was linked with the Jesuit journal, *La Civiltà Cattolica*, which began its activity in 1850. While serving as an editor and *paterfamilias* of this highly influential review—one of the main stimuli behind the publication of Pope Pius IX's Syllabus of Errors and the whole subsequent development of Catholic Social Doctrine—Taparelli produced numerous articles on the relationship of individuals, society, Church and State. Many of the most important of these were then collected together in 1854 in a book entitled *Esame Critico degli Ordini Rappresentativi alla Moderna*.

[†]   An address delivered in Spain in April 2013.

In order properly to appreciate Taparelli's discussion of the emergence and value of representative democracy, it is essential to realize that it is intimately connected with that broad but comprehensive guideline for all of human action that he provides his readers underneath the name of *diritto ipottatico*: a term that may be translated as Hypostatic; or perhaps better still, Incarnational Law. This is founded upon the belief that it is solely by keeping one's eyes focused firmly upon the full message of the Incarnation of the Second Person of the Blessed Trinity as Jesus Christ the God-Man that even those concerns which at first glance appear to be purely "natural" ones can properly be addressed. Why? Because it was only through the Incarnation's *supernatural* confirmation of the goodness of God's Creation that man was given sufficient intellectual stimulus and grace to courageously accept the importance of his *natural* gifts, to correct their sinful distortions and insufficiencies, to order them according to a proper hierarchy of values, and to put them to serious, harmonious, practical use in service of his final end, with human Reason at the top of the list of the tools so brilliantly mobilized.

A key lesson of *diritto ipottatico* is that the individual must be perfected in and through society. This truth is revealed by the call of all human persons, body and soul, to a new and higher life as sons of God, and the teaching that the "divinization" that such a new life makes possible *must* be achieved through membership in and submission to the "society" of Christ; a society which is continued in time by means of His Mystical Body, the Church.

Diritto ipottatico indicates that whatever is taught concerning the individual's direct relationship with the Creator and Redeemer also holds true with respect to his dealings with the entirety of God's handiwork. What this then signifies is that all things natural—each and every one of them confirmed as being essentially good and capable of "divinization" by the very fact of the Incarnation itself—can only be brought to fruition through cooperative social action; through the work of societies to which individuals on the path to perfection submit themselves; through associations which in turn submit to the society of the Church for that correction and transformation in Christ rendering them fully suitable to the task of benefitting human persons. Each of these many societies promotes some natural gift or value in a unique way, encouraging individual growth in virtue and avoidance of vice in ways that the others cannot do, thereby making all of them supremely useful to God's plan, and any arbitrary interference with their work supremely destructive.

But how are cooperative natural societies formed? Here, too, one learns the answer by looking to Christ. The society of the Church, based upon the innate truth, goodness and strength of the living God, was formed through the *authority* of her Founder. Similarly, the innumerable natural societies that aid the human race to use created things to move individual men from earth to heaven are formed through the social authorities that activate their innate truths and strengths, harmonizing them with divine wisdom so as to purify them of the flaws due to Original and personal Sin.

Authority, for Taparelli, thus can be defined as the "form" of the many societies to which human persons must submit *in time* to make their lives happier and perfect themselves *for eternity*. It is authority that makes societies "real" for the individuals who cannot help but benefit from them, naturally and supernaturally. And given the multiform society that the work of activating the multitude of diverse natural phenomena dictates, this means that the *fullness of social authority* ensures the fullness of personal protection from the ravages of lawless men corrupted by sin and the fullness of personal freedom to grow and develop in every natural and supernatural respect:

> When the right of command, or authority, is exercised in all its fullness, then all individuals, even the most weak, may use in all fullness their own rights; with the result that the fullness of liberty corresponds precisely to the fullness of authority, while, in contrast, the prevalence of either public force or of the multitude against right corresponds always to slavery.

Still, "authority" as such is a spiritual and intellectual principle. The Incarnation, the foundation for *diritto ipottatico*, teaches us that in order for such a principle to be proportioned to a world of individual human persons, it has to "take flesh." This can only come about through an historical action, as it did in the case of the God-Man Himself, by being born of a specific woman in a specific place at a specific time. An abstract spiritual authority could only be the ruler of an abstract "human nature." But such a human nature does not exist apart from human persons. Distinct creatures of flesh and blood required distinct leaders in order effectively to be moved by authority. This is why the common tongue equates the words "superior" and "authority," the former identifying the concrete aspect of the force that the latter term points to in the abstract. This is also why the Christian reveres possessors of authority, with the divine character of the natural function rendering the person wielding it somehow "sacred" as well. To avoid such "divinization" of authority, one would have to ensure that fleshly objects in no way spoke to man of the spirit, and that "the consecration of the sacrifice does not also render sacred the chalice in which it is offered." Yes, authority in and of itself is something different from its possessor in time and space. Yes, this authority must always be exercised in union with the laws of God and Reason for the ultimate benefit of those subject to it and be capable of being shown to do so. Nevertheless, authority can only *practically* serve as the "form" of a society when some historical event incarnates its beneficent powers in a given individual or group, and that authority is regularly obeyed as authority, separate from any day-by-day approval of each and every one of its actions on the part of its subjects.

In short, the right of command not naturally being in the hands of any person, it is necessary that it become his by means of some fact. This fact—the reason not for the authority but for his investiture with it—may often (whatever its opponents say) not depend on the will of him who obeys, whenever not obeying would be a violation of the rights either of the ordering Creator either naturally or supernaturally, or of man assisted by the usual laws of the natural order.

Specific historical facts can incarnate the authorities serving as the form of the many different societies of a highly complex universe in innumerable ways. If disobeying the commands of the historically incarnated authorities to which individual Catholics find themselves subject is detrimental to the good of the other members of the societies that they rule, then faithful followers of Christ cannot thwart them. Yes, they may discuss their flaws and even work to realize changes in them, but only with full respect for such authorities' pre-existing rights, and without withdrawing their obedience from them as such. This was especially true of the incarnate authorities of the State, which, for Taparelli, was the noble coordinating guarantor of the smooth functioning of all of multiform human society. And hence, despite a personal preference for hereditary monarchy, he was convinced that he had to accept any form of government incarnated by historical facts that was not "a living error" and regularly detrimental to the common and individual good as identified through *diritto ipottatico*.

Let us note that in discussing different forms of government, Taparelli did *not* contrast "democracy" with "hereditary monarchy." Hereditary monarchies had very often been shown to be deeply concerned with ascertaining and responding favorably to serious popular desires, thereby proving themselves to be eminently democratic in spirit and practice. What he *did* contrast with hereditary monarchy—along with a myriad of other possible historical incarnations of State authority—was a government that based possession of its specific right to command upon the will of some or all of the governed. Once again, when Taparelli saw that historical facts had created such systems; as, for example, with the Roman and the Venetian Republics, the Swiss Cantons, and the Kingdom of Belgium; and when he realized that disobedience of the commands of these incarnate authorities would regularly hinder attainment of the common and individual good, then he fully admitted that they too possessed an undeniable *droit de cité*. Aside from inevitable problems in some respects not dissimilar to those of hereditary monarchies—namely those connected with an electoral politics that could produce "an interregnum exposed to the assaults of a thousand ambitions"—nothing in and of itself prevented representative governments from responding to the demands of *diritto ipottatico*. Catholics, regardless of personal preference, were obliged to submit to them and obey them, working conscientiously, as they always must, for their purgation of any evils due to human sin.

For Taparelli, essential difficulties with respect to governmental forms emerge only through political visions that openly defy and reject *diritto ipottatico*, along with its emphasis upon the symbiosis of nature and the supernatural and the beneficent union of the individual and society. Unfortunately, he lamented, such visions dominated the modern political landscape, filling it with tyrannical, and ultimately untenable and self-destructive governmental debris. Anti-incarnational theories had been used to corrupt hereditary monarchies. And they could be and were continually used to corrupt the democratic representative governments whose genesis and development we are addressing here today as well.

Let us approach this deadly assault on *diritto ipottatico* on modern representative governments with reference to the insistence on the part of many of their proponents that their legitimacy be based solely upon "popular sovereignty." In one abstract sense only, Taparelli argued, could "The People" be said to be universally sovereign: they clearly indicated throughout all of history that they universally willed to be ruled by social authorities. But one could not make a statement regarding the origins of any given functioning government with an abstract concept lacking an historical bridge to the world of nature. A qualitative jump of this sort required a qualitative change in instruments. Some historical fact always had to incarnate social authority, that placing The People at the foundation of the system included.

Unfortunately, the *real* historical facts incarnating *attempts* to create governmental systems based upon "popular sovereignty" repeatedly reveal the truth that calls for "democratic" rule have regularly served merely as a useful cover for the satisfaction of some willful individual or oligarchic desire hostile to Reason as well as to Faith; i.e., the imposition of a power inimical to *diritto ipottatico*. This was already visible in the efforts of the Kings of France to use blatantly manipulated meetings of the Estates-General to orchestrate an outraged "popular opinion" supposedly mandating regal attacks on Boniface VIII, the Knights of the Temple, the Church and subsidiary societies in general. But the full reality of just what such "mandated response" to the "People's Will" actually entailed was made crystal clear through the anti-papal "conciliarist" movements of the fourteenth and fifteenth centuries. For practically all of the contradictory, pseudo-mystical and tyrannical consequences of the "democratic" arguments that one finds in a Jean-Jacques Rousseau can be found in one or the other theory regarding the "popular constitution" of the *res publica christiana* propounded in the late Middle Ages.

Take, for example, Marsilius of Padua's writings on behalf of the Emperor Louis IV in his battles against Pope John XXII. Here,

Marsilius argues that his master's ultimate political legitimacy lies in submission to the "Will of the Roman People." Now the real Roman People in the fourteenth century were a particularly wild, unreliable, flighty and downright treacherous bunch, but that was no particular problem for Marsilius. According to his theories, the task of the prince, aided by his intellectual advisors, was to awaken in that unfortunate mob the *kind* of popular will that he *might* want to respond to in the first place. Papal opposition to the political Will of the Roman People—as created by the prince and his advisors—could then be overcome by summoning a General Council representing the Will of the entire Christian population. Of course, this population's religious will, as expressed through the Council, also had to be "prepared" by theological experts to give the answers expected of it. And this could provide endless employment for hungry men of letters and ideologues of all stripes.

William of Ockham tells us clearly what really forms the political and religious "Will of the Roman and Christian People" as prepared by the prince and his advisors. It is certainly not the dictates of Faith and Reason as understood by Socratic philosophers and orthodox Catholic theologians. Instead, it turns out to be the individual, disconnected, strongly felt earthbound desires of the already existing authority, the Emperor, all of which are associated with the will of God and demands of Reason that he, like all extreme Nominalists, prohibits discussing logically lest such speculation degenerate into useless babble. Ockham's guide to the People's Will emerges as a political philosophy that is simultaneously blatantly materialist and irrationally mystical in character; a civil religion that in many respects foreshadows that of the American pluralist system of the twentieth century. "One comes to wonder," as Georges Lagarde notes, "if the justification at all costs of the established order is not the first and last word of this rather poor philosophy of society and history."

Political propagandists continued to exercise enormous influence as *real* powers behind further incarnations of governments *supposedly* based upon popular sovereignty in the centuries to come, although the primary open agent of their manipulation of the "Will of the People" in Taparelli's own day was no longer an individual king or emperor, but, rather, a wealthy bourgeois oligarchy. The men of ideas at the service of this oligarchy made sure that it always had arguments at its disposal to explain why that popular Will must reflect its own particular individual material desires, particularly its concerns for unlimited economic freedom. In one way or another, whether consciously or unconsciously, these arguments reiterate a theme most associated with Rousseau: namely, the need for mature, awakened, truly nature-focused individuals to speak for and guide those who were under the spell of retrograde, superstitious and unnatural principles such as those of *diritto ipottatico*, the majority of men though these poor deceived folk might actually be. Such arguments gave to individuals with the *right* ideas—that is to say, the members of the oligarchy—the justification for dismissing democratic votes that did not accord with what the popular will really *ought* to mean. This confirmed the oligarchy in its democratic mission as Vanguard of the People; in its role as unquestioned educator of the befuddled masses longing to support what they really should support, even if it did not benefit them one whit, temporally or eternally. Taparelli quotes with deep disdain an Italian Minister of Education representative of this mentality and therefore opposed to any and all retrograde and unnatural Catholic influence over the population, no matter how much support for such religious guidance the population expressed:

> But among us, the citizen is the property of the State. The law of conscription binds him to the soil of the fatherland during the most florid period of life. The State has, therefore, the right and the duty of exercising over him an almost parental tutelage. It scarcely would be able to hold itself responsible to the laws of the country if it had been delinquent, or permitted that its moral or political education be perverted by others. It would only half understand the office of legislator, if it did not claim for itself the domination of education.

Aside from making use of these ideas to deprive democracy of its sting, the dominant bourgeois oligarchies of the nineteenth century sought to pursue their goals by reducing the many possible forms of government that "popular sovereignty" might seemingly approve to one constitutional representative system imitating Whig/Liberal England. Once again, insofar as this system was based upon historical facts seriously incarnating it in its homeland,

Taparelli most certainly recognized its legitimacy, hoping that the inertia of Tradition might accidentally preserve a certain Catholic consciousness correcting its flaws.

Alas, these flaws were all too many, because the English model was sorely vitiated by a spirit that was detrimental to *diritto ipottatico*, reflecting Protestant ideals hostile to social authority that were rendered still more individualist, materialist and destructive of the full message of the Incarnation by the teaching of John Locke. Such a spirit, bad enough in its homeland, was still worse when the institutions it corrupted were exported to countries that had no experience of the historical facts incarnating them in Britain and possibly still mitigating their perversion. But it was precisely this anti-incarnational spirit and a-historical set of circumstances that made the popular sovereignty-based constitutional representative system suitable for promotion and manipulation by the oligarchies. For wherever such a spirit and such alien machinery went into operation, the beneficent influence of the Church over the State immediately disappeared and the system that was created became inhuman, ungovernable and tyrannical in consequence:

> Man being essentially one, though composed of two substances, whoever commands man must of necessity influence both parts substantially composing the same individual. To exclude the Church, therefore, from commanding the body, and the State from obliging conscience, is a separation against nature. The two powers will always find themselves on the same field, either united for the purpose of order, or combating and triumphing over one another. Those, therefore, who through hatred of the Church or out of a desire for unlimited freedom, promote separation cannot do anything other than permit either full anarchy of consciences or chain them under material force.

With the prime supernatural foundation for *diritto ipottatico* removed, all things natural lost their strength as well, and irrational, pseudo-mystical, late medieval, Protestant and Lockean individualism and materialism invaded the whole of the body politic. The government, even when democratically elected, could no longer represent anything substantive and useful to human beings. If any good could be accomplished by it, it had to be purely the result of accident or of the dying remnants of a Catholic spirit—anything but the product of the system itself. "Tell me frankly that the law is the expression of fortuitous combinations," Taparelli begged liberals, but "please {do} not tell me that in your system it represents the {true}will of the nation."

How could it be otherwise? Representation in the modern constitutional order was atomistic, based upon individuals separate from the societies and social authorities that seriously disclosed their needs, their virtues, their vices, and thereby perfected them. Such representation was as little reflective of true human persons and their concerns "as a calf would be by that heap of macerated flesh to which it is reduced by the knife of a butcher." How were such individual representatives supposed to be experts, simultaneously, on foreign policy, agriculture and commerce? Legislators could not appreciate society's final spiritual end, justly coordinate men as they actually are, body and soul, hear the messages of nature spoken by organic corporations, and think about what they might mean. Legislation was reduced to clashing vulgar interests in the eternal war of all against all accidentally and temporarily coalescing and shaping purely conventional state "laws" backed by force rather than Faith and Reason.

But the liberal State had no clear, effective, incarnate head to administer such arbitrary, force-backed pronouncements. The checks and balances created to deal with the *political* war of all against all evaporated the powers of the executive. These were hedged around with restrictions so effectively emasculating the Head of State that he ceased to be such in any practical sense. Even if he could overcome the limitations to his authority imposed by a legislature incapable of representing true popular will, his power and that parliament's self-interested "laws" would be contested by a judiciary viewing any action of social authority as pregnant with the destruction of all individual "liberty."

> This inference ... could be applied to everything a man has on earth and that is governed in society by authority. The language of the citizen, we could say, becomes useless, as soon as the sovereignty of the State can prohibit contumely and curses. Human action is destroyed from the moment that robbery and homicide are prohibited. The home is done for when it cannot be used to organize plots and fires. In sum, if the governor has the right to order society, if he possesses power, society becomes valueless [for the liberal].

Hence, despite its seeming potential for irrational tyrannical action, the history of democratic, constitutional representative systems is one of helplessness, lack of confidence, and paralysis, making any decisive action, arbitrary as well as just, almost impossible. But men desire order. In the democratic constitutional representative system described above, it is not the State *qua* State that can give it. It is the oligarchic party organized by the liberal bourgeoisie that provides men the order that they crave. Driven by a will to power, the party pulls the marionette strings of the democratic constitutional State. The executive, legislative and judicial branches of the State do what the party wants them to do with whatever authority the party gives them. The party tells the people that the government is implementing the popular will while it actually serves the oligarchy's interests. It sacrifices its helpless executive-legislative-judicial "ruler" puppets as expiatory victims should the population react against its oppression. The pointless liberal "State" is held responsible for the crimes that the *real* authority continue to perpetrate; that is, the liberal bourgeois oligarchy, operating through the pseudo-society of a political party.

Horrified as he was at the manipulation of the democratic representative system by liberal bourgeois oligarchies for their narrow self-interested purposes, Taparelli realized that maintenance of their power was by no means inevitable. On the one hand, their victory had only been made possible in union with philosophical and theological dreamers whose high-minded political theories actually tied unchained human will together with that of God and provided "democratic" arguments in support of any number of parochial materialist passions detrimental to the true well-being of the individual---not just those of liberal capitalist magnates. On the other, liberal ascendancy in recent times had most often been assured by alliance with Bonapartist and Sardinian-Prussian warmongers giving free rein to "might makes right" military ambitions that at least temporarily seemed to be "good for business." The Wilsonian visionaries could believe what they wished about the value of modern representative government, but the average man whose eyes were open to the world around him knew that the critic from the *Journey to the End of the Night* was right. When the word "democracy" rules the roost, the only certainty is that the average man has to "pay and march."

29

The Question of the
Res Publica Christiana in
Postconciliar Catholic Doctrines†

NEVER IN THE HISTORY OF CHRISTENDOM
has there been such an outpouring of rhetoric regarding
brilliant developments in the Church's understanding of her own
nature and her proper relationship with the world than since the
days of the Second Vatican Council. But a man of both Faith
and Reason who looks beyond this rhetoric of stunning progress
encounters a trinity of problems revealing a contemporary reality
that is anything but brilliant: 1) the transformation of the Church
into the plaything of passionate factions; 2) her abandonment of
any distinctly Catholic effort to influence either society at large
or the State in particular; and 3) the apparent disappearance of
all sense of "society" and "common good" that might, as in the
past, be used as a natural "seed of the Logos" that one could
baptize in the cause of constructing a true *res publica Christiana*.
Rather than a positive development, Catholics who respect both
Faith and Reason see a modern regression to an intellectual and
practical environment open neither to the message of Christ nor
to that of Solon the Lawgiver; a brave new world where believers
are led by "a willful Church subservient to a willful society."

Justice demands that we begin our examination of this contemporary return to Plato's cave by taking the claims of the proponents of a modern "development of doctrine" at face value; as
the considered judgments of men who have the well-being of the
Church at heart. No one's arguments are better suited to such a
friendly examination than those of John Courtney Murray, S. J.
(1904–1967), a *peritus* of New York's Francis Joseph Cardinal
Spellman, and a man whose influence on the final Declaration on
Religious Freedom, *Dignitatis Humanae*, was enormous. Knowledge of Murray's position is crucial, because it combines the serious

---

† Conference paper from Spring 2014 published in the Spanish journal *Verbo*.

reflections of a man of faith together with debatable historical judgments that he himself was aware could—and according to some progressive readings, *would have to*—cause more fundamental turmoil in the future.[1]

Murray argued that anyone seeking a complete understanding of the extraordinary development of Catholic Social Doctrine emerging from the Council had to study *Dignitatis Humanae* together with the Pastoral Constitution on the Church in the Modern World, *Gaudium et Spes*, as a comprehensive unit. He claimed that the advance they represent *in toto* is two-fold in character: 1) a transformation in mentality regarding the Church's awareness of how she is to approach dealing with the outside world that incalculably strengthens her age-old struggle to restore all things in Christ; and 2) a rooting of this broader and more effective evangelical consciousness in a much sounder ecclesiology than in the past.

Basically, Murray's thesis runs as follows. The Catholic Tradition clearly recognizes that the Church's mission is the salvation of individual human persons possessing reason and free will. It teaches that these individual persons make their pathway to their supernatural end by means of a natural world whose great riches are channeled to human use through a complex social order, a society composed of many different societies, one of which is the State. Because of nature's intrinsic limitations, as well as Original Sin and its consequences, the societies in which individuals develop and perfect themselves need the teaching and grace offered by the Church, the Body of Christ, to understand and fulfill their purpose effectively.

Unfortunately, the Church, in practice, has shaped her approach to the complex society of societies forming the whole of the individual person-friendly social order through her relationship with the State alone. She has done this by seeking spiritual

---

1 Murray's work is mostly in article form, including *We Hold These Truths.* For Murray and the Council, see J. Bryan Hehir, "Church-State and Church-World: The Ecclesiological Implications," *Proceedings of the 41st Annual Convention of the Catholic Theological Society of America* (1986), pp. 54–74, http://ejournals.bc.edu/ojs/index.php/ctsa/issue/view/278; Francis Canavan, S. J., "Religious Freedom: John Courtney Murray, S. J. and Vatican II," *Faith & Reason* (Summer, 1986), *https://www.ewtn.com/library/HUMANITY/ FR87203.TXT.*

and juridical ties with public political authorities that determine how and under what conditions she can engage the rest of society. This has regularly resulted in her co-option by authoritative political forces in the service of their own limited, distorted and sometimes openly anti-Catholic purposes. Even when she has sought to address the problems of the rest of society—as through the praiseworthy encyclicals of Leo XIII—the restoration of all things in Christ has nevertheless, in practice, ended up being treated as a kind of "second class" activity; a mere "extension" of her basic sacramental labor rather than a marching order emerging logically from the meaning of the Incarnation issued to every believer, clerical and lay alike.

Historically, therefore, the Church has found herself in the curious position of being simultaneously politicized, as the ally of States frequently using her as a cover for their earth-bound projects; and not political enough, through her denial of the innate need for every member of the entire Christian community to be completely free to serve the Incarnate Word and transform the whole society-rich Creation in Christ's image. Murray was convinced that this arrangement unacceptably sacralized the State at the expense of desacralizing the Church and the rest of society. We might say that he was convinced that it produced one Cardinal Richelieu after another, ready to work primarily for the glory of his nation, whatever the nefarious consequences for the Catholic cause in general, and not enough men like St. Vincent de Paul and his *dévot* followers in France, burning with zeal to use spiritual tools to fight evil in every realm of life.[2]

Let us pause for a moment to note that this position in many respects exactly parallels that of the great twentieth century Protestant theologian, Karl Barth (1886–1968).[3] Barth, horrified by the willingness of religious denominations to follow their various governments unquestioningly into the carnage of the First World War, attributed their slavishness to that same tradition of Church and State unity politicizing religion and crippling the Church's true supernatural mission to judge the world that Murray attacked.

---

2 See my article, "Can Anything Good Come From France?," (The Remnant, December 31st, 2004, http://jcrao.freeshell.org/GoodFromFrance.html).
3 On Karl Barth, see Center for Barth Studies, https://barth.ptsem.edu/theology/.

His leap *into* battle against the Nazis after having fled from the politicized religious world of the 1910s was in no way contradictory; it reflected his understanding of the independent and "God First" vantage point from which the Christian's *inevitable* political and social impact must emerge. Even Barth's refusal to fight the Communists after 1945 was logical. He felt that joining in the anti-Communist "crusade" would turn him into a political tool of a "Free World" whose secularism posed more dangers to Christianity's supernatural transforming mission in the long run. But, ironically, it was precisely to that American political experience providing the ideological guidance for the "Free World" anti-Communism so distrusted by Barth that Murray appealed, and as the very model for assuring liberation of the Church to fulfill her more vast and spiritually-rooted social mission.

At least to begin with, Murray argued that his judgment was based on simple historical and sociological observation. America, due to the ever more diversified waves of immigration reaching her shores, had become a land of many faiths and cultures: a "pluralist society." An application of the political developments inherited from the England of the Glorious Revolution to her own peculiar pluralist circumstances had led America to realize that the State's primary and God-given duty to preserve social peace and quiet required a governmental retreat from alliance or positive interference with the numerous religious denominations competing for her population's faith. She left them all free to pursue their independent development and fulfillment. Through this general governmental retreat, the Catholic Church had thereby been given the opportunity to engage and potentially Christianize the entire social order, to which it now finally had direct access. Yes, the same could also be said for opposing denominations; but Catholicism was strong enough to face and defeat them on its own two feet alone.

And anyone with eyes to see could judge the results for himself. Not only had the Church prospered and grown in the American context, but she had done so without the divisiveness and bloodshed that had characterized her fight for survival in the past, both when in alliance with the State as well as when openly opposed by it. The conclusion was that Catholics were morally bound to maintain a system that so clearly permitted the State, the Church and the rest of complex corporate society to carry out all of their diverse, specific missions so peacefully and so well.

Many factors contributed to spreading the prestige of the American pluralist system in the post-1945 world: European exhaustion and questioning of the dangers of all ideological rigor after two world wars and genocidal butchery, that of the anti-religious Enlightenment included; admiration of the contrasting stability, power and wealth of the United States; and, inevitably, comparison of Old World ecclesiastical failures with Church success on the other side of the Atlantic. Prestigious intellectuals like Jacques Maritain, himself personally well-acquainted with the situation in the United States, openly drew the consequences of America's "teaching" for the instruction of the Catholic world as a whole. Making reference to those "signs of the times" that indicated both a weakening of hostility to the Church on the part of a previously antagonistic but chastened liberal world, as well as a recognition of the need for a common anti-totalitarian front composed of everyone nurtured by a sense of "human dignity" that was rooted, historically, in Christian teaching, men like Maritain labored for the practical creation of a universal pluralist environment. They fostered the impression that the outside world was waiting breathlessly for Christ without really knowing it; that under a pluralist regime, men could finally open their arms fully to the Church, knowing that they were opening them to Faith as opposed to political expediency; to Jesus, rather than to Constantine. Hence, the call to a new *gaudium* and a new *spem*.

Let us begin our analysis of Murray's arguments by admitting that *aspects* of his critique of the Catholic past are all too accurate, beginning first of all with the question of *ecclesiology*, which is the theology of the Church and her "constitution." Ecclesiology, historically, has indeed been something of a neglected child in the Catholic family. This is not particularly surprising. It involves a subject that is intimidating in its all-encompassing complexity. More than that, historical circumstances of varied kinds have stood guard, like angels with fiery swords, preventing a full and proper treatment of the idea of the Church as such. Hence, the real progress in ecclesiology and understanding of the complexities of the social order that can be seen in the work of some of the thirteenth century scholastic theologians was stalled and then almost entirely buried alive by the blow to the prestige of the intellectual world brought about by the bitter battles of philosophical Realists and Nominalists. The consequence was that when the heretical ecclesiological writings of William of Ockham and Marsilius of Padua presented the vision of a Church-Empire wherein the sacral was indeed swallowed up by the secular realm, the response of a Papacy that was itself obsessed with temporal political issues proved to be painfully deficient; dominated by legalist canonical arguments as anti-intellectual as those of its opponents.

Only a renewed but also slow and haphazard "ascent of Mount Carmel" worked to pull together once again all of the elements necessary to understanding the "constitution" of the Church and her relationship to the world at large. Trent sought to tackle these questions, but could not do so because the theological complications of the papal-episcopal relationship and the demands of States jealous of religious prerogatives won in the late Middle Ages risked the shipwreck of the entire Council. After further Enlightenment-engendered setbacks, the Catholic revival movement of the nineteenth century was finally able to stimulate further advances. But here, too, a mixture of intellectual turmoil and international political pressures prevented the First Vatican Council from completing work on that comprehensive "constitution of the Church" and discussion of her mission to the world at large that had first been planned.

Secondly, even though the Roman Church's history is replete with efforts to make contact with the many communities that shape individual persons for the purpose of "restoring all things in Christ," let us also admit the claim that she has *tended* to focus her external concerns on her relationship to the State. It is certainly not difficult to understand why. The State was prior to her in time, greater than she was in power, and respected by her as a God-given institution. The Reformation, in its frontal assault on the Church and its panicked hunt for protection from the ensuing social convulsions, strengthened the position of the State still further. Enlightenment appeals to governmental aid in fighting organized religious influence over daily life, as well as that of "irrational" and "tyrannical" subsidiary social groups obstructing "progress" continued to feed the State's totalitarian potential. Trying to "bypass" the State to confront a social order that was itself in dire straits alongside the Church would have illustrated wishful thinking at best; destructive self-delusion at worst.

All this was complicated enough when power lay in the hands of ruling authorities traditionally tied to the idea of an international Christian order. It grew still more problematic when the many offshoots of the naturalist Enlightenment sought control over the swollen powers of the secular, national State. Precisely because all of these offshoots could make appeal to one or another distorted aspect of that Catholic European past from which they had confusedly emerged, any liberal, democrat, nationalist, socialist or Bonapartist faction willing to seek Catholic help could find some aspect of the Church's message that his party seemed to promote and that its enemies ignored. And just like monarchs of the past, partisan factions of more recent times could thereby press for public Catholic recognition of *their* "godly" mission.

Finally, there is no denying that the clergy—which, in addition to being the God-given authoritative force within the Mystical Body of Christ, also represents a human "interest group" all too ready to view the Church's relationship with the State from the standpoint of its own particular limited concerns—has often demonstrated a willingness to abandon the broader work of Christianization, leaving the powers-that-be untroubled in exchange for its own security in carrying out its basic sacramental activity.

Nevertheless, the clergy has been divided in the way in which it has pursued such "deals." Italian concerns have often pulled the Papacy and the Roman Curia to seek security in ways that have conflicted with national episcopacies cementing alliances with their local "sacred" States. Although the lower clergy in the modern world, angry at the co-option of its bishops by local government authorities, has indeed often taken up the cudgel of the broader Christianizing cause, it has regularly done so at the price either of exaggeratedly praising all papal decisions in these realms, or through a union with one or the other naturalist "party" that was happy to legitimize its activities in the eyes of believers through a clerical presence in its ranks. In any case, given both the propensity of the old monarchies to build alliances with moderate Enlightenment forces, as well as the atmosphere of panic created by the "parties of order" regarding the Red Menace, national episcopacies and Papacy alike moved generally down the direction of making their peace with and blessing the monarchical-liberal State, and whatever other allies it felt it had to make to fend off more radical challenges. In short, the social order was sacrificed to ensure that a clerical-dominated and sacramental "clubhouse" remain untouched.

Murray argued that the pluralist solution, in freeing the Church from all direct involvement with the State, liberated her from those totally unacceptable restrictions that the union of Throne and Altar had also placed on her ability to Christianize the entire social order. Leaving the highly limited Anglo-American State its secularism in its own narrow sphere, where it could do no harm to religion, society and the development of the human person, she now marched out to conquer the world under the banner of the dignity of man alone. She had nothing to fear in doing so, because she had given birth to that concept in the first place. Papal elaboration of its meaning in the recent past demonstrated her conviction that she understood what was required to develop and perfect it better than anyone else. And armed with a better ecclesiology underlying the responsibilities of each and every one of her children in the evangelical enterprise, she was confident that what she had to offer the world gave her an historical, rational and grace-backed superiority in a free dialogue with others that no role as the Established Church or Concordat could hope to equal in fruitful consequences.

As hopeful and tradition-friendly as Murray's prognosis may have sounded to many people, it sadly masqueraded two great dangers that were to lead to the post-conciliar dominance of teachings and actions totally destructive to any substantive sense of social order whatsoever, Christian or non-Christian. The first was the fact that the embrace of the American pluralist system burdened the Church with a new set of political and social luggage equipped with a ticking anti-Catholic and anti-rational "time-bomb." Secondly, commitment to pluralism facilitated the progress of that many-headed European personalist movement that was even more influential at the Council than anything coming from the American experience, and presented a much more clearly subversive alternative view of the Catholic future to boot. Let us explore both of these dangers in their common work for the banishment of Faith, Church and Reason from all discussion of State and society.

445

Murray himself knew that the success of the pluralist system actually depended upon it being not all that pluralist in reality, since it required a moral consensus "with regard to the rational truths and moral precepts that govern the structure of the constitutional state, specify the substance of the common weal, and determine the ends of public policy."[4] America maintained this consensus, at least for a time, due to any number of factors, including the powerful influence of ordinary human inertia and the presence of traditional institutions like the Catholic Church that served as militant counterpoints to logical ideas and practical behavior working to break down all rational and moral unity.

The destructive developments flowing from these ideas and this behavior were rooted in Protestantism, developed in conjunction with the so-called "moderate" Enlightenment and its response to disruptive religious conflict, and taught most completely and confidently from the time of the Glorious Revolution onwards by men like John Locke and his American disciples. Founded upon a consideration of the human person as an isolated atomistic being defined by his many material desires, these first worked primarily to construct a society that was friendly to the freedom of individual property owners, as well as the theorists defending their concerns. Constructing a property-friendly society demanded a weakening of coercive authorities dangerous to the two interests in question.

In the seventeenth century, these authorities were economy-disrupting Anglican and Puritan religious forces as well as the Stuart Monarchy, with its demand for taxes to support an ever-larger standing army and navy. Taming them in a way that did not foster a fearful Spinoza-like atheism and endanger basic social peace and quiet as well led to the call for "religious toleration" and the "necessary evil" of a government with "checks and balances." Religious toleration allowed freedom for so many different religious denominations to flourish that no one of them could succeed in dominating social life. While appearing to be religion-friendly and maintaining commitment to a common moral vision as yet contested by no one, it nevertheless turned one's religious faith into a purely "decorative" aspect of life; a personal consolation

---

4 John Courtney Murray, S. J., *We Hold These Truths* (New York: Sheed and Ward, 1960), pp. 72–73.

with no public significance.[5] The tendency was to make government as "decorative" as possible also. Both forces were shown their limitations by the real powers in the land—the men of property and their moderate Enlightenment intellectual allies—who shaped the social order according to *their* will.

All these developments, especially when translated into the New World environment, could seem, at first, to offer an opportunity for the Catholic Church and the subsidiary societies of a corporate order to prosper. After all, the attack on authoritative influence in life was aimed primarily at two Protestant entities and the power of the State alone. But the deeper teaching of the Anglo-American experience was its definition of the need for the individual, defined by Locke as a bundle of passions, to be "free." And with this principle as a guide, any social authority that stood in the path of the fulfillment of material "freedom" had to come under assault, Catholic and subsidiary as well as zealous Protestant and governmental in character. The use of coercive authority, which so many philosophers, throughout the ages, had seen to be an absolutely essential *rational* requirement for any effective social activity, had to be presented as somehow *unnatural* in character. What took its place was the raw power of the strong individual, whose will was thereby unchained to lord it over the weak.

Moreover, the individual "freedom" promoted could be of any kind whatsoever. Yes, the men of property and some of their intellectual allies may have wanted to limit "freedom" to economic concerns, utilizing concepts like "common sense" to try to shame others into "behaving themselves" for the maintenance of public order. Still, the ideas in play simultaneously took the call for liberty down different directions than purely economic ones. Proponents of other, assertive "freedoms" argued that public order was threatened due to a failure to accommodate the liberties they loved, and that "common sense" therefore demanded their acceptance.

In the long run, what this meant was that the strongest individual wills would ultimately be the arbiter of everything. And in America, where the system permitting such a triumph of the will was shored up by a "civil religion" that divinized the desires

---

5 See Blanford Parker, *The Triumph of Augustan Poetics* (Cambridge University Press, 1998) for the concerted effort to reduce religion to a personal, decorative element rather than a public force shaping society.

of its historical creators, the strong men found themselves obliged to tie their will together with that of the Founding Fathers. An ultimatum was thereby issued to Faith, Reason, Common Sense and all social institutions: the Church, now reduced to the level of a mere "religious denomination"; the emasculated State; and other corporate authorities. Either they publicly committed themselves to supporting the will to power of the strongest proponents of particular "freedoms," or they had to be paralyzed and relegated to a powerless, "decorative" role in life.

Gaudium et Spes argued that the "split between the faith which many profess and their daily lives deserves to be counted among the more serious errors of our age... Therefore, let there be no false opposition between professional and social activities on the one part, and religious life on the other."[6] American Catholics entering into the social arena to "Christianize" the world understood from their pluralist historical baggage and environment just how that "false opposition" could be erased. It was certainly not by bending society to the Catholic vision as traditionally understood. In order for the "true message" of Christ to triumph, those responsible for teaching it would have to read the American "signs of the times" that taught them the game of "Follow the Will" discussed above. And this showed that a new Catholic order of the ages would only come about by recognizing the catholicity of the will of the Founders as authoritatively defined by the strongest "freedom fighters" of the day, and obeying its dictates.

Therefore, if anything in pre-existing Catholic theology and the rational philosophy traditionally utilized in union with it stood in opposition to the will of the "Strong Men—Founding Fathers," then it was these discordant theological and philosophical elements that had to disappear. To make matters worse, the Council's "clearer understanding of ecclesiology" was also called upon to justify such a surrender. The Council's grant of "full citizenship" to the laity was said to be a sign that the Church was finally "catching up" to the spirit of that American democratic and pluralist environment which had proven to be so beneficial to Catholics in the United States. What was now needed was to carry a "pilgrim Church's" learning process to its obvious conclusions, as, bit by bit, the deeper spirit of the American experience taught her what

6 *Gaudium et Spes*, 43.

Christ really expected from her: a structural democratization favorable to baptizing as Catholic the dictates of individual "free consciences"; and a condemnation of the use of coercive social authority of any sort, even that of purely internal impact and devoid of physical penalties, as offensive to human dignity and the dignity of Sons of God. Both the Catholic Church and her Christianization of the world at large would thus be guided by supposedly Christ-like, but actually John Locke-shaped individual consciences; individual consciousnesses whose "liberation" was demonstrated by their slavish repetition of the demands of the latest willful interpretation of the willful Founding Fathers.

Did Murray expect or want this result? Given John F. Kennedy's insistence during the 1960 campaign that his Church, so respectful of Faith and Reason, would have no influence in shaping his individual conscience and behavior as president (What then would? Reading omens? Investigating tea leaves? Or simply playing the game of Follow the Will?), it hardly seems that such a development would have been surprising to him. A number of Murray's colleagues from Fordham University known to me personally (like Fr. Francis Canavan and the late Dr. William Marra) insisted that he was aware of the exaggerated emphasis upon individual freedom troubling the American experience and disturbed by its post-conciliar application to Church teachings and structure, both doctrinal and moral. But others create a different picture; that of a Murray arguing for a coercion-free development of the human conscience:[7]

> Murray had assiduously avoided joining the debate on religious freedom in society with the question of freedom in the Church. He did this for both theological and tactical reasons, contending that the conciliar text did not have the theological foundation to argue the internal issues, and that any attempt to revise the text in that direction would be a fatal mistake. After Vatican II had stated the Catholic position on religious liberty as a human and civil right, however, Murray commented: 'Inevitably, a second great argument will be set afoot—now on the theological meaning of Christian freedom. The children of God, who receive this freedom as a gift from their Father through Christ in the

7   Hehir, pp. 72–73, citing Murray in Walter Abbott, ed., *The Documents of Vatican II* (New York: Guild Press, 1966) 673).

Holy Spirit, assert it within the Church as well as within the world, always for the sake of the world and the Church. The issues are many—the dignity of the Christian, the foundations of Christian freedom, its object or content, its limits and their criterion, the measure of its responsible use, its relation to the legitimate reaches of authority and to the saving counsels of prudence, the perils that lurk in it, and the forms of corruption to which it is prone. All these issues must be considered in a spirit of sober and informed reflection.'

Conciliar embrace of the pluralist ideal also struck at a Catholic or Socratic vision of the authoritative teaching role for the Church through the practical assistance that pluralism gave to a current of thought, personalism, intellectually much more influential in the Rome of the 1960s than anything coming from America.[8] Twentieth-century European personalism developed out of a comparison of the failures of Catholic missionaries and activists with the continued vigor of non-Christian cultures and the successes of modern mass political and cultural movements. Among those influential in its growth were Emmanuel Mounier (1905–1950), editor of the journal *Esprit,* the proponents of the so-called New Theology emerging from the Dominican and Jesuit centers of Saulchoir, Latour-Maubourg, and Fourvières, and thinkers connected both with the French scouting movement as well as the specialized Catholic Action groups aimed at young Christian workers. Jacques Maritain, who served as host to personalist discussions in *soirées* at his home in interwar France, can be seen as a unique although rather critical bridge between their ideas and those of American pluralism, which he preferred.

A major center of the spread of personalist concepts was the *École des cadres* at Uriage in Vichy France, created to prepare a new elite for a new European order during the Second World War. Under the guidance of men like Pierre Dunoyer de Segonzac (1906–1968) and Hubert Beuve-Mery (1902–1989), the future founder of *Le Monde,* priests like Henri de Lubac, Jean Maydieu,

---

8   On the historical development of the influence of Personalism, see John Hellman, *Emmanuel Mounier and the New Catholic Left, 1930–1950* (University of Toronto Press, 1981); (John Hellman, *The Knight Monks of Vichy France: Uriage, 1940–1945,* McGill, 1997, p. 56); Emile Poulat, *Les prêtres-ouvriers: Naissance et fin* (Cerf, 1999),

Victor Dillard and Paul Donceour were brought to Uriage to teach. These men, in turn, introduced students to the writings of Félicité de Lamennais, Henri Bergson, Maurice Blondel, Marie-Dominique Chenu, Yves Congar, Karl Adam, Romano Guardini, Charles de Foucauld and, perhaps more importantly than anyone else, Pierre Teilhard de Chardin. Uriage also had links, direct and indirect, with Frs. Louis Joseph Lebret and Jacques Loew, founders of the Catholic social movement *Economie et Humanisme*, and, at least in Lebret's case, influential in the genesis of *Gaudium et Spes.*

Transformation of the world, according to the doctrine taught at Uriage, was dependent upon the creation of "persons" as opposed to "individuals." "Persons" were defined as men who responded to the call of "natural values" through participation in a community life elevating them above narrow individual desires. One knew that he was dealing with a valid community dedicated to a natural value constructing true persons whenever he saw that that community possessed a discernible, energetic "mystique," and that that mystique led its individual members to creative, self-sacrificing activity. One day, the "convergence" of all such mystiques would result in the establishment of a community of communities producing, in effect, super-persons, "the greatest transformation to which humanity has ever submitted." The nightmare of the twentieth century was actually "the bloody birth of a true collective being of men," mysterious indeed, but providential and eminently Catholic.[9]

Catholicism's role in this "convergence" was that of "giving witness" to the supernatural significance of every natural value, reflected in the mystiques of the active communities of self-sacrificing persons it saw around it, and helping each of them to come to its own innate perfection. It must not sit in judgment of them, because Catholicism itself could not fully know what it itself really was until everything natural had matured and converged. Catholicism was part of a multifaceted pilgrimage to God, linked together by intuition and action, whose destination was unclear. What was important at the moment was encouraging deeply willed commitment to self-sacrifice of all sorts.

Hence Uriage's stunning ecumenism, testified to in a myriad of ways. It began with Segonzac's ability "to form friendly relations,

9   Hellman, *Knight Monks*, p. 178.

on the spiritual plane, with Protestants, Catholics, Jews, Moslems, agnostics," since he "preferred (rooted) people . . . in their own setting, in their own culture."[10] It passed through the Uriage Charter's proclamation that "believers and non-believers are, in France, sufficiently impregnated with Christianity that the better among them could meet, beyond revelations and dogmas, at the level of the community of persons, in the same quest for truth, justice and love."[11] And it arrived, in Mounier, at full-fledged Teilhardian rapture over the strange growth of the "perfect personal community," where "love alone would be the bound, and no constraint, no vital or economic interest, no extrinsic institution":[12]

> Surely [development] is slow and long when only average men are working at it. But then heroes, geniuses, a saint come along: a Saint Paul, a Joan of Arc, a Catherine of Siena, a Saint Bernard, or a Lenin, a Hitler and a Mussolini, or a Gandhi, and suddenly everything picks up speed...[H]uman irrationality, the human will, or simply, for the Christian, the Holy Spirit suddenly provides elements which men lacking imagination would never have foreseen.
>
> May the democrat, may the communist, may the fascist push the positive aspirations which inspire their enthusiasm to the limit and plenitude.

As John Hellman explains, "Mounier's belief that there was an element of truth in all strong beliefs coincided with Teilhard's vision of the inevitable spiritualization of humanity."[13]

Uriage's message was not a rational one. Its ultimate justification was intuition and strength of will leading to creative action. Any appeal to logic, either in support or criticism of strongly willed commitment to natural values was dismissed as either belaboring the given, or as a dangerously decadent and individualistic scholastic pedantry. Better to bury the temptations of a sickly rationalism through the development of the obvious virtue of "manliness," again, defined in completely anti-intellectual ways: the ability to leap onto a moving streetcar; to ride a bicycle up the steep hill to the École like Jacques Chevalier; to look others "straight in the eye" and

---

10 Ibid., p. 83.
11 Ibid., p. 59.
12 Hellman, *Emmanuel Mounier*, p. 85, 90.
13 Ibid., p. 128.

"shake hands firmly"; to endure the sweat-filled regimen defined as *décrassage,* devised for Uriage students under the inspiration of General Georges Hébert; to sing enthusiastically around the evening fire in the Great Hall; to know how to "take a woman"; and, always, to feel pride in "work well done." Such manliness was said to have deep spiritual meaning, aspects of which were elaborated in lectures like de Lubac's *Ordre viril, ordre chrétien* and Chenu's book, *Pour être heureux, travaillons ensemble.*[14]

Finally, let us note that Uriage's teaching was unabashedly elitist, the particular mystique of the École being that of developing the natural value of leadership. "The select youth of Uriage" were said to be "the first cell of a new world introduced into a worn-out one,"[15] "entrusted with the mission of bringing together the elite from all of the groups that ought to participate in the common task of reconstruction in the same spirit of collaboration."[16] Since they were destined to reveal the eternal supernatural significance of the natural values witnessed to by the mystique of all virile communities, Uriage students were actually priestly figures as well. Each class was consecrated and given a great man's name as talisman. Segonzac especially "took upon himself a certain sacerdotal role, even regarding the wives and children of his instructors."[17] This entailed also a "separation between the leaders, the lesser leaders, the lesser-lesser leaders, the almost leaders and the not-at-all leaders," irritating some of the interns. "The central team," as one of them indicated, "were gods."[18]

The Uriage gods at first saw Fascism as the "monstrous prefiguration" of the new personalist humanity waiting to be born under their spiritual guidance. Nevertheless, Nazi racism never appealed to men who appreciated vitality in every people and culture, while Fascism in general proved its ultimate unworthiness by its very inability to succeed. Enthusiasm was then transferred to Marxism, another "monstrous prefiguration" promising a happier future. Here, the activity of the Uriage cadres was paralleled by the efforts of priests and bishops trying to understand

---

14 Hellman, *Knight Monks,* pp. 71–76.
15 Ibid., p. 65.
16 Ibid., p. 63.
17 Ibid., p. 90.
18 Ibid., p. 75.

the "mystique" of workers in labor camps and ordinary French factories, training for the latter purpose being offered under the patronage of the supra-diocesan *Mission de France*. Uriage teachers were themselves involved in these priestly activities – Fr. Dillard, for example, canonizing the Soviets he encountered in the labor camps, and insisting that all workers were "born" into their tasks with specific virtues denied to other people. But an Uriage-like openness was everywhere in the air. After all, there were "riches in modern disbelief, in atheist Marxism, for example, which are presently lacking to the fullness of the Christian conscience."[19] Enlightened spirits had "to share the faith in and the mystique of the Revolution and the Great Day (that of the total Christ),"[20] as did one priest who asked to die "turned towards Russia, mother of the proletariat, as towards that mysterious homeland where the Man of the future is being forged."[21]

The sons of Uriage retained their wartime sense of being a priestly nation, a people set apart, chosen to judge which mystiques were and were not acceptable on the pathway to "convergence." Objects of contempt offered themselves aplenty. Soviet apparatchiks did not seem to understand that Marxism was meant to be spiritually transcended. A Stalinist mystique, therefore, had to be jettisoned. American culture was even more hopeless. "The Americans," Beuve-Mery complained, "could prevent us from carrying out the obligatory revolution, and their materialism does not even have the tragic grandeur of the materialism of the totalitarians."[22]

Perhaps most of all, however, traditional Catholicism, which, from Uriage days, had feared the "insistence on bringing together men with different 'mystiques' while affecting a 'manly' irritation with clericalism, dogma and the orthodox,"[23] needed to be tossed onto the rubbish heap with contempt. "Tridentine" Catholicism, with its concern for individual sanctification and its emphasis upon private devotions to achieve it, was accused of crippling the development of the human person. A full grip on the Christian

19 Emile Poulat, *Les prêtres-ouvrières: Naissance et fin*, Cerf, 1999, p. 408.
20 Ibid., p. 386.
21 Ibid., p. 244.
22 Hellman, *Knight Monks.*, p. 213.
23 Ibid., p. 88.

message and a full perfection of personhood required self-loss and a complete donation to Christ as revealed in the vital, active community or communities around him.

Many of those experiencing the hostility or indifference to Catholicism on the part of soldiers and laborers from a myriad of social and ethnic backgrounds began to argue for a total immersion in the milieu to which the activist was sent. This immersion demanded a root and branch obliteration of all previous education and practice that gave the militant missionary a different character from someone from the milieu in which he was to operate; it was to be the total immersion in the specialized milieu that prepared a man properly for teaching the message of Christ. The awesome drama of the new kind of evangelization this would entail then was linked with faith in that evolution towards a greater universal knowledge and manifestation of the love of Christ prophesied by Teilhard de Chardin.

Tie personalism and the "new evangelization" together, and the missionary's program then becomes clear. He must "get out" of himself and his narrow presuppositions about Christianity, and give himself over to the vital, effective, cohesive, active group or culture to which he is sent. The spirit of Christ that is revealed by each of them is to be nurtured by him and brought to its innate perfection. In helping it along, he is "witnessing" to his presumably still more complete Christian faith in a quiet, humble and ultimately more successful way, and yet actually learning things about Christ that he could never otherwise have known outside the group in question.

Mounier is particularly instructive with respect to this growing dismissal of an authoritative Church. His vision had always logically involved the possibility of shelving whole realms of Christian scripture, theology and spirituality, should they clash with the "emerging convergence." By the last years of the war, "there was little place for sin, redemption and resurrection in the debate; the central acts of the Christian drama were set aside."[24] Nietzsche's critique of slavish Christianity now seemed to him to be unanswerable, and he "came to think that Roman Catholicism was an integral part of almost all he hated. Then, when he searched his soul, he

---

24   Hellman, *Emmanuel Mounier*, p. 255.

discovered that the aspects of himself which he appreciated least were his 'Catholic' traits."[25] Doing what one willed was the *unum necessarium*. Everything rational from the Greek tradition used to support Christianity and dampen the will was execrated as well. If there was anything valuable in the Greco-Christian heritage, it had to come from personalists rebuilding it from scratch; those appealing to the Catholic name and Catholic practice in his day required psychiatric diagnosis and medical help.

Mounier now flatly denounced traditional Christianity and Christians. Christianity, he wrote, was "conservative, defensive, sulky, afraid of the future." Whether it "collapses in a struggle or sinks slowly in a coma of self-complacency," it was doomed. "Christians," he castigated in even stronger terms in a rhapsodic style worthy of his new master (Nietzsche): "These crooked beings who go forward in life only sidelong with downcast eyes, these ungainly souls, these weighers-up of virtues, these dominical victims, these pious cowards, these lymphatic heroes, these colourless virgins, these vessels of ennui, these bags of syllogisms, these shadows of shadows..."[26]

Metaphysical speculation, Mounier declared, was a characteristic of "lifeless schizoid personalities." Mounier even referred to intelligence and spirituality as "bodily diseases" and attributed the indecisiveness of many Christians to their ignorance of "how to jump a ditch or strike a blow." ... "Modern psychiatry," Mounier wrote, had shed light on the morbid taste for the "spiritual," for "higher things," for the ideal and for effusions of the soul.... Thus, many forms of religious devotion were the result of psychosis, self-deception or vanity. Prayer was often a sign of psychological illness and weakness."[27]

Let us parenthetically note that worker-Marxist-Soviet mania from 1942 onwards increased the demand for a liturgy based on pastoral response to particular mystiques to fever pitch. Henri Godin's famous work, *France: Pays de Mission?* (1943), outlining worker dechristianization, had created a sense of a crisis that had to be overcome at all costs. Lack of any precise plan for diving into the worker mystique was attributed to genius and faith in the

---

25   Ibid., p. 190.
26   Ibid., p. 191.
27   Ibid., p. 192–193.

Spirit. One thing alone was certain: the liturgy and the priesthood were out of sync with the world of labor. All that was associated with what Paul Claudel called the "mass with one's back to the people" had to be abandoned. It had become the precious toy of little minds and bigots who could not understand the New Order coming into being around them. Hence the critique offered by Fr. Dillard, who both dismissed the difficulties of a total rejection of the past, and also took it for granted that the worker clientele would be able to sense the superior spirituality of what we would call a secularized clergy due to the *je ne sais quoi* emanating from its own new mystique:[28]

> My Latin, my liturgy, my mass, my prayer, my sacerdotal orna-
> ments, all of that made me a being apart, a curious phenomenon,
> something like a (Greek) pope or a Japanese bonze, of whom
> there remain still some specimen, provisionally, while waiting
> for the race to die out.
> Religion as they [the workers] knew it is a type of bigotry for
> pious women and chic people served by disguised characters
> who are servants of capitalism . . . If we succeed in ridding
> our religion of the unhealthy elements that encumber it, petty
> superstitions, the bourgeois "go to Mass" hypocrisy, etc. we
> will find easily with the Spirit of Christ the mystique which
> we need to re-establish our homeland.

Embrace of American pluralism in the giddy atmosphere of "joy" and "hope" characterizing the end and immediate wake of the Council gave personalists, with their highly developed intellectual agenda, a tremendous advantage in taking control of the evangelization of the entire social order that the break of Church and State supposedly guaranteed. The innate tendency of pluralism to treat social authority as dangerously suspect worked first of all to break down the authority and morale of the old guard at the Roman Curia, turning real power to implement the Council's decrees over to commissions, study groups, and journals dominated by those possessing the requisite "open spirit." Paul VI's *Octogesima adveniens* (1971) confirmed the pluralist approach on the ecclesiastical level by arguing that local churches would be better able than the Papacy to understand the peculiar natural

---

28   Poulat, pp. 329, 333.

Seeds of the Logos offered by their own lands and through their own corporate social institutions.

No one seems to have wanted to remember Karl Barth's warning of just how much more susceptible to politicizing and secularizing influences local authorities had historically proven to be. Bishops and episcopal conferences failing to respond to the "teaching" of the energetic local community were quickly condemned to learn this lesson anew. Moreover, the local corporate institutions, reduced by pluralism and personalism to being mere channels for "mystiques" instead of truly authoritative societies, learned that they could not perfect the "natural messages" they nurtured on their own steam alone. They were shown that the "witness" of elitist activists, whose spiritual superiority was made manifest by their abandonment of all traditional Catholic teaching and their willful arrogance in interpreting the deeper aspirations of the varied communities attracting their particular attentions, was required to bring them to their full perfection.

"Evangelizing the social order" under these conditions took different shapes, depending upon differing circumstances. The formerly Catholic social movements of Europe and Latin America were expected to continue their labors only on the basis of perfecting "natural values" that could be shared by believers and non-believers alike. Distinctly Catholic elements were not to be allowed to interfere with the development of social action in Africa and Asia where they had had little or no influence before, lest they somehow distort a Seed of the Logos in the process of development. Popular forces resisting the abandonment of Catholic ideas or the shape that social action was taking had to have their consciousness raised by superior spiritual guides appealing to the "spirit of the Council" in base communities and encounter groups. How else could backward souls come to know what their deeper aspirations really were?

The post-conciliar consequences of this type of "evangelization" have been disastrous. Insofar as there was an unprejudiced dive into the vital, active milieu in which the spirit of Christ was supposedly taught, this permitted no contact with the Christ of history outside and above it. The objective reality of the Incarnate God-Man was thus ultimately called into question, with the very concept actually being identified as merely a "western" understanding of the work of "the Spirit" in human life. Personalist men were left spiritually "barren in the face of a Ramakrishna," as Maritain, much too wedded to his Aquinas to go the whole personalist route, predicted they would be.[29]

Besides abandonment of Faith, none of the real Seeds of the Logos active in one culture were allowed the possibility of making an objective contribution to human life capable of influencing another. Greco-Roman civilization was especially stripped of all right to speak any message whatsoever, given its traditional use for precisely this supra-cultural mission in the past. All cultures became like ships passing one another in the night, with no philosophy, no theology and no Christ as polar star above them by means of which they might navigate with precious cargo safely from port to port. Reason and logical judgment lost all significance, denounced, as they were, as the useless baggage of crippled individuals seeking to stand above their more vital and spiritually exalted communities.

"Evangelization" of the social order under these circumstances is a code word for a conscious, determined burial in fallen natural desires and perceptions which *might* have been lifted up to God, had the tools for accomplishing that goal not been rejected, and an opening not been given instead to all the gross, banal and frequently inane fantasies to which human beings always feel their deepest pull. Moreover, no willful insistence upon their spiritual superiority could save those attempting to "witness" to such a false spiritualization from a depressing fall to earth along with the "vital energy" of their affections. Hence, the once deeply pious Fr. Dillard ended by concluding that his work in the factory was more important than his Mass, and, indeed, that the machine on which he labored itself actually had a soul.[30] Similarly, Mounier's Ascent of Mount Carmel jettisoned prayer for psychoanalysis. Meanwhile, the *Monde* milieu of Beuve-Mery helped mightily to build a technocratic Europe which is now marked by the same bland, materialist "diversity" of the American pluralist circus it so readily condemned at the end of the Second World War.

Numerous statements coming from the Vatican during the reigns of Pope John Paul II and Benedict XVI attempted to explain the

---

29 Hellman, *Emmanuel Mounier*, p. 42.
30 Poulat, p. 327.

Council's true meaning regarding its relationship with the outside world in ways that sought to correct the horrible consequences for Catholic Social Doctrine stemming from the victory of the pluralist and personalist mentalities. Nevertheless, the embarrassment attached to making such statements, due to the stigma accompanying recourse to the use of all forms of social authority whatsoever in the life of "free, dignified, individual modern man," has generally rendered such valuable theological corrections utterly meaningless in practice.

In practice, Church and State have never been more united than ever before in history—in a common commitment to allow fallen nature to have its way with society, against the dictates of both Faith and Reason. And, ironically, as so often in the past, it is renegade clergy, proclaiming the liberation of the laity and then preventing it from exercising its Faith and Reason in its proper spheres of political and social action, who have been most guilty in cementing this new union of Throne and Altar. The Church is still a "sign of contradiction," but, unfortunately, contradiction of her own divine character and mission, which has become nothing other than subservient to the voice of "the Promethean lust for material power that serves as the deepest common drive behind all modern Western cultures."[31]

Without the truly authoritative and coercive guidance of Faith, Reason, Church, State, and substantive corporate societies to lead it, the nature and limitations of a Catholic Social Order has to be defined by the strongest individual wills seeking the satisfaction of their strongest willful desires. They are the sovereigns, in Carl Schmitt's sense of the term, determining who are to be recognized as their friends and who their enemies. And, despite all of the continuing efforts of more leftist interpreters of energetic communities around the globe to provide a Marxist-sounding definition of Catholic Social Action, and claims that the present Roman Pontiff is on their side, I do not see Pope Francis presiding either over a serious worker priest charge into battle or even over a variety of totally contrasting guides to the Church's position—a *complexio oppositorum* a la Schmitt—concerning which he is capable of pronouncing final judgment.

---

31   Gawthrop, R., *Pietism and the Making of Eighteenth Century Prussia* (Cambridge, 1993), p. 284.

What I see the post-conciliar pluralist and personalist opening to the outside world to have achieved by 2014 is the equation of the *res publica Cristiana* with that form of individual willfulness that has proven itself to be the strongest: the willfulness coming from the moderate Enlightenment, John Locke-guided, "will of the Founding Fathers"-obsessed American experience. All of the Catholics involved in the struggles of contending factions in the United States—liberal, conservative, neo-conservative and libertarian—tie the defense of the Catholic cause together with the victory of American freedom and the will of the Founding Fathers as they interpret it. All have clergy active in their ranks. All of them work to convince people that there is no alternative for Catholics but support of the American Way. All actively exercise an enormous influence over Rome on behalf of their concerns for either a sexual or economic libertinism, with both ultimately tied together and weighted on behalf of the latter. So successful are they in their work that even Pope Francis, who perhaps thinks that he represents a more radical current of Catholic Social Doctrine, is going about his work of "reform" with the aid of American public relations companies and with the enthusiastic support of every contrasting faction in pluralist America. In short, the Catholic Church the world over is the slave, whether consciously or unconsciously, of American, Lockean, faithless, irrational, individual willfulness. To paraphrase the old slogan of Liberal Catholics, she is now a "willful Church in a willful Society." This was not what the personalists wanted, but this, I would argue, is what they were fatally destined to get.

To end on a positive note, I wish that I could say that I thought that resurrection of the hunt for a truly Catholic social order was just around the corner. If it is, it may be that it will be due to the aid of the kind of calamity which charity forces one to pray can still be avoided. Still, God cannot be mocked forever. Nature will turn against those who have used her name to abuse her. The destruction of history that has come along with the general attack on Tradition may wipe the memory of Enlightenment naturalism in general and John Locke in particular from the human mind. Demographic changes of drastic proportion may ensure the victory of Islamic Law, against which the Catholic faithful will have to fight or die. But in the meantime, all that we can do is what we are doing at the moment, keeping up the work of education and resistance provided by organizations such as this one. That work, while often highly frustrating to young people who want to act and win cannot be avoided. For as Ernst Jünger, a man of highly militant temperament himself, has noted:[32]

> Now battle had to be joined, and therefore men were needed to restore a new order, and new theologians as well, to whom the evil was manifest from its outward phenomena down to its most subtle roots; then the time would come for the first stroke of the consecrated sword, piercing the darkness like a lightning flash. For this reason individuals had the duty of living in alliance with others, gathering the treasure of a new rule of law. But the alliance had to be stronger than before, and they more conscious of it.

---

32 Ernst Jünger, *On the Marble Cliffs*, XX.

30

Monarchy as the Enemy of Oligarchy†

O NE OBVIOUS STARTING POINT FOR DIS-
cussing the value of a particular form of government is an
assessment of its ability to resolve serious temporal problems; not
just for a brief moment, but, rather, for a reasonably long period of
time. Many Catholics consider the most pressing problem facing
us today to be the threat presented by militant Islam. Although
I by no means wish to downplay that particular menace, I am
nevertheless convinced that the current Moslem peril is itself
the product of a still more powerful and persistent evil that only
a proper government can eliminate; an evil that has all too long
been central to our daily political and social life.

The evil in question is the domination of the West, and now
seemingly the entire globe as well, by an oligarchy whose victory
has been responsible for innumerable and willful ills, the regrettable strength of Islamic terrorism among them. To paraphrase Léon
Gambetta: *l'oligarchie—voilà l'ennemi!* And examination of the
character of this hostile oligarchy is a highly suitable introduction
to understanding the great value of the monarchical principle,
the unfortunate problems that often impede its beneficent anti-
oligarchical action, and how these flaws can be overcome.

Oligarchy's unforgiveable "sin against the Holy Spirit" lies in its
reductionism: its replacement of the pursuit of the common good
by a hunt for the satisfaction of the particular narrow interests
of an identifiable minority of the population. In principle, such
blatant and shortsighted self-serving should offer an easy target
for an assault by intelligent opponents. But this, sad to say, historically has not been the norm, at least in the western world, for
reasons that seem tied to the ever-troubling power of the strange
mystery of iniquity.

Ever since the Socratic elevation of political debate to a probing
beyond surface appearances for the purpose of uncovering the

---

† A talk given in April 2015 in Spain and published in the Spanish journal
Verbo.

deeper underlying meaning of things—their *logos*—western political leaders began to recognize the need to provide their exercise
of power with an intellectual "cover story." In other words, they
began to understand that the development of serious political
and social thought forced them more intelligently to relate their
possession of power to some higher justifying principle, or, in the
absence of any credible means of doing so, to claim that control
of society actually lay with others who were truly concerned with
securing the common good, thereby reducing their own extraordinary successes to a happy by-product of these others' decisions.

Clever thinkers and rhetoricians were required for elaborating
such an argument. Their labors became still more essential as a
result of the Incarnation of the *Logos* Himself in the God-Man
Jesus Christ, and that unification of the supernatural and natural
search for the deeper common good demonstrable in the construction of Catholic Christendom. And somehow the cover stories
presented by such subtle "word merchants" have proven to be
extremely seductive, even to the enemies of oligarchy themselves,
making exposure of the lies that they perpetrate often very half-
hearted and correspondingly unconvincing.

The cover story now protecting our modern western oligarchy is the most effective, seductive and fraudulent of these tall
tales to date, although its very strength reveals the contemporary
oppressor's Achilles Heel: the fact that it is a clique composed
of two distinct factions and therefore always a potential "house
divided against itself." On the one hand, it is an oligarchy built
upon the desire to make the world safe for material wealth in
general and financial investment in particular, with the life of the
mind and the spirit reduced to social and individual impotence
in consequence. On the other, it is an oligarchy in which the
thinkers and rhetoricians who have provided the justification for
the victory of money and finance form a distinct power in their
own right; a "word oligarchy" whose members play a major role in
both public as well as private institutions and their bureaucracies,
and precisely through cultivation of that very world of ideas that
is disdained by their plutocratic allies.

The "word oligarchs" in question are proponents of that
approach to understanding life that we call naturalism. As naturalists, they are intellectual reductionists; that is, ideologues,

disdainful of any knowledge that does not immediately impress itself upon one's physical senses or feelings. This emphasis upon the immediate makes them angry with the Socratic search for a deeper *logos* behind things natural aiming ever "upwards," and totally contemptuous of the supernatural wisdom offered through the *Logos* Incarnate. As naturalists, they have come to the aid of those seeking to liberate the effort to accumulate wealth from the critique of both natural and supernatural *logos*-hunters. Still, such thinkers can be much more thoroughgoing and logical in their far-reaching naturalist concerns than men with merely gold on their minds would want them to be. Hence, they have often promoted visions with long-term social and individual consequences that eclipse in importance and may even run counter to the goals favored by their rather thoughtless and therefore more short-sighted materialist allies. Such logical naturalism constantly threatens the exclusive pre-eminence of the money power over a world that it too wishes to be freed from the *logos*-hunters.

In sum, modern society is shaped by a joint plutocratic-ideological oligarchy, whose two component factions have either consciously or unconsciously leaned on one another to advance their own particular purposes. Despite their historically demonstrable cooperation, each has also shown a capacity for taking the other down a highway that it does not wish to travel. Plutocrats recognizing their need for an effective intellectual cover story have often been driven by their reliance on the word oligarchs to support broader naturalist policies whose logic they did not foresee and which could even bring about their own destruction, such as Communism. Meanwhile, ideologues who could only get the chance to ply their intellectual wares through the practical clout afforded them by the oligarchs of money, have often been pressed by the demands of their supporters and the highly seductive material environment created through their prominence to betray their own more logical principles; to limit the role of thought to that of cheerleading only for those "natural virtues" suitable to the accumulation of wealth.

It has not been at all unusual for members of one part of this strange coalition consciously to be converted to the more blatantly "gold digging" or "intellectually thoroughgoing" naturalism of the other. But the contradictions of the thoughtless and thoughtful plutocratic-ideological alliance are nevertheless all too real, and when they have rubbed harshly against one another, the unity of the oligarchy has exploded in violent "civil wars." In fact, unity among the bulk of the inhabitants of a house as potentially divided against itself as the modern oligarchy can only be maintained if the joint menace presented by a common foe can be kept constantly before the eyes of both of its component factions.

Georges de Lagarde, in his *Naissance de L'Esprit Laique au Declin du Moyen Âge*, has shown that this two-fold oligarchy has origins reaching back to the twelfth century, rooted ultimately in the desire of both thoughtless and thoughtful naturalists to be free from the direction of the *logos* hunters. Nevertheless, its most effective and sustained development began in the sixteenth century, with inspiration coming primarily from Germany, the Anglo-American world and France. It was then and there that property and money men seeking freedom from a "higher" guidance began to bond more clearly with a budding Republic of Letters whose complex Protestant, Pietist, Jansenist, Legalist and Enlightenment membership was also working in highly varying ways for liberation from the temporal consequences of the message of the Word Incarnate and its Socratic allies. But it was also then and there that the problems of the condominium of the thoughtless and thoughtful came brutally out into the open, forcing unexpected choices upon the sometime allies: with Evangelical "robber barons" and their fellow-traveling pastors separating themselves out from the "Enthusiasts" applying the full logic of Luther's principles; with the English propertied classes shedding their ties to the utopian Puritans of the Civil War and Commonwealth Era; with the bourgeoisie of the National Convention in 1794 repudiating Jacobin allies now committed to a root-and-branch purge of forces deemed detrimental to the perfection of a truly natural, Rousseau-inspired Republic of Virtue, property owners prominent among them.

Nineteenth century industrialism confirmed the dominant role of the plutocratic bourgeoisie in the constitution of the modern Double Oligarchy. 1794 had amply demonstrated the dangers of fishing for a cover story justifying bourgeois power in the waters of the Radical Enlightenment. This left reliance on the "argument" that came from the support of armed strength alone—whether that of the more conventional police and army of a Napoleon or the more radical fascist militias of a Mussolini and a Hitler—as a possible option for maintenance of its influence. But dependence upon raw force alone brought with it its own peculiar dangers to property in the form of warmongering and defeat, reinforcing recognition of the need for a more durable intellectual defense.

The favor of the money power thus fell upon the arguments of moderate Enlightenment thinkers like John Locke and Adam Smith, whose ideas had first proven their value in the United Kingdom of the Glorious Revolution of 1688 and its aftermath, and then found their Promised Land and most potent means of expression in the United States of America and the teachings of its Established Religion, American Pluralism. It is through the tall tale of American Pluralism that the "word oligarchs" exercise their influence over the Double Oligarchy most effectively today. And this cover story they spread globally through organizations both public and private, many of them fueled by endowments of astronomical proportions.

As tall tales go, that of American Pluralism seems to offer everything that the plutocratic oligarchy could desire. It dismisses "conspiratorial" claims of political control by the financial power, proudly proclaiming governmental authority to be the province of the Sovereign People, whose wisdom and choice alone lies behind the oligarchs' success. Then it praises the pluralist environment of religious toleration as demonstrative of the simultaneously individual, traditional and God-friendly character of the established order: its establishment of a marvelous free marketplace of ideas where the *logos*-hunters are as empowered as anyone else non-violently to make a case for their own vision. And finally, in stark contrast to those governing the wicked ages preceding its victory, it basks in the "peace that surpasses all understanding" that pluralist doctrines guarantee to all societies accepting its blessings.

Such a cover story has indeed allowed individual plutocrats the ability ruthlessly to do what one of its Founding Fathers, John Locke, said that they must do in order to protect themselves in a world that he, like Hobbes, viewed basically as one of merciless jungle struggle: gain and defend private property. For while it soothes defenders of the common good by claiming that power lies with the People; while it calms the *logos*-hunters by insisting that religious freedom allows them the chance to win converts to their position; it actually makes a practical mockery of any popular or philosophical or religious effort to block the advance of the money power. It "checks and balances" the governmental authority of the supposedly Sovereign People out of any practical ability to control the triumph of individual economic willfulness. It reduces the influence of serious *logos*-hunters eager to understand the true role of property and wealth to public meaninglessness, turning them into the actions of just one more private group, ultimately impotent amidst the horde of contradictory and mindless sects that religious freedom mobilizes for battle in a "liberated society." And it does this while relentlessly drilling in the argument that Locke's individualist, materialist philosophy is the sole possible key to a peace and prosperity that only the vicious and the insane would dare to oppose.

But unfortunately for the thoughtless plutocrats, the logic of the pluralist cover story allows for a great deal more than the unchaining of individual economic desires. Its effective destruction of the governing authority attributed to "the People"; its multiplication of religious factions to ensure a ruinous war of all against all preventing the *logos*-hunters from having a meaningful impact; its relentless promotion of individual materialist concerns: all this is used by other willful persons and factions for their own specific purposes, many of which do not fit in with the plutocrats' concerns. Hence, the strength of those individuals and groups pursuing sexual liberation agendas, those dedicated to whatever benefits the State of Israel, and those so in love with pluralism as such that their chief goal in life is to impose it by armed might the world over. Neo-liberal pluralists may lament neo-conservative warmongering "abuse" of pluralism as dangerous to commerce all that they wish, but they do not have a leg to stand on intellectually. For pluralism is a fraudulent cover story designed to allow such "abuse" to take place from the outset, with the victor in the struggle of wills upon which it rests defining what constitutes "abuse." And the fact that its value as a cover story is placed higher than the dangers that it offers is revealed by the way that the plutocratic oligarchs always rally to its defense whenever the most serious anti-pluralist and anti-oligarchical force threatens a resurgence of strength.

That force is the monarchical principle, which, when fully activated, confronts the narrow, self-interested Double Oligarchy with its own immensely powerful Dual Alliance: a Dual Alliance that unites all of the political and social forces concerned for the common good of the entire population with all of the spiritual and intellectual forces teaching the true meaning behind the superficial appearance of things; its *logos*. I stress the words "fully activated," because in total contrast to the modern pluralist system, whose results are *worse* the more faithfully its true character is realized, and *better* the more that it is violated, the ills of the monarchical principle lie in its haphazard application and their cure in stricter obedience to its underlying spirit. Unfortunately, there is no simple key mechanically guaranteeing such full activation. Maintaining it involves a constant labor of mind, soul and body. And it is the historical weakening and abandonment of that labor that explains the Double Oligarchy's current possession of an advantage that its own inherent contradictions really do not warrant it having.

"Every good and perfect gift comes from above, from the Father of Lights" (James 1:17). Our account of the value of the monarchical principle begins, accordingly, with the monarchical principle inherent in the Incarnation of the Divine Logos and its most important *temporal* teaching: the fact that the "Kingdom of God is at hand." That kingship demands changes in behavior on the part of social institutions and individuals alike, based not only upon the substance of the message that the King of Kings delivered but also on the very character of the Incarnation itself. Changes dictated by Jesus Christ as King are demanded *now* and not at the end of time, when Our Savior will come again to judge what we have done with His commands today. And these supernaturally-mandated changes also stimulate that good (though flawed and limited) natural hunt for Truth and perfection that unconsciously seeks to acquire the fullness of light offered through Revelation and Grace; a hunt the Church Fathers saw well reflected by Greco-Roman developments in philosophy, politics and law.

The brilliant nineteenth century movement of Catholic revival, fed by a variety of influences, including the literary and artistic meditations of chastened supporters of the Enlightenment, many of whom eventually converted, provides us with an incomparable fount of arguments concerning the nature-friendly and anti-oligarchical consequences of a monarchical principle deduced from the message of the Incarnation. Some of the finest of these arguments can be found in the pages of the Roman Jesuit journal, *La Civiltà Cattolica*, in the years between its foundation in 1850 and the promulgation of Blessed Pius IX's *Syllabus of Errors* in 1864. Particularly instructive in this regard are the articles of two of its Jesuit authors: Matteo Liberatore (1810–1892) and Luigi Taparelli d'Azeglio (1793–1862). And a set of Taparelli's *Civiltà* pieces then published under the title of *Esame Critico degli Ordini Rappresentativa alla Moderna* (1854) deal especially with the battle of monarchy versus willful minorities.

Their argument runs basically as follows. The Incarnation demonstrated that the final salvation and perfection of individuals lies in social union with, and obedience to, the flesh and blood authority of Jesus Christ. That flesh and blood authority is continued in the visible social authority of the Roman Catholic Church. The Incarnate Word's existence on earth as a visible "social institution" in and of Himself, and His continuation of this function in the Mystical Body of Christ, by its supremely authoritative example, points to the necessity of considering natural social institutions analogously, and utilizing them in union with their supernatural model. For membership in such societies enables individuals to learn and fulfill responsibilities that flow from living in the natural order created by God, and to gain assistance in avoiding the injustices made possible in the world due to sin. When the sinful actions to which these societies themselves are tempted are addressed and corrected through obedience to Christ in His Mystical Body, the Church, they are exalted far above their original function. They then serve not only to perfect individuals' temporal existence, but also to aid in opening them to God's grace and eternal life.

But natural social institutions can only fulfill this two-fold task effectively if, like the Incarnate Word Himself, they are understood to possess a certain reality of their own and are not viewed as pliable tools of their individual members. That reality is manifested through their possession of authority and the ability to enforce authoritative commands. It is possession of authority that marks these societies off as entities with an eternal significance, since the authority they wield can only come from the eternal God. As with Christ, that divine authority and its voice must be rendered clear for human eyes to see and for human ears to hear so that there can be no doubt as to who commands and what is being commanded. And given that there are human persons involved in the work of such institutions, including that of the Mystical Body of Christ, such clear authority is required to ensure that there can be no doubt regarding where praise for work well done and pleas for correcting a wrong-headed or sinful abuse of power must be directed. Such a clear authority, in its final expression, must also be univocal as well as visible, and hence monarchical in character. It must end in a monarchical supreme pontiff, king, president, father, rector or guild executive of some kind. There is no other way that the *common* need that the society in question addresses can impress itself as a reality upon creatures of flesh and blood. It must be "incarnated" to be made serious.

There is no need here to indicate all of the different types of social institutions, from that of the family upwards, which an ultimately univocal monarchical authority makes palpable. Suffice it to say that the growth of Catholic Christendom in the Middle Ages was accompanied by a corresponding intensification of intellectual awareness of the importance of society and social authority with an ultimately monarchical expression in all of the manifold realms of natural endeavor, and with respect to their joint supernatural and natural value.

Perhaps nowhere is this better seen than during the reign of Pope Innocent III. His recognition of the complexity of natural human action and the need to mobilize the kaleidoscope of human spheres of action in a militant crusade for transformation in Christ translated into a persistent effort to "incarnate" all of them in social institutions with visible authorities, themselves accepting correction coming from a monarchical Papacy in turn. An example of this concern is his deep respect for the role of the mind in uncovering the "logos of things," and his passion for giving intellectual activity solidity, direction and impact by confirming the visible structures of the University of Paris and the authority of its Chancellor. And even more interesting is his recognition of the fact that such authoritatively directed studies, together with the labors of the newly institutionalized mendicant orders, might serve to keep in proper bounds what many churchmen from the time of John of Salisbury onwards were noting with alarm: the exaggerated growth of a potentially anti-Catholic, oligarchic money power.

La Civiltà Cattolica was particularly insistent upon the need for the State and its authority to follow the monarchical example offered by the Word made flesh. Taparelli argued that this monarchical authority could and indeed must take many different forms depending upon historical circumstances. Despite the obvious flaws of hereditary monarchy, Taparelli believed that it did possess the great advantage of powerfully incarnating the State's acceptance of the primary importance of the family to life in general, as well as of the need to build current public policy upon the wisdom of past generations and in a way that looked to the long-term future. Moreover, it limited ambitions among competitors for the supreme authority and the evils springing from doubt regarding who the next ruler might be—a doubt that more often than not caused infinitely more woe than the actual failings of an existing superior; a doubt that was rendered permanent in systems where a "People" whom no one could see were said to reign.

Whatever the form that monarchical authority may take, submission to the overriding Kingship of Christ allows it to be purged of its sinful, self-divinizing tendencies. It clarifies the State's proper function—the coordination, in unity and harmony, of a society composed of many societies, through which men are capable of responding to higher truth but sorely tempted still to pursue parochial self-interests. In encouraging the State to respect the roles of all the other monarchical authorities in complex human society, it brings that State closer, democratically, to the true will of the People, limits is own need to appeal to centralized police action, and ensures a more ready compliance in those matters where coercive action is definitely required. And just as the monarchical authorities of all the societies below the State work for the general principle that they incarnate, thwarting narrow oligarchical interests in the process, the monarchical State perfects that love for the common good and ordered justice that a population can only fully appreciate when a flesh and blood ruler modeling himself after Christ incarnates their meaning and significance.

Still, as noted above, there is no mechanical way to describe and to guarantee the effective implementation of this full, *logos*-driven monarchical vision. The social complexity in question is stupefying. The individuals exercising and obeying such a complex of monarchical social authorities are all unique in their capacity for both good as well as for evil. And, finally, that social authority can impact upon the potentially saintly or wicked individuals wielding or submitting to it in endlessly unpredictable ways. One can only "see" how this vision works out in practice by entering into the full but fragile dance of life that it embraces as part of the nature of things, and with all the information given to us by Faith and Reason. That dance requires a non-ideological, non-mechanist state of mind, and a readiness to move out of the way gracefully each time a stumble rattles one's daily twirl around the ballroom floor, and perhaps differently each time a new stumble occurs. For those trying to maneuver according to the rules of this Christian dance of life will always be on the lookout for clumsy fools and remember they may sometimes bump into their neighbors themselves.

Maneuvering in good faith to avoid stumbles or to recover from their effects in a "ballroom" constantly subject to the ravages of sin can often involve irregular, exaggerated or theoretically unwanted interferences on the part of one (or many) of the monarchical authorities of a given society in the affairs of another (or many others): that of the Church in the life of the State, the State in that of the Church, or of a subsidiary society in that of Church, State or their fellow corporations. But this can only justly occur for the sake of securing the health of its fellow "monarchies," which may then find themselves called upon to return the favor in the future.

This "yin-yang" effect has a long and positive history behind it, especially (and not surprisingly) when oligarchies have threatened to subvert one or the other monarchical forces active in Christendom. Hence, to cite but the most famous examples, the Ottonian and Salian King-Emperors came to the aid of the Papacy to free it from the grip of local oligarchical control in the tenth and eleventh centuries, forcibly replacing the unfortunate figures then legitimately occupying the papal throne with more suitable pontiffs. The Emperor returned to the fray in the fifteenth century to save the Holy See from internal paralysis at the time of the Great Western Schism, totally violating the normal canonical rules in the process.

Would that the monarchies of State, Church and corporate society had always acted in such a positive fashion, strengthening one another through their irregular interventions! But, alas, the history of Christendom is replete with sinful, exaggerated uses of imperial, regal, papal and corporate authority designed not to confirm but to crush the just and necessary influence of the others. Sad to say, such actions have all too frequently involved stirring up the oligarchic forces most dangerous to the targets of such "power grabs" and encouraging recourse to their fraudulent cover stories to justify them. Not surprisingly, this has then proven, in the long run, to be detrimental to the monarchical principle in general.

Michel Antoine's exhaustive biography of *Louis XV* (Fayard, 1989, pp. 176–179) provides a valuable description of the non-ideological, non-mechanist, dance-like exercise of the monarchical authority of the State in pursuit of its mission of coordination of a corporate society of many societies, ultimately highly respectful of the Kingship of Christ. In doing so, he provides an interesting illustration of how two dance partners used to bumping into one another on the ballroom floor nonetheless recognized that they were on the same basic wavelength. This meant that a generally Gallican-minded Crown called in the special and normally unwanted aid of the Holy See to deal with that strange alliance of Jansenists, Legalists and the lower clergy that gravely threatened the authority of both king and pope in the seventeenth and eighteenth centuries. But it also shows just how cleverly this very coalition exploited external and internal threats to both the French and Papal monarchies, even winning them over, by the second half of the eighteenth century, to endorsing aspects of their cover stories as though they were friendly to them. The end result was that neither king nor pope was in position to aid the other in its ever more perilous crises of authority.

Whatever the varied routes to its emergence, the modern Double Oligarchy did come into being, and in such a way, by our own time, as to tie its plutocratic wing to the cover story provided by American Pluralism, the most effective expression of the moderate approach to Enlightenment change. As noted above, American Pluralism seems to achieve the goal of destroying the fullness of the *logos*-driven monarchical principle, replacing it with the naturalist individualism of John Locke, but gently, under the appearance of actually being in many respects friendly to religion and social authority and calming their adherents. But to reiterate what was said earlier, the religious liberty it proclaims is given under the condition that every faith, reduced to the level of a private, impotent clubhouse, merely testify to the sacred mission of America in its own particular "free" way. Meanwhile, the free corporate institutions that it appears to maintain see their palpable social authority broken down relentlessly in the name of the will of the sovereign individual. And the individual jungle warfare thus unleashed stands no chance of being controlled by a State whose various branches have the capacity to check and balance one another into total paralysis, as the current paralysis of the American government so clearly indicates.

Louis Veuillot satirizes the simultaneous paralysis and danger of the system with reference to its seemingly monarchical element, the Presidency:

> Through fisticuffs and slander, by means of a thousand frauds, they [the Americans] manufacture for themselves from day to day governmental tools made purposely to be worn out quickly...They take a workman, a corporal, a buffalo herder, a pig-skinner, a speculator in newspapers; they place him at the head of the country, under safe guard; they heap outrages upon him, he allows himself a thousand improprieties, and this lasts four years [sic], thanks to his trickery, when he has sufficient spirit to engage in it. When he departs, covered with spittle, another replaces him who just spat upon his predecessor, and upon whom someone else will soon spit. This works for them, and it will last until they have become too savage to retain the same leader for [four] years. They will then create dictators who will perpetuate their power, or they will devour one another, and the loveliest republic of the world will end by being a strongly disciplined hereditary empire, or a cave and a slaughterhouse.

Peaceful protection of property may have been the goal of the plutocratic component of the Double Oligarchy in adopting American Pluralism as a cover story, but the system has not functioned with particular gentleness or to the exclusive favor of the plutocrats even in its homeland. The smooth machinery of the Moderate Enlightenment has presided over the genocide of the Indians, a bloody Civil War with one million dead and wounded after merely seven decades of existence, and unjust conflict after expansionist conflict. Yes, it has indeed promoted the interests of the plutocrats, with the economic detriment to the bulk of the population limited only by benefits owed to its imperialism, and the accompanying impoverishment of the nation's cultural life. But that plutocracy's primary concern for wealth and still more wealth is threatened constantly by the demands of equally willful individual sexual perverts and the warmongering ideologues serving Israel, Revisionist Zionism and Trotskyite Neo-Conservatism for whom they have no built-in sympathy and often an outright loathing. And it is due to the strength of all of these willful forces, unchecked by social authority, that American Pluralism so effectively unleashes—the culture-killing plutocrats, the perverts, the warmongering Zionists and Neo-Conservatives—that the plague of Moslem terrorism itself is due.

Whatever their annoyance, the plutocratic oligarchs cannot free themselves from their pluralist cover story without turning for defense to the pure force that comes from a military or fascist dictatorship subjecting them to different dangers to their wealth than those presented by radical thinkers. The word oligarchs know this and keep them in line by constantly keeping the Nazi Threat before their eyes as the sole alternative to praise of Pluralism. On the other hand, the word oligarchs cannot be freed from the deadening threat of plutocratic reduction of each and every one of their willful causes to mining them for their wealth-producing possibilities. They are held to their materialist allies by a golden chain as thick as the ideological one that keeps their colleagues in check.

Rigorous Islam may bring this totally inhuman Double Oligarchy down, but it has no innate and long-term civilization-building capacity of its own, for the simple reason recently underlined by Pope Benedict XVI: Islam has no *logos*. It is only the hunt for the *logos* of things that can save us from rule by a Double Oligarchy that is doomed to bring itself and the world around us to ruin for exactly the same reason that Islam is at flaw. It is only the hunt for the *logos* of things, crowned by submission to the Word Incarnate, His Social Kingship, and its teaching on monarchical authority that can make the world safe for a truly human existence, valuing all that is natural and that leads men towards eternal life with God.

Effective battle against the Double Oligarchy obviously requires the vigorous action of a logos-focused papal monarchy respectful of the whole gamut of social institutions possessing authorities of monarchical strength. This, today, does not exist. Due to a variety of revolutionary influences, the Papal authority has been ravaged, with power in the Church devolving into the hands of arbitrary clerical factions that are themselves part of or manipulated by either the plutocratic or ideological wings of the reigning Double Oligarchy. The Holy See seems only to continue to exercise its authority today as a willing tool of that Oligarchy and in a correspondingly willful manner. Its actions work to break down the essence and authoritative expressions of the other societies it is supposed to strengthen, the family now among them. And, sad to say, there is no Holy Roman Emperor to intervene to get a wayward Rome to behave itself properly, with a Russian autocrat, Vladimir Putin, the favorite current target of the Double Oligarchy, appearing to be the nearest equivalent. The hunt for the Social Kingship of Christ has been replaced globally by the rule of whichever plutocratic, libertine or ideological expression of the individual materialism of John Locke happens to be the strongest in a given place at a given time.

In these sad days when the Church seems more interested in promoting the cause of the Double Oligarchy than the message of the *Logos*, papal encyclicals cannot be looked to for a pithy summary to a paper like mine. In seeking to find one, I came across the work of Seward Bishop Collins (1899–1952), a curious and rather eclectic American thinker of the interwar period; a man who proclaimed himself a fascist while saying many things that sound more Catholic than anything else. In any case, I cannot think of any better way to conclude our discussion regarding the work of monarchy against oligarchy than with this citation from Collins' "Monarch as Alternative" (1933), the first article of his New York journal, *The American Review* (1933–1937), with its references to very non-fascist English Distributist and Scottish royalist critics of the modern oligarchy:

> What is a monarch? A monarch is a man (a woman, or, formally, a child) in whom all governmental responsibility of a state is vested; he governs in the interest of the whole state, and in secular matters stands above all individuals and groups in the state. The ultimate sovereignty of the people is symbolized in him and is by him realized in action. In particular the leading function of the monarch, in the words of Hilaire Belloc, 'is to

protect the weak against the strong, and therefore to prevent the accumulation of wealth in few hands, {as well as} the corruption of the Courts of Justice and the sources of public opinion.'

It is worth noting that there is no essential conflict between the monarchical principle, however strongly present, and the full expression of the democratic principle. The democratic *form* is only one way of satisfying the democratic spirit. Those who insist on the absolute superiority of monarchy to other forms of government . . . put the case more emphatically: 'There is no People unless there be also a King.' [This phrase comes] from *Monarchy or Money Power*, the recent valuable book by the Scotch author R. McNair Wilson, who is a Royalist (that is, one who is attached not only to the monarchical principle, but also to its hereditary form and to a particular claimant). His whole passage is worth quoting:

'The story of the Middle Ages is the story of the fight for Kingship, in which the Church, no less than the laity, played a part. The object was to establish Kings secured in their office on the one hand by the grace of God, and on the other by the loyalty of the People, so that power might be assured wherewith to curb the intoxication of privilege and the influence of money. It is evident that the People cannot exert power of itself, for, in truth there is no People unless there be a King. Peoples without Kings are ever sundered into parties and factions of which the richest inevitably becomes the most powerful.' (Seward Bishop Collins, "Monarch as Alternative," *Conservatism in America Since 1930*, ed., Gregory L. Schneider, NYU, 2003, p. 22).

31

Half a Millennium of Total Depravity

1517, LUTHER, AND THE IMMINENT
APOTHEOSIS OF WILLFUL IGNORANCE†

O UR CIVILIZATION IS SO SICK THAT EVEN
the best efforts to prop up its few tottering remnants manifest the pathetic illness that step by step has brought the entire
structure crumbling down. The disease in question is a willful,
prideful, irrational and ignorant obsession with "freedom." But this
is a malady that gained its initial effective entry into Christendom
in union with the concept of the natural world as the realm of
"total depravity."

It is crucially important that we recognize both the ultimate
responsibility of this hideous willful liberty for the destruction of
our Classical and Christian culture as well as the historical role
played by the idea that "incarnated" it in our midst for two reasons.
The first is so that we can attempt seriously to rid ourselves of
their monstrous influence over our own minds, souls and bodies.
The second is because a massive attempt to masquerade the truth
regarding their real character and alliance will be mounted in conjunction with the five hundredth anniversary of Martin Luther's
devastating appearance on the public scene in 2017: and this for
the sake of maintaining their nefarious impact upon believers and
delivering the Faith its *coup de grace* as a meaningful social force.

Allow me to cite Philip Hughes regarding Luther and his
antecedents as a means of driving home the point that I wish to
make in this brief piece:

> All those anti-intellectualist, anti-institutional forces that had
> plagued and hindered the medieval Church for centuries,
> whose chronic maleficent activity had, in fact, been the main
> cause why—as we are often tempted to say—so little was done
> effectively to maintain a generally higher standard of Chris-
> tian life; all the forces that were the chronic distraction of
> the medieval papacy, were now stabilized, institutionalized

---

† Given in Gardone Riviera, June 27–July 8, 2016.

in the new reformed Christian Church. Enthronement of the will as the supreme human faculty; hostility to the activity of the intelligence in spiritual matters and in doctrine; the ideal of a Christian perfection that is independent of sacraments and independent of the authoritative teaching of clerics; of sanctity attainable through one's own self-sufficing spiritual activities; denial of the truth that Christianity, like man, is a social thing;—all the crude, backwoods, obscurantist theories bred of the degrading pride that comes with chosen ignorance, the pride of men ignorant because unable to be wise except through the wisdom of others, now have their fling. Luther's own special contribution—over and above the key doctrines that set all this mischief loose—is the notion of life as radically evil. (Hughes, *A History of the Church*, Sheed & Ward, 1949, III, 529).

Hughes eloquently stresses the central fact that our underlying problem is *pre-Lutheran* in origin. In other words, 1517 is *not* the *source* of our woe; any more, for that matter, than 1962 and the opening of Second Vatican Council was. All of the spiritual, intellectual, political and social diseases that had hovered for centuries about the Camp of the Saints had gathered together, ready for injection into the lymphatic system of Catholic Christendom as one "mega-malady," already long before that date. All of these ultimately reflected a revulsion over the need for the individual and his entire environment to be corrected, perfected and transformed under the Kingship of Christ with the aid of Faith, Grace and Reason on the one hand, and social authority, both supernatural and natural, on the other. Anyone in 1517 looking for a simple explanation for why he *should* reject these aids had available to him an embarrassment of arguments from a myriad of fonts indicating that the only thing that really mattered was the individual and his willful feelings; and that relying upon these alone was somehow the sole pathway to pleasing God.

Nevertheless, the conflicted mind of the Late Middle Ages clearly needed someone with the outlook and the talented rhetorical venom of a Luther effectively to inject this mega malady into the lymph of Christendom. Christian man was too aware of the reality of sin to leap *directly* into an adulation of his individual willfulness. Luther's concept of the "total depravity" of the individual and the world in which he lived after Original Sin gave Everyman the pious entry into the obsession with liberty that was required. After all, it seemed so humble to argue for each believer's personal need to rely solely on God's grace to save him; for his need to affirm that "freedom" from "enslavement" to "the despotism" of "the Law" that allowed him to avoid a "hopeless" and ultimately spiritually arrogant attempt to bend his individual, life long, workaday thoughts and actions to fall in line with the commands of Christ.

Still, it proved to be very easy over the course of a couple of generations for this *negative* definition of "liberty"—a "freedom" *from* the Law—to be transformed, in the Enlightenment, into the means for a *positive* new and redemptive order of things. In short, it did not take long for a freedom *from* restraints upon the lawless, individual willfulness of Luther's totally depraved mankind to be seen as the providential tool for molding unbridled human thoughts and actions into the building blocks of a new Age of Gold. In other words, the more that a freedom *from* restraints actually ensured that the truly sinful passions of mankind were all released in order to allow flawed individuals *truly* to became totally depraved, the more that that depravity was now looked upon as something intrinsically wonderful, good, and even pleasing to God.

It is precisely because this venomous attempt to build a civilization upon a freedom *from* efforts to fight Original Sin and its willful effects upon individuals is so tempting that it has infected almost all of us in some way or another. We almost all fall prey to the enticement simply to pick what "liberty" most appeals to our particular passion, declare it pleasing to God, willfully condemn whichever application of the same principle we find personally unacceptable when used by others, and ignore the innately poisonous nature of the entire concept. And, quite frankly, we almost all fall prey to the cynical temptation to mobilize the "total depravity" argument anew when we chuckle over the naïve, utopian vision of opponents who want to use law and authority to help make people virtuous in realms where we want "liberty." But blithely making common cause with "liberty" in a world that did not have to be totally depraved but is making every effort to become so is riding on the back of a willful monster, with the current self-destructive appeal to religious liberty at the top of the list. It is only the positive liberty to use our Faith, Grace, our Reason and the help of social authorities, both supernatural and natural, to correct and transform ourselves under the Social Kingship of Christ that can lead to a life worth living in this world and to eternal happiness in the next.

Sad to say, it is absolutely certain that most of our ecclesiastical leaders, foot soldiers of the *Zeitgeist* that they are, will turn 2017 into a year-long paean to the accomplishments of Luther & Company and "all those anti-intellectualist, anti-institutional forces"; "all the crude, backwoods, obscurantist theories bred of the degrading pride that comes with chosen ignorance; the pride of men ignorant because unable to be wise except through the wisdom of others" that Philip Hughes tells us lay behind them for centuries. It is our duty as Traditionalist Catholics to steel ourselves against the lies that are to come concerning the wonderful value of such hideous, willful principles that now have "had their fling" for five hundred years. It is our duty to hammer home the evil they have caused. Because that five hundred-year-old ignorant, willful, individualist cancer has spread everywhere throughout the lymph of Christendom into every institution and everyone's mindset, believing Catholics should spend the next two years helping those less aware among us to gird their loins. 2017—like 1517—is going to be a trial for all of us. And it is an awakening to this frightful nightmare that the 24th Annual Summer Symposium of the Roman Forum will seek to ensure.

32

He Who Loses the Past, Loses the Present[†]

PUTTING *DIGNITATIS HUMANAE* IN ITS FULL HISTORICAL CONTEXT

BEING NEITHER A THEOLOGIAN NOR A logician, my task here today is not that of entering directly into a discussion of whether the Declaration on Religious Liberty of the Second Vatican Council is or is not in contradiction to previous Church teaching on this topic of immense spiritual, political and social significance. My role is merely that of laying out the historical background in which that Declaration came to life.

Nevertheless, I do think that a broad consideration of the modern revolutionary context in which the current discussion of the question of religious liberty emerged offers an absolutely essential preparation for the more substantive dialogue to come. On the one hand, such a study demythologizes the claim by the most vocal proponents of the Declaration that their position called attention to a fresh development of Catholic doctrinal insight dealing with a political situation very different from that faced by believers even in the recent past. It does so by making it clear that the battle leading up to *Dignitatis Humanae* at the Council was actually nothing other than the second part of a contemporary drama whose nearly identical first act began a century and a half earlier, although it ended on a quite different note. On the other hand, contemplation of this broad historical picture demonstrates that the proponents of the 1965 teaching reflected what was, at best, an appalling ignorance or naiveté regarding the political and intellectual conditions under which the Catholic Church was operating in the period after the Second World War, and, at worst, an active participation in the work of rendering the cause of Christ sociologically and even spiritually meaningless.

---

† Norcia Conference on *Dignitatis Humanae* (October 2015).

Moreover, at least as far as I am concerned, a knowledge of both the long-term as well as the more immediate historical setting of the Declaration on Religious Liberty leads to two further conclusions: first of all, that an orthodox interpretation of the final text stood no chance of obtaining any serious practical hearing whatsoever; and, secondly, that the task of the believing Catholic lies not so much in glossing this document to death as in uncovering the horrific obstacles that the *Zeitgeist* dominating our lives in 2015—as in 1965 and the nineteenth century beforehand—places in the path of learning and acting in accord with Faith and Reason on any substantive issue of political and moral importance.

Act One of the religious liberty drama began with that nineteenth-century Catholic renewal whose main French, German and Italian-speaking centers were circles of clerics and laity seeking both to understand the reasons behind the disastrous attack on the faith in the French Revolution, as well as to find a means of reconstructing a new Christianity on the ruins of the old. All such circles came to confront a similar disappointment that greatly troubled them: the fact that the post-Napoleonic Restoration monarchies that prided themselves on their public support for religion, continued, in practice, to maintain frustratingly tight controls on Catholic evangelization.[1]

The hunt for an explanation of the restrictions muzzling full Church freedom by supposedly "Catholic" States led the circles in question to a deeper study of the tremendous complex of linguistic, psychological, political and material influences that shape a given society and the individuals living within it. Their labors brought them to understand that the radical Enlightenment naturalism that had proven to be so devastating to the faith in the 1790s had already gained an influence in a more moderate form over both Catholic monarchies as well as the Church authorities working in union with them well before the French Revolution. They then realized that the resulting changes had created a mesh of forces whose impact made it difficult for believers, the simple faithful and

---

1 Much of this discussion comes from my two books, *Black Legends and the Light of the World: The War of Words with the Incarnate Word* (Remnant Press, 2011) and *Removing the Blindfold: Nineteenth Century Catholics and the Myth of Modern Freedom* (Angelus Press, 2014). For the sake of brevity, I will only footnote direct citations, points that I believe need special emphasis, and, of course, any other works used.

their leaders alike, to appreciate that there was something dreadfully wrong with what still in many outward respects looked traditional and good; that the positive-sounding words "Catholic monarchy" actually masqueraded the emergence of a secularized counterfeit of a Christian society. In short, proponents of Catholic renewal realized that a *Zeitgeist* had been created whose hold on life prevented Church authorities and believers in general from grasping what the Christian mission *really* entailed, and effectively diverted them away from a recognition and examination of the sources that they needed to consult in order to regain a complete sense of it.

A conscious dive into the fullness of the Catholic Tradition awakened in these thinkers' minds and souls a theme that they perceived to have been put soundly to sleep by the relentless but measured advance of the eighteenth-century naturalist *Zeitgeist* in its more moderate form. This was the basic truth that the Church's role was not that of some "established" administrative machine fulfilling her humdrum "spiritual" obligations by helping to defend the existing social order, keeping civil records, and promoting openness to agricultural improvements and smallpox vaccinations. On the contrary, her task was that of being the Mystical Body of Christ, entrusted with the simultaneously supernatural-natural mission of continuing the life and work of the Incarnate Logos in a world deemed worthy of Redemption but badly wounded by sin. And this task she could only accomplish by seeking to make Christ the King of all of Creation, the very goal of all human existence:[2]

> God . . . has established one sole order composed of two parts: nature exalted by grace, and grace vivifying nature. He has not confused these two orders, but He has coordinated them. One force alone is the model and one thing alone the motive principle and ultimate end of divine creation: Christ. . . . All the rest is subordinated to Him. The goal of human existence is to form the Mystical Body of this Christ, of this Head of the elect, of this Eternal Priest, of this King of the immortal Kingdom, and the society of those who will eternally glorify Him.

Moreover, the Christ who came to free men from the bondage of sin had shown that the sole way this sublime goal could be achieved was through individual submission to His authority; a

---

2 "L'Enciclica dell'8 Dicembre," *La Civiltà Cattolica*, Series 6, Volume 1 (1865), 287–288.

submission possible only if men and women welcomed the authoritative guidance of His Mystical Body. But the men and women in question had to offer this submission through their daily lives in that natural world that God Himself had created and the Incarnation was intended to perfect rather than to abolish. Therefore, the Church had to recognize that all natural tools were intrinsically valuable to that work of saving and "divinizing" individual believers, which was her primary responsibility. Everything natural had to be rescued; that is to say, corrected and transformed by Christ's message and grace, to help bring about the ultimate liberation of the individual from sin that was essential to his final perfection. This meant that all the natural, authoritative, social institutions so crucially important to daily human life, from the family to the not-so-Catholic Restoration monarchies as well, were also central to this corrective and transforming goal. To paraphrase a nineteenth century American orator: human freedom, individual dignity and social authorities; now and forever; one and inseparable.[3]

To fulfill her mission, the Church needed freedom: an internal, "psychological," self-liberation from enslavement to a *Zeitgeist* that blocked her from recovering and cherishing the whole of a Tradition that a progressive secularization had hidden in shadowy and vilified places; an external, physical freedom for her to work efficiently to correct and transform the natural world in its entirety; and, finally, an equally public liberty for the faithful, as individuals, to follow her authoritative social teaching concerning where she must lead them.

Such freedom to exercise her full corrective and transforming influence would, as St. Justin Martyr had already indicated in the second century, place every natural gift and institution in its proper place in the hierarchy of values. A truly free Church would give to the work of Reason, and especially to philosophy, the help that it desperately needed both to avoid its ancient limitation to the role of "parlor sport" for "boys" or sophistic justification of the powers-that-be, as well as its modern Enlightenment mobilization

---

3   Some characteristic articles to consider in this regard, all from *La Civiltà Cattolica*, are "Il Restauro della Personalità pel Cristianesimo," 1, 2 (1850), 367–383; "Se la Personalità Umana Abbia da Temere dalla Chiesa," 1, 2 (1850), 518–541; "L'Autorità Sociale," 2, 4 (1853), 19–37, 175–189, 291–304, and "Dell'Elemento Divino nella Società," 2, 9 (1855), 129–140, 385–396.

for purely materialist and utilitarian purposes. A truly free Church would help simultaneously both to exalt the State in her proper role as the indispensable coordinator of all social authorities laboring for the attainment of man's natural and eternal end, as well as to humble her historical tendency to self-divinization. In short, a truly free Church would remove the blindfold placed by sin upon man's eyes regarding how to properly use all natural goods for human perfection. Everything natural was calling for the "light" that could make it fully see, and this could ultimately only arrive "from above, coming down from the Father of Lights" (James 1:17), by means of union with and completion in the Incarnate Word. Separation of Christ and Reason, Christ and State, Christ and family, Christ and each and every aspect of life as a whole were all, therefore, an insult to nature's deepest longings and needs, parochializing and blinding every one of its manifold elements.[4]

The above argument slowly developed in the first half of the nineteenth century. It was ultimately refined in the years following the Revolutions of 1848 in the many circles inspiring the Syllabus of Errors of Blessed Pius IX (1864), and, perhaps most systematically of all, in the literally thousands of pages published between 1850 and 1864 by the editors of the internationally influential Roman Jesuit journal, *La Civiltà Cattolica*. That polishing took place with much reference to ideas emerging from among the very ranks of the forces of renewal themselves: first those of the Abbé Félicité de Lamennais (1782–1854) and his followers—the men we know of as the Mennaisians—and then by thinkers and activists who after 1848 began to call themselves Liberal Catholics.

Lammenais, disillusioned by the chains imposed upon the full expression of the Catholic spirit through existing governments, like all those eager for true renewal, began to argue that only a clean separation of Church and State would put an end to the manipulative activity of fraudulent "sacred monarchies" and the *de facto* secularization of the clergy that slavishly worked together with them. Only then would the local episcopacy and clergy, united under the international direction of the Pope, be able to dedicate

---

4 Compelling in this regard are the Platonic themes emphasized by Werner Jaeger in *Paideia: The Ideals of Greek Culture* (Three Volumes, Oxford, 1986), and *Early Christianity and Greek Paideia* (Belknap Press, reprint of 1961 edition).

themselves freely to unleashing that still vital Catholic spirit and energy of believing peoples that had been unnaturally repressed by secularists, both revolutionary and monarchical alike. Only then would the Christianization of all of life be brought about; a Christianization of the State enabling its proper reunification with the Church included. "God and liberty," the motto of his journal, *l'Avenir*, founded in 1830, neatly expressed the gist of the broad Mennaisian program. A godly unity was its ultimate aim.

But episcopal opposition and condemnation by Pope Gregory XVI in *Mirari Vos* (1832) thwarted the progress of Lamennais' vision. In consequence, he became convinced that hidebound Church authorities enchained Christ's message just as willingly as those of the State. From this point on, Lamennais claimed that the only guide to the Faith and its meaning could be that which sprang from the Spirit of God operating in and through the faithful mass of believers. Unfortunately, the populace's awareness of that Spirit active in its midst would remain unconscious and mute unless it were awakened by Lamennais' own fully conscious prophetic witness. But once awakened, it would recognize the foolishness of its blind and ultimately impious leadership. It would realize that Christianity, as a variety of contemporary thinkers from the Saint Simonians to Polish nationalist poets exiled in Paris were insisting, was a *palingenesist* phenomenon—that is to say, a religion born anew in each age as the vital energy pouring forth from the believing population revealed to the world God's ever-evolving message; a message that popes and bishops clearly did not wish to accept.[5]

Those reformers who rejected Lamennais' teaching but wanted to continue to work for freedom from the oppressive chains of supposedly Catholic monarchies, focused on the need for a division of competence to ensure the correction and transformation of all things in Christ. According to them, Catholic political and social action should be left in the hands of lay pressure groups; dogmatic and moral guidance in that of the clergy. If the laity conducting the politics of the movement still did not follow the dogmatic and moral guidance of the clergy, at least this would not compromise

---

5   See J. Rao, "Lamennais, Rousseau, and the New Catholic Order," *Seattle Catholic* (1 February, 2005); also, J. M. Mayeur, ed., *Histoire du Christianisme* (Desclée, Thirteen Volumes, 1990–2002), Mayeur, X, 427–477, 628–906.

the Magisterium of the Church, confusing believers regarding the sacrality of this new kind of lay action the way that monarchies appealing to their impressive and long-lasting historical ties with Christianity might still do. The war cry of this post-Lamennais movement was "freedom of association." Freedom of association would guarantee the religious liberty necessary for understanding the mission of the Church and for teaching it accurately. It would assure a real chance for a Catholic transformation of State, society and individuals in Christ, instead of seeing the Church's mission perverted by a fraudulent union of sacred and secular subjecting the former to the latter.

But given the difficulties of obtaining freedom of association in the Restoration Era, battle conditions seemed to require a pragmatic alliance with Enlightenment-inspired political forces who demanded such liberty for their own particular purposes: that is to say, cooperation with liberals, democrats and nationalists; perhaps even with budding socialists. Lamennais had already looked to such collaboration with reference to the union of believers and liberals that had resulted in the creation of the Kingdom of Belgium in 1830. Still, those Catholics now working for "freedom of association" encouraged it from a practical as opposed to an ideological standpoint. Their hunt for non-Catholic allies made much progress, giving rise to the hope that mutual assistance might result in an honest dialogue revealing the intellectual differences with their pragmatic allies to be misunderstandings rather than real disagreements.

Such collaborative endeavors reached their peak in the first victorious stage of the Revolutions of 1848, especially in Italy and Germany. Still, it did not take long for bitter conflicts to arise among the victorious allies on the actual meaning of the freedom that had been won; conflicts that led very quickly to the suppression of religious orders, the call for a holy war of Catholic Italians against Catholic Austrians, and the exile from Rome of a pope who had committed himself sincerely to dialogue: all this in the name of obtaining "freedom."

One wing of the "cooperative movement" had as its most famous head the Count Charles de Montalembert (1810–1870), an ex-follower of Lamennais who had fought valiantly for Church freedom under the quite difficult conditions of the Liberal Monarchy born in France in 1830. Montalembert claimed that despite setbacks, Catholics must recognize that continued work with the liberal system of government under the divided religious and intellectual conditions of modern times was an absolute pragmatic necessity if freedom for the Church and individual believers were to be ensured. Yes, those who now came to be called "Liberal Catholics" argued, many non-believing liberals were ideologically hostile to religion, but this, to a large degree, was because the behavior of foolish believers had convinced them that the faithful were fawning admirers of an absolute monarchy that had not even been good for their own religious cause. Nevertheless, a truly liberal system could not help but guarantee the functioning of "a free Church in a free State." And if Catholics would only show that they respected such a system and had no desire to overturn it, even the fire-eaters' abusive anti-religious actions would eventually lose their appeal.[6]

Opponents of the Liberal Catholic approach included the above-mentioned editors of *La Civiltà Cattolica*. These were men who took the sad reality of contemporary religious and intellectual division as well as the appeal to pragmatic necessity to heart. A number of them, including their most famous member, Luigi Taparelli d'Azeglio (1793–1862), had vigorously supported cooperation with liberals at the beginning of the 1848 Revolutions, and were still willing to continue a dialogue with them. But given the disputes with liberals and supporters of other Enlightenment-inspired political movements that had once again been brought to the surface as the revolutions in question advanced, the *Civiltà* editors argued that any judgment regarding the possibility of substantive future interaction with such forces, liberalism included, had to be preceded by a much more systematic and critical study of the full meaning given to the words "individual," "freedom," "dignity," "social order," "dialogue" and "pragmatism" by all of the parties concerned. Moreover, it also had to be preceded by a more sober, rational examination of exactly how these words played out in practice under the form of government that Montalembert insisted was an *unquestionable* modern necessity and blessing for the Church.

Liberalism and the Liberal Catholic call to recognize the benefits of the "free Church in a free State" that ultimately went along with it did not come off well as the *Civiltà's* detailed study proceeded.

6   C. de Montalembert, *Des Interest Catholiques aux XIX Siècle* (Paris, 1852).

It is important for the Second Act of our drama to note that they did not come off well because their critique identified problems that the editors perceived as being imbedded in liberalism in its original and supposedly friendly and moderate Anglo-American form, not in some radically anti-religious perversion of its "true character." Already in the 1850s and 1860s, these problems were said to destroy the possibility of possessing the religious liberty that liberalism was supposed to ensure and to open wide the gates to the radical abuses that Liberal Catholics like Montalembert themselves honestly abhorred. And the editors insisted that any hope for defining and attaining the individual freedom and dignity fully obtainable only under the Social Kingship of Christ was obliterated in the process.

Allow me briefly to outline just enough of the *Civiltà* critique to indicate its acute awareness of those innate difficulties that were to be either ignored or purposely dismissed with the reemergence of the questions of religious liberty and separation of Church and State in the second act of our drama, to which we will soon come. It is a tribute to the acuity of their judgment that the *Civiltà* editors put so many of the pieces of the problem together, even without a full knowledge of all of that extraordinary *mélange* of esoteric, gnostic, nominalist, protestant, utopian, pietist and simply sinful, self-interested elements that played a role in the chaotic English Civil War era, leading to the formation of the Whig Alliance, the Glorious Revolution, Locke, Newton, and Anglo-American liberalism.[7]

Once again, the *Civiltà* did not deny that religious division presented a real problem for achieving the common good that budding liberalism justly sought to address, and exactly as one had to address it under such circumstances, with reference to the natural law alone. Still, it believed that it was necessary to admit that at the very best this was a tragic situation. For the natural law was a "paper tiger" without the aid that divine wisdom and grace gave to men to marshal their rational faculties properly and instill in them the courage actually to believe consistently what

---

7   Especially important to this critique was L. Taparelli d'Azeglio's *Esame Critico degli Ordini Rappresentativi nella Società Moderna,* which first appeared as a series of articles in *La Civiltà Cattolica* and then was published separately (Rome, Two Volumes, 1854). See, also, C. Hill, *The World Turned Upside Down* (Penguin, 1984) on the ideological battles of the English Civil War era.

their minds told them to be true.

Protestantism could not offer such assistance. It must always logically be suspicious of Reason, both because of its fundamental doctrine of the total post-lapsarian depravity of all things natural, as well as its dislike of the historic mobilization of Socratic Philosophy on behalf of Catholic doctrinal formulations. Neither could "religious liberty" do the cause of natural law a favor, even if it ungagged Catholics. . As Moderate Enlightenment thinkers like Voltaire joyfully recognized,[8] all that this general liberation accomplished was to encourage a cacophonous forum where competing voices from private religious "clubhouses" could babble ceaselessly, rendering what they had to say publicly impotent and, quite frankly, rather ridiculous to boot. When one added to the weakening of the mind the Enlightenment's reduction of the work of Reason to purely scientific or purely banal utilitarian tasks brought about by this stripping away of religious help in forming the human mind, it became ever more obvious that any concept of a substantive natural law capable of making universally applicable judgments on issues of moral importance was doomed. Under these circumstances, natural law could only survive as an historical memory, as a sociological codification of existing habits and customs, and one that was condemned to be eaten away more and more under the pressure of contempt for non-scientific metaphysical thought.

But the *Civiltà* was convinced that liberalism gave the *coup de grace* to natural law in two other telling fashions. One was through the *theoretical* support that its Protestant and Enlightenment roots provided for an *individualist* vision of materialist life. This vision understood such "law" to be nothing other than the "right" of men to build their private personalities on the basis of the many sensual passions that they experience in shrapnel-like fashion in the course of a lifetime, along with their "liberty" to do what these passions told them that they must do. Such rights were limited, once again, only by conventional agreements based on what, for the moment, people generally still "felt" to be good and bad. Their number and content would expand as the growing demand for more "freedom" ate away at existing "custom." That expansion was rendered even more inevitable due to liberalism's seeming conviction that some mysterious hand would harmonize the unleashing of individual

---

8 P. Gay, *The Enlightenment* (W. W. Norton, Two Volumes), I, 168–171.

expressions of Original Sin in pursuit of an overriding "common good"; a common good whose definition was just as materialist, convention-bound, shaky, and doomed to spiral downwards into meaninglessness as everything else in this catastrophic system.

A second, *practical* blow to any serious use of natural law came through the opportunity that was given by the purposefully weak liberal State for the strongest and most willful individuals or groups of individuals to dominate society as they saw fit. This opportunity emerged as that same disdain for authority that had worked for the abandonment of public religious coercion was applied to the construction of a system of division of powers guaranteeing the semi-paralysis of the government. And given that whatever ethos is publicly dominant exercises its influence over the rest of society as well, the anti-social spirit of the liberal State sooner or later translated into denigration of and assaults on the internal authorities of the now "private" religious denominations, along with those of families and every other kind of community as well. Unfortunately, as legitimate social *authority* was withdrawn from the public and private sphere, the naked and illegitimate *force* of powerful, immoral, irrational individuals and the passionate factions formed by them moved in to take its place. And these illegitimate forces, undeterred by their logical and moral savaging of the concepts of individual freedom and dignity that they always inscribed on their own banners, imposed new, self-interested, tyrannical controls upon the weaker elements of the community, precisely the sort of thing that liberal constitutionalism was supposed to prevent.

Although the editors realized just how much this system allowed the property owners and financiers historically active in creating it to manipulate defenseless society for their own private profit, it seemed logical to them that others would try to cash in on the golden opportunity provided by the emasculation of legitimate public and private authority. They thought that the liberal system gave all individuals and unnatural groupings of individuals dedicated to material and ideological passions of any type imaginable a chance to wreak their own special havoc.

All that these "others" had to do in order to press their advantage was to develop the innate logic of the liberal argument that worked to break down barriers to individual personality construction. After all, continued barriers were maintained solely by the mere habits and customs of the existing, illicit "powers-that-be," who irrationally defended them as the "obvious" dictates of "common sense." But in pursuing the satisfaction of their willful desires thoroughly, vigorously, and with tools that the current tyrants perhaps never imagined possible, the new oppressors would force their wishes upon a community lacking legitimate authority: either by violence, or by peaceful acceptance of their demands in the name of maintaining "public order." Ironically, such individuals and factions might eventually demand reactivation and illegitimate exaggeration of the powers of the State for the purpose of obtaining goals that were actually inimical to the original anti-authoritarian liberal program. This, the *Civiltà* argued, was precisely what happened in the new Kingdom of Italy, where budding totalitarians with warmongering nationalist obsessions happily used the apparatus of the liberal State to pursue policies that Montalembert insisted the liberal State had been created to thwart; and once again, all in the name of individual freedom and dignity.

Finally, it was quite clear to the editors that many liberals had a new, irrational, and ultimately unquestioningly "fideist" faith in the ability of the political system they adored to guarantee each and every one of the benefits that the *Civiltà* denounced as precarious at the very best. The articles of faith of this system were legion, although somewhat varied by place and time, depending upon what worked, practically, to allow its writ to run in one country as opposed to another.

One should add that insofar as religious-minded elements played a role in creating such fideism, as they very much did in Britain, its articles of faith included the pietist-inspired command to abandon "sterile" battles over doctrinal differences and replace them with efforts to find God through the practical exploitation of nature for the sake of that human material progress which was deemed the greatest aid to charity and public order. Such a policy was regarded as secure because it would be guided by an unchanging Christian morality that was by now unalterably rooted in men's minds and hearts and clearly crowned by God with practical success. Besides, adopting it was said to procure the further benefit of allowing believers to stay united in fighting the real enemy threatening them all: the naturalist atheism of Baruch Spinoza (1632–1677). Be that as it may, it gave to those who followed this path absolutely no

494

means of seeing just how much "unchanging Christian morality" actually was changing all around them. Such change proceeded as material "successes" in the natural order in war, commerce and sexual seduction seemed to indicate God's blessing on behavior that a consultation of "divisive" doctrine and the historical record of Church pronouncements would have revealed to have been regularly condemned as morally reprehensible.[9]

La Civiltà Cattolica, like Voltaire, thought that religious toleration under English historical conditions and in the materialist atmosphere of liberal Britain was sufficient to render Christianity gradually meaningless, without any violent assault upon it. This meant that there would be no need to press acceptance of the new liberal or liberal pietist faith forcefully in the United Kingdom. But wherever the memory of a "sacred government" might still be vivid, or where there were fewer religious divisions to exploit than in Britain, or where Catholic resistance to being rendered publicly impotent might still be vigorous, or where the ideological factions not yet in power felt the need to press their claims to control over rudderless society with every tool imaginable, the articles of this new faith would have to be more strictly preached and enforced. It was this that had happened in moderate form in the pre-revolutionary Kingdom of Prussia and the "sacred monarchies" that sought to combine the Enlightenment and Catholicism before 1789. And it was this that had happened much more radically in revolutionary France.

It is clear from the above comments that the editors would have thought that a prophet like Lamennais who might gain an influence over a different kind of society than that of liberal Britain would be likely to *impose* his palingenesist view of a changed Christianity upon that community as a whole, and through the power of the State as well. For contrary to what people generally think, a genuine Mennaisian can *never* really be in favor of the separation of Church and State. Lamennais was upset with the *old* State, because it blocked the victory of the religion it hypocritically claimed to support. But a new, democratically guided State could not suffer from the same flaw; where the voice of the Holy Spirit *must* infallibly be heard, once coaxed to the surface by a fully conscious prophet of

9 Interesting in this regard is R. Gawthrop, *Pietism and the Making of Eighteenth Century Prussia* (Cambridge, 1993).

ever-evolving Christianity. State, People, Prophet and Spirit would be united in transforming society as Christ wished it transformed at that moment in time. And woe to those Pharisees and Sadducees—popes, bishops and kings alike—who sought to maintain a faith in the Old Law when the New was now unmistakably upon them! They would ruthlessly be exposed as the enemies of God and "contemporary man" that they truly were.[10]

Reformed Mennaisian though he might have been in other respects, Montalembert also appeared to the *Civiltà* to be an irrational, fideist, Lamennais-like proponent of a liberalism that he proclaimed the infallible "pragmatic" tool for protecting the message of the Holy Spirit and Christ "in our time"; a tool against which the devil was himself somehow quite powerless. The editors repeatedly tried to explain to him why they believed that the only kind of "free Church" that liberalism permitted was one whose activity was limited to that of a private denominational clubhouse bickering impotently with an ever-increasing number of similarly castrated communities, while whatever illicit private powers were momentarily manipulating the "free State" went forward, uncontested, to define the meaning of life, the "Christian" moral virtues required to live it fully, and the "spiritual" role religion might yet have to play in service of its particular ideological or material interests. But Montalembert prohibited any rational questioning of the value of liberal propositions for the protection of Catholicism through an irrational ideological sloganeering: by condemning opponents as "intransigent" enemies of social peace, prosperity, progress, individual freedom, human dignity and Christianity itself, rather than responding frankly to their critique. Adopting his approach, the *Civiltà* editors submitted, entailed nothing other than a return to the enslavement of the Catholic vision to a partisan ideological position against which the movement for renewal had rebelled when it was supporters of "sacred monarchies" who had demanded it. The only thing that this would definitely ensure was that there would once again be no freedom to work to effect the real changes in State, social

10   See J. Rao, "Lamennais," *Op. cit.*; on the Mennaisian spirit, see A. Gough, *Romantic Catholics: France's Postrevolutionary Generation in Search of a Modern Faith* (Cornell, 2014); *Paris & Rome: The Gallican Church and Ultramontane Campaign, 1848–1853* (Clarendon Press, 1996).

and individual behavior that must come along with construction of the Social Kingship of Christ.[11]

Seeking the correction and transformation of all things in Christ was an innately daunting project even under extremely favorable conditions. Nevertheless, the editors of *La Civiltà Cattolica* were most troubled by the complex of problems posed for the whole endeavor by their own immediate and unfavorable *Zeitgeist*. This had now, for a century or more, taken control of the basic terms of all substantive debate, and had defined words like "Reason," "freedom," "individual dignity," "success," "progress," "authority," "tyranny," and even "peace," "Christian charity" and "pastoral efficacy" in reductionist and naturalist ways that soldiers for the Kingship of Christ would have to re-explain, from their most basic roots, in a fully Catholic manner. These definitions had been hammered into people's minds with all of the means that the *Zeitgeist* had at its disposal, including the press, the theater and popular song; means that Catholics were far less adept in using, but would have to learn to master for success. Moreover, the political and socially dominant enemies of correction and transformation in Christ possessed another "convincing" argument: their power to break believers' lives, ruining their careers and destroying their families, should they go about the business of questioning the existing order and reacquainting the world with a truly Catholic *paideia*.

Nevertheless, the *Civiltà* and its allies set to work, employing all of the tools utilized by their opponents, and pressuring the Papacy to exercise its universal teaching authority to instruct believers clearly regarding the truth and morality of contemporary political and social visions. They insisted that if such teaching were to be effective, it had to be absolutely crystal clear, naming the names of enemies as it condemned their ideas and actions. Ambiguities would only afford the *Zeitgeist*, with its overwhelming verbal and physical power, an opportunity to interpret them in a manner that was advantageous to its worldview. Inaction was not an option, for a drama of incalculable significance was unfolding before modern eyes. As one *Civiltà* article put it: either God would be King of the world, with true individual freedom and dignity, or man would be King, guaranteeing an irrational, willful, forceful reign of Original

---

11   See J. Rao, *Removing the Blindfold*, pp. 157–165.

Sin masqueraded as the victory of personal liberty and dignity.[12] The Syllabus of Pius IX, the partial but interrupted work of the First Vatican Council, and the development of Catholic Social Doctrine in the hands of the popes from Leo XIII onwards can be counted as confirmations of their work. And *nota bene*! It was this stiffening of the Catholic position, begun through the work of the laity and lower clergy earlier in the century, and only seriously involving the Papacy since 1848, that brought about the real "culture wars" of the nineteenth century, not some innate desire for battle on the part of a liberalism whose preference was always for work through subtle and subversive *palingenesis* rather than brutal straightforward assault.

The *Civiltà* was aware that fighting an existing *Zeitgeist* is always an uphill battle, and that the spirit of the times dominating the latter nineteenth century was in no way moribund. Worse still, the practical consequences of Enlightenment materialism in the form of its ever-increasing ability to divert the mass of the population away from consideration of substantive ideas to cheap entertainments or simplistic and demagogic arguments was rendering the problem of battling the enemy intellectually an infinitely more burdensome enterprise. And even if the reign of Pope St. Pius X might still be considered an integral part of Act One of our religious liberty drama, many of the new forces that would play an integral role in Act Two were already strongly present by that moment; chief among them being the Mennaisian conception of a Catholicism built on vital energy as it translated into at least one branch of theoretical and political Modernism, and the Americanist flip on the basic liberal vision.

What I would like to emphasize at this juncture, however, is the *demoralization* of those militants aroused to action by the drive to make Christ the King of the universe; a demoralization that was a primary factor in bringing an end to earlier, medieval efforts to achieve the Social Kingship as well.[13] A contributing element to this more recent demoralization was the confusion sown by those Church authorities who, while seemingly promoting the concept

12 "O Dio Re Colla Libertà o L'uomo Re Colla Forza," *La Civilta Cattolica*, 2, 3 (1853), 609–620.
13 See G. Lagarde, *La Naissance de L'Esprit Laique au Declin du Moyen Age* (Nauwelaerts, Five Volumes, 1958).

of transformation in Christ, repeatedly tended to belie it through their practical decisions. One serious example of such morally demoralizing decisions may be found in repeated expressions of papal and episcopal willingness to compromise with existing liberal forces that were terrified by the growing power of the Socialist Movement. Such compromises, which involved attenuating criticism of liberal errors, made liberalism seem as though it were actually a conservative and pro-Catholic force. They also tended to affirm a conviction that protection of the cult and the position of the clergy were the sole issues of moment to believers, thereby giving the impression that the Church was uninterested in the fullness of the Social Kingship, which she perhaps held to be for all intents and purposes unattainable and therefore even utopian in character. [14]

A second and perhaps much more powerful form of demoralization emerged from the recognition on the part of activists of their very slight impact on the world outside. This perception of insignificance was visible in innumerable settings: among leaders of Catholic political parties eager to escape from limitation to their narrow confessional base; amidst missionaries frustrated by their inability to make a dent in the cultural armor of some of the lands they wished to convert; in specialized Catholic Action organizations dealing with everything from youth to industrial workers, and shocked by confrontation of their meager numbers with the mass of the young, unchurched population in the trenches of the First World War; with men convinced that their nation must win the Great War, or that that war had given European populations the chance to purify their banal, materialist, prewar lives, and that one needed to bond with similar seekers of victory or war purification from non-Catholic backgrounds; in the company of enthusiastic liturgists aroused to find ways to attract modern men and women to a life of prayer after the ravages of the world conflict; among Russian *emigrés* as passionate to explain the reasons for the collapse of their Church in the aftermath of the Revolution as their Catholic counterparts had been a hundred years earlier; and finally, in the ranks of all religious-minded observers of the successes of popular atheist and pagan communist and fascist movements, wondering how to stir up such energy in their own anemic confessional ranks,

---

14 See J. Rao, "All Borrowed Armor Chokes Us," *Seattle Catholic* (9 July, 2005).

and ready to contemplate the ecumenical action of Christians everywhere to do so. [15]

Representatives of all the forces mentioned above took part in a more intellectual discussion of religious failure and what to do to reverse it that gave rise to the highly variegated phenomenon known as Personalism. Among those influential in Personalism's growth were Jacques Maritain (1882–1973), who served as host to debates on the subject for *soirées* at his home in Meudon in interwar France. These were attended by Russians like Nicholas Berdyaev (1874–1948), a representative of the Orthodox revival that placed a great deal of emphasis upon the nineteenth century Slavophile concept of the individual "finding himself" in community (*sobornost*), and Emmanuel Mounier (1905–1950), future editor of the Personalist journal, *Esprit*.

Catholic scouting groups were an important force for spreading concepts reflecting what Mounier called "Communitarian Personalism" before the Second World War, and the *École des cadres* at Uriage in Vichy France, which was created to prepare a new elite for a transformed European order once that conflict seemed to indicate a Nazi victory. Under the guidance of men like Pierre Dunoyer de Segonzac and Hubert Beuve-Mery, the future founder of *Le Monde*, priests like Henri de Lubac, Jean Maydieu, Victor Dillard and Paul Donceour were brought to Uriage to teach. These men, in turn, introduced students to thinkers connected with the so-called New Theology emerging from the Dominican and Jesuit centers of Saulchoir, Latour-Maubourg, and Fourvières. Writings of Lamennais, Henri Bergson, Maurice Blondel, Marie-Dominique Chenu, Yves Congar, Karl Adam, Romano Guardini, Charles de Foucauld and, perhaps more importantly than anyone else, Pierre Teilhard de Chardin (1881–1955), were examined here with care. Uriage also had links, direct and indirect, with Frs. Louis Joseph Lebret and Jacques Loew, founders of the Catholic social movement Economie et Humanisme, and, at least in Lebret's case, very influential in the genesis of *Gaudium et Spes*. [16]

---

15   See J. Rao, "The Good War and the Rite War," *Latin Mass Magazine* (Spring, 2001), pp. 34–38; "The Bad Seed: The Liberal-Fascist Embrace and its Postconciliar Consequences," *Latin Mass Magazine* (Fall, 2001).
16   On the historical development of the influence of Personalism, see J. Hellman, *Emmanuel Mounier and the New Catholic Left, 1930–1950*

Transformation of the world, according to the doctrine taught at Uriage, was dependent upon the creation of "persons" as opposed to "individuals." "Persons" were defined as men who responded to the call of "natural values" through participation in a community life elevating them above narrow individual desires. One knew that he was dealing with a valid community dedicated to natural values working to construct true persons whenever he saw that that community possessed a discernible, energetic "mystique," and that that mystique led its individual members to creative, self-sacrificing activity. One day, the "convergence" of all such mystiques would result in the establishment of a community of communities producing, in effect, super-persons, "the greatest transformation to which humanity has ever submitted." The nightmare of the twentieth century was actually "the bloody birth of a true collective being of men," mysterious indeed, but providential and eminently Catholic.[17]

Catholicism's role in this "convergence" was that of "giving witness" to the supernatural significance of every natural value, reflected in the mystiques of the active communities of self-sacrificing persons it saw around it, and helping each of them to come to its own innate perfection. It must not sit in judgment of them, because a "palingenesist" Catholicism itself could not fully know what it itself really was until everything natural had matured and converged through its witness. Catholicism was part of a multifaceted pilgrimage to God, linked together by intuition and action, whose destination was unclear. What was important at the moment was encouraging deeply willed commitment to self-sacrifice of all sorts.

Hence Uriage's stunning ecumenism, testified to in a myriad of ways. It began with Segonzac's ability "to form friendly relations, on the spiritual plane, with Protestants, Catholics, Jews, Moslems, agnostics," since he "preferred (rooted) people . . . in their own setting, in their own culture."[18] It passed through the Uriage Charter's proclamation—reminiscent of pietist claims regarding an unchangeable Christian morality anchored firmly in European

(University of Toronto Press, 1981); *The Knight Monks of Vichy France: Uriage, 1940–1945*, McGill, 1997, p. 56); E. Poulat, *Les prêtres-ouvriers: Naissance et fin* (Cerf, 1999).

17 Hellman, *Knight Monks*, p. 178.
18 Ibid., p. 83.

society—that "believers and non-believers are, in France, sufficiently impregnated with Christianity that the better among them could meet, beyond revelations and dogmas, at the level of the community of persons, in the same quest for truth, justice and love."[19] And it arrived, in Mounier, at full-fledged Teilhardian rapture over the strange growth of the "perfect personal community," where "love alone would be the bound, and no constraint, no vital or economic interest, no extrinsic institution":[20]

> Surely [development] is slow and long when only average men are working at it. But then heroes, geniuses, a saint come along: a Saint Paul, a Joan of Arc, a Catherine of Siena, a Saint Bernard, or a Lenin, a Hitler and a Mussolini, or a Gandhi, and suddenly everything picks up speed…[H]uman irrationality, the human will, or simply, for the Christian, the Holy Spirit suddenly provides elements which men lacking imagination would never have foreseen.
>
> May the democrat, may the communist, may the fascist push the positive aspirations which inspire their enthusiasm to the limit and plenitude.

As John Hellman explains, "Mounier's belief that there was an element of truth in all strong beliefs coincided with Teilhard's vision of the inevitable spiritualization of humanity."[21]

Uriage's message was not a rational one. Its ultimate justification was intuition and strength of will leading to creative action. Any appeal to logic, either in support or criticism of strongly willed commitment to natural values, was dismissed as either belaboring the given, or as a dangerously decadent and individualistic scholastic pedantry. Better to bury the temptations of a sickly rationalism through the development of the obvious virtue of "manliness," again, defined in completely anti-intellectual ways: the ability to leap onto a moving streetcar; to ride a bicycle up the steep hill to the École like Jacques Chevalier; to look others "straight in the eye" and "shake hands firmly"; to endure the sweat-filled regimen defined as *décrassage*, devised for Uriage students under the inspiration of General Georges Hébert; to sing enthusiastically around the evening fire in the Great Hall; to know how to "take a woman";

---

19 Ibid., p. 59.
20 Hellman, *Mounier*, p. 85, 90.
21 Hellman, *Mounier*, p. 128.

and, always, to feel pride in "work well done." Such manliness was said to have deep spiritual meaning, aspects of which were elaborated in lectures like de Lubac's *Ordre viril, ordre chrétien* and Chenu's book, *Pour être heureux, travaillons ensemble.*[22]

Finally, let us note that Uriage's teaching was unabashedly elitist; the particular mystique of the École being that of developing the natural value of leadership. "The select youth of Uriage" were said to be "the first cell of a new world introduced into a worn-out one,"[23] "entrusted with the mission of bringing together the elite from all of the groups that ought to participate in the common task of reconstruction in the same spirit of collaboration."[24] Since they were destined to reveal the eternal supernatural significance of the natural values witnessed to by the mystique of all virile communities, Uriage students were actually priestly figures as well. Each class was consecrated and given a great man's name as talisman. Segonzac especially "took upon himself a certain sacerdotal role, even regarding the wives and children of his instructors."[25] This entailed also a "separation between the leaders, the lesser leaders, the lesser-lesser leaders, the almost leaders and the not-at-all leaders," irritating some of the interns. Members of the "central team," as one of them indicated, "were gods."[26]

The Uriage gods at first saw fascism as the "monstrous prefiguration" of the new personalist humanity waiting to be born under their spiritual guidance. Nevertheless, Nazi racism never appealed to men who appreciated vitality in every people and culture, while fascism in general proved its supreme unworthiness by its very inability to succeed. Enthusiasm was then transferred to Marxism, another "monstrous prefiguration" promising a happier future. Here, the activity of the Uriage cadres was paralleled by the efforts of priests and bishops trying to understand the "mystique" of workers in labor camps and ordinary French factories, training for the latter purpose being offered under the patronage of the supra-diocesan *Mission de France.* Uriage teachers were themselves involved in these priestly activities—Fr. Dillard, for example, canonizing the

---

22   Hellman, *Knight Monks*, pp. 71–76.
23   Ibid., p. 65.
24   Ibid., p. 63.
25   Ibid., p. 90.
26   Hellman, *Knight Monks*, p. 75.

Soviets he encountered in the labor camps, and insisting that all workers were "born" into their tasks with specific virtues denied to other people. But an Uriage-like openness was everywhere in the air. After all, there were "riches in modern disbelief, in atheist Marxism, for example, which are presently lacking to the fullness of the Christian conscience."[27] Enlightened spirits had "to share the faith in and the mystique of the Revolution and the Great Day (that of the total Christ),"[28] as did one priest who asked to die "turned towards Russia, mother of the proletariat, as towards that mysterious homeland where the Man of the future is being forged."[29]

Communitarian Personalists employed familiar Mennaisian arguments to explain their desire to give witness to the work of the Holy Spirit in modern times through the triumphant energy of Marxism-Leninism. Still, the Zeitgeist-savvy nineteenth century editors of La Civiltà Cattolica would have understood that the mere physical victory of the Soviet Union in the Second World War was already an enormously powerful, non-intellectual, psychological weapon, fit for convincing the war-weary and demoralized European world—its Catholic population included—unthinkingly to attribute a superiority to the beliefs and system lying behind its success and the unquestionable necessity of making accommodations with them.

Neither would the Civiltà have been surprised that that same powerful but unthinking psychological reaction made itself apparent with respect to the other victor in the global conflict: the United States. When one adds the especially uncritical appeal that America might have to those truly suffering persecution under her Soviet partner in victory to the by now ingrained and unconscious influence of the Enlightenment "gospel of natural success" over modern western man as a whole, it becomes obvious that there would be a ready-made cheering squad for the politically stable and economically rich regime across the pond. But a rational analysis of the full impact of this second victorious force requires some mention of five particular themes and persons: the development of what by the late nineteenth century was called "Americanism"; the postwar ideological politics of the American government and Press; the role of John Courtney Murray, S. J. (1904–1967); the

---

27 Poulat, Op. cit., p. 408.
28 Ibid., p. 386.
29 Ibid., p. 244.

personalist Integral Humanism of Jacques Maritain (1882–1973); and, finally, the continuing impact of the demoralizing activity and inactivity of the Catholic clergy.

What is Americanism?[30] It is in one sense a by now all too familiar demand for an unquestioning *faith* in the *pragmatic* necessity of accepting the American system as the sole means of protecting liberty and public order *in our time*. Americanists addressing themselves to Christian believers build upon the anti-Spinoza arguments of earlier pietist promoters of doctrinal syncretism and tolerance. They insist upon their recognition that the American separation of Church and State and religious liberty are their best possible friend and indispensable defender versus contemporary atheism, something that after the Second World War was most clearly represented by Soviet Communism.

America's career as a redemptive and liberating faith—with a country accidentally attached to it—began in seemingly purely Christian form through the Pilgrim Fathers' description of their flight from an evil Catholic Europe to a New Jerusalem across the Atlantic. The Pilgrims saw the "city on a hill" that they were to construct in the New World as a beacon light that might eventually religiously illuminate the entire globe. New England preachers stirring up their parishioners to dramatic expressions of faith in Christ saw this light growing ever brighter under the direct impetus of the Holy Spirit in the Great Awakening of the 1700s.[31]

Many of these migrants soon lost their faith in the Christian God, but not their religious fervor. That fervor they transferred to the Enlightenment concepts that also had begun to exercise an influence over them, perceiving God's hand through His providential action in the natural world; that is to say, in the birth of the American version of the Glorious Revolution and its secularized vision of redemption through the spread of individual "freedom." Abraham Lincoln added immeasurably to the divinization of the American experiment by emphasizing earlier calls for a civil religion that would underline its peculiarly sacred character. Lincoln

30 For the following, see J. Rao, "Le Mirage Americain," in B. Dumont, ed., *Église et Politique, Changer de paradigme* (Artéges, 2013), pp. 227–257; also, *Americanism and the Collapse of the Church in the United States* (Tan Books, 1995).

31 M. Marty, *Pilgrims in their Own Land* (Penguin, 1985), pp. 107–128.

envisaged enshrining the Founding Fathers and the nation's foundational documents, the Declaration of Independence and the Constitution, in secular temples with eternal flames burning in their honor. His civil religion preached the message that through America, God and the Founders had provided the "last, best hope of mankind" for both peaceful social order and individual freedom.[32]

Unfortunately, faith in America hid the disturbing facts that the *Civiltà* had already brought to light in discussing the *mélange* of Moderate Enlightenment and liberal ideas that this system also enshrined: that the "free" and peaceful social order established by it was one in which the most passionate and most willful individuals and factions had the advantage over anyone continuing to play by the supposedly unchanging "Christian-common sense" rules that the regime always claimed to defend and obey. Freedom and peace were reconciled under its aegis, but by ensuring the construction of a pseudo-order guaranteeing the victory of the strong over the weak, with the weak expected to praise the liberty that oppressed them, and limit their own use of it in the interests of the strong. The will of the strongest—whose representatives could, of course, always change, should those on the hunt for power press their demands in ways that the "common sense" of the current elite would not have dreamed possible—thereby also came to interpret the "will" of the Founders and the "original intent" of the foundational "scriptures" along with "freedom," "social order," and what was considered to be acceptable "pragmatic action" in the public sphere. And given the need to placate a continuing American religious feeling unwilling to believe that the "unchangeable Christian moral code" was actually being subverted, the strong defined what the true wishes of God were as well.

Uncovering the variety of contradictory influences behind this victory requires precisely the complex doctrinal, philosophical, historical, sociological and psychological study of the *Zeitgeist* that the *Civiltà* editors encouraged. Unfortunately, "truly free and pragmatic citizens," living under the guidance of this spiritually and

---

32   Marty, *Op. cit.*, pp. xiii, 154–164, 221–224, 280–284; W. J. Wolf, *Lincoln's Religion* (Pilgrim Press, 1959), pp. 9, 98, 116–120, 143–144, 152–159, 193–194; P. F. Boller, Jr., *George Washington and Religion* (Southern Methodist University Press, 1963), pp. 66–115; Mayeur, *Op. cit.*, X, 479–538, XI, 853–932; Gay, *Op cit.*, II, 555–568.

intellectually stifling American Liberation Theology, are pressured by means of all the public and private tools available to manipulators of the spirit of the times to avoid just such an investigation. Besides condemning any thoughtful critique as unpatriotic and even downright treasonous, the spokesmen for the new civil religion say that it represents a divisive, impious, uncharitable and utterly impractical obstacle to the success of "the last, best hope of mankind" for peace and freedom. Morever, they argue that it simultaneously displays the misanthropic spirit of men and women envious of the material successes of their more energetic brethren, whose enrichment works charitably for the benefit of all. As always with "religious" defenders of the Moderate Enlightenment, they insist that it is only through the pragmatic exploitation of material nature that social peace, the fruits of liberty and the blessings of the Christian God Himself are to be obtained; not through a harping on spiritual and intellectual abstractions dear to the hearts of sterile, unproductive "losers" who bring all serious practical religion into disrepute.

One cannot underline this Americanist fideist approach strongly enough. Anyone opposing its pragmatically ideological civil religion is vilified as an enemy of public order, freedom, the practical material success that is the fruit of "real Christian virtue," and the only effective religious response to the evils of unbelief as well. He is, in short, branded as a "hater of mankind," both cynical and naïve at one and the same time. Sustained attempts to point out the contradictions in this heap of conflicting arguments do nothing but bring down upon the wretched critic yet another round of the usual exasperated invectives further peppered with the accusations of outright mental illness.[33]

A quantum leap in the preaching of the American civil religion and its self-conscious Liberation Theology took place in the 1890s. The need to "integrate" an enormous and highly diverse immigrant population that might not easily be able to digest what was, after all, a basically English medley of pietist, Newtonian and Lockean contributions to a new and "pragmatically ideological" Christianity dictated this more intense evangelization. Various pronouncements of President Woodrow Wilson concerning American goals of the

---

33   J. Rao, "Why Catholics Cannot Defend Themselves: The Religious and Cultural Suicide of a Conquered People," *Diocesan Report* (3/19/03).

First World War in 1917 and 1918 made the worldwide scope of such evangelization clear enough to anyone with ears to hear. True, American devotion to the international spread of the national Liberation Theology slowed in the 1920s and 1930s, due chiefly to a desire to purge it from any contamination that involvement with a war-torn, revolutionary (and, in "Christian" eyes, impious) Europe might have entailed, as well as to a domestic need to finish the massive immigrant population's incomplete indoctrination. But all that changed by the end of the Second World War, when Americans in general finally took the nation's global role as practical guide to the liberation of the universe as an unquestionable given, and prepared themselves to bring the light definitively into each and every dark foreign cave.

As they did the members of each and every religious denomination, Americanists told Catholics that the nation's sacred system gave all of them a freedom to pursue their faith that was incomparably greater and more beneficial than ever known beforehand. How could it not do so, given that the regime's providential charism enabled them to come to grips with and understand the true meaning of their own specific teachings with more clarity than popes, councils and scriptures could ever have provided? But what the Americanists did not openly admit was that the "freedom" that this providential system offered did not permit individual members of religious denominations to freely link their personal convictions with the public actions they required, since these were contrary to the self-interests of the dominant materialist oligarchy that defined what liberty really meant.

Leo XIII's attacks upon Americanism and its errors in the last decade of the nineteenth century were quite accurate. Nevertheless, they failed to halt the civil religion's progress among believers. The many reasons for this failure include the fact that Rome's attention was swiftly turned away from the United States to the battle against the Modernists, whose intellectual errors were—as more intellectual arguments always are—an easier target to identify than those of the Moderate Enlightenment. Americanism, which was rooted in just this moderate approach, could always hide behind a deceptive outward appearance of a "purely pragmatic" concern for solving "immediate practical problems." In the meantime, it had the opportunity to go about its more subversive work on behalf of its infallible and ironclad ideology, "defending religion" by castrating or transforming it beyond recognition.

A reading of the *Handbook* discussing the task of the National Catholic War Council created in 1917, subsequent NCWC documents, and the comments of Cardinal Gibbons in the copies of the New Testament given to soldiers going off to battle in the War to End All Wars all show how an uncritical commitment to "national principles" of democracy and freedom, as well as to ecumenical activities in pursuit of patriotic goals, inexorably advanced. A Catholic wartime ecumenical cooperation potentially "disturbing to pious ears" continued to be praised in popular interwar films. And the call for fraternal union of Catholics and non-Catholics on behalf of the American Liberation Theology, resurrected in the Second World War in the battle against National Socialism, reached a peak of frenzy due to the postwar conflict with Soviet Communism.[34]

Eager to guarantee a militant commitment of all men of faith to the primary battle against the Red Menace, Americanists sought to calm continued religious squabbling inside the United States. A major source of this bickering was the terror felt by a number of Protestant leaders at the high American Catholic birth rate. These Protestants feared that a future papist majority would forge a traditional Catholic union of Church and State, the anti-American evils of which they illustrated by pointing to the authoritarianism of the Spain of General Francisco Franco. Spanish authoritarianism was identified as a threat to the individual liberty central to the American system in everything from religious to economic matters, revealing a basic, inescapable truth: freedom was endangered by Catholic tyranny in a manner analogous to that of Soviet Communism.[35]

Americanist anti-communists could not escape the conclusion that such debilitating divisions had to be put to rest in a fashion that allayed Protestant fears: by making it clear that neither the

---

34   See *The Handbook of the National Catholic War Council* (NCWC, 1918); M. Williams, *American Catholics in the War: National Catholic War Council, 1917–1921* (Macmillan, 1921); see Pat O'Brien as Fr. Duffy in *The Fighting Sixty Ninth* (1940); Marty, *Op. cit.*, p. 409; Mayeur, *Op. cit.*, xiii, 833–924. Fr. John Ryan (1869–1945) is an interesting and much more nuanced critic of many aspects of the American system.

35   D. A. Wemhoff, *John Courtney Murray, Time/Life, and the American Proposition: How the CIA's Doctrinal Warfare Program Changed the Catholic Church* (Fidelity, 2015), pp. 143–149, 168–169.

union of Church and State nor Spanish authoritarianism could remain a praiseworthy model for Catholics. The Church had to be taught that her anti-communism must be the American form of anti-communism, and that since the "pragmatic" American system was the "last, best, hope" for the Church as well as everyone else to be free and really come to grips with her own message, adoption of the tenets of the American civil religion could not help but be beneficial to Catholicism.

Since Moderate Enlightenment methodology dictated a gentle rather than a violent path to impotence, this teaching had to proceed by means of seduction, preferably with the enthusiastic help of Catholics themselves.[36] Anyone interested in pursuing a study of this seductive emasculation has a variety of sources that he can consult. One of the most interesting is the recent work of David A. Wemhoff: *John Courtney Murray, Time/Life, and the American Proposition: How the CIA's Doctrinal Warfare Program Changed the Catholic Church.* Here, Wemhoff discusses in great detail the American government's creation of such agencies as the "Psychological Strategy Board" (1951) and the "Operations Coordinating Board" (1953), as well as the development of a "Doctrinal Warfare" program (1953) designed to destroy all *non-American* as well as anti-Soviet communist outlooks, with as much internal Catholic assistance as possible.[37]

Doctrinal warfare's propaganda campaign began appropriately enough by identifying America's "fundamental characteristic": Lockean liberalism. This revealed that she "values the individual as an end in himself."[38] An appreciation of individualism was said to explain America's "deep tolerance" and "the diversity of its doctrines and philosophies." Such dedication to individual freedom made the United States "a revolutionary nation" from its very birth. That revolution in the name of personal liberty continued globally in the postwar world, and "America, as the leader of the Free World, leads this revolution" because she "still is in the business of revolution."[39] Following the typical palingenesist pattern, however, the "revolution" in favor of individual

36 Ibid., pp. 52–53, 116–120, 143–149, 168–169, 235.
37 Ibid., pp. 151–318.
38 Ibid., pp. 305, 297.
39 Ibid., 449, 450–451.

liberty was simultaneously identified as being totally traditional in character. In truth, it was more traditional than Christian Tradition itself, which, once again, needed the aid of the American Way to achieve its full development and self-understanding. For American individualism began with the "Christian-Judaic religion which, in its very concept, recognized the dignity, worth and right to freedom of the individual, as do most of the other major religions of the world."[40]

It was unfortunate that there were dangerous forces that did not realize that Christian, Jewish and most major religions were all of them in one way or another nothing other than embryonic protagonists of Lockean individualism. These elements had to be destroyed by employing the method that James Madison in *The Federalist* indicated as being central to the standard operating procedure of the American regime: by multiplying factions inside the enemy's ranks. Hence, "[t]he program was to give voice to 'new and stimulating ideas, even contradictory ideas' because these 'have self-generative powers and are desired." Doctrinal Warfare had to "[c]reate, when advisable, deviationist movements designed to split organizations promulgating hostile ideologies," and "[e]xploit local divergences, heresies or policy disagreements within opposition systems." But, once again, this was for the ultimate benefit of the "opposition systems" in question, which could not help but prosper should they rid themselves of their own "totalitarian" tendencies and tap into the American vision that could truly set them free.[41]

Wemhoff's discussion of the personnel at work on these specific projects, as well as those active in the broader enterprises of the Central Intelligence Agency of the 1950s, also indicates clearly just how much government agencies interacted with the private world of the American Press on behalf of Doctrinal Warfare. Staff members regularly communicated with one another and moved back and forth in the employment of both. Henry R. Luce's (1898–1967) *Time/Life* network stands out in particular relief with respect to the program's concern for convincing religious denominations that the ethos of Locke Land enabled them to understand the inner striving of their visions better than by consulting their own history,

---

40 Ibid., p. 449.
41 Ibid., pp. 304–306.

thinkers, and heroes.[42]

Luce personally emphasized all of the themes indicated above. "The founding purpose of the United States," as he wrote in one article in *Time*, "was to make men free, and to enable them to be free and to preach the gospel of freedom to themselves and to all men."[43] Reiterating the ever-useful palingenesist concept, he insisted that America "is at once revolutionary and conservative, traditional and progressive."[44] Because America was so rooted in traditional religion, she was deeply concerned for fighting off atheism; for forging a "Holy Alliance with God."[45] Still, her advanced knowledge of what was best for believers showed her that this Holy Alliance had to unite "all people who believe in a Supreme Being" for "the promotion of confidence of people everywhere in religious truth."[46] Christian dogma, as Doctrinal Warfare also firmly agreed, could not enter into the redemptive picture.[47]

American wisdom also taught that the fight against atheism was equivalent to the battle for individual freedom, whose chief purpose Luce was candid enough to identify: the ability "to make all the money you can and 'to do as you damn please with your own'"; apparently, as his wife noted, without any concern for moral questions or right and wrong.[48] Luce's understanding of the real purpose of freedom was confirmed by a speaker at a conference he organized in Princeton on behalf of a "World Economic Plan" (1954) who defined it as "the capacity of the individual to produce more per capita, and to enjoy a greater degree of pleasure."[49] Meanwhile, the real purpose of the Holy Alliance was underlined at the 1955 meeting of the Luce-backed Foundation for Religious Action in the Social Order:[50]

> [O]ur Christian religion and our competitive business system [are] in themselves the two most revolutionary forces in the

42 Ibid., pp. 151–180, and *passim*.
43 Ibid., p. 576.
44 Ibid., p. 393.
45 Ibid., p. 373.
46 Ibid., p. 465.
47 Ibid., p. 294.
48 Ibid., pp. 172, 465, 551.
49 Ibid., p. 433.
50 Ibid., pp. 467, 53.

world today. Communism and socialism, which we frequently think of as revolutionary, are, in fact, reactionary movements, leading man back to the bondage from which he has only so recently emerged. What we call 'free enterprise' or 'competitive capitalism' or 'the American way of life'... upsets the old established order. Christianity endowed the individual with spiritual dignity; our American Constitution endowed the individual with political dignity; but it has remained for American industry to endow the individual with economic dignity.

One of the main participants at this same Foundation conference was John Courtney Murray, S. J., editor of *Theological Studies*, based in Woodstock College in New York. Murray, who in his earlier life had made rather vehemently anti-Americanist statements, became deeply involved with the whole governmental-*Time/Life* project, and an intimate friend of Henry and Claire Booth Luce as well. His career as apologist for the American Liberation Theology and the Catholic Church's duty to accommodate it, in the name of a pragmatic historical necessity that providentially assured her a more complete understanding of her own teachings and best interests, began through those wartime ecumenical stimuli central to many believers' "conversion" to the cause of "religious freedom" and syncretism everywhere.

Particularly significant in Murray's case was a Church and State symposium organized by the National Conference of Christians and Jews at the Biltmore Hotel in New York on April 26th, 1948. It was only after that date that he began publicly to propagate the argument on the relationship of Church and State and religious liberty for which he became famous, along with those themes so dear to the hearts of Doctrinal Warfare and Henry Luce. Once again, these themes were individualism, the religious syncretism required to defend it, and the exaltation of America as the sole key to a global solidarity essential for the defeat of atheistic evil (communism) and the victory of God and the good (free enterprise capitalism).[51]

Murray attacked the "historical union" of Church and State as an unfortunate, accidental product of circumstance, and one that had had the consequence of enchaining Catholicism, hindering

---

51   Ibid., pp. 122–276, 467, 505–509, 575, 746; Marty, *Op. cit.*, pp. 417–422.

its true mission of transforming all society in Christ. American constitutionalism had given the faith the chance to set itself free, permitting the Church to return to "the true Christian Tradition." He insisted that the American political system, with its division of powers and a still more clear separation of Church and State than in Britain, limited the competence of the government over social life, leaving Catholicism totally free to go about its work of evangelization. It thereby differed intrinsically from that nineteenth century Liberalism that had militantly worked against Christianity.

And how could it not so differ? After all, the Founding Fathers of the United States took for granted that basic Christian morality that no one could call into question precisely because it was an uncontestable given; an integral part of the natural law that every right-thinking man relying on human Reason could grasp.[52] Anyone with eyes to see could judge just how fruitful their system had been for the American Church. Adoption of the same approach by the Universal Church must bring about similar results elsewhere. For the contemporary world, burned by horrible experiences with ideological and tyrannical states, would then realize that Catholicism had nothing to do with governmental coercion. Modern man was more "sensitive," with "deeper insights into the needs of the human person," and ready to hear the message of the Church that historically guided him on his first shaky steps to the realization of his individuality and dignity under the only political conditions suitable to their fulfillment: those established by the Founders. Besides, America and America alone could fight the good fight against atheistic Soviet Communism. "For [the] Catholic Church cannot with full effectiveness oppose Communism as long as it is itself regarded as being in opposition to the American political system," "man's best, and possibly last, hope of human freedom," "that stands out most strongly against the spread of Communism."[53]

Most of this is very old indeed, beginning with Murray's complaints regarding the *abuses* of Church-State unions, which recall those of the militants of the early nineteenth century. The appeal for a defense of religion against the one common atheist enemy by means of a reliance upon natural reason rather than doctrine, the insistence on the uniqueness of the practical-minded American

52   Ibid., pp. 133–142,182–207, 220–221, 719.
53   Ibid., pp. 228, 235, 223, 147–148.

experience for allowing all traditional forces their sole chance to reinvigorate their real roots in modern times, and the focus on an individual freedom that ends up supporting the interests of the dominant group in society all recall Pietist, Whig, Palingenisist, Mennaisian, Liberal Catholic, and of course, early Americanist themes and their consequences. Similarly familiar is Murray's contemptuous distortion and dismissal of criticism and his failure to honestly confront certain basic practical problems, among them his *Time/Life* and Doctrinal Warfare allies' praise of the danger-ously revolutionary movements of the eighteenth and nineteenth centuries, which movements he attacked; and Leo XIII's critique of precisely this supposedly "fresh" and "different" American manifestation of liberalism.[54] All that is really different in Murray is the extent to which he as a Catholic priest became involved in the nexus of powerful governmental and private forces active in promoting principles destructive of true Catholic freedom.

Part of this nexus was Fr. Felix Morlion, O. P., the founder of the *Pro Deo* University (1944) in Rome, with financial assistance from "all the usual suspects" of governmental and private background.[55] Morlion used *Pro Deo* to apply "the solid and balanced work of the American Founding Fathers as expressed by their correspon-dence (1773–1776), by the Federalist papers, the Declaration of Independence and the Constitution of the U. S. A." to European practice. He did so because this "most realistic way of establishing a free but God-centered way of life" was "an inspiration for the Italian and other democracies."[56] Of course that faith-friendly way of life was not to be taken as specifically Catholic in character, for American principles were "profoundly united with the principles of living faith in God common to all authentic religious denomi-nations."[57] And there could be little surprise in the fact that *Pro Deo* understood that promotion of a system dear to freedom and to God very much entailed a "spreading of the philosophy of American Business."[58]

Luce, inevitably one of the main supporters of Morlion's project,

---

54   Ibid., pp. 52, 245–257, 270, 369–370, 418, 449, 488, 637–641.
55   Ibid., pp. 366–372.
56   Ibid., p. 368.
57   Ibid., p. 376.
58   Ibid., p. 371.

gave a speech before 4,000 persons, including Alcide de Gasperi, at the opening of the *Pro Deo* academic year on November 29th, 1953 entitled "The American Proposition." He consulted John Courtney Murray to ensure intellectual depth to his comments and admitted that he lifted much of the content directly from his response. Forgive me one last time if I summarize aspects of the Doctrinal Warfare-*Time/Life*-Murray effort to seduce Catholics with reference to this address.[59]

The "American Proposition" presented for *Pro Deo* was one that Luce summarized more succinctly in a *Time* article of 1963; namely one that "consists of a word, a tendency and a method. The word is liberty. The tendency is equality. The method is constitutionalism."[60] Its most practical element was said to be that of getting rid of governmental obstacles to personal belief and action, thereby making men ever more free. American freedom, in consequence, could "support much pluralism in religious beliefs, political opinions, and local customs," as well as, *mirabile dictu*, economic freedom and the encouragement of "business." Luce read from "our National Scriptures"—the Gettysburg Address—to back his argument, discussing various American governmental institutions, such as the Supreme Court, which he called the "Keeper of the Ark of the Covenant," with the same hushed, sacred awe.

Lest Catholics think that the individualist, anti-social authority approach of the American Way was somehow opposed to the Catholic Faith, Luce assured them that it was based upon the obvious dictates of the natural law and therefore could not be in any way anti-Catholic. In fact, it could not be anti-anything natural. The "intelligent American can legitimately long for a world in which all men will think his political thoughts and talk his political language," he explained, because insofar "as the American way of life rests upon these principles, understood in their Western traditional sense, it is exportable, but only because it is, or ought to be, indigenous everywhere."[61] And besides the natural law, the Founding Fathers had a deep commitment to God, reflected in the thoughts of the "Christian" John Adams (he was a Unitarian) and the Deist Thomas Jefferson, both of whom agreed that "God

59 Ibid., pp. 374–382.
60 Ibid., p. 381.
61 Ibid., p. 379.

reigned and, directly or indirectly, ruled."[62] But why refer to these sources when one could calm Catholic fears by citing the blessings of America as proclaimed by the Third Council of Baltimore in 1887, also mentioned by the *Handbook* of the NCWC in 1917: "We consider the establishment of our country's independence, the shaping of its liberties and laws, as a work of special Providence, its framers building better than they knew, the Almighty's hand guiding them."[63] In short, the Enlightenment understanding of man, enshrined most securely in America, was that of the traditional natural law and the best means of fulfilling Catholic along with all other human values. And anyone present at the talk knew from its tenor that the only possible alternative to the American Proposition was atheistic communism.

Murray, Luce, *Time/Life* and presumably those behind the Doctrinal Warfare Program as well were very pleased with Jacques Maritain's influence in spreading openness to the American Liberation Theology.[64] Although closely connected with the development of the personalist approach, Mounier's Communitarian Personalism did not appeal to Maritain. He believed that its total embrace of vital energy as a guide to the presence of the Holy Spirit meant abandonment of the unique significance of Catholicism, so much so that its supporters would find themselves helpless before *any* superficially vibrant phenomenon; spiritually "barren in the face of a Ramakrishna."[65]

Nevertheless, Maritain's Integral Humanism, and his treatment of the "person" as an ineffable being whose full spiritual dignity would be injured by coercion in that socio-political realm where man operated as a mere "individual," did call for a Mounier-like dialogue with others. The need for dialogue was confirmed by reading the "signs of the times." The signs of the times indicated that that indefinable creature known as "modern man," whose deep sense of "dignity" was ultimately rooted in the Christian heritage, and who still needed the witness of Catholic Truth, had perhaps temporarily leaped ahead of the Church in his longing to fulfill his destiny as a person. Contemporary perceptions and strengths

---

62 Ibid., p. 377.
63 Ibid., p. 378.
64 Ibid., pp. 220, 225, 235, 269, 506, 518, 627, 882, 943.
65 Hellman, *Mounier*, p. 42.

must therefore be cultivated.

Dialogue with sensitive modern man could involve many groups, from Marxists to previously antagonistic but now chastened, anti-totalitarian liberals. Maritain's experiences while living in the United States, expressed in his *Reflections on America* (1958), encouraged the conviction that her pluralist system represented another great leap forward whose appreciation would work for the benefit of Christianity. For the American Way permitted that free, non-coerced dialogue among all manner of sensitive "individuals" through which men unconsciously waiting for Christ could be opened up to the faith, certain that they would be getting the message of Jesus rather than that of Constantine manipulating religion through the power of the State. The unchanging project of Christianization could finally advance under the historically changed socio-political framework of liberating American Pluralism.

Maritain's apparent ignorance or naiveté regarding just how open to dialogue and true religion American society actually was in practice is regrettable. Among the peculiar benefits that he claimed came from it—benefits that slaves, Indians, Mexicans, exploited Latin American economies and anyone familiar with the Christmas shopping season might well have contested—was America's total freedom from any and all Machiavellianism, as well as a possession of many consumer "gadgets" that freed men to pursue more spiritual goals.[66] But no one can deny that, along with Father Morlion, *Pro Deo*, Luce, Murray and the American security apparatchiks, this great philosopher helped mightily in smoothing European acceptance of the American Way as the "last, best hope of Catholics." Just how much Maritain's book might have helped the Communitarian Personalists, who were initially very suspicious of American individualism, to see how a worldwide spread of liberal pluralism in Church and State might provide opportunities for prophets who were usurping control of the various "energetic mystiques" to which they supposedly "gave witness" to seize control of the authoritative vacuum it guaranteed, is up for debate.

One last element that needs briefly to be mentioned before sum-marizing the *Zeitgeist* at the time of the Council and its aftermath

---

66 Maritain, *La Fin de Machiavellisme* (NV, 1942), p. 125; Wemhoff, *Op. cit.*, p. 518.

is the ever more vociferously expressed anger of the main enemies of Murray and the *Time/Luce* project in the 1950s and 1960s over the inaction of the Roman and American ecclesiastical establishment in the face of the Americanist onslaught. Chief among these opponents were the two most important American theologians of the pre-Murray era, Mgr. Joseph Fenton (1906–1969), editor of the *American Ecclesiastical Review,* and Fr. Francis J. Connell (1888–1967), the central founder of the Catholic Theological Society of America.

Fenton and Connell understood that what actually was being promoted through the call for a rejection of the union of Church and State and an embrace of the principle of religious liberty was a divinization of a materialist American attitude towards life.[67] They were furious with the incessant propaganda for these ideas in the American Press, and even more so with the way in which the *Time/ Life* position was devoured and then slavishly copied by Catholic newspapers in the United States as well. Nevertheless, what most irritated both men was the increasingly obvious fact that nothing could arouse the vast majority of bishops to do anything serious about the subversion of the Faith. Fenton's diaries in particular indicate his ever greater demoralization; a demoralization similar to that discussed earlier, based upon a conviction that there was no real belief in the concept of the Social Kingship of Christ in Rome and America alike, and this because of a practical acceptance of the precepts of the same old liberalism in its latest and only deceptively new clothing. He finally came to the conclusion that Rome was run "by vain and money-hungry cowards who are afraid of the manifest opponents of the true faith within the ranks"; men who were easily seduced and bullied by materialist society in all its forms.[68]

> The inner circle here lives on a diet of steady promotion. . . . They go to foreign lands as diplomats mixing with and living like the richest of the rich. They occupy archbishoprics or fill-in posts. Then they return and drive around Rome in super-sized chauffeur-driven German cars, and, at the top of the ladder there is always the big prize . . . Here are members of the Church

---

67 Wemhoff, *Op. cit.,* pp. 514–516.
68 Ibid., p. 625; also pp. 191, 245, 247,418, 425, 493–494, 514–516, 607, 685–686.

who are obviously in a state of mortal sin. Some of them do not believe Our Lord's message at all . . . What nonsense!

In short, Fenton and Connell felt that the Blitzkrieg on behalf of a "free Church in a free State" providing a Catholic future brighter than any past was resulting in an enslavement of the authorities of the Mystical Body of Christ to exactly that hunt for purely material benefits that the illegitimate powers *really* guiding life in a pluralist system defined as both paramount and "spiritual." Supporters of Catholic renewal in the early nineteenth century would have understood what was happening. The freedom of the Church and Catholics was being subverted, and the pathway to true liberty and human dignity obscured by the *Zeitgeist*.

By the time the Council was called and met, pressure for a discussion of "religious liberty" was very strong indeed. This pressure can be divided into three parts—Communitarian Personalist, Integral Humanist and Americanist—and the greatest of these was the Americanist. That immense Americanist pressure was to be backed at the Council by a *Time/Life* press campaign of staggering consistency. Correspondents like Robert Blair Kaiser and Michael Novak were urged to take sides in this monumental battle of the "good guys" versus the "bad guys," with the good guys—Personalists, Americanists, Palingenesists, and Modernists in general+—rewarded with adulation not just in print but also through triumphal speaking tours of American universities. They were aided in their lobbying activities by inside information leaked through *periti* breaking conciliar rules of secrecy, and, to Fenton and Connell's horror, by the ever more obvious collaboration of the Catholic Press at home and the American bishops present at the Council itself.[69]

This meant that whatever the text of *Dignitatis Humanae* itself eventually said, it was the "rising expectations" of a *Zeitgeist* shaped by well-funded and self-proclaimed prophetic forces interpreting the "signs of the times" outside the Council—expectations to which Bishop Emile-Joseph de Smedt made passionate reference in pleading for a swift completion of work on the religious liberty decree—that would dictate what it was *permitted* to mean. It was the servants of the *Zeigeist* who would mobilize "the spirit of

---

69   Ibid., pp. 659–901.

Vatican Two"—a favorite Novak phrase—in righteous opposition even to the most obvious words of the Council's clearest documents, not to speak of its more ambiguous ones. And it was this *Zeitgeist* to which Church authorities with eyes and ears open to the "signs of the times" would submit again and again in the future.[70]

All this was totally predictable. Playing carelessly with the word "liberty," of whose *Catholic* sense very few "sensitive," "dignified" modern men possessed any inkling whatsoever, was like riding on the back of a monster. One needed only to consult the evidence from Act One of our drama to have an appreciation of what would happen by mounting this beast. But such rational consultation, under the "freedom" allowed by the "signs of the times" interpreted by those prophetic spirits awakening Catholics to their full dignity in a totally new stage in human history, was strictly prohibited. And the result was that the predictable did indeed come to pass.

Opening the Church to liberalism's innate tendency to treat social authority as dangerously suspect worked first of all to break down the authority and morale of the old Roman Curia, turning real power to implement the Council's decrees over to commissions, study groups and journals dominated by those possessing the requisite spirit. Under these circumstances, *any* strong-willed forces with a clear agenda gained a tremendous advantage in taking control of a Church apparatus left bereft of legitimate authorities.

Equation of the principles of the *Zeitgeist* with those of Christianity itself in the giddy atmosphere of "joy" and "hope" characterizing the end and immediate wake of the Council gave all of those forces which Maritain deemed eager to enter into a "dialogue" with Catholics a chance to do exactly what those "dialoguing" with the faithful did in 1848: demand a Catholic surrender on whatever issue was of deepest concern to them as the sole means of proving the Church's good will. The Integral Humanist project lacked a sufficient number of non-Catholic individuals prepared to respect believers' "personhood," and believers were easily cowed by their opponents' all too familiar strength of will. The reader will remember that it was precisely this sort of problem that *La Civiltà Cattolica* sought to address in that call for greater Catholic clarity that Montalembert labeled as hopelessly "intransigent."

---

70   Ibid., pp. 726–729, 797–798.

Meanwhile, the Communitarian Personalist approach bared its teeth. Bishops and episcopal conferences that failed to respond to the "teaching" of the energetic local community were quickly condemned. Other corporate institutions, reduced by pluralism and personalism to being mere channels for "mystiques" instead of truly authoritative societies, came to understand that they could not perfect the "natural messages" they nurtured on their own steam alone. They had to be guided by the "witness" provided through prophetic, elitist activists. The spiritual superiority of these witnesses was in turn made manifest by their abandonment of traditional Catholic teaching and their willful proclamation of its latest "reborn" lessons.

The formerly Catholic social movements of Europe and Latin America were now expected to continue their labors only on the basis of perfecting "natural values" that could be shared by believers and non-believers alike. Distinctly Catholic elements were not to be allowed to interfere with the development of social action in Africa and Asia where they had had little or no influence before, lest they somehow distort a Seed of the Logos in the process of development. Popular forces that dared to resist the abandonment of Catholic ideas or contest the shape that social action was taking had to have their consciousness raised in base communities and encounter groups by palingenesist guides appealing to the "spirit of the Council." How else could those trapped in the past come to know what God wished, and what their own deeper aspirations really were?

Disastrous is the only word that can be applied to the post-conciliar consequences of this new "evangelization." Insofar as there was an unprejudiced dive into the vital, active milieu in which the spirit of Christ was supposedly taught, this permitted no contact with the Christ of history outside and above it. The objective reality of the Incarnate God-Man was thus ultimately called into question, with the very concept actually being identified as merely a "western" understanding of the work of "the Spirit" in human life. Catholicism was indeed left spiritually "barren in the face of a Ramakrishna," as Maritain, much too wedded to his Aquinas to go the whole Mennaisian personalist route, had predicted it would be.[71]

---

71 Hellman, *Emmanuel Mounier*, p. 42.

"*Aggiornamento*" means getting the Church of 1965 up to where the US Constitution was in 1789," Murray had happily explained.[72] If this judgment was accurate, as the masters of the *Zeitgeist* were determined that it was to be—and as Pope Benedict XVI, speaking in 2005, apparently concurred[73]—then there was no surprise that the American Catholic experience after the Council would parallel that of the country's as a whole. This meant that if anything in pre-existing Catholic theology and the rational philosophy traditionally utilized in union with it stood in opposition to the American Way, it was these discordant theological and philosophical elements that had to disappear. The Council's "clearer understanding of ecclesiology" was indeed called upon to justify such a surrender. A pilgrim Church's learning process had to be carried to its obvious conclusions, as, bit by bit, the deeper spirituality of the American experience taught her what Christ really expected from her: a structural democratization favorable to baptizing as Catholic the dictates of individual "free consciences"; and a condemnation of the use of coercive social authority of any sort, even that of purely internal impact on the faithful and devoid of physical penalties, as offensive to human dignity.

Both the Catholic Church and her Christianization of the world at large thus came to be guided by supposedly Christ-like, but actually John Locke-shaped individual consciences; individual consciences whose "liberation" was proven by their slavish repetition of the demands of the latest willful interpretation or competing interpretations of the will of the willful Founding Fathers. And as believers' rational abilities deteriorated, the "obvious, common-sense dictates" of the natural law disappeared with them, all of these now seen as nothing other than private religious options rejected by large numbers of sensitive modern men with a deeper awareness of their individual dignity; discarded because unacceptable to the consensus needed to maintain public order. The drab, pragmatic, utilitarian and downright silly crochets of an America that was now the Master of the Universe became the only "spiritual" elements that the individual on his way to his full dignity as a "person" was allowed to take seriously in the course of his daily life. "Evangelization" of the social order under these circumstances became a code

---

72   Wemhoff, *Op. cit.*
73   Ibid., pp. 900–901.

word for a conscious, determined burial in fallen natural desires and perceptions. These *might* have been lifted up to God, had the tools for accomplishing that goal not been rejected, and an opening not been given instead to all the gross, banal and frequently inane fantasies to which human beings always feel their deepest pull.

No willful assertion of spiritual superiority could save those prophets attempting to "witness" to such a false spiritualization from a depressing fall to earth along with the "vital energies" closest to their hearts. Hence, the once deeply pious Fr. Dillard ended by concluding that his work in the factory was more import-ant than his Mass, and, indeed, that the machine on which he labored itself actually had a soul.[74] Similarly, Mounier's Ascent of Mount Carmel led him to jettison prayer for psychoanalysis. Meanwhile, the *Monde* milieu of Beuve-Mery helped mightily to build a technocratic Europe which is now marked by the same bland, materialist "diversity" of the American pluralist circus it so readily condemned at the end of the Second World War.

Murray's own "spiritual" trajectory could serve as a key to the whole downward spiral of American society. Already before the Council's end, he began to reject a Catholic right to intervene in the public square by means of verbal condemnations and economic boycotts of indecent films and literature. Any open Catholic oppo-sition to socially divisive issues such as birth control and abortion stood next in line for stigmatization. Daily contact with LSD started to look to Murray as though it might provide a definitive pathway to true sanctification. Both he and Clare Booth Luce occasionally took the drug with the blessing of an intimate friend and spiritualist guru, Gerald Heard, who not surprisingly lamented the nefarious influence of morality on business freedom and saw homosexuality as a sign of creative evolutionary development.[75]

And yet despite his descent into 1960s madness, Murray still felt his undegenerated religious and philosophical tendencies working upon him. Hence, he anxiously admitted the swift dissolution of that common understanding of the natural law which he once argued would be sufficient for preservation of a moral social order. "The thing we have not yet proved in the United States," he said in 1966 shortly before his death, "is that the social consensus, as

---

74 Poulat, *Op. cit.*, p. 327; Hellman, *Mounier*, pp.190–193, 255.
75 Wemhoff, *Op. cit.*, pp. 483–491, 535, 537–549, 858–895.

at least moral, can be maintained in the absence of religious unity, in the presence of radical divisions. There are signs that the consensus is eroding."[76] But he was wrong. The underlying American pluralist consensus was stronger than ever. The American Church was linked more closely to the American State and society than ever before in her demonstration of a willingness to bless whatever it was that the strongest forces controlling them all demanded that she accept and proclaim as integral to the Catholic Tradition.

Numerous statements coming from the Vatican during the reigns of Pope John Paul II and Benedict XVI attempted to explain the Council's "true meaning" on a variety of subjects, including both religious liberty as well as the Church's relationship with the State and outside world in general. All these sought to correct the horrible consequences for the Social Kingship of Christ stemming from the victory of the pluralist and personalist mentalities, making it clear that concern for "public order" could never be permitted to justify public and individual immorality. Nevertheless, the stigma attached to statements suggesting possible recourse to the use of any form of social authority in the life of "free, dignified, individual modern man," has rendered such valuable theological corrections utterly meaningless in practice. They are not backed up by serious consistent action.

How could they be? Accusations of everything from "opposition to the will of the Holy Spirit" to "cultivation of innate fascist sympathies" regularly bring closure not just upon effective action but coherent argument as well. And that coherent argument never seems to emerge. The root refusal to critique the pluralist vision of political and social life and to make an effort to understand whence it came remains painfully apparent. Fenton and Connell themselves do not appear to have understood the origins of the Americanist problem in the mesh of forces giving birth to the Glorious Revolution and the Whig interpretation of man and society. Nor could they bring themselves to admit that a Catholic order would alter the American Way of Life. Contemporary popes, bishops, priests and laity show almost no knowledge of Act One or Act Two of the drama outlined above. A mere expression of concern for gaining that knowledge would itself be a crime of *lèse majesté* against the glories of the contemporary *Zeitgeist*.

---

76   Ibid., p. 869.

Without the root problems being tackled, the tree that grows therefrom cannot be destroyed. That tree, once again, supports a society in which Church and State have never been more united in their common commitment to allow fallen nature to have its way against the dictates of Faith and Reason. Both illustrate a conscious or unconscious subservience to "the Promethean lust for material power that serves as the deepest common drive behind all modern Western cultures."[77] Neither the Church nor individual Catholic believers nesting in this tree possess true Christian freedom.

Yes, the Church is still a "sign of contradiction," but, unfortunately, contradiction of her own divine character and mission, which has become enslaved in a much deeper and complete sense than when abused by sacred monarchies still nurturing at least some flicker of Faith. A false tradition has become *the* Tradition. As Louis Veuillot indicated during Act One of our religious liberty drama, this false tradition, destructive of all Church and individual Catholic freedom, seeks irrationally to silence Christ's full message. Our true liberation can never come by following its pragmatic guidelines, defined in such a way as to fix a blindfold permanently over our own eyes. It can only be effected through a return to a full knowledge of Christ and the demands of His Social Kingship. All borrowed armor chokes us. [78]

> [F]erocious pride is correctly the genius of the Revolution; it has established a control in the world which pleases reason out of the struggle. It has a horror of reason, it gags it, it hunts it, and if it can kill it, it kills it. Prove to it the divinity of Christianity, its intellectual and philosophical reality, its historical reality, its moral and social reality: it wants none of it. That is its reason, and it is the strongest. It has placed a blindfold of impenetrable sophisms on the face of European civilization. It cannot see the heavens, nor hear the thunder.
>
> The right tactic for us is to be visibly and always what we are, nothing more, nothing less. We defend a citadel that cannot be taken except when the garrison itself brings in the enemy. Combating with our own arms, we only receive minor wounds. All borrowed armor troubles us and often chokes us.

---

77 R. Gawthrop, *Op. cit.*, p. 284.
78 L. Veuillot, *Mélanges, Oeuvres completes* (Paris, iii series, 1933) x, 45–46; v, 276.

33

Visions of Western and European Order†

HIGHWAYS FROM
CHRISTENDOM TO NOWHERE

"BELGIUM IS A KINGDOM; NOT A ROAD." IT was with that phrase, whether true or apocryphal, that King Albert I (1909–1934) is popularly said to have responded to the German request to cross his country to begin the attack on France in 1914. If accurately reported, what the king was expressing was a commitment to Belgium as a substantive reality and not a passageway to satisfaction of another nation's purposes. And Albert did, in fact, oppose the well-sculpted pre-war battle plan, with four years of bitter fighting and civilian suffering as the price his country paid for holding out against it.

Anyone who might wish to speak of the West as a "kingdom"; that is to say as a *substantive reality*, and seek to rally its troops against those attempting to use it as a mere "road" has a much harder task ahead of him than a monarch who had to mobilize normally very badly divided French- and Flemish-speaking Belgians. For the dominant naturalist vision of the West, just as that of Europe before it—not to speak of the contemporary pluralist world's obsession with a "global society"—is an empty one. It precisely *does* identify a "road" rather than a "kingdom," and one that leads to a terrible dead end. And it constructs this highway to nowhere because the seemingly exalted picture of a civilized international order that it paints has no connection other than a manipulative rhetorical one with the sole force that can prevent it from being what it actually is: a "cover story" for ideological or individual wills on the road to a self-destructive victory.

Catholicism, which once inspired and at least partially realized a truly international *res publica cristiana*, is the sole salvific force that can still give to Europe and the West—not to speak of the East

---

† A talk presented in Mexico (April 2016).

or "global society" as a whole—the ability to create and sustain a substantive civilization of flesh, blood and spirit. For attempts to build any of these upon a conscious rejection of Christ render all their natural building blocks unnatural, destroying the very people who initially seem to benefit from this secularizing labor along with those they unmistakably oppress as they go about their work. Only a Catholic order, with Christ as its King, can confidently adopt the motto "all that which is natural is ours," constructing ever more complex societies while cherishing and perfecting all of their contributing elements. Our greatest task as contemporary Catholics is to understand that the historical perversion of this Christian stimulus to rise above parochialism while saving all that is "particular" has been a long-term enterprise. Believers themselves have often accepted the claims of this perversion, generally without even realizing that they have been seduced by them.

Martin Luther occupies a crucial role in this project of hermetically sealing off nature and the societies through which nature's potential is developed from their necessary expansion, correction and transformation in Christ, thereby opening up the highway from Christendom to a willful, self-destructive nowhere. Nevertheless, he could not have played his part so well had others not already cleared the construction site on which he worked for some centuries before him. Allow me to cite the great English Church historian Philip Hughes to indicate broadly what I mean, and then to suggest a clarification that I believe is useful for grasping the particular importance of Luther's appearance on the scene:[1]

All those anti-intellectualist, anti-institutional forces that had plagued and hindered the medieval Church for centuries, whose chronic maleficent activity had, in fact, been the main cause why— as we are often tempted to say—so little was done effectively to maintain a generally higher standard of Christian life; all the forces that were the chronic distraction of the medieval papacy, were now stabilized, institutionalized in the new reformed Christian Church. Enthronement of the will as the supreme human faculty; hostility to the activity of the intelligence in spiritual matters and in doctrine; the ideal of a Christian perfection that is independent of sacraments and independent of the authoritative teaching

---

[1] P. Hughes, *A History of the Church*, Sheed & Ward, 1949, III, 529.

of clerics; of sanctity attainable through one's own self-sufficing spiritual activities; denial of the truth that Christianity, like man, is a social thing; all the crude, backwoods, obscurantist theories bred of the degrading pride that comes with chosen ignorance, the pride of men ignorant because unable to be wise except through the wisdom of others, now have their fling. Luther's own special contribution—over and above the key doctrines that set all this mischief loose—is the notion of life as radically evil.

It is this last phrase of Hughes that needs a slight elaboration. Yes, Luther did dramatically emphasize the notion of life as radically evil, but he was certainly not the first westerner to do so. The Catharists had already introduced that concept to Europe by the eleventh and twelfth centuries. What Luther did was to present the principle of the total depravity of life as the product of Original Sin, thereby placing the evils of the world squarely on the shoulders of men rather than some gnostic monster. It was this more "conservative," "humble," sinful man-flaying, and seemingly Christian-like argument that guaranteed him a hearing from late medieval believers overwhelmed by the seemingly incurable evils around them but still convinced that Creation was the product of a supremely good God. It was this more conservative *disguise* that permitted the concept of total depravity to be effectively incarnated in Western Christendom.

Luther's *incarnation* of the pseudo-Christian vision of the total depravity of the children of Adam and Eve could not help but corrupt and destroy social institutions of all kinds, along with the natural building blocks they nurture and perfect. It had to do so, because its central practical effect is to give flesh and blood reality to that irrational individual willfulness which Hughes rightly describes as long festering in the West, opening the door to all of the anti-social consequences that inevitably flow therefrom.[2] We must explore the way this irrational, parochial willfulness functioned in an already ailing Christendom in order to clearly grasp the very old historical roots of supposedly excitingly new projects for transforming a substantive international order into an empty "Europe," "West" or "Global Society."

---

2   On Luther's "incarnation" of a "principle of independence," see L. Taparelli d'Azeglio, "Il Protestantesimo," Series 1, Volume 2, *La Civiltà Cattolica*, (1850), 260–284, 377–400.

A *Consilium de emendanda ecclesia,* presented by a group of cardinals to Pope Paul III in 1537 concerning the causes of the Protestant Reformation, pointed to the fact that all too worldly, politically-charged actions on the part of the Papacy played a central role in preparing the disaster, awakening a cynicism regarding the very possibility of that "transformation of all things in Christ" which was the essential *raison d'être* for the mainline Catholic reform movement of the High Middle Ages. St. Bernard of Clairvaux had warned of the dangers of such a degeneration long beforehand. In a work entitled *De Consideratione* (c. 1150), he lamented to his former pupil, now Pope Eugenius III, just how much the medieval reform movement, infiltrated by the wrong spirit, was already becoming a "Catholic" cover for a basically secularist enterprise. Even a brief examination of Rome's thirteenth century obsession with "fixing" the situation in southern Italy according to precisely the right political contours gives credence to the claim that Sicily was the graveyard of the medieval Papacy. Under these circumstances, an international Christendom meant to reflect the love of Christ easily lent itself to being criticized as a poisonous recipe for disturbance of the European social order. [3]

Hence, the need to have recourse to a proper, international "defender of the peace," identified by Marsilius of Padua (c. 1275– c.1342) in his book of that name as the Roman Emperor, whose claim to such a title was much more venerable than that of the Pope in the first place. Support for this truly serious guarantor of European order was also promoted by Marsilius' allies, which included the Nominalist philosopher William of Ockham (c. 1287–1347) and the mystical and millennial-minded Spiritual Franciscans, all of them embittered by the "worldly" actions of the Papacy as guides of Christendom. A student needs no more than a summary of the consequences flowing from the cooperation of such varied critics of late medieval Christendom to have both the pre-Lutheran preparation of Luther handed to him on a silver platter, as well

---

3   E. Gleason, *Gasparo Contarini: Venice, Rome, and Reform* (University of California, 1993), pp. 129–185; St. Bernard of Clairvaux, *Five Books on Consideration* (Cistercian Publications, 1976); Mayeur, J. M., ed., *Histoire du Christianisme* (Desclée, XIII Volumes, 1990–2002), V, 542–543, 627–633; VI, 575–583; Hughes, II, 389–406, III, 22–56; D. Waley, *The Italian City-Republics* (London & New York: Longman, 1988), pp. 145–156; W. Ullmann, *The Origins of the Great Schism* (Archon, 1967), pp. 251–278.

as all the building blocks for our more recently opened European and Western highway to nowhere.[4]

On the one hand, this alliance appeared to encourage a deeply religious concern for the majesty and rights of a God whose clear and simple will, supposedly grasped quite easily by the apostolic church, had been obscured by a subsequent rationalist, legalist, speculative theological and philosophical perversion of religion manipulated by impious popes and their minions. Moreover, it coupled this concern for a return to simple, apostolic purity with another highly traditional appeal: a call for intercession on behalf of God's thwarted will through the work of the pious Catholic Emperor.

On the other hand, the alliance in question eliminated from the intellectual and spiritual baggage of the Emperor everything that could identify the divine will in a manner that might require a change of the human will of the "defender of the peace," with speculative theology, philosophy and basic logic as the main victims; or even merely distinguish the divine will from the human will. The will of God thus became whatever its earthly agent decreed that it was, with no consideration of the broader judgments of Faith and Reason regarding the divine plan recorded through the ages.

Just to make matters more complicated for the budding modern world, the will of an Emperor that had become practically indistinguishable from the will of God was then itself said to be dependent upon other willful earthly forces. For appeal to the Imperial Will was justified with reference to an underlying grant of imperial authority emerging from "the Roman People." Furthermore, this "People" was itself shown to be "formed" to provide the desired imperial authorization through the work of the Emperor's advisors; men who were also stripped of theological, philosophical and logical blocks to the equation of their arbitrary judgment with God's clear and simple will.

Now the "Roman People" of 1324, or any other "People" throughout history for that matter, was a motley, disorganized force, and the contemporary imperial power itself generally a rather shaky factor in European politics, widely contested in its

4 Lagarde, G. de, *La Naissance de l'Esprit Laique au Declin du Moyen Age* (Nauwelaerts, Five Volumes, 1958), III, 61–357.

claims when it did actually gain strength. Moreover, the thinkers defending the Empire, rather irrationally and nostalgically enamored of a "universal international institution" that the ceaseless Nominalist attack on man's ability to conceive "universal principles" completely undermined, were also so critical of authorities lacking demonstrable physical power that one could hardly be surprised if their love affair might collapse as time demonstrated real imperial impotence.

Given such circumstances, it seems that identification of the "clear and simple will of God" inevitably had to fall into the hands of whatever earthly power happened to be the momentarily strongest, with the intellectual and spiritual forces opposed to the "speculative" Catholic vision allying themselves with this *force de la nature* to justify its tyranny and then "form" the "People" to understand that they wanted it and to accept it. This meant that insofar as concern for some sort of overriding Christian order remained vivid in believers' minds—and it did—the possessor of pure physical power, however parochial in his willfulness he might actually be, still had to be justified by the intellectual and spiritual members of a Triple Irrational Alliance as the international, God-friendly, *Defensor Pacis*. In short, in a world still touched by aspects of the Christian message, the thug and the intellectual word merchant ultimately needed one another to go about their willful work, so as to rationalize an irrational victory. But the results might not be exactly what either party fully wanted, and they might, in consequence, constantly be on the lookout for a better deal with changed partners.

It was this *practical* union of the thug and the irrational but seemingly Christian ideologue, unsuccessful before Luther's time, that was effectively *incarnated* through his Protestant Reformation. It came about because Luther's humanist inspired preaching— convinced of its apostolic purity, rhetorically charged, powerfully vulgarized, and backed intellectually by an anti-rational Nominalist philosophical training—immediately unleashed a tidal wave of totally logical deductions that he personally considered stark raving mad. This led him to impose his individual and rather conservative will on the revolutionary movement he had generated, rejecting the radical scriptural interpretations of his opponents, justifying the injury he was doing to the logic of his position with reference to the need to affirm "Gospel paradoxes." While indeed calling a halt to radical developments in the lands subject to his arbitrary religious will, he nevertheless continued to feed them by nourishing the willfulness that gave them birth, butchering the Bible he claimed to honor when its words ran counter to his own heretical principle, forcing scripture to say what it means on the basis of his own passionate ideological desires.[5]

But stymying the "enthusiasts, as he called the wild men, while protecting his own "limited" but always potentially explosive radicalism (i.e., his "conservatism") required the help of practical physical force. A Catholic Emperor was obviously of no value in this regard. The German princes, terrified by the momentary boost given to the otherwise weak imperial authority by Charles V's vast accumulation of territory, had to be cultivated instead. These were more than pleased to become what Luther called "necessity bishops," crushing the various radicals he detested, happily appropriating the lands of the Church he had abolished in exchange, but also ready to call halt to any of the reformer's projects that did not fit with their own now liberated, parochial, political willfulness. They became his *defensores pacis* in the common project of enforcing God's "clear and simple will," with thug and intellectual word merchant each tugging the other down directions they did not necessarily wish to go, and with the international imperial authority that the "conservative" Luther actually still respected torn to shreds in the process.

We can now much more effectively return to the question of the collapse of even the veneer of an international Christendom and what it is that was to take its place. That order was shaken not just through Luther and his princely protectors, but also through the variety of other thug-intellectual arrangements of more radical or conservative-but-radical-encouraging flavor flowing from the Protestant Reformation, all of them constantly on the lookout for a "better deal." And with the failure of the also heavily politicized Hapsburg effort to restore a Catholic unity by the latter part of the Thirty Years War, confirmed by the Treaty of Westphalia (1648), the final nail was hammered into medieval Christendom's coffin.

---

5   See Cameron, E., *The European Reformation* (Oxford, 1991), pp. 136–144; H. Jedin, ed., *History of the Church* (Seabury, Ten Volumes, 1980), V, 3–301.

Gottfried Wilhelm Leibniz (1646–1716) was prominent among honorable men who sought sincerely to find a way out of the religious-political disunity and parochialism contributing mightily to the intellectual reductionism they perceived to be gaining ground in their day. Given that the confessional division could not be overcome, but the longing for an international unity that had also existed under pre-Christian conditions remained, it is no surprise that many of them began to envisage its restoration on the purely secular foundations favored by the seventeenth- and eighteenth-century Enlightenment.[6]

Unfortunately, anyone seeking support for a rational international order based on these foundations was to be sorely deceived. For the so-called Age of Reason was one that actually worked to humble and subject the rational mind to passion. Radical in its earliest formulation, like the Protestant Reformation, with its initial destructive teaching on total depravity, the Enlightenment also witnessed a widespread, "conservative," Luther-like recoiling from open embrace of its revolutionary consequences. But a two-fold and unfortunate development completed the analogy with the previous Lutheran model. For, in providing a seemingly more traditional and less threatening framework for nurturing the principles that it claimed to reject, the Moderate Enlightenment allowed their logical developments peacefully to mature under its aegis, gradually radicalizing its own intellectually vulnerable "conservative" camp. Nevertheless, the political and social forces with which the moderates were allied exercised their own powerful tug, pulling the application of *both* conservative *and* more radical ideas away from where their principled supporters might wish them to go.

What this all meant for international order was nothing other than the confirmation, in one way or another, of the dominion of the by now familiar thug and intellectual alliance, filled with tensions due to the pull of the partners towards their different favored goals, and their often disgruntled search for a "better deal," when the work they *really* wanted done was not accomplished. In other words, the hunt for international order on secularized grounds was

---

6   P. Riley, ed., *Leibniz: Political Writings* (Cambridge, 1972); M. Greengrass, *Christendom Destroyed: Europe, 1517–1648* (Penguin, 2014); J. Israel, *Democratic Enlightenment* (Oxford, 2012).

to produce a tug of war between two sorts of passionate, willful, irrational men: those of the mind on the one hand and those commanding the political and social "flesh" of life on the other, with the former providing the intellectual cover hiding the brutal struggle behind the scenes, and with both ready to change partners for a "better deal" on their joint road to materialist self-destruction.

Let us explore this situation just a bit more before bringing our discussion down to our own time, beginning with the influence of Baruch Spinoza (1632-1677), the real father of what historians call the Radical Enlightenment. Due to their highly subversive character, Spinoza's ideas had to be at first passed down mostly in disguised and often rather private ways. This involved the work of men like Pierre Bayle (1647–1706) with his *Critical Dictionary*, the Abbé St. Pierre (1658–1743), founder of the highly influential Entresol Club during the Orléan Regency in France (1715–1723), and Denis Diderot (1713–1784), the chief editor of the Encyclopedia.[7]

For the atheist and materialist Spinoza, a grant of *droit de cité* to the passions generated by the eternal machine of nature in all of us without exception was a "rational" necessity. In union with the thought of Thomas Hobbes (1588–1679), this underlined at one and the same time the common character of individual human machine parts everywhere.

Spinoza and his followers, unlike Hobbes, generally believed that the way to prevent one person's passions from dominating those of his fellow men was by democratically unleashing all of them, a liberation that nature's machine would inevitably cause to work for the common good. Democratic though this vision was, its recognition of the enormity of the labor required to fulfill it, and especially the need to destroy the political impact of passionate "Christian" men who had successfully encouraged belief in their non-existent God to gain power over others, demanded wariness of the gullible mob. That mob was in need of a rigorous "re-education" to avoid succumbing to proven Christian guile. As men the globe over marched to their liberation, the states that re-educated them had to crush self-interested religious trickery,

---

7 N. Childs, *A Political Academy in Paris 1724–1731: The Entresol and Its Members. Studies on Voltaire and the Eighteenth Century* (Voltaire Foundation, 2000); J. Israel, Op. cit. and *Radical Enlightenment* (Oxford, 2001), pp. 331–341, 573–574; *Enlightenment Contested* (Oxford, 2006), pp. 781–793.

with obedience to such governments' commands being treated as the highest moral good. As some of the central British, Dutch and French Huguenot members of the so-called Hague Coterie that arranged for publication of pro-Spinoza books such as *The Three Imposters* argued, the purely natural and democratic state, whose enormous powers were designed to break down obstacles to the freedom of all individuals, ought to be worshipped by means of a secular and liturgically rich civil religion, the historical precedents for which could be found in Druidic societies.[8] Analogous arguments regarding the sacred democratic state were provided by Jean-Jacques Rousseau (1712–1778) and were put into practice in the civil ceremonies organized by Maximilian Robespierre (1758–1794) and Louis Antoine de St. Just (1767–1794) during the Revolution.[9] In short, one had to create an absolute state power and the apparatchiks needed to employ it, with both guided by prophetic priest-like intellects conscious of what must be destroyed and what must be encouraged in order for the machine of nature to triumph. And though historical circumstances might cause this enterprise to begin in the Dutch Republic or revolutionary France, the universality of its underlying principles made completely understandable an Anacharsis Cloots' (1755-1794) discussion of its European and worldwide implications in his *Bases Constitutionnelles de la République du Genre Humain.*[10]

Spinoza's thoroughgoing, materialist mechanism was too horrifying for contemporary Europeans generally to accept. Men like Robert Boyle (1627–1691), John Locke (1632–1704), the members of the Royal Society of London and Isaac Newton (1642–1727), its most famous President, reacted vigorously against it. They sought to preserve the idea of a Creator God but encouraged pious men and women to worship this God in a "truly Christian" and "rational" fashion. Such piety entailed a backing away from divisive and unproductive doctrinal disputes as well as philosophical "system building," and then seeing and doing the divine will by exploiting

8   Margaret Jacob, *The Radical Enlightenment* (Cornerstone, 2006), 183–222 and *passim*; J. Billington, *Fire in the Minds of Men* (Basic Books), pp. 52–123.
9   C. Blum, *Rousseau and the Republic of Virtue* (Cornell, 1986); J. Billington, *Op. cit.*, pp. 52–123; S. Schama, *Citizens* (Knopf, 1989), pp. 827–836.
10   A. Baillot y A. Yuva, eds., *France-Allemagne: Figures de l'Intellectuel, Entre Révolution et Reaction, 1780–1848* (Septentrion, 2014), p. 187; J. Israel, *Democratic Enlightenment, passim.*

the machine of nature that the Almighty had created and kept in existence. Such work, they argued, would inevitably be charitable in character, bringing benefit to everyone, its successes demonstrating God's blessing upon it, unlike the divisive and "idle speculation" of both doctrinal fanatics and the Spinozists.[11]

Eighteenth century "conservatives" of the Newton-Locke school tried to work within the existing, familiar order of things as much as they could. After the radical interval of the French Revolution, their project was carried on by nineteenth century liberalism—particularly that "conservative" liberalism of the post-1848 era, terrified as this was by the socialist manifestation of Radical Enlightenment thought in action. This conservative liberalism continues to exercise an enormous impact today. And it was this manifestation of the Moderate Enlightenment with its outwardly "pious" face that many Roman Catholics from the top on down have been tempted to accept as the only alternative to radical atheism since Newton's so called "physico-theological" approach to nature was first known.[12]

But the Moderate Enlightenment, "conservative," or "conservative liberal" project, God- and Reason- friendly as many of its supporters may sincerely want to be, cannot free itself from its fundamental radical baggage. It cannot have its cake and eat it too. In effect, it promotes a perfunctory Sunday worship of a God it actually finds and adores on a day-to-day basis through its work with the natural machine it claims that He created, reinterpreting everything from Christian miracles to morality with reference to its mechanical twists and turns; seeing God's "clear and simple" will in whatever successes men obtain through manipulating it.

Moreover, its dominant Locke-inspired teaching understands the practical working of that machine to be founded purely upon individuals responding to nothing other than the material stimuli upon them, ultimately humbling "Reason" to the role of slave to their impact, though without wanting to admit this openly lest it sound too Spinoza-like and therefore "ungodly." Locke Land understands the individual good to be gained through society's retreat from hindrance to the accumulation of that property which

11   J. Israel, *Enlightenment Contested*, pp. 201–222.
12   J. Israel, *Enlightenment Contested*, pp. 344–405, 700–793, *Democratic Enlightenment*, pp. 326–348, 374–410.

is needed to satisfy his material needs and perfect himself as a person. It then sees the common good guaranteed by nothing other than Bernard Mandeville's (1670–1733) Spinoza-like clash of passions as they work inevitably to achieve harmony. It envisages social problems being resolved through "sensible" agreements of "sense-driven," property-owning strong men, who "know" that "true Christianity" and "solid Reason" would be harmed if anyone dared to be divisive enough to evoke doctrinal concerns or non-mechanical, Socratic Philosophy to question the whole basis of the Moderate Enlightenment approach to securing the Triumph of the Will.

In short, a "God-fearing" world had to be created by sweeping everything out of the passionate individual's path as he used the machine of nature to gain property and success through its power. And although work towards this end might begin in a country like England or the United States, its principles were universal and potentially applicable to Europe, the West, or the Globe in its entirety. But wherever this vision was implemented, the outcome was to be the same: the victory of one or the other version of the familiar thug-intellectual alliance noted above; and perhaps to satisfy even more radical individual passions than those dreamed possible by the purely property hungry empiricists originally promoting it. All this, with the aid of believing Roman Catholics who thought that failure to accept the "moderate" approach meant falling into the hands of atheism.[13]

Two final and very important points must be stressed. When anyone foolish enough to do so brings serious, doctrinal, Roman Catholic Christianity and the rational thought allied with it through the ages to bear against the basic Enlightenment commitment to the machine of nature and the machine-like passions guiding it, the moderate springs into action alongside his radical counterpart to "crush the infamous thing." Clear and simple Godliness and Reason in the Enlightenment mode cannot ever include Roman Catholic Godliness and Socratic Reason. The most significant contemporary secular historians of the Enlightenment have discussed how this "no enemies to the Left" policy has repeatedly functioned, with the budding Freemasonic movement in the late seventeenth and

---

13   Sobre Mandeville, Locke, and l'Illustration Católica, J. Israel, *Radical Enlightenment*, pp. 477–627; *Enlightenment Contested*, pp. 344–405, 700–793, and *passim*; *Democratic Enlightenment*, pp. 326–348, 374–410.

eighteenth centuries offering a major example thereof. Nevertheless, the irrational "wills" unleashed by the movement, both ideological and material, operating through a divinized state or a society open to property- and passion-driven individuals, cooperate though they might against a common enemy, differ, clash and betray one another to achieve their particular goals.[14]

This is not the place to enumerate all the plans for some type of supra-national European order that emerged in the eighteenth, nineteenth and twentieth centuries. Some of these were still religious in character; Pietist, millenarian or Catholic in inspiration, about which more in a moment. Many of them were motivated by serious secular recognition of a growing economic interdependence, common interests vis-à-vis outside powers such as the United States or an "Asiatic" Russia, and the very real danger of European self-destruction due to the power of modern weaponry.

Moreover, it is undeniable that idealists honestly committed to naturalist Enlightenment concepts sincerely believed that the liberating influences of free trade, technocratic application of modern scientific knowledge, universal national self-determination, or democratic socialism would lead to a regeneration of the various peoples of Europe inevitably involving their natural union. And recognition of a need "to abandon nationalism to take one's place in the European community with honor," because a "new Europe of solidarity and co-operation among all its people will find rapidly increasing prosperity once national economic boundaries are removed," something that "the countries of Europe are too small to guarantee" became more and more common as the twentieth century proceeded.[15]

How such plans transformed into a focus on the West instead of Europe is primarily due to two factors, one of which is the colonial movement of the nineteenth and early twentieth centuries. Yes, it is true that Europe was the chief catalyst for this development. But certainly from the standpoint of countries like Japan, and in its own quite distinct way, Latin America, colonialism and its

---

14   J. Rao, *Removing the Blindfold* (Angelus Press, 2014), pp. 33–133, 156–177.
15   Jean Monnet, in A. Ertl, *Toward an Understanding of Europe* (Universal Publishers, 2008), p. 75; Mark Mazower, *Dark Continent: Europe's Twentieth Century* (Knopf, 1998); H. C. Chopra, *DeGaulle and European Unity* (Abhinav, 1974), pp. 4–6.

consequences had to be expanded to include the United States as well. The "National Doctors" that the government of the Meiji Restoration sent out after 1867 to learn what needed to be done to survive in the modern world went to "the West" in general, studying at American and European universities. Such a readjustment of "us" and "them" was also deemed necessary by colonialists like Cecil Rhodes, more than tinged with racial thought, whose vision of the defense of civilization actually excluded almost all of Europe while demanding the participation of America in the march to progress the globe over.[16]

Secondly, more importantly, and once again speaking now purely on the "idealistic" plane, the perception on the part of many educated Americans of a common, God-friendly Moderate Enlightenment intellectual and cultural heritage, coupled together with an awareness both of the dangers that threatened its survival and progress as well as the ever-growing strength of the United States as its chief defender, led to an emphasis upon the concept of "the West" as opposed to that of "Europe." This played its role in Wilson's understanding of America's mission in Europe in World War One and the need for a permanent League of Nations afterwards. It served as the framework for the basic instruction of students in the United States from the 1920s onwards: an approach that underlined "Western History" with the omnipresence that "Global History" now enjoys. America as Europe's partner in an expanded vision of "the West" celebrating a "common intellectual and political heritage" in a way that could even include non-European nations like Japan became still more intense with the exclusion from the club of a powerful "Asiatic Russia" committed to a godless Radical Enlightenment in the form of Communism.

Popularization of the theme of "the West" as a cultural entity encompassing everything from Plato to NATO, all understood in its conservative, secularist, but somehow God-friendly mode, with the United States as the shield of the common heritage, can be seen in the work of American journalists from Walter Lippmann

16   A. Bonnet, *The Idea of the West* (Palgrave, 2004), R. Hancock, *America, the West, and Liberal Education* (Rowman & Littlefield, 1999); I. Nish, *The Iwakura Mission to America and Europe: A New Assessment* (Routledge, 2008); P. Kramer, "Empires, Exceptions, and Anglo-Saxons: Race and Rule between the British and United States Empires, 1880–1910", *The Journal of American History* (Vol. 88, No. 4, March, 2002), pp. 1315–1353.

(1889–1974) to Clarence Streit (1896–1968) to Henry Luce (1898–1967). One finds in the arguments of the latter in particular a Moderate Enlightenment-inspired insistence that the American-guided West is the sole defense against godless radicalism, and that any divisive, doctrinal or rational argument standing in America's way plays the godless radical game to the detriment of "true Christianity" and "charity" towards all men. This vision obviously had its enthusiastic supporters on the other side of the pond, devastated by two world wars, desperately longing for a noble United States to protect it from its woes, and seemingly gaining American support for European union in the process. That it gained American and significant European *Catholic* support is also obvious, and that such support could actually serve as a "cover story" for secularization had already been made clear by St. Bernard long, long ago. [17]

Both religious and secular sincerity have never been lacking in many of those trying to build Europe and the West out of a civilization in which certain long festering ills were incarnated by Luther and passed down to us by the naturalism of the seventeenth and eighteenth centuries in a more intensified form. It is not such people's personal integrity that is in question, but their wisdom; their failure to perceive the historical and sociological reality of the intellectual-thug alliance and their susceptibility to its seductive propaganda, especially when accompanied by conservative, Moderate Enlightenment assurances of "friendliness" to both Religion and Nature.

Taparelli d'Azeglio, S. J. (1793–1862), the most significant of the founding editors of the Jesuit journal, *La Civiltà Cattolica*, is important in consult in this regard. He was perhaps the most prominent of those Catholics of his day who were convinced that Europe had to come to terms with practical realities *incarnating* its need for a common international order soon to encompass the entire globe. Not only did he present a very clear picture of a growing European and global economic and political union that could only guarantee

---

17   P. den Boer, P. Bugge, eds., *The History of the Idea of Europe* (Routledge, 1995); R. Bavaj, "'The West': A Conceptual Exploration," *European History Online / Europäische Geschichte Online* (2011); A. Hartmann, *A War for the Soul of America: A History of the Culture Wars* (University of Chicago, 2015); K. Weisbrode, *The Atlantic Century* (Da Capo, 2009); D. Gress, *From Plato to NATO* (Free Press, 2004); J. Rao, "Le Mirage Américain," in *Église et Politique: Changer de Paradigme*, ed. Bernard Dumont (Artege, 2013).

respect for the particular nations entering into it under the umbrella of Christ as their King; the Catholic motto, in effect, being *De Uno, Plures* rather than *E Pluribus Unum*. Alongside Georges de la Garde, through his book, *La naissance de l'Esprit Laique au Declin du Moyen Age*, he was also the thinker who opened my own eyes to the entire historical argument that I have outlined here:

• Luther as the "conservative" agent for incarnating the long-emerging intellectual-thug alliance with its liberation of willful, arbitrary passion;

• The greater efficiency of the secularist but "conservative" Moderate Enlightenment for making what guarantees the reign of force acceptable to traditionally minded men, "God-fearing" Catholics included;

• The way in which both of these "conservative" historical forces, born themselves of a radical vision, actually aid and abet the logic of the radicalism they claim to dispel;

• Their turning of substantive nations and international orders, whether European, Western or Global, into mere "roads" for the satisfaction of irrational, arbitrary intellectual or physical passions, either through the power of a divinized state and its apparatchiks or unchained individuals in societies bereft of authorities capable of controlling them;

• The internal battling of intellectuals and thugs among themselves and with their partners, and their willingness to change allies at the drop of the opportunistic hat;

• Conservative condemnation of doctrinal and rational objections to their program as nothing but fruitless and divisive speculation serviceable only to the godless, the unsuccessful and the uncharitable;

• The utter self-destructiveness of this entire, reductionist, mental and material justification of the triumph of the strongest wills billed as the sole protector of God and/or Nature.[18]

Taparelli's articles in *La Civiltà Cattolica* provide many illustrations of the thuggish irrational force triumphing under the intellectual "cover stories" of nation- and Europe-building, with the partners in the enterprise changing and destroying one another when they prove no longer useful to their desires. It is no surprise to him that

---

18   See J. Rao, *Removing the Blindfold*, pp. 33–133, 156–177; *Black Legends and the Light of the World* (Remnant Press, 2012), 220–233.

more powerful proponents of universal liberation would guillotine an unprotected ideologue like Anacharsis Cloots. Nor that Napoleon, while in exile, depicted his appalling career of armed mayhem as a struggle for a unified Europe of free nations open to both past and future, thereby providing a justification for future military agents of Order and Progress. Nor that a Holy Alliance and a Concert of Europe, fueled by a mindless mystical syncretism and a concern for "legitimacy," hypocritically ignored these whenever the political demands of the victorious powers of Russia, Austria, Prussia and England require. Nor that democratic nationalists, convinced that a united "Young Europe" built out of purified nation-states, in fact destroyed their peoples' culture, replacing it either with a passion-driven lust for political power and racial cleansing or the creation of yet another Lockean land of liberal individualism unconcerned for internal or international social justice.[19]

Taparelli's ally in this exposé was the French journalist and literary critic Louis Veuillot (1818–1883). Veuillot was equally convinced that those who were pursuing a naturalist, secularist program in a moderate and outwardly God-friendly fashion, claiming that failure to approve their labors through divisive doctrinal criticism merely aids the cause of the radicals, were providing the most effective cover story for a *global* triumph of the will. In an article entitled "Le Canon Rayé," published in 1859, he insisted that the alliance of raw physical power—a thuggery benefiting arrogant nations and anti-social money men—with the ideological drive for a naturalist "re-education" of the population guided by governments and apparatchiks was working towards the establishment of a universal state. This, he felt would ultimately be headed by a charismatic dictator, whose power would rest upon a bureaucratic elite skilled in techniques of manipulation, but catering to individual passions:[20]

> Everywhere the conqueror will find one thing, everywhere the same, the only thing that war and the Revolution will nowhere have overturned: bureaucracy. Everywhere, the bureaus will have prepared the way for him, everywhere they await him with a servile eagerness. He will support himself on them,

---

19 Rao, *Removing the Blindfold*, pp. 33–133; *Black Legends and the Light of the World*, pp. 429–631.
20 L. Veuillot, *Mélanges* (*Oeuvres Complete*, iii series, 1933), viii, 366–367.

the universal Empire will be the administrative Empire par excellence. Adding without end to that precious machinery, he will carry it to a point of incomparable power. Thus perfected, administration will satisfy simultaneously its own genius and the designs of its master in applying itself to two main works: the realization of equality and of material well-being to an unheard-of degree; the suppression of liberty to an unheard-of degree.

Men ruled by this system would be much more easily oppressed than at any time in the past. Such facility would be due not so much to the fact that new weapons would give the dictator undreamed-of instruments of control as to the sad reality that stupefied machine man would approve of his chains, and a dull-witted intelligentsia would bless them. "These forces, which today's man possesses," Veuillot wrote, "possess him also; they engage him in weaknesses as unmeasured as his pride; weaknesses which succeed in changing him completely."[21] Men now really were being totally depraved, unable to desire the destiny outlined for them by the Gospel, "too powerful to control the taste for pleasure."[22] The universal Empire would enslave such creatures by satisfying their most banal individual passions,[23]

> The police will take care that one is amused and that its reins never trouble the flesh. The administration will dispense the citizen of all care. It will fix his situation, his habitation, his vocation, his occupations. It will dress him and allot to him the quantity of air that he must breathe. It will have chosen him his mother, it will choose him his temporary wife; it will raise his children; it will take care of him in his illnesses; it will bury and burn his body, and dispose of his ashes in a record box with his name and his number.

A task which, as time went on, would become simpler and simpler. For a decline in human imagination would entail a destruction of the taste for a variety of pleasures:[24]

> But why would he change places and climates? There will not be any more different places or climates, nor any curiosity

---

21   Veuillot, *Mélanges*, viii, 364.
22   Ibid.
23   Ibid., 369.
24   Ibid.

anywhere. Man will find everywhere the same moderate temperature, the same customs, the same administrative rules, and infallibly the same police taking the same care of him. Everywhere the same language will be spoken, the *bayadères* will everywhere dance the same ballet. The old diversity would be a memory of the old liberty, an outrage to the new equality, a greater outrage to the bureaus which would be suspected of not being able to establish uniformity everywhere. Their pride will not suffer that. Everything will be done in the image of the main city of the Empire and of the world.

Contemporary students of Taparelli or Veuillot, myself included, would find no problem applying their analysis to later developments as well. Taparelli's colleagues at the *Civiltà* saw that the Paris Peace Conference of 1919, while flying the American Messianic flag of the "war to end all wars," sacrificed the defeated powers to victorious Entente material interests, readily denying justice to weaker states or the rest of the globe in the short-lived League of Nations.[25] Who can resist noting that some of the calls for European union cited above came from Nazi leaders and those physically compelled to deal with their all-too-naturalist attempt to build a New Order on the old continent violently? Or that the other pleas on behalf of Europe came from men sometimes forced and sometimes eager to shape the post-war unification movement in submission to the Moderate Enlightenment principles of American Pluralism, with its doctrines of doctrinal and social emasculation "making the world safe for individualist materialism"?

These were "arguments that could not be refused" by the post-war builders of Europe because of the need for American economic aid as represented by the Marshall Plan and for American military power as provided through NATO and what the United States wished NATO to signify. And, once again, these were arguments backed by the typical "conservative" claim that any divisive religious or rational criticism of Pluralism could do nothing other than destroy the "common western heritage" and ensure the victory of Soviet radicalism or the rebuilding of Auschwitz.

---

25 *La Civiltà Cattolica*, "Il Grido di Dolore delle Piccole Nazionalità Oppresse," 1921, iii, 245–248; "Feste e Lutti di Guerra," 1921, iv, 289–296; "L'Europa Senza Pace," 1922, i, 311–319; "Nuovi Fallimenti della Plitica," 1922, I, 101; "Patria e Patriotismo," 1923, iv, 486.

Taparelli and Veuillot's students could also easily demonstrate that the liberation theology that American Moderate Enlightenment Pluralism preaches—and was ready to adopt a "global" vision to promote when the concepts of "Europe" or "the West" no longer served its purposes—itself bears the deeply-rooted radical germ of irrational, arbitrary willfulness permitting whichever force is stronger to determine exactly what Pluralism means. As usual, the thugs manipulating this preaching can and do differ, and the preachers allied with them as well.

Hence, depending upon the ups and downs of the American political and social scene, the call for "Europe," "the West," and "Global Society" may reflect Neo-Liberal insistence upon a libertarian and individual-friendly economic order detrimental to the "European," "Western" or "Global" common good; or the Neo-Conservative demand to make the world safe for Israel, regardless of the impact on the international orders in question; or the libertine crusade for individual sexual rights destroying the understanding of man and woman and morality deeply rooted in European, Western, or Global societies. All those societies are expected to accommodate the "will" of the latest Pluralist "strongman," who does not have to justify his choices because of all of the arguments adduced since the time of Marsilius of Padua, with "American Exceptionalism" thrown in for good measure. And this, with the support of believing Americans, Catholics at the forefront, all of them convinced that abandoning Pluralism can only allow something awful to triumph, like Godless Communism or Islam. But to paraphrase Iago in Shakespeare's *Othello*, American Pluralism "is not what it is," or, rather, what it appears to be. In the name of protecting freedom for religion as well as protection for Europe and the West, it turns the Church and the globe at large into a road for the strongest passions to march down on their path to nowhere.

St. Augustine in his *City of God*, horrified by a Roman Empire that was becoming nothing other than a road for German barbarians, knew that the key to the rebuilding of a new and just international order would be openness to the teaching and grace of the Mystical Body of Christ. He could never have imagined the magnificence of medieval European Christendom, but he did know that Christ's and the Holy Spirit's will was for a substantive Kingdom to be built, and for that City of God to take its message on the road, to the ends of the earth; not for the lands in which Christians already lived to become mere "spaces" for willful ideologues and thugs to exploit. He would have understood that if taking that substantive pilgrim route, which was man's highway to eternal life, brought on not merely the four years of misery faced by Belgians refusing to be "walk-overs," but another fifty or a hundred or five hundred years of misery for those who love what Christendom must really mean, then this was what one had to do.

Alas, the enemies of "Global Society," "the West," and "Europe"; *that is to say, the enemies of Christendom*, are strong. Like Iago, when he is recognized as being demonic and assaulted, they, when attacked, tend "to bleed, but not to die." But this is understandable, for the enemy is basically unchanged since the time of Marsilius of Padua and his allies and has had many centuries to perfect his seductive "tall tale."

We Catholics, on the other hand, are physically weak. It is good for us to realize the extent of our physical weakness so as not to entertain vain hopes for an easy return to sanity in any regard. But it is also essential for us to realize where our true strength lies, and that is not with the "borrowed armor" of the false "conservative" accepted as our guide for fear of something worse. Our strength lies in looking directly at the face of Christ, which one sees through the sacraments, and also by looking at and accepting the fullness of what our Tradition has taught and accomplished through the ages; through the work of Catholic cultures and Catholic heroes; through comparing these, with all of their admitted sins and imperfections, with the ideological and individualist triumph of the strongest will that the Pluralist Regime guarantees. Making that comparison provides more than sufficient fuel for a *spiritual* break with that Regime and its "borrowed armor" which has a powerful impact on those we know, even if we do lack the power to make serious political and social changes right now.

Mexico, with all its imperfections, past and present, still offers the Catholic who wants to look at the face of Christ much that can lead him to make that kind of spiritual break. It was this look to Christ through its culture that caused Irish immigrants serving in the American Army engaged in an unjust war with Mexico to realize that their true Catholic identity required a change of heart and, in their case, military allegiance. They formed the

Saint Patrick's Brigade, fighting on Mexico's side and dying for their choice. Would that we could have that courage on the purely spiritual plane in front of friends and relatives fooled by cover stories promising protection for a Europe or a West or a Global Society that offers nothing other than a highway for willful men to walk down on their path to nowhere. Would that we will go to our graves telling the intellectuals and thugs dominating our world today, "you cannot fool me. Viva Cristo Rey!"

34
Rediscovering the Obvious[†]
HAVING CHRIST AS KING REQUIRES
A CATHOLIC SOCIAL DOCTRINE

A LEXANDER SOLZHENITSYN ONCE NOTED
that it was very difficult for anyone who had grown up under
the Soviet regime to escape both the general influence of Marxist-Leninist presuppositions as well as the way in which these
impacted on the definition of words and the conclusions one drew
from them. The same is true for those who have been raised in
the liberal western pluralist world, Roman Catholics included.

Even we who call ourselves traditionalists and firmly believe
that Christ is meant to be King of the universe as a whole find
anti-Christian presuppositions regarding the individual, society and
the concept of freedom so much part of our historical baggage that
we are often tempted to define what that regal authority means
in a way that satisfies what are really crippling naturalist limitations upon it. Like Solzhenitsyn in his battle with Enlightenment-
inspired Marxism-Leninism, we, too, find it difficult to shake off
the remaining chains wrapped around our minds, hearts and souls
by our Enlightenment-inspired pluralist environment; chains that
prevent our recognition of basic truths that should really be obvious for a believer.

Among these "obvious" but generally only partially accepted
basic truths is the fact that proclaiming Christ as our King binds
us to the work of building a world quite different from the fallen
one which does not permit Him to reign. It is the explanation,
promotion and defense of this arduous but essential work of transformation of all things in Christ that has come to be known to us
as Catholic Social Doctrine.

Even a brief glance at the history of Christendom indicates a
swift awareness on the part of both ecclesiastical as well as political authorities that acceptance of the Faith requires substantive

---

† First published in *The Angelus* (July 2016).

social changes reflecting the ultimate sovereignty of Christ as King. Yes, many dramatic and attention-catching caesaro-papist battles illustrated both continuing imperial resistance to such changes as well as efforts to control and secularize them. Nevertheless, a steady conquest of the public forum, backed by imperial authority, characterized the bulk of the fourth century, while the Theodosian (438), Justinian (529–534), and Ecloga (726) law codes proceeded more and more to regulate all manner of social concerns, from marriage to economics to entertainment, in a Christian spirit markedly different from that of the imperial past.

Meanwhile, barbarian rulers eager to gain legitimacy by demonstrating a commitment to Catholic Christianity sought to outdo their imperial predecessors in their assault on various practices of their pagan societies. One sees this clearly in the revision of the Salic Law under Pippin the Short in 763, not to speak of the much more comprehensive legislation of Charlemagne and Louis the Pious. Some of them, such as Czar Boris of the Bulgars (852–889) in his correspondence with Pope Nicholas the Great (858–867) in 866, requested detailed ecclesiastical instructions on exactly what social changes were demanded of a converted people, and how these might most effectively be accomplished.

Perhaps most importantly of all, there is no way that one can truly understand the history of the High Middle Ages as a whole without recognizing their superhuman effort to ensure Christ's kingship over a world desperately in need of supernatural correction. It was this attempt to shake off the dead weight of the "business as usual" mentality that shaped the preliminary attempts to change fallen human men and institutions undertaken by the Abbots of Cluny and their allies in war-torn tenth and eleventh century Europe; it was this that propelled the manifold political, social and general cultural deductions taught and put into practice throughout the remaining "Christian centuries" by so many popes, bishops, monks, mendicants, scholars, princes, guilds and saintly souls; it was this, in short, that developed a body of ideas and standard operating procedures suitable for uniting individuals and the innumerable corporate societies in an ascent of Mount Carmel, turning sons of Adam into sons of God.

Nevertheless, the actual term "Catholic Social Doctrine" is modern, and the first person who appears to have actually utilized it was Luigi Taparelli d'Azeglio (1793–1862), one of the editors of the Jesuit journal *La Civiltà Cattolica*. In an article of 1855 entitled "On the Divine Element in Society," he describes that "doctrine" as something that the Church would inevitably have to develop more systematically and more dogmatically in modern times.

> It will come, there is no doubt about it. A day will come in which social and juridical theory will shine forth with that certitude with which morality shines forth in the Church today, defined in precepts and canons. But before this hoped-for progress can be realized, long studies must be pursued on the nature of society; studies in which the human intellect . . . prepares the material for the infallible voice of the Church: that Church which leaves research and discussion to its learned ones before proclaiming {as in councils} that 'it seems good to the Holy Spirit and to us' {to proclaim a Catholic dogma} . . . . (Series II, Volume 9, 1855, 390).

Taparelli believed that the Church required a conscious development of her Social Doctrine for two reasons. The first of these was the clear need to answer the violent and sustained Enlightenment attack upon the claim that Christian teachings must impact upon all natural social and individual conduct by means of an equally self-conscious and complete Catholic mobilization of every intellectual and practical tool at the Church's disposal. He was convinced that such an all-out Catholic "social" counteroffensive had to be founded upon an elaboration of the doctrines of the Incarnation and the Mystical Body of Christ that was more profound than any previously known to Church History. Taparelli insisted that a love and nurturing of these two specific doctrines were the only solid means of grasping exactly why a good but fallen nature was dependent upon the life and grace of Christ in order to fulfill and surpass its original *raison d'être*, and why the individual must walk down the pathway to salvation and his personal "divinization" through membership in and submission to authoritative social bodies: first and foremost, in and through Christ and His Church; and secondly, in and through all other natural social organizations willing to accept Christ's corrective and transformative kingship over them.

This *coeur di cri* for a full awareness of the meaning of the Incarnation and the Mystical Body leads us directly to a second reason for securing the development of Catholic Social Doctrine in modern times: the ease of Catholic cooption by Enlightenment propaganda without it. For Taparelli saw just how readily proponents of anti-Catholic ideas and institutions could seduce believers down the naturalist path through calls that mimicked the concerns of the faith while actually turning them into impotent accessories to the victory of irrational, arbitrary human will over truth and justice. He saw this because he himself had once experienced their pseudo-Christian sirène call, and did not wish to succumb to it ever again:

> I will candidly add that in the past I experienced in myself the force of social influences that rendered plausible and just to me many of those institutions; the fallacy, insufficiency, contradiction and iniquity of which I see today so plainly, and have seen ever since, the facts of experience constrained me to bring a new light of examination to the principles that inform them. ("The Modernizers of the Papal States," Series II, Volume 11, 1855, 176).

Experience, Taparelli believed, had shown that Catholics easily succumbed to Enlightenment propaganda by taking seriously the claims of naturalists to promote on the one hand a seemingly Christian-like appreciation for the basic unity and equality of all men, and on the other a seemingly Christian approval of the liberty and dignity of the individual. The Abbé Félicité de Lamennais (1782–1854) and his disciples and allies demonstrated a propensity to follow the first path, and the so-called "Liberal Catholics" the second; their acceptance of whose seductive arguments were the cause of Taparelli's lamentation. Neither group saw that they both were obsessed with a truncated understanding of man; totally social on the one hand and totally individualist on the other. Neither saw that they therefore created an unnatural "human nature" guaranteed to build an order of things that was deaf to the complete message of the Incarnation and the Mystical Body with its unification of society and the individual for the earthly benefit of both and the supernatural salvation of the second. Neither was willing to admit that freedom, justice and equity in everything from the family to education to economic life required more from them than they wished to give: the social-minded to the individual and the individual to society.

Catholic Social Doctrine was indeed developed much more profoundly from the nineteenth century onwards, from the reign of Blessed Pius IX through that of Pius XII and even in some limited respects up until the present day. Unfortunately, the chief movers and shakers of the world we live in have been either the equality- or liberty-obsessed Enlightenment forces, the Marxists and the Pluralists, to which the disciples of Lamennais and of the Liberal Catholics (whose heirs, in admittedly different ways, include both American liberals and conservatives) accommodate themselves.

It is these forces who control the environment in which we live and the language with which that environment is defended. It is they who forge the cultural bonds that we in the Pluralist West find as difficult to break as Solzhenitsyn noted in the old Marxist East. One means of breaking those bonds is by diving into the liberating teachings of Catholic Social Doctrine, to be found in the encyclicals of a century of noble pontiffs and the writings of those men who inspired such popes and were inspired by them. There is no justification whatsoever for Catholic men and women to neglect that "bath" in times still more perilous than those in which Taparelli wrote. I would suggest that every traditionalist do so. We have nothing to lose but our chains.

35

Pious Mugging

LEGITIMATE AUTHORITY, ARBITRARY POWER AND PROTESTANTISM[†]

LEGITIMATE AUTHORITY IS A RATIONAL and good thing, beneficial both for the maintenance of temporal societies as well as for the flourishing and even the sanctification of all their individual members. The power wielded by a mugger over his victims is quite a different matter: egotistical, irrational, arbitrary, and devastating to the dignity of every human person, the criminal included. Traditional Catholic Christendom, using both supernatural and natural tools, taught the meaning of legitimate authority very clearly and promoted its proper use at all levels of social organization. Dominant modern naturalism, in contrast, teaches and promotes the art of an anti-social and anti-individual mugging as the height of human progress.

If the men and women of the ascendant Christian society of the past had been told of the victim fate that was in store for them should they swallow the full message of modernity, they might well have instantly spat it out of their mouths like a piece of tainted meat. Alas, many of them gorged on this poison instead. They were tempted to do so because of the sugarcoating applied to it in the early stages of its confection by Martin Luther and his progeny. For Luther and Company made the path to becoming mugging victims seem downright lovely, by associating it with their understanding of a true Christian piety; one that was said to be rejected by the wicked Papists. In short, he and his Protestant followers promoted a social vision sanctioning a "pious mugging," with legitimate authority in a Catholic Christian sense as its first intellectual target, and with each and every society, along with all of its individual members, as its ultimate day-to-day victims.

This is not the place for a full discussion of the Catholic understanding of legitimate authority, which was itself heavily

---

[†] First published in *The Angelus* (November–December 2017)

influenced by prior rational Greek influences. Suffice it to say for
the moment—and this with reference not just to pre-Reformation
thought but also to the insights of nineteenth and twentieth century
writings dealing with the question in the aftermath of Luther, the
Enlightenment and the French Revolution—that Catholics understood legitimate authority to be valuable for two complementary
reasons. On the one hand, the ravages of sin indicated to them
the individual's "negative" need for social guidance and correction to fend off the evils he inflicted upon himself and his fellow
man. On the other, the reality of a Redemption that was offered
to men only through their incorporation into Christ's Mystical
Body demonstrated to Catholic thinkers the individual's "positive"
dependency upon social authority for his personal perfection and
eternal wellbeing. If there were no submission to Christ and His
Mystical Body there would be no passage to becoming sons of God.
And if there were no submission to the complex mesh of temporal
social institutions capable of imitation of the example of Christ
and His Mystical Body, there would be no recognition that the
Incarnation confirmed the crucial importance of all things natural,
and the role that the authorities of the entire "society of societies"
constituting Christendom, from family to state, was meant to play
in teaching men their duties and leading them to heaven.

A Catholic understanding of the value of all of nature, society and social authority included, had its enemies from the first
moments of Church History. These became ever more vocal
as the full meaning of a complex Christian society came into
focus, along with all of the mistakes, sins and hypocritical actions
of Church leaders and believers claiming to promote it. And
yet despite such deep roots, it was only when "all those anti-
intellectualist, anti-institutional forces that had plagued and hindered the medieval Church for centuries" were "institutionalized
in the new reformed Christian Church" that they truly were to
begin to "have their fling" (P. Hughes, *A History of the Church*,
Sheed & Ward, 1949, III, 529).

There are two major reasons explaining this long gestation, the
first of which was the fact that the original anti-incarnational attack
was a Manichean one, based upon an outright condemnation of a
material Creation whose goodness was confirmed by God through
the Incarnation and Redemption. This assault was too shockingly

direct to get a serious grip on Catholic spirits. It went straight for the jugular, in a way that St. Francis of Assisi, with his popularization of such practices as that of the construction of a Christmas crèche—something the anti-materialist Manicheans with their loathing of the body were bound to despise—was able to defuse.

What Luther did was to present the principle of the wickedness of life as the product of Original Sin, thereby placing the responsibility for the total depravity of the world squarely on the shoulders of men rather than the Christian God. Man had to be humiliated so that God could be exalted. It was this much less radical, much more pious-sounding, God-friendly and sinful-man-flaying argument that guaranteed him a hearing from late medieval believers overwhelmed by the seemingly incurable evils around them, but still convinced that Creation was the product of a supremely good Trinity.

Luther's "pious" incarnation of what was actually a deadly, anti-Christian vision of the total depravity of the man-corrupted natural world could not help but undermine the validity of temporal social institutions of all kinds. After all, the human authorities guiding them would logically have to be considered subject to the same hopeless corruption as men engaged in other endeavors from the very outset of their activity. And yet this supposed exaltation of God and humbling of human pretensions was to prove to be the key to unleashing that truly sinful, irrational, individual willfulness, long festering in the bowels of the medieval western world alongside the attack on the Incarnation, and ensuring the modern replacement of legitimate authority with the arbitrary power of the mugger.

The second reason for the long gestation was the fact that Luther simply happened to be the right man in the right place at the right time. In fact, the broad strokes of what was to happen were already crystal clear in the thought of some of the fourteenth century precursors of Luther and his progeny, from whom much of their "pious mugging" ideas and practices was taken. The precursors in question were Marsilius of Padua (c. 1275–c.1342), the Nominalist philosopher William of Ockham (c. 1287–1347), and the mystical and millennial-minded group of Franciscans called the Spirituals, all of them embittered by the worldly actions of a wicked Papacy abusing Christendom in the name of transformation in Christ.

556

Their alliance appeared to encourage a deeply pious concern for the majesty and rights of a God whose clear and simple will, supposedly grasped quite easily by the apostolic church, had been obscured by a naturalist perversion of things spiritual, manifested in rationalist, legalist, and theological and philosophical speculation, manipulated by impious popes and their arrogant, earth-focused minions. Moreover, it coupled this concern for a return to spiritual purity by a call for intercession on behalf of God's thwarted will through the work of the pious Holy Roman Emperor; the man that Marsilius' most famous book labeled *The Defender of the Peace.*

Unfortunately for the cause of Truth, the alliance in question eliminated from the intellectual baggage of the supposedly pious Emperor everything from speculative theology, philosophy and basic logic that could identify the divine will in a manner that might require some change of the human will of the "defender of the peace," or even merely distinguish the former from the latter. The will of God thus clearly became whatever its earthly agent decreed that it was, with no consideration of the broader judgments of Faith and Reason regarding the divine plan recorded through the ages.

Just to make matters more complicated for the inevitably more pious world to come, an imperial will that for all practical purposes had become indistinguishable from the will of God was then said to be dependent upon still other willful earthly forces. The appeal to the pious imperial will was itself justified with reference to an underlying grant of imperial authority emerging from "the Roman People." Furthermore, this "People" was then shown to be "formed" to provide the desired imperial authorization through the work of the Emperor's intellectual and mystical advisors; men who, however, were equally stripped of theological, philosophical and logical blocks to the equation of their arbitrary judgment with "God's" clear and simple will.

Nominalists like Ockham and politicos like Marsilius saw themselves as "no-nonsense" men, and this made them contemptuous of authorities lacking demonstrable physical power. Given such circumstances, it seems that identification of the "clear and simple will of God" inevitably had to fall into the hands of whatever earthly power happened to be momentarily strongest. The intellectual and mystical forces opposed to the arrogant, naturalist, speculative

Catholic vision would ally themselves with this "strongest force" and then justify its tyranny, "forming" the "People" to understand that its victimization was actually just what they always wanted and that they must happily accept it.

Such an argument meant that insofar as concern for some sort of overriding Christian order remained vivid in believers' minds—and it did—the possessor of pure physical power, however parochial his willful desires might actually be, nevertheless still had to be justified by the more intellectual and spiritual members of a Triple Irrational Alliance as a God-friendly "Defender of the Peace." In short, in a world still touched by aspects of the Christian message, the intellectual word merchant, the mystic and the thug ultimately needed one another to go about their willful work, so as to rationalize an irrational victory. But the results might not be exactly what any of the parties to the arrangement fully wanted, and they might, in consequence, constantly be on the lookout for a better deal with changed partners.

It was this supposedly pious union of the intellectual word merchant, the mystic, and the thug—whose victory historical circumstances had rendered hopeless in the fourteenth century—that was effectively *incarnated* through the Protestant Reformation. That incarnation was effected in three steps. First of all, Luther's God-exalting, man-humbling, anti-rational, and ultimately anti-incarnational Nominalist philosophical training was transformed by his conversion to the use of Humanist methodology. It was then transmitted to the world in a rhetorically charged and vulgarized form, exuding conviction of its godly, apostolic teaching regarding the total depravity of sinful humanity. Secondly, Luther's anti-incarnational position not only met with opposition from the Roman Church, but also immediately unleashed a tidal wave of totally logical deductions concerning the wickedness of man and nature that he personally considered stark raving mad. This led him to wish to impose his individual, quite illogical and rather conservative will on the logic of the revolutionary movement he had generated, and simultaneously to reject both the Catholic position as well as the radical interpretation of his principles by his opponents.

Finally, stymying the "Papists" and the "enthusiasts," as he called the wild men, while protecting his own "limited" but always potentially explosive radicalism (i.e., his "conservatism") required the help of practical physical force. The current emperor, Charles V, Marsilius' favored "Defender of the Peace," was of no value in this regard. He had made his anti-Lutheran Catholic convictions all too clear. On the other hand, many German princes, terrified by the unusually great strength of the contemporary Empire, and on the hunt for some justification for opposing it, were more than pleased to become what Luther called "necessity bishops" and to take the steps required to construct a new and more pious Christian world. These involved crushing the wicked Roman Church with its incarnational vision, appropriating the lands of the Whore of Babylon to build up their own anti-imperial power in the process, and also happily eliminating the various radicals that the more conservative reformer detested.

But the German princes were also ready to call halt to any of Luther's projects that did not fit with their own now liberated, parochial, political willfulness. They became his "Defenders of the Peace" in the common project of enforcing God's "clear and simple will," by tugging him down directions he did not necessarily wish to go, and with the international imperial authority that the "conservative" Luther actually still somehow respected rendered more and more impotent and unable to control them in the process.

Moreover, while bitterly upset by various princes' manipulation of his message to suit their own parochial material purposes, Luther's own teaching demonstrated that his bile was, once again, ultimately illogical in character. For he himself had logically deduced that the totally depraved natural world had to be controlled by the arbitrary will of the state authorities to prevent what he personally deemed to be an unacceptable anarchy. And, despite his eagerness to unleash these princes to call a halt to religious developments he disliked, he nevertheless continued firmly to maintain the basic anti-incarnational principle that allowed the radicals to drive home their more logical commitment to its full implications. This guaranteed the survival of radical insistence on the total depravity of the very state power that was being used against them. It guaranteed their continued hunt for protection of their "pious" cause from different thugs whose power they would, in turn, be unable logically to defend when still more logical and more radical forces "piously" opposed to their will condemned them. And the unfolding of the social consequences of the anti-incarnational principle of total depravity would then continue—as we know that it has continued—until all the legitimate authorities of all legitimate societies open to correction and transformation in Christ were assaulted with a myriad of different thugs, backed by their intellectual and mystical propagandists, all convinced of their "piety" (or its equivalent naturalist virtue), emerging to replace them.

Philip Hughes, in the same passage briefly cited above illustrating the effects of Luther's incarnation of the anti-incarnational principle long gestating in medieval Christendom, accurately notes what it is upon which our modern naturalist world is firmly constructed: "Enthronement of the will as the supreme human faculty; hostility to the activity of the intelligence in spiritual matters and in doctrine; denial of the truth that Christianity, like man, is a social thing; all the crude, backwoods, obscurantist theories bred of the degrading pride that comes with chosen ignorance, the pride of men ignorant because unable to be wise except through the wisdom of others . . . ."

And it is this construction that makes it obvious that when Christ is not King of the Universe, with His earthly reign guided through legitimate societies ruled over by legitimate authorities ranging from the Church through the State and down to the family, His throne is usurped by muggers and time-serving intellectuals and mystics willing to work in union with them to do the necessary work of praising the "piety" of their man-destroying tyranny.

Martin Luther: thanks, but no thanks.

36
The Three Estates and the
Counterrevolutionary Vocation[†]

CATHOLICS GENERALLY THINK OF MOD-
ern revolutions in conjunction with the religious persecu-
tions that have frequently accompanied them. But if believers
wish to fight systematically against such horrors; that is to say, if
they wish to engage in militant counterrevolutionary action, they
should first seek to understand the underlying principles shaping
the more Catholic political and social order that the revolutionary
vision ravaged.

Those principles were not more suitable for promoting Catholic
Christendom because of any supposedly unbreakable connection
with hereditary monarchies. Such monarchies could indeed be
legitimate and good, but they did not always act for the benefit
of Christian order. The superiority of the pre-revolutionary vision
was really owed to its innate sense of respect for the political and
social dimension of human vocations in life. And it is for this reason that I would argue that it is an absolutely essential part of the
vocation of any counterrevolutionary activist who is concerned for
a substantive restoration of Christendom to recapture the broader
understanding of that concept that I am referring to here.

Normally, when we speak of vocations we think of these on a
personal level, with regard to a specific individual's basic career
choice. In the Catholic world, this is usually even more limited
to treatment of a personal decision for the priesthood or religious
life. But here, too, we are quite used to recognizing the fact that
a particular individual vocation emerges out of a social context;
out of an environment that nurtures and encourages a growing
child's inclination to enter the clergy or a convent. That fact alone
underlines the truth that the social institution called the family
has a vocation, part of which involves preparation of their children
for making proper lifetime choices that could involve responding
to the call of God.

---

† First published in *The Angelus* (May–June 2018).

But the family and its individual members live and perfect themselves under the authority of a variety of other societies, all of which, insofar as they address legitimate physical and spiritual needs, have the right to exist. One of these societies is the State, whose vocation is to stand as earthly guardian over all the other social organizations that enable men and women to live humanly and justly in this world of nature and pursue their personal perfection. Still, for the State to perform its vocation of overall guardianship properly, it is compelled to gain knowledge of what the vocations of all of these many other societies demand. For if it did not do so it would be operating as a cripple, with only a partial appreciation of all of man's needs.

Western Catholic States displayed an awakening to this aspect of their vocation in their theoretical, and often quite practical, recognition of their need to consult with representatives of the other social authorities in Christendom, grouped together under three fundamental headings: those of the clergy, the nobility and the commons. This was because, despite the many diverse social entities composing each of these groups, each could be seen as possessing an internal unity of a basic life pattern. Each of the three called attention to a distinct "station" in life; or, to use the proper legal term, a distinct "Estate," reflecting its own particular vocation. A State open to the message of its own vocation as the guardian of social order knew that it had to hearken to those vocational messages coming from these three basic sources of truth about man and the God who knows what man needs.

Awakenings sometimes emerge from unexpected stimuli. The concept of the Three Estates is one of them. It was first brought up by several prelates trying desperately to keep alive the broken institutions of Charlemagne's Empire in the bad times of the Tenth Century. What their discovery of the three basic stations in life taught them was the necessity of a total separation of the tasks of clergy, what at this point must be labeled "soldiery," and commons into those of men who "pray, fight, and work." The only exception to this rule in their minds was that accorded to the Emperor, who, while primarily engaged in the task of fighting in command of his soldiers, also joined with those who prayed because of his special anointing with sacred oils. Everyone else was relieved of the responsibility of contributing to the sanctification of the social order and, quite frankly, of working for his own personal salvation as well. Those who prayed took care of that duty for them.

This vision of the Three Estates was transformed due to the victory over the Catholic mind won by the chief enemies of the prelates in question: the monks of Cluny and their allies in other monasteries. While in no way denying the particular *functions* of the three stations in life, the message of Cluny was that each of them had to perform their tasks in a meaningful, vocational, spiritual context supporting their ultimate sanctification. That meant that each of them inevitably had to contribute to the lifting up of the social order as a whole. And it was this message that won its way into the policies of the Roman Pontiffs and those reforming Catholic Emperors and Kings of the High Middle Ages whom we most revere.

What did their specific vocations teach the State, the guardian of the social order as a whole? The character of the clerical vocation is plain enough. It testified to the supreme supernatural end of all men giving life on earth its meaning, and for this existential reason, the clergy was given pride of place as the First Estate. The commons, the last of the trio, while most diverse in its composition, nevertheless bore vocational witness to the necessity of that daily labor, in all its forms, that is required for the very physical survival of men destined for an eternity with God.

Particularly interesting was the social message coming from the vocation of the soldiery forming the Second Estate. This teaching was two-fold in character. On the one hand, it spoke to the State of the need for manly strength, the fighting spirit, without which a world subject to sin cannot maintain itself against the all too powerful forces of evil. On the other, it instructed it regarding the immense importance for the stability of the social order of family and the family's cultivation and respect for continuity.

It developed this second message as a kind of accident of history, due to Cluny's efforts to redirect the rather nasty soldiery of the time to the service of the just war, and the pride with which those knights won over to the call to a crusading vocation passed down a sense of the need to maintain their initial dedication to their descendants, generation after generation. Through this consecration of their families to crusading justice, a Second Estate that had been a rapacious soldiery became a respectable nobility, the definition of the latter being a class that "knows" what it is and where it comes from; in this case, from Christian obligations rooted in the family past.

All three of these Estates taught their specific vocational messages to the State and the society it guarded by means of an education proper to their different stations, rendered visible to the world outside by variance in dress, language and *esprit de corps*. Moreover, given that the work of the monks of Cluny was first aimed at teaching the soldiery the spiritual dimension of its vocation, the sense of crusading militancy that the Second Estate developed tended to hover over all of the reform movement of the High Middle Ages. This gave to the vocations of the clergy and the commons a Catholic crusading spirit as well. In short, the State learned of the need to be spiritual, militant, and respectful of family, tradition and work, all at one and the same time.

If the guardian of social order were to be guided solely by the First Estate, it could, at worst, become a mere clerical tool, and, at best, degenerate into an ethereal entity incapable of defending or feeding itself. If it were placed purely in the hands of the nobility, it could become an impossibly warmongering force obsessed with family lineages and their class pride. And if the commons were in uncontested control, it could dedicate itself purely to a soulless and unmanly concern for an endless work of supplying goods that could be consumed. The sinful tendencies of all groups and their individual members always made the usurpation of power to serve but one corrupted vocation possible. The vocation of the guardian of the social order was to beat these down and allow all three together to keep the ship of State on its proper course.

It is precisely this hearkening of the State to the messages of the three authoritative social vocations that the modern revolutionary spirit cannot permit to function. For the essence of the Revolution politically is its reduction of the social order to being a plaything of sovereign individuals, stripped of the militant guidance coming from the vocations teaching the need for a *unified* submission to messages regarding the importance of Revelation, the family, tradition and work, and thereby left defenseless before the demands of their fallen personal desires and wills. It was this *de facto* abolition of any substantive reality of authoritative social institutions that turned the French Estates General into a National Assembly publishing a Declaration of the Rights of Man, confirming that it was now the naked individual whose fallen liberty guided the ship of State. And just in case one thinks that that revolutionary spirit was limited to France alone, it is important to note that it was the same atomistic (and materialist) individualism that John Locke handed down to the American revolutionary experiment, the political logic of which was really only made known to the colonists through Thomas Paine's incendiary pamphlet, *Common Sense*.

What this liberation of the individual meant became swiftly clear for anyone with eyes to see and ears to hear. It meant first of all handing over the State to the guidance of the majority of individuals; that is to say, the commons. One of the first proponents of a French National Assembly, the Abbé Sieyès, already indicated in his famous pamphlet, *What is the Third Estate*, that this exaltation of the commons required the divinization of its vocation, productive work, as the sole force capable of guiding the properly constituted State.

It is no wonder, in consequence, that our revolutionary society is contemptuous of a world where the "unproductive" clergy and nobility played a significant role in the life of the State. It is no surprise that it understands the word "corporation" to signify a business enterprise alone, rather than all social organizations, the family included, as our pre-revolutionary ancestors did. It stands to reason that it thinks of an aristocracy only in terms of money. There can be no shock in its promotion of a university education that denigrates Theology and the Liberal Arts, offering a cornucopia of "productive" Doctorates in Real Estate and Finance in their place. Should anyone be amazed that the urban pre-revolutionary experience of all three Estates living together even in the same buildings dissolved into money-segregated neighborhoods? Or that our revolutionary world lost interest in the family, whose needs, traditions and continuity were subordinated to iron-clad demands of production and consumption, long before any Red assault upon it, as Marx himself indicates in his *Communist Manifesto*?

But the mention of Marx brings up a further development of the social silencing of the messages coming through the vocations of the Three Estates. For, alas, all productive flesh and blood members of the commons proved not to be equal. "Freeing" atom-istic individuals actually meant liberating the weak among them to become the tools of the strongest, "productive," personal passions and wills. This meant unjust subjection first of all to the rich, the moneymen, the bourgeoisie, and their particular property concerns. Behind them came the productive working classes, who were led to demand not a just control, but full control over society under the influence of the will of atomistic, materialist, Marxist intellectuals. And running alongside of both capitalists and workers came the productive entrepreneurs ready to supply the atomistic, materialist demands for satisfaction of every moral perversion known to man as well as the consequences flowing from them. Why should they not have their chance to dominate the social order? After all, an American Supreme Court justice said not so long ago that everyone had the right to create his own reality.

States in our revolutionary society have lost their vocation of proper guardianship of the social order that had been nurtured by an openness to the messages delivered to them through respect for the vocations of all the social institutions in whose bosom individuals truly grow and gain a perfection to be completed in eternity. These social institutions were those grouped, historically, in the West under the heading of the Three Estates. The result is that the "nations" that Christ wished to accept the Gospel can no longer be converted, and the naked "individuals" who become the sole object of evangelization become correspondingly less likely to respond to a teaching that, after all, itself comes through submission to an authoritative society: the Church, the Mystical Body of Christ.

Yes, we still have our personal vocations to nurture, but we cannot be guided to understand and nurture these properly until the complete concept of vocation is regained. We desperately need a revival of all of our social institutions and their flesh and blood incarnation of their specific vocations for our own benefit, begin-ning, most importantly, with the Church and the clergy. Fighting for this revival is the vocation of the counterrevolutionary. And, as Ernst Jünger tells us in his remarkable novel, *On the Marble Cliffs*, that counterrevolutionary must go out into battle today with a better knowledge both of his duty as well as the character of his enemy than ever before in history:

566

Now battle had to be joined, and therefore men were needed to restore a new order, and new theologians as well, to whom the evil was manifest from its outward phenomena down to its most subtle roots; then the time would come for the first stroke of the consecrated sword, piercing the darkness like a lightning flash. For this reason individuals had the duty of living in alliance with others, gathering the treasure of a new rule of law. But the alliance had to be stronger than before, and they more conscious of it. (*Auf den Marmorklippen*, Chapter XX)

37
Not At All What a
Vain Modernity Thinks†
TRANSFORMATION IN CHRIST AND
NINETEENTH CENTURY SPIRITUALITY

THERE IS NO DOUBT THAT THE ARCHI-
tects of our ever more rapidly collapsing "modern" Church
were correct in their chastisement of pre-conciliar Catholic weaknesses in the study of history. Nevertheless, it also has to be said
that any valid hopes for a much-needed improvement in the understanding of the Christian past have, in practice, been buried alive
under the quite unhistorical demands that their ideological vision
of modernity impose upon the current powers-that-be regarding
what they are willing to tell the world actually happened before
their regrettable rise to dominance.

Such mischief with respect to the distortion of the history of
nineteenth century Catholicism has been particularly grotesque,
the achievements of both the clergy and the laity in this era often
being totally ignored or misrepresented to enhance the reputation
of whatever "forward looking" forces are deemed to have been
precursors of the open, modern Church. Just as knowledge of
the greatness, immensity and variety of lay Catholic Action in
the nineteenth century has been buried under the mantra of an
awakening of the laity only first begun in the 1960s, that same
period's spirituality has been brutally raked over the coals as painfully lacking in both substance and good taste.

Let us "give the devil his due" and concede that much devotional
literature of the age, particularly that of the first part of the century,
does confirm aspects of these accusations. Still, one must remember
that the majority of writings concerning every human activity, along
with the public record of the practical results achieved by men
and women engaged in each of them, is always less than desirable.
I certainly can vouch for that fact of life in my own field of high

† First published in *The Angelus* (March–April 2020).

education. Moreover, the evangelical—and, I might add, truly democratic—necessity of bringing the message of salvation and the means to attain it to all of humanity inevitably, at all times in history, has had to involve extraordinary differences in intellectual and aesthetic presentation that range from the most sophisticated to the most popular, in ways that must end by providing at least something unpalatable to everyone.

A more suitable standard for judging the nature and quality of a given age's spirituality is whether its basic spirit actually moves men closer to God or not. And the nineteenth century, rejecting the preceding era's tendency to emphasize a naturalist, *Poor Richard's Almanac's* grasp of spirituality—a spirituality wherein cleanliness was next to godliness, and the chief guide to life was getting to bed early to be healthy, wealthy and wise—cannot be faulted in this regard. Both its theologians and its spiritual writers, men as diverse as the Tübingen scholar Johann Adam Möhler (1796–1838), Cardinal Louis Edouard Pie (1815–1880), Bishop of Poitiers, and his auxiliary, Msgr. Charles Gay (1819–1892), preached ever more firmly, with ever more varied references to historical sources ranging from the Greek Fathers to more recent and often neglected mystics, and to an ever more universal audience the need and real possibility for a fundamental transformation of the individual, society and nature as a whole through cooperation with supernatural truth and grace within the Mystical Body. With all due respect to that great pontiff, rather than St. Pius X's motto of "restoration of all things in Christ" being an innovative call to arms, it can more accurately be described as a summary of the essence of the spirituality of the century in which he was born.

Let us explore this badge of honor with reference to the immensely powerful devotion to the Sacred Heart of Jesus. This cult, whose importance was discussed in depth by the Jesuit theologian Giovanni Perrone (1794–1876), a disciple of Möhler, was instinctively understood by many ordinary believers to be the obvious counterpoint to the naturalism of the Enlightenment and the disasters brought about by subsequent revolutionary movements. It was this popular appreciation of its meaning that caused the leaders of the counterrevolutionary revolt of the Vendée in 1793–1794 to plant an image of the Sacred Heart on their otherwise plain white banner, their later French counterparts to build a church on Montmartre bearing its name to expiate for the nation's sins against the rights of God in the 1870s, and Gabriel Garcia Moreno (1821–1875) to place his attempt to Catholicize the political and social life of Ecuador under its patronage at the same time. Popular commitment to the devotion was such that Pope Pius IX and Leo XIII both enhanced the importance of its Feast Day, the latter ending the century in 1899 by consecrating the entire human race to the Sacred Heart.

What does the devotion ultimately teach? It demonstrates that Christ's fully human heart, the most important symbol of a man's vitality and openness to altruistic love, was rendered sacred through its union with His divine nature in the Second Person of the Blessed Trinity, the Word of God. This then pointed to the way in which all things human and natural could be rendered sacred, or "divinized," to use the language of the Greek Fathers appropriated by the editors of the influential nineteenth century Roman Jesuit journal, *La Civiltà Cattolica*, through participation in the life of Christ and His Mystical Body.

An awareness of the magnificence of this truth, the centrality and urgency of the call to individual transformation in Christ, and the need to mobilize every possible tool for achieving the glory it entailed, immeasurably increased the century's focus upon the chief means of gaining supernatural grace. It is therefore no real surprise that it was accompanied by an enhanced appreciation of the Eucharist and the frequent reception of Holy Communion. The names of St. Peter Julian Eymard (1811–1868), Mgr. Gaston de Ségur (1820–1881), and the layman Marie-Marthe Tamisier (1834–1910) must be evoked here, with Eymard providing spiritual stimulus to the practical work done by de Ségur and Tamisier to promote adoration of the Blessed Sacrament and reception of the graces coming therefrom through the organization of ever more influential and popular International Eucharistic Congresses, beginning in the 1880s.

The longing for an individual transformation in Christ that was understood to be as difficult a task as it was urgent also increased an appreciation for the need to mobilize other forces from His Mystical Body within whose embrace this "divinization" must take place. Hence, the massive reinvigoration of devotion to every relic associated with Jesus, to the Blessed Mother, to the saints, and to pilgrimages to all of their many shrines, both old and new. Such devotions had been forcefully downplayed by the powers-that-be of the previous century, with their common-sense driven *Poor Richard's Almanac* understanding of godliness.

Enemies of these developments, still steeped in such a humdrum moralism, were stunned by the mass of believers, educated and uneducated, that came to revere the seamless robe of Christ, deemed to be in the possession of the Cathedral of Triers, when pilgrimage to it was revived by the local bishop in the 1840s. Moreover, they were horrified that pilgrims utilized the modern tool of the railroad, which was supposed to lead them more rapidly to the performance of merely naturalist tasks, to undertake this supernatural journey. They were no more pleased by the popularity of the rediscovered writings taking people away from earthly concerns that theologians and preachers were making known to the ordinary Catholic, one of the most significant being Louis Grignon de Montfort (1673–1716), whose *Treatise on True Devotion to the Blessed Virgin* was finally published in 1843.

Assistance for individual transformation in Christ needed the support of a natural order that propelled men and women to seek this goal and not to treat it as a fanciful theological speculation diverting the population from the more practical labor of building personal economic prosperity or national political power. It was the recognized need and urgency for the family, the school, the workplace and the political institutions of each and every land to open themselves fully to Christ to push the individual believer to his supernatural goal, fed by nineteenth century spirituality, that fueled the truly impressive counterrevolutionary Catholic Action movements of the day in so many different countries. Such activity then worked back to stimulate the spirit still further. "Almost every Catholic meeting which I attended at that time," a witness of Austrian political activity noted, "was a fiery furnace for the souls, from which a torrent of sparks and flames of holy enthusiasm was generated; a powerful forge, in which the armaments were hardened for a battle for the Cross which now threatened from all sides" (S. N. Kalyvas, *The Rise of Christian Democracy in Europe*, Cornell, 1966, pp. 97–98).

Anyone unfortunate enough to take seriously the distortions of the past promoted by the dominant forces in the Church today, who seem to argue that Catholic History began in 1962 with the opening of Second Vatican Council, will believe a lot of ultimately very contradictory facts about nineteenth century spirituality which I cannot fully explain in an article of this length: that it was somehow simultaneously both exaggeratedly intellectual and yet maudlin, daintily feminine and childlike in character, in a fashion that should alarm both those concerned for democratizing the Gospel as well as those embarrassed by what this might practically entail; that it was simultaneously too obsessed with individual sanctity and yet constantly seen by the world at large to involve grand popular pilgrimages, public International Eucharistic Conferences, and mass Catholic political action.

Once again, "giving the devil his due," all of this has some truth to it. Nineteenth century spirituality does display all these aspects, because it was truly Catholic, and therefore "all things to all people," in a proper manner, not "in a way that a vain modernity thinks." It displayed all of these seemingly contradictory elements in a unified spirit that dealt with humanity in an honestly, and not selectively, democratic fashion, recognizing the incredible diversity necessary to take seriously to find how to lead everyone to transformation in Christ. In short, it offered something for everyone in aid of the same uplifting goal: eternal life in union with God through incorporation into Our Lord and Savior's Mystical Body. And, thankfully, given its rejection of the previous century's cultivation of a gloomy Jansenism suspicious of the possibility of doing God's will on earth, and its enthusiastic promotion of Alphonsus Liguori's (1696–1787) moral theology and spiritual teaching, it actually gave living men and women a real hope that they just might succeed in joining Christ, Mary and the saints in heaven after all.

38

Vital Error[†]

ENERGY, PERSONALISM, PLURALISM AND THE TRIUMPH OF THE WILL

NINETEENTH AND EARLY TWENTIETH
century Catholicism was rich in militant initiatives pursuing
global evangelization outside the older borders of Christendom as
well as spiritual and socio-political revivification of the troubled
lands within them. These initiatives were stimulated by a general
movement of Catholic revival vigorously opposing an Enlightenment-inspired secularization of European and American lands
that had already begun before 1789, and which was intensified
and spread still further due to the violence and warmongering of
the French Revolution.

Spokesmen for this general revival insisted upon the reality of
a dramatic "culture war" with enormous consequences for earthly
life and the salvation of souls being waged between those proclaiming Christ as their King and the adherents of a soul-killing
revolutionary naturalism. Global evangelists and militants inside
ancient Christendom took their words to heart. They felt compelled to do everything in their power to achieve success in this
conflict as fast as possible. But that passion for success, laudable
though it was in and of itself, was destined to lead a number of
them to give their support to what I am calling a "vital error"
equating Catholicism with the triumph of the arbitrary but "energetic" human will.

Let us begin our tale by calling up the "noonday devil" of
demoralization that always lay there lurking, waiting to pounce
upon the drooping spirits of zealous nineteenth and early twentieth century activists. This demon crept from its den to plague
militants of all types at just those moments when a sense of failure
to obtain any truly serious impact upon the populations that they

† First published in *The Josias* (July 7, 2020).

had targeted for swift conversion and transformation in Christ began to overwhelm them.[1]

Such perception of lack of success was already noticeable in certain militant circles before the First World War, with some of the "Outer Missionaries"—those dealing with non-Christian lands—expressing deep frustration over their inability to make a telling dent in the armor not just of the seemingly impregnable Moslem world, but even in that of their beloved and long-lived Chinese field of operation. They were joined in their brooding by a number of influential members of European Catholic political parties grappling with their own "Inner Mission" limitations, conscious as they were of having painfully little impact outside their narrow confessional base.

World War One and its troubled aftermath increased the influence of this noonday devil immensely among those militants laboring in one of the fields of the "Inner Missions" known as "Specialized Catholic Action," whose organizations focused on youth in precise types of industrial and agricultural labor. The meager fruits of their work were especially driven home to them upon mingling with a young population of overwhelmingly un-churched fellow soldiers in the trenches. They were further shocked by discussions with some of the more articulate of these comrades in arms who were convinced that the war had indeed given European peoples the chance to purify and spiritualize their banal, materialist, prewar lives, but through bonding together with their mates in the front lines without any concern whatsoever for their previous religious backgrounds and aspirations. Yet a third and perhaps even more powerful stimulus to demoralization came at the conflict's end, when this small band of committed Inner Missionaries marched

---

1 For the entire following argument on the missions, Russian Orthodoxy, and Personalism, see Mayeur, J. M., ed., *Histoire du Christianisme* (Desclée, Thirteen Volumes, 1990–2002), XII, 87–158, 259–345, 451–522, 617–694, 769–779, 813–819; Jedin, H., and Dolan, J. *History of the Church* (Crossroad, Ten Volumes, 1981), X, 229–409, 458–488, 583–600; J. Hellman, *Emmanuel Mounier and the New Catholic Left: 1930–1950* (U. of Toronto, 1981); *The Knight-Monks of Vichy France: Uriage, 1940–1945* (McGill, 1997); Cholvy, G., *Jeunesses Chrétiennes au XXE Siècle* (Ouvrières, 1991, III, 19–66; Meinvielle, J., *De Lamennais à Maritain* (La Cité Catholique, 1949); pp. 89–262, 281–300, 134–142; Zernov, N., *The Russians and Their Church* (St. Vladimir's Seminary, 1978), pp. 134–187; Ware, T. K., *The Orthodox Church* (Pelican, 1993).

home in the ranks of masses of their battle-scarred fellow soldiers who were now displaying a willingness to devote themselves, body and soul, to atheist Marxist and budding neo-pagan Fascist Faiths.

Once the activists returned, some of them began openly to hunt for reasons explaining the failure of their apostolic endeavors in a world where others were having great success enticing converts to sacrifice themselves for their relatively recently born or utterly new anti-Catholic creeds. They hoped that knowledge of these reasons would allow them to correct what must only be "pastoral" errors in their approach, given their consciousness of possessing a Catholic Faith as solid as the rock of Peter. Their attempts to provide answers enabling them to address and remedy these crucial *pastoral* as opposed to *faith* problems brought them together with other Christian "seekers" whose passion for success intersected with their own.

One of these groups of seekers was composed of the Outer Missionaries and influential members of Catholic political parties working with the Inner Missions already mentioned above. Another was formed by promoters of liturgical renewal exploring ways of attracting the mass of modern men and women to a life of prayer and peace that could calm the individual and social ravages brought about by the world conflagration before these ignited a new inferno. A third group involved dedicated members of the growing ecumenical movement, concerned lest Christians remain divided in their private, limited efforts to fend off what to them was the greater and obviously more imminent threat posed by contemporary atheism and neo-paganism.

Among those prominent in bringing together Christian intellectuals for extensive discussion of theoretical problems, practical failures, and pastoral projects that might enable them to snatch spiritual victory from demoralizing defeat, was Jacques Maritain (1882–1973). Maritain served as the host of regular gatherings probing such subjects at his home in Meudon, near Paris, after the papal condemnation of the Action Française in 1927 removed him from the camp of Charles Maurras (1868–1952) and his Integral Nationalists with their slogan of *politique d'abord*.

Supporters of all of the western forces noted above attended these soirées, but the Christian East made its presence felt there as well. For also visiting Meudon were men from among that Russian Orthodox diaspora which was so visible in Paris, London and

Oxford, particularly the philosopher-theologian Nicholas Berdyaev (1874–1948). Thinkers like Berdyaev brought with them as great a passion for finding an explanation for the collapse and a hope for the revival of *their* Church in the aftermath of *their* Revolution as that which had stimulated zealous anti-revolutionary Catholics a hundred years earlier.

One of the names given to the intellectual and practical "programs for success" discussed at the Meudon soirées was Personalism. Personalism, whose story encompasses more than just the Meudon experience, must be defined as a tendency rather than a program, its name being used by a wide range of thinkers reflecting a myriad of contrasting nuances, with Maritain's own "practical philosophy" of Integral Humanism among them. But whatever their particularities and nuances may be, I would argue that these varied forms of Personalism all owe an essential debt to a late eighteenth, nineteenth, and early twentieth century emphasis upon the importance of the "vital energy" of "natural forces and values" as a guide to the truth and its transmission into practical action.

Central to the introduction, further development, and dissemination within the Catholic world of this emphasis upon vital energy was the thought of the Abbé Félicité de Lamennais (1782–1854).[2] Lamennais' work was consciously or unconsciously carried on by a segment of the Modernist camp condemned by St. Pius X (1903–1914). This "Mennaisien" heritage, reinvigorated through the meditation of our Inner Mission veterans upon the puzzling question of how soldiers who had been hopelessly divided at home before the war successfully created a fraternal unity at the front, then entered into the conclusions elaborated by the various Personalists and their fellow travelers at Meudon and elsewhere.

What emerged was a recipe for escaping Catholic failure in the dramatic modern culture war and more swiftly gaining that victory for Christ that every militant, firm in the Faith, desired. Unfortunately, however, it is this recipe that constitutes the "vital error" leading to the equation of the triumph of that Faith with the

---

2 For this argument, see Blum, C., *Rousseau and the Republic of Virtue* (Cornell, 1986); Billington, J. H., *Fire in the Minds of Men* (Basic Books, 1980), pp. 125–364; Mayeur, X, 427–477, 628–906; Jedin and Dolan, VII, 261–292; Meinvielle, Op. cit.; Cranston, M., *The Romantic Movement* (Blackwells, 1994). pp. 94–97. Also, J. Rao, "Lamennais, Rousseau, and the New Catholic Order."

dictates of the strongest successful will. Let us explore the transformation of this hunt for success into a divinization of effective but mindless will, destructive of the Catholic Faith, by focusing on what I think to be the most logical of the many contemporary forms revealing this development: Communitarian Personalism.[3]

Communitarian Personalism was the brainchild of one of Maritain's Meudon guests, the French philosopher-journalist, Emmanuel Mounier (1905–1950), founder in 1932 of the Parisian journal promoting his vision, *Esprit*. Mounier maintained contacts with a kaleidoscope of thinkers, outside as well as inside the Meudon circle: Jean Guitton (1901–1999), who would one day become a close friend and advisor to Pope Paul VI; Henri Daniel-Rops (1901–1965) and his fellow members of the organization *Ordre Nouveau* (New Order); Jean Danielou (1905–1974), the future cardinal; Belgians inspired by the "spiritualized socialism" of Henri de Man (1885–1953); proponents of European cooperation like Otto Abetz (1903–1958), Nazi ambassador to fallen France in the 1940s; and a group of "revolutionary National Socialists" who gathered in the early 1930s around the Hitler rivals Gregor (1892–1934) and Otto Strasser (1897–1974).

Mounier sees a successful Catholic conquest of society as emerging from the transformation of limited "individuals" into full-fledged community-minded "persons." For him, an individual on his own is a living dead man, "trapped" by his private intellectual mind games and atomistic behavioral concerns. To become a full person, capable of realizing his deepest potential and fulfilling his true God-given destiny, the individual must find a way to get out of himself and his deadening introspective existence. He can only accomplish this by diving into the richer life provided by communities, the most important of which, on the supernatural level, is the Church, the Mystical Body of Christ.

But the Mystical Body of Christ, having taught the value of nature, also points out the need for enriching and perfecting one's existence by immersing oneself in the life of "natural communities" and the "natural values" they incarnate. Which natural communities? Which natural values? The answer is those communities the beauty of whose natural values is demonstrated by the "vital mystiques" they exude; vital mystiques revealed by the energetic

---

3 See footnote 1, particularly with respect to the two works by Hellman.

action to which they move the individuals embracing them and the successes that they obtain through them over the world at large. Committed adherence to such vital mystiques and their demands, together with acceptance of the vital mystique of the Catholic Church, would transform crippled, atomistic individuals in need of what they have to offer into truly fulfilled and successful persons.

For Mounier, the Catholic believer who approached the Faith of his own supernatural community and its vital mystique as a set of intellectual precepts to be studied and put into practice on the individual level was just that sort of self-crippling, introspective atomist that he loathed, a man in desperate need of awakening to full personhood. Such an awakening would ultimately require shaking him out of an obsession with whatever parts of his heritage blocked his opening to the energetic pursuit of the natural values of whatever vital communities his life needs called upon him to join. This was particularly true with respect to any rigidly intellectual spirit of theological, philosophical and legal dogmatism that could dampen his commitment to spontaneous, natural, energetic action.

We will have much more to say about this topic below, but for the moment let us simply underline Mounier's conviction that an individual Catholic's acceptance of and immersion in the vital mystiques of the energetic and successful communities around him were essential not only to the full perception of the natural values that they reflected, but also to the spiritual perfection of Christian personhood and the pastoral success of the Faith themselves. Yes, he admitted, the successful vital mystiques of a number of contemporary communities and the movements they engendered that he was urging Catholics to join might appear at first glance to reflect *purely* natural values and dubious ones, seemingly dangerous to the spiritual life, to boot. Nevertheless, the energies that they unleashed, and the successes that they were clearly obtaining demonstrated that there was something supernatural at work through them: the providential action of the Holy Spirit developing Christ's teaching and bringing it to fruition in history.

Hence, to tie the argument back to our main theme, what this all meant on the practical level was that any militant who was engaged in the work of the Outer or Inner Missions and understood the crucial need for victory for Christ, had to pursue that undoubtedly laudable goal through a pastoral methodology of immersion in the energetic, vital mystiques of successful communities. This entailed no longer seeing their natural characters as potentially flawed forces whose erroneous characteristics had to be overcome, but as trustworthy reflections of the obvious presence of the Holy Spirit within them. The Outer and Inner missionary's task was that of "witnessing" to his Catholic Faith by humbly listening to the voice of the Holy Spirit through the vital mystique in question and helping Him to nurture it and bring it to its innate natural perfection. Such immersion and abandonment demanded a pastoral strategy of root and branch abandonment of any educational or practical activity that gave the militant missionary the perspective and appearance of an alien trying to dampen the natural value that he was confronting.

One day, the Holy Spirit would guarantee the "convergence" of all the seemingly contradictory, vitally energetic, age-old or recently emerging communal mystiques and natural values to which such militant missionaries were witnessing. The result would be the establishment of a unified Catholic "community of communities" capable of producing what would, in effect, be super-persons, "the grandest transformation to which humanity has ever submitted."[4] Once again, the key to achievement of this goal was that Catholic believers witnessing to mystiques on the path to convergence must never sit in judgment of them as "outsiders." For they could not even fully know what the Catholic Faith they were trying to transmit entailed, and what the Holy Spirit was seeking to do with it, until the natural values that the various mystiques enshrined had all completely blossomed and merged together. Hence, the violent, secular, twentieth century communal movements hostile to the Faith that were encountered by returning Catholic activist soldiers had to be viewed in the long run not as enemies to be fought and defeated, but as splendid, Spirit-guided organisms calling men and women to an "eminently-Catholic" perfection of their varied natural values.

A number of the activists of the Outer or Inner Missions attentive merely to the key words of Mounier's thought, perceived in them a confirmation of what they, with their, *at that time,* much more traditional goals in mind, were also trying to do: follow in the footsteps of Matteo Ricci (1552–1610) by "getting under the skins" of the various peoples or groups they were trying to evangelize or

---

4   Hellmann, *Knight Monks*, p. 178.

revitalize and "inculturate" the Faith. Thus, he could be seen as simply urging the Christian missionary to "go native" and thereby soften the opposition of potential converts and facilitate their willingness to accept the True Faith. The names of Charles de Foucauld (1858–1916), Vincent Lebbe (1877–1940), and their disciples are very important with respect to this "going native" outlook in the Outer Missions, while their parallel in the Inner Missions can be seen in the work of men like Fr. (later Cardinal) Joseph Cardijn (1886–1967), probably the most important proponent of the Specialized Catholic Action with which we are already familiar.

That strange mixture of Anglicans and members of the Russian Orthodox diaspora working together in various postwar ecumenical projects also could and did connect with and further influence Communitarian Personalist ideas. Its organs were dedicated to promoting a supposedly superior Eastern spirituality and recipe for Christian living to be found in the mystical writings of the *Philokalia* and in those of the Slavophiles dealing with the relationship of the individual and the community referred to by the term *sobornost*. Both these types of writings were used by them to drive home two criticisms of the "Roman" school of Catholic Christianity much related to those of Mounier: 1) that it crippled souls through an intellectually rigid theological, philosophical and legal dogmatism under the micromanagement of the Supreme Pontiff; and 2) that it could never truly be "successful" in the fight against Enlightenment naturalism because it shaped atomistic individuals working for sanctification totally on their own, rather than the fully spiritual Christian persons formed by individual immersion in and obedience to community as understood by the teachers of *sobornost*.

The French Catholic scouting movement, filled with a youthful energy that was both anti-atomist and communal in spirit, as well as possessed of a very clear and distinctive mystique of its own, offered a fruitful soil in which Communitarian Personalism, often in union with the ideas of the missionaries and ecumenists just mentioned, could plant its tents.

Moreover, scout troops also served as regular centers for experimentation with that branch of the liturgical renewal movement rooted in a number of monasteries and intellectual circles in Northern Europe nurturing Mounier-like ideas. One person worthy of mention in this regard is Fr. Jean-Augustin Maydieu (1900–1955), who celebrated mystique-friendly masses for the scouts during which he faced his congregation so as to better connect with its needs, providing it with a French narration of the advancing liturgical action in the process. Another is Fr. Paul Doncoeur, S. J. (1880–1961), who, terrified that Catholics had lost touch with vital life forces, had become enthusiastic for pastoral liturgical developments in Germany that were seeking a closer linkage with "deeply felt reality" as early as 1923. He honed in on the French scouting movement's concern for communal games and sports for a cue to teaching a better understanding of the liturgy that might perhaps influence its future development throughout the Catholic world:[5]

> Games can also be an excellent preparation for worship, which to the little ones appears to be very little different from a game. This should not scandalize us. The word game is not in the child's vocabulary, and particularly in the realm of scouting, it is a synonym for diversion. A game is an action, passionate insofar as it is sincerely played. Well, official worship is eminently sincere. Children sense this. They find satisfaction in this atmosphere of truth. They savor this serious action, wherein all participate, body and soul, this collective and ordained action, similar in nature to those grand modern sports events wherein modern youth finds its discipline and sometimes its mystique. But the little faithful heart senses well that worship is more noble than sports. Worship is the Big Game, the Sacred Game which is being played for the Chief of Chiefs .... Among the troops the Mass is generally a Dialogue Mass at which all actively participate. Certain among them make the offering. The cadets which Father Doncoeur leads each summer with knapsacks across France's roads also have the Dialogue Mass. Gathered before the altar, they respond to the liturgical prayers, {and} make the offering of the host which will be consecrated for them at the Offertory ....

Many supporters of Communitarian Personalism, convinced of the innate weaknesses of the atomistic, individualist, "Established Disorder" of the liberal, bourgeois western world, were highly sympathetic to Fascist movements. Fascism clearly revealed an appreciation for vital, energetic, virile manliness, combined with self-sacrifice to the community through obedience to its charismatic

---

5   J. Duquesne and Abbé Aigrain, quoted in Didier Bonneterre, *Le Mouvment Liturgique* (Fideliter), pp. 38, 39.

leader. While flawed, Fascism was nonetheless said to be a "monstrous prefiguration" of the new humanity of truly unified and faith-filled communal persons waiting to be born. The initial German victories of the Second World War were, in consequence, in no way surprising to such sympathizers, who insisted that liberal bourgeois defeat at Fascist hands had to be looked at from a hopeful perspective. What really concerned Mounier and his followers was whether Catholicism could find a way to turn what to the superficial observer seemed to be an apocalyptic situation to the advantage of the higher, long-term good. By "witnessing" to the construction of the German-guided, European-wide New Order, it would turn that budding super society down the direction that the Holy Spirit—who, unbeknownst to the Nazis, was the force that *really* stood behind their successes—ultimately wanted it to go.

Marshal Philippe Pétain's (1856–1951) so-called National Revolution, born out of the defeat of the Third Republic in June of 1940, was appreciated by the Communitarian Personalists both because of its condemnation of liberal bourgeois individualism and its freedom from what they understood to be the more grossly materialist aspects of Nazism. They hoped to make Vichy France a wartime laboratory for educational and evangelical schemes designed to reshape the world in the more vitally energetic spiritual manner that the Holy Spirit so obviously demanded.

One major example of educational experimentation combining the ideas of Communitarian Personalists and their fellow travelers discussed above together with those coming from National Socialist *Ordensburgen*—castle training centers for the new elite of German youth—was the École Nationale des Cadres at the Château Bayard above the village of Uriage, near Grenôble. Founded in the waning months of 1940, this institution became especially significant by June of 1941, when the Vichy regime determined to require a session at the *École* for all future high government functionaries.

The teachings of a vast array of contemporary Catholic luminaries destined for an influential future were marshaled under the banner of the National Revolution to play a role at Uriage. Under the day-to-day direction of Pierre Dunoyer de Segonzac (1906–1968) and the Study Bureau of Hubert Beuve-Mery (1902–1989), Mounier's Communitarian Personalism was very much central to this labor. This was true even after political problems led to

Mounier's personal removal from the Uriage staff. For his vision continued to prosper through the similar teaching of his friend, Jean Lacroix (1900–1986), and their common master, Jacques Chevalier (1882–1962), a professor at the university in Grenôble and sometime Vichy Minister of Education.

Allied with Communitarian Personalism at Uriage was the radicalizing influence of the budding New Theology, itself also sharing many aspects of the common Mennaisien "vital energy" approach. This arrived via the Dominican houses of Saulchoir and Latour-Maubourg, the Jesuit center at Fourvières in Lyons, journals *La vie intellectuelle, Sept,* and *Temps present,* and French scouting, liturgical, and Specialized Catholic Action groups also open to Communitarian Personalist and New Theology teachings. Segonzac and Beuve-Mery had frequented such circles before the war. They happily brought to Uriage priests like Henri de Lubac (1896–1991) and Victor Dillard (1897–1945), along with the above-mentioned Abbés Jean-Augustin Maydieu (1900–1955) and Paul Donceour (1880–1961). Uriage also had links, direct and indirect, with Frs. Louis Joseph Lebret (1897–1966) and Jacques Loew (1908–1999), founders of the Catholic social movement, *Economie et Humanisme,* which was destined for a significant "progressive" future both in Latin America as well as in Europe after the Second World War.

Through all these sources, students were introduced directly to the writings of Lamennais, as well as those of Henri Bergson (1859–1941), Maurice Blondel (1861–1949), Charles Péguy (1873–1914), Marie-Dominique Chenu (1895–1990), Yves Congar (1904–1995), Karl Adam (1876–1966), Romano Guardini (1885–1968), Charles de Foucauld and, perhaps more importantly than anyone else, Pierre Teilhard de Chardin (1881–1955). Their instruction combined Communitarian Personalism together with currents of biblical, philosophical, historical, spiritual, liturgical and ecumenical thought that, while marginal at the moment, would become immensely powerful and instrumental in guiding the Second Vatican Council and the "spirit" of the post-conciliar Church. The names of Congar, Chenu and Lebret (who was an author of the Pastoral Constitution *Gaudium et Spes*) are alone sufficient to make that point obvious. And this team, "ensconced in a chateau up in the mountains with a commission to completely rethink and transform the way France educated its young people," was even then absolutely and enthusiastically convinced that it was *the* prophetic guide to *witnessing* and perfecting the vital mystiques of numerous groups and natural values backed by the vigor of the Holy Spirit.[6]

A stunningly broad Uriage "ecumenical" commitment to the value of all forms of vital communal mystique and energy was testified to in a myriad of ways. One could note Segonzac's ability "to form friendly relations, on the spiritual plane, with Protestants, Catholics, Jews, Moslems, agnostics," since he "preferred (rooted) people . . . in their own setting, in their own culture."[7] Uriage's Charter proclaimed the truth that "believers and non-believers are, in France, sufficiently impregnated with Christianity," so that "the better among them could meet, beyond revelations and dogmas, at the level of the community of persons, in the same quest for truth, justice and love."[8] And Mounier, "whose belief that there was an element of truth in all strong beliefs coincided with Teilhard's vision of the inevitable spiritualization of humanity,"[9] prophesied the mysterious and convoluted growth of the "perfect personal community," where "love alone would be the bond" and "no constraint, no vital or economic interest, no extrinsic institution" would play a role:[10]

> Surely [development] is slow and long when only average men are working at it. But then heroes, geniuses, a saint come along: a Saint Paul, a Joan of Arc, a Catherine of Siena, a Saint Bernard, or a Lenin, a Hitler and a Mussolini, or a Gandhi, and suddenly everything picks up speed... [H]uman irrationality, the human will, or simply, for the Christian, the Holy Spirit suddenly provides elements which men lacking imagination would never have foreseen.
>
> May the democrat, may the communist, may the fascist push the positive aspirations which inspire their enthusiasm to the limit and plenitude.

---

6 Hellman, *Knight Monks*, p. 56. Courrier de Rome, *La 'Nouvelle Théologie'* (Courrier de Rome, 1994); Mayeur, XII, 168–186, 451–522; Jedin and Dolan, X, 229–336; Cointet, M., *L'Église sous Vichy* (Perrin,1998), pp. 140–161; Cholvy, III, 19–66, 107–166; Also, J. Rao, "The Good War and the Rite War," *Latin Mass Magazine* (Spring, 2001), pp. 34–38; "The Bad Seed: The Liberal-Fascist Embrace and its Latin Postconciliar Consequences," *Latin Mass Magazine* (Fall, 2001).

7 Hellman, *Knight Monks*, p. 83.

8 Ibid., p. 59.

9 Ibid., p. 128.

10 Hellman, *Mounier,* pp. 85, 90.

We have seen that intellectual rigidity was considered to be a bad thing by Communitarian Personalism, and the message taught at Uriage was definitely not a rational one at all. What counted most was the deeply felt intuition of the teachers giving prophetic witness to the future, and their strength of will in leading the young men under their control to a creative action; a creative action, once again, formed by taking seriously the Holy Spirit-backed messages of all of the varied vital mystiques contributing to the construction of the coming New Order. Any appeal to critical logic questioning the existential or moral appropriateness of aspects of successful mystiques and the natural values they represented was dismissed as dangerous, decadent, crippling, atomistic, scholastic pedantry blocking the obvious will of the Holy Spirit for the future.

Better to bury the critical temptations emerging from a sickly rationalism through the development of the obvious virtues of a vitally energetic "manliness"—virtues defined in completely anti-intellectual ways: the ability to leap onto a moving streetcar; to ride a bicycle up the steep hill to the *École* like Jacques Chevalier; to look others "straight in the eye" and "shake hands firmly"; to endure the sweat-filled regimen labeled *décrassage* devised for students under the inspiration of General Georges Hébert (1875–1957); to sing enthusiastically around the evening fire in the Great Hall; to know how to "take a woman"; and, always, to feel pride in "work well done." Such vitality was said to have deep intellectual and spiritual meaning in and of itself on the more developed "personal" level, aspects of which were elaborated in lectures like de Lubac's *Ordre viril, ordre chrétien* (*Virile Order, Christian Order*), and Chenu's book, *Pour être Heureux, Travaillons Ensemble* (*For Happiness, Let Us Work Together*).[11]

Finally, let us stress that Uriage's teaching was unabashedly elitist. In fact, the particular mystique of the *École* was that of developing the natural value expressed through Fascism by means of the Leadership Principle. "The select youth of Uriage" were said to be "the first cell of a new world introduced into a worn-out one,"[12] "entrusted with the mission of bringing together the elite from all of the groups that ought to participate in the common task

11   Hellman, *Knight Monks*, pp. 4–52, 68–92, 139–162.
12   Ibid., p. 65.

of reconstruction in the same spirit of collaboration."[13] Students had to learn to lead others in witnessing to the development of the Spirit-guided future.

Since they were destined to reveal the higher supernatural significance of the natural values in the mystiques of all the vitally energetic communities to which they must give witness, Uriage students had to be trained as priestly figures. Each class was "consecrated" and given a great man's name as a talisman. But, once again, learning to lead came through future leaders first learning to obey their own infinitely more priest-like, intuitive, prophetic teachers. Segonzac especially "took upon himself a certain sacerdotal role, even regarding the wives and children of his instructors."[14] This entailed a "separation between the leaders, the lesser leaders, the lesser-lesser leaders, the almost leaders and the not-at-all leaders." "The central team," as one of the interns indicated, "were gods."[15]

According to the doctrine taught at Uriage, the National Revolution ultimately had to be judged upon its *success* in the creation of "persons" open to communal life with many varied "others" as opposed to shriveled atomistic "individuals." Liturgy would be central to this process, and Uriage was permeated with a spirit of "pastoral concern," through the liturgists active in its ranks. In fact, Uriage turned the entire day into a vital, energetic, and therefore liturgical experience. Bonfires were lit, backs slapped, virile poems and hymns composed, and special pageants mounted. All these were said to be inspired by the "deep feeling" coming from vital mystiques requiring the participation of the still atomistic-minded but developing Uriage persons. Failure to participate in the communal liturgies of the entire Uriage day would be a breach of *Volksgemeinschaft* equivalent to an individualistic sin against the Holy Spirit and the super-personhood of the future. And all of this new, "natural," participatory, creative—and expensive—liturgical life emerging "from the bottom up" as guided by priest-like leaders was elaborated at the same time as Frs. Maydieu, Doncoeur, Chenu, Congar and others were bringing into existence what would become the extremely influential "Center for Pastoral Liturgy," designed to effect similar liturgical changes in the life of ordinary parishes.

---

13   Ibid., p. 63.
14   Ibid., p. 90.
15   Ibid., p. 75.

Yes, Fascism, with its exaltation of individual abandonment to the vital energy and will of a community guided by its charismatic leader or leaders, and with its denigration of sickly, individual, rationalist criticism, was intensely appealing to Uriage. Nevertheless, Fascism's dominant National Socialist strain was unavoidably tied to the racial vision of the *Volksprinzip*, and Mounier, his followers, and Personalists in general never accepted the ideology of modern racism. After all, different races could be just as energetic in the support of their beliefs and traditions as the Nazis were of Aryan supremacy. It is not surprising therefore, that important Personalists of all types courageously and openly opposed National Socialist *racism* from the very outset.[16] And whether it was their growing horror over the intensification of Nazi racial persecution, or their increasing awareness as the war went on that the Fascists possessed less "vital energy" than their United Nations Alliance opponents, Personalists in general came to realize that any flirtation with the ever less successful Nazi regime had to be jettisoned.

Nowhere was this need to flee National Socialist racism and military failure more felt than at Uriage.[17] The deportation of French youth to forced labor camps, the tightening German control of internal Vichy affairs, and the outright takeover of the Unoccupied Zone in the latter part of 1942, had already moved its leadership closer to the growing Resistance Movement, long before allied success in combat was assured. This tendency matured by December of that fateful year, when the enemies of the project at Vichy managed to have the *École* expelled entirely from the Château Bayard.

Uriage never did anything haphazardly. Building upon its sense of constituting a modern band of crusading knights, the exiled *École* leadership now created a 'Chivalric Order" whose inner circle was bound by spiritual vows of a character that Fr. Maydieu compared to those of matrimony. Members of the Order were to sally forth to show the various communities composing the Resistance how to perfect their "mystiques" and "natural values" in the Uriage manner. Thus, high-level emissaries were dispatched to contact de

---

16   Chelini, J., *L'église sous Pie XII* (Fayard, Two Volumes, 1983, 1989), pp. 213–311; Poulat, E., *Les prêtres-ouvriers: Naissance et fin* (Cerf, 1999), pp. 179–375; Cholvy, III, pp. 67–125.
17   Hellman, *Knight-Monks*, pp. 182–254.

Gaulle, and "flying squadrons" into the countryside to guide the Communist *maquis* so that both of their deficient mystiques could be "transcended spiritually" and "converge" in the construction of the better world of the Teilhardian Omega Point.

The enthusiasm with which this labor was undertaken was genuine, but especially so with respect to the Marxist component of the Resistance Movement. Most Uriage men felt a preference for the vital energy of Marxism-Leninism. Despite its anti-spiritual Enlightenment mechanist foundation, the Marxist "communal" emphasis, as reflected in the Soviet collective experiment, was much more satisfying to their own pronounced social sense than the natural value shaping the vital mystique of the other crucial community forming the United Nations Alliance: the Lockean individualism of the United States. Complained Beuve-Mery, who ultimately moved from Uriage to the management of the highly influential postwar French newspaper, *Le Monde*, "The Americans could prevent us from carrying out the obligatory revolution, and their materialism does not even have the tragic grandeur of the materialism of the totalitarians."[18] Round Two of the creation of super-persons through super-communities was thus to involve "witnessing" to the vital, successful energy of the Marxist Mystique as another monstrous prefiguration of a happier future coming into being with the aid of the Holy Spirit.

One sees this outlook expressed not only among members of the Uriage Chivalric Order, but also in the writings and labors of priests trying to understand and witness to the Marxist mystique of the proletariat in two different contemporary settings. One of these settings was the German labor camps to which these priests had either themselves been deported or chose voluntarily to move as an apostolic service to the exiles. The other venue was that of ordinary French factories, where experiments were being conducted to address the problem of the industrial population's manifest de-christianization, as outlined by Fr. Henri Godin (1906–1944) in his famous text: *France: Pays de Mission?* (1943). Under the patronage of the supra-diocesan *Mission de France*, set up in response to this book, "worker priests" were given systematic preparatory training for "witnessing" to that

---

18　Hellman, *The Knight Monks*, p. 213.

energetic French industrial "proletarian mystique" whose energy also revealed the presence of the Holy Spirit calling out for Catholic aid to perfect.[19]

In any case, a cleric like Fr. Dillard canonized the Soviet citizens he encountered in the camps in which he labored, insisting that all the workers slaving therein were endowed with specific virtues denied to ordinary people outside the compounds. Other priests praised the "riches in modern disbelief, in atheist Marxism, for example, which are presently lacking to the fullness of the Christian conscience."[20] They urged enlightened spirits "to share the faith in and the mystique of the Revolution and the Great Day (i.e., when all spiritually valid approaches would converge together)."[21] One cleric asked to die "turned towards Russia, mother of the proletariat, as towards that mysterious homeland where the Man of the future is being forged."[22]

Personalist-Marxist-Soviet-Worker fervor inevitably increased the hunt on the part of liturgical reformers for a pastoral response to the particular mystique in question. Those committed to the factory workers said that the liturgy and the priesthood were completely out of sync with the vital energy of the proletarian world. The Mass was clearly nothing other than the precious toy of atomistic, bourgeois minds that could not understand the spiritual beauty of the entire Marxist mystique. Hence, the critique of Fr. Dillard, who dismissed the dominant "anachronistic" definition of the Catholic priestly mission as useless. He insisted that his proletariat clientele was able to sense the superior spirituality of what pathetically limited old-style Catholics might be tempted to label a secularized clergy pandering to its audience. This ability was due to a *je ne sais quoi* emanating from that "new" clergy's fresh sacerdotal adoption of the Marxist mystique. A more complete and effective Catholicism was thereby in the making.[23]

> My Latin, my liturgy, my mass, my prayer, my sacerdotal ornaments, all of that made me a being apart, a curious phenomenon, something like a (Greek) pope or a Japanese bonze, of whom

19 See Poulat, *Les prêtres-ouvrières, passim.*
20 Ibid., p. 408.
21 Ibid., p. 386.
22 Ibid., p. 244.
23 Ibid., 329, 333.

there remain still some specimen, provisionally, while waiting for the race to die out.

Religion as they [the workers] knew it is a type of bigotry for pious women and chic people served by disguised characters who are servants of capitalism . . . . If we succeed in ridding our religion of the unhealthy elements that encumber it, petty superstitions, the bourgeois "go to Mass" hypocrisy, etc. we will find easily with the Spirit of Christ the mystique which we need to reestablish our homeland.

But there were many problems blocking success in this mission of witnessing to the voice of the Holy Spirit as expressed through the Marxist Mystique. Those peoples who ultimately came under Soviet control, exercised through a party dictatorship backed by the military strength of the Red Army, did not show themselves as open to the charms of Marxist-Leninist vital communal energy as its Uriage-engendered supporters had been. Moreover, Communist General Secretaries did not seem as responsive as they ought to have been to the witnessing mission of the priest-prophets sent to raise their monstrous pre-figuration of a new world to the seventh heaven. And these hopeless leaders were even less receptive when "security for the apparatchiks" became the Party's chief goal under Leonid Brezhnev, solidifying both the advantages of a petty bureaucratic elite as well as the general cynicism regarding Marxism of the peoples under its disappointing yoke.

This difficulty aside, there was also no denying that the vital mystique and energy of the United States on behalf of its own "natural value" of individualist materialism combined with spiritual and intellectual indifferentism—once referred to as Americanism, but now marketed under the more suitably globally applicable term of Pluralism—had also been "successful" in the war against the Fascists. Using the innate and often unconsciously felt power and prestige that came from "success," the United States had been hugely effective in reshaping the heritage of Western Europe to fit pluralist demands; and, unlike the Soviets, with voluntary support from the peoples of the Old World.

Moreover, Jacques Maritain, one of the historic pillars of the many-headed Personalist hunt for Catholic success, rejected the skepticism of men like Beuve-Mery regarding the value of diving into the American mystique. His experience in the United States led him to realize that its Pluralism was an immensely powerful *revolutionary* force suitable for breaking down many petrified traditions—if only Catholics witnessed to it and aided the work of the Holy Spirit within it properly. The pluralist offer of a practical, "pastoral method" for dealing with the diversity and divisions of modern life by guaranteeing freedom for all beliefs and cultures amounted to an Emancipation Proclamation for each and every natural value and vital mystique. Their Long March to convergence for the perfection of Catholic personhood could not help but be promoted through an embrace of American Pluralism.

Maritain argued that the pluralist vision, in permitting liberty even for the natural communal values represented by the Marxist mystique to thrive, could promote that necessary spiritualization of its mission under the guidance of the Holy Spirit that had been so badly botched by the Soviets. And some of the "usual suspects," including Mounier, Chenu, Lebret and Maritain himself, saw hopes for a fresh chance for open minds and hearts to freely witness to and perfect those aspects of the Marxist mystique that they most appreciated coming out of Latin America in the postwar era. A number of Personalists and fellow travellers with connections to Uriage grew especially excited when the Cuban Revolution unleashed by Fidel Castro (1926–2016) and Che Guevara (1928–1967) was crowned with "success" at the beginning of 1959, thereby proving the blessing of the Holy Spirit upon its own vital energy. Subsequent events in Chile confirmed their hopes for the future in this regard.

Meanwhile, step by step, making their way to the center of the world stage, were so many other vital communal mystiques representing natural values to which Catholics heeding the voice of the Holy Spirit must witness, uplift and allow to converge with one another. These included not just the mystiques of different Faiths, whose inner meaning Outer Missionaries—*now reflecting Mounier's thought much more than that of Ricci*—were claiming much better to appreciate, but those of all the cultures of the newly independent nations of Asia, Africa and Oceania as well. Perhaps even more exciting was the recognition of the existence of communities inside the borders of old Christendom composed of people energetically promoting the needs of specific gender, sexual and psychological mystiques. Embrace of the revolutionary message of

American Pluralism could allow the thousand vital flowers of all these manifold mystiques to blossom, as well as Catholic freedom to "witness" to the natural values that the Holy Spirit wished to uplift and bring to fruition through them.[24]

But before the priest-prophets of the various Personalist camps could do their work of Christian witnessing to a new form of Marxism, the religions and cultures of a "Third World," and the hitherto neglected mystiques of gender and sexual character, with or without the aid of American Pluralism, something much more obstructive had to be destroyed: Traditional Roman Catholicism itself. Mounier and Uriage had already denounced "frozen" teachings and rituals that "feared the insistence on bringing together men with different 'mystiques.'" They had long felt "a 'manly' impatience with clericalism, dogma and the orthodox."[25] Before the end of the war, Fr. Dillard had reached the point of saying that his work in the vibrant forced labor factory was more important than his Mass under any form whatsoever, and indeed, that the very machine on which he toiled itself actually had a soul of its own.[26]

Mounier is particularly instructive with respect to this ever-intensifying dismissal of the whole of the Church's traditional teaching and practice as an obstacle to the voice of the Holy Spirit. His vision had always logically involved the possibility of shelving entire realms of Christian scripture, theology and spirituality, should they clash with embracing the energies of the "emerging convergence." By the last years of the war, "there was little place for sin, redemption and resurrection in the debate; the central acts of the Christian drama were set aside."[27] Nietzsche's critique

---

24 For the union of the Soviet and American "magisterium" see Meinvielle, pp. 216–39, 257, 260, 291; On the atmosphere in the Catholic world down to the opening of the Council, see Chiron, Y., *Paul VI: Le pape écartelé* (Perrin, 1993), pp. 77–168; Scaglia, G. B., *La Stagione Montiniana: Figure e Momenti* (Studium, 1993); Cholvy, III, 127–255; Jemolo, A. C., *Chiesa e Stato in Italia dalla Unificazione agli Anni Settanta* (Einaudi, 1970), pp. 283–310. On Latin America, see Mayeur, XII, 941–1022; XIII, 509–577; Jedin and Dolan, X, 672–750; Letamendia, P., *Eduardo Frei* (Beauchesne, 1989), pp. 13–182.

25 Hellman, *The Knight Monks*, p. 88; also Meinvielle, pp. 224, 262.

26 Poulat, p. 327.

27 Hellman, *Mounier*, p. 255.

of slavish Christianity now seemed to him to be unanswerable, and he "came to think that Roman Catholicism was an integral part of almost all he hated. Then, when he searched his soul, he discovered that the aspects of himself which he appreciated least were his 'Catholic' traits."[28]

Not surprisingly, everything *rational* from the Greek tradition that had been used to support Christianity to critique and often dampen the vital will and its energy as often both wrongheaded and immoral, was execrated alongside Catholicism. The Socratics, for Mounier, were indeed Seeds of a Logos that confirmed the importance of the work of the energy-taming intelligence; and, as such, had to be driven into the wilderness with a fiery sword. Philosophical thought was as dangerous an enemy as theological speculation. Both blocked that "going with the vital flow and the willful energy stimulating it" that was the *unum necessarium* of the New Catholicism of the Holy Spirit.

Mounier's denunciations became increasingly vitriolic. Christianity, he wrote, was "conservative, defensive, sulky, afraid of the future." Whether it "collapses in a struggle or sinks slowly in a coma of self-complacency," it was doomed. Christians were castigated as "these crooked beings who go forward in life only sidelong with downcast eyes, these ungainly souls, these weighers-up of virtues, these dominical victims, these pious cowards, these lymphatic heroes, these colourless virgins, these vessels of ennui, these bags of syllogisms, these shadows of shadows ... "[29] Metaphysical speculation was a characteristic of "lifeless schizoid personalities." He referred to intelligence and spirituality as "bodily diseases" and attributed the indecisiveness of many Christians to their ignorance of "how to jump a ditch or strike a blow." "Modern psychiatry," Mounier wrote, had shed light on the morbid taste for the "spiritual," for "higher things," for "the ideal and for effusions of the soul ... " Thus, he dismissed many forms of religious devotion as the result of psychosis, self-deception or vanity. Psychiatric treatment must address the psychological illness revealed by obsession with doctrine and prayer, although vigorous exercise would help to cure some of this as well.[30]

---

28   Ibid., p. 190.
29   Ibid,, p. 191.
30   Ibid., pp. 192–193.

How was it that the powerful influence of the American mystique over postwar Europe created the conditions under which its Pluralist vision could facilitate the projects of all the above-mentioned Personalist forces and their fellow travellers? How did they come to mold the Second Vatican Council and place people of their kind of outlook in charge of the implementation of its many non-dogmatic, pastorally-focused, dangerously ambiguous "mission statements" and decrees? It would require an entire book to demonstrate this in sufficient detail.[31] At the moment I can only assert that they actually did gain such control, and that the consequence has been the victory of the "vital error" posited at the start of this article.

That vital error is the reconstruction of the Catholic Faith upon a foundation that is fundamentally Fascist in character. For this reconstructed Catholicism is built upon nothing other than the Leadership Principle and the need for obedience to the triumph of the strongest arbitrary wills rejecting all reference to anything outside of their deeply felt intuition: namely, the interpreters of the "Spirit of Vatican Two," whose charismatic dictates lesser believers with their obstructive appeal to Faith and Reason in defiance of the obvious demands of the Holy Spirit are allowed no means of criticizing whatsoever.

Such an outcome was totally predictable, and, in fact, a number of precisely those thinkers who inspired the militants of the nineteenth-century Catholic revival who so desperately wanted "success" as quickly as possible foresaw it. Obviously, they did not use the word "Fascism" to describe the "rough beast slouching towards Bethlehem to be born" since the time of Lamennais. On the other hand, they very much saw where the logic of his arguments was going, and it was these arguments and that logic that continued to be central to the *ideas* of the Personalists and the *pastoral stimulus* offered by their Pluralist facilitators.

For all of the main features of this Catholicism-as-Fascism mystique are present in Lamennais; the subsequent contributions of radical Personalists like Mounier being little more than refinements on the original theme, with those of more moderate thinkers

---

31   See Rao, J., "He Who Loses the Past, Loses the Present: Putting *Dignitatis Humanae* in its Full Historical Context," in Dignitatis Humanae Colloquium (Dialogos Institute).

such as Maritain, whose Thomism caused him to see the dangers lurking therein, merely offering intellectual warnings regarding an end result that his Integral Humanism and Pluralism nevertheless make "pastorally" inevitable. All we need to do to make the Fascist end game palpable is briefly to sketch the personal trajectory of its founder, Lamennais.

Exactly like his twentieth century heirs, Lamennais was desperate for Catholic success against the foe. This, he felt, could easily be achieved if the vital energy of the believing Catholic People, who knew, by instinct, what the Faith was all about and what needed to be done with it, were free to fight the obvious evils perpetrated by the enemies of God around them. But instead of unleashing that energy, bishops and popes collaborated with political forces that wanted to control this absolutely reliable source of the Faith. Worse still, the believing Catholic People, acquiescing in their continued chains, did not themselves display the energy that it obviously innately possessed.

Hence, the need for the believing Catholic People to be awakened and put into energetic action by means of the witness that was being given to their central role by a prophetic figure who saw what the Holy Spirit demanded of them. That figure was, of course, Lamennais himself. Upon being attacked by a Papacy making reference to traditional doctrines to justify its condemnation, he began to argue that the *sole* source of the Faith came through the believing Catholic People, *under his prophetic guidance,* even if it pronounced itself against what the Papacy and Sacred Tradition had always taught and were teaching anew. Moreover, he began to claim that that Faith was evolving under the action of the Holy Spirit expressing Himself through the voice of the energetic People *in general,* not just that which at the moment called itself Catholic. This voice had to be heard, witnessed to and uplifted by the prophet to create the Faith of the future, as Lamennais's friend, Giuseppe Mazzini, reminded him when, at times he seemed still too intellectual in his approach at the expense of energetic action:[32]

> Why do you only write books? Humanity awaits something more from you ... Do not deceive yourself, Lamennais, we need

---

32   Mayeur, X, p. 893.

action. The thought of God is action; it is only by action that it is incarnated in us ... So long as you will be alone, you will only be a philosopher and a moralist in the eyes of the masses; it is as a priest that you must appear before it, a priest of the future, of the epoch which is beginning, of that new religious manifestation of which you have a presentiment, and which must inevitably end in that new heaven and new earth which Luther glimpsed three centuries ago without being able to attain it, since the time had not yet come ...

It is this same principle that the Personalists and their Pluralist facilitators adopted and expanded upon by dividing The People up into many mystique-driven communities, all of which, in their non-rational, Tradition-hating wisdom, they charismatically understood how to allow to converge to obtain the victory of the Holy Spirit. All theological and philosophical tools for distinguishing between a good and bad manifestation of the communal energy promoting a specific "natural value," and how to put it into practice, were now *verboten*. No existing theology, no philosophy, and no contact with the vital, active historical Christ outside of and above the energy and will of the People as interpreted by the charismatic prophet guiding it to the Omega Point was permitted.

The "success" that was to be won for the Catholic Faith is thus won for a Catholic Faith that defines itself solely through abandonment to passionate energies and arbitrary wills. Someone among our own dominant Priest-Prophet Leaders who is actually sincere in giving way to the vital mystiques he encounters, thereby finds himself to be incapable of rejecting any energetic fraud; "barren in the face of a Ramakrishna," as Jacques Maritain—whose love of Pluralism nevertheless precisely encourages, in practice, this surrender—quite justly lamented.[33] But we have now reached the stage where it is difficult to believe that the hunt for "success" through the nurturing of "vital mystiques" and the natural values they energetically promote is in the hands of Church leaders who are anything other than hypocrites and Judas-priests who know fully well that they are blatantly betraying Christ.

---

33 Hellman, *Mounier*, p. 42.

39

These Ruins are Inhabited

CATHOLIC CIVILIZATION VERSUS
"THE LIBIDO FOR THE UGLY"†

"HERE, DULL AND DREARY PEOPLE INHABIT a dull and dreary landscape." This was the sole line written to me by a downcast friend on a postcard depicting what had to be labeled a "zone of habitation" rather than an honest-to-goodness city. Jobless, the poor wretch had been forced to take up work and lodgings amidst these ruins of civilization for the punishment of his sins. Abandoned to his barbaric, atomistic fate without any *sursum corda* from the zone of habitation around him was already sufficient torture on its own. Still, what pained him much more was the fact that his fellow citizens took such blind pride in their soulless environment that they actually marketed it on the souvenir card that he posted to me.

Students of Church History know that a somewhat equivalent "postcard" is available to them for their research purposes, this one "mailed" to them from varied circles of zealous nineteenth century European Catholic clerics and laymen, particularly those working out of Germany, France and Italy. All these circles depict in their academic postcard a body of Christendom in ruins, its soul extracted from it not only by the Revolution and the spirit of the Enlightenment lying behind it, but also the rather pathetic acquiescence of the Catholic Establishment to the work of naturalist destruction, already in the decades before 1789.

There is, however, one obvious and crucial way in which this "postcard from the past" differs from the one sent me by my friend in our time. Its picture was meant to evoke revulsion over the reduction of Christendom to a "zone of habitation." Those nineteenth century thinkers and activists who marketed it hoped to stir up anyone contemplating what it depicted to a massive work of rebuilding the kind of civilized Catholic society needed to help

---

† First published in *The Angelus* (July–August 2020).

the human person "lift up his heart" to the truth, goodness and beauty of things eternal rather than lower it into the swamp of fallen nature.

Such a rebuilding project, they argued, could only be undertaken properly when men's eyes were aimed on Christ, His Incarnation, His Mystical Body, and the truth and grace provided through them. This was because "every good and perfect gift is from above, coming down from the Father of lights" (James 1:17). The Incarnation's confirmation of the innate value of God's Creation coming from above, made them recognize that the contemporary ruins of Christendom could not be completely destroyed; they were "still inhabited," offering some building blocks for the work at hand. With eyes aimed upwards, they hoped to nurture the existing, indestructible goods of nature while correcting their sinful failings and transforming them in Christ, thereby constructing a new Catholic world on the rubble of its butchered predecessor. In this new Christendom, the state, the economic order, and, as the Nazarenes, a group of artist-converts founded by Johann Friedrich Overbeck (1789–1869) and working in Rome fervently claimed, even the beauty expressed by the painter, the sculptor, the architect, the musician, and the poet, playwright and novelist could rise to the highest level imaginable (George Goyau, L'Allemagne Religieuse, I, 237, 248), providing the best possible natural civilization suitable for lifting up the hearts of individuals seeking eternal life.

Such Catholic builders of the new Christendom issued two practical warnings regarding this work, the first of which was that no one could take for granted that it could somehow be mechanically guaranteed, since the constant temptation to sin in a fallen universe would remain a basic fact of life for each and every one of us until the end of time. Moreover, the naturalist, Enlightenment, revolutionary insistence on having us look for "every good and perfect gift" from *below* rather than from *above* had politically and socially intensified the enticement to reject transformation in Christ wherever it had gained a foothold. A naturalist project of this kind worked overtime to put man and society "to sleep" regarding the pull of sin, encouraging a "spirit of independence" from the truths of reality that could not help but fuel a kind of "libido for the ugliness" of wickedness, spiraling farther and farther away from the beauty of God and God's Creation, and ending in the construction of "zones of habitation" rather than civilized societies. This citation from the "circle" around the Jesuit journal *La Civiltà Cattolica* makes that point nicely:

> Starting with the words "I am free" and their newly found spirit of independence, men began to believe in the infallibility of whatever seemed natural to them, and then to call "nature" everything that is sickness and weakness; to want sickness and weakness to be encouraged instead of healed; to suppose that encouraging weakness makes men healthier and happy; to conclude, finally, that human nature {conceived of as sickness and weakness} possesses the means   to render man and society blissful on earth, and this without faith, grace, authority, or supernatural community . . . since "nature" gives us the feeling that it must be so. (*La Civiltà Cattolica*, I, 6 ,1851, 497– 498)

A second "builders' warning" concerned the proper hierarchy of values. Crucially important as the construction of a civilized Catholic society was in aid of the *sursum corda* individuals seeking eternal life with God need to get from the environment in which they live, the effort to reconstruct Christendom as such had to be understood as an *indirect* endeavor. "Seek ye first the Kingdom of God" had to be the activist's order of the day, since it is only through the human person *primarily* aiming at his transformation in Christ that the rest of the world could *secondarily* go through the crucially necessary purgation provided by the truth and the grace of the Incarnation at his hands. To cite *La Civiltà Cattolica* once more, there would be a real perfection of the world around us only when it was "transfigured vitally through individuals," "by means of the individual operation of each member of the faithful . . . divinized by grace" (*La Civiltà Cattolica*, ii, 9, 1855, 134–135; iv, 3, 1859, 414–426).

In other words, Christ's mission was not to build a civilization but to make men Sons of God who, in following His teaching could not help but work to that civilizing end anyway. Christianity was not to be taken seriously because a beautiful civilization bore its name; this was the error of a contemporary of the circles we are considering, René de Chateaubriand (1768–1848). Rather, it was to be taken seriously because it was true, and it created a beautiful civilization because its faithful took these truths to heart and followed them. To think and act otherwise would be to invert the hierarchy of values and set oneself up for the kind of fall that we will address below.

One poignant way of coming to grips with the complex hopes of the project under discussion, along with the perils of neglecting the "builders' warnings" concerning how its foundation might collapse, is by taking a closer look at one of the most important among the circles involved in this work. This was the Congregation of St. Peter, which the charismatic Abbé Félicité de Lamennais (1782–1854) assembled at his estate of La Chênaie to study methods for resuscitating dormant Christendom through vigorous Catholic Action. The *Mennaisiens*, as their opponents contemptuously labeled them, included in their ranks a large number of men who were to play major roles in all fields, clerical and lay, for many decades to come, often vociferously so.

Lamennais was primarily an activist, with the real theologian and "all around intellectual" of the operation being the Abbé Philippe-Olympe Gerbet (1798–1864), who from 1854 onwards served as the Bishop of Perpignan. Gerbet always remained deeply inspired by his mentor's initial zeal for transforming the world in Christ. In 1836, along with several other former members of the La Chênaie circle, he founded a religious, philosophical, scientific and literary monthly review of eighty pages an issue entitled *L'Université Catholique* (*The Catholic University*), designed to serve as an institution of higher education for the faithful, substituting for the state structures, which were highly secular. Through forty published volumes in the nearly twenty years of his involvement with it, this journal offered courses in five realms deemed necessary to building the New Christendom, from letters and the arts to religion, philosophy, psychology, physics, mathematics and the social sciences. In the last of these categories, discussions of the nature of a Catholic economic order were particularly important and destined to have a wide influence in the future.

The circle at La Chênaie was very much concerned with freeing the effort to build a new Christian civilization through transformation of all things in Christ from the political constraints that even self-proclaimed Catholic states, reflecting the continued influence of both ancient Regalism and Enlightenment Naturalism upon them, still sought to maintain. The tragedy of Lamennais lay in the fact that his passionate concern for breaking through these chains caused him to join the chain makers himself, forging these in a new and yet more insidious naturalist fashion that earned him excommunication in 1834 but survived to emerge triumphant in our own time.

His chain-making error was connected with the nineteenth century concept of historical "palingenesis" or successive "rebirth." The Comte Henri de Saint-Simon (1760–1825) and the school of thought founded by him are the most famous promoters of the palingenesist vision. Horrified by the destructiveness of the Revolution, the Saint-Simonians argued that valuable forces in the progress of human life could never be tossed into the rubbish heap of history. Christianity was perhaps the most important of these. Even when there have been moments in time that it looked as though it were disappearing, it has always been reborn anew, but in different form, preserving what is of eternal value to it at base.

Since the Saint-Simonians believe man and society to be in a continuous progress from theological to philosophical to "positive" (i.e. naturally demonstrable) scientific, technological modes of expression of the truth, Christianity, in our present, positive, sci-entific, technocratic "third age of humanity" must be reborn again to reflect its requirements. Christianity, Science and Technocracy must all work as one. In other words, the modern rebirth of the religion of the Father of Lights has to take on its contemporary expression by looking downwards rather than upwards, and by baptizing the mechanical, technocratic civilization that will come into being under its banner as just as spiritual and beautiful as past Christian cultures.

Lamennais did not become a palingenesist in Saint-Simonian form. In his passion to be freed from the constraints upon trans-forming all things in Christ imposed by obviously politically moti-vated governments and the all too many clerical forces painfully subservient to them, he came to the conclusion that the libera-tion of the Catholic voice required a new rebirth of society in which Church and State would be totally separated from, and therefore incapable of corrupting, one another. This new society would nevertheless be much more Christian than its predecessor, because it would be guided and governed by the Voice of the vital, energetic Catholic People, expressed democratically, whose vitality and energy could not help but transmit the infallible will of the Holy Spirit.

How far we still are from that religion of devotion, of self-forgetfulness for the good of all; in sum, of that fraternity of which one speaks so much! I only find it in the People; the People surround the cradle of the future, just as the shepherds at Bethlehem surrounded that of the God about to be born. Blessings on the little ones, the simple of heart. It is those who will save the world. (Mayeur, *Histoire du Christianisme* x, p. 866)

But to his dismay, Lamennais could not rouse even the Catholic People of his day to do its God-given work of giving birth to a new Christian Commonwealth. It remained for Lamennais, who knew himself to be the Prophet of the Will of the People once awakened, to be the energetic, vital, popular Voice of the Holy Spirit in the meantime. Giuseppe Mazzini (1805–1872), another democratic revolutionary who had no interest in the Catholic Faith as such, worked to bolster him in his palingenesist mission:

Why do you only write books? Humanity awaits something more from you . . . Do not deceive yourself, Lamennais, we need action. The thought of God is action; it is only by action that it is incarnated in us . . . So long as you will be alone, you will only be a philosopher and a moralist in the eyes of the masses; it is as a priest that you must appear before it, a priest of the future, of the epoch which is beginning, of that new religious manifestation of which you have a presentiment, and which must inevitably end in that new heaven and new earth which Luther glimpsed three centuries ago without being able to attain it, since the time had not yet come. (*Mayeur, X, p. 893*)

Ironically, the Abbé and then Bishop Gerbet played a major role in identifying the problem with his former mentor's thinking, both through his elaboration of a Catholic Social Doctrine separating the wheat from the chaff in the project of rebuilding Christendom, as well as by being one of the early promoters of what was to become Blessed Pius IX's Syllabus of Errors of 1864. Like other activists in Catholic circles committed to the project that many of them had begun at Lamennais' side, they knew where his error lay. His eyes were no longer aimed upwards towards the Father of Lights to gain guidance for "every good and perfect gift" necessary to construction of a Catholic civilization, but downwards towards the "vital, energetic will" of the purely natural "Voice of The People," whose desires, interpreted during its dogmatic slumber by The Prophet, were equated with the commands of the Holy Spirit. In making this dreadful choice for uncorrected humanity, Lamennais had deprived himself of all means of judging whether what he was listening to in himself as the agent of the slumbering People was really the Voice of God or that of man's fallen nature spiraling ever downward into a positive libido for the ugliness of sin incapable of a *sursum corda* of any kind.

Nineteenth-century Catholics hungry for rebuilding Christendom indeed found that revolutionary Enlightenment naturalism had gained a foothold every, and was a hard enemy to overcome. Nevertheless, they at least knew by the time of Blessed Pius IX, that they had the ecclesiastical authorities on their side. This, of course, is no longer the case. For despite its initial condemnation, Lamennais' downward looking "reborn" Catholicism, never died out and has come to dominate the *Zeitgeist* friendly pastoral" vision of social order and civilization of the Modern Church, which interprets following the Spirit of the Times and the State authorities enforcing it as the Voice of the Holy Ghost. It is the swamp rather than the heavens that fuel the construction of "Catholic Civilization" today.

"This is Venice; my house is not a grange!" Brabantio shouts down to Rodrigo and Iago in Shakespeare's *Othello,* thereby dismissing straightaway their loud and wicked call to take immediate action upon what are but slanderous lies. Brabantio's instinct is not to heed them, precisely because everything in his environment gives him an initial "push" to look upwards to determine the truth, goodness and beauty of what is being said before acting upon it. Othello later lacks this crucial push when left to his own devices in Cyprus. The awful result is that he looks downwards into himself and believes the absurdities that Brabantio in "Venice"—and that is to say, in the atmosphere of the truly civilized Catholic city, lacking the libido for the ugly—was first inclined to spit out like a piece of tainted meat.

Othello in Cyprus is operating without restraint in the fallen "civilization" that St. Augustine called the "City of Man." This City of Man will tempt the human race to join its ranks until the end of time. Why it should have such seductive powers over us is part of the incomprehensible mystery of iniquity. For it ultimately operates with that bizarre libido for the ugly that the naturalism of the Enlightenment and the Revolution, the palingenesist vision of Lamennais, and the dominant forces in the Church in our own time have made the guide for contemporary man and contemporary civilization. To paraphrase a line from H. L. Mencken, whose biting essay on the subject of the "libido for the ugly" gave me the title for this essay: "Enlightenment naturalism has chosen to build its clapboard horror of a civilization with its eyes open, and having chosen it, let it mellow into its present shocking depravity. It likes it as it is: beside it, the Parthenon would no doubt offend it."

Nineteenth-century Catholics knew men were meant to be part of the civilization of what St. Augustine calls the City of God. They knew that seeking to create this on earth as far as was humanly possible in a universe that would be subject to sin until the end of time was a duty that flowed from their primary task of gaining their personal salvation. And they knew that if they did not work to their utmost to give flesh to this project, nations would be comprised of nothing but "dull and dreary people populating dull and dreary zones of habitation."

40

Le Sillon, Modernism, and Catholicism as Democracy[†]

E UGÈNE DE RASTIGNAC IS A PRINCIPAL character in that series of novels dealing with the Restoration and July Monarchy (1815–1848) Era that Honoré de Balzac linked together under the title of *La Comédie Humaine* (The Human Comedy). He first appears in *Le Père Goriot* (Old Man Goriot, 1835) as a sympathetic, young, poor student from the provinces who nevertheless wants to "make it" in Parisian high society. While he does indeed turn down an offer of direct help from the devil, incarnated in another recurring figure of the series by the name of Vautrin, Rastignac flees from this satanic temptation, but only to pursue the same goal by other means. *"A nous deux, maintenant!"* ("It is between you [Paris] and me now!") he proclaims at the end of the novel as he confirms his quest for "conquest" of the city through his own personal sell-out to its moral corruption.

Far be it from me to suggest any exact comparison of Rastignac with Marc Sangnier (1873–1950), the founder in 1894 of the movement called Le Sillon (The Furrow). Even though the all too hagiographic discussions of Sangnier's life almost make one want to find in him some hidden personal flaw, it is clear that he, like Rastignac, also never made a direct deal with the devil. Moreover, Sangnier did not even share the moral weaknesses of Balzac's fictional nineteenth century social climber. He was too much of a practicing believer for those flaws. Still, he, too, did not abandon his dangerously obsessive goal—a Catholic marriage with modern democracy—but pursued it though the use of other tools: in his case, dubious and ultimately blinding "intuitive" ones.

It was in the crypt of the College Stanislas in Paris in 1894 that the polytechnic student Sangnier, born into a Catholic family wealthy enough to allow him eventually to dedicate himself entirely to his apostolic labors, first founded Le Sillon. Designed for the promotion of Leo XIII's program of political and social engagement

---

[†] First published in *The Angelus* (September 2020).

as expressed in *Rerum Novarum* (1891) and *Au Milieu des Sollic-itudes* (1892). The Furrow's first "study circle" rapidly expanded in number, bringing into its orbit not just students, but also priests, seminarians, and office and industrial workers, both in the provinces as well as throughout Paris. By 1905, after a good number of cardinals and bishops had given Sangnier's efforts their blessing, following pilgrimages to Rome where he and his followers were welcomed by two popes, and having established fruitful friendships with a variety of other Catholic activist organizations, Le Sillon claimed as many as 10,000 participants in 640 study circles.

Nevertheless, only one year later, in 1906, when internal debates had revealed some serious differences of opinion among its members, Sangnier decided to transform the movement he had created into something "new," now giving it the name of Le Plus Grand Sillon: "The Greater Furrow." But anyone familiar both with the personality of the man as well as the *modus ope-randi* of the organization's meetings and militant actions cannot really be surprised by the "development of doctrine" character-izing this supposedly new course. For Sangnier and Le Sillon had from the very outset exuded that overheated embrace of the importance of an irrational "vitality" as the prophetic key to Catholic Teaching promoted earlier in the century by the highly influential but eventually excommunicated Abbé de Lamennais (1782–1854); an approach that in the case of both men ended in confounding Catholicism with a passionate, energetic, "vitalist" commitment to democracy.

François Mauriac's 1913 novel, *L'Enfant Chargé de Chaines* (*Young Man in Chains*) described his experiences while tempo-rarily under the spell of Le Sillon, later summarizing Sangnier's cultivation of "vitality" very succinctly: "Everything about him was intuition, aspiration and movement of the heart." (See Hughes Petit, *L'Eglise, le Sillon, et l'Action Française*, Nouvelles Édtions Latines, 1998, p. 128; also for the material below). Jeanne Caron, author of another useful book on the movement, underlines his anti-rational, charismatic, Lamennais-like character still more clearly, indicating that he "made his choices with the light of intuition, inventing his path as he went along ... The modes of his action made reference to an interior certitude most often without passion for the mediation of discursive thought" (Ibid., 128).

Henry du Roure (1883–1914), one of Sangnier's closest lieutenants, gives an explanation as to why both the ordinary members of the movement as well as the activists known as the *Jeune Garde* breathed with "one common spirit in one common goal." This was because, although the discussions at the study circles appeared to observers to be free flowing, unguided, and almost anarchistic in character, all his devoted followers felt "the necessity to believe in Marc's providential vision and vow to him an absolute and unconditional confidence" (Ibid., p.17). For as with Lamennais, the vision of the prophetic leader dominated all, and neither of the two men was particularly willing to treat favorably disagreement from anyone else.

Deeper implications of Sangnier's unsurprising "development of doctrine" were very much emphasized by members of an organization with which he had at first had quite friendly relations: l'Action Française (French Action). Charles Maurras (1868–1952), its founder, responded to his "new course" criticism in a book entitled *Le Dilemme de Marc Sangnier* (*The Dilemma of Marc Sangnier*, 1906). Here, Maurras rejected Le Plus Grand Sillon's argument that Catholic social justice and modern democracy with its conception of the need to "free the individual" from "authority" were necessary partners, along with its attack on l'Action Française for its failure to recognize this indisputable truth by preferring the governance of the traditional French Monarchy. He noted that Sangnier reached his conclusions by completely overturning the movement's hierarchy of values. Democracy and liberty in the modern revolutionary sense of the terms had become his supreme guides as to what was defined as "Catholic" and "socially just": even though an historical study of what those pilot lights had actually accomplished since the 1700s proved that they destroyed the well-being of people at large for the benefit of a small elite that hypocritically waved the banner of liberty, equality and fraternity.

Maurras predicted that Sangnier—who to him appeared to spout off all-too-disputable slogans rather than logical thoughts designed for rational discussion, somewhat in the manner of Flaubert's "Dictionary of Received Ideas" in *Bouvard et Péchuchet*—would find that was "easier to agitate democratically than to get a Catholic result from it" (Ibid., p. 145). And referring to one of the most important new features of Le Plus Grand Sillon, the opening of its ranks to Protestants, Freethinkers and Socialists alongside believing Catholics, another Action Française supporter, Mgr. Anatole De Cabrières (1830–1921), the Bishop of Montpellier, perceived it as already having embraced heretical principles:

> ... the novelties, the unclear formulas, the chimerical hope of baptizing and canonizing even opinions that are far removed from the true Faith; that entire complex of confused notions in the bosom of which the intelligent minds of our times struggle, that modernism, in one word, that elusive Proteus of multiple forms, must profoundly disquiet us because they menace religion with the greatest peril. (Ibid., p. 158)

All critics of Sangnier insisted that Catholic social justice teachings were based upon the Kingship of Christ and Natural Law, and were in no way tied to any specific form of government, least of all one that had a tainted record with regard to openness to any supernatural and even rational guidance whatsoever. Yet Le Plus Grand Sillon took it for granted as a given that the morally good and just order emerged not from obedience to Christ and the world that conformed to and corrected itself according to His unchangeable message, but from democratic structures whose "passion" and "vital action" constituted the actual and sanctifying grace that moved men irresistibly heavenwards and in changing ways as well. Heresy? Impossible! For their democratic fervor on its own would prevent its Catholic followers from falling into doctrinal error, even though they seemed to be altering traditional definitions of human nature, liberty, and the meaning of "progress" along the way. Its goal, as the journal of "social action," *Democratie,* that the movement began raising funds for creating in 1908 was designed to promote, was the development in France of a "truly" democratic republic, where individuals were freed from all oppressive authority, and this as the clear fulfillment of the will of Christ. For, as Sangnier himself said:

> A man rose up who, working against political barbarism, allowed the democratic regime to prevail; a doctrine was founded which every day made oppression and nature herself back off before the Holy Liberty of souls; that doctrine is the Christian Doctrine ... that man is Christ Jesus, our God! He alone founded, He alone maintains the democratic principle. (Ibid., p. 201)

Two immediate effects of the creation of Le Plus Grand Sillon alarmed bishops who had once been friendly to and even quite active in their support of Sangnier's movement. One was the abandonment to their own devices of those study circles that were most closely connected to their particular dioceses and not prepared for a union with non-believers and even anti-Catholics through the fraternal glue supposedly provided by the grace of a common vital commitment to democracy. The other was the enthusiasm for the "new course" shown by a number of priests and seminarians who, utilizing the arguments provided through the movement, criticized episcopal efforts to dissuade them as the sort of oppressive authoritative behavior that would soon be discredited as anti-Catholic anyway under the development of doctrine desired by the Divine Founder of Democracy.

Opposition in both France and Italy rapidly mounted, with friends and foes of both Le Plus Grand Sillon and l'Action Française fueling the ever more public debate. But given the anti-Modernist campaign in Rome, it was inevitable that Pope St. Pius X would intervene in this clash of vitality and Tradition on the side of the opponents of Sangnier. His assault came with *Notre Charge Apostolique* (*Our Apostolic Duty*) on August 25, 1910, just as the movement's standard bearing journal *Democratie* had finally appeared on the scene. While praising "the happy days" of the original Sillon and urging a return to its path, Pius went on to condemn the principles of its "greater" successor along exactly the same lines we have already indicated above. True liberty, equality and fraternity, he explained, do indeed come from Our Lord, but at the end of the process of obedience to natural and supernatural laws and not through the mediation of an ever more democratic liberation of individuals from authorities that will remain valid until the last days; through transformation in Christ and not through some new form of democratic libertarian "grace" superior to that initially offered by the Savior. For St. Francis of Assisi was not somehow less of a model of the holy, free and charitable Christian man because he lived in a society that did not possess the tools of sanctification only unleashed through democracy.

Yes, it is true that Charles Maurras and l'Action Française were not without serious problems of their own vis-à-vis Church teaching. Nevertheless, their practical defense of the Catholic Faith at this time period was undeniable, and their particular critique of Le Plus Grand Sillon was spot on. While the l'Action Française was, to begin with, an association "of non-believers which, because it had taken up the defense of the Church in a number of circumstances, found itself joined by a number of Catholics to such a degree that these latter then occupied the key posts within it," Sangnier's group was one "founded among Catholics that opened up to unbelievers, and which, by that fact alone, gave proof of a certain softness in the fight versus anti-clericalism" (Ibid., p. 152).

Once again, Sangnier himself was devoted to the Catholic Faith. His real dilemma, contrary to the one that he posed to Maurras regarding the sole compatibility of social justice and an order of things accepting the principles of 1789, was that his utter faith in modern political democracy blinded him to the battles between the two. He was a man who suffered from what St. Cyril of Alexandria called *dypsychia*, the possession of two souls leading in opposite directions, as this great Eastern Church Father saw all too vividly among Christians of his own day still bound to pagan practices.

The founder of Le Sillon did, indeed "submit" to Pope St. Pius X's condemnation of his "new course." He did so, however, not by returning to its earlier "happy days," which always contained the seeds of its further development within them anyway. Instead, dissolving Le Plus Grand Sillon, he dedicated himself in 1912 openly to politics as such, through a movement called *Jeune République*, totally democratic in its aspirations. But Sangnier's star began to rise again, especially from the late 1920s onwards, closely connected with the intensification of the problems of l'Action Française with respect to the Church mentioned above. We, to our misfortune, have lived to see the way in which Sangnier's political modernism, basically canonized by the mainstream Church in our own time, has so overturned the hierarchy of values that the Democratic Catholicism preached around us today would most certainly offend the believing Catholic psyche of the founder of Le Sillon himself, whatever his *dypsychia* might have been. For "Paris" in the form of Democracy has today conquered "Rastignac" in the figure of Sangnier and Le Sillon, and seemingly the Catholic world as a whole, and the battle is now "between us and this monster from hell." It is a battle through which that monster can do a great deal of damage to souls, but one that in the final analysis it cannot win.

41

Tough Environments
Breed Militant Catholics†

PROTESTANT SECULARIST AUSTRALIA
AND "BOB" SANTAMARIA

"EVERYTHING IN AUSTRALIA IS TRYING TO kill you." That was the ominous title of a video I once watched that outlined in chilling detail all of the shabby ways that native animals, insects and flora, from the familiar kangaroo down to organisms totally unknown to me beforehand, were out to ruin human life "down under."

Little did I suspect at the time that these life-threatening organisms would come to include the government of the State of Victoria, the anti-Covid measures of which seem designed to liquidate the entire social nature of mankind. And little did I imagine that that State harbored a number of elements deadly to Catholic life in particular, from long before the irrational, degrading and politically manipulated Reign of Terror raging there today. But tough environments seem to stimulate the emergence of brave men ready to take the steps necessary to deal with them. And no one battled against the difficult anti-Catholic problems in Australia in a more persistent and influential manner than Bartolomeo Agostino Santamaria (1915–1998).

Born of Sicilian immigrants living in Melbourne, the capital and largest city of Victoria State, "Bob"—as Santamaria was always known to friend and foe alike—experienced all the anti-Catholic prejudice that Anglo-Saxon, Protestant and secularist-Freemasonic Victoria could toss at him. He fought against these not just privately, but, much more importantly, publicly, because of their dire effects in the socio-political and economic realms, becoming one of the model Catholic militants of the twentieth century.

What made Bob so exemplary was his clear awareness that effective "transformation of all things in Christ" had to be

---

† First published in *The Angelus* (March 2021).

founded on two fundamental pillars: on the one hand, a total loyalty to sound Catholic doctrine which could never be sacrificed for "success," but did indeed have to be applied—always with risks—to the change and confusion of a "practical" daily life lived by flawed, sinful men, who did not necessarily act rationally and consistently; and, on the other, upon the cooperation of a militant laity committed to Catholic Action with a militant teaching clergy that guided it theologically and encouraged its daily activist battle with the foe.

Bob's brilliant career was to unfold precisely because the model cleric ready to make this second pillar of effective Catholic Action a reality was ready to launch it: Daniel Mannix (1864–1963), Archbishop of Melbourne from 1917 until his death in 1963. Mannix, a prelate who understood, in the immortal words of an old friend of mine, that the job of a bishop was "to bish," something that he often did with a great big stick, nevertheless paired powerful episcopal leadership with the deepest respect for the unique role of the laity and the wide autonomy in many questions of practical socio-political action that this required.

Santamaria came to Mannix's attention in 1937, when Bob was only 22 years old, due to the impact that the young man made in a famous public debate with prominent Leftists on the Spanish Civil War. Already well-grounded in Catholic Social Doctrine, and particularly interested in the ideas of the English Distributists, he fervently promoted the need for believers to build an economic system that rejected the materialism and injustices of both unrestricted Capitalism and Marxist or Marxist-Leninist Socialism. A member of the recently founded Campion Society and editor of an Australian review, *The Catholic Worker*, at least partly influenced by that of Dorothy Day in New York, Bob still presumed that his main work would be a career in law.

Mannix changed his plans dramatically. He enticed Santamaria into becoming one of two members of the new National Secretariate of Catholic Action, which began its work in 1938. It must be said that in making this choice, the archbishop thereby also demonstrated his freedom from another prejudice that plagued men and women like Bob: the general disdain of his fellow Irish-Australian Catholics for believers of Italian background. Having won him over to full time militancy, Mannix's protégé was made responsible for preparing almost all of the Annual Social Justice statements of the Australian Episcopacy between 1941 and 1956.

Bob's foundation of the National Catholic Rural Movement in 1939, designed to promote small farm ownership, was certainly dictated by both intellectual and practical concerns, very much reflecting contemporary Distributist ideas. Nevertheless, nothing illustrates his insistence upon that joint commitment to sound doctrine and the reality of the need to make risky choices in implementing its vision under confused daily realities constituting the first fundamental pillar of effective lay action than the creation of the Catholic Social Studies Movement in 1941.

Catholic Social Doctrine clearly rejected both the atomistic, individualist materialism of classical liberal capitalist thought, as well as the collectivist materialism of Marxist Socialism most effectively represented after the First World War by Marxist-Leninist Communism. Some Catholics, due to a primary fear of the latter, inclined towards supporting the Australian Liberal Party, which was anti-Communist but not on the same wavelength as the Church regarding the problems of capitalist society. A large number of working-class believers, suffering from economic injustices, saw greater hope coming from the Labour Party, which was, however, quite subject to anti-Catholic and outright Communist influences. Unfortunately, given the general lack of intellectual formation regarding Catholic Social Doctrine, both Liberal- and Labour-leaning believers tended bit by bit to gravitate towards the unacceptable teachings prevalent in both parties.

"The Movement" was to a large degree a machine for overcoming practical obstacles to the achievement of integral Catholic goals in economic life through a specific targeting of the working classes and the Labour Party they supported. It pursued its aim through the "Groupers," who were "Movement" members who became part of "Industrial Groups" which fought to rid trade unions of Communist domination and guide them down a Catholic direction. So successful was the work of the Groupers that the trade unions, all but of two of which were under Communist control in 1949, were almost entirely in Catholic-influenced hands by 1952.

Although we have seen that the Labour Party, which was under the leadership of Herbert Vere Evatt (1894–1965) from 1951 onwards, was no friend of Catholics, support of the trade unions was central to its political life, and Grouper effectiveness led it openly to seek Santamaria's support for the General Election of 1954. When it lost that election, and control over Victoria as well, remaining out of power over the central government of Australia down to 1972, Evatt openly and violently blamed Santamaria and the Catholics for the defeat.

Any possible leadership opening to the Groupers was now closed, and the Labour Party suffered what was called "The Split," with Catholics expelled from its ranks and forming their own Democratic Labour Party under Santamaria's influence to carry on fighting for the cause. So pathologically outraged was Evatt over the consequent inability of Labour to regain power over the central government that Santamaria and his pursuit of Catholic influence over Australian political life became for him public enemy number one.

Although Bob moved forward with his work through the Democratic Labour Party, trouble was brewing for his profound understanding of Catholic Action and Catholic Social Doctrine. This was not due to competition from those Catholics, with powerful clerical backing in New South Wales, who supported cooperation with the Liberal Party. It was rather a direct result of the revolution in the Church brought about by Vatican Council Two and its aftermath. For that revolution overturned the two pillars upon which Santamaria had built his work: accepting the risks of practical action *only if in union with sound doctrine*, and guiding a militant laity that could count upon the support of a vibrant teaching clergy respectful of that laity's distinctly active role in promoting the Christian mission. What went wrong?

In supposedly "liberating" the realm of the "practical" from the supernatural guidance of doctrinal truth, all that the "spirit of Vatican Two" achieved was to allow for exactly what anti-Liberal, anti-Pluralist Catholics since the nineteenth century had predicted would happen: 1) the giving of carte blanche to the strongest worldly passions successfully to proclaim their right to dominate Church life, unguided and uncorrected by supernatural truth and grace; and, 2) the creation of a craven episcopacy eager to give its blessing to whatever "worked" according to the standards of willful fallen men, thereby wreaking havoc with the entire project of a corrective 'transformation of all things in

Christ." To make matters worse, just as this evil was unfolding, Bob's protector and soulmate, Archbishop Mannix, went to his eternal reward.

One victim of the revolution was the Democratic Labour Party, which now suffered internal divisions of its own and ceased to function. Still, Bob soldiered on for many, many years to come, working more and more in ways that avoided the emasculating control of real Catholic Action coming from an arrogant episcopacy that ironically was in practice an increasingly puppet-like servant of the goals of powerful but morally corrupt lay forces. He fought on by means of organizations like the National Civic Council and the Australian Family Association, as well as through his writing and a long-lived television commentary called "Point of View." Moreover, his Thomas More Centre and its literary voice, *AD2000*, gave support to the causes of the growing Traditionalist Movement, which alone was seriously defending the kind of Catholic Action he had approved of all of his life.

One man deeply influenced by Santamaria is George Cardinal Pell (1941–2023). Bob died in March of 1998 during Pell's tenure as Archbishop of Melbourne (1996–2001), and it was he who delivered a panegyric at the Funeral Mass.

Calling attention to the great opposition and outright hatreds that Bob had aroused, along with his inevitably risky and not necessarily successful battles for control of the social sphere, Pell praised Santamaria most for having made it clear that the battle of Catholicism with the world, the flesh and the devil was a deadly serious one:

> We are told that the sure mark of the false prophet is that all people speak well of him. In death, as in life, Bob Santamaria has triumphantly escaped such a fate... Thanks to Bob Santamaria, much more of this struggle is now in the open, with the issues available to public scrutiny. This represents progress. He could not remove or much deflect the mighty forces damaging faith and morals in the Western world, but he has managed to alert an increasing number of us to the folly of embracing the forces seeking our destruction.

Tough environments breed militant Catholics who pass the torch on to others inspired by them. Cardinal Pell himself now knows the price one must be prepared to pay for following in

Bob's footsteps. For the forces against which Santamaria fought in Victoria State and elsewhere have struck at him as well. But he knows from Bob that this was to be expected not just in Australia, but all across the globe. Because in our time especially, it seems that not just "down under," but everywhere "everything is trying to kill Catholics."

42

The Roman Question†

I. A TALE OF TWO SYLLABI

If I were forced to choose a single papal document representing everything that the friends of "modernity"—both those who also call themselves Catholic as well as men of purely naturalist convictions—have consistently chastised as being most regrettably obscurantist, I cannot imagine that they would fault me for placing the *Syllabus of Errors* of Pope Pius IX, promulgated on December 8th, 1864, at the top of their list. Pilloried down to our own day for its lamentable reactionary content, most contemporary critics of the Syllabus were also convinced that the Syllabus was nothing other than a politically motivated papal response to the latest attempt of Pius' opponents to resolve the dilemma of the Temporal Power; to deal with "the Roman Question."[1]

This "Roman Question" had gained ever greater importance since the 1790s due to three factors: the repeated violation of the Papal States as a result of the invasions of the peninsula accompanying the French Revolution and the Napoleonic Wars; the Restoration Era debates over Italian unity and what it would mean for the Papacy; and, finally, the further disruptions to the Church's territories brought about by the violence of the so-called Risorgimento. Such disruptions, beginning with the Pope's flight from the Eternal City and the establishment of the Roman Republic of 1848, were temporarily ended by French military intervention the following year. They became more threatening with Napoleon III's sudden adoption of a pro-Risorgimento foreign policy and the Kingdom of Sardinia's interpretation of its alliance with him against Austria in 1859–1860 as one giving permission to overrun papal lands outside the old Patrimony of St. Peter. At least as the argument of the critics ran, it was the Emperor Napoleon's

---

† First published in the Spanish journal *Verbo* (November–December 2021).

---

1 Hence, the response of Msgr. Dupanloup, *The Convention of 15 September and the Encyclical of 8 December* (1865): See J. Rao, *Removing the Blindfold* (Angelus Press, 2014).

September Convention with the new Kingdom of Italy in 1864, justifying removal of the French troops still remaining in the Eternal City in exchange for the rather dubious promise of the Italian government to fix its capital permanently in Florence rather than in what was supposedly to remain a papally-governed Rome, that caused a suspicious Pius IX to vent his clearly political frustrations through the promulgation of the Syllabus.

Catholic friends of "modernity" and their moderate-minded naturalist allies insist that thankfully there has been a happy ending to this sad nineteenth-century tale in our own times. For Catholicism in the present age is guided by the teaching of the Second Vatican Council, whose "spirit" they praise as having created a new and quite different kind of "Syllabus"; a "Counter-Syllabus." By means of this "Counter-Syllabus," a disposition towards positive embrace of the good to be found in the modern worldview has replaced the negative obscurantism of Pius IX's document. Encouraged by prophetic Catholics tragically crushed by the reactionary papal teachings of the nineteenth century, a major consequence of this change of spirit has been the raising of hearts and minds from exaggeratedly earthly affairs to truly supernatural concerns. Hence, the assertion by Cardinal Angelo dell'Acqua, the representative of Pope Paul VI at the hundredth anniversary of the conquest of the Eternal City on September 20th, 1970, that the end of the Temporal Power—the conclusion of the "Roman Question"—was an event of providential, positive significance for the life of the Catholic Church.[2]

The modern "Roman Question," from 1798 down not just to 1870 or 1970 but to today as well, is indeed a spiritual one. Nevertheless, an appreciation of its complexity and a proper judgment regarding the "providential" character of its supposedly more spiritual conclusion cannot be gained and made through the arguments provided by the ideologues of modernity. For the defense of the Temporal Power provided by the supposedly politically-inspired Syllabus of 1864 was actually shaped by a profound nineteenth century religious revival viewing all things natural in the light of the transformative, supernatural grace of the Incarnation, while the Counter-Syllabus of the 1960s has actually guaranteed the burial of the spiritual realm under the dead weight of materialist temporal powers, creating a wrong-headed union of Church and State tighter than anything

2 *Avvenire*, September 20, 2000.

that ever existed in the past in the process. Moreover, commitment to that Counter-Syllabus has placed a blindfold over the eyes of contemporary Catholic man, preventing him from doing what he needs to do to learn the truth regarding the Roman Question; a blindfold that we will now proceed to remove.

II. THE FIRST SYLLABUS AND THE CATHOLIC REVIVAL: TRANSFORMATION OF ALL THINGS IN CHRIST

Far from being a document bound to the highly specific concerns of the September Convention of 1864, Pius IX's Syllabus of Errors had a universal spiritual purpose and had been in serious preparation since 1851. Among those thinkers and activists most significant to its genesis, completion and interpretation were the editors of the Roman Jesuit journal, *La Civiltà Cattolica*. A really solid understanding of the Syllabus and what it meant for the Roman Question demands an exploration of the influences upon and character of this multi-disciplinary periodical, founded in 1850 with the express goal of providing a comprehensive Catholic critique of the revolutionary mentality based upon the fullness of the Faith. It appeared in hefty biweekly installments filled with theological, philosophical, historical, sociological and literary articles.[3]

Along with many other contemporary critics of revolutionary change, the *Civiltà* editors realized that that fullness of Faith had been lost due to the enormous success that eighteenth century Enlightenment ideas had had in dragging religious thought and activity down to a depressingly naturalist level; a success that is generally unknown to most Catholics in our own day. This secularization of spirit had left the Church badly alienated from her rich, supernaturally rooted reality; her only true source of justification and serious effectiveness, both intellectually as well as on the practical level.

---

3   Taparelli, "Dell'Elemento Divino nella Società," *La Civiltà Cattolica* (henceforth, C. C.) ii, 9 (1855), 390, A. Dioscordi, "La Rivoluzione Italiana e la *Civiltà Cattolica*," *Atti del XXXII Congresso del Risorgimento Italiano* (Rome, 1956), p. 94; Calvetti, "Congruenze Sociali di una Definizione Dogmatica sull'Immacolato Concepimento della B. V. M.," i, 8 (1851), 377–396. See also E. Papa, *Il Sillabo di Pio IX e la Stampa Francese, Inglese, e Italiana* (Rome, 1968); and E. Avogadro della Motta, *Saggio Intorno al Socialismo e alle Dottrine e Tendenze Socialistiche* (Turin, 1851). *Memorie della Civiltà Cattolica*, p. xlvi. G. Martina, "Osservazione sulle varie relazioni del Sillabo," *Chiesa e stato nell'ottocento*, iv, ii, 437.

Such alienation prevented Catholics from understanding the central consequence of the Incarnation: its offer of an eternal participation of the individual person in the life of God made possible only by means of the Hypostatic Union. This "divinization"—the term used by the Greek Fathers of the Church to describe it—was to be obtained by life-long personal labor through the complex network of *natural* human societies and under their various *visible* authorities, all rooted firmly in the teaching and grace of Christ's *supernatural* Mystical Body. Moreover, the obviously corporeal message of the Incarnation showed that each and every one of these authoritative societies, the Church included, had to employ every tool that the physical world created by a loving and redeeming Creator had given them. The individual and society, the spiritual and the physical: all stood firmly together in the incarnational plan for man's storming of Heaven.

Failure to understand this truth would thwart the whole mission of the God-Man at any time in history, but it had especially disastrous consequences in a world that was troubled by the ideas of the naturalist Enlightenment; the world of the Italian Risorgimento. For this world illicitly appropriated much Christian language regarding individual freedom, dignity and perfection for its intrinsically anti-incarnational purposes, assuring not the "divinization" of the individual in Christ, but the triumph of the strongest, fallen, sinful, self-destructive human wills in the process.

All these themes reflect the Christocentric focus of the European-wide Catholic revival movement of the first half of the nineteenth century, both in thought as well as in piety, with study of the patristic doctrine of the Mystical Body of Christ and devotion to the cult of the Sacred Heart central to our discussion.[4] One of the most impressive examples of this trend was the work of the Tübingen professor, Johann Adam Möhler (1796–1838). Möhler's *Symbolik* (1832) avoided discussing the Church in the naturalist manner, as a purely juridical structure, and treated it, instead, "from the standpoint of heaven," as the continuation of the Incarnation, a perpetual manifestation of God made man.[5] His influence

---

4   R. Aubert, *Le pontificat de Pie IX* (Histoire de l'Eglise, xxi, Paris, 1952), 43.
5   G. Goyau, *L'Allemagne Religieuse: Le Catholicisme* (Four Volumes, Paris, 1905), ii, 38–39. The subtlety of Möhler's argument in this regard helped

extended to Italy, where men like Giovanni Perrone (1794–1876), the influential Roman Jesuit theologian, praised and defended him. Perrone was also a proponent of the cult of the Sacred Heart, which made the reality of God's influence upon the natural order as a whole palpable to the average pious believer. In his theological writings on this devotion, Perrone insisted that society and the individuals composing it were meant to be elevated in union with Christ and Christ's Church, analogous to the manner in which Christ's human nature, represented by His Heart, was made sacred in union with the Word, the Second Person of the Blessed Trinity.[6]

Perrone's friends and fellow Jesuit editors at *La Civiltà Cattolica* developed these specific ideas in impressive detail and variegated form.[7] Three of them should especially be mentioned, given their importance to my discussion: Carlo Maria Curci (1809–1891), Matteo Liberatore (1810–1892), and Luigi Prospero Taparelli d'Azeglio (1793–1862). Both Curci and Liberatore had been students of Taparelli while the latter was teaching in Naples. Already well known for his *Saggio Teoretico di Diritto Naturale Appoggiato sul Fatto*, published in the 1840s, their teacher exercised "a kind of moral dictatorship" over the entire Italian Catholic camp through the *Civiltà*.[8] A step-by-step discussion of the central argument

to make him a precursor of all types of schools, from the most orthodox to the most heretical.

6   Aubert, *Op. cit.*, 464–466; G. Perrone, "Tractatus de Cultu Sanctorum. De Devotione in Erga Sacratissimum cor Jesu," *Theologiae. Cursus Completus*, ed., J. P. M. (9th ed., Paris, 1841), viii, 1478–1491.

7   See, for example, Taparelli, Carteggi, 142–144, 161–162, 393–395.

8   P. Droulers, *Chiesa e Stato nell'Ottocento*, iii, i, 146. Aubert, *Op. cit.*, 226; Jemolo, *Op. cit.*, pp. 188, 199. Curci, *Memorie*, pp. 38–50, 88–205; *Memorie della Civiltà Cattolica*, pp. xix–xxiv; T. Mirabella, *Il Pensiero Politico di P. Matteo Liberatore ed il suo Contributo ai Rapporti tra Chiesa e Stato* (Milan, 1956), pp. 39, 70–73; C. Piccirillo, "Le 'Idee Nuove' del Padre Curci," *Chiesa e Stato nell'Ottocento* (Italia sacra, iii–iv, 1964), iv, ii, 608–611. Mirabella, *Op. cit.*, pp. 3, 5n, 39–42, 45, 84–89, 223, 328, 350; P. Droulers, "Question Sociale, État, Église dans la *Civiltà Cattolica* a ses débuts," in *Chiesa e Stato nell'Ottocento*, iii, i, 123, 123n. See Jacquin, *Op. cit.*, pp. 1–66. Taparelli d'Azeglio was born of an aristocratic Piedmontese family, another of whose sons, Massimo (1796–1866), is well known to Italians as a major liberal leader of the independence movement, the so-called Risorgimento. His fame primarily rested on his work as an educator in Naples, Palermo, and as Rector of the Roman College (1824–1829) along with his widely used *Saggio Teoretico di Dritto Naturale* ("Theoretical Essay on Natural Law," 1840), published during his stay in Sicily.

unifying all of the editors' concerns leads us straight from the individual human person through the complex network of societies in which he perfects himself to the issue of the Temporal Power and the "Roman Question." Once again, that unifying argument is the insistence that the Incarnation had had the effect of "shocking" Creation to its very depths, revealing to nature its mission of working in union with grace to join everything together in Christ's Mystical Body for the sake of the adoration of the Creator God.[9]

> God . . . has established one sole order composed of two parts: nature exalted by grace, and grace vivifying nature. He has not confused these two orders, but He has coordinated them. One force alone is the model and one thing alone the motive principle and ultimate end of divine creation: Christ . . . All the rest is subordinated to Him. The goal of human existence is to form the Mystical Body of this Christ, of this Head of the elect, of this Eternal Priest, of this King of the immortal Kingdom and the society of those who will eternally glorify Him.

III. THE INCARNATION AND THE TEMPORAL POWER

The Incarnation confirmed the importance of everything natural by showing that God so loved the world that He was ready to send His only begotten Son to die for it. It drove home the truth that nothing is superfluous to God; that the messages of nature all have something valuable to say and must be attended to if the full goal of life is to be known and fulfilled. All such natural messages must be preserved and cherished if man is to live life fully and gain perfection.

The highest of nature's messages is the reality that human beings exist as individual creatures of flesh, blood and soul, and not as abstract "human natures." What effect does the Hypostatic Union have on individual human beings possessing only a human nature and only a human personality? Like Möhler and Perrone, the *Civiltà* editors insisted that participation in the life of Christ offered the believer a prize that "a person could scarcely conjecture in the abstract"; that of attaining "a perfection that surpasses all that is innate in him,"[10] becoming "a participant in

---

9 Liberatore, "L'Enciclica dell'8 Dicembre," C. C., vi, 1 (1865), 287–288.
10 Ballerini, "Il Progresso," C. C., iii, 12 (1858), 432; See, also, Liberatore, "Il Restauro della Personalità," C. C., i, 2 (1850), 369, 536; Berardi, "La

Christ,"[11] "in a sense, initiated into his substance,"[12] "the living image of the Nazarene."[13]

"Divinized" men thus see the whole of Creation from the transcendent position of God; from the very ground of Being Himself. Through the gift of supernatural grace bestowed by the one, true, transcendent God, men do more than gain divinity: they also come into the full possession of their humanity. "Divinized" individuals thus become the chief agents of passing the rest of the world through its purgation from sin, allowing nature in its entirety to "put on Christ." As Bertrando Spaventa (1817–1883), an Italian Hegelian enemy of the *Civiltà* ironically, but correctly, commented: "in a theocracy, it is God Who dominates; in the system of the Jesuits, it is man considered as God who dominates."[14] There would be a true improvement of the world only as it was "transfigured vitally through individuals," "by means of the individual operation of each member of the faithful," "no longer by the finger of God, but [indirectly] by that of man, divinized by grace."[15] But this work continues unabated until the end of time due to the ever-present danger of sin and the reality of man's free will.

All of the other messages of nature, the *Civiltà* argued, are arranged hierarchically to serve the individual human person as he seeks to learn life's meaning, and thereby have life more abundantly. But natural messages for natural creatures of flesh and blood as well as soul require bodies or societies with visible, effective natural authority to incarnate them. Each natural authoritative society does an immense service for men, pinpointing in

Passione di Gesù Cristo," C. C., vi, 2 (1865), 42; Also, Liberatore, "Se la Personalità Abbia da Temere dalla Chiesa," C. C., i, 2 (1850), 533; Taparelli, *Carteggi*, 115; "Dell'Elemento Divino," C. C., ii, 9 (1855), 134; "La Stampa Libera," C. C.,i, 4 (1850), 256–257.

11   Ballerini, "Il Vero ed il Falso nel Progresso," C. C., iv, 3 (1850), 176.

12   Liberatore, agreeing with a book reviewed in the journal, "Della Differenza e della Somiglianza tra Dio e l'Uomo. Cenni Bilico-Cattolici di Don Placidio Talia," C. C., iii, 3 (1856), 688.

13   Taparelli, C. C., "Un Raggio di Luce," iv, 10 (1861), 315, 315–325; Also, "Il Pedagogo Supremo della Chiesa e del Mondo," C. C., v, 2 (1862), 449; Ballerini, "Il Vero ed il Falso nel Progresso," C. C., iv, 3 (1859), 176; Ibid., 548.

14   Spaventa, "La Teocrazia," in *La Politica dei Gesuiti nel Secolo XVI e nel XIX*, ed., Giovanni Gentile (Milan, 1911), p. 96.

15   Taparelli, "Dell'Elemento Divino nella Società," C. C., ii, 9 (1855), 135, 134; Ballerini, "Il Vero ed il Falso," C. C., iv, 3 (1859), 414–426.

a different, physically concrete way the meaning of virtue. Each makes it possible to "see" moral duties more vividly; each manifests the precise material and emotional assistance it offers the individual striving for perfection. The more thoroughly the natural truth in question is embodied by the society concerned, the greater the likelihood of the truth being understood, and the more perfect the imitation of God, Who taught "as one having authority" for "those who have eyes to see and ears to hear."[16]

Membership in the "society" of Christ and subjection to His authority stands at the pinnacle of this hierarchy of authoritative social bodies. Christ's first disciples encountered Him directly. We, their posterity, encounter Him through submission to what St. Augustine calls the "whole Christ"—the Christ encompassing the glorified God-Man in heaven and His visible Body on earth: the Church. She is, literally, Christ-alive-on-earth, acting for us here below, through human persons and with human as well as divine tools. The Church "is Jesus Christ, but Jesus Christ spread out and communicated by means of charity and faith in the totality of the Sons of God"; "a perpetual and universal sacrifice offered to God by the great Priest who offered Himself"; "a second Incarnation of the Son of God." Hypostatically united with God, the Church in its simultaneous humanity and divinity confuses and enrages the world in the same way that Christ confused and enraged the Jews.[17]

> Christ, then lives in the Church as the principle of the life of this Church, and as a principle so joined that it yields an image of the Hypostatic Union, producing, accordingly, a human-divine life, in imitation of the life that Christ Himself led on the earth, not withstanding the continued existence of the human elements in their entirety.

---

16   See, among many others, Taparelli, "Teorie Sociali sull'Insegnamento," C. C., i, 1 (1850), 26–51, 129– 157, 257–274, 369–380; "La Società," C. C., ii, 3 (1853), 225–242; Liberatore, "Valore del Razionalismo Intorno alla Civiltà," C. C., i, 1 (1850), 159–182; Taparelli, "Il Superiore," C. C., ii, 10 (1855), 5–20, 241–256, 369–383; Taparelli, "L'Autorità Sociale," C. C., ii, 4 (1853), 19–37, 175–189, 291–304; "Trasmissione dell'Autorità," C. C., iii, 3 (1856), 369–378; "Il Superiore," C. C., ii, 10 (1855), 5–20, 241–256, 369–383; "Ordini Rappresentativi," C. C., i, 6 (1851), 497–518, 641–652.

17   Liberatore, "Se la Personalità Abbia da Temere dalla Chiesa," C. C., i, 2 (1850), 535; Berardi, "La Passione di Gesù Cristo nella sua Chiesa," C. C., vi, 2 (1865), 41, 42, 43 (extended quotations).

[The Incarnation] is a miracle repeated in a manner equally ineffable, although diverse, in the great body of the Church, divinized by the life that Jesus Christ lives in her, and still left with all the human characteristics, because composed of men. And thus, things are also true of her that seem contradictory, but are only opposites. In this way, it can be understood that Christ is united with His Church not like any other founder with respect to a society of men ... but in the way the head is joined together with the body in a man, and thus blended as the vital principle with a living thing.

Not just individuals, therefore, but the authoritative social bodies that transmit nature's messages to them must submit to the active "cleansing" guidance of the Church for their own perfection.[18] This includes the State, which is purged of the false glory accorded it by men believing it to be a god holding the key to all truths, divine as well as human.[19] It also includes that powerful and harder to define entity that we call our homeland, our *patria*, with all of its authoritative familial, linguistic and customary influences upon us. So dreadful is its power when gone astray that those under its influence—as everyone certainly is under its influence with respect to the common language and prejudices of his homeland—will generally not even know how to phrase their complaints against it. The Church must show the patriot that his immediate homeland is good but flawed and not infallible; that it is only a partial homeland; that he has another, permanent homeland in the Mystical Body, in God, through Christ, in heaven; a homeland with its own language, customs and affection in the form of divine love to guide it. The patriot must be taught that patriotic love and sacrifice for the glory of his nation has moral limits; that the spirit and authority of a specific place and time must bend to Christ.

And this also involves recognizing that each *patria* is part of the unity of all men in an international, worldwide fraternity, which the Church has the mission of solidifying, and which may even exist politically, as it did, at least in part, in the Middle Ages, guided by the Roman Pontiffs. The idea of a just international order—a just homeland for all mankind in which both his common nature

---

18   Curci, "Esclusività," C. C., i, 3 (1850), 476.
19   Taparelli, "Trasmissione dell'Autorità," C. C., iii, 3(1865), 177–178.

and his true national differences are simultaneously respected—was far more than merely "helped" by Christianity. It was only within Catholic Christendom, headed by the Papacy, that it first became an effective natural force at all; an effective natural force designed for the benefit of individuals seeking divinization through submission to Christ.[20]

It is this entire Incarnation-focused substructure that supported the *Civiltà*'s defense of the Temporal Power. The Mystical Body's supernatural teaching and grace were meant for the benefit of the divinization of social individuals of flesh, blood, and soul. Her ineffable supernatural mission did not merely justify but actually required the use also of all natural, material tools available to her for fulfillment of her task. If it did not so require, she would be condemned to rule over nothing but inhuman, disembodied spirits, just as natural social authorities deprived of her spiritual guidance would rule over lifeless robots.[21] By giving flesh to spiritual principles with which even the supreme political authority, much less a given *patria*, could not meddle, she dealt illicit, degrading force "a mortal and irreparable blow."[22] She confirmed the value of all social authorities ready to rise up against a willful oppressor in defense of the specific truths they each incarnated. She gave the individual human person such a sense of his dignity and the path to its perfection that he would not readily accept his enslavement by any earthly force. And she backed all this up with the Church's provision of supernatural grace, the chief antidote to the natural as well as the eternal wages of sin.[23]

If the practical, historical development of this divinizing work, whose central physical authority was the Roman Pontiff, had proven to entail the possession of some small slice of territory in central Italy that appeared to allow him a basic independence of action, then this territory "is a right of Christ, whose Mystical Body is the Church, and it is to Him which rightly belongs all

---

20   See, for example, Taparelli, "La Separazione della Chiesa dallo Stato," C. C., i, 1 (1850), 652–654; "La Tregua di Dio," C. C., iv, 2 (1859), 529–541.
21   Taparelli, "La Separazione della Chiesa dallo Stato," C. C., i, i (1850), 657–669; Taparelli, "Le Armi Spirituali a Difesa del Temporale," C. C., iv, 6 (1860), 249–265; Ibid., 255; Taparelli, "Lo Stato Separato dalla Chiesa," C. C., i, 7 (1851), 263.
22   Liberatore, "Il Restauro della Personalità," C. C., i, 2 (1850), 377.
23   Taparelli, *Carteggi*, 132.

of her property."[24] If one would only understand the Temporal Power in this incarnational perspective, Liberatore said, then everything, even "the very carriages of the cardinals, would change their appearance in your eyes."[25] The divinization of the Christian individual of flesh, blood and soul by means of authorities of flesh, blood and soul amply justified it.

IV. THE ROMAN QUESTION & THE TRIUMPH OF THE IRRATIONAL WILL

However justifiable it was, the editors of *La Civiltà Cattolica* never deemed the maintenance of the existing Papal States to be a Catholic dogma. Taparelli's understanding of the many ways that authority is incarnated and becomes legitimate very much accommodated the reality of historical change and the need to accept and respond to it in a proper way. Liberatore insisted that even without the historical Papal States the Church would survive due to the strength of "the omnipotent Word of God mystically incorporated in her; her internal principle, which is Christ."[26] The dogmatic necessity, in their minds, lay in admitting a temporal, physical impact to the spiritual authority of the Papacy that definitely would permit the possibility of papal claims to authority over an earthly domain as well as outrage over its robbery. But this did not preclude a theoretical debate over just how useful possession of the older States of the Church actually had been to its central spiritual-temporal mission in the past, and a practical one regarding what good its retention would serve in a contemporary world of mega-states of vast military and economic power.

Both dogmatically and practically speaking, the loss of the temporal impact of the spiritual authority of the head of the Roman

---

24 Liberatore, "La Passione di Cristo e l'Epoca Presente," C. C., v, 2 (1862), 5. Berardi, "La Passione di Gesù Cristo," C. C., vi, 2 (1865), 40; Taparelli, "Un Raggio di Luce," C. C., iv, 10 (1861), 293; Liberatore, "Il Principato Civile Dei Papi Tutela della Dignità Personale," C. C., i, 3 (1850), 99, 210.
25 Liberatore, "Roma e il Mondo," C. C., i, 7 (1851), 533; See, also, Taparelli, "Il Pedagogo Supremo del Mondo e della Chiesa," C. C., v, 2 (1862), 449; Liberatore, "Proposta di Dimostrazione Cattolica per gl'Italiani," C. C., vi, 3 (1865), 523; Piccirillo, "Il Prete e il Sacerdozio Cattolico Considerato in Tutte le sue Glorie per l'Abate P. A. Turquois," C. C., iii, 8 (1857), 87.
26 Liberatore, "Il Principato Civile Dei Papi Tutela della Dignità Personale," C. C., i, 3 (1850), 99, 210.

Church would be an unmitigated disaster, for the consequence would be that "*il mondo ricadrà nella prisca superstizione, nelle lurida corruttela del gentilesimo.*"[27] It was precisely this disaster that threatened the specific, historical, temporal subjects of the Pope at the hands first of the Sardinian and then of the new Italian Kingdom in the 1850s and1860s. Disaster threatened them due to the fact that both these kingdoms were guided by the ideology of naturalist modernity, with its refusal to treat supernatural truths with any respect whatsoever, and, most particularly, by a militantly naturalist, and ultimately self-contradictory nationalism. It was this dreadful threat that made the *immediate* answer to the "Roman Question" the unquestionable duty of the current pontiff to do his utmost to protect the individuals on the path to divinization living in the existing Papal States, however non-dogmatic in character the possession of a Temporal Power might be, from the ravages a naturalist victory would ensure.

For what would the "freedom" coming through this agent of the naturalist Enlightenment mean for his subjects but the replacement of a "participation in Christ" with a burial in the fallen, unredeemed, passionate, willful perversion of his true natural character alone? Naturalist man looks into a mirror that reflects a lower animal without wisdom; and from the distorted image he sees, he extrapolates a theory of nature and strikes out on the road of "progress." In doing so, he must call evil good, encourage more evil when he does not achieve the particular wicked goal that he has attempted to reach, and constantly reject all medicines that might heal his sickness. He must relentlessly move from blindness to blindness, "curing" his lack of sight by tightening the bonds that hold the blindfold on him and prevent him from seeing his true state.[28]

> Starting with the words "I am free" and their newly found spirit of independence, men began to believe in the infallibility of whatever seemed natural to them, and then to call "nature" everything that is sickness and weakness; to want sickness and weakness to be encouraged instead of healed; to suppose that encouraging weakness makes men healthier and happy; to conclude, finally, that human nature [conceived of as sickness and weakness] possesses the means to render man and society

27 Ibid., p. 210.
28 Taparelli, "Ordini Rappresentativi," C. C., i, 6 (1851), 497–498.

blissful on earth, and this without faith, grace, authority or supernatural community . . . since "nature" gives us the feeling that it must be so.

There was only one brief and highly instructive moment when Pius IX hesitated in his commitment to maintenance of the existing Papal States. This was just after the foundation of the Kingdom of Italy, when Cavour, building his argument upon a memorandum from conciliatory Catholic sources within the country, offered to the pope the total renunciation of interference in ecclesiastical affairs: "a free Church in a free State" (March 27, 1861). As E. E. Y. Hales notes, "Cavour understood that for the Pope the issue was entirely one of principle, a matter of conscience, and that he would never yield his standpoint on the inalienability of the Temporal Power unless he could be convinced that superior spiritual advantages would be won for the Church by sacrificing it."[29]

Why, then, did Pius IX reject the offer? Because, as the Count de Montalembert, himself a supporter of the principle of a "free Church in a free State," said, what actually was being offered the pope was nothing better than "a despoiled Church in a spoliative State,"[30] and this, as we have seen, would erect a block to individual transformation in Christ. For Cavour and the Kingdom of Italy, brutally introducing anti-Catholic Sardinian legislation into newly annexed provinces at the very moment the offer of liberty was being made, quite clearly indicated what the word "free" actually was allowed to mean: whatever they willed.[31] Arturo Jemolo underlines the madness of Cavour's actions even when viewed from a purely pragmatic standpoint if he meant his theoretical offer to be taken seriously by Pius IX at all.[32]

> He could well have delayed the extension of the Piedmontese ecclesiastical legislation to the annexed province; there would have been no harm in the convents conserving their juridical personality for a few months longer; Pantaleoni [a liberal Catholic], who is certainly not to be suspected of tenderness for the cause of the religious, gave warning on the 13th March, how difficult it was to make it acceptable at Rome that no religious corporation

29   E. E. Y. Hales, *Pio Nono* (New York, 1954), p. 223.
30   Ibid.
31   Hales, p. 224.
32   Jemolo, 230, 231, in Hales, p. 224.

should have a juridical personality. Nor can it be claimed that it was simply a matter of weakness on the part of the government in the face of the party of action [the more revolutionary Left]: was it not Cavour himself who, in the late autumn of '60 wrote to Pepoli, the commissioner in Umbria: 'Put into force energetic measures against the friars. You have done well to occupy some of the convents to recover there the emigrants from Viterbo. Go on like that so as to heal the leprosy of monasticism which infects the territories remaining under the Roman domination'?

As far as the editors of the Civiltà were concerned, this was what was inevitably to be expected from the naturalist, liberal nationalist ideologues dominating the new Kingdom of Italy. They talked a wonderful talk about freedom, progress and obedience to the will of the people. But what all these things actually meant in practice was whatever their naturalist, liberal nationalist "Party-State" said that they meant. Antonio Gallenga, writing in *Il Cimento* in 1855, had already made this crystal clear, insisting that everyone must be bound to the type of education determined by the powers in control of the State, regardless of whether they approved of that education or not. Why? Because men had not yet been given "the discernment of good from bad." The population was still in thrall to Catholicism. Until national regeneration had been completed, Gallenga continued, "let us say it frankly," there had to be a "tyranny of education." Sardinia needed to have "united in one person the attribute of supreme magistrate and supreme pontiff." Freedom in a country still subject to "evil Catholic influences" had to involve restraints. Restraints on liberty, one might ask? God forbid! These are merely restraints on Catholic slavishness. It is for the sake of "helping" people to be free that the Party-State conceived the need to become absolute teacher.[33]

> But among us, the citizen is the property of the State. The law of conscription binds him to the soil of the fatherland during the most florid period of life. The State has, therefore, the right and the duty of exercising over him an almost parental tutelage. It scarcely would be able to hold itself responsible to the laws of the country if it had been delinquent, or permitted that its moral or political education be perverted by others. It would

---

33 Antonio Gallenga, "Sviluppo di Uno Statuto Morale in Piemonte," *Il Cimento*, v, 12 (1855), 1079, 1080.

only half understand the office of legislator, if it did not claim for itself the domination of education.

From the Inquisition of the Church, which was based on a firm belief in truth, one moves to the pseudo-Inquisition of the Party-State, which suppresses its enemies in the name of pseudo-truths it admits it could never really know nor define for each and every individual. The dominant faction crushes any supposed opposition of true popular will to its desires in the name of the very People in question. This the party does by claiming that an expression of popular will contrary to the actions of the State is a manifest absurdity. By definition, the State machinery already guarantees perfect representation of the people's will. Any "apparent" expression of popular will contrary to the wishes of the Party-State is then easily explicable: it is merely an indication of the continuing influence of irrational and superstitious forces frightening the People into acting against its own real desires. Rather than giving in to this unpurged popular will, the forces manipulating it—Church and corporate institutions in all likelihood—must be chastised anew. In the name of the future educated population, it is necessary to oppose what amounts to a vulgar and ignorant mob. An enlightened populace a generation hence will thank the Party-State for what it has done.[34]

> 'Each people has the right to govern itself. The people is defined as that minority which thinks the way that I do; all the rest who wish to enjoy the fruits of peace must be illuminated as we are. Until they are illuminated, their vote has no value.' Can he [Gallenga] express with more splendid candor the theory of a despotism of a small faction over a whole people? If the 'obscurantists' made this discourse, calling themselves alone

---

34   "Libera Chiesa in libero Stato," *Il Mediatore*, i (1862), 1278; "Cronaca Contemporanea," ii, 4 (1853), 577. Taparelli, *Un Carteggio Inedito*, p. 105; Taparelli, "Teorie Sociali," C. C., i, 1 (1850), 269, 372; "Cronaca Contemporanea," C. C., iii, 6 (1857), 246, Curci, "I Principii dell'Ottantanove," C. C., v, 10 (1864), 687; Taparelli, "Teorie Sociali," C. C., i, 1 (1850), 274n; "Il si ed il no del Regno dell'Opinione," C. C., iv, 6 (1860), 666; "Petitzioni in Piemonte," C. C., iii, 7 (1857), 19–35; Taparelli, "O Dio Re Colla Libertà o l'Uomo Re Colla Forza," C. C., ii, 3 (1853), 618; Liberatore, "Se la Personalità Abbia da Temere dalla Chiesa," C. C., i, 2 (1850), 540–541; "Di Una Nuova Filosofia del Diritto," C. C.. ii, 9 (1855), 383– 384; Taparelli, "Epilogo," C. C., i, 11 (1852), 438.

the active and intelligent population, God knows with what invectives they would be excoriated.

The answer to the "Roman Question," both in its broader meaning as well as in its more specific sense of defense of the remainder of the existing Papal States in the years between the first Sardinian assault on their territory and 1870, had to be one that clarified exactly what was at stake in the war of the Catholic and naturalist Enlightenment world views. Hence, on the one hand, the *Syllabus of Errors*, along with the manifold articles of *La Civiltà Cattolica*, underlined its opponents' willful, materialist destruction of the temporal freedom, progress and civilization, historical Italian civilization included, of which they claimed to be the sole defender.[35] Hence, on the other, there was an anti-nationalist emphasis on the worldwide international impact of a Christianity possessing Papal Rome as its universal capital; a project promoted through the great celebrations surrounding the canonization of the Japanese Martyrs in 1862, the calling of the First Vatican Council in 1870, and, perhaps in the most "fleshly" manner of all, by means of the strengthening of a globally-recruited Papal Army.[36]

V. RESPONSE TO THE HISTORICAL TRANSFORMATION OF THE ROMAN QUESTION: ADMIRABLE DOCTRINAL RIGOR OFFSET BY A PROBLEMATIC PRAXIS

Modernist critics of any union of Church and State have correctly pointed out how much officially Catholic monarchies abused that association for purely political ends through much of history. On the other hand, they are apparently ignorant of the fact that this was one of the primary complaints of practically every representative of the nineteenth century revival, the editors of *La Civiltà Cattolica* included. The constant threat of a political misuse of the Church-State connection to crush the spiritual independence of the Mystical Body and thereby thwart its attempts to effect temporal changes in sinful behavior was all too clear to them. So was the historical weakness of the Papacy in resisting such threats, even when in possession of the States

35   See, for example, Taparelli, Il Protestantesimo, C. C., I, ii (1850), "Gli Ospiti di Casorate," C. C., ii, I (1853); Curci, "L'Italia Una nel 1861," C. C., iv, ix (1861)

36   See, for example, Guenel, J., *La Dernière Guerre du Pape* (PUR, 1998).

of the Church. But the dangers of life in a fallen world in no way impaired their recognition of the inevitability of the very union that could be so distorted for the guidance of men of flesh and blood.

Fr. Carlo Curci, one of the most important editors of *La Civiltà Cattolica*, figured among a number of prominent clerics and prelates who, over time, and especially after the death of Pius IX, became convinced that the "fact" if not the justice of the creation of the Kingdom of Italy had to be recognized and the answer to the "Roman Question" altered accordingly. Leo XIII (1878–1903), Pius' successor, along with his most famous Cardinal Secretary of State, Mariano Rampolla di Tindaro (1843–1913), rejected their argument. From the very outset of his reign, the new pontiff proclaimed his determination to conduct a "grand politics," maintaining the temporal influence of the Church's spiritual authority in a myriad of ways that still involved commitment to the reestablishment of the stolen Papal States.[37]

Occasional but quickly dispelled indications of a possible Italian-Papal détente aside, Leo repeatedly sought the help of one or the other of the Great Powers to achieve his temporal goal. Despite pronounced efforts to influence Bismarck, who kept papal hopes for support alive for quite some time, the new German Empire failed him. It was failure in Germany that brought Leo to pursue what proved to be another dead end: the enticement of France to aid the cause of papal restoration through his encouragement of a Catholic *Ralliement* for the maintenance of the Third Republic. Still, as Pope St. Pius X's (1903–1914) Cardinal Secretary of State Merry del Val (1865–1930) later admitted to the Austro-Hungarian ambassador to the Holy See, even Leo openly said that his policy regarding the Roman Question was based not upon dogmatic commitment to the idea of a revived Papal States, but simply upon his inability to see any other pathway to maintaining some form of independence for the Holy See to pursue its spiritual-temporal mission.[38]

---

37   See Launey, M., *La Papauté à l'Aube du XX Siècle* (Cerf, 1997).; Also, Mayeur, XI, 473–481; Jedin, H., and Dolan, J. *History of the Church* (Crossroad, Ten Volumes, 1981)., IX, 3–25.

38   Friedrich Engel Janosi, The Roman Question in the First Years of Benedict XV, *The Catholic Historical Review*, Vol. 40, No. 3, October, 1954, pp. 269–285.

Pius X, already long known to the government of Italy as "a man with whom one can work," saw further insistence upon a return of the Papal States as being utterly pointless. "*Se il Re mi mandasse a dire di riprendere possesso di Roma, perché egli se ne parte e me la lascia,*" he said, "*io gli farei rispondere: resti al Quirinale e se ne parlerà un'altra volta. Ci mancherebbe altro per la Santa Sede.*"[39] Even a miniscule Temporal Power would be a horror in his eyes. "What would we do if they would hand us over the administration of the Leonine City?" Merry del Val asked. "We would be very embarrassed as to how to administer it."[40] Nevertheless, like his predecessor, he could not see the answer to the dilemma, and looked to Divine Providence for its solution.

Governments outside of the peninsula, while not necessarily interested in maintaining the Vatican's temporal influence, were concerned that any attempt by the Holy See to solve the Roman Question through sole negotiation with the Kingdom of Italy would involve a further Italianization of the Papacy they wished to avoid. In German and Austrian minds in particular, only a European-wide agreement could avoid this danger. World War One complicated the solution to the Roman Question enormously. Pope Benedict XV's (1914–1922) efforts to exercise papal influence to bring the conflict to a conclusion found him battling Catholics in all of the belligerent countries who were convinced that their particular nation's position was unquestionably the sole spiritually "just" one.[41] Moreover, he had to try to bring his supernatural authority over temporal matters to bear from inside an Italy part of whose price for joining the Entente through the Treaty of London in 1915 was her partners' agreement to allow the Holy See no participation whatsoever in any peace settlement.[42]

Benedict's experience in the War helped mightily to convince him that the future temporal influence of the Holy See and the Church in general lay in the cultivation of a new Christendom outside of a Europe dedicated to its self-destruction. Nevertheless, his last words included a hope that his successor might finally bring the immediate Roman Question concerning the political position

39 Gianparolo Romanato, Pio X (Rusconi, 1992), p. 269.
40 Janosi, Op. cit.,, p. 274.
41 A major exception was Charles Maurras, who openly defended Benedict.
42 See Janosi, op. cit.

of the pope in Italy to an end. Pius XI (1922–1939), who signaled his own desire to pursue this goal by giving the first external blessing to the City of Rome since 1870 upon his election in 1922, seemed to have fulfilled Benedict's wish with the Lateran Accords of 1929, reconfirmed, with the end of the Kingdom of Italy, by the Republican Constitution of 1947. These Accords, as everyone well knows, reestablished the Temporal Power in the form of a City of the Vatican and its extraterritorial holdings, gave the Papacy certain financial satisfactions, and, most importantly from the standpoint of the argument of the editors of *La Civiltà Cattolica*, a serious temporal influence in daily life through its recognition of Roman Catholicism as the religion of the nation.

On both the doctrinal as well as the practical level, one might, at least at first glance, have considered the Roman Question thereby resolved. One could argue that reduction of the Papal States to Vatican City saved the principle of the moral validity of *some* Temporal Power as an independent base of practical action for the spiritual authority in a manner that made it clear that the Church was not putting any misplaced hopes in playing Great Power politics. A historian might also make the claim that the sovereignty of the Holy See was perhaps better respected in World War Two than it had been when the Roman Pontiffs were in possession of the fullness of the Papal States in the balance of power wars of the eighteenth century. And in that realm where the older *Civiltà* editors believed the real Roman Question truly coincided with doctrine, the Papacy seemed to be teaching exactly what it was supposed to teach: with Pius XI demanding recognition of the sovereignty of Christ as King over the entire universe, and both he and his successor, Pius XII (1939–1958), urging a Gramsci-like effort to dominate all cultural spheres as a means of gaining spiritual influence over physical nature as a whole.

Nevertheless, the response to the "Roman Question" on the level of actual clerical praxis brings up some serious grounds for concern. While admitting the nuances called for in a case-by-case discussion of the interaction of local temporal issues and ecclesiastical policy, I do not feel great alarm over the Vatican's theoretical cold shoulder to political parties and movements that either openly or in an indirect manner claimed to be the "Catholic" agent for protecting the common good, both spiritual and temporal. Rome's fear of identifying the Faith with the inevitably complex and potentially anti-Catholic demands of modern political forces in their search for popular support and utilization of state authority was entirely understandable, especially when clerics were involved in leading and guiding them. In fact, this fear could be considered as simply a manifestation of the heightened awareness of dangers of this kind signaled by the nineteenth century revival, with potentially secularizing Catholic Parties serving as the modern equivalent of secularizing Kings of the past.

However, what is alarming is what appears to have been a "preferential option for compromise with existing authorities," whatever these powers might be. In the twentieth century, this has resulted in a myriad of agreements with openly non-Catholic political parties and governments who have promised to protect the clergy, the cult, and the private teaching of the catechism in exchange for a practical ecclesiastical abandonment of the pursuit of the Social Kingship of Christ. But what I have been arguing here is that it is precisely in the open insistence upon the full temporal impact of the Church of Christ under the guidance of the Holy See that the real essence of the Roman Question reveals itself.

It seems to me that there is a world of difference between the action taken by Pope St. Pius X in totally rejecting the conditions accompanying the French Third Republic's denunciation of the Concordat in 1905 and the active support given by him to Italian Liberals through the Gentiloni Pact of 1913. In this second category also lies Pius XI's Arreglos with the Mexican Government ending the revolt of the Cristeros in 1929, and even much of the actual substance of the Vatican response to Mussolini's violations of the Lateran Agreements throughout the 1930s. The first type of action, while indeed, in effect, accepting the consequences of the French Government's unilateral separation of Church and State, in practice left the Holy See free to pursue her mission as she saw fit. The second set of examples all seem to share a willingness to accept the idea that the Roman Question is one of simply maintaining order in the sacristy, the church building, and the catechism classroom, while the world outside is left to endure its subjection to continued secularization. And unfortunately it would prove not to take long for churchmen to demonstrate that the step turning prudential sacrifice of pursuit

of the Social Kingship of Christ into its theoretical abandonment
was an easy one to take.

VI. THE COUNTER-SYLLABUS AND THE ROMAN QUESTION: PALINGENESIS AND THE DEFORMATION OF TRANSFORMATION IN CHRIST

Promoters of the "Counter-Syllabus" dominating the Church
since the time of the Second Vatican Council have given an
answer to the "Roman Question" that the supporters of the Syllabus of Pius IX would have understood to be both theoretically
unacceptable as well as practically disastrous. They have done
so by means of the transformation of an officially "pragmatic"
pastoral approach to dealing with contemporary conditions into
a dogmatically rigid weapon effectively preventing the Roman
Pontiff and any bishop, priest or layman believing in the traditional Magisterium of the Church from exercising a real spiritual
influence over the temporal order. The result has been exactly
what the editors of *La Civiltà Cattolica* would have predicted it to
be: a renewed surrender to the naturalist, secularizing temptations
of the eighteenth century that the men of the Catholic revival of
the 1800s fought so hard to overturn.

Collaboration with naturalist Enlightenment secularism has
once again ensured—and in much more craven form—a replacement of the search for a true *transformation* in Christ with a
commitment to the *deformation* of the individual, by depriving
him of the authoritative guidance of spiritually enlightened social
institutions necessary to his sanctification. Through this abandonment of the Roman mission to dedicate nature to the greater glory
of God, Catholics are called upon to lower things spiritual to the
level of the fallen temporal world the Savior came to redeem;
to decline the invitation to a banquet nourishing a supernatural
divinization and to dine, instead, upon an earthly "mess of pottage."

Many critics of the revolutionary Counter-Syllabus have noted
a dramatic liturgical illustration of the change of emphasis. This is
the movement of the Feast of Christ the King, designed by Pius XI
to take place at the end of October, just before that of All Saints,
to indicate the *temporal* labor required of each and every *spiritually* healthy Christian in our earthly realm as the pathway to his
eternal reward, to the last Sunday of the ecclesiastical year, thereby

identifying a Kingship of Christ that can only come at the end of time, in the supernatural world. And yet this "spiritualization" of Rome and the Roman Church has had precisely the opposite effect, uniting the Papacy with the fallen temporal realm under the latter's own terms, more tightly and more perversely than Church and State have ever been united in the past.

This is not the place to outline all of the various influences bringing about the victory of a transformed and deformed answer to the Roman Question in full detail. Let us limit ourselves here briefly to indicating the central role that has been played in this sea-change, not by the atheism of the Enlightenment of Spinoza and Diderot, but through the much more effective and seemingly more religious-minded Enlightenment of two otherwise contrasting means of burying redeeming grace under the muck of fallen nature: those provided by Jean Jacques Rousseau's "democratic" general will and by the "individualist" pluralism of the Anglo-American world.

Although totally earth-bound in his approach, Rousseau's emphasis on the overriding importance of non-rational feeling and passion in human life does give his "natural world" a certain intangible, mysterious glow. It has, therefore, since the very outset been seen even by some Catholics as open to sacred influences that a positivist, mathematical, scientific, experimental approach to understanding the universe cannot allow. Those enchanted by his position have even gone so far as actually to limit the very essence of the spiritual to the kind of "tingle" given by Rousseau's vision, equating the presence of God and His blessings only with the existence of strong internal feelings and the vital, energetic, conquering kind of action that they release. This was ultimately the real point of the Abbé Felicité de Lamennais' (1782–1854) formative *Essay on Indifference* (1817), which was not a call for devotion to the external Deposit of Catholic Faith, but, rather, a condemnation of half-hearted or lazy commitment preventing the internal "felt" witnessing to the truth that alone could truly do God's work.

Lamennais passed this ultimately Rousseau-steeped teaching to his Catholic descendants in union with the popular nineteenth century concept of *palingenesis*. Formed from the Greek words "again" and "birth," palingenesis was the notion that a new age of humanity was emerging out of ancient and Christian traditions that modern men thought erroneously to be dead. Palingenesis was appealing to all defenders of modern ideas, such as the followers of Henri de Saint Simon (1760–1825), who still possessed a spiritual sense, did not want to jettison the entire Christian baggage of European civilization, and were therefore horrified by the violence of the French Revolution.

Sharing this vision and critiquing what he viewed to be the moribund Catholicism in his day, weighed down by a union of the Church with the time-bound State deadly to the internal spiritual enthusiasm needed for sanctity, Lamennais lamented "how far we still are from that religion of devotion, of self-forgetfulness for the good of all; in sum of that fraternity of which one speaks so much!"[43] But this death of the spirit could not last. A moribund Catholicism would be reborn in a new and better form that would place the existential choice of belief or nihilism before everyone. "There will be no more middle way between faith and nothingness," Lamennais wrote to Joseph de Maistre with respect to the decision to be made in the world that was coming into being. "Everything is extreme today. There is no dwelling place in between."[44] Still, an elitist guide to this Promised Land would be necessary. Rousseau's recognition that the democratic will of all "passionate, deeply feeling, natural men" that should guide society was prevented from exercising its beneficent impact due to the continued power of existing oppressive forces over ordinary folk led him to the conclusion that people's real desires had to be interpreted though his own infallible, prophetic insight. Lamennais, following his path, felt that the spiritually "dumb," contemporary Catholic episcopacy and papacy, all too dependent upon union with the temporally powerful State, had to be awakened to the true spiritual message of the Gospel through the imposition of his personal, prophetic Magisterium.

Unfortunately, Lamennais' "separation" of Church and State, rooted in the convoluted reasoning of a Rousseau-like naturalism, guarantees the perpetration of the monstrous fraud that the editors of *La Civiltà Cattolica* so accurately identified. What it actually ensures is the placing of the authority of both institutions

---

43   Mayeur, J. M., ed., *Histoire du Christianisme* (Desclée, Thirteen Volumes, 1990–2002), X, 866.

44   Billington, J. H., *Fire in the Minds of Men* (Basic Books, 1980), p. 123.

in exactly the same hands: those of the prophet. The prophetic individual—or, more generally, the party of disciples to which his vision gives birth—understands God as well as the believing People's true character and desires. He (or it) can therefore answer the "Roman Question" properly. Should Lamennais' advice be taken, the Church would no longer have to worry about clashes with the State on matters where their jurisdiction over creatures of body and soul might intersect, because in his system such a collision cannot possibly take place. How could there be any tension of authorities when all power was invested in the God-People-Prophetic agent, from whose judgments only an enemy of everything spiritual and temporal might think of making an appeal? In the final analysis, it is prophetic, energetic passion and vital will which are the King in the land shaped by the new Christianity that this union represents. Moreover, that will is truly absolute; not bound by a Tradition enshrined in Scripture and decisions of the Magisterium throughout history like the individual will of a particular Roman Pontiff.

Despite his condemnation by Gregory XVI, Lamennais' influence went underground, and has come back again and again to haunt the Catholic world. Its latest re-emergence, since the 1920s and 1930s, has come through varied forms of Personalism, with their intangible, mystical adulation of the freedom either of the passionate, feeling individual or the passionate, feeling fraternal community, always, as usual, instructed regarding the true meaning of that feeling by a prophetic spiritual elite. Given "scientific" evolutionary support by Teilhard de Chardin (1881–1955), and expanded upon in the writings of morally relativist, Liberation and "Third World" theologians, it was this *intellectual* influence that "drafted" the palingenesist Counter-Syllabus of the 1960s; the so-called "Spirit of Vatican Two." Each time this vision returns, it announces itself to be strikingly new, startlingly energetic, invincible, and yet, predictably, the humble victim of overpowering, earthly-minded, persecuting forces. Ever time it appears, it raises the banner of the primacy of the Holy Spirit over the wrong-headed, traditional, earthly concerns of the Roman Church, and then, in practice, proceeds to reduce the Christian mission to a set of pressing temporal imperatives. Over and over again, it insists that it is ushering in an age of Christian victory

and Christian freedom, although the greater its successes, the less
there is anything distinctly Christian about it, the more that the
very word Catholic tends to disappear entirely from its lexicon,
and the more that the individual believer is reduced to becoming
a helpless tool of the ideological prophet.

But this *intellectual* influence could not have provided its
answer to the Roman Question without the aid of the individualist-
pluralist Anglo-American domination that came through the
power and influence gained by the United States as a result of
its victory in the Second World War. By 1945, Catholic Europe,
tired of the seemingly endless, bloody, spiritual and ideological
wars that had characterized the past two hundred years, was
ready to hear an answer to the Roman Question abandoning the
difficult search for truth and real human greatness offered by the
transformation of all things in Christ. Into the breach of post-war
demoralization walked Moderate Enlightenment individualism,
fathered by John Locke, nurtured by the British Whigs and the
American Civil Religion, baptized at the end of the Second World
War by Christian Democrats like Jacques Maritain (1882–1973),
and now preached to the world through the praxis-as-dogma
teaching called pluralism.[45]

According to the pluralist Magisterium, people should accept
the practical reality of diversity, and pragmatically tolerate one
another's incompatible beliefs and ways of life, allowing all of
them their freedom so as to procure an end to a hatred and
bloodshed that in no way can be pleasing to the Incarnate God.
E pluribus unum is pluralism's "common sense" motto: freedom
and a temporal peace, prosperity and unity are all to emerge from
society's practical embrace of diversity. Through this eminently
peaceful and supposedly purely pragmatic approach, the Papacy
would also finally be totally free to pursue its mission in a way
that it had never really been free to do through the past union
of Church and State. What could possibly be the objection to
pluralism's promise of the Golden Age?

---

45 Luigi Sturzo and Angeline Helen Lograsso, "The Roman Question
before and after Fascism," *The Review of Politics* (Vol. 5, No. 4 (October,
1943), pp. 488–508; Pietro Pavan. *Le Metamorfosi della Dottrina Sociale
della Chiesa Durante il Pontificato di Pio XII* (il Mulino, collana "Santa
Sede e Politica nel 1900," Bologna 2012).

The objection is that what it really promises is a political and social order and a fulfillment of individual human dignity through a total surrender to Original Sin. Rather than simply urging men pragmatically to accept the reality of human diversity, it presses them positively to multiply differences of belief and moral behavior to prove the validity of their pluralist credentials. It renders fallen nature the teacher of man and society and declares the redemptive transformation of all things in Christ unnecessary and unwanted; in fact, the cause of social evil and individual slavery. Through its subtle transformative influence over Catholics and the Church, the pluralist Blitzkrieg inspired the calling of a "pastoral" and "purely pragmatic" synod that, in practice, was utilized by the palingenesist, prophetic, dictatorial elites that have shaped and interpreted its guidance into the only truly dogmatic Council in the history of the Church; the only acceptable Council for the new Catholic man. But given that this prophetic elite is not actually united in what it deems most significant in life, and given that the multiplication of factions is ensured by the individualist pluralist mentality, the Counter-Syllabus has made certain that the "Holy Spirit" shapes Catholicism according to the temporal wishes of whatever the strongest party in a given land wants the Paraclete to teach.

What the Counter Syllabus has done, without officially changing doctrine, is radically deform the life of Catholics—the rhythm of their weeks and years, the nature of their feasts and fasts, their private devotions, their public worship, and the appearance of their churches—and in doing so taught them the new doctrine of surrender to the fallen natural world more subtly and effectively than might otherwise have done. It has changed everything while claiming to change nothing. All the ideas of the world have become acceptable, and the Catholic faithful have been taught to acquire the habit of being open to them. The only unacceptable thing is the ancient mode of life, the Catholic mode, which has been dismantled, its devotees condemned as semi-fascist at the very best. This modern answer to the Roman Question seems to me to have its symbolic ending in the tragic video seen by all of us in the midst of this dreadful worldwide virus, showing a Roman Pontiff friendly to the Counter-Syllabus preaching to an empty Piazza San Pietro.

ABOUT THE AUTHOR

JOHN C. RAO obtained his doctorate in Modern European History from Oxford University in 1977. He worked in 1978–1979 as Eastern Director of the Intercollegiate Studies Institute in Bryn Mawr, PA, and was Associate Professor of European History at St. John's University in New York City from 1979 to 2021. Dr. Rao is also director of the Roman Forum, a Catholic cultural organization founded by the late Professor Dietrich von Hildebrand in 1968. He writes for numerous French, German, Spanish and Italian journals. Perhaps the most important of his works are *Americanism and the Collapse of the Church in the United States* (Roman Forum Press, 1995), *Black Legends and the Light of the World* (Remnant Press, 2012), *Removing the Blindfold* (Angelus Press, 2014), a discussion of Catholics rediscovering their own heritage in the post-French revolutionary era, and *A Centenary Meditation on a Quest for "Purification" Gone Mad* (Arouca Press, 2019). He has also written a companion volume to his collected works, *The Unrepentant Catholic's Cautionary Calendar* (Arouca Press, 2022).

www.ingramcontent.com/pod-product-compliance
Lightning Source LLC
Chambersburg PA
CBHW020914140626
46545CB00015B/7